DATE DUE

BRODART, CO.   Cat. No. 23-221-003

Comparative Education

Comparative Education

The Dialectic of the Global and the Local

Edited by
Robert F. Arnove
and
Carlos Alberto Torres

ROWMAN & LITTLEFIELD PUBLISHERS, INC.
Lanham • Boulder • New York • Oxford

ROWMAN & LITTLEFIELD PUBLISHERS, INC.

Published in the United States of America
by Rowman & Littlefield Publishers, Inc.
4720 Boston Way, Lanham, Maryland 20706

12 Hid's Copse Road
Cumnor Hill, Oxford OX2 9JJ, England

British Library Cataloguing in Publication Information Available

Library of Congress Cataloging-in-Publication Data

Comparative education : the dialectic of the global and the local / edited by Robert F.
Arnove and Carlos Alberto Torres.
    p.   cm.
    Includes bibliographical references and index.
    ISBN 0-8476-8460-1 (cloth : alk. paper). — ISBN 0-8476-8461-X
(pbk. : alk. paper)
    1. Comparative education—Philosophy.   I. Arnove, Robert F.   II. Torres,
Carlos Alberto.
LB43.R44   1999
370.9—dc21   98-52849
                                               CIP

Printed in the United States of America

♾ The paper used in this publication meets the minimum requirements of American
National Standard for Information Sciences—Permanence of Paper for Printed Library
Materials, ANSI/NISO Z39.48—1992.

Contents

Introduction

Reframing Comparative Education
The Dialectic of the Global and the Local

Robert F. Arnove

This book reflects the forces shaping comparative education at the turn of the twenty-first century. These forces are internal as well as external to the field of comparative education. Within the discipline, theories and methods for studying school-society relations undergo change in accordance with advances in knowledge, shifts in paradigms, and increases in capacity to process and analyze large data sets in more sophisticated ways. Conceptual and methodological frameworks, in turn, are constantly being reshaped by events on the world stage and corresponding changes in economic, social, and educational policies.

A central thesis of this book is that the workings of a global economy and the increasing interconnectedness of societies pose common problems for educational systems around the world. These problems relate to the governance, financing, and provision of mass education; they relate to issues of equality of educational opportunities and outcomes for differently situated social groups, especially those who historically have been most discriminated against—women, ethnic minorities, rural populations, and working-class people. Although there are common problems—and what would appear to be increasingly similar education agendas—regional, national, and local responses also vary. As the title of this book indicates, a dialectic is at work between the global and the local. Understanding this interactive process, the tensions and contradictions, is central to recasting or "reframing" the field of comparative and international education. I believe that the adoption of a focus on globalization contributes to a greater understanding of the dynamics of school-society relations as well as the potential and limitations of education systems to contribute to individual and societal advancement.

Globalization

Globalization can be defined as "the intensification of worldwide social relations which link distant localities in such a way that local happenings are shaped by events occurring many miles away and *vice versa*."[1] Various adjectives may be used to describe the different dimensions of this process. Certainly economic and cultural globalization are foremost among the descriptors used for the processes by which societies are increasingly linked in real and virtual time.[2] Economic globalization, the result of major transformations in the processes of producing and distributing goods and services, is integrally related to changes in the international division of labor. One of the central characteristics of this highly globalized capitalism is that the factors of production are not located in close geographic proximity. At the same time, however, national economies are increasingly integrating into regional ones. The era of "Fordist" mass-scale production within national boundaries has been replaced by "just-in-time Toyotism."[3] The fragmentation and reintegration of economies is facilitated by concurrent revolutionary improvements in telecommunications and computerization, all made possible by quantum leaps in the production of scientific and technological knowledge. The ease by which individuals can communicate via satellite, and by which products can be assembled and disseminated, has its cultural counterparts in the so-called "Coca-Cola-ization" and "McDonaldization" of the world, the spread of television programs and movies from the West and North to the rest of the world.[4] These trends are paralleled by the increasing use of English as a language of scholarly production and advanced studies, as well as the language of business and diplomacy, "Study English and Computers," found on flyers distributed at the most frequented transportation hubs and commercial centers of major cities around the world, is promoted as the surest and quickest way to find a job and enter the global economy.

In the realm of education, as the various authors in this book point out, globalization also refers to the closely intertwined economic and education agendas promoted by the major international donor and technical assistance agencies, namely, the World Bank, the International Monetary Fund, and national overseas aid agencies such as USAID (United States Agency for International Aid), CIDA (Canadian International Development Agency), and JICA (Japan International Cooperation Agency). Similar prescriptions are being offered by these powerful agencies for enhancing the equality, efficiency, and quality of education systems.[5] These reforms are being implemented by education policy makers who often have little choice but to do so in exchange for access to needed funds.

These common prescriptions and transnational forces, however, are not uniformly implemented or unquestionably received. As the title of this book suggests, there is a dialectic at work by which these global processes interact with national and local actors and contexts to be modified and, in some cases, transformed. There is a process of give-and-take, an exchange by which international trends are reshaped to local ends. Just as scholars from the developing world have challenged dominant research paradigms and conceptual frameworks of the industrialized North to propose more relevant theories related to dependency as well as education for critical consciousness and liberation,[6] so have local people appropriated and transformed the language of the former colonizers. Hickling-Hudson, for example, has illustrated how the English language is received and reshaped by Creole-speaking Jamaicans into something beautifully and poetically different.[7]

The impact of globalization on education systems has significant and manifold implications that are studied in this volume. They include questions such as, Who has access to what levels of education and with what outcomes? What types of jobs will be available for whom?[8] Will decentralization and privatization of education—promoted by international donor agencies as well as by national elites—lead to greater equality, efficiency, and quality? What will be taught and in what language? These various transnational forces raise significant questions about the viability of the nation-state and the role of public education systems in creating citizens.

As the loci of economic production, political decision making, and group identity are transformed, so too do our understandings of the nature of public education in contributing to citizenship formation and economic development come under challenge. These changes on the world stage call for new ways of viewing education-society relations. Comparative education, which traditionally has taken as its subject matter the macro- and microlevel forces shaping education systems around the world, is a field ideally situated to study the dynamic interactions between global trends and local responses. This volume represents an attempt to "reframe," or shift the foci of, the field to this interplay between the global and the local. It seeks to provide generalizable propositions and useful insights into the forces shaping the origins, workings, and outcomes of education systems.

Evolution of the Field

Although the origins of the field of international and comparative education can be traced to the pioneering work of Marc-Antoine Jullien and César August Basset in the first half of the nineteenth century, its institutionalization as a field of study and research in universities is largely a phenomenon of the post-World War II period.[9] Closely tied to major shifts in geopolitical realities and changing views of education's role in advancing personal enlightenment and social progress, the comparative study of education systems initially attempted to explain, in the words of Watson, the "beginning of a new world order in Europe" in the aftermath of the Napoleonic Wars.[10] Since then, the comparative study of education has been concerned with attempting to explain the role of education in contributing to nation-state building as well as to totalitarian or democratic forms of government. Major expansion in the field occurred in the 1960s, when, according to Altbach and Tan, "higher education in the industrialized nations was expanding rapidly, and . . . the major powers were preoccupied not only with Cold War rivalries, but with understanding the newly emerging nations of what came to be called the Third World."[11] The emergence and widespread acceptance of notions of education's contribution to human capital formation and the economic growth of nations further fueled an interest in comparative education. More recently, the belief that there is a causal relationship between the "excellence" of a school system, as measured by national standardized examinations, and the economic success of a country in global competition has revived the interest in the relationship between education systems and national productivity. Finally, the end of the Cold War, the breakup of the former Soviet Union with the emergence of newly independent republics, often microstates, and the outbreak of ethnic conflict in various regions of the world has, once again, led to renewed interest in the relationship of education to political stability and development.

The Dimensions of Comparative Education

Historically, the field of comparative and international education has comprehended three principal dimensions or thrusts, which I call the scientific, pragmatic, and international/global understanding. These dimensions are closely related, and, as I shall argue, are converging to an even greater extent.[12]

The Scientific Dimension[13]

One major goal of comparative education has been to contribute to theory building: to the formulation of generalizable propositions about the workings of school systems and their interactions with their surrounding economies, polities, cultures, and social orders. As Farrell has noted, all sciences are comparative. The goal of science is not only to establish that relationships between variables exist but to determine the range over which they exist.[14] As Bray and Thomas have further pointed out, comparison enables researchers to look at the entire world as a natural laboratory to view the multiple ways in which societal factors, educational policies, and practices may vary and interact in otherwise unpredictable and unimaginable ways.[15]

The value of a comparative perspective is illustrated in a question that education researchers pose frequently: What is more important in determining academic achievement—school-related characteristics or the socioeconomic background of the student? Research conducted in the United States by Coleman et al. and Jencks et al., as well as by Plowden et al. in England, in the 1960s and early 1970s concluded that forces largely beyond the control of schools, namely, the characteristics of students and their families, are more significant determinants of what students learn.[16] However, studies conducted in places as far apart as Uganda and Chile reach different conclusions.[17] Schools do matter, but perhaps to a greater extent in less industrialized countries. Cross-national data over time indicate that as societies industrialize and social class formation solidifies, socioeconomic status increasingly becomes important in determining access to the highest levels of an education system and the most prestigious institutions of learning and to better jobs.[18] Given the great disparities in school resources in low-income countries, in which rural schools as well as many urban ones may not have the most basic amenities and equipment, provision of textbooks and the presence of a competent teacher who can work with well-designed learning materials can make a difference.[19] This research has played a role in convincing major international technical assistance and financial aid agencies such as the World Bank that certain key inputs (e.g., well-prepared textbooks) can contribute to substantial gains in student academic achievement. (For further discussion, see chapter 6 in this volume.)

The value of cross-national, longitudinal data is also apparent in calculating social rates of return to investments in education. Psacharopoulos and others have argued that the best education investment for a country is at the primary school level, followed by secondary, and lastly by higher education.[20] These conclusions by prominent economists working for the World Bank have led this lender agency, as well as other bilateral aid agencies such as USAID, to propose that higher education institutions charge tuition fees representing a more substantial share of costs. The policies favored by these agencies also have led to a greater emphasis on the privatization of education. Yet the social rate of return is usually higher to primary education because the costs are minimal relative to secondary and tertiary levels of schooling. The important point is that a diminishing social rate of return to primary education occurs as access becomes nearly universal. Comparative data suggest that in some countries secondary education now has the highest rate of return. A recent review of the literature by Carnoy indicates that social rates of return in many of the so-called NICs (Newly Industrializing Countries) rise with higher levels of schooling.[21] Moreover, higher education leaders in developing countries have argued that what these societies need are not poorly funded universities but well-endowed, first-rate institutions capable of conducting the type of scientific research that helps them overcome their dependency on the metropolitan countries of the North, whose technologies often are inappropriate for them.[22]

The value of gathering comparative data guided by theory to reach reasonable propositions about the workings and outcomes of education systems in relation to their social and historical contexts is particularly pertinent to a consideration of the second dimension of the discipline.

The Pragmatic Dimension

Another reason for studying other societies' education systems is to discover what can be learned that will contribute to improved policy and practice at home. Altbach has referred to the processes involved in the study and transfer of educational practices among countries as "lending" and "borrowing."[23] Countries may alternately or simultaneously be involved in both processes, as evidenced by the cases of Japan and the United States.

One of the earliest examples of educational borrowing occurred in A.D. 607, when the Japanese court sent a mission to China to study the empire's education system. According to Kobayashi, one outcome of this visit was the establishment of Japan's first national school system.[24] At the turn of the twentieth century, Japanese education authorities looked to the West for guidance as they attempted to modernize their school system. In turn, countries such as China and Thailand found the Japanese model to be appropriate in their attempts to develop economically without abandoning their cultural traditions.

The United States, similarly, has undergone various phases of borrowing and lending. In the nineteenth century, the country was a "borrower." Academics from the United States studied the higher education systems of other European countries, particularly that of Prussia, as a basis for establishing research-oriented graduate schools (Johns Hopkins University being the first such institution). Many U.S. postbaccalaureate students completed their graduate studies in Europe. Today, the flow of students and scholars has been reversed, with the United States being a principal destination for advanced scholarly studies in major research universities. Hundreds of U.S. educators now are involved in the process of "lending," sometimes transplanting (whether appropriate or not) educational policies and practices to other countries. But since the 1970s, the United States has been fascinated with the so-called Japanese education miracle—the high levels of achievement of Japanese students in mathematics and sciences on the various tests administered as part of the studies of the International Association for the Evaluation of Educational Achievement (IEA). This fascination with the Japanese school system, which has a much longer academic year, has led to increases in the number of days of schooling across the United States and sometimes to longer school days. These modifications of the school calendar have been based on the problematic assumption that extending the time involved in learning would necessarily lead to improved scores on standardized achievement instruments, regardless of the ways in which that time was used or the quality of the teaching. Moreover, to the amazement of a past Japanese Ministry of Education official who visited Washington, D.C., in the mid-1980s, the U.S. secretary of education noted that his office was contemplating the recommendation of the establishment of cram schools (*jukus*) much along the lines of the Japanese parallel education system. The secretary's comment was made at a time when the Japanese were seriously attempting to minimize the influence of jukus and shorten the academic calendar. While the United States was attempting to instill elements of the more rigorous and standardized Japanese curriculum and school system, reform-minded Japanese educators were looking at the more child-centered and progressive elements of the U.S. system.[25] In other words, each system was enviously eyeing the other's system and attempting to borrow elements of it.

However, as comparativist scholars of Japanese and U.S. education have pointed out, the school system of each country reflects the corresponding sociocultural systems within which they are embedded.[26] One cannot simply uproot elements of one society and expect them to flourish in the soil of another society.[27] But as Cogan points out, certain principles may be deduced from the study of school systems in other societies that may be applicable to another country. These principles, however, are very general ones, such as the greater the status accorded to a teacher, the shorter the time period or obstacles required to obtain a teaching license, and the more opportunities for in-service professional development, the greater the likelihood that highly competent individuals will be motivated to select a teaching career and stick with it.[28]

Moreover, the most important principles to be derived from studying the history of educational borrowing and lending is that there is no one best system, that all systems have strengths as well as weaknesses. Also, education systems, as I noted above, reflect their societies—their many tensions and contradictions. Perhaps more can be learned from lessons of failure—what not to do—than from stories of success. However, I do not believe that it is necessary to experience failure in order to succeed. If understanding is to be advanced as to what works and what does not work in a country, then such study must be guided by knowledge of that country, by familiarity with its history and unique qualities as well as by recognition of what it shares in common with other societies.[29]

The role of the systematic accumulation of knowledge or guiding principles and theories (i.e., the scientific dimension) of comparative education is central to the pragmatic and ameliorative thrust of the discipline—to improve educational policy and practice. However, there has often been a separation or tension between these two components. Reviews of pioneering work in the field commonly trace two different approaches to the field—one more scientific and one more historical. In the early part of the nineteenth century French scholar Marc-Antoine Jullien called for the development of "detailed research guidelines and checklists for foreign studies in education."[30] As Crossley and Vulliamy note, Jullien's initiative is seen as the "inspiration for the twentieth century development of international databases for education" and as the beginnings of an attempt at establishing a scientific basis for identifying "the one best policy and practice for all contexts." They further point out that an alternative path was marked by Sir Michael Sadler, who drew "attention to the dangers and dilemmas of international transfer, and to the importance of contextual factors in the analysis and development of education."[31] In his study of nineteenth-century Germany, Sadler noted:

> In the educational policy of a nation are focussed its spiritual aspirations, its philosophical ideals, its economic ambitions, its military purpose, its social conflicts. For a German or for an Englishman to speak of his own country's educational aims is to speak of its ideal, of its hope and fears, of its weakness as well as of its strength. To attempt even this is not an easy task, but to speak of another country's education system from the standpoint of a foreign observer is to hazard more and to risk misunderstanding.[32]

Following in the footsteps of Sadler, Isaac Kandel, a leading figure in the field of comparative education during the first half of the twentieth century, observed:

> In order to understand, appreciate and evaluate the real meaning of the education system of a nation, it is essential to know something of the history and traditions, of the forces and attitudes governing its social organizations, of the political and economic conditions that determine its development.[33]

In later sections of this chapter I further discuss the evolution and permutations of these different approaches to the comparative study of education systems. At this point, I indicate how these two paths relate to the third dimension of the field—education for international understanding and peace.[34]

International Education: The Global Dimension

A third and significant (but previously underemphasized) dimension of the discipline is that of contributing to international understanding and peace. This dimension will become a more important feature of comparative education as processes of globalization increasingly require people to recognize how forces from areas of the world previously considered distant and remote impinge upon their daily lives.[35]

The study of cross-national currents and interactions is closely linked to notions of global education and, in many ways, to world-systems analysis. In 1980, I called for increased emphasis on the international dimensions of our field. As I noted, studies of the ecology of educational institutions and processes often failed to take into account an international context of transactions. Most macrostudies of education accepted the nation-state as the basic unit of analysis. But I argued that an examination of the international forces impinging upon education systems was no less essential than an examination of the international economic order would be to an understanding of the dynamics of economic development or underdevelopment in any one set of countries.[36]

For those attempting to introduce international perspectives not only into scholarly research but into teaching at all levels of education (i.e., suffuse curricula with content and activities that enable oncoming generations as well as adults to understand the increasingly interconnected world in which they live), a global set of lenses is absolutely essential. Global education, as defined by Alger and Harf, is differentiated from international education. They contrast international education, which they view as largely area studies or descriptive accounts of discrete countries and regions of the world, with global education, which they distinguish as emphasizing values, transactions, actors, mechanisms, procedures, and issues.[37]

Briefly, values education teaches that people around the world have different ways of viewing the world, ways that are equally valid and reflective of their life circumstances, which they call "consciousness perspective" (based on the work of Hanvey). It also recommends seeking out and building upon what interests people have in common.[38] (An example of this is Piscitelli's use of art to point out the common concerns of children all around the world—their fears and hopes—and also their differing societal contexts—why a Vietnamese eight-year-old might draw a picture of children working on a tea plantation as something very natural.)[39] In pointing out the importance of actors and transactions, Alger and Harf call attention to the multiplicity of actors (at all levels from the international to the local, governmental as well as nongovernmental) involved in diverse interactions across national boundaries in areas ranging from telecommunications, meteorology, emergency relief, health, and education. The study of the mechanisms and procedures provides insights into what, for example, an international agency like the International Monetary Fund, an important transnational actor, does when it enters a country experiencing debt and currency crises and attempts to stabilize the economic situation. Issues are those that face all of humanity—environmental destruction, the spread of disease, the proliferation of weapons of mass destruction, as well as the increasing impoverishment of populations and the growing disparity of wealth among regions and within nations.[40]

The economic crises, commencing in 1997, in the four Asian nations of Indonesia, Korea, Malaysia, and Thailand illustrate very concretely the value of a global perspective (as outlined by Alger and Harf). The interconnected nature of the global economy has meant that as the currencies of these countries were greatly devalued, banks collapsed, and investors withdrew capital, economies all around the world were negatively affected. Headlines not only warned of the loss of jobs in export industries and tourism resulting from the Asian crisis but how university student enrollments abroad would diminish.[41] Some university officials in countries ranging from Australia to the United States lamented the damaging budgetary effect of a decrease in fully paying students, others scrambled to see how they could assist international students who were in dire financial need and were under great economic stress. In the

meantime, mechanisms and procedures for coping with the economic instability in the four nations—the conditionalities imposed by the International
Monetary Fund—were, at the time this chapter was written, leading to food ri-
ots and ethnic violence in Indonesia, followed by the toppling of the Suharto
government.

The contributors to this volume contend that teachers, at all levels of formal
as well as nonformal education, need to educate their students about the causes,
dynamics, and outcomes of these transnational forces and actors and that comparative and international education can play a vital role in teacher education.
Although Brembeck in his 1975 Comparative and International Education Society (CIES) presidential address expressed concern about the distancing of our
field from teacher education, and Heyneman in his 1993 presidential address
warned of the possibility that comparative education could become a marginalized field irrelevant to the knowledge needs of policy makers, we believe that
comparative education will become even more relevant to both teacher education and policy making.[42] Theisen in his 1997 CIES presidential address called
on comparative educators to link the knowledge building, or scientific, dimensions of the field to better informed and effective educational policy and practice. Among the contributions he proposed were the study of how various institutions (nongovernmental as well as governmental technical assistance
agencies) could better coordinate their efforts while incorporating grassroots
organizations to resolve pressing education problems.[43]

These problems relate to the need to expand access to education to all groups
in a society, promote effective learning, and, simultaneously, achieve greater
efficiency in the running of school systems. Systems all around the world confront these problems. At the same time, the prescriptions proposed by powerful transnational actors such as the World Bank may not always be the correct
medicine. The application of market mechanisms—including privatization,
charging user fees for services previously offered free of charge, decentralizing highly centralized state bureaucracies—to resolve problems of equality of
educational opportunity may lead to inequitable consequences and may actually be counterproductive.

About the Book

This chapter (as well as this book) is a call for efforts to unite the three strands
of comparative and international education so that all work together to contribute to improved theory, policy and practice, and the conditions for greater
equity in schooling and society that contribute to global peace and justice. The
initial chapters in this book address topics pertinent to (1) what theoretical and
methodological frameworks promise to offer more effective ways to study education systems cross-nationally and cross-culturally (chapter 1 by Welch); (2)

the importance of examining the assumptions, workings, and outcomes of major international financial and technical assistance agencies (chapter 2 by Samoff); (3) the need to reconceptualize the role of the nation-state as the basic unit of collective identity and educational provision as well as the importance of studying social movements in relation to education for social change (chapter 3 by Morrow and Torres); and (4) the relevance of the study of culture and personal identity formation to continued inquiry in the field of comparative education that contributes to theory building and improved educational policy and practice (chapter 4 and chapter 5, by Masemann and Fox respectively).

The various chapters in the middle section of the text examine current challenges to education systems around the world and offer new ways to study the limitations as well as emancipatory potential of different reform efforts. This section includes chapters on changing notions of equality of educational opportunity and outcomes (chapter 6 by Farrell), the significance of studying gender and social movements (chapter 7 by Stromquist), different ways of conceptualizing centralization and decentralization of education systems (chapter 8 by Bray), the role of nonformal education and literacy programs in fostering social change (chapter 9 by Hickling-Hudson), how neoliberal and neoconservative agendas are reshaping higher education internationally (chapter 11 by Shugurensky), and all levels of education in specific contexts, particularly in Australia, the United Kingdom, and the United States (chapter 10 by Berman).

A final section examines how global economic currents and convergence in educational reform proposals play out in specific world regions, namely, Latin America (chapter 12 by Arnove et al.), Asia (chapter 13 by Su), the Middle East (chapter 14 by Christina et al.), the former republics of the Soviet Union and Eastern and Central Europe (chapter 15 by Bucur and Eklof), and Africa (chapter 16 by Samoff). Limited space prevents the editors from giving separate chapters to North America, Western Europe, and the South Pacific, although various chapters in the text make reference to or give special attention to specific countries within these regions.

Current Trends and New Directions

A review of educational change in the above regions indicates that the field of comparative education is particularly pertinent to an understanding of the common issues and subregional, national, and local differences that education policy makers and practitioners face. Familiarity with developments in the field further suggests that higher education institutions are offering courses and instituting programs in recognition of the relevance of our field. Although some comparative programs may have been cut back or integrated into larger policy studies units of schools of education in various countries, evidence of its continued vitality and growth is found in a number of countries, especially in Asia.

In a 1994 global survey of the field, Altbach and Tan identified eighty-one university programs and centers in twenty-one countries on all continents that had at least one full-time equivalent staff member and taught at least four graduate courses in comparative and international education.[44] The researchers listed 450 scholars teaching comparative courses. Although the survey was the most comprehensive one to date, it was by no means all-inclusive. Listings for European, North American, and Asian programs and centers tended to be complete, but information on Latin America, the Middle East, and Africa failed to capture the growing interest and activity in the field.

Europe and North America (with 29 different centers and 162 and 159 scholars, respectively) dominate the field. However, the most significant expansion of centers and scholars over the past twenty years has taken place in Asia. As Bray points out in his review of the status of comparative education in that region, "the Japan Comparative Education society (JCES) and the Chinese Comparative Education Society-Taipei (CCES-T) each have over 600 members and the Korean Comparative Education Society (KCES) has over 300 members."[45] In comparison, the British and Canadian societies have fewer than two hundred members each. On a per capita basis, the Taiwanese society is, according to Bray, "probably the largest in the world."[46]

There also has been a growth in national and regional societies in recent years. Although the Altbach and Tan survey failed to locate academic programs in the following countries, the February 1997 listing of national associations belonging to the World Council of Comparative Education Societies includes representatives of Argentina, Brazil, Bulgaria, Colombia, Egypt, Hungary, India, the Netherlands, Nigeria, Poland, Portugal, Russia, and Spain. Slovakia has formed a joint society with the Czech Republic; and the Comparative Education Society of Asia (CESA), which held its first meeting in Tokyo in 1996, serves, according to Bray, "as a mechanism through which scholars and practitioners in countries which would otherwise have no national infrastructure can meet in a regional setting."[47] These countries include the Philippines, Singapore, Malaysia, Thailand, and Vietnam as well as Brunei Darussalam, and Pakistan. CESA further would include the newly independent states of Kazakhstan, Kyrgyzstan, Mongolia, Tajikistan, and Uzbekistan. Scholars from Australia and New Zealand, with an already well-established society, ANZCIES, are likely to wish to play a role in CESA in the future, as these countries increasingly view themselves as Asian nations.

A central issue in the formation of the newly independent states of Eastern and Central Europe and Asia is the language of government and instruction. This issue is attracting a general interest in comparative education on the part of policy makers and scholars. The growing interest in English as an international language of communication represents a fascinating subject of study for the field of comparative and international education.

The dominance of English as the language of scholarly communication and publication is both a fact and a point of contention. Although many scholars recognize that English will continue to be the primary language for scholarly research, dissemination, and exchange, there is also a marked growth in Chinese,[48] as well as in Spanish language publications, and a substantial literature in Russian. Well over 80 percent of communication over the Internet is in English, followed by French, but programs now exist to provide for translation of texts among many other languages. A challenge to the field will be to find ways to provide adequate outlets for articles in major scholarly journals in languages other than English or abstracts of such articles, at the very least.

The growing body of literature from different regions of the world, whether in English or not, will continue to expand the existing theoretical and conceptual framework of CIE, eventually transforming the very boundaries of the field. Just as Latin American scholarship has contributed dependency theory and Freirean notions of education for critical consciousness and liberation, the literature of Asia and Africa will help offset the hegemony of European and North American scholarship.[49] What does teaching and learning mean in societies imbued with Confucian, Taoist, and Zen notions? How, for example, can North American and European art educators learn from traditional Japanese and Chinese forms of instruction in these areas? And conversely, what can Asian educators learn from new curricular approaches to art education in the West?[50] What can North American universities attempting to achieve greater diversity in education, as well as inclusion of minority students, learn from the example of historically white higher education institutions in South Africa as they attempt to incorporate students of color, especially black South Africans, who constitute a majority population? Are the experiences of North American universities attempting to desegregate their institutions pertinent to South African higher education institutions?[51]

What is being advocated here is not only the need for different perspectives, based on different cultural traditions, to be infused into the literature but, ultimately, a multidirectional flow of scholarship and ideas to improve not only educational policy and practice but also our ability to generalize about education-society interactions.

In his chapter, Anthony Welch asks whether comparative education is more science or more history? Similarly, the theoretical and pragmatic thrusts of education, at various times, have gone their separate ways or have been at odds with each other.[52] The answer to Welch's question is that comparative and international education, at its best, should be both science and history, contributing to theory building and to more informed and enlightened educational policy and practice. Although eclecticism may be viewed as "a disease that can be cured by taking a stand,"[53] the contributors to this volume believe in the value of a variety of epistemologies, paradigms, methods, and approaches to studying education systems across national boundaries and at various levels—from the global to the local.

Bray and Thomas provide a useful framework for attempting to link different geographical/locational levels, nonlocational demographic groups, and aspects of education and society. They note that comparative education typically has focused on countries as the locational unit of analysis but that the units may range from that of the world/regions/continents to that of schools/classrooms/individuals. The nonlocational democraphic groups may range from ethnic/age/religious/gender groups to entire populations. The aspects of education are those typically studied: curriculum, teaching methods, educational finance, management structures, as well as others. Their article recommends that comparativists can make their greatest contribution to improve theory and policy by attempting to introduce as many levels of analysis as possible to portray the complex interplay of different social forces and how individual and local units of analysis are embedded in multiple layered contexts.[54]

We believe that the vitality of our field depends upon strengthening dialogue with one another and welcoming diverse approaches to gathering and analyzing data on education-society relations. These approaches are qualitative and quantitative, case oriented and variable oriented.[55] Theory building depends on attempts to generalize from case studies while also building on and contextualizing large-scale cross-national studies.

Case studies are likely to continue to be the most commonly used approach to studying education-society relations. Given the limited resources of most researchers working in the academy, the tendency of most individuals is to study areas that are familiar. More than just a convenience, Ragin argues, the comparative method is essentially a case-oriented strategy of comparative research.[56] In case studies "outcomes are analyzed in terms of intersections of conditions, and it is usually assumed that any of several combinations might produce a certain outcome."[57] By contrast, "Sometimes quantitative cross-national studies have an unreal quality to them—countries become organisms with systemic distress, for example—and the data examined have little meaningful connection to actual empirical processes. More concrete questions—relevant to the social bases and origins of specific phenomena in similarly situated countries and regions—do not receive the attention they deserve."[58]

Ragin's orientation is toward macrolevel comparative studies and causal analysis. Others, such Bradshaw and Wallace, view the value of case studies as residing in their contribution to the refinement and modification of extant theory, and ultimately to the creation of new theory when existing explanatory frameworks are not applicable. They find much of existing social science theory, formulated in a few select countries of the North, to be inappropriate to much of the world.[59] Their concern is not so much with achieving generalizable propositions concerning causal relationships as with understanding, much in the tradition of Weber, the patterning of relationships in different types of historical and social configurations.[60]

Some recent examples of promising studies along the lines suggested by Brad-shaw and Wallace are those by Slaughter and Leslie, Mundy, and Christina. In these studies, different levels of government, the relationship between the state and the private sector, the interplay of the global and the local are brought out.

One of the most sophisticated studies of what is occurring in higher educa-tion in developed industrial countries is Slaughter and Leslie's examination of the "entrepreneurial university" in Australia, Canada, the United States, and in the United Kingdom. In addition to focusing on common patterns as well as variations within the four countries with regard to strong cross-national forces promoting privatization of universities and gearing them more closely to mar-ket demands, the researchers examine two very different cases within Australia to determine how closeness to the market affects research funding, program de-velopment, and faculty rewards.[61]

Mundy's study of the nature of literacy programs and their outcomes in Tan-zania, Zimbabwe, and Botswana critically examines extant theories in the light of world-systems theory. As she impressively documents, the extent of literacy provision and achievement is greatly influenced by the degree of incorporation of each country into the global economy at the time of its independence and the subsequent development paths that the governments choose.[62]

Christina, using a world-systems analysis, examines how current interna-tional notions concerning early childhood education are implemented at the na-tional and local levels in the West Bank and Gaza, and how policies result from the interactions between nongovernmental organizations and the Palestine Na-tional Authority. She displays how these multiple forces affect the decisions of individual, institutional, and group actors in specific contexts. Studies such as Christina's demonstrate the alliance and bridge building that comparative edu-cators can engage in to improve educational access, curriculum development, and teacher upgrading, among other things.[63]

Case studies, however, have their limitations and pitfalls. Ragin, Bradshaw and Wallace, and others, are well aware there is a danger in attempting to gen-eralize from one case to other instances that are not appropriate and to view the world only from the lens of that which is most familiar. Major funding agen-cies for international research also tend to favor quicker, quantitative studies that meet the exigencies of immediate decision making and present the facade of being more scientific.[64]

Large-scale variable-oriented studies, whatever their limitations, also have great value in contributing to theory building as well as more informed and en-lightened policy making. We see great utility in studies such as those conducted as part of the International Evaluation of Educational Achievement. As Husén and others have pointed out, the great range of examples provided by such stud-ies enables researchers and policy makers to examine the effects of introduc-ing different subject matter (e.g., foreign languages) at certain points in the cur-riculum, of permitting early specialization in certain disciplines (such as mathematics and sciences), or of taking different pedagogical approaches to instruction (e.g., inquiry-oriented versus more didactic science education).[65] Large-scale research can reveal, for example, what conditions favor the educational careers and life chances of females,[66] or successful literacy and adult basic education program.[67] Although such studies are useful in illuminating general patterns, we also believe the general tendencies revealed by them need to be studied in greater detail through individual cases of educational institutions and programs within their unique contexts.[68]

Conclusions

The June 1998 Western Region meeting of the CIES was called "Dance on the Edge." It was organized to "celebrate Comparative and International Education at the Cusp of the 21st Century." I quote at length the promotional brochure for the conference because it so cogently (and delightfully) captures the state of our field at the dawn of a new century:

> Comparative and international education is enjoying a renaissance. Globalization has infused the ever-present need to learn about each other with an urgency and emphasis like no other in history. At the same time, the postmodern attack on meta-narratives and totalizing discourses has infused our scholarship and practice with doubt about much orthodox wisdom. Even the meaning of "comparative" and "international" is in question, accompanied by vigorous contests over who will control "education." For some, education is an instrument of social justice and bulwark against cultural hegemony. For others it is a commodity to be bought and sold on a "free market." [69]

Yes indeed. There is vigorous debate within our field. We would also question a central point made in the above announcement. As the various chapters in this volume underscore, "metanarratives and totalizing discourses," although under attack, continue to be alive and well; rumors of their demise (to paraphrase the American humorist Mark Twain) are much exaggerated. Moreover, if they are to be challenged, their continued prevalence, workings, and implications need to be understood.

If there is a constant in the field of comparative education, it is its constantly changing nature. Since its institutionalization in the academy, our field has undergone marked shifts in paradigms and approaches to the field—from modernization theory and structural functionalism combined with attempts to create a science of education based on the rigorous gathering of comparative data to test theoretically based hypotheses, to neo-Marxist, world-systems, and dependency theories of school-society relations, to ethnomethodological and ethnographic approaches, to a variety of isms—poststructuralism, postmodernism, and postcolonialism coupled with feminist perspectives.[70] New developments in comparative education include incorporation of theories of multiculturalism, social movements, and the state as well as Critical Race Theory and Critical Modernism.[71] The field has undergone a shift from a macrofocus on the role of schooling in contributing to such outcomes as social mobility and stability, political development, economic growth, cultural continuity and change to a microfocus on the inner workings of schools and on what is learned and taught in school. These shifts do not have clearly demarcated dates. The trends have tended to overlap. At times advocates of these different approaches have been at odds with one another, sometimes in dialogue with one another. Now more than ever, there is a need to learn from one another, to view the strengths and limitations of different theoretical and methodological approaches to the study of education. Small-scale case studies and large-scale research demonstrate increasing sophistication in attempting to combine different levels of analysis (from the world-system to the local context), quantitative and qualitative data to reach more precise conclusions about the nature of what is being studied and what may be generalized. If a discipline is based on systematic, cumulative increases in knowledge, with studies building on previous research to refine and expand our understanding of the social world, comparative education is indeed becoming more of a discipline that can contribute to improved policy and practice.

The continued growth of a systematic, codified body of theory and knowledge, however, does not mean homogeneity or even a consensus about the boundaries of the field or the best way to go about studying education across countries and cultures. In a predecessor to this text, Gail Kelly noted that

> research in the field has been and will in the future be diverse, focusing on a range of topics which at times seem tenuously connected, like school finance, illiteracy among women, textbook publishing practices, colonial schools . . . and so forth. The field—has no center—rather, it is an amalgam of multidisciplinary studies, informed by a number of theoretical frameworks. Debates in the field will likely over time shift as educational policies and practices and needs change and the trust placed in particular theories, social systems, or reforms prove themselves valid or lacking in validity. The fact that the field has not resolved these debates about culture, method, and theory may well be a strength, rather than a weakness and point to the viability of the field and its continued growth.[72]

In the same text Arnove, Altbach, and Kelly noted that although comparative education was a loosely bounded field, it was held together by a "fundamental belief that education can be improved and can serve to bring about change for the better of all nations."[73] In this chapter and text, the various authors state the belief that our field can contribute to positive change efforts in education and society. One way in which comparative education can help effect change is by contributing to a more realistic and comprehensive understanding of the transnational forces influencing all societies and education systems–both their potentially deleterious as well as beneficial features. Also, members of our field can become more directly involved in teacher education and educational reform initiatives—infusing programs and efforts with international/global perspectives.[74] We believe that comparative education can—and *should*—play a significant role in contributing to the possibility that coming generations will use their talents on behalf of international peace and social justice in an increasingly interconnected world.

Notes

The author wishes to acknowledge the editorial and substantive contributions to this chapter made by Mark Bray, Stephen Franz, Yun-Suk Oh, Toby Strout, and Carlos Alberto Torres.

1. David Held, ed., *Political Theory Today* (Stanford, Calif.: Stanford University Press, 1991), 9.

2. For further discussion, see Malcolm Waters, *Globalization* (New York: Routledge, 1995); Anthony D. King, ed., *Culture, Globalization and the World System: Contemporary Conditions for the Representation of Identity* (Minneapolis: University of Minnesota Press, 1997); and Raimo Vayruynen, *Global Transformation: Economics, Politics, and Culture* (Helskini: Finnish National Fund for Research and Development, Sitra, 1997).

3. On "Foridism" and "Toyotism," see Wilford W. Wilms, *Restoring Prosperity: How Workers and Managers Are Forging a New Culture of Cooperation* (New York: Times Business/Random House, 1996); also Ladislau Dowbar, Octavi Ianni, and Paulo-Edgar, *Resende, Desafiós da Globalização* (Petropolis, Brazil: Editora Vozes, 1998).

4. Benjamin Barber, *Jihad vs. McWorld* (New York: Times Books, 1995).

5. UNESCO (the United Nations Educational Scientific, and Cultural Organization) and UNICEF (the United Nations International Children's Emergency Fund) are important international technical assistance agencies working in the field of education, but they are not following the neoliberal economic agenda similar to that of the World Bank (WB) and the International Monetary Fund (IMF), and their educational goals often differ in a number of respects from the WB and IMF.

6. See, for example, Fernando Enrique Cardoso and Enzo Faletto, *Dependencia y desarrollo en América Latina* (Mexico City: Siglo Veintiuno, 1969); Fernando Cardoso, "The Consumption of Dependency Theory in the United States," *Latin American Research Review* 12, no. 3 (1977): 7–24; Theotonio Dos Santos, *Dependencia ecónomica y cambio revolucionario* (Caracas: Nueva Izquierda, 1970); Theotonio Dos Santos, "The Structure of Dependency," *American Economic Review* 60, no. 2 (1970): 231–236; and the seminal work by Paulo Freire, *Pedagogy of the Oppressed* (New York: Continuum, 1970).

7. Anne Hickling-Hudson, "When Marxist and Postmodern Theories Won't Do: The Potential of Postcolonial Theory for Educational Analysis" (presented to the annual conference of the Australian Association for Research in Education, Brisbane, 1–4 December 1998).

8. See Stanley Aronowitz and Jonathan Cutler, eds., *Post-Work: The Wages of Cybernation* (New York: Routledge, 1998); Peter F. Drucker, *Post-Capitalist Society*

(New York: Harper Business, 1993); and Robert Reich, *The Work of Nations: Preparing Ourselves for 21st-Century Capitalism* (New York: Knopf, 1991).

9. Philip G. Altbach and Eng Thye Jason Tan, *Programs and Centers in Comparative and International Education: A Global Inventory,* rev. ed., Special Studies in Comparative Education, no. 34 (Buffalo: State University of New York at Buffalo, Graduate School of Education Publications, 1995), ix. Published in cooperation with the Comparative and International Education Society.

10. Keith Watson, "Memories, Models, and Mapping: The Impact of Geopolitical Changes on Comparatives Studies in Education," *Compare* 28, no. 1 (1998): 6. For the nineteenth-century origins of the field, see Erwin H. Epstein, "Comparative and International Education: Overview and Historical Development," in *The International Encyclopedia of Education,* 2d ed., ed. T. Husen and T. N. Postlethwaite (Oxford: Pergamon, 1997), 2:918–923.

11. Altbach and Tan, *Programs and Centers,* ix.

12. These dimensions also resonate with the three knowledge interests discussed by Jürgen Habermas in his *Knowledge and Human Interests,* ed. and trans. Jeremy J. Shapiro (Boston: Beacon, 1971). The three knowledge interests are the empirical-technical, the historical-hermeneutic, and the emancipatory.

13. The term "scientific" in relation to the field of comparative education is most frequently associated with the work of Max Eckstein and Harold Noah, particularly their *Toward a Science of Comparative Education* (New York: Macmillan, 1969).

14. Joseph P. Farrell, "The Necessity of Comparisons in the Study of Education: The Salience of Science and the Problem of Comparability (Presidential Address)," *Comparative Education Review* 23, no. 1 (February 1979): 3–16.

15. Mark Bray and R. Murray Thomas, "Levels of Comparison in Educational Studies: Different Insights from Different Literatures and the Value of Multilevel Analysis," *Harvard Educational Review* 65, no. 3 (Fall 1995): 486.

16. James S. Coleman et al., *Equality of Educational Opportunity* (Washington, D.C.: U.S. Office of Education, 1966); Christopher Jencks et al., *Inequality: A Reassessment of the Effect of Family and Schooling in America* (New York: Basic Books, 1972); Bridget Plowden et al., *Children and Their Primary Schools: A Report of the Central Advisory Council for Education, England* (London: Her Majesty's Stationery Office, 1967).

17. Stephen P. Heyneman, "Influences on Academic Achievement: A Comparison of Results from Uganda and More Industrialized Societies," *Sociology of Education* 49, no. 3 (July 1976): 200–211; and Joseph P. Farrell and Ernesto Schiefelbein, "Education and Status Attainment in Chile: A Comparative Challenge to the Wisconsin Model of Status Attainment," *Comparative Education Review* 29, no. 4 (November 1985): 490–506.

18. Heyneman, "Influences"; Lois Weis, "Education and the Reproduction of Inequality: The Case of Ghana," *Comparative Education Review* 23, no. 1 (February 1979): 41–51; and Abby R. Riddell, "Assessing Designs for School Effectiveness Research and School Improvement in Developing Countries," *Comparative Education Review* 41, no. 2 (May 1997): 178–204.

19. It also is very likely that the emphasis on textbooks reflects a lack of faith in teachers as adequate sources of information as well as in the power of international textbook publishing conglomerates to determine what constitutes official knowledge. See

Michael Apple, *Official Knowledge: Democratic Education in a Conservative Age* (New York: Routledge, 1993); and David C. Korten, *When Corporations Rule the World* (West Hartford, Conn.: Kumarian, 1995), esp. 165–166.

20. George Psacharopoulos et al., "Comparative Education: From Theory to Practice. Or Are You A:\neo.* or B:*.ist?" *Comparative Education Review* 34, no. 3 (August 1990): 369–380.

21. Martin Carnoy, "Rates of Return to Education," in *International Encyclopedia of the Economics of Education,* 2d edition, ed. M. Carnoy (Oxford: Pergamon, 1995), 364–369.

22. Xabier Gorostiaga, "New Times, New Role for Universities of the South," *Envío* 12, no. 144 (July 1993): 24–40.

23. Philip G. Altbach, "The University as Center and Periphery," in *Comparative Higher Education,* ed. P. G. Altbach (Norwood, N.J.: Ablex, 1998), 19–36; and Gita Steiner-Khamasi, "Transferring Education, Displacing Reforms," in *Comparative Studies,* ed. Jürgen Schriewer (New York: Lang, 1998).

24. Tesuya Kobayashi, "China, India, Japan and Korea," in *Comparative Education: Contemporary Issues and Trends,* ed. W. D. Halls (London: Jessica Kingsley; Paris: UNESCO, 1990), esp. 200; cited in Mark Bray, "Comparative Education Research in the Asian Region: Implications for the Field as a Whole," *Comparative Education Bulletin* [Comparative Education Society of Hong Kong] 1 (May 1998), 6.

25. Nancy Ukai Russell, "Lessons from Japanese Cram Schools," in *Education in Eastern Asia: Implications for America,* ed. William K. Cummings and Philip G. Altbach (Albany: State University of New York Press, 1997); and Walter Feinberg, *Japan and the Pursuit of a New American Identity: Work and Education in a Multicultural Age* (New York: Routledge, 1993), 153–170.

26. John J. Cogan, "Should the U.S. Mimic Japanese Education? Let's Look before We Leap," *Phi Delta Kappan* 65, no. 7 (March 1984): 463–468; Joseph J. Tobin et al., "Class Size and Student/Teacher Ratio in the Japanese Preschool," *Comparative Education Review* 31, no. 4 (November 1987); William K. Cummings, "From Knowledge Seeking to Knowledge Creation: The Japanese University's Challenge," *Higher Education* 27, no. 4 (June 1994): 399–415; Susan Ohanian, "Notes on Japan from an American Schoolteacher," *Phi Delta Kappan* 68, no. 5 (January 1987): 360–367.

27. Harold J. Noah, "The Use and Abuse of Comparative Education," *Comparative Education Review* 28, no. 4 (November 1984): 558–560.

28. Cogan, "Should the U.S. Mimic?" 466–468.

29. Keith Watson, "Memories, Models and Mapping: the Impact of Geopolitical Changes on Comparative Studies in Education," *Compare* 29, no. 1 (1998): 5–31, 10–12.

30. Michael Crossley and Graham Vulliamy, "Qualitative Research in Developing Countries: Issues and Experience," in *Qualitative Educational Research in Developing Countries,* ed. M. Crossley and G. Vulliamy (New York: Garland, 1997), 7; and Stewart Fraser, *Jullien's Plan for Comparative Education, 1816–1817* (New York: Columbia University, Teachers College, 1964).

31. Fraser, *Jullien's Plan,* 7–8; also see Michael Crossley and Patricia Broadfoot, "Comparative and International Research in Education: Scope, Problems, and Potential," *British Educational Research Journal* 18, no. 2 (1992): 99–112.

32. M. E. Sadler, "The History of Education," in *Germany in the Nineteenth Century: Five Lectures by J. H. Rose,* ed. C. H. Herford, E. C. K. Gooner, and M. E. Sadler (Manchester: At the University Press, 1912), 125.

33. Isaac L. Kandel, *Studies in Comparative Education* (Boston: Houghton and Mifflin, 1933), xix; cited in Crossley and Vulliamy, *Qualitative Research,* 8.

34. For a discussion of the relationship of comparative education to international education, see David N. Wilson, "Comparative and International Education: Fraternal or Siamese Twins? A Preliminary Genealogy of Our Twin Field (Presidential Address)," *Comparative Education Review* 38, no. 4 (November 1994): 449–486; also Gary Theisen, "The New ABCs of Comparative and International Education (Presidential Address)," *Comparative Education Review* 41, no. 4 (November 1997): 397–412.

35. Noah ("Use and Abuse," 553–554) has pointed out how a country's education system provides a "touchstone" for examining what values are most cherished.

36. Robert F. Arnove, "Comparative Education and World-Systems Analysis," *Comparative Education Review* 24, no. 1 (February 1980): 48–62; also see Carlos Alberto Torres, *Education, Democracy, and Multiculturalism: Dilemmas of Citizenship in a Global World* (Boulder: Rowman and Littlefield, 1998); and the 1996 CIES presidential address of Noel F. McGinn, "Education, Democratization, and Globalization: A Challenge for Comparative Education," *Comparative Education Review* 40, no. 4 (November 1996): 341–357.

37. Chadwick F. Alger and James E. Harf, *Global Education: Why? For Whom? About What?* (Columbus: Ohio State University, 1986). ERIC Document EN 265107.

38. Robert Hanvey, *An Attainable Global Perspective* (Denver: Denver University, Center for Teaching International Relations/New York Friends Group Center for War/Peace Studies, 1975).

39. Barbara Piscitelli, "Culture, Curriculum, and Young Children's Art: Directions for Further Research," *Journal of Cognitive Education* 6, no. 1 (1997): 27–39; B. Piscitelli, "Children's Art Exhibitions and Exchanges: Assessing the Impact," *In SEA News* 4 (1997): 1.

40. Alger and Harf, *Global Education.*

41. Randal C. Archibold, "Economic Troubles Back Home Squeeze Asian Students in U.S.," *New York Times,* 8 February 1988, 1, 10.

42. Cole S. Brembeck, "The Future of Comparative and International Education," *Comparative Education Review* 19, no. 3 (October 1975): 369–374; also see Stephen P. Heyneman, "Quantity, Quality, and Source (Presidential Address)," *Comparative Education Review* 37, no. 4 (November 1993): 372–388.

43. Theisen, "New ABCs."

44. Altbach and Tan, *Programs and Centers,* ix.

45. Bray, "Education in Asian Region," 8.

46. Bray, "Education in Asian Region," 8.

47. Bray, "Education in Asian Region," 7–8.

48. Bray, "Education in Asian Region," 9.

49. Elizabeth Sherman Swing, "From Eurocentrism to Post-colonialism: A Bibliographic Perspective" (paper presented at the annual conference of the Comparative and International Education Society, Mexico City, 1997); Vandra Masemann, "Recent Directions in Comparative Education" (paper presented at the annual conference of the Comparative and International Education Society, Mexico City, 1997); Bray, "Education in Asian Region," 9; and Abdeljalil Akkari and Soledad Pérez, "Educational Research in Latin America: Review and Perspectives," *Educational Policy Analysis Archives* 6 (March 1998).

50. Lynn Webster Paine, "The Teacher as Virtuoso: A Chinese Model for Teaching," *Teacher College Record* 92, no. 1 (Fall 1990): 49–81; Allan Mackinnon, "Learning to Teach at the Elbows: The Tao of Teaching," *Teaching and Teacher Education* 12, no. 6 (November 1996): 633–664; Robert Tremmel, "Zen and the Art of Reflective Practice in Teacher Education," *Harvard Educational Review* 63, no.4 (Winter 1993): 434–458; Melanie Davenport, "Asian Conceptions of the Teacher Internship: Implications for American Art Education" (unpublished paper, School of Education, Indiana University, May 1998).

51. Kimberly Lenease King, "From Exclusion to Inclusion: A Case Study of Black South Africans at the University of the Witwaterland" (Ph.D. diss., Indiana University, 1998).

52. See Epstein, "Comparative and International Education"; and Watson, "Memories, Models."

53. This is a quip of Jerome Harste of the Language Education Department of the Indiana University School of Education, Bloomington. Harste, a leading proponent of whole language education, has difficulty with people who claim to be eclectic in their approaches to teaching reading and writing.

54. Bray and Thomas, "Levels of Comparison."

55. See, for example, Rosemary Preston, "Integrating Paradigms in Educational Research: Issues of Quantity and Quality in Poor Countries," in *Qualitative Educational Research in Developing Countries,* ed. M. Crossley and G. Vulliamy (New York: Garland, 1997); Charles C. Ragin, *The Comparative Method: Moving Beyond Qualitative and Quantitative Strategies* (Berkeley: University of California Press, 1987); and Robert K. Yin, "The Case Study as a Serious Research Strategy," *Knowledge: Creation, Diffusion, and Utilization* 3 (1981): 97–114.

56. Ragin, *Comparative Method,* 16.

57. Ragin, *Comparative Method,* x.

58. Ragin, *Comparative Method,* ix.

59. York Bradshaw and Michael Wallace, "Informing Generality and Explaining Uniqueness: The Place of Case Studies in Comparative Research," *International Journal of Comparative Sociology* 32 (January-April 1991): 154–171.

60. Max Weber, "The Fundamental Concepts of Sociology," in *Max Weber: The Theory of Social and Economic Organization,* ed. Talcott Parsons (New York: Free Press, 1964), 87–157.

61. Slaughter and Leslie, *Academic Capitalism.*

62. Karen Mundy, "Toward a Critical Analysis of Literacy in Southern Africa," *Comparative Education Review* 37, no. 4 (November 1993): 389–411.

63. Rachel Christina, "State-NGO Dynamics in Palestinian Early Childhood Education: Local Innovation in an Internationalizing System" (unpublished paper, Indiana University, School of Education, 1998).

64. See, for example, Michael Crossley and J. Alexander Bennett, "Planning for Case-Study Evaluation in Belize, Central America," in *Qualitative Educational Research in Developing Countries,* ed. M. Crossley and G. Vulliamy (New York: Garland, 1997), 221–243.

65. Tosten Husén, "Policy Impact of IEA Research," *Comparative Education Review* 31 (February 1987): 29–46 in the special issue on the second IEA study; also see David A. Walker with C. Arnold Anderson and Richard M. Wolfe, *The IEA Six Subject*

Survey: An Empirical Study of Education in Twenty-One Countries (Stockholm: Alquist and Wiksell International; New York: Wiley, 1976); T. Neville Postlethwaite and David E. Wiley with the assistance of Yeoh Oon Chye, William B. Schmidt, and Richard G. Wolfe, *The IEA Study of Science II: Science Achievement in Twenty-Three Countries,* 1st ed. (Oxford: Pergamon, 1992); and John W. Meyer and David P. Baker, "Forming Educational Policy with International Data: Lessons from the Sociology of Education," *Sociology of Education* 69 (1996): 123–130. Extra issue for 1996.

66. Abigail J. Stewart and David G. Winter, "The Nature and Causes of Female Suppression," *Signs: Journal of Women in Culture and Society* 2 (Winter 1977): 531–555.

67. Warwick B. Elley, ed., *The IEA Study of Reading Literacy: Achievement and Instruction in Thirty-two School Systems,* 1st ed. (Oxford: Pergamon, 1997).

68. On the need to contextualize IEA data, see Gary L. Theisen, Paul P.W. Achola, and Francis Musa Boakar, "The Underachievement of Cross-National Studies of Achievement," *Comparative Education Review* 27, no. 1 (February 1983): 46–68.

69. "Dance on the Edge," 1998 CIES (Western Region) Conference, Department of Educational Studies, University of British Columbia, Vancouver B.C., Canada.

70. See Gail P. Kelly, "Debates and Trends in Comparative Education," in *Emergent Issues,* ed. Robert F. Arnove, Philip G. Altbach, and Gail P. Kelly (Albany: State University of New York Press, 1992), 13–22; and Philip G. Altbach, Robert F. Arnove, and Gail P. Kelly, "Trends in Comparative Education: A Critical Analysis," in Altbach et al., eds., *Comparative Education,* 505–533.

71. For further discussion of these critical theories, see Carlos Alberto Torres and Theodore R. Mitchel, eds., *Sociology of Education: Emerging Perspectives* (Albany: State University of New York Press, 1998).

72. Kelly, "Debates and Trends," 21–22.

73. Robert F. Arnove, Philip G. Altbach, and Gail P. Kelly, introduction to *Emergent Issues,* 1.

74. See 1992 CIES presidential address of Mark B. Ginsburg with Sangeeta Kamat, Rajeshwari Raghu, and John Weaver, "Educators/Politics," *Comparative Education Review* 36, no. 4 (November 1992): 417–445.

Chapter 1

The Triumph of Technocracy or the Collapse of Certainty?

Modernity, Postmodernity, and Postcolonialism in Comparative Education

Anthony Welch

In this chapter I argue that the theoretical trajectory of comparative education, for much of the twentieth century, has paralleled that of the social
sciences in general, initially describing an arc that was based upon a faith in
broadly technocratic social science concepts of modernity, drawn largely
from functionalism. More recently, this theoretical arc has been breaking up,
revealing an increasing fragmentation of purpose, and perhaps failure of
vision, which has paralleled, once again, that of the social sciences—if
somewhat more slowly. This chapter traces some of the principal lines of that
theoretical trajectory, beginning with an outline of the technocratic elements
within a broadly modernist, positivist functionalism, and then tracing the
recent tendency toward theoretical fragmentation and the associated collapse
of certainty. In tracing this theoretical trajectory, I create links between the
literature of comparative education and that of the social and natural
sciences. I argue that the more recent failure of vision, and increasing
fragmentation, which is in turn a response to wider movements in fin de
siècle industrialized nations, and perhaps the world system, is not entirely
necessary. Some alternatives are advanced in the conclusion, based on arguments as to the ethical dimensions and responsibilities of comparative
education.

From History to Science?

As Imre Lakatos[1] (inter alia) has reminded us, hindsight allows a distinct, and arguably more complete, vantage point from which to evaluate competing theoretical perspectives, which the protagonists of the time may have seen rather differently. From the perspective of the end of the twentieth century, then, it is easy to be somewhat skeptical as to the brash ebullience of comparative education of the 1960s, as new and more positivistic forms of comparative education were elaborated by an emerging generation of authors who variously asserted their independence from the "factors and forces" traditions of more historically oriented predecessors: inter alia, Nicholas Hans,[2] Isaac Kandel,[3] and Friedrich Schneider.[4] Notwithstanding substantial differences between such emerging figures of the 1960s as Brian Holmes,[5] Max Eckstein and Harold Noah,[6] and George Bereday,[7] however, the promise of scientific methodology was generally held to ensure a more certain and precise future for comparative education, in which "knowledge" and "facts" would play a major and determinate role in educational reform. Neither of these two concepts were yet much problematized, and it is in this sense that it can be argued that debates in comparative education in the 1960s were mostly conducted within the parameters of a positivistically based modernism.

What is meant by positivism here? Briefly, the view that the methods of the social sciences were coextensive with, indeed drawn from, those of the natural sciences, whose methodological development was generally assumed to be at a more mature stage of development than the newly developing social sciences. Although the term "positivism" is widely debated (and much abused), it is nonetheless possible to distil several broad strands that underpin positivistic forms of social science: a belief that methods of inquiry are monolithic (the so-called unity of method), a belief in lawlike generalizations in the social sciences, a technical relation between theory and practice (which thus brackets out any consideration of ethics in social theory), and the belief in value-free social inquiry, in which "facts" and "knowledge" were the basis for progress and were rigidly separated from "values," which were not the concern of the (social) scientist. This restricted form of self-understanding of science and knowledge, which informed modernism, was inherited from at least the French Enlightenment (toward the end of the eighteenth century), and arguably earlier. Although it was by no means the only theory of knowledge or science, its prominence constricted the development of alternatives, in both the natural and social sciences.[8]

The *Methodenstreit* (methodological dispute) among comparativists of the 1960s, then, largely occurred *within* the bounds of that modernist faith described above, that is, in the capacity of science and technology to underpin social reform and progress, including in education, and the ability of an epistemology (theory of knowledge) entirely bounded by the philosophy of the natural sciences to root out errors in any area of knowledge. Debates thus turned largely on the question of which particular position in the philosophy of the natural sciences was superior. Holmes's more explicit attempt to base claims for a new science of comparative education upon Popperian hypothetico-deductive foundations was paralleled by the more or less explicitly inductive approaches of Bereday, and Noah and Eckstein. All ultimately fell victim to the principal tenets of the broad positivist tradition sketched above, which underpinned so much of modernist social science and was thought would herald the same golden age of progress and discovery that had been achieved in the natural sciences of the seventeenth and eighteenth centuries.[9]

It is in this sense, as Habermas has argued, that "the concept of enlightenment functions as a bridge between the idea of scientific progress and the conviction that the sciences also serve the moral perfection of human beings,"[10] a view that stems directly from figures such as Condorcet and others in the Enlightenment, that false moral and political views are a product of false understandings of nature. Science itself was believed to be a form of enlightenment, which once perfected, would deliver the same rapid advances in knowledge to the moral sciences that had already been demonstrated in the natural sciences. In common with many social scientists of that era, then, major methodologists in comparative education of the 1960s were heirs to a belief, stemming from at least the Enlightenment, if not from the birth of modern science in the seventeenth century, that a base of scientific reason was a secure foundation for the epistemological, and, by extension, the social and moral, renovation and improvement of society.

The major theorists of comparative education in the 1960s made no attempt to problematize scientific reason or to subject its social effects to critical scrutiny, despite the fact that powerful critiques of the social distortions caused by the uncritical adoption of scientific reason in the human sciences by social theorists such as Herbert Marcuse,[11] Alfred Schutz[12] and Max Horkeimer and Theodor Adorno,[13] and in earlier eras, by Edmund Husserl[14] and Wilhelm Dilthey, already existed.[15] In the philosophy of science too, at least by the 1970s, scholars such as Thomas Kuhn[16] and the late Paul Feyerabend[17] had outlined a much more sociological profile of scientific change and development, from which none of the methods of the sciences had proved immune. Indeed, according to Feyerabend's withering critique of claims to a scientific methodology that would hold good in all instances, the only rule is that there are no (final) rules, that is, "there is no 'scientific method'; there is no single procedure, or set of rules that underlies every piece of research and guarantees that it is 'scientific' and, therefore, trustworthy."[18]

Despite these parallel attacks upon the adequacy of scientific reason, in its own sphere, and even more so in the social sciences, the "modernists" in comparative education of the 1960s viewed science and scientific reason, in its various forms, as a beneficent force, which, if it were only adopted fully and implemented rigorously, would herald the dawn of a more precise and more certain science of comparative education. It is in this sense that the major figures of the 1960s were children of the positivism of the Enlightenment and heirs to the rationalist ideology of perfectibility—the increasing subjection of the world to the dictates of a technology of reason would promote a more rational and more morally perfect world. Despite vigorous internecine disputes among several of the high priests of the scientific faith, such as Brian Holmes, Harold Noah and Max Eckstein, and George Bereday, the notion of the progressive rationalization of education, via the increasing methodological perfection of the science of comparative education, was common to major theorists of this era.

Perhaps one of the better-known instances of the role of scientific reason in comparative education is provided by functionalism (sometimes called structural functionalism), arguably the most prominent and persuasive form of scientism to hold sway in the postwar era and for much of the twentieth century. Not merely was (structural) functionalism arguably the most prominent of the range of grand theories that laid claim to the mantle of "social science," but a broadly functionalist ethos underlay most of the major positions in comparative education of the 1960s, as indeed among the social sciences more generally.[19]

Stemming from the work of such founding fathers as Auguste Comte in the nineteenth century and Emile Durkheim in the early twentieth, functionalism held that "sociology," a term invented by Comte, should be modeled closely upon the methods of the natural sciences. A functionalist social science then, like its natural science forebears, should be lawlike and socially integrative (as the quote from Francis Bacon, below, reveals). Functionalism was influenced by other movements in the natural sciences too, however, notably the nineteenth-century scientific theory of evolution, from which was incorporated the view that social change should be, just as with biological change, slow and accretive rather than swifter and/or large scale. In other words, the model of social change within functionalism was evolutionary rather than revolutionary. Lastly, functionalism asserted a supposedly value-free social science in which researchers should simply seek out and present the facts, eschewing questions of ethics or the moral dimensions of the knowledge they developed. (In practice, however, technicist values of efficiency and economy were dominant within functionalist forms of social science, if often implicitly.) Here once again, functionalism revealed its positivist heritage, drawn from the modernist presumptions of the Enlightenment and the origins of modern experimental science in the seventeenth century.

In comparative education, the functionalist tradition was arguably most clearly expressed in the substantial literature of the 1950s and 1960s that was devoted to the theme of modernization, particularly the elaboration of the role that education played in the renovation of traditional societies. A common, broadly positivist agenda, based upon the technocratic values sketched above, of efficiency and economy, and a strong system concept, was often present in this literature. As well, a reified notion of social needs, evolutionary progress, social integration rather than social change, and a reliance upon supposed laws of society was evident. The basic aim was continuous with that of Comte,[20] Durkheim,[21] Talcott Parsons,[22] and others: the devising of a science of society modeled upon the natural sciences.[23] And, just as with those theoretical fountainheads, functionalism embodied the aim of control. Just as the natural sciences had already brought nature under control, so too, it was argued, would the science of society, this time in the guise of functionalism, bring society under control. In this sense, functionalism was a direct heir to modernist presumptions, indeed it represented a modern form of sociological positivism.

Education was of major significance within functionalist theories of modernization and was generally accorded two principal roles. First, as a prime site for the inculcation of integrative, stabilizing values, education systems were perceived to be of signal importance in this sedative process, not merely in "modern" societies but also, crucially, in the reformation of societies that were "developing" or "modernizing." In this sense too, as was argued above, functionalism was direct heir to the positivist faith, in which the twin aims of the advancement of knowledge and an increase in social control were intertwined. Already in the seventeenth century, the great scientist-philosopher Francis Bacon had compared science and learning to a harp that would quiet the otherwise tumultuous and mutinous crowd, thus making them more politically malleable: "it is without all controversy that learning doth make the minds of men gentle, generous, maniable and pliant to government; whereas ignorance makes them churlish, thwart and mutinous."[24]

The second role that accorded particular significance to education within functionalism was, of course, the provision of adequate numbers of skilled personnel to service the needs of the various branches of the workforce: both of these functions worked to ensure the ongoing stability of society.

The triumph of modernity was expressed with particular clarity in the articulation, and defense, of the unilinear process whereby societies became "modern." Third world or developing countries were always assumed to be at an early stage of progress toward the same inevitable end point: a technological, industrial, advanced bureaucratic, and pluralist society, which when examined, bore an uncanny resemblance to the United States or the United Kingdom, or other societies from which the authors of these works stemmed. Modern advanced capitalist societies were always seen as, in effect, the ultimate goal toward which the economies and politics of the former colonies of the third world must be redirected, no matter how much this disrupted traditional cultures and values. Evolutionary assumptions, common to functionalist social science, were once again adopted from biological theory, via figures such as Durkheim, and implied a specific conception of historical development that divided the world into two camps: "Advanced" societies were seen as "core," whereas the former colonies of Asia, Africa, or Latin America were, in effect, viewed largely as "periphery." Clearly discernible, then, if not always stated, was "a teleological notion of history, which views the knowledge and ways of life in the colony as distorted or immature versions of what can be found in the 'normal' or Western society."[25] Modernization was, in effect, westernization. These unilinear evolutionary assumptions were of particular relevance to modernization theory and embodied, as I have already pointed out, a distaste for swift or systematic social change or political value systems that were not consonant with modern, advanced capitalism. In this sense, modern functionalism is heir to Durkheim's goal of the establishment of an integrative social science: modern society's "civil religion."[26] To repeat, however, the evolutionary direction that lay at the center of modernization theory was always a one-way street—toward the attainment of Western capitalist structures and values—and presaged profound changes to traditional institutions and ideologies. Moreover, the process of evolution toward a state of modernity was based solidly upon a foundation of modern science, which was assumed to be able to advance the rate of human progress significantly: "Man [sic] in this century of science can move forward in leaps instead of steps."[27] Once again, this faith in the potential of science and technology to advance the perfectibility of humanity is a further echo of Enlightenment faith in the power of reason as *techne,* that is, embodiment of modern, technocratic society, in which instrumental reason overwhelms ethical constraints and mores.[28]

McLelland,[29] Coombs,[30] and Harbison and Myers,[31] among others, saw modernization as either directly or indirectly an example of the Weberian rationalization of society, whereby traditional social mores and institutions such as kinship were replaced by a "coldly rational"[32] modernist action orientation more suited to complex, bureaucratic societies of the twentieth century. More broadly, rationalization meant "a lessening of mystical or supernatural orientation towards life, an increase in striving, orderliness, rigidity, orientation to work without reward, and other such features which Weber saw (as) characteristic of modern capitalist orientations."[33]

Indeed McClelland specifically adapted Talcott Parsons's reformulation of Weber's ideas to develop his "need achievement" index of modernization. The concept, as its name implied, comprised a composite index of modernization and argued that to achieve an increase in economic growth and to become truly modern, developing nations needed to reorient both ideologies and institutions, while individuals needed to become more achievement oriented. The suggested changes centered around the institutionalization of structural features like the increased division of labor and more contractual social relations allied with a reorientation of values, for example, the substitution of material for spiritual forms of satisfaction, as well as a lessening in spiritual influences generally. Here again, we see evidence of a means-ends style of rationality in which economic efficiency is, at least implicitly, accorded the status of a prime value.[34]

Little or no consideration was given to alternative value systems, least of all that held by people from the "modernizing" society. The end point of this process of evolution was always that of advanced capitalist society.

The Role of Western Culture

Positivism, often including a broadly evolutionary perspective, however, has been only one of several common assumptions underlying much modernist empirical and theoretical work in comparative education. But its influence is linked to (and helps to explain) others. The fact that modern science was an artifact associated with the rise of the West helps to explain another given within the traditions of mainstream, modernist comparative studies of education: Western culture as the apex of civilization. A common assumption of nineteenth- and early twentieth-century anthropology, this view remained pervasive and influential in comparative education during at least the first half of the twentieth century. Like many of their colleagues and contemporaries in political science and other social science disciplines, Coombs, McClelland, Harbison and Myers, and others in both comparative education during the period up to and including the 1950s and 1960s tended either to view "other" societies from a generally Western perspective, or in the case of modernization theorists, to situate non-Western nations at a point somewhere along the road that culminated in the attainment of "westernization." In a sense, the fact that the field of comparative education largely grew out of Western scholarly foundations, and most of its founding figures were from Europe and America, made this assumed trajectory of social development unsurprising and goes some way to explain the critique that modernization was in fact coextensive with westernization. Nonetheless the minimal value accorded the principle of difference, and the rich and long-standing traditions associated with such non-Western cultural traditions, was not a good base for a field of study that purported to analyze cultural difference.

The Nation-State as Unit of Analysis

A further assumption of traditional comparative education was that of the nation-state as the prime unit of analysis. To some extent, this reflected the genesis of comparative education as a social science that, like others, grew to maturity during the heyday of the growth and rivalry of the nation-state in the nineteenth and early twentieth centuries, and to some extent was dependent upon major international organs such as UNESCO (United Nations Educational, Scientific, and Cultural Organization) and OECD (Organization for Economic Cooperation and Development), whose statistics were collected along national lines. Although some earlier comparativists analyzed the construction of political identity[35] or the educative role and function of mission schools,[36] even these more thematic analyses fell largely within heuristic traditions in which the dominant unit of analysis was still the nation-state. Even Holmes's well-known problem approach[37] did not realize its theoretical possibilities to undermine the convention of the nation-state as the analytic unit of choice within comparative education. Indeed, the final section of Holmes's most well-known and original work of 1965 was devoted to national case studies. Not even Noah and Eckstein's programmatic statement that "a comparative study is essentially an attempt as far as possible to replace the names of systems (countries) by the names of concepts (variables)"[38] succeeded in checking the prominence of the nation as a given within the literature of comparative education. Not all comparative education scholars of the time were trained as area specialists (Bereday was first and foremost a Soviet specialist, but neither Holmes nor Noah and Eckstein were so disposed), but the nation-state still figured as the analytic unit in the majority of comparative research.

Tributaries

Although the above elements characterized mainstream comparative education during the period of intense development of comparative methodologies from the 1960s, there were also important tributaries that diverged significantly. Some of these have since gone on to become significant currents. Not all comparative education of the postwar decades shared the view that the further development of comparative education was dependent upon debates in postrelativity physics, nor the view that Western culture should be assumed to be the unproblematic end point of all civilizations.

Two developments challenging the ubiquitous emphasis upon scientism in comparative methodology drew upon more interpretive, anthropological traditions: ethnomethodology and ethnography. The first was largely exemplified through the work of Canadian-American scholar Richard Heyman, who (in a series of articles in the late 1970s and early 1980s) deliberately articulated an alternative stream of work to the scientistic ethos of prevailing methodological discourse. In common with the ethnomethodological scholars upon whom he drew, Heyman decried the influence of the natural sciences upon the methodological development of the social sciences. Following the mandate of his mentors, he proffered instead a "non-science of comparative education."[39]

For ethnomethodologists, context was vital and thus knowledge, and the language with which it was described, was "indexical," or situationally mediated. In stark contrast with most scientifically based methodologies, there was no independent reality that each individual must accept according to the dictates of a transcendental, abstract method, and irrespective of individual background or interests. Indeed, the very assumption of a scientific method of detached observation that produced objective insights into social phenomena was simply erroneous, on this account. On the contrary, every observation was itself a construction, one of many possible constructions, each of which could be further deconstructed, or subjected to further interpretation.[40] Indeed, an account of a social phenomenon was coextensive with accounting for a phenomenon. Observation equaled interpretation, meaning that interpretation was, in principle, endless. Each account could be subjected to yet another interpretation, and so on. Indeed, what Anthony Giddens accurately characterized as the hermeneutic vortex[41] at the core of ethnomethodology was embraced by its followers as a feature of social interpretation.

Heyman's application of such precepts to the renovation of comparative education led him to press for a focus on the microprocesses of school life via intensive study of audio- and video-taped interactions. In itself this was unexceptionable; but to go on to argue that other forms of educational investigation should be postponed pending the provision by ethnomethodologists of "a reasonable picture of the essential processes of education"[42] was both unreasonable and chimerical. Equally, although claiming to be strongly antipositivist and postulating an epistemology that celebrated the concrete and different ways in which social reality was constructed, it nonetheless claimed to produce its own facts, which were somehow prior to other interpretations. By claiming, at least implicitly, to provide a kind of epistemic bedrock upon which other researchers might then rely, it also fell victim to the selfsame positivism it critiqued.[43] The other problem that dogged ethnomethodological prescriptions for comparative research in education was its field of vision. As it concentrated on the microcosm of classroom interaction, with its myriad small details, it often lost the connection to the wider world (including the often powerful ways in which this macrocosm influenced the small-scale world of the classroom). Indeed, one of the more insistent and powerful critiques of ethnomethodology was its failure to embrace or analyze power relations, particularly the important ways in which power structures in the larger world, including relations based on social class, pervaded the microcosm of the classroom. In a real sense, it could be argued that, in gaining one class, ethnomethodologists had lost another.

The Canadian connection was strengthened in Vandra Masemann's pregnant and important elaboration of critical ethnography,[44] which avoided many of the pitfalls listed above and provided an important challenge to the scientism of much contemporary comparative research:

> Is it the task of social scientists to seek ever more diligently to define objective methods of researching the social world (or education), with possibilities for change seen as simply the result of "reading out the data" and making choices on the basis of some cost-efficient or technological rationale?[45]

For Masemann, critical ethnography offers not merely a renewed emphasis on "participant observation of the small-scale . . . with an attempt to understand the culture and symbolic life of the actors involved"[46] but also "insists upon a level of agency which is persistently overlooked or denied."[47] Plumping for a form of ethnography, which sited the micro within the context of a macrotheory of social organization, Masemann argued that "it should be possible to . . . investigate the lived life in schools while not necessarily limiting the analysis to the actors' perceptions of the situation."[48] It is only in that way, she argued, that the practices by which a hegemonic rationality are imposed upon students could successfully be revealed and analyzed. By connecting the macro to the micro, she avoided the problems of ethnomethodologists, whose bracketing out (i.e., methodological exclusion) of larger structures and ideologies rendered them unable to analyze power very successfully, if at all.

Examples of other theories that diverged from mainstream assumptions include work that challenged the conventional Western-centric view of much research and/or proceeded from rather different political assumptions about the international political arena and the relationship between powerful and relatively disempowered groups in education, including the role of philanthropic agencies in fostering dependency.[49] Turning the functionalist assumption of a unilinear path to a monolithic Western modernity on its head, several of these scholars articulated a core-periphery model, often paying some allegiance to currents of the Marxist tradition, which emphasized the capacity of wealthy and powerful Western nations, as well as lending and other programs of agencies such as the International Monetary Fund (IMF) and World Bank, to deepen the dependency of third world nations.[50] Drawing upon the theoretical work of scholars of Andre Gunder Frank,[51] Immanuel Wallerstein,[52] and others, key comparative scholars cast a critical eye on the influence of colonialism and on relations between the first and third world. Martin Carnoy's important early book was succeeded by Philip Altbach and the late Gail Kelly's important work on colonialism,[53] which did not merely examine the educational influence of Western colonial incursions in Africa, Latin America, and the Asia Pacific region but also included an important early study of internal colonialism in the education of indigenous minorities, which applied the work of such figures as Harold Wolpe to the analysis of education among American Indian peoples.

Robert Arnove's application of world-systems analysis stemmed naturally out of his work on the ideological penetration of philanthropic organizations, especially in the third world.[54] Issuing a clarion call for an international approach to understanding educational systems rather than the traditional reliance upon the nation-state as the basic unit of analysis, Arnove explored the benefits of setting educational analysis in the context of international economic, political, and social developments. The effects of colonial and neocolonial influences on areas such as Africa, Latin America, and Oceania were obvious instances of the necessity of such approaches. They underlined too the ongoing difficulties faced by these regions in overcoming an often long-standing history of dependency, fostered by the colonial relationship and often changing only in form well beyond the formal end of the colonial era. As Arnove explained, the international ideological penetration of colonial and postcolonial nations also extended within nations in the third world:

> Dependency theory basically articulates a descending chain of exploitation from the hegemony of metropolitan countries over peripheral countries to the hegemony of the center of power in a Third World country over its own peripheral areas. Closely related to such notions of center and periphery are the concepts of Wallerstein concerning convergence and divergence in the global system.[55]

Altbach's analysis of neocolonialism and dependency also articulated the processes that developed and sustained what he termed "servitude of the mind"[56] both among and within nations, a process not merely fostered by disparities of economic wealth and power but also reflecting the fact that third world nations

> find themselves at the periphery of the world's educational and intellectual systems. . . . The world's leading universities, research institutions, publishing houses, journals, and all the elements that constitute a modern technological society are concentrated in the industrialized nations of Europe and North America.[57]

Fin de Siècle Fractures

If the above theoretical development represented a divergence from mainstream scientism of modernist comparative education, the picture had altered again by the 1990s. By then, the ebullience of the postwar decades was well and truly on the wane. The oil crisis of the 1970s, as well as periods of intermittent recession thereafter, led to the advent of mass unemployment, especially among the young, in many parts of the world. The widening gap between rich and poor (both within and among countries) and the increasing deregulation of many economies evidenced a more general decline in government activity and intervention in social and economic affairs. In the social sciences, the confident certitudes of earlier decades were falling increasingly into disarray. Economically, politically and epistemologically, the zeitgeist of the 1990s was considerably less certain and confident than it had been some thirty years previously, and debates in the social sciences, including comparative education, reflected that changing context.[58] The rise of poststructuralist thought, with its rejection of much of the modernist platform, represented a considerable challenge, but not the only one.

Globalization and the Decline of the State

By the 1990s, however, the assumed centrality of the nation-state as the unit of analysis in comparative education was under increasing challenge. This was reflected in the theoretical literature and politically in terms of the changing boundaries of both the nation-state and our understanding.[59] Diffuse international economic and political changes at the end of the twentieth century pushed older conventions aside. Both centripetal and centrifugal forces substantially reshaped the boundaries of postcommunist Eastern Europe,[60] as new regional trading blocs, in part sustained by international trading and political agreements, challenged the traditional emphasis on the nation-state. The European Union (EU), North American Free Trade Agreement (NAFTA), and Asia Pacific Economic Community (APEC) often, interestingly, spawned educational infrastructure to support internationalization of education, at least within their region.[61]

Despite a considerable divergence of views on the meaning of globalization, and a fair degree of hyperbole, some definite trends were discernible, including the massive global movement of capital in the context of a more deregulated international economic environment and the huge growth in international communications. Each of these has had an impact on fostering more regional economic alliances, as well as on global manufacturing and financial enterprises. The process of internationalizing previously more nationally based economies grew apace, while the massive growth in electronic forms of communication also represented a challenge to national borders (including in education), at least for those who had access to the technology.[62] Despite much of the rhetoric about a reorientation of understanding toward developing broader forms of understanding not bounded by the nation-state (as Roland Robertson put it, making "the world a central hermeneutic"),[63] and substantial differences as to the real meaning of the much debated term "globalization" notwithstanding, it is possible to argue that the effects are principally economic rather than theoretical.

Analysts such as Huntington now postulate a "clash of civilizations"[64] between, for example, Islam, China, and the West, which has overtaken the preceding era of nationalist rivalries. In fact, the supposedly newer thesis of the clash of civilizations had more in common with theories of nationalist rivalries, or even earlier eras, than was usually supposed in that both were predicated on an essentialism that is simply mistaken.[65] In Huntington's case, neither "the USSR" nor "Islam" is a unitary entity:

> The key weakness of Huntington's analysis is that, like the early Cold Warriors, he has fallen into the trap of depicting the enemy as a monolith. . . . At the outset of the Cold War, the Communist countries were depicted as the vanguard of a movement dedicated to the triumph of an international communist utopia. . . . In like fashion, Huntington depicts the Islamic countries as part of a wider pan-Islamic movement, united in their hostility to the West and the United States.[66]

Clearly, as with globalization, it is unarguably the case that more sophisticated analysis is needed here. It is important that scholars of comparative education contribute to such clarification and analysis because in the midst of this rapidly changing scene and despite the substantial implications for comparative education of both globalization and the clash of civilizations thesis, they are yet to figure all that largely in the literature. Approaches that integrate political economy perspectives with education and social theory are more likely to be successful here, particularly if combined with a multilevel approach,[67] which does not merely examine the effects at an international, macro level but also investigates local, small-scale effects.

Equally, and notable exceptions notwithstanding,[68] it can fairly be said that theorizing the implications of the changing role of the state for education, as well as correlative issues such as privatization, has, in the 1980s and 1990s, remained underdeveloped in the literature of comparative education, relative to the collection of case studies that chart the effects of privatization, including (at times) access and equity in education.[69] Some scholars from within (and rather more from without) comparative education have marked the effects of the progressive erosion of the former postwar democratic settlement in advanced capitalist states such as the United Kingdom, Europe, and Australia, including its implications for education.[70] But fewer have located such accounts within the context of a systematic analysis of changes in the form of the state[71] and in international economic patterns and relations (see chapter 10 in this volume). Given the significance of the shift from what has been characterized as the welfare state (in which it was widely accepted that it was the state's responsibility to ensure that good-quality education, health, and welfare were available to all) to what has been termed the competition state (the state intervenes only to heighten national or international economic competitiveness, individual success or failure being an individual or family responsibility),[72] this general omission is somewhat disturbing. Arguably, thoroughgoing analyses of this development have much to offer studies of educational change, not merely in the industrialized West but also in the former socialist nations and in various third world contexts.

From Positivism to Post-ism

Many of the changes described above, however, left major assumptions of modernism largely unchallenged. But if an adherence to many of the principles of positivism characterized much modernist comparative education of the two or three decades after World War II, the gradual growth of poststructuralist thought in the West toward the end of the century gave rise to challenging postmodern critiques in the social sciences and, somewhat later, in comparative education.

What is meant by poststructuralist thought? Briefly, structuralist theories such as (structural) functionalism and the more determinist forms of Marxism emphasized the central explanatory role of structure in determining societal outcomes. The central importance that such theories accorded to the social system meant that individuals were powerless to struggle against a powerful, deterministic set of structures that shaped their social destinies. In a sense, it can be argued that such theories were akin to the religious doctrine of fatalism, which held that people were powerless to struggle against the fate that God had allocated them. Against such views, poststructuralist theories, including those in education, held that social reality was shaped by people and the meanings they variously allocated to the world they inhabited. Social reality was, according to such views, a matter of negotiation. It was not monolithic but was constructed in different ways, according to how people and groups positioned themselves in the world. In principle, such views allocated more space to "agency" (people's ability to act upon the social world to change it) as compared with the more deterministic social theories described above, which emphasized "structure." Poststructuralist theories are quite mistrustful of the pretensions of large-scale "grand theory," which purport to explain how society works overall.

Work by scholars such as Paulston, Coulby, Coulby and Jones, and Cowen[73] has undermined many prior assumptions, such as the objectivity of knowledge or the centrality of scientific methodology, upon which much recent research in comparative education had been predicated. Postcolonialism too has begun to exert an influence, if perhaps more indirectly, and the joint insistence on heterogeneity and mistrust of grand theories informs both, and poststructuralist thought generally: "The post-colonial distrust of the liberal-humanist rhetoric of progress and universalizing master narratives has obvious affinities with post-structuralism."[74] Nonetheless, there are significant differences between postmodernism and postcolonialism, which are explored below.

Postmodern critiques are of relatively recent origin in comparative education, effectively dating from Rust's CIES presidential address of 1991.[75] In itself, this relatively late onset of the debate within comparative education (and indeed the relative lack of engagement since) is interesting, given the potential consonance of the supposed insistence upon heterogeneity by postmodern critics and the supposed centrality of cultural diversity to comparative education. But, as with Winnie the Pooh, all was not necessarily what it seemed.[76] Just as the above argument has proposed that modernism represented, inter alia, the triumph of science over diversity (including cultural diversity), so it will be argued that postmodernism was less about the celebration of difference than was commonly supposed.

This was for two reasons, arguably. One of the original aspirations of postmodernity was to site difference at the center stage of (social) theory in an effort to overcome the universalizing, monolithic tendencies of modernist thought. In itself this was laudable and was potentially a valuable corrective to the closed tendency of modernism to hew out a unilinear path and to dismiss those who diverged from it as aberrant rather than different. As part of this celebration of difference, the aim to give voice to silenced ethnic and gender minorities, for example, was enunciated. Both of these aims were reasonable, given the record of modernism, in particular its intolerance of difference. Regrettably, however, they rapidly became overwhelmed by an increasingly arcane language, in which esoteric terminology and language games/tropes rendered these original intentions largely invisible and unintelligible. In practice, difference, like other social artifacts, became textualized and hence suppressed, buried under an avalanche of recondite discursive devices. It is one thing to underline the importance of language in describing social difference, but quite another to argue that there is nothing beyond language. Postmodernism falls into the latter camp and thus

> operates on an abstract (quasi-systemic) model of "opposition" and "difference" where those terms are deprived of all historical and experiential content, and treated, in effect, as linguistic artefacts, or products of discursive definition.[77]

> There is . . . a danger of textualising gender, denying sexual specificity, or treating difference as merely a formal category rather than having an empirical and historical existence.[78]

In other words, instead of confronting and opposing social distortions and the oppression and marginalization of particular social groups, as certain forms of Marxism and feminism had tried to do, postmodernism increasingly consigned difference to a linguistic artifact, remote from the everyday world and the concerns of those marginal groups they originally claimed to be interested in. Difference became "difference."

Second, postmodernism's celebration of image(s) meant that it came to be increasingly criticized for being more concerned with style rather than substance, with how things looked rather than with their importance or faddishness. Having divested itself of a solid standpoint from which to analyze events, postmodernism was rendered unable to develop a position from which to make ethical judgments. Knowledge is divorced from commitment (the latter of which is reduced to the status of one value, among a potentially limitless number of others), and knowledge and meaning are made devoid of ethics.[79] Thus even if difference is encompassed (and there are considerable doubts about this), there is no longer any basis to judge this difference. As an abstract category without a moral base, the "difference" expressed by white supremacists such as the American Nazi Party is of the same inherent worth as that of the cultures they seek to oppress, such as that of African Americans or Jews. Indeed, in some recent works, the only resort with which to complete the promise of postmodernity has been to connect it to some of the moral stances of feminism and African-American literature, as in the work of Henry Giroux.[80] Some theorists of postmodernism make much of its capacity to map the terrain.[81] By eschewing any moral compass, however, postmodern theories leave us unable to chart the direction.

Vis-à-vis the so-called modernization of third world states, postmodern theories (which resist easy categorization, and of which there are now a considerable variety) appear to offer a substantial critique of the assumptions of functionalist modernization theories, in particular of the supposed correspondence of the modernization process with westernization and the notion that the social and economic progress of third world states depends on advanced science and technology, as well as scientific modes of rationality. Postmodern critiques of the totalizing reason of science or other modes of universalistic reason seem to offer space for alternative views of development and for marginalized groups to position themselves more centrally in development processes. Increasingly, however, the lived reality of oppressed rural peasantry is not seen, except though several layers of arcane and obscure, densely theoretic forms of language that render the experience of those individuals unrecognizable to themselves and invisible to other readers. Not only is the line between people's history and fictional accounts blurred, as Morrow and Torres argue, but the whole notion of domination and hegemony, by which forms of oppression have been identified and opposed, is abandoned. Instead, according to theorists such as John O'Neill and Christopher Norris, people are disattached from their history, floating free in a semiotic world of myriad images and signs. Equity and equality, according to postmodern theories, make up just one set of values, to be placed alongside all other sets of values. They indeed may have less importance than most, given the individualizing tendencies of postmodern theories, which tend to reject acting for the collective good. Ultimately, this offers little by way of substantive critique of the concrete processes of modernity, which often destabilize long-standing cultural traditions (e.g., matriarchy) and oppress less powerful social groups (e.g., small landholders and peasants). A more progressive resolution can be achieved by allying postmodern critiques with forms of feminism and race: "Few theorists of race and gender would succumb to throwing out general theories of domination in the name of a pluralist celebration of difference."[82]

Postmodern or Postcolonial?

As indicated above, postcolonial theories share with postmodern critiques an insistence on the centrality of difference. However, work by scholars such as Homi Bhaba and Tejaswini Niranjana[83] forms some sort of corrective to the moral vacuum at the heart of postmodernity by incorporating the political dimension into their understanding of difference. Central to this work is an opposition to the domination of male, white, heterosexual, and Western forms of reason and to practices associated with this form of logic. Niranjana illustrates this thesis via an extended discourse on the ways in which translation is used as a medium to create an exotic and uncivilized "other" in need of the fruits of Western civilization, including the taming influence of education. In this sense she is an ally of Edward Said, whose analysis of orientalism also showed how the process of translation was deployed in colonies such as India to serve "to gather in, to rope off, to domesticate the Orient and thereby to turn it into a province of European learning."[84]

Comparativists are familiar with the problems of translation. The experience of lawyer-novelist Louis Begley, who encountered some of his own characters in a recent translation (in a language with which he was familiar), strikes a chord:

> Not so long ago, I came across some of my personages in a translation, who were standing on the sidewalk, outside their New York City hotel, in the hope that someone would bring them a lemonade with a great deal of water in it. "How strange," I said to myself, and checked the original, to find out that in English the poor chumps were waiting for their stretch limo.[85]

The confusion of "lemo" for "limo" is one of the less serious problems of translation, which, as Niranjana indicates, can also reveal implicit or explicit strategies of portraying the Other. Indeed, representations of the Other often reveal as much about the interests of the translator as they do about the translated and need to be understood in the context of strategies of intercultural communications[86] and the effects of colonialism and imperialism.[87] An illustration Niranjana provides of the work of eighteenth-century scholar and translator (Sir) William Jones is based not so much on his direct translations of key Indian classics as on his prefaces, speeches, poetry, and the like. Finally, Niranjana distills the most significant elements of Jones work into the following:

1. The need for translation by the European, since the natives are unreliable interpreters of their own laws and culture
2. The desire to be a lawgiver, to give the Indians their "own" laws
3. The desire to "purify" Indian culture and speak on its behalf[88]

In these strategies are revealed key elements of the discourse of colonialism, in which the colonial Other is characterized as a "submissive, indolent nation, unable to appreciate the fruits of freedom, desirous of being ruled by an absolute power . . . (and) incapable of civil liberty."[89] It is but a small step from here to justify the perpetuation of paternalistic forms of administration and governance that serve to speak for the colonial Other and keep them in their place. By recognizing this distortion of power as a key motif of colonialism, postcolonial theories are better placed to oppose such paternalistic and oppressive practices.

History can be a willing teacher—if we are willing to learn. The Enlightenment assisted the replacement of the older Christian religions, based on faith, with the revealed religion of Bacon, Descartes, Galileo, and Newton, based on a blend of empiricism and codified rationality. The priests of old were replaced with the new, and often equally doctrinaire, priesthood of science, thereby failing in many ways to fulfill the promise of the Enlighteners to free humanity from the constraints of a hidebound social order and sclerotic epistemology. Despite its revolutionary potential, science, instead of heralding a new rational order of equality and human rights, was often pressed into service to sustain existing stratified societies, at times providing the basis for making the existing social hierarchy more scientific. Nonetheless, the Enlightenment was the era in which the dignity and rights of man[90] (if not yet entirely of women)[91] were clearly and passionately articulated. Although modernity did not fulfill its early promise, there was much positive potential that was available to be harnessed to the creation of a more just social order.

The contemporary rush by theorists of both left and right to jettison all of the features of modernity shows little appreciation of the complexity of this history and to some extent becomes captive to a somewhat naive understanding of it. The simplistic critiques of the history of epistemology characteristic of much poststructural thought are most clearly evident in the literature of postmodernism. Here modernist thought is often mistakenly oversimplified and demonized as a field littered with grand, broken dreams, which were responsible for much of the problems and misdirections of late twentieth-century humanity. The wholesale retreat from questions of social justice (dismissed as just another such dream) therefore follows quite logically, if mistakenly, from such misconceived assumptions. There is much that may be salvaged from the detritus of modernity, and much from its agenda that needs urgent and powerful rearticulation at the end of the twentieth century, when such economically and socially fissiparous tendencies as neoliberalism, globalization, and xenophobia are widening the already existing gap between rich and poor, white and black, rural and urban, male and female, both within and among nations and regions of the world.[92]

Yet much poststructural thought, in particular postmodernity, leaves us rudderless in a sea of blasé ironic detachment. We drift along as passive observers of the social world, watching the rising tide of imagery but unable to distinguish between images of third world poverty, on the one hand, and the star-studded funeral rites of haute couturiers such as Gianni Versace or Princess Diana, on the other. Images all.

The methodological trajectory I have traced reveals that the preoccupation with making a science of comparative education of the 1960s fulfilled much of its modernist, positivist mandate, despite some oppositional crosscurrents. Although poststructuralist theories were slower to have an influence in comparative education than in other social sciences, the decade leading to the passing of the twentieth century is finally showing some of their effects. However, I have argued that postmodernity is an unsatisfactory response to some of the admitted shortcomings of modernist theories and that postcolonialism is in many respects a more solid starting point for comparative methodology, not just because it sites difference at center stage but also because it rejects speaking for the other. Whether postcolonial theories are the base from which such an ethical stance begins or another standpoint is adopted,[93] a refusal of paternalism and an assumption of mutuality and reciprocity (such as is found in social theorists such as Hans-Georg Gadamer and Jürgen Habermas) is an important starting point for intercultural theories such as comparative education.[94]

Notes

1. Imre Lakatos, "The Methodology of Scientific Research Programmes," in Imre Lakatos, *Philosophical Papers,* vol. 1 (Cambridge: Cambridge University Press, 1974).

2. Nicholas Hans, *Comparative Education: A Study of Factors and Traditions* (London: Routledge and Kegan Paul, 1949).

3. Isaac Kandel, *Studies in Comparative Education* (London: George Harrap 1933); Isaac Kandel, *The New Era in Education* (London: George Harrap, 1955).

4. Friedrich Schneider, *Triebkräfte der Pädagogik der Völker* (Salzburg: Otto Muller, 1947); Schneider, *Vergleichende Erziehungswissenschaft* (Heidelberg: Quelle and Meyer, 1961).

5. See Brian Holmes, *Problems in Education: A Comparative Approach* (London: Routledge, 1965); Holmes, *Comparative Education: Some Considerations of Method* (London: Allen and Unwin, 1981).

6. Harold Noah and Max Eckstein, *Towards a Science of Comparative Education* (London: Macmillan, 1969).

7. George Bereday, *Comparative Method in Education* (New York: Holt, Rinehart, and Winston 1964); George Bereday, "Reflections on Comparative Method in Education 1964–6," in *Scientific Investigations in Comparative Education,* ed. Max Eckstein and Harold Noah (New York: Macmillan 1969).

8. See, inter alia, G. H. von Wright, *Explanation and Understanding* (Ithaca, N.Y.: Cornell University Press, 1971); and Anthony Giddens, "Positivism and Its Critics," in *A History of Sociological Analysis,* ed. Tom Bottomore and Robert Nisbet (London: Heinemann, 1979), 237–286; Jürgen Habermas, "Technology and Science as 'Ideology,'" in *Toward a Rational Society* (London: Heinemann, 1970), 81–122. Despite corrosive criticism, such techniques still flourish, albeit less commonly. For a more egregious example, see George Psacharopoulos, "Comparative Education: From Theory to Practice, or Are You A Neo:/* or B/*ist?" *Comparative Education Review* 34, no. 3 (1990): 369–380. The World Bank's adherence to a technicist and quasi-empiricist, currently based on rate-of-return analyses, is another example: see, inter alia, Phillip Jones, "On World Bank Education Financing," *Comparative Education* 33, no. 1 (1997): 117–129, and his earlier *World Bank Financing of Education* (London: Routledge 1992); Steve Klees, "The World Bank and Educational Policy: Ideological and Inefficient" (paper presented at the Comparative and International Education Society annual conference, Williamsburg, Va., March 1996); and Joel Samoff, "Which Priorities and Strategies for Education?" *International Journal of Educational Development* 16 (1996): 249–271.

9. Robert Cowen, "Last Past the Post: Comparative Education, Modernity and Perhaps Post-modernity," *Comparative Education* 32, no. 2 (1997): 151–170.

10. Jürgen Habermas, *A Theory of Communicative Action* (London: Heinemann, 1984), 147.

11. Herbert Marcuse, *One-Dimensional Man* (New York: Sphere, 1968).

12. See Alfred Schutz, *The Problem of Social Reality,* vol. 1 of *Collected Papers* (The Hague: Martinus Nijhoff, 1964); Alfred Schutz, *The Phenomenology of the Social World* (Evanston, Ill.: Northwestern University Press, 1967); Alfred Schutz, "Commonsense and Scientific Interpretations of Human Action," *Philosophical and Phenomenological Research* 14, no. 3 (1953): 3–47.

13. Max Horkheimer and Theodor Adorno, *The Dialectic of Enlightenment* (New York: Continuum, 1972).

14. Edmund Husserl, *Phenomenology and the Crisis of European Philosophy* (New York: Harper, 1965); Edmund Husserl, *Cartesian Meditations,* trans. D. Cairns (The Hague: Martinus Nijhoff, 1960).

15. Wilhelm Dilthey, *Gesammelte Schriften,* vol. 9, *Pädagogik* (Leipzig: Teubner Verlag, 1934); Wilhelm Dilthey, "Über die Möglichkeit einer allgemeingültigen pädagogischen Wissenschaft," in *Gesammelte Schriften,* vol. 6 (Leipzig: Teubner Verlag, 1926).

16. Thomas Kuhn, *The Structure of Scientific Revolutions* (Chicago: University of Chicago Press, 1970); and Thomas Kuhn, "Reflections upon My Critics," *Criticism and the Growth of Knowledge,* ed. Imre Lakatos and Allan Musgrave (Cambridge: Cambridge University Press, 1974).

17. Paul Feyerabend, *Against Method* (London: New Left Books, 1975); Paul Feyerabend, "On the Critique of Scientific Reason," C. Howson, *Method and Appraisal in the Physical Sciences* (Cambridge: Cambridge University Press, 1976); Paul Feyerabend, *Science in a Free Society* (London: New Left Books, 1978). For a more social scientific view, see also Habermas, "Technology and Science as Ideology," and his later *Knowledge and Human Interests,* 2d ed. (London: Heinemann 1978).

18. Feyerabend, *Science in a Free Society,* 98. "The validity, usefulness, adequacy of popular standards can be tested only by research that violates them" (Feyerabend, *Science in a Free Society,* 35).

19. See, for example, Roger R. Woock, "Integrated Social Theory and Comparative Education," *International Review of Education* 27, no. 4 (1981): 411–426; and Jerome Karabel and A. H. Halsey, "Educational Research: A Review and Interpretation," in *Power and Ideology in Education* (Oxford: Oxford University Press, 1977).

20. Auguste Comte, *The General Philosophy of Auguste Comte,* 2 vols., trans. Harriet Martineau (London: Trübner, 1853); Auguste Comte, *A General View of Positivism,* trans. J. Bridges (Paris: 1848, Academic Reprints, n. d.).

21. Emile Durkheim, *The Rules of Sociological Method* (London: Collier Macmillan, 1964).

22. Talcott Parsons, *The Structure of Social Action* (New York: Free Press, 1949); Talcott Parsons, *The Social System* (Glencoe, Ill.: Free Press, 1951); Talcott Parsons, *Societies: Evolutionary and Comparative Perspectives* (New Jersey: Prentice-Hall, 1966).

23. Giddens, "Positivism."

24. F. Bacon, *Of the Proficience and Advancement of Learning* (London: J. W. Parker, 1861), 14. Note that "maniable" is not used in all editions.

25. Tejaswini Niranjana, *Siting Translation: History, Poststructuralism and the Colonial Context* (Berkeley: University of California Press, 1992), 11.

26. E. Tiryakin, "Emile Durkheim," in *A History of Sociological Analysis,* ed. Tom Bottomore and Robert Nisbet (London: Heinemann, 1979), 188.

27. F. Harbison and C. Myers, *Education, Manpower, and Economic Growth* (London: McGraw-Hill, 1964), 1.

28. Jürgen Habermas, *Knowledge and Human Interests,* 2d ed. (London: Heinemann, 1978), Marcuse, *One-Dimensional Man.*

29. David McClelland, *The Achieving Society* (London: Van Nostrand, 1961), 174.

30. Philip Coombs, *The World Educational Crisis: A Systems Analysis* (Oxford: Oxford University Press, 1968).

31. Harbison and Myers, *Education, Manpower and Economic Growth;* and F. Harbison and C. Myers, *Education and Manpower* (London: McGraw-Hill, 1965).

32. McClelland, *Achieving Society,* 174.

33. Anthony R. Welch, "The Functionalist Tradition in Comparative Education," *Comparative Education* 21, no. 1 (1985): 11.

34. For further detail, see Welch, "The Functionalist Tradition"; and Anthony R. Welch, "La Ciencia Sedante: El Funcionalismo como Base para la Investigación en Educación Comparada," in *Educación Comparada: Teorías, Investigaciones, Perspectivas,* ed. J. Schriewer and F. Pedro (Herder: Barcelona, 1991).

35. Isaac Kandel, *The Making of Nazis* (New York: Teachers College Press, 1935).

36. Brian Holmes, ed., *Educational Policy and the Mission Schools* (London: Routledge, 1967).

37. Holmes, *Problems in Education.*

38. Harold Noah, "Defining Comparative Education: Conceptions," in *Relevant Methods in Comparative Education,* ed. Reginald Edwards, Brian Holmes, and John Van de Graff (Hamburg, UNESCO, 1973), 114.

39. Richard Heyman, "Towards a Non-Science of Comparative Education" (paper presented at the annual conference of the Comparative and International Education Society, Ann Arbor, Mich., March 1979), 1–17.

40. "Every procedure which seems to lock in evidence, thus to claim a level of adequacy, can itself be subjected to the same kind of analysis that will in turn produce yet another indefinite arrangement of new particulars or a rearrangement of established particulars" (Aaron Cicourel, *Cognitive Sociology* [London: Penguin, 1974], 124).

41. Anthony Giddens, *New Rules of Sociological Method* (London: Hutchinson, 1976), 166.

42. Richard Heyman, "Ethnomethodology: Some Suggestions for the Sociology of Education," *Journal of Educational Thought* 14, no. 1 (1980): 46. In the same article Heyman refers to further essentialist claims to provide "knowledge about education" or "what schooling is all about."

43. Anthony Welch, "A Critique of Quotidian Reason in Comparative Education," *Journal of International and Comparative Education* 1 (1986): 37–62.

44. Vandra Masemann, "Critical Ethnography in the Study of Comparative Education," *Comparative Education Review* 26, no. 1 (1982): 1–14; Vandra Masemann, "Ways of Knowing," *Comparative Education Review* 34, no. 4 (1990): 465–473.

45. Masemann, "Critical Ethnography," 1.

46. Vandra Masemann, "Critical Ethnography in the Study of Comparative Education," in *New Approaches to Comparative Education,* ed. Philip Altbach and Gail Kelly (Chicago: University of Chicago Press, 1986), 23.

47. Paul Willis, *Learning to Labor: How Working Class Kids Get Working Class Jobs* (Westmead, U.K.: Saxon House, 1977), 194, cited in Masemann, "Critical Ethnography," 23.

48. Masemann, "Critical Ethnography," 23.

49. Robert Arnove, *Philanthropy and Cultural Imperialism: The Foundations at Home and Abroad* (Bloomington: Indiana University Press, 1980).

50. Martin Carnoy, *Education as Cultural Imperialism* (New York: Longmans 1974); Martin Carnoy, "Education for Alternative Development," in *New Approaches to Comparative Education,* ed. Philip Altbach and Gail Kelly (Chicago: University of Chicago Press, 1986), 73–90.

51. Andre Gunder Frank, "The Development of Underdevelopment," *Dependence and Underdevelopment: Latin America's Political Economy,* ed. James Cockcroft, Andre Gunder Franck, and Dale Johnson (New York: Doubleday/Anchor, 1972), 3–18; Andre Gunder Frank, *Capitalism and Underdevelopment in Latin America* (New York: Monthly Review Press, 1969).

52. Immanuel Wallerstein, *The Modern World System* (New York: Academic Press, 1979).

53. Philip Altbach and Gail Kelly, eds., *Education and Colonialism* (New York: Longmans, 1978); see also the second revised edition, *Education and the Colonial Experience* (New Brunswick: Transaction, 1984). Katherine Jensen wrote the chapter on internal colonialism, "Civilization and Assimilation in the Education of American Indians." The work alluded to earlier was by Harold Wolpe, "The Theory of Internal Colonialism: The South African Case," in *Beyond the Sociology of Development,* ed. I. Oxaal et al. (London: Routledge and Kegan Paul, 1975), 229–252. Theories of internal colonialism have since been used to analyze the education of other indigenous minorities: Anthony Welch, "Aboriginal Education as Internal Colonialism: The Schooling of an Indigenous Minority in Australia," *Comparative Education* 24, no. 2 (1988): 203–217. See also the relevant chapter in Anthony Welch, *Australian Education: Reform or Crisis?* (Sydney: Allen and Unwin, 1996), 24–53.

54. Robert Arnove, "Comparative Education and World Systems Analysis," in *Comparative Education Review* 24, no. 1 (1980): 48–62.

55. Arnove, "Comparative Education," 49.

56. Philip Altbach, "Servitude of the Mind? Education, Dependency, and Neocolonialism," in *Comparative Education,* ed. Philip Altbach, Robert Arnove, and Gail Kelly (New York: Macmillan, 1982).

57. Altbach, "Servitude of the Mind," 470.

58. Robin Burns and Anthony Welch, eds., *Contemporary Perspectives in Comparative Education* (New York: Garland, 1992).

59. See Kenichi Ohmae, *The Borderless World: Power and Strategy in the Interlinked Economy* (London: Fontana 1991); Kenichi Ohmae, *End of the Nation State: The Rise of Regional Economies* (London: HarperCollins, 1995); Roland Robertson, "Mapping the Global Condition: Globalization as a Central Concept," in *Global Culture,* ed. Roland Robertson (London: Sage, 1994), 15–30; Anthony Giddens, *Beyond Left and Right: The Future of Radical Politics* (Oxford: Polity, 1994).

60. Anthony Welch, "Class, Culture, and the State in Comparative Education," *Comparative Education* 29, no. 1 (1993): 7–28.

61. For some examples in higher education, see, inter alia, Anthony Welch and Brian Denman, "The Internationalization of Higher Education: Retrospect and Prospect," *Forum of Education* 1 (1997): 14–29. For more specific analyses of regional educational schemes, see, inter alia, Guy Neave, "The University of the Peoples of Europe: A Feasibility Study," in *The Open Door: Pan-European Academic Co-operation* (Bucharest: UNESCO European Center for Higher Education, 1991), 85–150; Ulrich Teichler, *Experiences of ERASMUS Students, ERASMUS* Monographs, no. 13 (Kassel: Wissenschaftliches Zentrum für Berufs-und Hochschulforschung der Gesamthochschule Kassel, 1992); UNESCO, Asia-Pacific Programme of Education for All (APPEAL) (Bangkok: UNESCO Regional Office for Education in Asia and the Pacific, 1986); International Development Programme for Australian Universities (IDP), *Curriculum Development for Internationalization,* Australian Case Studies and Stocktake (Canberra: IDP, 1995).

62. For the effects on China–Hong Kong relations, see Gerard Postiglione, "The Academic Profession in Hong Kong: Maintaining Global Engagement in the Face of National Integration," *Comparative Education Review* 42, no. 1 (1998): 30–45. For a wider discussion of the phenomenon, see, inter alia, Pasi Rutanen, "Learning Societies and Global Information Infrastructure (GII) Global Information Society (GIS)" (keynote speech delivered at the OECD/IMHE conference, Institutional Strategies for Internationalization of Higher Education, David C. Lam Institute, Hong Kong, December 1996).

63. Robertson, "Mapping the Global Condition," 19.

64. Samuel Huntington, *The Clash of Civilizations and the Remaking of World Order* (New York: Simon and Schuster, 1996).

65. The notion of an uncivilized and monolithic "other" arguably provided the major rationale for the twelfth-century Crusades, for example.

66. Syed Maswood, "The New 'Mother of All Clashes': Samuel Huntington and the Clash of Civilizations," *Asian Studies Review* 18, no. 1 (July 1994): 19.

67. Mark Bray and R. Murray Thomas, "Levels of Comparison in Educational Studies: Different Insights from Different Literatures and the Value of Multilevel Analyses," *Harvard Educational Review* 65, no. 3 (1995): 472–490.

68. Martin Carnoy, *The State and Political Theory* (Princeton: Princeton University Press, 1984); Carlos Alberto Torres and Adrianna Puiggros, "The State and Public Education in Latin America," *Comparative Education Review* 35, no. 1 (1995): 1–27; Robert Arnove, "Neoliberal Education Policies in Latin America: Arguments in Favour and Against," in *Latin American Education,* ed. Carlos Alberto Torres and Adriana Puiggrás (Boulder: Westview, 1997), 79–100; Anthony Welch, "Class, Culture, and the State"; and Anthony Welch, *Australian Education: Reform or Crisis?* (Sydney: Allen and Unwin, 1996). Also published as *Class, Culture, and the State in Australian Education: Reform or Crisis?* (New York: Peter Lang, 1997).

69. Ka-Ho Mok, "Privatization or Marketization: Educational Developments in Post-Mao China," *International Review of Education,* special double issue, "Tradition, Modernity, and Post-modernity in Comparative Education," 43, no. 5–6 (1998): 547–567; Gholam Abbas Tavassoli, K. Houshyar, and Anthony Welch, "The Struggle for Quality and Equality in Iranian Education: Problems, Progress and Prospects," in *Quality and Equality in Third World Education,* ed. Anthony Welch (New York: Garland, 1997)

70. Anna Yeatman, "Corporate Managers and the Shift from the Welfare to the Competition State," *Discourse* 13, no. 2 (1993): 3–9.

71. See P. Cerny, *The Changing Architecture of Politics: Structure, Agency, and the State* (London: Sage 1990); Claus Offe, "Ungovernability: On the Renaissance of Conservative Theories of Crisis," in *Observations on the Spiritual Situation of the Age,* ed. Jürgen Habermas (London: MIT Press, 1984); Claus Offe, "Interdependence, Difference, and Limited State Capacity," in *New Approaches to Welfare Theory,* ed. G. Drover et al. (Aldershot: Edward Elgar, 1993); Jürgen Habermas, *Legitimation Crisis* (Boston: Beacon, 1976); Michael Pusey, *Economic Rationalism in Canberra: A Nation Building State Changes Its Mind* (Cambridge: Cambridge University Press, 1991).

72. Anna Yeatman, *Bureaucrats, Technocrats: Femocrats and Essays on the Contemporary Australian State* (Sydney: Allen and Unwin, 1990); Cerny, *Changing Architecture.*

73. See Rolland Paulston, *Social Cartography: Mapping Social and Educational Change* (New York: Garland, 1966); Rolland Paulston and Martin Liebman, "An Invitation to Postmodern Social Cartography," *Comparative Education Review* 38, no. 2 (1994): 215–252; David Coulby, "Ethnocentricity, Post Modernity, and European Curricular Systems," *European Journal of Teacher Education* 18, nos. 2–3 (1995): 143–153; David Coulby and Crispin Jones, "Post-modernity, Education and European Identities," *Comparative Education* 32, no. 2 (1996): 171–185; and Robert Cowen, "Last Past the Post: Comparative Education, Modernity, and Perhaps Post-modernity," *Comparative Education* 32, no. 2 (1996): 151–170.

74. Niranjana, *Siting Translation,* 9.

75. Val Rust, "Postmodernism and Its Comparative Education Implications," *Comparative Education Review* 35, no. 1 (1991): 610–626.

76. Winnie the Pooh, it will be recalled, lived under the name of Sanders, that is, he had the name Sanders above his door, and he lived under it.

77. Christopher Norris, *The Truth about Postmodernism* (Oxford: Basil Blackwell, 1993).

78. Peter McLaren, "Schooling the Postmodern Body: Critical Pedagogy and the Politics of Enfleshment," in *Postmodernism, Feminism, and Cultural Politics,* ed. Henry Giroux (Albany: State University of New York Press, 1991), 144–173.

79. Norris, *Truth about Postmodernism,* 16–28. See also Ben Agger, *A Critical Theory of Public Life* (London: Falmer, 1991); and Robert Young, "Comparative Education and Post-modern Relativism," *International Review of Education,* special double issue, "Tradition, Modernity, and Post-modernity in Comparative Education," 43, no. 5–6 (1998): 497–505.

80. Giroux, ed., *Postmodernism;* and Henry Giroux, *Border Crossings: Cultural Workers and the Politics of Education* (London: Routledge, 1992).

81. Paulston, *Social Cartography.*

82. R. Morrow and C. A. Torres, *Social Theory and Education: A Critique of Theories of Social and Cultural Reproduction* (Albany: State University of New York Press, 1995), 421.

83. Homi Bhaba, *Nation and Narration* (London: Routledge, 1991); Niranjana, *Siting Translation.*

84. Edward Said, *Orientalism* (New York: Penguin, 1995), 78.

85. Gordon Bilney, "Why Do We Got a Problem with Some Words?" *Sydney Morning Herald,* 24 May 1997, 18.

86. Robert Young, *Intercultural Communication: Pragmatics, Genealogy, Deconstruction* (Clevedon, U.K.: Multilingual Matters, 1996).

87. Edward Said, *Culture and Imperialism* (London: Vantage, 1994).

88. Niranjana, *Siting Translation,* 13.

89. Niranjana, *Siting Translation,* 14.

90. See, for example, Tom Paine, *The Rights of Man* (London: J. S. Jordan, 1791) and also his *Common Sense* (London: H. D. Symonds, 1793), which were influential in eighteenth- and early-nineteenth-century debates in the United States about independence and democracy.

91. Mary Wollstonecraft, *A Vindication of the Rights of Woman* (London: J. M. Dent, 1929).

92. Arnove, "Neoliberal Education Policies"; A. Boron and Carlos Alberto Torres, "Education, Poverty, and Citizenship in Latin America: Poverty and Democracy," *Alberta Journal of Educational Research* 42, no. 2 (1996): 102–114; Anthony Welch, "Introduction: Quality and Equality in Third World Education," in *Quality and Equality in Third World Education,* ed. Anthony Welch (New York: Garland, 1997).

93. Adrian Snodgrass, "Asian Studies and the Fusion of Horizons," *Asian Studies Review* 15 (1992): 81–94; Welch, "Class, Culture, and the State."

94. See, for example, Hugh J. Silverman, ed., *Gadamer and Hermeneutics* (New York: Routledge, Chapman Hall, 1991); and Hans Georg Gadamer, *Truth and Method,* 2d ed. (New York: Crossroad, 1989).

Chapter 2

Institutionalizing International Influence

Joel Samoff

Their mass is truly astounding—thousands of pages, many of them tables, figures, and charts. These externally initiated studies of education in Africa undertaken during the early 1990s are most striking for their similarities, their diversity—of country, of commissioning agency, of specific subject—notwithstanding.[1] With few exceptions, these studies have a common framework, a common approach, and a common methodology. Given their shared starting points, their common findings are not surprising. African education is in crisis. Governments cannot cope. Quality has deteriorated. Funds are misallocated. Management is poor and administration is inefficient. From predominantly Islamic Mauritania in the western Sahara to the mixed cultural, colonial, and political heritage of Mauritius in the Indian Ocean, the recommendations too are similar: Reduce the central government role in providing education. Decentralize. Increase school fees. Expand private schooling. Reduce direct support to students, especially at the tertiary level. Introduce double shifts and multigrade classrooms. Assign high priority to instructional materials. Favor inservice over preservice teacher education. The shared approach of these studies reflects a medical metaphor. Expatriate-led study teams as visiting clinicians diagnose and then prescribe. The patient (i.e., the country) must be encouraged, perhaps pressured, to swallow the bitter medicine.

For the most part, learning disappears from view, buried by the focus on finance. Theory and method, for example, human capital theory and rate of return analysis, are assumed and asserted, not proposed, considered, assessed, defended, and adapted. Nearly all studies lament the gaps and problems in the available education data, yet few collect their own information. Fewer still develop strategies for using reasonably the data that are available.

Education is perhaps the most public of public policies. Yet most of these major studies of education, explicitly commissioned to guide policy decisions, have very limited circulation. Designated "confidential" or "restricted," Africa's education sector studies are generally available only to the commissioning agency and a few government officials. Unpublished, they do not appear in available bibliographies and source lists.

The volume of these studies, their central role in the aid relationship, and thereby their influence on objectives and priorities in African education is the most visible manifestation of the evolution of the international role in education: the institutionalization of international influence. Individually, none of these studies, or perhaps even the aid programs that spawned them, is likely to prove very consequential over the longer term. But as a group, these studies outline and provide insights into changing patterns of international influence in education. In this discussion I trace that evolution briefly, concerned especially with the experiences of the world's poorer countries and particularly those that became independent during the second half of the twentieth century.

Exploring commonalities amid diversity is a powerful tool for exploring both what is—education in different places—and how we know what is—research and the sociology of knowledge. The field of comparative education frets about its central concerns, sometimes focused on what appear to be universal patterns and sometimes oriented toward the unique and exotic. Its enduring challenge is to employ each perspective to illuminate the other.

Global Convergence

Throughout human history societal interactions have involved both borrowing and conquest. Perhaps because educational achievement has often been associated with elite status, the organization and focus of education nearly everywhere in the modern era reflects international influences, some more forceful than others.

Higher education provides one clear example. Instructors regularly employ what they term the Socratic method, more or less accurately seeking to capture the intellectual master-apprentice relationship associated with classical Greece. Students of education in Asia find persisting influences of Confucian patterns and ideas, not only in revolutionary Communist China but in other countries in the region as well. As Altbach points out, universities nearly everywhere are modeled on institutions created in thirteenth-century France.[2] Professor centered and relatively autonomous even when state funded, that model has withstood academic, social, religious, and political challenges in diverse settings. There have, of course, been significant additions to the pattern. As individual institutions became advocates and enforcers of a single truth with universal validity, they came to be called universities. At least since the nineteenth century, notions of nation and nation building have tightened the links between universities and the countries in which they are located and have nurtured the expectation that contributing to national development is one of the responsibilities of higher education institutions. Those responsibilities have come to include research, commonly organized into a set of disciplines that are surprisingly similar across the world. The institutions themselves vary, including a range of more-or-less vocationally oriented postsecondary institutions, many with aspirations to become fully recognized universities. The general point is clear. Notwithstanding diverse roots, different settings, and local variations, the commonalities stand out, from basic features of organization and governance to pedagogy to claims of autonomy and academic freedom. Rather like their predecessors, though now generally detached from religious doctrine, more or less confidently they assert the universality of their ways of knowing—academic standards and scientific methods. Altbach concludes, "Regardless of political system, level of economic development, or educational ideology, the expansion of higher education has been the most important single postwar trend worldwide."[3] We see in this example international influence as imposition and as emulation, with both coercion and rewards.

Colonial rule provided the setting for a particular sort of international influence in education: the implantation of metropolitan education institutions in the colonized world. Emulations, models, replicas, or overseas branches, these institutions often reproduced not only the curriculum, pedagogy, and hierarchial organization of their European models but even their architecture and staff and student codes of conduct. Both the intentions of the colonizers and the aspirations of the colonized elite they socialized insisted that the new education institutions appear to resemble as closely as possible their models. Still, they remained distinctly colonial institutions. Their charge was to equip a segment of the colonized society with the skills needed to administer the colonial enterprise. In practice, they were fully integrated into neither the local society nor the metropolitan education system. Even the special schools that served expatriates and an emerging national elite were generally truncated copies of their metropolitan counterparts.

Both borrowing and imposition have occurred. In the modern era, with few exceptions, the direction of influence is from European core to southern periphery. Institutional arrangements, disciplinary definitions and hierarchies, legitimizing publications, and instructional authority reside in that core, which periodically incorporates students and professors from the periphery, of whom many never return home. There are, to be sure, challenges to this dominance. The end of the twentieth century finds Japan a strong claimant to core status, with a widely respected university system. Several middle-tier, rapidly industrializing countries have invested heavily in higher education, developing recognized centers of research and innovation. Occasionally an academic debate initiated in the periphery (e.g., dependency in Latin American, oral history in Tanzania) becomes a critical concern for core institutions, perhaps supporting the view that the weakest links of the global system are those at the periphery.[4] Intellectual challenges rooted in the core regularly include advocates from outside the core.[5]

Twentieth-Century Education Reform

In many respects, the twentieth century has been a period of education reform initiatives with roots in several different national settings. Early in the century U.S. education reformers sought to link schools more closely with their communities and to reinforce the organic connections among learning, schooling, and work. The Bolshevik Revolution provided an opening for rethinking the role of education, though in practice Soviet educators drew heavily on the thinking of the U.S. education reformers as they emphasized technical education and sought to link schooling even more closely to employment needs and opportunities.[6] The decolonization era following World War II saw experiment and ferment in education. For the newly decolonized countries of Africa and southern Asia, the transfer of sovereignty offered the hope and possibility of charting new directions. For parts of Latin America and China, regime transitions provided space for education innovators. The competition of capitalism and socialism, especially the efforts of the United States and the Soviet Union to extend their influence in the southern hemisphere, created maneuvering room for experimentation. At the same time, the widespread student and worker militancy of May 1968 highlighted a parallel upheaval in the North Atlantic. Students asserted their political role, condemning their education and the societies whose expectations and values it transmitted. Although the national mobilizations generally fell short of their political objectives, education itself became both the focus of intense reform efforts and the vehicle for broader challenges to the political order. This trajectory is especially clear in South Africa in the mid-1970s. Students protesting an education issue—the government's decision to require instruction in Afrikaans—quickly escalated their challenge to focus on disadvantaged education and the entire structure of white rule.

Similarities

Still, it is the similarities across national settings that have most intrigued scholars of comparative education. Especially striking has been the relatively rapid movement in most countries from education as the privilege of a small elite to mass education as a responsibility of the state. Many analysts have sought explanations for that transition within particular societies. In specific settings scholars have attributed the national decision to develop mass education to the importance of schools as mechanisms of social control, to the role of education as a desired good able to win public support in the conflict among competing interest groups and political coalitions, to schooling as a common experience essential to developing social solidarity and national identity, to the perceived need to prepare the labor force for industrial society, and to the belief that education promotes national development. Other scholars have sought to elucidate the theories of the state embedded in national philosophies of education[7] and to understand education in terms of the national and global political economy.[8] Refining their earlier argument about the correspondence between state and school, Bowles and Gintis argue that education necessarily reflects, and simultaneously is in tension with, the structure of the national political economy.[9]

Challenging that national orientation, Boli and Ramirez interpret the rapid implementation of compulsory schooling in diverse societies as the global consequence of a distinctly Western set of values and cultural practices.[10] In their view the nineteenth century produced revised understandings of the individual, the state, and social organization, which in turn required the transition from elite to mass education. Drawing on notions of modernization[11] and world system,[12] they argue that the widespread adoption of mass education reflected a global diffusion of Western cultural values, including a focus on an improved material standard of living, a sense of the individual as the fundamental social unit and the ultimate source of value and authority, and an expanded state responsible for social welfare.

Other authors focused on the agency of that diffusion in the postcolonial era. Arnove and Berman explored the critical roles of national commissions of inquiry and philanthropic foundations in specifying the organization of the social sciences, that is, the acceptable procedures for studying society.[13] Westernization did not mark inexorable and inevitable progress toward a universal modernity but rather reflected a conscious process of creating and shaping institutions. Born in the changing organization of production and accompanied by the expansion of monotheistic religions and the creation of the nation-state, the development of capitalist hegemony was not a conscious design in the manner of the construction of precapitalist empires. Rather, it occurred through the actions of particular individuals and institutions. Education was both cause and consequence.

My concern here is to build on this foundation, maintaining the notion that deeper structural relationships and pressures operate through and are thus visible in specific institutional arrangements. Within that context, I explore education and development in terms of the conjunction of international organizations, increased dependence on aid, and the development of a particular role for research.

Context

By the late twentieth century, development and aid had become inextricably linked. Modernization provided the theoretical underpinnings, interpreting human progress as more or less linear progression always characterized by a fundamental distinction between the more and the less modern.[14] Colonial rule crystallized the we/they, modern/primitive categorization and reached to notions of social obligation (colloquially, the "white man's burden") to justify the often harsh imposition of European rule and rules. Following World War II, the new United Nations system incorporated the idea of trusteeship even as it became an arena for challenging and terminating colonial rule. At the same time, the link between development and aid was formally institutionalized in the creation of the International Bank for Reconstruction and Development. Charged with supporting the rebuilding of Europe, generally in alliance with the International Monetary Fund, another institution responsible for facilitating orderly international exchange, the World Bank dispensed both funds and advice.

Education was no exception. If education was associated with economic progress, then surely it had to be a prominent component of development aid. As a large number of former colonies became independent, many of them very poor and with little investment or infrastructure to support autonomous development, it became commonplace that improving education required foreign assistance. After an initial period of high expectations and apparently rapid progress, education in poorer countries became a story of decay, crisis, and dependence instead of development and independence. Indeed, as the century ends, there is a cry for the return of colonial rule—"some states are not yet fit to govern themselves"—a proposal that might be regarded as outrageous but in fact seems sufficiently legitimate to feature in prominent publications.[15]

This, then, is the context for the discussion that follows: education, aid, the funding and technical assistance agencies that manage the aid relationship, and the scholars and scholarship that have become essential to its operations and legitimacy. First, however, it is important to elaborate that context briefly, beginning with its politics and transformations in the organizations of the international system.

Socialist Disarray and U.S. Triumphalism

Not so long ago, "alternative strategies of development" featured prominently in university course catalogues and internationalist bookshops. No longer. That notion of alternative approaches and the scholars who employ it have become anachronisms, heirlooms that may be interesting but no longer have any great utility.

The precipitous dissolution of communist rule is interpreted as the inevitable victory of the United States over the Soviet Union, capitalism over socialism, the market over planning, indeed, good over evil. Capitalism prevailed because it is inherently better. What better proof could there be than its unequivocal victory? Everything that can be linked to socialism, however tenuous the link, is clearly flawed, precisely because of that link.

The arrogance of U.S. triumphalism is palpable and unceasing:

We're the only country complicated enough, sophisticated enough, big enough to lead the human race.[16]

There is a grand—and instructive—irony in a triumphalism that is politically and ideologically centered in the United States. As Przeworski puts it,

Neoliberal ideology, emanating from the United States and various multinational agencies, claims that the choice is obvious: there is only one path to development, and it must be followed. . . . Yet if a Martian were asked to pick the most efficient and humane economic systems on earth, it would certainly not choose the countries that rely most on markets. The United States is a stagnant economy in which real wages have been constant for more than a decade and the real income of the poorer 40 percent of the population has declined. It is an inhumane society in which 11.5 percent of the population—some 28 million people, including 20 percent of the children—lives in poverty. It is the oldest democracy on earth, but has one of the lowest voter-participation rates in the democratic world, and the highest per capita prison population in the world.[17]

Where socialism can provide neither useful ideas nor instructive experiences and where only one strategy of development is worth considering, the lessons are clear. Third World poverty is a Third World phenomenon. Where poverty is the result of poor policies, policy reform—structural adjustment—is the essential remedy. The prescription follows from the diagnosis: "getting macroeconomic policies right" (especially reducing budget deficits, increasing tax revenues, eliminating barriers to international exchange); "taxing agriculture less"; "putting exporters first"; ("rationalizing import barriers," "privatizing public enterprises," and "financial reform" (especially "reducing financial repression, restoring bank solvency, and improving financial infrastructure").[18]

This triumphalism has (at least) two powerful consequences for the relationship between aid and policy making. Those who have triumphed need no longer listen. Since they know what is right and since it is their power (rather than negotiation) that secures their interests, they can instruct rather than learn. As well, since the triumph, they believe, proves the correctness of their perspective, they need not feel reticent or guilty about telling others what to do.

Like its 1960s incarnation, late twentieth-century developmentalism takes the global political economy as given, rather like a complex weather pattern. Africans cannot change the intertropical convergence zone that dominates much of the continent's weather. Monsoon rains and droughts are simply beyond their control. So the world system—imposing, inexorable, and largely out of reach. That understanding itself fosters impotence. Consciously and forcefully, late twentieth-century developmentalism directs attention away from efforts to conceive of the world system as a web of nation-states and corporations linked in complex but understandable and modifiable ways. Countries and companies, after all, are organized and managed by people and can be changed by people, sometimes even the lowest-level laborers and poorest citizens. At issue here is not a contest between external/foreign and internal/national explanations for the Third World's problems. Rather, it is the internalization within the Third World of the relationships and understandings of that larger environment, the internationalization even of ways of knowing, that has largely been excluded from the analytic and policy agendas.

Resuscitation of Modernization

This late twentieth-century developmentalism also reflects the resuscitation of modernization theory, which insists now, as it did a half century ago, that the causes of the Third World's problems are to be found within the Third World: its people, resources, capital, skills, psychological orientation, child-rearing practices, and more. That analytic framework is seductive and often is assumed uncritically. Just as poverty is to be explained by the characteristics and (in)abilities of the poor, so the explanations of problems of Third World education are to be found within and around Third World schools. Institutionalized in the centers of financial, industrial, and academic authority, this fundamental misunderstanding is sheltered from the challenge that the primary sources of contemporary problems are to be found in the process by which most Third World countries have been incorporated into the global economy. The international relationships are acknowledged and are at the same time treated as part of the policy environment. They are the furniture, the paint on the walls, the air in the room—a part of the setting and thereby not a principal concern for policy attention. As normal and largely unexceptional features of the structure of international interactions, those relationships are assigned a low priority in the search for explanations and strategies for change. In this way what may matter most warrants little explicit attention. The explanatory framework and research agenda that dominate the aid relationship largely exclude from active consideration the analytic perspective that emphasizes global integration. The powerful critique developed by the dependency and world-systems literature—that explaining poverty in the contemporary Third World requires attention to the role of particular countries in a world system and the institutionalization of those global connections within those countries—is widely noted and, except in its broadest sweep and most superficial form, commonly ignored. The international order is a given, a background condition. To take as given what are potentially primary causes is to exclude them from the policy (and research) discourse. What is unseen and undiscussed will surely not be the focus of policy attention or public action.

Changing Roles in the United Nations System

Especially striking has been the reorientation of roles and responsibilities among the organizations of the United Nations system. In its 1980 Education Sector Policy Paper, the World Bank highlighted the role of UNESCO (United Nations Educational, Scientific, and Cultural Organization) as the international education technical assistance agency, crediting it for what has become the World Bank's holy grail, the focus on primary education.[19] By 1995, the World Bank's most recent major education sector overview barely mentions UNESCO and certainly does not indicate that it or anyone else will rely on UNESCO for technical assistance and expertise in education, science, and culture, a reflection of changed roles in the international system.[20] In the post-World War II mood of reconstruction, education was understood as the principal vehicle for remaking the world. Capitalists and socialists agreed. Education had to be central to rebuilding and social transformation, whether in the countries shattered by war, in those recently decolonized, or in countries in which socialism was to become the ideal to be achieved and the engine of development. In many minds, there really was no alternative. Education was an essential antidote to the horrors of the experiences of the recent past, the Holocaust, trench warfare, and nuclear devastation. In hindsight, the optimism was nearly unbounded.

In that understanding, countries were policy-making domains and educators were to be the critical education policy makers. The newly fashioned international system had a distinctly developmental thrust. International economic organizations were to stabilize currency flows (and thus both international trade and national growth) and to support the reconstruction and development of Europe. Special U.N. councils were charged with economic and social development and with overseeing what were clearly the final days of the colonial system. For education, science, and culture, UNESCO was to provide technical expertise and assistance. It was structured to be responsive to its member states, less constrained by the major power vetoes of the Security Council and the rich country dominance of the financial organizations.

Whereas thirty years ago it was powerful nations that sought to impose the will of the international system on former colonies, by the 1990s the international financial institutions had become the principal enforcers of global dictates. Surprisingly rapidly, structural adjustment became both the description and the content of the imposition of that external control. Effectively, structural adjustment offered access to capital in exchange for the adoption of externally specified national policies and the surrender of some national autonomy. Although the specific mix of policies termed structural adjustment varied from one setting to another, the general strategy was similar across diverse countries. Special foreign aid not linked to specific projects and increased foreign assistance in general became available, on the condition that the recipi-

ent government adopt a series of economic policies (often termed liberalization!). Commonly those policies emphasized substantial devaluation, decreased direct government role in the economy, especially in productive activities, reduction in the size of the civil service, encouragement of foreign
investment, and support for privatization of many activities, including public
services. Nearly everywhere the implementation of these policies meant new
or increased fees for social services (e.g., medical treatment) and increased
prices for consumer goods (often through the elimination of subsidies for staples). For impoverished countries and dysfunctional economies, structural adjustment was stick as well as carrot.

Although their rhetoric seemed to call for a sharply curtailed role for the state
in all spheres, structural adjustment programs in fact required a state sufficiently strong to implement highly unpopular measures, especially austerity
and reduced price supports for basic food and other staples. Conditionalities—
providing debt relief, currency support, and aid only when explicit conditions
were met—meant that their own governments assumed major responsibility for
the dependent integration of poor countries into the global political economy.
"Effective governance" became the preferred terminology, with emphasis on
administration, management, and appropriate technology. Wearing the cloak of
science and resting on the staff of research, this orientation dismissed alternative perspectives as political and nonscientific, especially those that emphasized raised consciousness of inequality and exploitation, mass mobilization,
and citizen participation.

In that context international financial institutions increasingly characterized
themselves as development advisory services. To some extent, funds provided
earlier to the more affluent countries of the North had always been accompanied by advice. By the 1990s, however, they were increasingly seeking to play
that role for the poor countries of South. In the process, funding organizations,
especially but not only the World Bank, effectively eclipsed technical assistance institutions like UNESCO. Reviewing the evolution of UNESCO is beyond the scope of this discussion. It is important to note, however, that the U.N.
organization institutionally most directly responsive to the majority of its
members (no major power veto, no votes weighted by affluence) has come to
be regarded by much of the world as less able to provide effective education
advisory services than the World Bank.

The institutionalization of this relationship, and particularly of the World
Bank's role, takes several forms, in part because there is a fundamental tension between international control and national implementation. Having analyzed the problems and prescribed the solutions, the international agencies
commonly assume they must direct events. At the same time, education reform
is the responsibility of national authorities. Where they perceive the agenda to
be imposed and perhaps inimical to their interests, national leaders are unlikely to pursue energetically the prescribed reforms. For the international

agencies, the challenge in this setting is to find strategies for exercising influence while encouraging national commitment to and implementation of the recommended reform strategy.

A major international conference, little known outside the circle of those most directly involved in Third World education but likely to be a point of reference, and perhaps legitimacy, for many years to come, was one response to that challenge. With appropriate substance and ceremony a distinguished group of educators and political leaders met in Jomtien, Thailand, in March 1990 to declare their support for making education available to everyone on the planet. Initiated and guided by the World Bank, the World Conference on Education for All had several formal sponsors: United Nations Development Programme (UNDP), United Nations Educational, Scientific and Cultural Organization (UNESCO), United Nations Children's Fund (UNICEF), and the World Bank. Amid formal ceremonies, official statements, and research reports, some 1,500 participants from 155 governments, 20 intergovernmental bodies, and 150 nongovernmental organizations adopted by acclamation "A World Declaration on Education for All" and "A Framework for Action." Other resolutions adopted by acclamation reflected the conference title. All people must have access to basic education, both because (basic) education should now be considered a right of citizenship and because development, however conceived, requires an educated populace. A series of follow-up conferences and monitoring agencies are intended to support continued progress toward universal access to basic education. It is far from clear, however, that this conference has in fact changed much behavior. Countries already committed to basic education have continued to support it. Others have neither increased their allocations to education nor transferred funding within education from other levels to basic education. Similarly, those funding agencies that already had major basic education support programs have continued them. The programs of others reflect different priorities. There is little evidence of the massive increase in global aid estimated to be necessary to achieve education for all.[21] Here, then, is a major initiative to institutionalize international influence. Rhetoric of collaboration and partnership notwithstanding, the agenda was largely that of the World Bank and other agencies. They sought to use this mechanism to persuade reluctant governments to reorder their priorities toward basic education. In a few settings, the conference and surrounding activities provided additional maneuvering room and perhaps leverage to education advocates. Elsewhere, beyond a tacit acquiescence in the World Bank's authoritative leadership, little changed. Indeed, some countries charged that the preference for basic education was intended to undermine support for higher education and thereby confine poor countries in their poverty. Without the development of advanced skills and research capacity, poor countries are relegated to the intellectual periphery, perpetually dependent on ideas and technologies (and, more importantly, ways of understanding) developed elsewhere. Impoverishing universities, the principal institutions for educating teachers and teacher educators, eventually undermines even the commitment to basic education.

At about the same time, the World Bank sought to institutionalize its leadership position among the funding and technical assistance agencies with support programs in Africa. The World Bank also supported the creation of Donors to African Education (DAE). Committed to promoting cooperation and coordination among the agencies and between the agencies and African education ministries, DAE became the umbrella for a series of working groups, each focused on a particular education level or problem and each led by one of the funding and technical assistance agencies. Several of the other aid agencies with major Africa support programs did agree for a time to follow the World Bank's lead, though others dragged their feet. To assure both impact and legitimacy, this initiative also required committed African participation in the form of explicit collaboration with African education ministers. Over time, that may transform the organization. By the mid-1990s, its leadership and secretariat had moved out of the World Bank and the African education ministers had begun to play a more energetic and influential role. A name change, the Association for the Development of Education in Africa (ADEA), reflected efforts to redefine coordination and partnership.

Two observations are appropriate here. First, these two initiatives employed the language of collaboration and joint effort as they created an institutional apparatus for the leading role of international organizations, especially the World Bank. In practice, both reinforced particular understandings about education and development (e.g., that spending on basic education is a very sound and very high priority investment in national development) and thus institutionalized influence by making it unexceptional. Conventional wisdom on analyzing and understanding education came to reflect the perspectives of economists and bankers. That education ought to be considered an investment and that education funding should be analyzed with the tools used to assess investments in other settings become commonplace, framework assumptions that were hardly noticed. Thus what otherwise might seem to be controversial issues that warrant extended discussion escape critical attention. Major assumptions that might be sharply contested if highlighted are embedded in the ostensibly uncontroversial tools. The active debates focus on which investment yields a higher return rather than on the utility of the investment metaphor as an analytic construct for understanding education.

Second, both initiatives reflect the nature of education as contested terrain. Influence is not unchallenged control. In some circumstances, institutions created for one purpose can be redirected toward another. Although the patterns of power and dominance are clear, it would be incorrect to presume that influence moves in only one direction or to ignore the ways in which the ostensible victims of the global system in fact assert initiatives and influence courses of action.

Organizations of Several Sorts

The discussion thus far has been concerned primarily with the ways in which the international system interacts with national governments that are responsible for education throughout the world. Since what I have termed loosely the international system has several components, all with their own interests, forms, and strategies, a brief categorization is useful.

Some organizations are juridically international, especially those that constitute the United Nations system, for example, UNESCO, UNICEF, UNDP, and the World Bank. Commonly the members of those organizations are countries, though there are important variations. Membership in the International Labor Organization, for example, includes countries, unions, and employers' groups. Governance rules also vary. Majority rule in the United Nations General Assembly is constrained by the veto power of the permanent members of the Security Council. Although UNESCO decisions are taken by majority rule, voting in the World Bank is proportional to the member countries' level of investment. Often these organizations are termed "multilaterals" to reflect their multinational composition and relationships.

Occasionally and somewhat misleadingly termed "bilateral" to distinguish them from the "multilaterals," some organizations are distinctly national, for example, the U.S. Agency for International Development and the Canadian International Development Agency. Often formally located within the foreign ministry, these organizations were created to serve national interests, including the provision of financial and technical assistance overseas. Even those that most energetically assert their role in providing development aid must defend their programs and budgets in terms of their contribution to the national economy and polity.

The term "nongovernmental organization" has come to refer to a very wide range of groups, including some that operate within countries or even small local areas, others that are national in origin and operate international programs, and still others that have an international constitution. Some nongovernmental organizations depend so heavily on contracts with national governments and international organizations that functionally they might reasonably be regarded as quasi-governmental organizations.

International and national agencies have initiated and supported continental, regional, national, and local organizations that assume particular education responsibilities. The World Bank, for example, has spawned the Capacity Building Foundation and the African Economic Research Consortium. Organizations of that sort may reflect a conflicted identity. Born with the values, orientations, and objectives of their parent or foster agencies, they also seek to establish their own independent existence and legitimacy.

The grid of internationally active education organizations and their affiliates is dense, many with overlapping memberships. Efforts of education researchers to establish enduring links with their colleagues and strengthen their voices through cooperative and collective action have resulted in the creation of several regional networks, including those that group scholars in Latin America, eastern and southern Africa, western and central Africa, and Southeast Asia, as well as education researchers in the industrialized north concerned with education, aid, and development.[22] Often still dependent on external funding and constituted by scholars themselves dependent on contracts with external agencies, those networks find it difficult to assert an effective autonomous voice and play a strong independent role.

Calls in many countries for global education standards have spawned a series of cross-national efforts to measure achievement in several subjects at different levels. Although they claim sensitivity to the unique characteristics of specific national and local settings, by design those assessments seek to use and thereby institutionalize internationally particular assumptions about both the content and the process of learning and teaching. The results of the assessment measures may contribute to improving the quality of education in some settings, but their more powerful role is to reject the education philosophy that associates effective learning with education objectives and measures that are debated and decided locally.

Education strategies that are regarded as effective in one country have provided models for initiatives elsewhere. Folk high schools in the Nordic countries, for example, have inspired Folk Development Colleges in Tanzania and parallel initiatives elsewhere. Southern African education activists seeking to link education and training and to provide learning opportunities for out-of-school youth and unschooled adults have drawn on national qualifications frameworks developed in Australia and New Zealand.

Churches and other religious groups are generally also termed nongovernmental organizations. Several have a long history of involvement in education, maintain extensive education departments and programs, and support an education agenda that is sometimes more, sometimes less closely related to religious doctrine and proselytization.

Several philanthropic foundations, most but not all with headquarters in the United States, have also played important roles in education and development. As I have already noted, the Carnegie, Ford, and Rockefeller Foundations have all explicitly sought to influence the development of the social sciences at home and abroad. Among the non-U.S. foundations with education activities in the Third World are the Gulbenkian Foundation and the Aga Khan Foundation.

Increasingly, international academic organizations have sought to influence the development of their disciplines globally. As the International Political Science Association, for example, functions to propagate the fundamental assumptions and orientations of the U.S. political science mainstream, it plays a role in promoting a global convergence of understandings and ways of knowing. Similarly, a small set of internationally recognized journals in each discipline functions to impose standards and set the terms through which Third World scholars must establish their legitimacy.[23]

Aid Dependence

How do external events and forces influence what happens within particular countries? Pulled by popular demand and pushed by the need for highly educated and skilled personnel, education can quickly become an insatiable demand for resources. Especially as economic crises succeeded earlier developmental optimism and structural adjustment replaced rapid development as the realistic short-term objective in Third World countries, there was strong pressure to assign the highest priority for available funds to directly productive activities, which often did not include education. How then to educate the teachers, develop new textbooks, or equip the science laboratories? Or more commonly, how to fix the leaking roof? The common recourse was to external funding. For many (though of course not all) Third World countries the external provision of assistance funds has become the center of gravity for education and development initiatives. Over time, it has come to seem not only obvious but unexceptional that new initiatives and reform programs require external support, and therefore responsiveness to the agenda and preferences of the funding agencies.

Although foreign aid to Third World education is substantial, its influence often far exceeds its volume. Since its first education loan in 1963, World Bank has increased its education funding significantly, tripling in volume between 1980 and 1995 and doubling its share in total World Bank lending. By 1990 the World Bank's allocation of nearly US$1.5 billion made it the largest single source of external financing for education in developing countries.[24] That large share, however, amounted to less than .5 percent of total spending on education in developing countries. Accordingly, the World Bank insists that its "main contribution must be advice, designed to help governments develop education policies suitable for the circumstances of their countries. Bank financing will generally be directed to policy change."[25]

Economic crisis and structural adjustment affect resources and how they are used. Commonly, the response to both resources and their use has focused primarily on reducing government expenditures. Sometimes the press of circumstances makes it possible to overcome entrenched resistance to cutting spending and reallocating resources in ways that contribute to the general health of the economy and the well-being of the populace. Often, however, the focus on spending less, ostensibly to use resources more efficiently, effectively, and equitably, becomes an end in itself. When it does so, the campaign to cut often obscures important objectives and rearranges priorities.

Most studies of the impact of crisis and adjustment have been concerned primarily with reduced public spending on education. Perhaps even more important, however, are rather less visible but more enduring influences on both the national education agenda and how it is set.

As the reliance on foreign funds increases, so does the influence of both the finance ministry and the external agencies. Representing the government in negotiations with those agencies, the finance ministry tends to become much more directly involved in policy and programmatic details across all government departments. That increased role may well suit the external agencies. Especially concerned with reducing government spending, those agencies are likely to see the finance ministry as their ally, in contrast with ministries of, say, health or education, whose general mandate requires them to be more concerned with spending than with saving. The alliance between external agency and finance (and perhaps planning) ministry may be structured as a powerful lever for influencing national policy.

Dependence on (rather than simply use of) external funds leads to both explicit conditions imposed by the funding organizations and more subtle influences. Sometimes that relationship is aggressively manipulative. The funding agency may condition the provision of support on the adoption of specific policies, priorities, or programs. Support for vocational schools, for example, may be contingent on the implementation of a strategy designed to increase female enrollment in the technical curriculum. Occasionally influence flows in the other direction. To secure resources for a preferred program, the national leadership may mobilize support and bring pressure to bear on the funding agency in its home. For example, where the goal is to acquire microcomputers, the national leadership may communicate directly with individuals and organizations in the prospective funding agency's home country who are energetic advocates of the instructional use of microcomputers.

At other times that relationship is less directly influential. The funding agency may, for example, finance research intended to support its preferred programmatic orientation. Or Third World educators may tailor their requests, more or less explicitly, to fit within the funding agency's agenda. In their planning discussions, for example, they may begin by exploring the funding agency's current high priority goals and then consider how to develop a request for assistance congruent with that priority. Occasionally the paths of influence are far more circuitous. A desire to win support for a high priority goal in one project may promote a willingness to accommodate a low priority goal in another.

Case studies of national responses to economic crisis indicate both the forms of aid dependence and differences among countries. Heavily dependent on foreign assistance, Sénégal and Tanzania have repeatedly modified education and training policies and programs in ways that reflected the priorities and preferences of the funding agencies.[26] By the end of the 1980s, for example, the planning director in Tanzania's education ministry characterized his work as "marketing."[27] His task, he said, was to advertise and market broad ideas and specific projects in the hope of finding a sponsor—an external assistance agency—to fund them. Over time priorities were set less by government and party leaders and more by what foreign governments and their aid organizations were willing to finance. The power brokers in education had once been those who could put together coalitions of people influential in Tanzania's public and private life. By the late 1980s they had become those who were most successful in securing foreign funding, those who seemed to have the most reliable access to embassies in Dar es Salaam and institutional headquarters in London, Washington, Stockholm, Paris, and elsewhere.[28]

Marketing may be a reasonable, as well as reasonably successful, coping strategy in an adverse setting. It may provide a vehicle for securing additional resources in times of economic distress. It may even permit national elites and their foreign partners to put off yet a bit longer confronting major problems and undertaking serious economic, political, and social transformation. At the same time, when marketing is the prevailing orientation, innovation is limited to whatever the funders are willing to finance.

As countries have become more dependent on external funding to support new projects and even recurrent expenditures, planning has acquired an increasingly external focus. Economic and financial crises energize the search for additional revenue sources. As manufacturers look for new customers, educators seek benefactors. Providing education assistance has become a big business.

National patterns of course vary. Aid dependence does not always secure compliance with the recommendations and expectations of the international financial institutions. "A small country has no choice." Asked why his relatively affluent Third World country had accepted the conditions attached to foreign assistance, the former Costa Rican president insisted he had no alternative.[29] Already deeply in debt, economically dependent on export sales to the countries that control most of its external aid, resisting with difficulty entanglement in efforts to overthrow a neighbor government, Costa Rica acquiesced to pressures to adopt structural adjustment policies and maintained that orientation through governments led by different political parties. What else could this small country do, its leaders argued. In practice, however, Costa Rica not only secured massive external assistance but also managed to maintain a good deal of its own agenda, protecting many of the social services—including education and training—targeted for reduction. A combination of its regional role, its history of stable democratic government and limited civil strife, its economic base and relative affluence, and the broad legitimacy of its national political system enabled Costa Rica to retain a good deal of policy autonomy even as it acceded to externally imposed conditions. Another example of local resistance and ability to retain control over local decisions were the teachers unions and militant student organizations who became allies to block the implementation of staff reductions and other austerity measures in Sénégal's structural adjustment program.[30]

Consequences

The exceptional assertions of national autonomy should not lead us to under-estimate the extent and durability of external influence on education policy and practice in the Third World. By the end of the 1980s, the collapse of the Soviet Union, U.S. triumphalism, and the reorganization of the system of international organizations provided the setting for the institutionalization of international influence on education, in large part in the form of aid conditions, with the World Bank as the advisory, oversight, and sometimes managing agency. In that process, education comes to be regarded as an investment and a manufac-turing process, with significantly decreased attention to learning as a process and to the other social and political goals generally expected of education sys-tems (equality, equity, national unity, citizenship). Expanded attention to in-ternational comparisons based on rather narrowly drawn measures of education results may presage efforts to institutionalize international standards for edu-cation, especially as a parallel trend in the most decentralized education sys-tem, the U.S. system, is articulated by the national leadership.

Education as Investment

Amid alternative perspectives on education, those of economics and finance have come to dominate the discourse on education and development. For the World Bank, the starting point is human capital theory: Education ought to be regarded as an investment in developing a country's human resources. In its 1995 education policy review the assertion of its superiority is unqualified: "Human capital theory has no genuine rival of equal breadth and rigor."[31] The East Asian[32] experience proves the value of investing in education, the World Bank argues, since it is precisely that investment that differentiates the suc-cesses from the failures. Within this framework, the primary mechanism for choosing among alternative patterns of investment is rate of return analysis.

Far from universally accepted, both human capital theory and rate of return analysis are intensely debated. Other funding agencies and the World Bank's own staff are among the critics:

> Traditional cost-benefit studies of education have tended to indicate the advan-tages of investment in education at various different levels, based on analyses of the social return which each produces. Recent studies have shown this method to be both fallacious and limiting.[33]

Much of the concern with education as an investment self-consciously ignores the process of education. Adopting an economic systems approach, it focuses on inputs and outputs, leaving inside the opaque black box most of what those involved in education do every day. In education, however, process is itself an output.

Schools select and socialize. For both society and individuals, schooling frequently matters more than learning. Although specific circumstances vary, the education system everywhere is central to constructing and maintaining a particular sort of social order. Often it is equally central to challenging and transforming it. To ignore the ways in which curriculum entrenches and legitimizes inequality, examinations reinforce and justify patterns of social stratification, or textbooks privilege some perspectives over others is to render meaningless findings about the number of graduates and their subject specializations. Limiting the specification to the relative values of alternative inputs and outputs permits developing a linear analysis and proposing global solutions. But in practice, education is interactive, replete with discontinuities, and always locally contingent. Even bankers and their economic advisers cannot develop feasible priorities and strategies for education by ignoring societal objectives and the learning process, however disorderly, partially understood, and contested they may be.

A second consequence of treating education primarily as a social investment is a disjunction between the issues deemed most important and the objectives articulated by Third World governments and educators. The mass of studies and recommendations that emanate from the funding agencies reflect little or no attention, for example, to fostering an inquiring and critical orientation among learners, eliminating discrimination and reducing elitism, promoting national unity, preparing young people for the rights and obligations of citizenship, equipping them to work cooperatively and resolve conflicts nonviolently, or developing among learners a strong sense of individual and collective competence, self-reliance, and self-confidence. Yet these objectives have featured prominently in statements of Third World leaders and ministers of education over the past three decades. These objectives are of course more difficult to quantify and measure than, say, building classrooms or increasing the availability of instructional materials. How can we know if a particular instructional program has reduced racial or gender discrimination? How can we determine whether or not conflict resolution skills have improved or ethnic favoritism has declined? Whatever increased tolerance and mutual respect schooling can foster may be overwhelmed by divisive powerful social forces. It is certainly difficult to be confident about what role education has played in pursuing these broader societal objectives. But if we do not ask, we shall certainly never know. To ignore these objectives entirely is to delete them from the education agenda that the World Bank and other funding and technical assistance agencies explicitly set.

Education as Production

A second metaphor commonly used to explain and reform schooling is education as production, which in turn leads to a focus on efficiency. But what exactly is efficiency in education?

In manufacturing, efficiency seems clear. To produce bottles or cars efficiently, for example, requires finding the lowest-cost raw materials, reducing waste and breakage, training workers to do their jobs quickly and accurately, installing machinery that is reliable, ensuring low energy cost, keeping maintainance simple, and making sure that expenditures on marketing are exceeded by income from increased sales. That is, efficiency in manufacturing has to do with reducing the costs of production.

Though the production metaphor is occasionally useful, education is fundamentally different from manufacturing. In an interactive process, the distinction between inputs and outputs is consciously blurred. Bottles do not contribute to their own manufacture. Students do contribute to their own education. Cars do not suggest improvements in the assembly process or reject the old way of doing things. Learners are active participants in their education, not only suggesting improvements and rejecting received wisdom but taking the initiative to chart new paths.

On the face of it, ever larger classes would increase an education system's efficiency. When the teacher's salary is spread across more and more students, the unit cost goes down. But of course the appropriate unit of education is not the student but learning. What matters most in an education system is not how many students there are per teacher or even how many teacher hours are allocated to each student who completes a particular level, but rather how much and how well those students have learned.

Beyond those problems, it is far from clear that efficiency, however defined, is or ought to be the primary goal to be maximized. Like those responsible for space travel, educators in poor countries may assign higher priority to redundancy. Suppose they discover that every school, or every subject, has its own duplicating machine. To maximize efficiency they might create a central duplication facility serving several departments or schools. Concentrated at a single site, duplicating machines and their associated supplies would be easier to manage and maintain. Economies of scale might permit reducing staff and purchasing materials at advantageous prices. But a power failure at that site, equipment breakdowns, or the lack of key supplies would mean that no school could get duplicated materials. The less-efficient alternative, each school or subject with its own duplicating machine, achieves reliability through redundancy. When one school has a power failure or exhausts its supplies, others may continue to function and to provide services for the schools temporarily unable to do their own duplicating. The point here is straightforward: whether efficiency, redundancy, or some other goal should have the highest priority cannot be assumed but must be determined. That determination is likely to be situationally specific, especially where setting priorities involves, as it should, people within each setting.

Notwithstanding the problems of using efficiency as an analytic construct in education, much of the current education and development writing is intensely concerned with what are commonly termed the internal and external efficiency of education systems. "Internal efficiency" is regularly used to refer to student progress through school, teacher-student ratios, use of physical facilities, and measures of achievement, commonly all summed in the unit cost per student. Little explicit attention is given to the ways in which that language structures understanding, in this case converting a matter of education policy (under what circumstances is repetition pedagogically, socially, politically, even economically desirable) into a technical or administrative concern. "External efficiency" is regularly used to refer to the relationship between schooling and the labor market, commonly assessed in terms of the percentage of students who pass, graduate, and secure employment, with little explicit attention to what can or cannot be said confidently about whether or not reforms within formal schooling can or do affect postschool employment. Like cost-benefit analysis, notions of efficiency focus on achieving particular goals with the smallest expenditure. Schools whose spending per pupil (or per student who completes the education cycle) is low are considered to be internally more efficient than schools whose per pupil expenditures are higher. In this example, internal efficiency may be improved by either spending less per pupil or reducing dropouts and repetition, or both. Increased employment rates among graduates are the principal indicators of greater external efficiency.

Commonly, in their concern with repetition and attrition, studies of internal efficiency consider what they term supply side (quality of instruction) and demand side (parental need for children's labor) factors. Rarely, however, does the analysis proceed to consider the ways in which the education system pushes students out. There is little attention to the magnitude and consequences of various eviction rules, for example, the common requirement that pregnant schoolgirls be expelled. Generally this orientation ignores the design of the education system itself, which in most countries is explicitly structured to screen and filter students out of the system. Most education systems are designed to restrict progress to an ever smaller elite. That the pyramid is smaller at the top than at the bottom is not an aberration, a mistake, or a problem to be overcome but is an intentional objective. The clearest example is systems in which the paucity of places at the next level means that in addition to a traumatic selection point (at which even many of those who have scored well on the selection examination are precluded from preceding), there are recurring discouraging moments. Students who do not excel in the terms the system sets, formally and informally, are likely to receive periodic negative messages. Although the apparent proximate cause for attrition may have to do with test results, family circumstances,[34] or distance to school, the underlying context is one of discouragement. "Why continue the drain on my family, or deal with the inconvenience, or feel like a failure if I am never going to succeed?" By ignoring the systemic sources of attrition, this approach makes it difficult to conceive of, let alone discuss coherently, the sort of policies required to transform an exclusive education system into an inclusive system whose guiding principle is education for all.

In three important ways the constructs internal efficiency and external efficiency focus policy attention in the wrong direction. Concern with reducing the
unit cost per student is likely to be far less fruitful than focusing on increasing the
effectiveness of each unit of expenditure. As the World Bank itself regularly
points out, many African countries currently allocate far less of their national
budget and spend far less of their gross domestic product on education than do
countries in much of the rest of the world. Second, since pass and graduation rates
are largely the consequences of general education and national policy and therefore not of either student or school achievement, it seems particularly obfuscat-
ing to characterize the decision to promote few students as internal inefficiency.

Third, recognizing that the charter of schooling is far broader than (and may
not even include) vocational preparation requires discarding efforts to assess
education's external efficiency from rates and types of employment. And since
it is far from clear that in-school and skill-specific vocational training make better employees, unemployment rates cannot provide even a rough measure of a
more limited notion of employment, preparation efficiency. Efficiency may be
assessed in terms of learning rather than expenditures, but that is rarely done.
When the pressure to quantify confronts the problems in measuring learning, it
is learning that is ignored.

Put simply, if the primary goals of schooling are to develop literacy, numeracy, and social consciousness and to foster curiosity, creativity, and critique, if
educators know relatively little about the sort of early in-school training that
leads to better mechanics, managers, or teachers, and if it is likely that adults
will work in several different occupations, then the rate-of-employment yard-
stick is a problematic and probably inappropriate tool for evaluating schooling.

From this perspective, to focus on internal and external efficiency as commonly defined is to undermine education's efforts to achieve the broader goals
with which it has been charged. It is also important to note here that to use this
terminology—internal and external efficiency—is to cast what are fundamentally issues of public policy as problems of administration and management,
presumably amenable to technical solutions.

A corollary to stress on efficiency is insistence on feasibility and practicality.[35] At first glance that orientation may seem quite reasonable, but in practice
it constrains both education and development. Innovations are inherently risky.
Attempts to change roles (for example, teachers and students as curriculum de-
velopers), quality measures (the mix and weights of student portfolios, continuous assessment, and standardized examinations), pedagogy (learner-centered
instruction, mixed ability groups), and links with the world of work (education
with production) may fail or interfere with other objectives. Since innovations
are risky, funding and technical assistance agencies generally require using
older, ostensibly proven and reliable approaches. A major consequence of that
orientation, to return to the production metaphor, is that creative departures and
the production of new means of production take place in the affluent countries.

Those who are poor scramble to catch up as they watch those who are more af-fluent discard the approaches and technologies they are told to use. In practice, poverty is deemed to preclude fundamental innovation, which in turn is likely to perpetuate the poverty.

Education as Delivery System

Aid dependence entrenches policy and programmatic change as something done to rather than by Third World education. In most of the education and de-velopment literature, learning is understood as information acquisition. The common construct is what Paulo Freire has termed the banking model of edu-cation. Learners are like empty bank accounts. More or less formally, teachers and others with the relevant capital, wisdom, make deposits into those ac-counts. Successful students save their resources and complete their education with heads full of knowledge on which they can subsequently draw. At least for younger learners, learning is understood largely as a passive process. Teach-ers *give* or *provide* or *offer,* and students *receive.* Where students play a some-what more active role, they acquire knowledge and skills. But what of the ex-tensive thinking, experimentation, and research on education and learning that regard learning as something substantially larger than information acquisition? What of the notion that what learners do is not simply acquire but generate, master, develop, and create knowledge? Educators who understand learning as an active process, who situate learners at the center of that process, and for whom learning involves the appropriation, manipulation, and integration of in-formation have little voice in the policies and programs developed using the economists' tool kit.

In part, this narrow view of education reflects an approach that limits its purview to what can reasonably be measured. Measuring education quality is of course problematic. The difficulties stem both from divergent understandings of what education is and what it is to accomplish and from problems of measure-ment. Degrees, certificates, and other earned credentials provide one set of mea-sures. Examinations provide another. Indeed, since examinations play a very prominent role in most education systems, it is common to take examination re-sults as the principal (or sometimes sole) measure of education quality. For all their flaws, examinations are a standardized and widely recognized measure. There is no comparable measure of progress toward national unity or improved conflict resolution skills. Reliance on examination results has several advan-tages, both theoretical and methodological. It also seems to leave the determi-nation of what matters (i.e., what is examined) to national authorities instead of imposing a foreign standard.[36] Still, educators everywhere understand the limi-tations of national and other standardized examinations as measures of educa-tion quality. They also understand that what is not examined is generally ex-cluded from quality assessment. Learning as process, information use rather than acquisition, concept formation, development of analytic skills, and the like are apparently only rarely included in quality measures. Other expectations of the education system, for example, developing a common national identity, preparing young people for effective citizenship, nurturing cooperative skills, reducing social inequalities, and resolving conflict, are included in quality measures even less often.

The terminology used is both instructive and formative. In the documents of the funding and technical assistance agencies education reforms are regularly termed interventions, that is, insertions from outside rather than initiatives from within. Externally funded, externally guided, and often externally managed, specific reform projects are rarely directly responsible to the settings—whether teachers, students, or the local community—in which they function. How are Third World educators to become owners of those reforms when they are the objects of the surgery, not the surgeons? Education is termed a delivery system, not an organic process in which learners are the doers rather than the receivers. How do recipients become owners? In practice, this combination of a vantage point external to education (whether national or foreign) and very limited accountability generally proves fundamentally disempowering.

When Does Aid Not Help?

Among the numerous studies of foreign aid and its problems,[37] including attention to the role of the International Monetary Fund and the World Bank,[38] there has been relatively little systematic attention focused directly on aid and education,[39] and especially on the links between the large-scale agenda and activities of the international and national aid agencies and the small-scale decisions and activities of education decision makers and educators.

Advocates of aid argue that the situation would have been much worse in the absence of assistance and that education in particular settings has clearly benefited from foreign support. Critics argue equally passionately that although there have been some benefits, on balance aid has been more harmful than helpful. They point to funds allocated to projects that have shown no significant benefit, to promising projects begun but not sustained long enough to bear fruit, to periodic and abrupt shifts in priorities among the aid agencies, and to a general preference for large-scale and high-tech efforts that are often situationally inappropriate. Their critique is also structural. In its very conception, foreign aid is fundamentally disempowering. Notwithstanding the widespread use of terms like cooperation, partnership, and empowerment, in practice aid generally functions to undermine local authority and initiative. By substituting external decisions for local autonomy, it reduces rather than builds capacity. Education is a sufficiently complex process that project or programmatic evaluations are unlikely to resolve this debate. Rarely is it possible to associate specific outcomes with particular reforms, whether locally generated or externally recommended. And even as they criticize particular aid programs and insist on their national autonomy, most Third World governments are anxious to secure as much education assistance as they can get, generally accepting the accompanying conditions.

The Role(s) of Research

Earlier I referred to the Jomtien conference and apparent consensus on education for all. Few would disagree with this noble goal, even though many countries lack the resources to achieve it rapidly. But why? Why is universal mass education the highest priority? And if it is, why focus primarily on basic (primary) education in schools, rather than, say, adult and other education programs outside school settings?

There are many answers to those and related questions, but the answer that seems the most important in the 1990s, especially to those who disburse funds to support education in the Third World, is that research shows that investing in primary education yields the best return. Support for this focus on primary education rests on the claim that research has persuasively demonstrated that investing in primary education promises the greatest progress toward development (however defined).

It is not the specific conclusion that is most striking here. I have already noted problems with uncritical reliance on rate-of-return analysis. The history of public discourse on education suggests that every broadly accepted observation is eventually discarded as partial, misleading, incorrect, or all three. A successor truth will emerge, advocated just as ardently. Rather, what is remarkable here is the implicit consensus on research as the principal determinant of education policy. The Jomtien resolutions are but a single example of the privileged position of research (or, more accurately, claims about research and its findings) in debates on education policy. Research may inform and guide policy, rationalize and justify policies adopted for other reasons, or be quite irrelevant to policy. But claims about what research shows constitute the core of the development discussion. Without the claim of research support, policy proposals lose credibility. Similarly, policy critiques that do not cite supporting research are easily ignored. Prospective participants in the policy debate must demonstrate an adequate supply of relevant research simply to have their voices heard.

The formulation "research shows that" and its synonyms are ubiquitous. Policy makers have probably always claimed that observation and experience (i.e., more or less formal research) support their decisions. The prominence and pervasiveness of the claim that "research shows" within the development arena, however, reflects a powerful contemporary phenomenon: the emergence of a financial-intellectual complex spawned by the development business. It is important to recognize both the unique characteristics and the shorter- and longer-term consequences of that combination of research and funding. That in turn requires understanding the ways in which the increasing importance of external assistance and the privileged position of research combine to condition and constrain education's substantive content.

The Evolution of the Social Sciences

To understand what people do and why, we need to know something about what they have done. Rarely, however, do social scientists directly observe all of the events that interest them. Hence, most often we rely on information that someone else has collected, more or less systematically, usually for some other purpose. The behavioral revolution in the social sciences, with its shrill cries of "falsifiability!" and "reproducibility!" has pushed us toward the sort of information that can be recorded and stored in quantitative form. It has pushed us as well toward increasingly complex, and perhaps sophisticated, techniques for exploring relationships within that information.

The Facade of Precision[40]

Note here the powerful but often little recognized influence of prevalent computation strategies. To the present, most computing in the social sciences has been digital. High-speed combinations of relatively simple bimodal choices—on/off, yes/no, either/or—permit the manipulation of massive volumes of information. Miniaturization and other technological advances have produced extraordinary increases in speed and capacity. Beyond the raw processing capabilities, digital representation of information seems to have important advantages for social scientists. For example, ambiguities in categorization are either explicitly precluded or organized into contingent connections through which individual paths are unambiguous. Events or relationships of interest can be more readily distinguished from similar phenomena and random variations. Yet the analogue world is at best imperfectly captured in its digital representation. However sophisticated the sampling techniques, some information is lost. Similarly, when social scientists are constrained to construct categories that are mutually exclusive, the disadvantages of excluding inconsistency and ambiguity may outweigh the value of the apparent resulting clarity. The variations in temporal and spatial context that go unrecorded because they are smaller than the units of measure employed may prove to be critical to inference and interpretation.

Of course, even the most advanced techniques can at best provide only partial remedies for inaccuracies and inconsistencies in the original data. Indeed, careful scholars regularly include a caveat at the beginning of their publications, calling readers' attention to gaps and other problems in the data they use. Unfortunately, often even careful scholars proceed to ignore their own reservations, developing arguments that rely on data characteristics and/or a level of precision not found in the original data.

Many, perhaps most, reported national statistics for the Third World, for example, have a large margin of error.[41] Enumerating the multiple sources of that large margin of error is beyond the scope of this discussion. But the immediate implication of taking seriously that margin of error, that is, treating national statistics as rough approximations, is clear. Small observed changes may be more apparent than real and must be treated as such. Even changes on the order of 5 to 10 percent (or more) may reflect nothing more than random fluctuations, annual variations, and flawed statistics. Consequently, apparent changes of that magnitude are a weak foundation for broad inferences and for public policy.

To be useful, analytic categories need to be larger and rougher (for example, rounded to the nearest 10 rather than to the nearest hundredth, tenth, or even unit). Quantification permits computerization. Although that may make them more defensible, it does not automatically produce better results.

A second implication is that both researchers and policy makers must reject statistics whose underlying assumptions require a level of precision, linearity, or continuity that the data do not reliably support. A profusion of numbers neither makes a particular interpretation more valid nor renders a policy proposal more attractive. Indeed, the numeric shroud may well obscure far more than it reveals.

Widespread acknowledgement of the uncertainty in the available data notwithstanding, the canons of social science impel those who conduct research, those who support research, and those who rely on research to justify their actions to overstate the precision of their findings and to attach to them an unrealistically high level of confidence.

Economics as Social Science

Accompanying and fueling the inclination to quantify has been the emergence of economics as the modal social science. This increasingly influential and powerful role for economics stands on two legs, one within the academy and the other outside it.

In their ideal form, the methods taught in basic economics courses correspond well to the direction social science has been moving over the past several decades. The focus is on causal relationships, established by drawing on lawlike statements about patterned regularities and exploring the connections among precisely defined factors. Whatever is deemed extraneous to the relationship may be ignored. Factors that may affect the relationship being studied are either assumed not to vary ("other things being equal") or to vary randomly (thereby having no systematic influence). Or they are directly or indirectly controlled by the researchers. Finally, the restricted set of factors to be examined (the "variables") can be studied. Ideally, those factors can be changed in some orderly way, either by careful choice of locations, times, or observations or by simulating the variation based on the information available. Expectations about causality (hypotheses) can then be rejected or supported. The longer-term goals are to increase the number of lawlike statements that are generally accepted as sufficiently well supported to serve as the foundation for research and perhaps policy and to broaden their field of applicability.

For many scholars, this orientation defines the social scientific method. The ultimate standard is the controlled experiment in which all of the factors can be manipulated by the experimenter. Since that is rarely possible for social scientists, the challenge is to approach that ideal as closely as possible.

The current preeminence of economics also stems from its role as the social science deemed to have the most important practical consequences. Many people, both inside and outside the academy, understand the value of social science primarily in terms of what used to be called social engineering: how to make society function better—how to improve people's lives, resolve conflict, or reduce environmental degradation. Especially in regard to sustained efforts to secure public funding for research and higher education more generally, researchers resort to liberal utilitarian defenses of what they do. Commonly, economics is perceived as the branch of social science that has the most to say (or the most to say that is useful) about the standard of living. Other disciplines fall short.

Research as Currency or Perhaps Ammunition

At the same time, research has become the currency of development planners and decision makers, used to assign value to alternative and often competing projects. Wealthier proposals and programs—those that can claim greater research support—are more likely to be approved and funded.

Surely that is desirable. Research guides decisions. Expertise rather than politics prevails. Researchers have long complained that decision makers pay too little attention to research. Finally they are listening to us, say the academics. But are they? This idealized model of the allocation of development assistance is deceptive in several ways.

First, the common view that competent policy makers base their decisions on a careful review of relevant research is simply inaccurate. In development, as in most other policy-making arenas, research enters the decision-making process through multiple, often indirect pathways. One begins well before any particular decision. The research to which decision makers have been exposed during their education and socialization informs the frameworks within which policies are considered and decisions are made. That is, long after their schooling has been completed, decision makers draw on their academic learning (and of course their practical experience) to formulate questions, select the proposals worth pursuing, specify evaluative criteria, and make decisions. That indirect influence may be very subtle and is often not apparent to the decision makers themselves.

Second, policy makers who are largely guided by research focused on the issue to be decided do not necessarily make better decisions. The research that is deemed relevant is generally instrumental and relatively narrowly gauged, since it takes the existing patterns of economic, political, and social organization as givens. Yet effective and appropriate public policy cannot ignore interests, preferences, and politics. Making public policy is not, after all, an antiseptic, sheltered, apolitical process. Successfully implemented policies must confront and engage, not avoid, the conflict of interests and the tensions among the organization of production, the structure of power, and patterns of social differentiation.

Third, research enters the policy process as justification for decisions already made. Especially in the public discourse of a bureaucratic environment, in which decision makers are charged to emphasize rationality and deemphasize politics and favoritism, the claim that research supports a particular course of action is the most powerful defense against all challengers. Put crudely, in the policy shoot-out, the gunfighter quickest to draw the research pistol and best supplied with research ammunition is most likely to emerge victorious. Even a slow draw with limited ammunition may insure survival.

Fourth, as I have argued, the conjunction of development assistance and research transforms both research and its role in the policy process, to the detriment of both. That research influences policy indirectly and that research is used to justify decisions are not necessarily problematic. In the contemporary development business, however, the same agencies are increasingly responsible for decisions, funding, and research, and thus it is timely to explore critically the roles of education research and researchers.

When Research Becomes Consulting

In much of the Third World education research has become inextricably intertwined with the needs, interests, and preferences of external assistance agencies. Currently, for example, directly and indirectly those organizations employ more researchers and commission more studies of African education than any African research institution and perhaps more than nearly all of them combined. Informed and well-grounded policy is, of course, desirable. So indeed is dialogue between policy makers and researchers. Yet just as their funds seat foreign aid organizations at the education policy table, so too do those funds secure powerful influence over research and the research process. Little anticipated and not yet well understood, this conjunction of external funding and education research is only beginning to be studied systematically. The major outlines of this relationship have become sufficiently clear, however, to warrant concern among both researchers and policy makers. To put the issue sharply, research and policy are both at risk.

When public funding for education is inadequate, public funding for education research hardly exists. Just as education and training decision makers and

planners look overseas to fund innovation and development, especially as their
real incomes have stagnated or declined and as their institutions struggle to
maintain even a minimum level of service, so do scholars look abroad for support for their research. They quickly learn that unencumbered research grants
are scarce and difficult to obtain. More readily available are contracts with external assistance agencies, that is, funding for commissioned research on all or
parts of the education sector. With those commissions come specifications of
appropriate approaches, methods, and analytic framework. Hence, education
research too becomes part of the aid relationship, with senior researchers regularly shuttling between cramped offices and empty libraries on the one hand
and on the other the computers, cellular telephones, and substantial fees of
client consulting.

The manifestations, consequences, and problems of this conjunction of funding and research are multiple. Since I have addressed them at length elsewhere,[42] let me simply note here several of the most visible and significant of
those outcomes: insisting on a detached, clinical perspective that devalues the
local role; influencing and constraining the education and development discourse; legitimizing weak propositions; entrenching flawed understandings by
according them official status; seeding and fertilizing theoretical and analytic
fads; treating education primarily as technique and administration; mystifying
knowledge and power relations; and promoting orthodoxy at the expense of
critical inquiry. Combined, these outcomes privilege a particular understanding of education and development, thereby diverting attention from and often
precluding alternative understandings and perspectives. What ought to be the
subjects of policy debate come to be regarded as the normal, unexceptional, and
largely unalterable features of the policy environment.

With low basic salaries, individual researchers are highly motivated to become consultants to the external agencies. Unable to pay a living wage or to
provide direct research funding, universities are inclined to tolerate, often encourage, that practice. Obliged to justify their programs and allocations and
chastised for relying so heavily on expatriate researchers, the funding and technical assistance agencies eagerly recruit local education researchers. Research
becomes consulting. That has several problematic consequences.

First, generally the contracting agency selects the topic to be studied and often the methodology to be used. It is of course reasonable for an agency to initiate and commission research to meet its needs. When that arrangement is the
only source of research funding, however, the topics studied do not emerge or-
ganically from interactions among educators, teachers, learners, and the community. Nor for the most part are the topics specified independently by those
who manage the education system or defined by the debates among researchers
and other educators. Similarly, the methodology employed is also generally determined by the contracting agency, commonly a methodology perceived to
have international legitimacy and considered credible by those to whom the

agency must report. Rarely does the methodology reflect the experiences of the researcher, methodological debates among researchers within the country, or the nationally developed critiques of dominant methodological orientations.

Second, commissioned research[43] generates reports that are sent to the contracting agency and perhaps the government. Only very rarely are findings subjected to academic and practitioners' peer review. As a result, what are taken as authoritative results and recommendations may be partial, seriously flawed, skewed, or all three.

Third, since the reports of commissioned research rarely enter the academic literature, they do not contribute to integrating the results of multiple investigations into common understandings, adapting findings to local circumstances, or incorporating them into instructional programs. Rather than the cumulation and sifting and winnowing that are central to the creation of knowledge, commissioned research produces largely disconnected lonely trees, some robust but many quite frail, scattered across the desolate plain of bookless schools and deskless classrooms.

Fourth, research as consulting transforms the academic reward system. Africa again provides the sharpest examples. In a few African universities, promotion remains important and requires publication. In most, however, promotion in university rank is less important and far less remunerative than securing another consulting contract. A month's work can yield a year's pay or more. It is consulting contracts, not university lecturing, that make possible computers, cellular telephones, four-wheel-drive vehicles, and international travel.

Fifth, even as commissioned studies do make it possible for there to be research, their disconnectedness functions to undermine the research institutions. Effectively unable to set their own agenda or to control the principal reward systems for their staff, research institutions are buffeted by the fickle winds of agency priorities and preferences.

Sixth, the current penchant for reducing government functions reinforces the privatization of research. Beyond their individual consulting contracts, in many countries researchers have formed local consulting firms that market their services to foreign funding and technical assistance agencies. In itself, that is not problematic. The existence of multiple and competing research centers may enhance both the quality of research and its utility for policy making. As the privatization of research has developed, however, it leads more toward the multiplication of parasitic organizations entirely dependent on one or several foreign patrons than toward the development of the institutional capacities and the autonomy that enable research centers to establish and sustain solidly grounded high quality research programs. Retaining their university posts and thus their academic legitimacy, researchers reconstitute themselves beyond the university's reach. That is, though they rely on the university's resources and credibility, they contribute little to the longer-term development of the university as an institution whose mission includes research. Often employing former senior civil servants, ostensibly independent research consulting firms contribute to the construction of research as a proprietary endeavor, hidden behind walls of confidentiality, secrecy, and ministerial privilege rather than shared widely and exposed to broad review and critique.

The creation of knowledge is always a complex and spasmodic process. The boundaries between the university and other knowledge-generating arenas are often productively ambiguous. And it is certainly not unique in human history to insist that knowledge creation be utilitarian or to find knowledge creators dependent on those with disposable funds. When research as consulting functions to determine how problems are specified and addressed (often with economics and its perspectives and assumptions privileged and elevated to be the mother of social science), national dependence is institutionalized well into the future.

Methodological Orthodoxy Stymies Critical Inquiry

That the external assistance agencies have influenced education policy is clear. Less clear but equally troubling has been their influence on research. Although there are of course debates and disagreements among those involved in commissioned research, the conjunction of external funding and research fosters a methodological orthodoxy. Quite simply, some theories and methods are deemed acceptable (a determination that is justified by terming them "scientific") while others are rejected. To be heard, to influence outcomes, and to be employed by the funding and technical assistance agencies requires operating, for example, within the world of human capital theory and rate-of-return analysis. As local researchers develop their skills within that orthodoxy, their critical edge is dulled. The presumed universalism of the accepted research canons treats efforts to depart from the mainstream in order to tune approach and method to the local setting as simply poor social science.

In this way, the combination of foreign assistance and commissioned research functions to disseminate globally not only particular understandings of education and development but also how those understandings are created, revised, and refined. Effectively, although its origins of course preceded the recent period of economic disarray and foreign assistance, financial crisis and structural adjustment have reinforced and entrenched the globalization of a particular sort of social science.

The Mystification of Knowledge and Power Relations

It is striking that individual scholars may orient their work very differently in the academic and financial-intellectual spheres of operation. In the former, the relevant audience is institutional and disciplinary, academic peers and university chairs and deans, whereas in the latter the officials of the employing agency constitute the audience that matters. They are more likely than the general body of academics to have shared preferences about method, approach, and findings. Much more easily than is possible at most universities and research institutes, funding agencies can readily terminate their relationship with a particular scholar.

In the conjunction of funding and research, scholarship becomes a proprietary process. The investors have the determining voice in the selection of topics, researchers, and methods, limit access to source materials, and often control the dissemination of findings. Consequently, the process of knowledge creation is obscured, mystifying the power relations embedded in the research and thereby in the programs it supports. Perhaps not entirely aware of their own role, scholars become advocates not only for particular understandings of development and underdevelopment but also for a particular sort of global order.

Knowledge is power in this setting. Education initiatives and reforms, even maintaining the schools, require resources. Securing funds requires research findings. Those who can provide research findings gain influence, often control, over decisions and programs. Those who determine the sorts of research that are acceptable secure even broader influence and control. More troubling, that systemic ability to constrain and set agendas and priorities is barely discernible and thus generally inaccessible, since it is embedded in ostensibly apolitical and neutral rules and procedures of research. How are peasants to challenge the scientific method? Are their teachers, or the teachers of their teachers, any more likely to do so? Power relations that might be regarded as profoundly problematic if they were seen clearly are so enmeshed in everyday practices that they become invisible. Research intended to clarify education functions to mystify power and authority.

Education and Development

What progress, then, over the past few decades? The World Bank regularly suggests that we know more about education and development, thanks to an improved and expanded research base. Schools, meanwhile, have deteriorated, and the number of people not reached by education systems has increased. International organizations and national authorities are apparently unable to translate greater knowledge into useful practices.

Cause and effect are very difficult to establish clearly in education, which is an intricate web of processes, some integrally related and others distantly connected. Mapping those links is a frustrating and usually contentious undertaking, especially where the concern goes beyond ostensibly standardized measures like examinations to explore learning and its consequences. It is therefore not surprising that the relationships between aid-supported curricular and instructional reforms on the one hand and specific developmental outcomes on the other are complex and difficult to discern. Confounding and compounding factors are numerous and often not readily apparent. The links between education and development more generally are still harder to establish. However daunting the challenge, though, it is essential to inquire about what education assistance programs have accomplished, at both the smaller and larger scales. Some, perhaps much, of what countries initiate or do not initiate in education is directly or indirectly the result of advice received from the World Bank and other agencies.

Sometimes those organizations radically change their advice. Earlier, for example, the World Bank energetically supported vocationalizing secondary education. Subsequently it came to reject that advice, arguing that the additional costs of vocationalized secondary education far exceed its benefits. Some countries seem to have suffered from that transition. Tanzania's educators initially opposed the recommendation to vocationalize their secondary education system and then acquiesced, largely to secure continued funding. Having barely begun the transition, they were told that since the World Bank's major study,[44] for which Tanzania was a principal case, had concluded that the benefits of diversified secondary education did not warrant the additional investment, they should give it up. From their perspective, they were saddled with an externally encouraged, even demanded, program and costs, for which the original external assistance was no longer available.

A related concern about the role of external funding agencies has to do with the net capital flow consequences of education aid. Critics regularly charge that foreign assistance results in a net outflow. There has been, it seems, very little analysis of that claim in terms of education aid. Foreign assistance is generally presented as a transfer of resources from more to less affluent countries. To be sure, the transfer is less than the total amount of aid, since much of the aid received must be spent on products, services, and personnel from the granting country. Still, the assumption is that there is a clear benefit, including increased resources, for the recipient country. The apparently expanding gap between the most and least affluent countries and the rapidly increasing debt burden of many of the world's poorest countries toward the end of the century challenge that assumption.

It seems clear to most of the education community that effective reform requires agendas and initiatives with strong local roots and the broad participation of those with a stake in outcomes, including not only officials but also students, parents, teachers, and communities. Unless the beneficiaries of the reform become its bearers, it is likely to be stillborn. For external agencies to support that process, they must conceive their role in terms of development cooperation rather than providing philanthropy or determining directions. Many studies of education and development and the recommendations based on them, however, function in practice not to foster and facilitate dialogue, but to undermine and discourage it. Seeking to provide clear and firm findings, they announce and pronounce. They set terms. They declare. Sheltered by specialized language and the strictures of confidentiality, they remain largely inaccessible outside a very small circle. Though they talk about capacity building, far too often they are incapacitating.

Notes

1. For a detailed inventory and analytic overview of studies undertaken within the context of the aid relationship, see Joel Samoff, with N'Dri Thérèse Assié-Lumumba, *Analyses, Agendas, and Priorities in African Education: A Review of Externally Initiated, Commissioned, and Supported Studies of Education in Africa, 1990–1994* (Paris: UNESCO, 1996).

2. Philip G. Altbach, "Patterns in Higher Education Development: Toward the Year 2000," in *Emergent Issues in Education: Comparative Perspectives,* ed. Robert F. Arnove, Philip G. Altbach, and Gail P. Kelly (Albany: State University of New York Press, 1992), 39–55.

3. Altbach, "Patterns in Higher Education Development," 44.

4. A perspective developed by Samir Amin from earlier works, *Accumulation on a World Scale: A Critique of the Theory of Underdevelopment* (New York: Monthly Review Press, 1974) and *Unequal Development: An Essay on the Social Formation of Peripheral Capitalism* [New York: Monthly Review Press, 1976]), through more recent works, for example, *Empire of Chaos* (New York: Monthly Review Press, 1992).

5. As, for example, the composition of the Gulbenkian Commission on the Restructuring of the Social Sciences, chaired by Immanuel Wallerstein, *Open the Social Sciences: Report of the Gulbenkian Commission on the Restructuring of the Social Sciences* (Stanford, Calif.: Stanford University Press, 1996).

6. Martin Carnoy, "Education and the Transition State," in *Education and Social Transition in the Third World,* ed. Martin Carnoy and Joel Samoff (Princeton: Princeton University Press, 1990), 91ff. and n. 12.

7. Martin Carnoy, *The State and Political Theory* (Princeton: Princeton University Press, 1984); and Martin Carnoy, "Education and the State: From Adam Smith to Perestroika," in *Emergent Issues in Education: Comparative Perspectives,* ed. Robert F. Arnove, Philip G. Altbach, and Gail P. Kelly (Albany: State University of New York Press, 1992), 143–159.

8. For example, Samuel Bowles and Herbert Gintis, *Schooling in Capitalist America* (New York: Basic Books, 1976).

9. Samuel Bowles and Herbert Gintis, "Education as a Site of Contradictions in the Reproduction of the Capital-Labor Relationship: Second Thoughts on the Correspondence Principle," *Economic and Industrial Democracy* 2 (1981): 223–242.

10. John Boli, Francisco O. Ramirez, and John W. Meyer, "Explaining the Origins and Expansion of Mass Education," *Comparative Education Review* 29 (YEAR): 145–170; Francisco O. Ramirez and John Boli, "The Political Construction of Mass Schooling: European Origins and Worldwide Institutionalization," *Sociology of Education* 60 (1987): 2–17; Francisco O. Ramirez and Richard Rubinson, "Creating Members: The National Incorporation of Education," in *National Development and the*

World System: Educational, Economic, and Political Change, 1950–1970, ed. John W. Meyer and Michael T. Hanan (Chicago: University of Chicago Press, 1979); John Boli and Francisco O. Ramirez, "Compulsory Schooling in the Western Cultural Context," in *Emergent Issues in Education: Comparative Perspectives,* ed. Robert F. Arnove, Philip G. Altbach, and Gail P. Kelly (Albany: State University of New York Press, 1992), 25–38.

11. For example, Alex Inkeles and David Smith, *Becoming Modern: Individual Change in Six Developing Countries* (Cambridge: Harvard University Press, 1974).

12. Immanuel Wallerstein, *The Modern World-System; Capitalist Agriculture and the Origins of the European World-Economy in the Sixteenth Century* (New York: Academic Press, 1974); Immanuel Wallerstein, *The Modern World-System II: Mercantilism and the Consolidation of the European World-Economy, 1600–1750* (New York: Academic Press, 1980); Immanuel Wallerstein, *The Modern World System III: The Second Era of Great Expansion of the Capitalist World-Economy, 1730–1840s* (San Diego: Academic Press, 1989).

13. Robert F. Arnove and Edward H. Berman, "Neocolonial Policies of North American Philanthropic Foundations" (paper presented at the annual meeting of the Fifth World Congress of Comparative Education, Paris, 2–6 July 1984); Robert F. Arnove, "The Ford Foundation and the Transfer of Knowledge: Convergence and Divergence in the World System," *Compare* 13, no. 1 (1983): 17–18; Robert F. Arnove, ed., *Philanthropy and Cultural Imperialism: The Foundations at Home and Abroad* (Boston: Hall, 1980); Edward H. Berman, *The Ideology of Philanthropy: The Influence of the Carnegie, Ford, and Rockefeller Foundations on American Foreign Policy* (Albany: State University of New York Press, 1983).

14. Talcott Parson's pattern variables provided a scientific legitimacy for that differentiation; see *Structure and Process in Modern Societies* (New York: Free Press, 1963). Valentin Y. Mudimbe explores how those who saw themselves as modern required an "other" to define themselves, inventing it as necessary, in *The Invention of Africa: Gnosis, Philosophy, and the Order of Knowledge* (Bloomington: Indiana University Press, 1988); and Talcott Parson, *The Idea of Africa* (Bloomington: Indiana University Press, 1994).

15. "Some states are not yet fit to govern themselves." Paul Johnson, "Colonialism's Back—and Not a Moment Too Soon," *New York Times Magazine,* 13 April 1993, 23.

16. Newt Gingrich, Speaker of the U.S. House of Representatives, 7 June 1995, quoted in the *New York Times,* 8 June 1995.

17. Adam Przeworski, "The Neoliberal Fallacy," *Journal of Democracy* 3, no. 3 (July 1992): 45–59.

18. World Bank, *Adjustment in Africa: Reforms, Results, and the Road Ahead—Summary* (Washington, D.C.: World Bank, 1994), 10–13, drawing on the full report, World Bank, *Adjustment in Africa: Reforms, Results, and the Road Ahead* (Washington, D.C.: World Bank, 1994), 184–196.

19. World Bank, *Education: Sector Policy Paper* (Washington, D.C.: World Bank, 1980), 79.

20. World Bank, *Priorities and Strategies for Education: A World Bank Review* (Washington, D.C.: World Bank, 1995), a document to which I shall return shortly.

21. Christopher Colclough with Keith Lewin, *Educating All the Children: Strategies for Primary Schooling in the South* (Oxford: Clarendon, 1993).

22. Noel F. McGinn, ed., *Crossing Lines: Research and Policy Networks for Developing Country Education* (Westport, Conn.: Praeger, 1996).

23. Edmundo F. Fuenzalida, "The Reception of 'Scientific Sociology' in Chile," *Latin American Research Review* 18, no. 2 (1983): 95–112.

24. *Priorities and Strategies in Education,* 14, 146, table 12.1. Note that in this report the World Bank expands its definition of "developing countries" to include the countries of (Eastern) Europe "in transition from command to market economics" as well as those the World Bank usually terms "less developed countries."

25. *Priorities and Strategies in Education,* 14–15.

26. Two case studies of the impacts of economic crisis and structural adjustment on education and training commissioned by a UNESCO-ILO task force, reported in Joel Samoff, ed., *Coping with Crisis: Austerity, Adjustment, and Human Resources* (London: Cassell/UNESCO, 1994).

27. Joel Samoff with Suleman Sumra, "From Planning to Marketing: Making Education and Training Policy in Tanzania," in *Coping with Crisis: Austerity, Adjustment, and Human Resources,* ed. Joel Samoff (London: Cassell, 1994), 134–172.

28. I review the successive strategies for formulating education policy in Joel Samoff, "Education Policy Formation in Tanzania: Self-Reliance and Dependence," in *Education Policy Formation in Africa: A Comparative Study of Five Countries,* ed. David R. Evans (Washington, D.C.: U.S. Agency for International Development, 1994), 85–126. Additional case studies of education policy making in Africa are reported in *Association for the Development of African Education, Formulating Education Policy: Lessons and Experiences from Sub-Saharan Africa* (Paris: Association for the Development of African Education, 1996).

29. Former Costa Rican president Arias, quoted in Martin Carnoy and Carlos A. Torres, "Educational Change and Structural Adjustment: A Case Study of Costa Rica," in *Coping With Crisis: Austerity, Adjustment, and Human Resources,* ed. Joel Samoff (London: Cassell, 1994), 92.

30. Michel Carton and Pape N'Diaye Diouf, with Christian Comeliau, "Budget Cuts in Education and Training in Sénégal: An Analysis of Reactions," in *Coping With Crisis: Austerity, Adjustment, and Human Resources,* ed. Joel Samoff (London: Cassell, 1994), 121–133.

31. Quoting Mark Blaug, World Bank, *Priorities and Strategies for Education: A World Bank Review* (Washington, D.C.: World Bank, 1995), 21. The citation attached to this sweeping claim (Mark Blaug, "The Empirical Status of Human Capital Theory: A Slightly Jaundiced Survey," *Journal of Economic Literature* 14 [1976]) is misleading, since Blaug's more recent writing, for example, "Where Are We Now in the Economics of Education?" *Economics of Education Review* 4, no. 1 (1985): 17–28, rejects the unqualified accolade and many of the common uses of human capital theory.

32. "East Asia" is a recurring reference in *Priorities and Strategies for Education,* presumably used to refer not to a geographic region but to the countries (and then colonies) widely regarded to have experienced rapid economic growth: Singapore, South Korea, Taiwan, and Hong Kong.

33. Overseas Development Authority, *Into the Nineties: An Education Policy for British Aid* (London: ODA, 1990), 7. For the use of rate of return analysis to reach the opposite conclusion—in Kenya, secondary, not primary, education has the higher rate of return—see John B. Knight and Richard H. Sabot, *Education, Productivity, and Inequality:*

The East African Natural Experiment (Oxford: Oxford University Press/World Bank, 1990).

34. Note that deficit theory (the underdevelopment of a child's intellectual ability and poor school results are attributed to deficiencies in the home and community environment) gains a renewed lease on life here.

35. Even as the aid agencies stress feasibility and practicality, their own studies are regularly criticized for their inattention to context and feasibility. The former functions to limit critique and innovation while the latter permits them to promote a general set of recommendations across diverse settings.

36. Note, though, the increasingly forceful assertion of the importance of international comparisons. In practice, that becomes another vehicle for imposing and institutionalizing standards generally developed outside the poor countries. Discussions among educators, parents, and policy makers rapidly come to focus on levels of achievement, and the standards themselves become immune to critical scrutiny.

37. Among them, Susan George, *A Fate Worse Than Debt: A Radical New Analysis of the Third World Debt Crisis* (London: Penguin, 1988); Jacques Hallak, *Negotiations with Aid Agencies: A Dwarf against a Giant,* IIEP Contributions no. 19 (Paris: UNESCO, 1995); Cheryl Payer, *Lent and Lost: Foreign Credit and Third World Development* (London: Zed, 1991); and Roger C. Riddell, *Foreign Aid Reconsidered* (London: James Currey, 1987).

38. Among them, Kevin Danaher, ed., *Fifty Years Is Enough: The Case against the World Bank and the International Monetary Fund* (Boston: South End, 1994); Susan George and Fabrizio Sabelli, *Faith and Credit: The World Bank's Secular Empire* (Boulder: Westview, 1994); Dharam Ghai, ed., *IMF and the South: The Social Impact of Crisis and Adjustment* (Atlantic Highlands, N.J.: Humanities, 1991); Bade Onimode, ed., *The IMF, the World Bank and the African Debt* (London: Zed, 1989); and David N. Plank, "Aid, Debt and the End of Sovereignty: Mozambique and Its Donors," *Journal of Modern African Studies* 31, no. 3 (September 1993): 407–430. Among the recent studies of World Bank Africa education policies have been Birgit Brock-Utne, "Education Policies for Sub-Saharan Africa as Viewed by the World Bank: A Critical Analysis of World Bank Report No. 6934," in *Education in Africa: Education for Self-Reliance or Recolonization?* Pedagogist Forskningsinstitutt, Rapport no. 3 (Oslo: Universitetet I Oslo, 1993); Lene Buchert, ed., *Education and Training in the Third World: The Local Dimension* (The Hague: Centre for the Study of Education in Developing Countries, 1992); Lene Buchert and Kenneth King, eds., *Learning from Experience: Policy and Practice in Aid to Higher Education* (The Hague: Center for the Study of Education in Developing Countries, 1995); Christopher Colclough, "Who Should Learn to Pay? An Assessment of Neo-Liberal Approaches to Education Policy," in *States or Markets? Neo-Liberalism and the Development Policy Debate,* ed. Christopher Colclough and James Manor (Oxford: Clarendon, 1991), 197–213; Kevin Danaher, ed., *Fifty Years Is Enough;* Joel Samoff, "The Reconstruction of Schooling in Africa," *Comparative Education Review* 37, no. 2 (May 1993): 181–222; and Joel Samoff, "Which Priorities and Strategies for Education?" *International Journal of Educational Development* 16, no. 3 (July 1996): 249–271.

39. Among recent contributions, see Lene Buchert, "Education and Development: A Study of Donor Agency Policies on Education in Sweden, Holland, and Denmark," *International Journal of Educational Development* 14, no. 2 (1994): 143–157; Lene

Buchert, *Recent Trends in Education Aid: Towards a Classification of Policies* (Paris: UNESCO/International Institute for Educational Planning, 1995); Lynn Ilon, "Structural Adjustment and Education: Adapting to a Growing Global Market," *International Journal of Educational Development* 14, no. 2 (April 1994): 95–108; *Philip W. Jones, World Bank Financing of Education: Lending, Learning and Development* (London: Routledge, 1992); Kenneth King, *Aid and Education in the Developing World: The Role of the Donor Agencies in Educational Analysis* (Harlow, Essex, U.K.: Longman, 1991); François Orivel and Fabrice Sergent, "Foreign Aid to Education in Sub-Saharan Africa: How Useful Is It?" *Prospects* 18, no. 4 (1988): 459–469; and Birgit Brock-Utne and Tove Nagel, eds., *The Role of Aid in the Development of Education for All,* Institute for Educational Research, Report no. 8 (Oslo: University of Oslo, 1996), including Joel Samoff, "Aid and Education-Transforming the Policy Making Process," 5–72.

40. For a fuller development of this argument and examples, see Joel Samoff, "The Facade of Precision in Education Data and Statistics: A Troubling Example from Tanzania," *Journal of Modern African Studies* 29, no. 4 (December 1991): 669–689.

41. Problems with the reported data and their major causes are well-known. The basic data deficiencies are often compounded by careless use of what is available (e.g., assuming that budgeted allocations are approximately the same as actual expenditures or comparing budget data in one year with expenditure data in another).

42. For a recent overview, see Joel Samoff, "Chaos and Certainty in Development," *World Development* 24, no. 4 (April 1996): 611–633.

43. Here I conflate commissioned research (studies initiated and funded by an external agency) and consulting (individual and occasionally institutional contracts for services rendered) because that is the common usage among the practitioners.

44. George Psacharopoulos and William Loxley, *Diversified Secondary Education and Development: Evidence from Colombia and Tanzania* (Baltimore: Johns Hopkins University Press, 1985).

Chapter 3

The State, Social Movements, and Educational Reform

Raymond A. Morrow and Carlos Alberto Torres

The task of this chapter is to consider the relationship between the state, social movements, and education from a comparative perspective. Though this constellation of issues may appear to be an obvious foundation for understanding comparative education, the relationships between social movements and education have rarely been explicitly addressed theoretically (as opposed to individual case studies), let alone taken up in relation to theories of the state.[1] In the first section, we introduce the problematic of the state, culminating in a conception of a critical theory of the state that we shall use as the framework for analyzing two contrasting policy orientations for understanding the state and education: the classic welfare state model and the neoconservative alternative to it. Then we shall introduce the theory of social movements, giving particular attention to the contrast between old and new social movements. In contrast to the class-based form of the traditional working-class movements that were crucial for the institutionalization of mass education, the new social movements, we shall argue, have rather different implications for educational policy, especially in struggles over curricular content and the organization of learning. Finally, we shall suggest that the impact of globalization provides a challenge for understanding the changing contexts for educational policy and its relationship to the state and social movements. The discussion will draw primarily upon examples and research based on European, North American, and Latin American experiences.

Before taking up the state and social movements, we shall make a few comments about the particular complex of problems at issue here. The unifying theme of this chapter can best be situated in terms of the question of the relationship between education and *cultural reproduction,* a problematic that highlights the question of the relationships between social movements and the state. Models of cultural reproduction begin with the premise that society needs to be understood as a complex and contradictory whole within which dominant institutions primarily serve to reproduce the basic form of social order.[2] Ordinarily, this process of reproduction requires extensive changes in society and culture, which are very selective even though they may involve major reforms. They are selective in that normally they do not challenge the overall continuity of a given form of society. Yet this reproduction is never completely smooth and encounters various forms of opposition and resistance, ranging from individual acts to massive mobilizations organized by social movements. Such forms of collective behavior thus become the source of conflicts that the democratic state attempts to manage and control. Though often viewed as disruptive and as a threat to the status quo, social and cultural movements are also the primary source of change and innovation in society. In the context of education, the primary sites of such conflict are schools and educational policy at all levels. Histories of education typically present the celebratory history of policy making as a progressive process based on "reforms" culminating in the present. From the perspective of the more fundamental claims and challenges of social movements, however, such reforms can often be revealed to distort the understanding of change. In this respect such reforms may serve to conceal ongoing social conflicts and dominant interests as well as reinforce the cultural capital of the professionals charged with legitimating and organizing.[3] Accordingly, the problematic of educational reform must be situated in the context of the contested relations between the state and social movements in the overall process of cultural reproduction and change.

Theories of the State

The liberal conception of the state—and the commonsense basis on which most people consider themselves to be democratic citizens—is centered on the notion of separate public powers (for the government and the governed). The state is conceived as the supreme political authority within precise limits.[4] This liberal notion of political authority needs to be reconsidered from the perspective of contemporary political science and political sociology. There is a dominant tradition of liberal political analysis that primarily addresses the question of state sovereignty and citizenship, that is, the formation of the citizen and the political culture of the nation. Such accounts provide the basis for official definitions of democracy in the primary and secondary curricula of liberal democracies.

A second tradition, that of liberal democratic theory, is more critical. It questions problems of political representation and accountability, that is, how the actions of individuals, institutions, and the state itself are subject to controls and checks and balances. This is particularly relevant in regard to the actions of individuals, institutions, corporations, and state agencies in the constituting of the democratic pact and in the extent to which their actions damage or betray the democratic pact. One influential stream of thought questions the effects of excessive individualism and calls for a more communitarian conception of public philosophy.[5]

A third tradition, Marxist social theory, focuses on the power of the state, especially those aspects related to the relationship between social class structure and the forces and instruments of political coercion. This analysis supposes that obtaining consensus and implementing measures that guarantee the fair representation of interests is not outside the realm of pressured persuasion or coercion, nor outside the realm of social relations of domination and exploitation.

Finally, the perspective of political sociology, with the extraordinary contributions of Max Weber, focuses on the study of the institutional mechanisms of the operation of the state, and especially on the exercise of the authority of the state and the relationships among nation-states.[6]

Despite their differences in theories of democracy, neo-Marxism and political sociology open new dimensions in the discussion of the state. As a theoretical point of departure, the notion of *the state* appears as a heuristic instrument, as a concept that differs radically from the classical notions of political regime, government, or public power found in pluralist democratic theory. Its usefulness is based on how the notion of the state includes the idea of the *condensation of power* and force in the society, a process that renders deeper levels of power invisible. The exercise of the power of the state occurs by the exercise of actions of power and co-action over *civil society* (i.e., nonstate institutions and voluntary associations) by means of specialized state apparatuses. This notion of the condensation of power also refers to another central aspect of the state—the notion that the state may exercise power relatively autonomously. This power may thus be independent of the major social actors (rather than merely represent their aggregated interests), even though on occasion it is exercised according to specific interests represented in society, for example, state action on behalf of specific elites. Thus the power of the state can reflect a specific political project, a class alliance, or a coalition of specific economic, social, cultural, or moral interests. The state appears as an alliance or a *pact of domination.*[7]

From the perspective of the critical theory of the state linking neo-Marxian and Weberian insights—the perspective that informs the following discussion— the state is also an arena of confrontation for conflicting political projects. As an arena of confrontation, it not only reflects the vicissitudes of social struggles and the tensions inherent in agreements and disagreements between social forces, but it also reflects the contradictions and difficulties of carrying out unified and coherent actions that are within the parameters of a specific political project. Every public policy, even though it is part of a project of domination, reflects an arena of struggle and a sounding board for civil society and its inherent tensions, contradictions, political agreements, and disagreements.

Approaching the state strictly as an actor in the struggle between social classes de-emphasizes other important variables related to social action. In addition to class distinctions, other aspects of race, ethnicity, gender, geographical location, or ethical-moral or religious differences among individuals produce social relations and social actions that require the state to legislate, sanction, manage, and punish. According to Claus Offe, perhaps the leading German proponent of a critical theory of the state, one of the central issues related to the state is the contradiction between the state's need for capitalist accumulation and the legitimacy of the capitalist system itself.[8] Offe proposes an analytical approach, based on systems theory, that complements and extends Gramscian analysis and Poulantzas's interpretation. For Offe, the state is a mediator in the crisis of capitalism, and it acquires specific functions in the mediation of the basic contradictions of capitalism—the growing socialization of production and the private appropriation of surplus value. In order to measure this fundamental contradiction, the state is obliged to increase its institutional functions, a process especially evident in the field of education.[9]

For Offe, the state is a self-regulating administrative system that reflects a group of institutional rules, regulations, and conventions that have historically developed in capitalist societies. Furthermore, the capitalist state does not necessarily respond directly to those who temporarily exercise power (the government of a particular political regime or party), nor does it directly respond to the dictates of particular social sectors (economic interests) or dominant classes. Given that the state appears as a pact of domination that mediates and attempts to prevent the recurrent crises of the capitalist system from affecting the conditions of production and reproduction of that system, the class perspective of the state is not based on representing specific sectoral interests, nor does it reflect the policies of the dominant classes or of a specific political group that may control governmental institutions.[10]

In sum, the state, as a pact of domination and a self-regulated administrative system, plays a central role as mediator in the context of the crises of capitalism, especially regarding the contradictions between accumulation and democratic legitimation. The discussion of theories of the state are particularly important for education for several reasons. First, the origins and specific characteristics of mass public education can only be understood in relation to a theory of the state and its relation to social movements. Second, the definition, interpretation, and analysis of contemporary educational problems and their solutions depend to a large extent on theories of the state that justify and underlie the diagnostic and solution. Finally, the new kinds of state intervention, often defined as the neoliberal state, reflect a substantial change in the logic of public action and involvement of the state. At the same time, this change in the character of the state can also reflect new visions about the nature and limits of the democratic pact, and of the character and role of education and educational policy in the global spread of capitalism.[11] From the perspective of critical theory, the normative implications of the erosion of democratization have been discussed in terms of the notion of the decline of democratic public sphere.[12]

The following two sections discuss two antinomical visions and practices of the state—the welfare state and the neoliberal state—two visions and practices that offer distinct options in regards to educational policy. Subsequently, using a political economy of education approach, we link the discussion of the neoliberal state to the globalization of capitalism. We outline some questions about the implications of globalization to state-society relationships and the challenges to social movements in the concluding section of this chapter.

From the Welfare State to the Neoliberal State

The welfare state represents a social pact between labor and capital. Its origins can be found in the institutional reorganization of capitalism at the beginning of the century in Europe, especially in the European social democracies, such as the Scandinavian countries.[13] More recently, the New Deal engineered during Franklin Roosevelt's administration in the United States represents a form of government in which the citizens can aspire to reach minimum levels of social welfare, including education, health, social security, employment, and housing. Such public provisions are considered a right of citizenship rather than charity.[14]

Another central aspect is that this model operates under the assumption of full employment in an industrial economy following Keynesian models. For many reasons, such as populist experiences and the extreme inequality of income distribution in Latin America, state formations with a strong element of intervention in civil society have some similarities with the model of the welfare state. However, there is also an important divergence, especially the lack of state unemployment benefits. This state, which plays an important role as the modernizer of society and culture, is also a state that undertakes protectionist activities in the economy, supports the growth of internal markets, and promotes import substitution as a central aspect of the model of articulation between the state and society.

It is important to point out that the expansion and diversification of education took place in states very similar to the welfare state—interventionist states that considered educational expenditures an investment, expanded educational institutions, including the massification of enrollments, and enormously expanded educational budgets and the hiring of teachers. The role and function of public education was expanded, following the premises of the nineteenth-century liberal state that consolidated the nation and markets. In this liberal model of the state, public education postulated the creation of a disciplined pedagogical subject, and the role, mission, ideology, teacher training models, as well as

the founding notions of school curriculum and official knowledge, were all profoundly influenced by the predominant philosophy of the state, that is, a liberal
philosophy that was, despite its liberal origins, state oriented.[15]

Premises of the Neoliberal State

Neoliberalism and the neoliberal state are terms used to designate a new type
of state that emerged in the region in the past two decades. Tied to the experiences of the neoconservative governments, such as those of Margaret Thatcher
and John Major in England, Ronald Reagan in the United States, and Brian
Mulroney in Canada, the first significant case of neoliberalism implemented in
Latin America is the neoliberal economic program carried out in Chile after the
fall of Allende under the dictatorship of General Pinochet. More recently, the
market models implemented by the governments of Carlos Saúl Menem in Argentina and Carlos Salinas in Mexico represent, with the particularities of the
Argentinian and Mexican circumstances, a neoliberal model.[16]

Neoliberal governments promote notions of open markets, free trade, reduction of the public sector, decreased state intervention in the economy, and the
deregulation of markets. In the context of developing countries, neoliberalism
has been philosophically and historically associated with structural adjustment
programs, whether initiated locally or though international pressures.[17] Structural adjustment is defined as a set of programs, policies, and conditionalities
that are recommended by the World Bank, the International Monetary Fund,
and other financial organizations. Although the World Bank distinguishes
among stabilization, structural adjustment, and the policies of adjustment, it
also recognizes that the use of these terms are "imprecise and inconsistent."[18]
These programs of stabilization and adjustment have given rise to a number of
policy recommendations, including the reduction of state spending, the devaluation of currencies to promote exports, the reduction of tariffs on imports, and
an increase in public and private savings. A central aspect of this model is a
drastic reduction in the state sector, especially via the privatization of state enterprises, the liberalization of salaries and prices, and the reorientation of industrial and agricultural production toward exports. In the short run, the purpose of these policy packages is to reduce the size of the fiscal deficit, public
debt, inflation, exchange rates, and tariffs. In the long run, structural adjustment
is based on the premise that exports are the engine of development. Thus structural adjustment and stabilization policies seek to free international exchange,
reduce distortions in price structures, do away with protectionism, and facilitate the influence of the market in the Latin American economies.[19]

The premises of the neoliberal state can be synthesized as follows. The political rationale of the neoliberal state encompasses a mixture of theories and
interest groups that are tied to supply-side economics, monetarism, neoconser-

vative cultural sectors, groups opposed to the redistributive policies of the welfare state, and sectors worried about the fiscal deficit at all costs. In other words, it is a contradictory alliance. These state models respond to fiscal crises and the crisis of legitimacy (real or perceived) of the state. In this way, citizen crises of confidence are important crises for the exercise of democratic representation and confidence in governments. In this culturally conservative and economically liberal model, the state, state interventionism, and state enterprises are part of the problem, not part of the solution. As has been pointed out on several occasions by neoliberal ideology, the best state is the small government.

The prevailing premises of the economic restructuring of advanced capitalism and the premises of structural adjustment are highly compatible with the neoliberal models. They imply the reduction of public spending, reduction of programs considered waste and not investment, sale of state enterprises, and mechanisms of deregulation to avoid state intervention in the business world. Together with the aforementioned, it is proposed that the state should participate less in the provision of social services (including education, health, pensions and retirement, public transportation, and affordable housing) and that these services should be privatized. The notion of "private" (and privatizations) is glorified as part of a free market. It implies total confidence in the efficiency of competition because the activities of the public or state sector are seen as inefficient, unproductive, and socially wasteful. In contrast, the private sector is considered to be efficient, effective, productive, and responsive. Because of its less bureaucratic nature it has the flexibility needed to adapt to the transformations occurring in the modern world. Free trade agreements, such as MERCOSUR or NAFTA between the United States, Mexico, and Canada, lead to production for export and the reduction of quota barriers, which are two central elements for the global circulation of capital. This is why (in contrast to the model of the welfare state in which the state exercises a mandate to uphold the social contract between labor and capital) the neoliberal state is decidedly probusiness, that is, it supports the demands of the business world. Nevertheless, as Schugurensky rightly points out, this departure from state interventionism is differential, not total.[20] It is not possible to abandon, for symbolic as well as practical reasons, all of the state's social programs. It is necessary to diffuse conflictive and explosive areas in the realm of public policy. That is why there are programs of social solidarity in Costa Rica and Mexico, or why Brazil and other Latin American countries have passed legislation that protects street children. Thus the modification of the schema of state intervention is not indiscriminate but is a function of differential power of the clientele, which leads to policies of solidarity among the poorest of society as well as subsidies and the transfer of resources for the middle and dominant sectors, including those who are fundamentally against protectionism. Furthermore, the state does not abandon the mechanisms of discipline and coercion, nor populist strategies of distribution of wealth (or promises of such), in order to obtain electoral consensus, especially during electoral campaigns. That is, the dismantling of the public policies of the welfare state are selectively, not indiscriminately, directed at specific targets.

A central element for understanding the development of neoliberalism is the *globalization* of capitalism. The phenomenon of globalization is based on the transformation of capitalism, which alters the principles of the functioning of capitalism, whether petty commodity production, imperialist expansion as the ultimate phase of capitalism (in the vision of Lenin), or the notion of monopoly capitalism analyzed by theoretical currents tied to the New Left in the United States (Paul Baran and Paul Sweezy) or what Claus Offe has denominated late or disorganized capitalism.[21] From a postmodern perspective, Fredric Jameson defines the characteristics of postmodernism as the cultural logic of late capitalism.[22] The important element to retain is the idea of globalization in a post-Fordist world. It is central to understanding the transformations of capitalism and the transformations of the neoliberal model of the state.[23]

Before turning to the question of the state and social movement, we wish to emphasize the main conflicts between the neoliberal model and the neoconservative model. These tensions are reflected in various domains. On one hand, the neoliberal model promotes individual autonomy (i.e., possessive individualism). On the other hand, it suggests that all citizens have public responsibilities, a position not reconcilable with possessive individualism. In the economic realm, a similar dilemma exists in regard to promoting individually conceived preferences and the search for an alternative selection of public policies based on "rational public social choice." If, following the paradox proposed by economist Kenneth Arrow, markets are aggregates of individual preferences totally independent of any notion of the public good, this mechanism only functions — irrespective of the form of democracy — when there is considerable convergence in the order of preferences of individuals. This model of political philosophy cannot easily reconcile individuals with autonomous individual preferences and the state as an arena of negotiation of such preferences. Furthermore, it is impossible to advance this reconciliation with presuming that there is a set of stable norms of behavior supported by a mature state structure, a formally rational public policy based on a legal-rational model, and in the context of consensual bases that are widely accepted in the political culture of society. These conditions are obviously rather different from the everyday reality of the majority of the countries in the world.[24]

Theories of Social Movements

Paradoxically, state theories have not generally been coupled with adequate conceptions of social movements: "Surprisingly little attention has been paid to the interaction between social movements and the state."[25] The reasons for this neglect vary with the type of state theory. Though classical Marxism was in key respects primarily a theory of revolutionary social movements, it tended to reduce them to class movements, identifying the working class as the only "true" one and thus dismissing other forms of movements. Furthermore, classical Marxism was based on a simplistic conception of the objective position of class as necessarily determining the outcomes expressed as collective class consciousness culminating in revolutionary action. More recent attempts to conceptualize education in terms of a model of social reproduction linking education and economy in terms of a correspondence principle typically conclude that educational outcomes are primarily a product of structural imperatives that nullify class resistance.[26]

In contrast, other forms of liberal pluralist state theory, related functionalist conceptions of society, and elitist theories of the state tend to be concerned with problems of order and legitimation, viewing social movements primarily as disruptive forms of protest to be controlled and contained. In this context interest groups are viewed as the legitimate form for advancing political claims, whereas social movements are implicitly branded as fanatical expressions of extremist ideologies. In the case of pluralist liberal theories this strategy has led to a focus on social movements as a form of interest group destined to be assimilated into existing or new political parties or, in the worst case scenario, threats to be contained through strategies of "counterinsurgency."

The neglect of social movements in educational sociology reflects their more general marginality in theories of society that have tended to be preoccupied with the basis of order. Though this tendency is most obvious in functionalist theories of society, it has been paradoxically reinforced by structuralist conflict theories preoccupied with explaining hegemony and cultural reproduction. Though these theories have more recently made resistance to hegemony in education a central thematic, this concern has largely been focused on forms of expressive behavior associated with the diverse standpoints articulating identity politics, rather than a historically specific account of actual social movements.

In short, taking the topic of social movements seriously requires giving more explicit attention to collective behavior and collective action, terms referring to the range of more or less spontaneous activities (ranging from crowd outbursts to revolutionary movements) that challenge the structures of existing institutions and cultural norms.[27] By exception, the social theory of French sociologist Alain Touraine has made social movements central to a theory of society and change.[28] The stricter meaning of social movements as a challenge to existing institutions should be clearly differentiated from the more diffuse notion of resistance as well as from the quite different notion of "reform movements" in education, which for the most part have little to do with politically threatening mass mobilization outside normal political channels. The following definition of social movements captures the key issues:

A social movement is a collective actor constituted by individuals who understand themselves to have common interests and, for at least some significant part of their social existence, a common identity. Social movements are distinguished from other collective actors, such as political parties and pressure groups, in that they have mass mobilization, or the threat of mobilization, as their primary source of social sanction, and hence of power. They are further distinguished from other collectivities, such as voluntary associations or clubs, in being chiefly concerned with defending or changing society, or the relative position of the group in society.[29]

Paradoxically, early social movement theory was characterized by a split between those who followed psychological theories of the "crowd," which emphasized the irrational and destructive side of collective action (here following Le Bon and Freud), as opposed to conflict and Marxist sociology, which analyzed it as a rational response to exploitation and political powerlessness.[30] Nevertheless, the problematic of social movements has long been one of the underdeveloped issues of classic Marxist theory, which was based on utilitarian assumptions about individual economic interests. On this basis it was assumed that class mobilization based on subjective class consciousness was a natural outcome of the objective conditions of class exploitation. Various explanations were first advanced in the 1930s to take into account the weak class basis of twentieth-century social movements, especially their failure to culminate in revolutionary consciousness. For the Italian Marxist Antonio Gramsci the response was to take into consideration how the cultural hegemony of the dominant classes restricted the development of working-class consciousness; similarly, the Frankfurt School tradition of Critical Theory proposed that the cultural industries of the new media along with the internalization of authoritarian personality structures in the working class had similar immobilizing effects.

The revitalization of social movement theory from the 1960s onward developed in several new directions, especially in response to the worldwide emergence of radical student movements culminating in 1968 with dramatic confrontations in Paris, Mexico City, and elsewhere. It refused to understand collective action as irrational, and various approaches radically revised the analysis of self-interest in social movement mobilization. One body of social psychological research was based on a reduction of collective action to *relative deprivation theory,* a thesis based on the important observation that collective outbursts are more likely to be a response to frustrated rising expectations than to absolute levels of impoverishment or deprivation.[31] But such approaches have little to say about either the structural conditions that produce deprivation or the factors that allow some movements to mobilize and others not.

Another tradition of research attempted to reformulate the implications of a utilitarian conception of mobilization based on a drastic revision of the economic argument that informed Marx's conception of social interests. According to *rational choice theory,* the logic of collective action is paradoxical because if human motivation is essentially based on individual self-interest, members of a collectivity have no rational interest in making sacrifices for collective gains when they can achieve the benefits without participation. The resulting "free-rider" effect has the consequence of making mobilization extremely difficult given the weakness of ideals to motivate activism for the vast majority of movement members. In this respect, rational choice theory has been more successful as a critique of classical Marxism and an account of social movement failure than as an explanation of why and when they do occur.[32]

The most influential recent sociological approach has been *resource mobilization theory,* which puts particular emphasis on the organizational bases of social movement success and failure. From this perspective, both psychological and social structural determinants recede into the background, and the organizational dynamic of movements takes on a life of its own as an explanatory hypothesis.[33] However useful as a corrective, such approaches also fail as a general theory of social movements, downplaying both the role of the state and ideological factors in movement mobilization.

The State and Social Movements

Where as the preceding social movement theories tended to focus on psychological processes and movement organization, another line of inquiry has focused on the macrosocial context through a focus on the state. Three basic positions have been influential here: classic pluralism and neopluralism; class elitist, state-centered theories; and classic Marxism and neo-Marxism.[34] Pluralist models view the state as a relatively passive and neutral umpire between competing interest groups whose motivation was often viewed in terms of rational choice theory. Elitist theories focus on the question of "state capacity" and view social movements as an expression of state weakness. Finally, classic Marxist perspectives viewed the state as an instrument of class power challenged by class-based oppositional movements.

The most recent developments have drastically revised Marxist approaches through a selective appropriation of insights from resource mobilization theory, as well as focusing on ideology and culture. These developments are associated with the concepts of both post-Marxist and critical social theory. From this perspective the terrain of civil society opens up as the central arena of democratic debate and change. Social movements represent the dynamic actors in civil society in challenging the state, and they are often facilitated by various kinds of nongovernmental organizations (NGOs) that have become significant actors in educational and other contexts. The resulting theory of *new social movements* has broken with classical Marxist theory in attempting to understand the relative shift from the politics of distribution to social movements concerned as well with identity politics and the quality of life. Discussion has centered around the contested thesis of the distinctiveness of "new social movements," a conception of largely European origin that puts greater emphasis on cognitive and ideological factors, as well as the importance of *civil society* (as opposed to the state) as an arena for change.[35] This approach arose from the attempt (beginning in the late 1960s) to make sense of protest movements that appeared to focus on distinctive issues and drew upon new types of participants: student movements, peace and environmental movements, the women's movement, and so on. According to this perspective, the new social movements differ in key aspects with respect to ideology (quality of life, as opposed to growth and redistribution); basis of support (diverse interests and emergent networks, as opposed to social classes related to industrial labor, agriculture, or race); motivations for participation (more idealist, as opposed to objective social interests); organizational structure (decentralized, as opposed to bureaucratic); and political style (extraparliamentary, as opposed to integrated into neocorporatist processes of negotiation).[36]

Old and New Social Movements and Educational Reform

The neglect of the relations between states and social movements has reinforced the even greater lack of explicit attention given to the relationship between education and social movements. Though educational change and reform are central to histories of education, functionalist approaches have tended to focus on the imperatives of differentiation as an autonomous process, as opposed to the dynamics of struggle between states and collective movements.[37]

The problematic of social movements touches on the educational field in various contexts of conflict theories of educational change. First, theories of educational practice (e.g., pedagogies) have often been the basis of cultural reformist movements that have often been aligned with broader social movements. More typically, the affiliation of educational theories with social movements has remained more marginal, for example, the twentieth-century "modern school" movement inspired by Spaniard Francisco Ferrer was closely related to the anarchist movement in the context of the United States.[38] Today, the "back to basics" movement in education is broadly affiliated with New Right political movements, much as "critical pedagogy" has ties with New Left movements.

Second, the problematic of student movements is largely associated with contexts in which the university itself (and occasionally secondary educational institutions) becomes the site of social movement activity. Such student movements have had periodic influence in advanced industrial societies (e.g., the revolutionary uprisings in Europe after World War I; confrontations in Europe involving fascists, socialists, and communists in the 1930s; and the worldwide student revolts of the late 1960s).[39] In many underdeveloped contexts, student movements have continued to be a source of agitation against more or less authoritarian states that serve to reproduce vast inequality of income and opportunity. In these settings, struggles over university "autonomy" have been in part triggered by the political threats posed by student movements.

Third, educational policy may be an explicit part of a general social movement, as in the case of "old" social movement theory concerned with working-class mobilization. The classic example here is the role of education played as one of the demands of European labor movements in the nineteenth and twentieth centuries.[40] The rise of public schooling in the West can be broadly described as the outcome of the struggles of class-based social movements to gain state support for inclusion as part of a universal citizenship.[41] Some of these have been associated with major social transformations. Following the Mexican revolution, for example, educational reform was officially linked with extensive efforts to expand rural schooling and assimilate the campesino and indigenous populations.

With the decline of various single-factor theories of educational growth (e.g., human capital theory, modernization theory), more comprehensive models of educational expansion have stressed the competitive struggle between institutionalized corporate and potential primary actors, that is, those capable of collective action.[42] One general conclusion of such research is that "the cause of the initial period of educational expansion is found in the behavior of the self-consciously marginal. An essential precondition is the erosion of one's location in the traditional social order."[43] In the European case the contention between Protestants and Catholics provided the initial impetus for primary action, whereas class-based movements emerged later in response to the industrial revolution. For example, the English case represents a complex process in which the Chartist and Owenite movements played an important role in the development of public education.[44] Similarly, in this century aspirations for basic educational rights have typically been part of modern urban and agrarian class-based movements (largely composed of peasants) in so-called third world contexts.

One of the few explicit contemporary attempts to link the state, social movements, and education as part of a general theory can be found in Carnoy and Levin's "social-conflict" theory of the state, which "provides a framework for developing a dialectical analysis of education in capitalist society, because it views social movements as playing a vital role in affecting educational policy."[45] On this basis an effort can be made to "predict" educational reforms and assess the potential and limits of struggles over schooling. Nevertheless, this approach remains largely within the framework of the class-based assumptions of "old" social movement theory, ignoring the peculiarities of the new social movements.

Finally, new social movement theory has provided the basis for a dramatic shift in understanding the relationship between social movements and education. A distinctive characteristic of new social movements is their cognitive and ideological focus on rethinking preexisting social and cultural paradigms as part of a politics of identity. As a consequence, one of their key strategies is broadly educational as opposed to political. Although they have experienced numerous setbacks at the level of dramatic changes in policy in response to new social movement demands, they have been more successful in their educational efforts, a process reflected in significant shifts in public opinion on various issues such as gender, race, the environment, peace, and sexual orientations. In the case of the racially based civil rights movement in the United States, the dismantling of segregated schools constituted perhaps the most fundamental and far-reaching demand linking race and education.[46] Virtually every new social movement has also been characterized by the advocacy of curricular change and has generally found a few sympathetic listeners within teacher education and among education policy makers. Moreover, the pluralist mandate of public educational systems in most liberal democracies requires ongoing updates of the agenda of "legitimate" issues to be presented as part of mass education. Such effects increase dramatically at the higher levels, thus precipitating recent debates about "political correctness" on university campuses, especially in the United States.[47] To a great extent, this whole debate can be viewed in terms of the significant success of new social movements in reforming—if not fundamentally transforming—the content of higher education in the humanities, and to a lesser extent the social sciences (which have long been more attuned to inputs from social movements). For the most part these changes have proceeded along the lines of the single-issue demands often typical of identity politics. One consequence has been the need to rethinking the relationships between race, class, and gender in education.[48]

Efforts to link and integrate new social movements with educational reform from the 1980s onward are most closely associated with the cultural movement most commonly identified with the term "critical pedagogy." Known variously as "postmodern," "multicultural," and "postcolonial" education, critical pedagogies have attempted to articulate "the language of possibility" that could unite such diverse oppositional movements.[49] In this context the notion of a "postmodern" or "postcolonial" pedagogy is evoked as a diffuse reference point for an epoch in which Western universalisms and scientific certainties are called into question from diverse perspectives as a particular Eurocentric and masculinist view of the world.

The general failure of critical pedagogies to effect significant change has elicited various forms of criticism. Most fundamentally, it has been argued that such efforts to develop a general critical pedagogy and apply it to stimulating counterhegemonic resistance in schools is inconsistent with Gramsci's theory of hegemony concerned with "social and political movements, as in 1968 in France and Mexico or in 1970 in the United States."[50] More negatively, it has been argued that the failures of critical pedagogy—as a "transformative pedagogy in general"—stem precisely from the lack of a historically specific relation to social movements:

The effect of critical pedagogy is to further distance new sociologists from past, contemporary and emergent social movements; to replace with generality, the specific requirements of an educational politics; and, finally, to diminish social understanding that prohibits flight from history and politics.[51]

Nevertheless, under the impetus of postmodernist and multicultural debates, critical pedagogy has consistently attempted to incorporate a multiplicity of voices from new social movements as part of the struggle against "the disconcerting proliferation of separatist forms of identity politics."[52]

Though critical pedagogies have not had a major impact on educational policy, they inform various social movements and in several developing societies have played a significant role as part of a process of political mobilization. On the one hand, there are the revolutionary experiences of Cuba, Nicaragua, and Mozambique. On the other, attempts at educational reform played a crucial part in the failure of socialist movements in Allende's Chile and, in a very different context, became the basis for innovative policies in São Paulo in Brazil.[53]

The Challenges Ahead: The Globalization of Capitalism, the State, and Social Movements in Education

From the perspective of emerging relationships between the state, social movements, and education, the theoretical problematic of *globalization* provides a more grounded and empirically analyzable set of questions than the slippery formulations associated with postmodernism and postcolonialism. Consequently it has been argued that "just as postmodernism was *the* concept of the 1980s, globalization may be *the* concept of the 1990s, a key idea by which we understand the transition of human society into the third millennium."[54] Though globalization in general has a long history, its specific meaning today is linked to the increasingly linear acceleration of the processes associated with it in the mid-twentieth century. In this respect globalization overlaps with processes variously described as postindustrialization, postmodernization, post-Fordism, and the information society. In sum, it can be defined as "a social process in which the constraints of geography on social and cultural arrangements recede and in which people become increasingly aware that they are receding."[55]

Economic globalization is the result of a worldwide economic restructuring that involves the globalization of economies, science, technology, and culture, as well as a profound transformation in the international division of labor.[56] Along with this transformation in the international division of labor there has been a readjustment of economic integration among nations, states, and national and regional economies.[57] In large part, this globalization is a result of changes in communications and computer technology that increase the productivity of labor, replace labor with capital, and lead to the development of new areas of high productivity (e.g., software technology, which helped people like billionaire Bill Gates and the Microsoft Corporation have a world reach). These changes are redefining relations between nations. They involve the mobility of capital via international exchanges as well as short-term, high-risk financial instruments. There is an enormous concentration and centralization of capital and production at the international level.[58]

Labor markets in contemporary capitalism are not homogeneous. The segmentation of labor markets implies that there are at least four kinds of markets: (1) a market that responds to the demands of monopoly capitalism, usually transnational; (2) a market that responds to the demands of competitive capitalism, representing the secondary labor market; (3) a market that is the public sector, one of the few labor markets relatively protected from international competition; and (4) a rapidly growing marginal labor market that includes everything from illegal transactions (such as narcotics trafficking) to self-employment, domestic work, family enterprises, small-scale subsistence production, and numerous other economic activities, which have been called marginal, underground, or informal work.

A central characteristic of this highly globalized capitalism is that the factors of production are not located in close geographic proximity. Furthermore, marginal profit rates are growing because of continuing increases in per capita productivity (which continues to increase in advanced capitalism) and a reduction of costs (via layoffs, intensification of production, replacing more expensive workers with less expensive ones, or replacing labor with capital). With the growing segmentation of labor markets in which the primary markets offer more income, stability, and perquisites, the hourly wage has been replaced by piecework. This creates a clear distinction between the nominal and real salaries and wages of workers and the social wage via indirect loans and state actions. At the same time, this set of transformations implies the decline of the working class and a reduction of the power of organized labor in negotiating economic policies and in the constitution of the social pact underscoring state domination. Over the last three or four decades, the service sectors have continued to grow, reducing the importance of the gross national product in the primary sector and manufacturing. There are clear indications that technology is replacing many "middlemen," which is demonstrated in the declining importance, for example, of travel agents and real estate agents.

These changes in the global composition of labor and capital are taking place at a time when there is an abundance of labor, and conflicts between labor and capital are decreasing. The increase of supernumerary workers is also associated with an increase in international competition and the conviction on the part of the working class and labor unions that it is not possible to exclusively pressure the companies in search of more and better social services or salaries. This is impossible because of the abundance of labor, as well as the awareness of the falling profit margins of companies in the transnational and competitive environments, and the resulting loss of jobs and the accelerated migration of capital from regional markets in advanced capitalistic countries to areas in which labor is highly skilled and poorly paid. The threat of free-trade agreements such as NAFTA or the new arrangements proposed by GATT mark the limits of protectionist policies. For example, engineers and computer experts from India enter payroll information of North American companies into databases for a fraction of the cost of employing white collar workers, or low-cost mass production by Chinese workers, sometimes subject to forced labor. In order to deal with falling rates of profits, transnational capitalism is attempting to achieve more productivity per capita or the reduction of the actual costs of production, as well as transferring its production activities to tax-free zones characterized by cheap and highly skilled labor, limited organized labor, and easy, efficient, and cheap access to natural resources.

This new global economy is very different from the former national economy. National economies were previously based on standardized mass production, with a few managers controlling the production process from above and a great number of workers following orders. This economy of mass production was stable as long as it could reduce its costs of production (including the price of labor) and retool quickly enough to remain competitive at the international level. Because of advances in communications and transportation technology and the growth of service industries, production has become fragmented around the world. Production is moving to areas of the world with either cheaper or better-trained labor, favorable political conditions, access to better infrastructure and national resources, larger markets, and tax incentives.[59]

The new global economy is more fluid and flexible, with multiple lines of power and decision-making mechanisms, analogous to a spider's web, as opposed to the static pyramidal organization of power that characterized the traditional capitalist system.[60] Although the public education system in the old capitalist order was oriented toward the production of a disciplined and reliable workforce, the new global economy requires workers with the capacity to learn quickly and to work in teams in reliable and creative ways. Reich defines these workers as symbolic analysts who will make up the most productive and dynamic segments of the labor force.[61]

Along with the segmentation of labor markets, full-time workers have been replaced with part-time workers (with a substantial reduction in the cost of labor due to fewer employer contributions to health, education, social security, etc.), an increase in female participation in labor markets, a systematic fall in real salaries, and a growing gap that separates salaried workers from the dominant sectors of society. A similar international phenomenon can be identified in the growing social and economic gap between developing countries and advanced capitalistic nations. The only exceptions are the newly industrializing countries of Asia.

In order to understand the changes in educational reform trends in the age of globalization, it is necessary to consider the implications of theories of the state and theories of social movements. Cultural globalization presents important issues with respect to social movements in various ways. One expression is the increasing international links between new social movements, a process also evident in religious movements. It has been argued that globalization has contradictory effects in provoking fundamentalist religious and ethnic movements that challenge the secularization of education and at the same time encouraging other ecumenical tendencies that force religious and ethnic movements to "relativize" their positions through the discovery of common principles.[62] But the primary impact of globalization—whether political, economic, or cultural—is reflected in a broad shift toward an international standardization of educational curricula and credentials that goes beyond (though has not altogether escaped) earlier forms of educational colonialism.[63]

The relationship between globalization and education remains an emergent form of inquiry. One promising line of analysis builds on the concept of the *creolization* of culture, a notion drawn from linguistics that provides a more empirically grounded basis for issues that have been taken up in the postcolonial literature under the heading of hybridity.[64] Hannerz stresses that "the cultural processes of creolization are not merely a matter of constant pressure from the center toward the periphery, but a more creative interplay."[65] In short, "creolist concepts also intimate that there is hope yet for cultural variety. Globalization need not be a matter only of far-reaching or complete homogenization; the increasing interconnectedness of the world also results in some cultural gains."[66] In the context of peripheral societies, cultural flows are framed primarily by the state and markets. On the one hand, the most common focus of attention is on how states typically use education to construct citizens as well as inculcate "an almost universally replicated set of basic skills, including literacy and numeracy."[67] But there is also a very different process whereby the state serves as a "transnational cultural mediator" through which education becomes the filter between the metropolitan culture and the indigenous culture that remains more marginally influenced and necessarily appropriates global culture on its own terms (see, for example, chapter 9 by Hickling-Hudson in this volume). Though the state channels transnational influences, it cannot fully control their relation to local practices. Those with higher levels of formal education reflect the rhetoric of globalization as market-based homogenization in their consumption patterns; less visible are the opposite processes: "creolized musics, art, literature, fashion, cuisine, often religion as well, come about through such processes."[68] Clearly such issues should become the basis of a research agenda concerned with globalization, education, and cultural change.

Economic globalization has provided an impetus for efforts to reorganize education and teacher's work and curricula along lines that the New Right claims reflect the imperatives of the new world economy, a process reinforced by the pressures of international organizations such as the World Bank. As a consequence, the demands of local, movement-based struggles can often be marginalized in the name of strategies of "national" development that just happen to co-incide with the longer-term interests of global, transnational capital. Though most obvious in the case of underdeveloped countries under pressure from international agencies, such processes can also be seen at work on a more voluntary basis in neoliberal, "post-Fordist" educational policies in advanced societies.[69]

There are five questions that suggest future research agendas:

1. Does globalization mean that the nation-state has lost its power to control social formation and therefore to create conditions for socialization, citizenship, and the promotion of a democratic environment?

2. Did social movements decline in the 1980s and 1990s and will demobilization continue with the process of globalization, thus eroding the capacity of social movements to open up new cultural and social possibilities?

3. Can we aptly characterize the rise of right-wing social movements in education, for instance, those presented in the analysis of Apple and Oliver,[70] as emblematic of the crisis of the state and suggestive of the impossibility of social movements re-emerging as progressive, transformative forces?

4. Given the intersection of state crises with the apparent weakness of social movements—old or new—in the age of globalization, what are the implications for socialization, education, citizenship, and democracy?

5. How will processes of global creolization affect metropolitan and peripheral societies, especially with respect to educational stratification, elite formation, and cultural change?

Notes

This chapter was presented to the Comparative and International Education Society Conference (CIES), Mexico City, 19–23 March 1997.

1. See, for example, Robert F. Arnove, Philip G. Altbach, and Gail P. Kelly, eds., *Emergent Issues in Education: Comparative Perspectives* (Albany: State University of New York Press, 1992). The section on "contemporary reform movements" is misleading in that it focuses on reform processes driven by state bureaucracies rather than on the social movements that may have either contributed to new agendas or might oppose them. The problematic of social movements is thus largely absent from this volume.

2. Raymond A. Morrow and Carlos A. Torres, *Social Theory and Education: A Critique of Theories of Social and Cultural Reproduction* (Albany: State University of New York Press, 1995).

3. Thomas S. Popkewitz, *A Political Sociology of Educational Reform: Power/ Knowledge in Teaching, Teacher Education, and Research* (New York: Columbia University, Teachers College Press, 1991).

4. David Held, *Political Theory and the Modern State* (Stanford: Stanford University Press, 1989), 12.

5. E.g., Michael J. Sandel, *Democracy's Discontent* (Cambridge: Harvard University Press, 1996).

6. Held, *Political Theory and the Modern State,* 11–55; David Held, ed., *Political Theory* (Stanford: Stanford University Press, 1991); Heinz Rudolf Sonntag and Héctor Valecillos, *El estado en el capitalismo contemporáneo* (México: Siglo XX Editores, 1977); David Held et al., eds., *States and Societies* (Oxford: Martin Robinson/The Open University, 1983); Andrew Vincent, *Theories of the State* (Oxford: Basil Blackwell, 1987).

7. Fernando H. Cardoso, "On the Characterization of Authoritarian Regimes in Latin America," in *The New Authoritarianism in Latin America,* ed. D. Collier (Princeton: Princeton University Press, 1979), 33–60. The term "domination" here is employed in the sense suggested by Max Weber's theory of *Herrschaft,* a German term referring to modes of relations between ruling and ruled, and variously translated as authority or domination. Hence a "pact of domination" alludes to the ways in which those ruled voluntarily accept the legitimacy of the ruler, thus producing ostensibly "legitimate" authority.

8. Claus Offe, *Contradictions of the Welfare State,* ed. John Keane (London: Hutchinson, 1984).

9. Carlos Alberto Torres, "The Capitalist State and Public Policy Formation: A Framework for a Political Sociology of Educational Policy-Making," *British Journal of Sociology of Education* 10, no. 1 (1989): 81–102; and Morrow and Torres, *Social Theory and Education,* chap. 12.

10. Martin Carnoy, *The State and Political Theory* (Princeton: Princeton University Press, 1984), 131–140.

11. Carlos Alberto Torres, "La Universidad Latinoamericana: De la Reforma de 1918 al Ajuste Estructural de los 1990," in C. Torres et al., *Curriculum Universitario Siglo XXI* (Facultad de Ciencias de la Educación, Universidad Nacional de Entre Rios, Paraná, Entre Rios, July 1994), 13–54.

12. Craig Calhoun, ed., *Habermas and the Public Sphere* (Cambridge, Mass.: MIT Press, 1992).

13. Gøsta Esping-Andersen, *The Three Worlds of Welfare Capitalism* (Princeton: Princeton University Press, 1990).

14. Harold R. Wilensky, *The Welfare State and Equality: Structural and Ideological Roots of Public Expenditures* (Berkeley: University of California Press, 1975); Harold R. Wilensky, *The New Corporatism: Centralization and the Welfare State* (Beverly Hills: Sage, 1976); Thomas Popkewitz, *Political Sociology of Educational Reform.*

15. Margaret S. Archer, *The Sociology of Educational Expansion: Take-Off, Growth, and Inflation in Educational Systems* (Beverly Hills: Sage, 1982); Adriana Puiggrós, *Democracia autoritarismo en la pedagogía argentina y latinoamericana* (Buenos Aires: Galerna, 1990); Adriana Puiggrós et al., *Sujetos, disciplina y curriculum en los orígenes del sistema educativo argentino* (Buenos Aires: Galerna, 1992).

16. Without attempting to make a theoretical excursus, it is useful to point out that the notions of neoconservativism and neoliberalism have been identified by Michael Apple as two factions of the same movement of the right. See Michael Apple, *Official Knowledge: Democratic Education in a Conservative Age* (New York: Routledge, 1993). Apple's position and some of the differences between the two ideologies have been discussed in Carlos Alberto Torres, *Democracy, Education, and Multiculturalism: Dilemmas of Citizenship in a Global World* (Lanham, Md.: Rowman and Littlefield, 1998).

17. Larissa Lomnitz and Ana Melnick, *Chile's Middle Class: A Struggle for Survival in the Face of Neoliberalism* (Boulder: Lynne Rienner, 1991), 9–47.

18. Cited in Joel Samoff, "More, Less, None? Human Resource Development: Responses to Economic Constraint" (unpublished paper, Palo Alto, Calif., June 1990), 21.

19. Sergio Bitar, "Neo-Conservativism versus Neo-Structuralism in Latin America," *CEPAL Review* 34 (1988): 45.

20. Daniel Schugurensky, "Global Economic Restructuring and University Change: The Case of Universidad de Buenos Aires" (Ph.D. diss., University of Alberta, 1994).

21. Claus Offe, *Contradictions of the Welfare State.* See also Scott Lash and John Urry, *The End of Organized Capitalism* (Madison: University of Wisconsin Press, 1987).

22. Fredric Jameson, *Postmodernism or the Cultural Logic of Late Capitalism* (Durham, N.C.: Duke University Press, 1991).

23. For a detailed discussion of the post-Fordist model of education, see Carlos Alberto Torres, *Education, Power and the State: Dilemmas of Citizenship in Multicultural Societies* (Lanham, Md.: Rowman and Littlefield, 1998), chap. 2.

24. Michael Williams and Geert Reuten, "After the Rectifying Revolution: The Contradictions of the Mixed Economy," *Capital and Class* 49 (Spring 1993): 82.

25. J. Craig Jenkins and Bert Klandermans, "The Politics of Social Protest," in *The Politics of Social Protest: Comparative Perspectives on States and Social Movements,* ed. J. Craig Jenkins and Bert Klandermans (Minneapolis: University of Minnesota Press, 1995), 5.

26. It should be noted that the correspondence theory of social reproduction developed by Samuel Bowles and Herbert Gintis in their *Schooling in Capitalist America* (New York: Basic Books, 1976) attempted to interpret the history of American education in terms of the class contexts of educational reform movements.

27. E.g., Charles Tilly, *From Mobilization to Revolution* (New York: Random House, 1978).

28. Alain Touraine, *The Voice and the Eye: An Analysis of Social Movements,* ed. by Alan Duff (Cambridge: Cambridge University Press, 1981).

29. Alan Scott, *Ideology and the New Social Movements* (London: Unwin Hyman, 1990), 6.

30. Clark McPhail, *The Myth of the Madding Crowd* (New York: Aldine de Gruyter, 1991).

31. Ted Gurr, *Why Men Rebel* (Princeton: Princeton University Press, 1970).

32. Mancur Olson, *The Logic of Collective Action* (Cambridge: Harvard University Press, 1965).

33. John McCarthy and Mayer Zald, "Resource Mobilization and Social Movements," *American Journal of Sociology* 82 (1973): 1212–1241; Aldon D. Morris and Carol McClung Mueller, eds., *Frontiers in Social Movement Theory* (New Haven: Yale University Press, 1992).

34. J. Craig Jenkins, "Social Movements, Political Representation, and the State: An Agenda and Comparative Framework," in *The Politics of Social Protest: Comparative Perspectives on States and Social Movements,* ed. J. Craig Jenkins and Bert Klandermans (Minneapolis: University of Minnesota Press, 1995), 14–35; for Latin America, see, for example, Susan Eckstein, ed., *Power and Popular Protest: Latin American Social Movements* (Berkeley: University of California Press, 1989); Willem Assies, Gerrit Burgwal, and Ton Salman, *Structures of Power, Movements of Resistance: An Introduction to the Theories of Urban Movements in Latin America* (Amsterdam: Center for Latin American Research and Documentation, 1990).

35. John Keane, ed., *Civil Society and the State* (London: Verso, 1988); Jean L. Cohen and Andrew Arato, *Civil Society and Political Theory* (Cambridge, Mass.: MIT Press, 1992); Joe Foweraker, *Theorizing Social Movements* (London: Pluto, 1995); Klaus Eder, *The New Politics of Class: Social Movements and Cultural Dynamics in Advanced Societies* (London: Sage, 1993).

36. Russell J. Dalton, Manfred Kuechler, and Wilhelm Búrklin, "The Challenge of New Movements," in *Challenging the Political Order,* ed. Russell J. Dalton and Manfred Kuechler (New York: Oxford University Press, 1990), 1–20.

37. Fritz Ringer, introduction to *The Rise of the Modern Educational System,* ed. Detlef Müller, Fritz Ringer, and Brian Simon (Cambridge: Cambridge University Press, 1987), 1–14; Neil Smelser, "Evaluating the Model of Structural Differentiation in Relation to Educational Change in the Nineteenth Century," in *Neofunctionalism,* ed. Jeffrey Alexander (Beverly Hills: Sage, 1985), 113–130.

38. Paul Avrich, *The Modern School Movements: Anarchism and Education in the United States* (Princeton: Princeton University Press, 1980).

39. Alfred Willener, *The Action-Image of Society: On Cultural Politicization,* ed. A. M. Sheridan Smith (London: Tavistock, 1970); Seymour M. Lipset, *Rebellion in the University* (Boston: Little, Brown, 1972).

40. Brian Simon, *The Rise of the Modern Educational System* (Cambridge: Cambridge University Press, 1987); Brian Simon, *Education and the Labour Movement: 1870–1920* (London: Lawrence and Wishart, 1965); Julia Wrigley, *Class Politics and Public Schools* (New Brunswick, N.J.: Rutgers University Press, 1982).

41. John Boli and Francisco O. Ramirez, with John W. Meyer, "Explaining the Origins and Expansion of Mass Education," *Comparative Education Review* 29, no. 2 (1985): 145–170.

42. Margaret S. Archer, "Introduction: Theorizing about the Expansion of Educational Systems," in *The Sociology of Educational Expansion,* ed. Margaret S. Archer (Beverly Hills: Sage, 1982), 3–64; Margaret S. Archer, *Social Origins of Educational Systems* (London: Sage, 1984).

43. John E. Craig and Norman Spear, "Explaining Educational Expansion: An Agenda for Historical and Comparative Research," in *The Sociology of Educational Expansion,* ed. Margaret S. Archer (Beverly Hills: Sage, 1982), 133–160.

44. A. E. Dobbs, *Education and Social Movements, 1700–1850* (1919; New York: Augustus M. Kelley, 1969).

45. Martin Carnoy and Henry M. Levin, *Schooling and Work in the Democratic State* (Stanford: Stanford University Press, 1985), 46–47.

46. Ron Eyerman and Andrew Jamison, *Social Movements: A Cognitive Approach* (Cambridge: Polity, 1991).

47. Michael Bérubé, *Public Access: Literary Theory and American Campus Politics* (London: Verso, 1994).

48. Raymond A. Morrow and Carlos Alberto Torres, "Education and the Reproduction of Class, Gender and Race: Responding to the Postmodern Challenge" *Educational Theory* 44, no. 1 (1994): 43–61.

49. Henry Giroux, *Border Crossings: Cultural Workers and the Politics of Education* (New York: Routledge, 1992); Henry Giroux, ed., *Postmodernism, Feminism, and Cultural Politics: Redrawing Educational Boundaries* (Albany: State University of New York Press, 1991).

50. Carnoy and Levin, *Schooling and Work,* 160.

51. Philip Wexler, *Social Analysis of Education: After the New Sociology* (London: Routledge and Kegan Paul, 1987), 87–88.

52. Peter McClaren, *Critical Pedagogy and Predatory Culture: Oppositional Politics in a Postmodern Era* (London: Routledge, 1995), 187. For an excellent survey of the relationship between local struggles and educational reform in the United States, see Catherine E. Walsh, ed., *Education Reform and Social Change: Multicultural Voices, Struggles, and Visions* (Albany: State University of New York Press, 1996).

53. See Pia Linquist Wong, Pilar O'Cadiz, and Carlos Alberto Torres, *Education and Democracy: Paulo Freire, Social Movements, and Educational Reform in Sao Paulo* (Boulder: Westview, 1998).

54. Malcolm Waters, *Globalization* (London: Routledge, 1995), 1.

55. Waters, *Globalization,* 3.

56. David Harvey, *The Condition of Postmodernity* (Cambridge: Blackwell, 1989); Anthony Giddens, *The Consequences of Modernity* (Stanford, Calif.: Stanford University Press, 1990).

57. Carlos Alberto Torres, *Education, Power, and the State: Dilemmas of Citizenship in Multicultural Societies* (Lanham, Md.: Rowman and Littlefield, 1998).

58. Martin Carnoy et al., *The New Global Economy in the Information Age: Reflections on Our Changing World* (University Park: Pennsylvania State University Press, 1993).

59. "Your New Global Workforce," *Fortune,* 14 December 1992, 52–66.

60. Several political scientists have analyzed these changes. For example, Adam Przeworski, *Democracy and the Market: Political and Economic Reforms in Eastern Europe and Latin America* (New York: Cambridge University Press, 1991); Kenichi Ohmae, *The Borderless World: Power and Strategy in the Interlinked World Economy* (New York: Harper Business, 1990); Robert B. Reich, *The Work of Nations* (New York: Vintage, 1991); Lester Thurow, *Head to Head: The Coming Economic Battle among Japan, Europe, and America* (New York: William Morrow, 1992).

61. Reich, *Work of Nations.*

62. Roland Robertson, *Globalization* (London: Sage, 1992).

63. Martin Carnoy, *Education as Cultural Imperialism* (New York: David McKay, 1974).

64. E.g., Homi K. Bhabha, *The Location of Culture* (London: Routledge, 1994), 112ff.

65. Ulf Hannerz, *Transnational Connections: Culture, People, Places* (London: Routledge), 68. There are also forms of creolization in the metropolitan urban centers.

66. Hannerz, *Transnational Connections,* 66.

67. Hannerz, *Transnational Connections,* 71.

68. Hannerz, *Transnational Connections,* 74.

69. See, for example, Victor Soucek, "Public Education and the Post-Fordist Accumulation Regime: A Case Study of Australia," *Interchange* 26, no. 2 (1995): 127–159, and from a comparative perspective, Victor Soucek, "Education Policy Formation in the Post-Fordist Era and Its Implications on the Nature of Teachers' Work" (Ph.D. diss., University of Alberta, 1996).

70. Michael Apple and Anita Oliver, "Why the Right Is Winning," in *Sociology of Education: Emerging Perspectives,* ed. Carlos Alberto Torres and Ted Mitchell (Albany: State University of New York Press, 1998).

Chapter 4

Culture and Education

Vandra Lea Masemann

Education can be seen through a quite different lens from the anthropological perspective than from the perspective of other disciplines. In addition, the depth of field and the focus are very different from those in large-scale comparative studies. The scope of the studies and the unit of analysis are usually much smaller, and the findings are less generalizable than in other kinds of comparative studies. The ethnographic methodology commonly used in this approach both constrains and liberates the researcher in the kinds of analysis and findings that are possible. Moreover, the voices of marginalized or peripheral populations can be heard in ways that are muted or never even listened to in large-scale comparisons.

In this chapter, the possibilities that anthropological theory and method hold for comparative education are explored. This chapter outlines the fundamental concepts of the cultural approach to the study of comparative education, shows the links between education and culture, and explores ways in which the anthropological perspective is useful in educational research. The main thesis of the chapter is that although the ethnographic approach is necessary to explore the workings of culture in the classroom, school, and administrative system, it should not constrain the researcher mainly to phenomenological approaches or ones in which the focus is only the subjective experience of the participants. It is argued that a critical or neo-Marxist approach is necessary to delineate the connections between the microlevel of the local school experience and the macrolevel of structural forces at the global level that are shaping the "delivery" and the experience of education in every country in even the most remote regions. In addition, a cultural approach to the study of comparative education is important to counter some increasing trends in the economistic analysis of school effectiveness that rest on productivity-oriented criteria, an analysis that is used on every level of education from early elementary school up to the tertiary level.[1]

This chapter opens with a brief summary of the central concepts used in the study of education and culture, followed by a discussion of the relationship of cultural values to education. Then the connection between culture, educational philosophy, and social class is examined. The role of evolutionism and colonialism and their relationship to the anthropological study of education is discussed and then the relationship of anthropology to functionalism and scientism is examined. The contribution of neo-Marxist approaches is considered, and, finally, the rise of school ethnography and its contribution to comparative education is presented.

The Concept of Culture

The foundation stone of the anthropological approach is the concept of culture. There are many different definitions of culture, but one I find useful says that culture is "concerned with actions, ideas, and artifacts which individuals in the tradition concerned learn, share, and value."[2] Culture refers to all the aspects of life, including the mental, social, linguistic, and physical forms of culture. It refers to ideas people have, the relationships they have with others in their families and with larger social institutions, the languages they speak, and the symbolic forms they share, such as written language or art/music forms. It refer to their relationship with their physical surroundings as well as the technology that is used in any society.[3] Considerable criticism has been leveled at earlier definitions of culture in their unquestioning assumption of homogeneity and the seeming denial of plural perspectives in any one social group. There is still, however, support for the idea that although groups of people may not exhibit identical forms of behavior, they may possess similar kinds of "control mechanisms—plans, recipes, rules, instructions . . . for the governing of behavior."[4]

Other related terms are "enculturation" and "socialization." "Enculturation" refers to the process of learning how to be a competent member of a specific culture or group, and "socialization" is considered by some anthropologists to refer to the general process of learning human culture.[5] "Acculturation" refers to the process of cultural transfer from one group to another.[6] All of these terms have relevance for the study of education, since it is important to delineate which aspect of culture is being transmitted or transferred from one group to another, whether it be a cross-generational transmission or a cross-group transfer of knowledge, skills, values, or attitudes. The terms "intercultural" and "multicultural" also carry a connotation of cross-group transfer and, in some cases, a political connotation of redrawing cultural lines to include a more pluralistic combination of what had previously been considered separate groups. All of these terms rest on the fundamental assumption that education has a cultural component and is not simply an information transfer.

Margaret Mead went so far as to define education as "the cultural process, the way in which each newborn human infant, born with a potentiality for learning greater than that of any other mammal, is transformed into a full member of a specific human society, sharing with the other members a specific human culture."[7] She thus defined all of the processes that a human undergoes as "education," whereas Yehudi Cohen and many educators distinguish between the processes of socialization and formal education. (As many professors of anthropology know, it is almost impossible to dislodge the popular meaning of "socialization" among college students as "partying.")

In Cohen's view, "socialization and education are two fundamentally different processes in the shaping of the mind—found in all societies, albeit in different proportions."[8] He defined socialization as "the activities that are devoted to the inculcation and elicitation of basic motivational and cognitive patterns through ongoing and spontaneous interaction with parents, siblings, kinsmen, and other members of the community" and education as "the inculcation of standardized and stereotyped knowledge, skills, values, and attitudes by means of standardized and stereotyped procedures" and hypothesized that "the quantitative role played by socialization in the development of the individual is in direct proportion to the extent to which the network of kin relations coincides with the network of personal relations."[9] Thus he argued that it is the nature of the wider social structure that provides the setting in which the socialization and education processes can be played out. This perspective is at the heart of this chapter, for it provides the anthropological and ultimately philosophical justification for seeing educational processes of any kind as inextricably linked with the social structure that gives rise to them. Thus the process of ethnographic study of education cannot be carried out without an acknowledgment of the setting in which the educational processes are taking place and the cultural content of the form of educational transmission.

Cultural Values

Another fundamental characteristic of culture is that it expresses the value system(s) of a particular society or group. In her classic work on dominant and variant value orientations, Florence Kluckhohn states that "there is a systematic variation in the realm of cultural phenomena which is both as definite and as essential as the demonstrated systematic variation in physical and biological phenomena."[10] She links her argument to a defense of the concept of cultural relativism and explores the range of value systems that answer five basic questions common to all human groups.

First, what is the character of innate human nature? It may be (1) evil—mutable or immutable, (2) neutral—mutable, (3) mixture of good and evil—immutable, and (4) good—mutable or immutable. In other words, human beings are seen as being born evil, neutral, or good and having the possibility of changing or not. Depending on the prevailing value system in the culture, the goals of education or socialization will be aimed at trying to enforce an orientation that is considered unchangeable or at changing the child into a better person (although changing for the worse is also theoretically possible in this schema). A third possibility is not to interfere at all with what is perceived to be the essential nature of the child or the person that the child will become.

Second, what is the relation of human beings to nature (and supernature)? They may be (1) subjugated to nature, (2) in harmony with nature, and (3) dominant over nature. These values are expressed in an emphasis on learning to accept whatever nature brings, to attempt some sort of collaboration with nature, or to want to triumph over nature.

Third, what is the temporal focus of human life—past, present, or future?

Fourth, what is the valued modality of human activity—being, being-in-becoming, or doing?

Fifth, what is the valued modality of people's relationship to other people—lineality, collaterality, or individualism?[11] In other words, do people value their ties to their ancestors, to those who are living in their own generation, or basically to themselves?

The answers to these five questions form the underlying assumptions of any system of socialization or education, formal or informal, in any society. The content of what is taught through socialization or education reflects the basic value orientations of any culture, mostly with variant value orientations as well that allow for a range of required and permitted variation within the system. For example, the emphasis on the practical value of education as an investment for the future in modern universities is counterbalanced (but not equally) by the aesthetic values of the arts curriculum or the humanistic contribution of the liberal arts. Moreover, the valuing of athletic superiority is also counterpoised to the valuing of the more intellectual aspects of the university enterprise.

Kluckhohn also argued that these dominant and variant value orientations could coexist and were complementary and that they would shift under external pressure to a varying extent. Thus she saw values as not the individual psychological attitudes of an individual but as socially structured orientations that were patterned in relation to the strictures of the society in which people played out their roles. She saw that people could shift in their value orientations away from one set of values into another set of equally sanctioned or perhaps even preferable values, as in the case of socially mobile persons in American culture.[12]

Although this schema can be applied to the analysis of culture as it was traditionally seen by anthropologists, it can also be applied to the analysis of the cultural foundations of education, to the study of formal curriculum and policy documents, and to the analysis of classroom. In addition, it can be applied to the study of the "hidden curriculum" of the school, which resides in the unintended cultural messages of the school experience.[13] Any ethnographic study of schools can show the cultural messages that the educational experience transmits, both intentionally and unintentionally. To the educational anthropologist, all the observed behavior in the classroom and all the printed and electronic information carry their own form of cultural knowledge, whether it is overtly or covertly expressed and whether it is formally articulated or part of the informal social life of the school.[14] Thus the link between what educators call "curriculum" and culture is clearly established.

Culture and Educational Philosophy

Kluckhohn's schema can also be applied to the analysis of changes in educational philosophy in Europe and North America (via Comenius, Rousseau, Pestalozzi, Froebel, Steiner, Montessori, and Dewey) in the last two centuries, in the shift from teacher-centered pedagogy to student-centered pedagogy as a result of changes in the conceptualization of the child from evil to good and from a creature to be dominated to one that should be nurtured, or at least allowed to develop as naturally as possible.[15] There are, of course, structural changes in the organization of society and work itself that have been concomitant with these changes in values. The perceived need for a more highly skilled workforce and the necessity for students to keep studying for a much longer number of years makes it necessary for the experience of schooling to be somewhat more endurable than in times when most people's educational biographies were relatively short.

This change of paradigm has also had a profound effect on the education of adults all over the world, and it is expressed most articulately in the work of Paulo Freire. He has proposed a "pedagogy of the oppressed" that is forged with individuals or peoples in "the incessant struggle to regain their humanity."[16] The philosophy of enabling adults to formulate their own path of learning is not, of course, a statement that they are in a situation in which there is no external authority and oppression, but that they can use their newly aroused consciousness to resist forms of external authority that they find oppressive and that they "must perceive the reality of oppression not as a closed world from which there is no exit, but as a limiting situation which they can transform. . . . The oppressed can overcome the contradiction in which they are caught only when this perception enlists them in the struggle to free themselves."[17]

This is quite different from the situation in a middle-class school in which the students are treated as if they were not really being controlled while actually being socialized into believing that they have the freedom to control their lives and the lives of others. Basil Bernstein has commented on this seeming contradiction, that student-centered pedagogy (which he designates as "invisible") appears to be based on the assumption that there is no external form of control to which the child must succumb, when in fact it is mainly middle-class students in progressive primary schools who are spared the most oppressive forms of teacher-centered pedagogy. He states that changing the code (underlying principle) that controls education transmission involves changing the culture and its basis in privatized class relationships. In other words, it is not possible just to teach students a new form of speech and writing in order to change society, since that results only in the social mobility of one individual or group of individuals. It is instead necessary to change the structural basis of society in which certain dialects or speech patterns are associated with certain forms of privilege or social class status, which have their basis in the economic, not the linguistic, order of society.

However, because integrated codes (those found in situations of invisible pedagogy) are integrated at the level of ideas, they do *not* involve integration at the level of institutions, such as school and work. He states that "there can be no such integration in Western societies (to mention only one group)" because the abstracting of education from work, such as in the tradition of liberal education, "masks the brutal fact that work and education cannot be integrated at the level of social principles in class societies."[18]

This is a position derived from Durkheim, that the division of labor in society is the fundamental characteristic that determines the shift in the principles of social integration through schooling, as exemplified in "the movement away from the transmission of common values through a ritual order and control based upon position or status, to more personalised forms of control where teachers and taught confront each other as individuals."[19] This is the classic shift from mechanical to organic solidarity, in Durkheim's terms, in the shift from an appeal to shared values, group loyalties, and ritual to the recognition of differences among individuals as they play out individualized, specialized, independent social roles. However, it is the social class position of the students that ultimately determines how they experience any form of pedagogy. The seeming variations in values are not merely cultural but are class-based.

Thus the link is made between education, culture, and class in every society. The cultural foundations of every form of socialization or education are made explicit in all the multiplicity of admonitions and rewards that kinfolk bestow on children as they are growing up and in the content of the curriculum and the classroom practices that are experienced by students in the formal education systems worldwide. Their experience of and reactions to their education are not grounded only in culture and values that are perceived in the liberal tradition as unconnected to the material basis of their society (the world of work), but these experiences are fundamentally shaped by the economic basis of their neighborhood, community, region, or country and ultimately the global economy.[20] However, the relationship of education, culture, and economics is not a simple one, and the ethnographic study of education in various countries can illuminate its dimensions. I turn now to a consideration of the colonial experience as an example of this complexity.

Evolutionism and Colonialism

Early conceptualizations of society by anthropologists such as Edward Tyler, Lewis Henry Morgan, and Herbert Spencer were based on a theory of "evolutionism" in which societies went through a series of stages, on the basis of increasing rationality, improved technology, or a progression similar to biological organisms, from the simple to the complex.[21] Thus societies based on hunting and gathering, pastoral nomadism, agriculture, herding of domesticated animals, feudalism, and industrialism were no longer seen as static entities (labeled and classified like so many butterflies in a museum case and interesting each in its own right and unrelated to the others) but as stages through which every society had to pass in order to progress further up the evolutionary ladder.

The rise of evolutionism in the nineteenth-century context of growing belief in rationality, human perfectibility, progress, and the promotion of technological advancement laid the foundations of the belief in "development" that reached its apogee in the twentieth century. The promulgation of Darwin's theory of biological evolution reinforced this theory of social evolution, with its attendant notions of "survival of the fittest" and an underlying assumption that all societies had to progress through the stages in the same order. No longer were the "armchair anthropologists" sitting in Europe simply applying labels to other cultures and groups; they were now proposing that all other peoples were evolving to more complex levels of society. Eventually, education was seen as the major means of forcing this evolutionary process to speed up.

Even though anthropological theorizing has become far more eclectic since those early days, and probably is characterized now by a willingness to study societies from a much more pluralistic perspective, education as a field has clung to this implicit evolutionary schema for a much longer period of time. As anthropologists were developing their "stages of society" schemata, educators were developing the beginnings of comparative education. These early comparativists were not searching for any kind of relativism, however, but for "borrowing from abroad useful educational devices for the improvement of education at home."[22]

This implicit evolutionary schema has not persisted merely as a heuristic device or some lingering trace of a firmly entrenched tenet of teacher ideology, however. The foundations for the growth of the development idea were firmly laid during the last several hundred years of colonial education. It has been held in place by the history of the colonial relationships between the major European countries and the rest of the world, the newer neocolonial relationships that emerged after the "granting" of independence to the former colonies, and the creation of new forms of fiscal dependency of poor countries on the major international lending agencies. Kelly and Altbach note that forms of internal colonialism still exist in the case of "populations still dominated by foreign nations existing within the same national boundaries"[23] (such as the case of native peoples of the Americas and South Africa at the time the book was written). There is also the case of populations still dominated by elites within their own national borders (such as women, African Americans, and the working class in America).

In colonial situations, education took on various forms. It was not just a simple matter of the colonial powers establishing schools so that the colonies produced citizens who resembled their colonial masters. Gail Kelly notes that colonial schools were sometimes quite removed from the metropolitan experience and were meant to produce subjugated people who could not function in the metropole. In other cases, they produced a distorted version of education in the metropole, particularly in relation to gender roles. Kelly describes vividly, for example, the classes for the teaching of English to Vietnamese refugees in the United States, in which women who were previously independent, income-earning fisherwomen were taught gender-stereotyped phrases (in American terms) for performing domestic duties and passing their time in leisure pursuits.[24]

This imposition of gender-stereotyped expectations is also reflected in curriculum materials in colonial (or formal colonial) countries. Masemann gives examples of a home economics curriculum in a West African girls' boarding school, in which the exercises were entirely based on the operation of a European-style household, with cooking and laundry activities being performed by a wife in a nuclear family. In fact, the presence of domestic servants and various relatives as well as a hired laundryman from the home village usually meant that well-educated women were not expected to perform these duties. Thus even the everyday life of the students outside of school was distorted in its curriculum representation in school.[25]

Johann Galtung's work on center-periphery theory deals with colonial education as part of the process of penetration of the dominant country into the countries to be dominated in such a way that "structural power really becomes operational when one nation gets under the skin of the other so that it is able to form and shape the inside of the nation."[26] Galtung distinguishes between the processes of subversion (from the bottom or periphery) and supervision (from the top). In the latter process, the education system is a key institution in the production of elites. Through being educated either in elite schools in the colonized country or in the metropole itself, colonial elites have more in common with their colonizers than they do with the peripheral populations in their own country. This process also fragments the peripheral populations, as Galtung believes that the relative affluence of the peripheral elites of the major colonial countries results in their having a greater political loyalty to their own national interest, and to the international bourgeoisie, than to the world proletariat of which they are a part.

He sees structural domination as made up of three processes—exploitation, fragmentation, and penetration—and notes that it is still in place wherever the

Western model of technical-economic development is accepted and the periphery depends on the center to supply something that the periphery thinks is indispensable and unavailable elsewhere. Moreover, "the Periphery thinks these things are indispensable because it has been taught to think so, because it has adopted and adapted to the culture of the Center."[27]

Although the direct colonial relationship has been altered since the political independence of many countries, this form of domination continues. However, the metaphor of evolution has changed, and the metaphors of educational development have become increasingly technicized, as if a new rationality had been invented that could make the old evolutionary processes speed up. Absent is any politicized discourse that might include notions of social justice or equity. Moreover, it is not only the process itself that is accelerated but the definition of time itself is linear and industrial. Christine Fox describes the dimensions of the new metaphors as being based on

> economic, structural images of building models, drawing analogies to the formulation of ground plans, making a blueprint for program implementation, delivery of materials, the sending "in" of a "team," the tight time line, inputs, and outputs, product flow, monitoring and so on. . . . The language used by consultants "in the field" is often particularly distorting, since they move within the "packaged" time frame, speaking of strategic planning and delivery, while their counterparts move within the more fluid and broader cultural framework of their ongoing educational context, speaking of people's lives.[28]

A similar point is made by Shen-Keng Yang in his analysis of the cultural assumptions underlying the passage of time in educational research and policy planning studies, and the way ordinary people experience or plan their lives. He refers to the concept of "time institutionalized" and points out that the railroad and now latterly the development of information technology are the means by which ordinary people experience the speeding up of institutionalized time.[29] In the preindustrial concept of time, the length of the task at hand and the repetitive cycle of the days, the week, the months, and the seasons of the year formed the basis of a nonlinear sense of time that was incorporated into the rituals of the culture and the sense of the worth of an individual human life span. In the industrial concept of time, human actions are arranged and connected in a linear sequence that is conceived of as having a purpose and a goal. The imposition of one concept on the other leads to the frustration of planners at the seeming lack of impact of their ideas, as well as bafflement on the part of the planned-for about the seeming impatience of such highly educated but apparently impractical people.

Arturo Escobar refers to development as

> a powerful and encompassing discourse which has ruled most social designs and actions of those ["underdeveloped"] countries since the early post-World War II

period . . . [that has] shaped in significant ways the modes of existence of Third World societies, mediating in a profound sense the knowledge they seek about themselves and their peoples, mapping their social landscape, sculpting their economies, transforming their cultures.[30]

Writing from the perspective of an anthropologist, he states that "there is an acute need to assert the difference of cultures, the relativity of history, and the plurality of perceptions"[31] in order to negate the view that more Development (his capitalization) is needed.

He presents an analysis of the debacle of the development idea, in which grassroots and other social movements "are opening the way for the creation of a politics for an alternative Development anchored in the grassroots and . . . providing new possibilities for satisfying human needs (including foods, nutrition, and health)."[32] He points to the importance of local knowledge in this process and notes that "a new dialectic of micro-practice and macro-thinking seems to be emerging, one which is advanced by intellectuals and activists engaged in processes of social transformation."[33]

Johann Galtung explicated this relationship still further in his analysis of the education of the elites of the countries of the center and the periphery. He noted that the interests of the elite in the center were well served by having the elite of the periphery educated either in elite colonial schools that were able to reproduce the social relations of the center in the peripheral country or in the elite schools of the center itself. Kelly's analysis fits in with Galtung's more in relation to the education of the peripheral populations of the periphery. She is mostly dealing with peripheral populations that have been colonized by representatives of the center, either by external colonizers (as in the case of classical colonialism) or by internal colonizers (as in the case of internal colonization).

Freire's analysis of mental colonialism takes the analysis still further. He postulated that the main effect of colonial education was to produce a mindset in which the colonized took on the mentality of the colonizer and judged himself or herself and others from the viewpoint of the colonizer.[34] This perception was the essence of the "neo-colonial mentality." African leaders such as Kwame Nkrumah used to fulminate against it in their public speeches, warning their countrymen not to continue to think like their former colonial masters. Even West African schoolchildren in the 1960s were well aware of the danger of having a neocolonial mentality (Masemann, personal recollection).

However, as Archie Mafeje has pointed out, the dangers of the neocolonial mindset went far deeper than comparing one's appearance, one's art, or one's politics to those of Europeans. Instead, the epistemology of European functionalist, positionistic thought became embedded in the pursuit of knowledge, which was a far more insidious mechanism for depriving Africans of their birthright.[35](Also see chapter 1 in this volume.) Mafeje saw the major epistemological links as being between the bourgeois colonial mind, on the one hand, and functionalism and scientism, on the other.

Functionalism and Scientism

Functionalism was a major strand in the development of anthropological and sociological thought. The two anthropologists most commonly associated with functionalism in anthropology were Bronislaw Malinowski and A. R. Radcliffe-Brown. Malinowski's version of functionalism focused more on the cultural needs approach—societies had to have institutions that functioned to meet the various needs of human beings. He saw ethnographies as showing how any society was able to meet the needs of its members. Radcliffe-Brown's version of functionalism was more of an analogy that compared the social system with a functioning human body, the various social institutions playing their respective roles in the healthy functioning of the whole. There was an underlying sense of harmoniousness in both models; conflict and social change did not fit well in these models of societal function.[36]

Functionalism formed the foundation of quantitative social science in the twentieth century and became very popular as the foundation of research in the "applied" areas of social science such as education. It was also the foundational research paradigm for educational research and statistics. Therefore, it has had an impact on educational research, which has been even stronger, perhaps, than on its own original disciplines.

It is not possible in this chapter to outline all the criticisms that have been leveled at the functionalist school in anthropology. Archie Mafeje does an excellent job of this in his article on the subject. He states primarily that anthropology, functionalism, and positivism were the handmaidens of colonialism and bourgeois social science in that they were an essential part of the imperialist enterprise:

> Their decision to leave their desks and disappear into the jungles of Africa, South America and Asia were not determined by love of unknown natives, but rather by the imperatives of European development, including intellectual curiosity and growing impatience with speculative theories of the nineteenth century evolutionists.[37]

He continues his argument with a discussion of the contradiction in many liberal anthropologists' position on subject-object relations and of their conception of knowledge itself:

> The harder the positivists insist on their conception of science as a guarantee for a closer and closer relation between knowledge and the real, the more they exacerbate the anomaly. In their belief that knowledge grows by secretion and that it is a result of specialized subjects (the scientists) who are able to extract knowledge from an object-world, they have overlooked the important principle of the reversibility of the subject-object relation in knowledge-formation.
>
> If at first it seemed that "positivist science" was making the world, it is now the same world that is forcing a crisis in positive science by throwing up contradictions

and anomalies in real life. . . . As a consensus model, it is inherently incapable of dealing with contradiction and revolution except in negative terms. These terms are not a problem of syntax but of ideology which precedes and predetermines possible forms of knowledge.[38]

He thus concludes that anthropology is

generically a child of imperialism [which] has been a systematic extension of bourgeois economic, political, intellectual, and cultural forms. From the twenties onwards anthropologists became embroiled in colonial affairs with the best intentions but with identical results as those of their soldier-administrator brethren.[39]

The implications of these arguments for the field of comparative education lie in the relationship between the forms of knowledge developed throughout the colonial and imperial experience and the spread of formal schooling in many countries, particularly after the end of the Second World War. The "comparison" was implicitly between the kinds of school systems developed in the European context and all other forms of schooling. Moreover, the rise of a scientistic culture allied with evolutionary notions of development coincided with the independence of a number of countries in the post–World War I period. Not surprisingly, their newly established education systems became linked with a world educational research enterprise firmly embedded in a functionalist framework. This research endeavor was primarily linked to European and North American publishing houses and later to the development of the computer. The implicit positivistic bias of the computer in its facilitation of the analysis of "more data" meant that the emphasis shifted from anthropological interest in indigenous cultures to a more sociological preoccupation with collecting statistics on the new or expanding social institutions in newly developed states.

The result has been the increasing homogenization of the culture of education on a worldwide scale, with the accompanying assumption by educators that there is only one valid epistemology. From a functionalist perspective, there is an assumption that the most scientifically reputable view has prevailed.

School Ethnography

Following the logical implications of Mafeje's conclusions concerning the "culture of positivism," the "new" sociologists of education such as Michael Young[40] and others during the 1970s rejected that culture and based their accounts of schooling on the experiences of those who were the participants in the daily life of the schools. This approach opened the way for the development of ethnographic approaches to educational research that harked back in a methodological sense to the heyday of anthropological fieldwork. It was an approach that could be carried out effectively in schools anywhere, whether at home or abroad. The work of George and Louise Spindler in the United States was also a pioneering effort in making the workings of schools in many different cultural contexts the focus of anthropologists' interests.[41]

Madan Sarup, in a review of anthropological studies in education from a neo-Marxist perspective, notes that these educational ethnographers could not ground their accounts of education in an objectively available social world because that world itself would be a feature of their method. Sarup asks, "What, then, is the justification of their own theorizing and how do they ground their accounts? What are the 'auspices' of their theorizing and on what grounds is their own enquiry better or more adequate?"[42] He suggests that their orientation to political egalitarianism is the particular interest in which their accounts are grounded. These are questions that deserve further consideration.

In my earlier work on the utility of anthropological approaches to the study of comparative education, I outlined the various ways in which ethnographic studies could be useful. First, the cross-cultural study of socialization can provide information on the kinds of values and cognitive categories that children in various cultures learn before they even enter school. It can illuminate the study of learning in natural settings from a natural-history participant-observer approach, and it can provide detailed accounts of the cross-cultural study of cognition.

Second, the comparative study of schooling, as well as the interface between socialization and the formal demands of the school system, is enhanced by the holistic ethnographic study of schools in their communities. Third, the ethnographic study of the workings of schools themselves as formal institutions can yield valuable comparative insights into current issues, such as "underachievement" of concern to educators, and can provide the grounded theoretical perspectives from which more large-scale survey-type studies can be developed.[43]

In terms of the theme of the chapter, immanent functionalism, all the suggestions above about the use of ethnography in comparative education seem to be tied to an implicitly functionalist paradigm. Subsequently, I examined constraints on the development of a neo-Marxist school ethnography. I argued that "school ethnography today is limited . . . in the same way early colonial anthropology was limited. It is essentially microcosmic, and can be carried out by researchers who see education as an essentially autonomous and isolated phenomenon."[44] (Thus the dialectic of the global and the local comes back to haunt us again. If ethnography is based on the liberal distinction that education and work are separate, then there is no need to postulate that education is related to the "outside" world.)

I asked if the trend to ethnographic studies could be likened to a metaphoric shift from "hard" to "soft" educational research in which, from a Bernsteinian perspective, educational researchers themselves had been socialized into an "elaborated code" of research, "with its shades of meaning, the ambiguities, the ambivalences, the unwillingness to judge, the interest in social relations, the emphasis on context."[45] In other words, just as Bernstein had postulated that the middle class is more likely to be socialized into a code of language production that includes elaborate distinctions and complex syntax and lexicon, so also the ethnographers have become socialized into a more complex form of educational research in which their findings cannot be easily synthesized into "results." Similarly, whereas members of the middle class are thus less likely to make judgments based on ideology because they are so overwhelmed by the complexity of all the knowledge they can discuss, members of the working class have a certainty about ideology that is made possible by the form of discourse they command, in which answers are somewhat more sharply defined as positive or negative choices. I concluded that the success of education itself leads to the inability of middle-class persons to think in ideological terms because they are involved in a form of knowledge production in which issues of ideology become subverted by issues of technique or, in this case, methodology. Thus school ethnography has become a technique widely used in colleges of education, but it has become deracinated from its place in the history of anthropological theory.

I concluded that school ethnography with a neo-Marxist perspective would be unlikely to proliferate because the power of statistical research itself will increase with the spread of formal education, which is associated with the concept of "modernization." However, I also concluded that the value of neo-Marxist approaches to ethnography lies in the researcher's eschewing the assumptions of neutrality and objectivity of functionalist positivistic approaches and assuming the autonomy and isolation of the school and classroom. Neo-Marxist approaches, instead, call for researchers to seize the opportunity of doing a political analysis in which their role, as well as that of the teacher, the student, and educational equality itself, is defined in new ways.[46]

In a further examination of the role of critical ethnography (studies that use a basically anthropological methodology but rely on a body of theory deriving from critical sociology and philosophy) in the study of comparative education, I raised the following issues:

> Is it the task of social scientists to seek ever more diligently to define objective methods of researching the social world (or education), with possibilities for change simply seen as the result of "reading out the data" and making choices on the basis of some cost-efficient or technological rationale? Or is it their task to attempt to understand as accurately as possible the subjective understandings that actors have of their own version of "social reality"? Or, third, is there some way of seeing social science in Marx's terms that would forever blur the objective/subjective distinction and thus make necessary the redefinition of social research itself?[47]

After a discussion of sociological and interpretive approaches to educational research, I examined the value of critical approaches in their treatment of social conflict and structuralism: "Neo-Marxist interpretations of school life have questioned the established categories of education and have raised fundamental questions about the social control functions of schools and the social contradictions they create or participate in."[48] Douglas Foley's work has been particularly noteworthy in this respect, in his studies of student alienation in Texas. He noted that critical ethnology offers the only way to study the techniques that schools and teachers use to organize, model, practice, and reward the behaviors that socialize students into technological rationality.[49]

I concluded by suggesting various uses to which critical ethnography could be put in comparative education: the study of socialization of students into preferred language dialects or national languages, national political cultures, or elite values; the study of the penetration of dominant ideology or imported "innovative" rationality; comparative studies of systems of student credentialing, and the penetration of computer technologies. Finally I suggested the study of "rationality" itself could be an interesting new focus of comparative education.

Since these papers were written, a great deal of ethnographic research has been done in educational settings, most prolifically in the United States and Great Britain. It is doubtful if the majority of these studies have been done from a critical perspective. Ethnographic method has been adopted as a tool of educational research, but in many cases its theoretical basis has been eschewed. Bradley Levinson, Douglas Foley, and Dorothy Holland have summarized the major work in critical educational research in the last two decades, and their book also provides a very complete bibliography of the most recent works in this field.[50] In their introduction, they review the more recent developments in critical educational studies: social reproduction, cultural reproduction, the cultural difference approach, ethnography and cultural reproduction, and cultural studies and the cultural production of the educated person. They also examine the Western schooling paradigm in global context and explore "how concepts of the 'educated person' are produced and negotiated between state discourses and local practice."[51] Their work provides a very comprehensive and forward-looking assessment of the state of the art of critical educational studies.

Conclusion

In conclusion, I return to the major themes of this chapter, particularly the relationship between culture and comparative education. Gail Kelly raised the question in 1986: "Vandra Masemann and Douglas Foley urged the field to engage in qualitative research that seeks to understand educational processes. No debate followed, nor for that matter did much research of a qualitative nature on school processes. The field neither accepted nor rejected the challenge; it simply acted as if it were never made."[52] I am not so lugubrious as Gail Kelly. She measured the acceptance of research by its appearance in the major journals in comparative education. As Levinson, Foley, and Holland's book documents, a great deal of ethnographic research was done in the 1980s and 1990s. It is generally published in journals such as the *Anthropology and Education Quarterly*.

Other questions, however, arise about the context in which critical perspectives thrive. From a Marxist perspective, there is a curious absence of focus on the dialectical struggle in comparative education, as if somehow the only struggle had been between East and West, when the epistemological struggle is being waged at a deeper cultural level between the North and the South and between industrial forms of culture and the more local, rooted forms of culture. Since schools are inherently sites of local cultural formation, this phenomenon should come as no surprise.[53] Moreover, the struggle of cultural groups that have not accepted the major epistemological assumptions of scientism has been widely ignored in the field of comparative education. The first Commission on Indigenous Education, for example, was held at the Ninth World Congress of Comparative Education in Sydney, Australia, for the first time in 1996.[54]

Although the cultural differences in education in industrial countries are perceived to be diminishing and the forces of standardization are growing ever stronger, even if only in the interests of "sharing data on education,"[55] the struggle is still being waged between those who do not share the scientistic epistemology of the world and those who assume their view has triumphed. Some protests can be heard, for example, from the growing numbers of home schoolers who resist state domination of educational systems, from religious and linguistic minorities, from feminists, from philosophical alternative schools, and from aboriginal and indigenous minorities worldwide. The growth of this plurality of voices is addressed in other chapters in this book that address the impact of critical theory and postmodernism on education.

With their emphasis on studying other cultures as complete wholes, as well as on cultural relativism, anthropologists attempted to ignore the impact of the colonial endeavor itself on cultural change. Moreover, the colonial enterprise was so laden with racist assumptions about the "other" people in the world that it became part of a convenient fiction to philosophize about human progress and perfectibility in order to implement cost-efficient forms of government such as Indirect Rule in West Africa and other areas, while at the same time providing forms of education that kept colonial subjects from competing academically on the same terms as their metropolitan masters.

On the other hand, attempts to equalize educational opportunity on a global scale have led to the ignoring of local cultural values and traditional forms of knowledge and ways of thinking, which are in danger of becoming extinct. Anthropological studies of education in every country and setting can help bear witness to the rich diversity of modes of cultural transmission and the great variety of experiences that can be called educational.

Notes

1. Jan Currie and Lesley Vidovich, "The Ascent toward Corporate Managerialism in American and Australian Universities" (paper presented at the Ninth World Congress of Comparative Education, Sydney, Australia, 1996).

2. Felix M. Keesing, *Cultural Anthropology: The Science of Custom* (New York: Rinehart, 1960), 25.

3. Thomas Rhys Williams, *Introduction to Socialization: Human Culture Transmitted* (St. Louis: Mosby, 1972), 125.

4. Clifford Geertz, quoted in Stanley Barrett, *Anthropology: A Student's Guide to Theory and Method* (Toronto: University of Toronto Press, 1996), 239.

5. Williams, *Introduction to Socialization,* 1.

6. Keesing, *Cultural Anthropology,* 28.

7. Margaret Mead, "Our Educational Emphases in Primitive Perspective," in *From Child to Adult: Studies in the Anthropology of Education,* ed. John Middleton (Garden City, N.Y.: Natural History Press, 1970), 1.

8. Yehudi Cohen, "The Shaping of Men's Minds: Adaptations to Imperatives of Culture," in *Anthropological Perspectives on Education,* ed. Murray Wax, Stanley Diamond, and Fred Gearing (New York: Basic Books, 1971), 21.

9. Cohen, "Shaping of Men's Minds," 22.

10. Florence Kluckhohn, "Dominant and Variant Value Orientations," in *Variations in Value Orientations,* ed. Florence Kluckhohn and Fred L. Strodtbeck (Westport, Conn.: Greenwood, 1961), 3.

11. Kluckhohn, *Variations in Value Orientations,* 12.

12. Kluckhohn, *Variations in Value Orientations,* 39.

13. Young Pai and Susan Adler, *Cultural Foundations of Education* (Upper Saddle River, N.J.: Prentice-Hall, 1997).

14. George Spindler, *Doing the Ethnography of Schooling: Educational Anthropology in Action* (New York: Holt, Rinehart, and Winston, 1982).

15. Robert Ulich, *Education in Western Culture* (New York: Harcourt, Brace, and World, 1965), chaps. 5–7.

16. Paulo Freire, *Pedagogy of the Oppressed* (New York: Seabury, 1974), 33.

17. Freire, *Pedagogy of the Oppressed,* 34.

18. Basil Bernstein, *Class, Codes, and Control,* vol. 3, *Towards a Theory of Educational Transmissions* (London: Routledge and Kegan Paul, 1977), 145–146.

19. Bernstein, *Class, Codes and Control,* 69.

20. Lynn Ilon, "Structural Adjustment and Education: Adapting to a Growing Global Market," *International Journal of Educational Development* 14, no. 2 (1994): 95–108.

21. Barrett, *Anthropology,* 51.

22. Harold J. Noah and Max A. Eckstein, *Toward a Science of Comparative Education* (New York: Macmillan, 1969), 112.

23. Gail Kelly and Philip Altbach, introduction to *Education and Colonialism,* ed. Philip Altbach and Gail Kelly (New York: Longman, 1978), 1.

24. Gail Kelly, "Vietnam," in *International Feminist Perspectives on Educational Reform,* ed. David Kelly (New York: Garland, 1996), 146.

25. Vandra Masemann, "The 'Hidden Curriculum' of a West African Girls' Secondary School," *Canadian Journal of African Studies* 8, no. 3 (1974): 479–494.

26. Johann Galtung, *The European Community: A Superpower in the Making* (Oslo: Universitetsforlaget; London: George Allen and Unwin, 1973), 43.

27. Galtung, *European Community,* 46.

28. Christine Fox, "Metaphors of Educational Development," in *Social Justice and Third World Education,* ed. Timothy J. Scrase (New York: Garland, 1997), 60.

29. Shen-Keng Yang, "*Shih* and *Kairos:* Time Category in the Study of Educational Reform." Reprinted from *Proceedings of the National Science Council, Part C: Humanities and Social Sciences* 1, no. 2 (1991): 253–259.

30. Arturo Escobar, "Reflections on Development: Grassroots Approaches and Alternative Politics in the Third World," *Futures* 24, no. 2 (June 1992): 411–412.

31. Escobar, "Reflections," 412.

32. Escobar, "Reflections."

33. Escobar, "Reflections."

34. Freire, *Pedagogy of the Oppressed,* 29–30.

35. Archie Mafeje, "The Problem of Anthropology in Historical Perspective: An Inquiry into the Growth of the Social Sciences," *Canadian Journal of African Studies* 10, no. 2 (1976): 307–333.

36. Barrett, *Anthropology.*

37. Mafeje, "Problem of Anthropology," 317–318.

38. Mafeje, "Problem of Anthropology," 325.

39. Mafeje, "Problem of Anthropology," 326–327.

40. Michael Young, *Knowledge and Control* (London: Collier Macmillan, 1971).

41. George Spindler and Louise Spindler, eds., *Interpretive Ethnography and Education: At Home and Abroad* (Hillsdale, N.Y.: Erlbaum, 1987); also see Spindler, *Doing Ethnography.*

42. Madan Sarup, *Marxism and Education* (London: Henley; Boston: Routledge and Kegan Paul, 1978), 33.

43. Vandra Masemann, "Anthropological Approaches to Comparative Education," *Comparative Education Review* 20, no. 3 (October 1976): 368–380.

44. Vandra Masemann, "School Ethnography: Plus ça Change?" in *Anthropologists Approaching Education,* ed. Adri Kater (The Hague: Centre for the Study of Education in Developing Countries, 1981): 85–99.

45. Basil Bernstein, *Class, Codes, and Control,* vol. 3 (London: Henley; Boston: Routledge and Kegan Paul, 1973).

46. Masemann, "School Ethnography," 94.

47. Vandra Masemann, "Critical Ethnography in the Study of Comparative Education," *Comparative Education Review* 26, no. 1 (February 1982): 1.

48. Masemann, "Critical Ethnography," 11.

49. Douglas E. Foley, "Labor and Legitimation in Schools: Notes on Doing Ethnography" (paper presented at a meeting of the Comparative and International Education Society, Ann Arbor, Mich., 1979). Also see Douglas E. Foley, *Learning Capitalist Culture: Deep in the Heart of Tejas* (Philadelphia: University of Pennsylvania Press, 1990).

50. Bradley Levinson, Douglas E. Foley, and Dorothy C. Holland, *The Cultural Production of the Educated Person: Critical Ethnographies of Schooling and Local Practice* (Albany: State University of New York Press, 1997).

51. Levinson, Foley, and Holland, *Cultural Production,* p. 18.

52. Gail Kelly, "Comparative Education: Challenge and Response," in *International Feminist Perspectives on Educational Reform: The Work of Gail Paradise Kelly,* ed. David H. Kelly (New York: Garland, 1996), 99.

53. Michael Apple, *Cultural Politics and Education* (New York: Teachers College Press, 1996).

54. Vandra Masemann and Anthony Welch, eds., *Tradition, Modernity and Post-Modernity in Education* (Amsterdam: Kluwer, 1997).

55. UNESCO, *Report on Education* (Paris: UNESCO, 1995).

Chapter 5

The Question of Identity from a Comparative Education Perspective

Christine Fox

> *The logic of binary oppositions is also a logic of*
> *subordination and domination.* (Benhabib 1992, 15)

This chapter explores a perspective of comparative education that focuses on the intersection of cultural identity and education as it affects our understandings of different educational systems. These concerns particularly affect that curious breed of educators—international educational consultants—who are confronted and immersed in contexts other than their own but claim some kind of universal authority to speak about educational change and development. I am an educational consultant as well as a teacher-educator in my native Australia, and so this exploration is partly autobiographical. Nevertheless, I claim that it is possible, as well as desirable, to reach uncoerced understandings interculturally that do not fall into Benhabib's logic of subordination and domination. The coming together of difference signals a potential to construct binary opposites; and where there are perceived opposites there are power games. The coming together of common ideas signals a potential to construct meaning; and where this occurs, there is transformation in education.

Colonizers and Colonized: A Brief Foray into the Literature of Intercultural Interaction

Comparative education has traditionally been a search for similarities and differences in educational systems or activities, ideas, and ideologies. Early attempts to compare are reminiscent of early narratives, or travelers' tales, which presented vivid descriptions of groups of peoples recognizing that they, like us, had intriguing differences in lifestyles. However, the tales of distant places soon became a mechanism for legitimating conquest and the stories expunged the humanness of colonized people (Pratt 1992). In the nineteenth and early twentieth centuries, anthropological research came into its own, epitomizing Eurocentric interpretations of the Other, making much of the contrasts between two supposed opposites. Metaphors of "primitive" or "savage" placed the Other firmly in another world from the "civilized" (Geertz 1973). Educational research, as well as educational planning in "developing" world settings, tended to be dictated by European perceptions of what was good for the Other.

In more recent times, the subtleties of linguistic and philosophical dilemmas of translation are often confused with a binary process of substituting one set of meanings for another. In education, the complex process of intercultural interaction has been analyzed by Western educators as a one-way adaptation and integration of the Other into the dominant educational norm, rather like Young Yun Kim's theory of adaptation of strangers into a host society (Gudykunst 1983; Kim 1988).

With the challenge of postmodernism, the notion of fundamental norms and values, or generalizable interests, has lost its appeal. It is increasingly being recognized that there are multiple voices and that diversity can be celebrated. The danger of course lies in a belief that diversity is an indicator that no common agreements on values or ethics are realizable, that all is culturally relative. The upshot of that argument is to claim that no authentic communication is possible across cultures. Now if this is the case, it may be argued that comparative education and international education are dead disciplines, particularly when educators come from diametrically different cultural backgrounds. This chapter posits the opposite argument, that the visibly embodied difference of the Other is a boundary that can and must be crossed and that in regard to education such boundaries are artificial, founded for the most part on historical racism.

The theoretical background of this chapter draws on some key issues arising from Jürgen Habermas's communicative action theory. Habermas posits a hypothetical "as if" ideal speech situation, coercion-free, in which interlocutors can develop a mutual understanding through a rational dialogic process (Habermas 1984). Laudable as it is, Habermas's theory assumes that there must be a common cultural background between communicators for this to happen. He thus dismisses most forms of communication in a postmodern, intercultural world (Fox 1992). Is this a paradox, then, and is this another case for dismissing comparative educational approaches? No, it is not. Procedures of communicative interaction can indeed be created which are sensitive to multiple modes of reasoning and to multiple differences of identity (Fox 1996).

Authenticity in cross-cultural professional communication about education is not only desirable, it is possible. An authentic communicative situation is an honorable kind of conversation based on mutual trust and a respectful sharing of intended meanings. It requires a sense of resonance between those who seek to reach agreement and understanding — intuitively, poetically, or experientially — by identifying shared moral values or through rational discourse, or a bit of each. The idea that cultural incompatibility is more or less inevitable is a logocentric view that stereotypes the Other and marginalizes those who identify with nondominant cultures. The ideas explored in this chapter show how people from contrastive worldviews can indeed bridge deep chasms of discursive difference if they work together to create authentic intercultural communicative situations, that is, if they create their own intercultural space.

What a pessimistic, and dangerous, view it is to dismiss the possibility of creating situations in which two people (or groups of people) from very different cultures can get together and achieve real understanding. It is almost like saying that incompatibility is inevitable and communication is therefore impossible, and that a peaceful solution to any conflict cannot be brokered. The disastrous consequences of failing to find compatibility between values and goals of groups of people has seen whole nations and ethnic groups oppose each other with violence and hatred. Atrocities committed in the name of a group or an ideology are a violation of any human value system.

Similar doubts have been raised by anthropologists and sociolinguists for a long time now, possibly for different reasons. Westerners used to feel that cultures from less industrialized countries were less complex and that Western concepts could not be adequately translated into languages used by so-called traditional societies. And yet, as Said (1978, 1983, 1993), Spivak (1990), and others have noted, this marginalizing of the Other stems from erroneous assumptions based on stereotyping of culture and language less known to a European, as well as racially motivated feelings of superiority over others. Just as feminist critiques of a supposed dichotomy between the public sphere and the private sphere show up a gender blindness, so does the author critique any supposed dichotomy between the West and the third world as culture blindness. Surely, if two cultural groups were perceived as equally powerful, and their values and beliefs able to be equally expressed without coercion, there would be scant reason why an "authentic" discussion about those differences could not take place — with sincerity, truthfulness within one's own position, and a willingness to accept and engage in different expressive discourse practices.

The idea of incompatibility tends to come mainly from an ideological construction of unequal relationships of power between two cultures. As Homi Bhabha says:

> An important feature of colonial discourse is its dependence on the concept of "fixity" in the ideological construction of otherness. Fixity, as the sign of cultural/historical/racial difference in the discourse of colonialism, is a paradoxical mode of representation: it connotes rigidity and an unchanging order as well as disorder,

degeneracy and daemonic repetition. . . . The stereotype . . . is its major discursive strategy. (Bhabha 1994, 66)

Authentic communication implies, as Hans-Georg Gadamer states, the opening of oneself to the full power of what the Other is saying. He shows that such an opening does not entail agreement but rather the to-and-fro play of dialogue (Gadamer 1989). It is this potential that comparative educators and international educational consultants can pursue, just as social ethnographers have achieved.

The implication for educators is that in each particular context, in each particular situation, and within particular activities the participants can agree to the same set of principles that have been deemed reasonable and fair in the context. Seyla Benhabib calls this "core intuition" (Benhabib 1992, 37), a process that is not to be mistaken as an outcome from linear rationality.

Intercultural Communication, Education, and the Notion of Identity

Over many years, and in particular over the past five years, I have been involved in a number of educational projects that have raised important issues about the influence that formal education has on the development of individual identity—compared with, say, developing the nation, developing human resources, or developing participation rates in schooling. These projects have included research into the development of education in Western Samoa (Fox 1992); the degree to which students from language backgrounds other than English are expected to participate in society (Iredale and Fox 1994; 1997), the participation of girls and women in education in Papua New Guinea (Fox 1995; forthcoming), the development of curriculum in Sri Lanka (Fox 1997), and, most recently, working with a doctoral student on the experiences of Spanish-speaking students in some Australian schools (Plaza, Wright, and Fox 1997). What these projects have indicated, and what my daily teaching at the university also indicates, is that the interplay of culture, education, and the state economy tends to create or support structural inequalities that mediate against the transformation of society into a just and peaceful place. And yet, within these structures, there are enormous possibilities for cultural change through the agency of those who refuse to be relegated to the margins.

In this chapter I discuss some of the issues that arise for those who feel they are marginalized individuals and/or belong to subordinated groups. At stake here is how education has influenced the ways people construct their cultural identity and how others construct that identity for them. It is posited that schooling is not necessarily unchangeable and is not merely a site for social and cultural reproduction. Rather, it presents possibilities for transformation, even if those possibilities are today being attacked more than ever before by economic rationalism and globalization. If such a transformation does take place, then it is postulated that it takes place largely through a reconceptualization of the identity of those who see themselves as agents of their own destiny, as resisters in a struggle to redefine who they are. The process itself transforms individuals, yet it takes place in a context of cultural identification of Other. The process challenges the conventional wisdom of the inevitable reproduction of inequality.

Education, Identity, and Transformation

The explanations of cultural reproduction have changed as researchers focus more on documenting the transformative experiences of the heretofore invisible or silenced minorities. Well-known writings by Paulo Freire and others on development and literacy have pointed to ways in which education can be transformative—as a process of conscientization. In a similar vein, the case study example in this volume by Anne Hickling-Hudson points to new theories of how such a transformation takes place. Other comparativists have been influenced by a body of ethnographic literature, such as the work of Clifford Geertz and other anthropologists. A significant collection of ethnographic examples of the interplay of culture, identity, and schooling has been compiled and edited by Bradley A. Levinson, Douglas E. Foley, and Dorothy C. Holland in *The Cultural Production of the Educated Person* (1996), illustrating how subordinated groups seek to use schools as sites for cultural politics and challenges. Through the production of cultural forms created within the structural constraints of sites such as schools, subjectivities form and agency develops (Levinson, Foley, and Holland 1996, 14).

Some of the empirical examples that I discuss raise further issues about the formation of identity and identities. Identity is not fixed, nor is identity a single definable "condition." Yet the construction of identity can be the construction of inequalities, as well as a powerful force in transforming the structures that seek to reduce the identity of Otherness to a single, stereotyped dimension. Thompson explains:

> While it is certainly true that modern societies are interconnected in many ways and at many levels both nationally and internationally, it is also the case that a great deal of diversity, disorganization, dissensus and resistance exists, and is likely to continue to exist, within modern societies. (Thompson 1990, 107)

The "Silent Indian"

An illustrative case discussed by Douglas Foley (1996) is that of the "silent Indian" stereotype that emerged in earlier literature on the experiences of Native Americans in schools set up by, and usually taught by, the dominant white majority in the United States. Foley revisited the myths and stereotypes of Native American schoolchildren by providing a close and personal "inside view" of how, and why, some Native Americans might choose silence as a resistant discourse, "a political retreat into a separate cultural space and identity far from the white world" (Foley 1996, 88). He interviewed a number of leading members of the Mesquaki community with whom he had gone to school several years before. He found that a number of the interviewees had successfully used silence as resistance so that they could avoid conflict and gain space, in other words, to create possibilities for their own development of an identity separate from domination. Earlier assumptions that this "silence" was a cultural trait were simplistic explanations for a multifaceted cultural "performance" in the Bakhtinian sense. Even so, such a widespread myth tended to be reinforced by the potential for the resisters to lose opportunities for future educational participation. Foley's analysis indicates how wrong it is to portray silence as a cultural stereotype instead of listening to how local actors articulate their own history.

The "Ethnic" Australian

Despite nearly twenty years of multicultural policy in the schools of most states of Australia, a notion persists of students from overseas, or students from language backgrounds other than English (LBOTE), somehow failing to match up to the standards and culture of the dominant culture. The "ethnic" Australian has been stereotyped as nonparticipative, possibly dull witted and unimaginative. LBOTE students who have left school and reflect on their schooling have said that their participation was limited when English as a Second Language programs tended to peter out after a couple of years of tuition, whereas curricula continued to draw much of their "knowledge" base from a fairly narrow band of cultural understandings that were confusing at best for someone unfamiliar with them, as well as disempowering and isolating (Iredale and Fox 1994).

In a study of the experiences of Spanish-speaking students from Uruguayan, Chilean, and Spanish families in three high schools in New South Wales, David Plaza (1998) has shown how the students try to resist the image they present in their schools of lacking ability through an approach similar to that of the "silent Indian," that is, projecting a concept of themselves as bored and withdrawn. Yet, when interviewed, students proffered a number of differing explanations. One girl in a Year Ten class commented that she did not like to read aloud in her English class because she was never encouraged and was afraid she might make a mistake and be ridiculed. The teacher's explanation was that the girl was not interested in the subject and seemed unmotivated to try to move up to a higher level.

Another girl in the Plaza study maintained that it was not much use to participate in class because of a general sense of negativity by teachers toward her and her friends, most of whom the girl classified as "wogs" or "ethnics":

En la clase no hay australianas, es un grupo de "ethnic" people y muchas veces el te trata como si tu no eres nada, muchas veces dice que tu no te sacas buenas notas porque eres esto o lo otro. (In the class there are no Australian girls; it is a group of ethnic people and many times he treats you as if you were nothing; many times he says you don't get good marks because you are this kind of person or that.) (Plaza 1998)

On the other hand, many of the students celebrated their multiple identities, being Uruguayan, Chilean, or Spanish at home, "wog" at school, and "gringo" (white foreigner) when visiting their parents' country of origin. They lived in two worlds in Australia, isolated on the one hand by their minority culture but participating in a variety of ways at school, particularly if they were born in Australia and were bilingual. Plaza found that many of the differentiating characteristics of their minority group depended not just on how dark their skin was, but on the accent detected in their English by the dominant group and in the extent to which the family remained in what Plaza calls their "cultural bubble." The children could go beyond the bubble and could go on to fulfill at least some of their dreams through various forms of both resistance and compliance.

The "Gendered" Papua New Guinea Woman

In 1995, a team of consultants (including the author) undertook an exploratory study of the levels of participation of females in Papua New Guinea in education and training (Fox 1995). In the course of this visit, the consultants interviewed a number of women to discuss their perceptions of the ways in which girls and women were able to participate in schools and in further education and university. The structural inequalities were obvious—girls' participation was far lower than boys', their job opportunities were fewer, and their status in society on the whole was far lower than for boys and men. It appeared that the greatest negative influence on female participation was an overwhelming and systemic subordination of women in much of Papua New Guinea society.

Some of the men interviewed during this same visit claimed that the subordination of women is a time-honored cultural factor in Papua New Guinea society. These interviewees claimed that any transformation of the role and status of women in society was a Western imposition of their concept of equity and equality, which went against traditional culture. When pressed, even those in high-status positions who were responsible for implementing gender equity in the education system and agreed in principle with the policy maintained that yes, cultural traditions were stronger than school-based ideas. Thus the perpetuation or reification of the image of a gendered Other tended to institutionalize the unequal state of affairs to the public "as if it were permanent, natural and outside of time" (Thompson 1990, 65). The illusion was reinforced by images of women depicted by the local media, in the community, in schools and other educational institutions, and in the workplace.

However, this claim was disputed by the women who were interviewed and by other men interviewed who supported equity. The women maintained that it was merely convenient for the men to lock women into a subordinated position in order to maintain their power and that it could hardly be "culturally" determined if only the male half of the population were in agreement. They saw the dangers of being determined by cultural or gendered relativity. Labeling and fixing the Other is a form of colonial discourse that perpetuates unequal relationships of power, and it is perhaps nowhere more overt than in Papua New Guinea between the male as powerful and the female as Other.

In spite of the powerful structural inequalities, several of the women interviewed in Papua New Guinea described how they had redefined their identity by establishing their voice through increased economic and educational participation and thereby creating spaces for a more powerful voice to transform their subordinated image in the community. For example, the women responsible for presenting their situation to the Beijing Conference of 1995 were survivors, and victors, in a struggle to go beyond the stereotyping, to provide ways of transforming the life chances of women who were currently in the higher levels of schooling.

One way in which women had been able to use the school site to transform female experiences was in a particular girls-only secondary school managed by a Catholic nun, who explained in the interview that she was deliberately teaching the girls at the school to be independent thinkers, conscious of the need to combat discrimination and violence against them when they went on to further education. This approach to the construction of a gendered identity can be compared to that described by Skinner and Holland (1996) in their study of Nepalese females who challenged the so-called traditional compliant identity of girls in society. In this account, the authors describe how the Nepalese school was a forum for the development of critical discourses on the legacies of caste and gender privilege. The students had their own ways of constructing their new identities and self-understandings, in this case by writing their own end-of-year revue of skits and songs focusing on their anger and resistance.

The "Educated" Sri Lankan

Over twenty years ago Ronald Dore published his well-known study of educational credentialing in four countries, *The Diploma Disease* (1976). Among the case studies was one on Sri Lanka and its education system, in which Dore showed that per capita levels of education were among the highest in the world, and yet employment and "development" were not as high as would have been expected at that time. In the 1990s, the proportion of graduates from education systems is still extremely high, although there are continuing concerns in industry and in government that the "educated" person is not necessarily employable. The identity of the educated person remains fixed on the white-collar worker, whereas the needs of the economy point to the desirability of greater emphasis on technological skills and competencies for the workplace, a need emphasized in 1943 by educational reformer C. W. W. Kannangara (Molligoda 1997).

Sri Lanka is fortunate in having successive governments that placed a high priority on education, even though there are inequalities in the supply of resources and access to higher education. The participation of females and males in the formal sector is fairly even; participation between rural and urban is far less even, with fewer opportunities for employment in rural areas and fewer resources supplied to schools.

Information gleaned from the curriculum development training project in which the author is involved suggests a discrepancy between the concept of the "educated person" as one who has knowledge and the "educated person" as one who can deal with change, manage resources, and learn how to learn, as stated in the new education reform program in Sri Lanka. This complex and seemingly contradictory positioning is multifaceted and is by no means an either/or situation. It rests on the definition of an educated person, and what characteristics pertain to such a label. As Dore said a generation ago, it rests on the form taken by the examinations, which are seen as the gateway through which the educated person must walk.

Tackling the Issue of Identity as a Social Justice Issue

The various studies briefly mentioned in the previous section are meant to illustrate how the notion of identity construction is closely connected to the construction of a socially just society. They call to mind other studies of education and equity in multicultural societies, and they are reminiscent of more recent studies of citizenship and identity (e.g., Castles and Miller 1993), in which the discourse considers who is included and who is excluded from being a citizen.

For members of ethnic minorities, culture plays a key role as a source of identity and as a way of organizing resistance to exclusion and discrimination. Reference to the culture of origin helps people maintain self-esteem and personal identity in a situation in which their capabilities and experience are undermined (Castles and Miller 1993, 33).

David Plaza's analysis of identity is pertinent to this discussion. Plaza places the construction of identity in its social context, showing how it is both a self-reflexive and an interactional process, one that is never determined and fixed, but is bound in time, culture, and location (Hall, Held, and McGrew 1992). They agree with Bhabha (1996), who puts forward the notion that separating the public from the private identity or the psyche from the social is a false dichotomy. Plaza's account tallies well with the thesis put forward by Levinson et al. (1996), who see the construction of the educated person as culturally and contextually defined and by no means a "common" process in Western or Western-influenced societies.

Hall et al.'s notion of identity tends to draw on the idea of cultural relativity, developing beyond the ideas of the subject as an individual unfolding from inside and beyond the concept of subjects forming their identities through the interaction of self with society. Identity becomes a moveable feast formed and transformed continuously in relation to the ways individuals are represented or addressed in the cultural systems that surround them. It is historically, not biologically, defined. The subject assumes different identities at different times, identities that are not unified around a coherent self (Hall et al. 1992, 275–277).

Plaza notes that Hall and du Gay (1996), when talking about identity and the great forced and "free" immigration movements that have taken place in the last fifty years, describe the present era as a period in which identity has been "marginalised, fragmented, disadvantaged and dispersed" for migrants—the "unhomely" (Bhabha 1994) denizens of the contemporary world. This, according to Hall et al., is a process of migranthood: "A sense of moving from a certain predictable world into one of unpredictability and change—what some have referred to as the 'post-modern' condition" (Hall et al. 1992, 33).

Migration is considered the most important experience of this century. Bammer uses the term "displacement" to refer to the phenomenon of people being separated from their native culture either through physical dislocation (as refugees, immigrants, exiles, or expatriates) or through the colonizing imposition of a foreign culture (Bammer 1994, xi).

Identity construction works in both directions. In the case of immigrants living in English-speaking countries, local people sometimes see them as intruders. In response, the immigrants cluster themselves in groups, creating a kind of vicious circle in which interactions reinforce preconceived ideas. Thus when the local and the migrant interact, the former positions the latter as disadvantaged and marginalized and in a situation that is peripheral to the main activities. The local sees the migrant as the Other and vice versa. In that way the metaphor of Otherness perpetuates the effects of cultural difference (Bhabha 1994).

An important element that contributes to the construction of immigrants' cultural identity is their home culture. Validation of their culture would eliminate sentiments of inferiority, which sometimes make immigrants feel so different. For some adolescent students in David Plaza's study, this was certainly the case. They found themselves caught between two cultures. A Year Twelve Spanish-Australian girl said,

> It is very difficult because I don't know what you should be called: Spanish, Australian or what? It is like being in the middle of both. At home I always speak in

Spanish, and so I call myself Spanish, but as I live in Australia and I was born in Australia, then I'm Australian; it is very difficult. (Plaza Coral, 1998).

Of course, some of the construction of identity forms around the language people use. The relationship between language and diversity, and between language and equity in schooling, is clear but complex. This observation brings me back to the first part of the chapter and completes the connection between identity, power, and communication. Intercultural communication is heavily influenced by relative positions of perceived power of the speakers, whether in their individual positioning or by dint of their positioning in the context (Fox 1992). Several comparative educators are involved in comparative studies of language policy in various countries, including the ways in which language policy can be used to create inequities of power (Corson 1993).

As Plaza notes, immigrants who have emigrated to an English-speaking country and can barely communicate in English feel themselves jeopardized by their lack of competence in the language. They are negatively stereotyped because of their perceived linguistic deficiency and usually have to take low-skilled jobs because these are the only positions available for them (Castles 1992). Australia, with a population of immigrants coming from practically every corner of the world, faces the great challenge of helping these linguistic minorities to overcome the linguistic isolation and the emotional consequences that it produces in their everyday lives:

> There is no language change without emotional consequences. Principally: loss. That language equals home, that language is a home, as surely as a roof over one's head is a home, and that to be without a language, or to be between languages, is as miserable in its way as to be without bread. (Kaplan 1994, 63)

The relationship between language, identity, education, and social justice (or the lack of them) is thus closely intertwined. In the 1990s many countries have attempted to transform society through more equitable systems of education, for example, South Africa, Sri Lanka, Papua New Guinea, Mexico, and Ecuador. Earlier attempts were made in, to name a few, Grenada, Nicaragua, Vietnam, Tanzania, Zimbabwe, Peru, Western Samoa, Jamaica, and Cuba. Social change, educational change, and transformation must encompass the issue of social and cultural identity in specific contexts; the social justice issue must address the needs of particular groups of people as well as tackle the inequalities in the "system" in general.

References

Acknowledgment is given to David Plaza, one of my doctoral students at the University of Wollongong, who has supplied some of the discussion on identity, and to Janice Wright, his cosupervisor.

Bammer, A., ed. 1994. *Displacements: Cultural Identities in Question*. Bloomington: Indiana University Press.

Benhabib, S. 1992. *Situating the Self*. Cambridge: Polity.

Bhabha, H. K. 1993. *The Location of Culture*. London: Routledge.

Bhabha, H. K. 1994. "Frontlines/Borderposts." In *Displacements: Cultural Identities in Question*. Edited by A. Bammer. Bloomington: Indiana University Press.

Bhabha, H. K. 1996. "Unpacking My Library . . . Again." In *The Post-Colonial Question: Common Skies, Divided Horizons*. Edited by I. Chambers. London: Routledge.

Castles, S. 1992. "Australia Multiculturalism: Social Policy and Identity in a Changing Society." In *Nations of Immigrants: Australia, the United States, and International Migration*. Edited by I. Chambers. Melbourne: Oxford University Press.

Castles, S., and M. Miller. 1993. *The Age of Migration: International Population Movements in the Modern World*. Basingstoke, U.K.: Macmillan.

Corson, D. 1993. *Language, Minority Education, and Gender: Linking Social Justice and Power*. Philadelphia: Multilingual Matters.

Dore, R. 1976. *The Diploma Disease: Education, Qualification, and Development*. London: Allen and Unwin.

Foley, D. 1996. "The Silent Indian as Cultural Production." In *The Cultural Production of the Educated Person*. Edited by Bradley A. Levinson, Douglas E. Foley, and Dorothy C. Holland.

Fox, C. 1992. "A Critical Examination of Intercultural Communication: Towards a New Theory." Ph.D. diss., University of Sydney.

Fox, C. 1995. "Listening to the Gendered Other: Participation of Girls and Women in Education and Training in Papua New Guinea." Paper presented at the Oxford Conference on Comparative Education, Oxford, U.K.

Fox, C. 1996. "Listening to the Other: Social Cartography in Intercultural Communication." In *Social Cartography*. Edited by R. Paulston. New York: Garland.

Fox, C. 1997. "Sri Lanka Curriculum Program: End of Course Report." Report prepared for the University of Wollongong, Wollongong, and the Illawarra Technology Corporation, Wollongong.

Fox, C. Forthcoming. "Education, Gender, and Development: The Construction of Gendered Identity in Papua New Guinea." In Gender, Education, and Development. Edited by C. Heward and S. Bunwaree. London: Zed.

Gadamer, H.-G. 1989. *Truth and Method*. 2d rev. ed. Translation revised by J. Weinsheimer and D. Marshall. New York: Crossroad. Originally published as *Wahrheit und Methode*. Tübingen: Mohr, 1960.

Geertz, C. 1973. *The Interpretation of Cultures*. New York: Basic Books.

Gudykunst, W. 1983. "Towards a Typology of Stranger-Host Relationships." *International Journal of Intercultural Relations* 7: 410–413.

Habermas, J. 1984. *The Theory of Communicative Action*. Vol. 1. Translated by T. McCarthy. Boston: Beacon.

Hall, E. T. 1966. *The Hidden Dimension: Man's Use of Space in Public and Private*. London: Bodley Head.

Hall, E. T. 1983. *The Dance of Life: The Other Dimension of Time*. New York: Anchor.

Hall, S., and P. du Gay, eds. 1996. *Questions of Cultural Identity*. London: Sage.

Hall, S., D. Held, and T. McGrew, eds. 1994. *Modernity and Its Futures*. Cambridge: Polity Press/Open University.

Hickling-Hudson, A. 1995. "Adult Education and Literacy in Grenada." Ph.D. diss., Queensland University of Technology, Brisbane.

Iredale, R., and C. Fox, with T. Shermaimoff. 1994. *Immigration, Education, and Training in New South Wales.* Canberra: Bureau of Immigration and Population Research/Australian Government Publishing Service.

Iredale, R., and C. Fox. 1997. "The Impact of Immigration on School Education in New South Wales, Australia." *International Migration Review* 23, no. 3: 655–669.

Kaplan, A. Y. 1994. "On Language Memoir." In *Displacements: Cultural Identities in Question.* Edited by C. Heward and S. Bunwaree. Bloomington: Indiana University Press.

Kim, Y. 1988. *Communication and Cross-Cultural Adaptation: An Integrative Theory.* Clevedon: Multilingual Matters.

Levinson, B., D. Foley, and D. C. Holland. 1996. *The Cultural Production of the Educated Person: Critical Ethnographies of Schooling and Local Practices.* Albany: State University of New York Press.

Molligoda, L. V. P. 1997. "Enhancement of the Vocational Abilities of Students of Home Economics in the Secondary Education System in Sri Lanka." Paper presented to the University of Wollongong Faculty of Education. Sri Lanka Curriculum Program Project Reports. Wollongong: Faculty of Education.

Oddou, G., and M. Mendenhall. 1984. "Person Perception in Cross-Cultural Settings: A Review of Cross-Cultural and Related Cognitive Literature." *International Journal of Intercultural Relations* 8: 77–96.

Plaza Coral, D. 1998. "Experiences of Spanish Speaking Students in Australia: A Case Study." Ph.D. diss., University of Wollongong.

Plaza, D., J. Wright, and C. Fox. 1997. "The Experience of Spanish-Speaking Students in Secondary Schools in a NSW Region." Paper presented at the AARE Conference, Brisbane, November 1997.

Pratt, M. 1992. *Imperial Eyes: Travel Writing and Transculturation.* London: Routledge.

Said, E. 1978. *Orientalism: Western Conceptions of the Orient.* Harmondsworth, U.K.: Penguin.

Said, E. 1983. *The World, the Text, and the Critic.* Cambridge: Harvard University Press.

Said, E. 1993. *Culture and Imperialism.* London: Chatto and Windus.

Skinner, D., and D. Holland. 1996. "Public Education in Nepal." In *The Cultural Production of the Educated Person.* Edited by Bradley A. Levinson, Douglas E. Foley, and Dorothy C. Holland.

Spivak, G. 1990. *The Post-colonial Critic: Interviews, Srategies, Dialogues.* Edited by S. Harasym. New York: Chatto and Windus.

Thompson, J. B. 1990. *Ideology and Modern Culture.* Cambridge: Polity.

Chapter 6

Changing Conceptions of Equality of Education

Forty Years of Comparative Evidence

Joseph P. Farrell

Debates about (and occasional action on) educational reforms, which are common currency in the late 1990s (e.g., decentralization, privatization, education for "global competitiveness," use of "new technologies" such as the Internet) have a considerable history. They are in many fundamental respects current manifestations of debates and reform efforts that have spanned, in one form or another, the past four to five decades, and in some cases longer. To think seriously about the possible import of currently fashionable reform movements for equality of education, particularly for the most marginalized members of various societies, requires that we review and try to make some sense of that history. That is the intent of this chapter. Comparative education, as a field of scholarly inquiry and as an applied discipline, has been central to what has been learned.

Background: The Optimistic Reforms of the Sixties

The twenty-five years following the end of the Second World War was an epoch of great and widespread optimism regarding questions of educational and socioeconomic equality. It was assumed generally that the evident gaps in wealth and power *among nations* could be rather quickly eliminated; that those already industrialized and "developed" nations that had been devastated by the war could be quickly put "back on their feet"; and that those nonindustrialized

or generally poor nations (whether newly independent from European colonialism or long independent) could rather quickly and easily be placed on the
"road to development," and that obvious gaps in access to income and power
among individuals and collectivities within nations could be equally quickly
reduced. It was also assumed that more general acquisition of education (understood mainly as the provision of formal schooling) was essential to the lessening of inequalities among and within nations. Increasing provision of education was seen as a major (in some views the most important) engine that would
drive the world to a more equal provision of access to wealth, power, and opportunity. Poverty and inequality (absolute or relative; individual, collective,
national or international) came to be seen widely as relatively easily solved policy problems rather than necessary, unavoidable and/or unresolvable human
conditions.

The advent of human capital theory in the late 1950s and early 1960s put education even more squarely in the center of this optimistic vision. Education
was no longer seen as simply one among many competing consumer goods to
be acquired individually (for personal gain) or collectively (through taxes for
perceived collective gain) to the extent that it could be afforded. Rather, education was constructed as an investment opportunity. Public expenditures on
increasing the availability of education would produce net social benefits, increasing the total amount of wealth in a society and improving its distribution.[1]
The confluence of these events and ways of understanding them led to enormously increased expenditures on education around the world, a major increase
in access to education (in poor nations, access to primary education and adult
basic education; in richer nations, which had already achieved nearly universal
primary education, in access to secondary and tertiary education), and major
educational reform efforts attempting to make it more accessible and effective
for marginalized or disadvantaged individuals or groups.

In rich nations primary education was already effectively compulsory and
universal, and secondary and tertiary education was relatively widely available.
There educational reforms focused on increasing the proportion of age-eligible
youth who completed secondary schooling and went on to some form of postsecondary education, and on improving the educational "chances" of specifically targeted "educationally disadvantaged" groups, whether the disadvantage
was based on race, ethnicity, socioeconomic status, gender, geographical location, or some combination of these. In many such nations there was a massive
expansion of secondary education facilities, with the policy target often being
universal access and usually universal completion. Existing universities expanded rapidly, large numbers of wholly new universities were created, and in
many nations entire new systems of nonuniversity, technically oriented postsecondary institutions were established.[2] In the United States massive resources and political energy were devoted to attempting to end racial segrega-
tion of schooling and to develop and implement changes that might increase the

educational success of disadvantaged groups. In much of Western Europe, "academic" secondary schooling led to university (e.g., the English grammar school, the French *lycée,* the German *gymnasium*) and served a small proportion of the eligible age-group—predominantly the children of already privileged families. Major attempts at "comprehensivization" of secondary schooling took different forms in different nations, but the general goals were to increase the proportion of youngsters who had access to a form of secondary schooling that could lead to university and to equalize the opportunities to access to such education across social groups.[3]

In developing nations, many children had no access to primary schooling and most adults were illiterate (although this varied dramatically from nation to nation). The main educational-change focus was on simple quantitative expansion, and many nations mounted national literacy "campaigns." In the early 1960s UNESCO convened a series of regional meetings of ministers of education that set broad targets for quantitative growth designed as a framework for national educational planning. The general aim was to move as quickly as possible (and it was assumed that this would be quickly indeed) to "universal primary education" and universal literacy, both seen as necessary components of national development. During this epoch scholars fiercely debated the precise nature of "national development," but a fairly general consensus developed that it entailed at least three main components: (1) the generation of more wealth within a nation (economic development), (2) the more equitable distribution of such wealth or at least more equitable distribution of opportunities for access to that wealth (social development), and (3) the organization of political decision-making structures that would be close approximations of those prevalent in "developed" nations (political development). More widespread and equitable provision of formal schooling was seen as essential to all three. Massive enrollment increases resulted from the application of this general view to educational policy in developing nations. Between 1960 and 1975 the number of children in school in developing countries increased by 122 percent; the proportion of age-eligible children in primary schooling increased from 57 to 75 percent during the same fifteen-year period, with corresponding increases at the secondary level (14 percent to 26 percent) and postsecondary level (1.5 percent to 4.4 percent).[4]

Results: Much Less Than Anticipated

However, by the early 1970s it was already apparent to many observers that this massive worldwide effort at educational reform in the name of growth and equality was not producing the expected results. As early as 1968 Coombs wrote the aptly titled book *The World Educational Crisis: A Systems Analysis.*[5] The structural reforms in Western Europe were seldom fully implemented, if at all, and were not, in most cases, significantly changing the social composition of academic secondary schooling. In the United States desegregation programs and other attempted reforms were not significantly improving the educational success of African Americans and other marginalized groups. In both instances some individuals benefited, but the overall pattern of structural inequality remained intact. In developing nations, because population was growing rapidly relative to the rate of educational expansion, the absolute numbers of primary-aged children out of school grew from 109.2 million in 1960 to 120.5 million in 1975.[6] The same pattern held for adult literacy. Overall literacy rates were increasing (in some cases quite rapidly), but the absolute number of illiterate adults was increasing as well. Moreover, it was becoming clear that the rates of educational expenditure increase that had occurred during the 1960s and drove the expansion of school places could not be sustained over a longer period. Beyond this, although many developing nations had been experiencing economic growth, the already wealthy nations were for the most part growing even faster, creating an ever widening gap between rich and poor countries. Furthermore, the gap between richer and poorer groups within many nations was also increasing, although this was a very mixed pattern.[7]

Within schooling systems themselves, in nations rich and poor, distributional inequalities were generally persisting, in some cases getting better and in some, worse. In many societies urban children benefited more than rural children from increased educational provision. In other societies particular ethnic, tribal, or religious groups benefited more. In many societies boys received more of the newly available schooling than did girls. In most societies newly available school places, whether at the primary, secondary, or tertiary level, were occupied mainly, or almost exclusively, by children of the already well-to-do.

The data available in the 1970s regarding all of these patterns were not especially systematic, coming primarily from unconnected case studies of different nations at different points in time, with very little systematic time-series data available, and they were interpreted differently by different scholars. Nonetheless, the newly available evidence led to a significant modification—for many a complete rejection—of the earlier optimistic view that had guided the actions of policy makers and advisers in rich and poor nations. Claims about the power of schooling to equalize the life chances of children who are born into very different social and economic circumstances generally became much more cautious. Don Adams once characterized this mood shift as the change from the "optimistic sixties" to the "cynical seventies."[8]

As the comparative evidence continued to accumulate through the 1980s and into the 1990s, it strengthened and reinforced the "cynical" view established in the 1970s. It became increasingly clear that educational reforms aimed at increasing equality were very difficult to enact and implement successfully, and even when implemented reasonably well seldom had the intended effects on comparative life chances of the children of various social groups within and among nations. There were some success stories but far more examples of partial or complete failure. In many developing nations the situation was made even more difficult by the fiscal crises produced by the oil shock of the 1970s and the debt crisis of the 1980s. In most rich nations the difficulty was aggravated by economic restructuring, which produced significant reductions in public educational expenditures and severe reductions in the numbers of middle-class jobs that had been the traditional target occupations for youngsters from marginalized groups who had managed to use education as a vehicle for social mobility (it is hard to be mobile if there are few jobs into which to be mobile!). In 1997 I summarized the experience of the past three decades as follows:

> One general lesson is that planning educational change is a far more difficult and risk-prone venture than had been imagined in the 1950s or 1960s. There are far more examples of failure, or of minimal success, than of relatively complete success. Far more is known about what doesn't work, or doesn't usually work, than about what does work. . . . Moreover, when planned educational reform attempts have been successful, the process has usually taken a very long time, frequently far longer than originally anticipated. There are in the experience of the past decades a few examples where an unusual combination of favorable conditions and politically skilled planners has permitted a great deal of educational change to occur in a relatively brief period, but these have been rare and ideosyncratic.[9]

Theoretical Accounts of Reform Failure

Partly as a result of this experience, a very complex and confusing theoretical debate has developed. Although the details of the debate are discussed elsewhere in this book, some of the main features that pertain directly to the theme of this chapter are discussed below. Core aspects of the debate for present purposes can be framed by the title of George Counts's famous book from the 1930s, *Dare the School Build a New Social Order?*[10] To pose the question at all assumes a positive answer to a previous question: *Can* the school build a new social order? The optimism of the 1960s was founded on a positive answer to that question. The schools could do it and we collectively should dare to do it, by marshaling nationally and internationally the appropriate mixture of knowledge, resources, and political will. One major set of theoretical explanations of and proposed remedies for the subsequent widespread failure continue to assume a positive answer. Schools *can* build a new social order. The problem is that we haven't yet "gotten it right." First, we have been operating from an incomplete and/or imperfect and/or badly interpreted knowledge base and, second, a wrong or incomplete set of political actors and stakeholder groups have been involved in the policy development and implementation process. The "problem" is a matter of technique and knowledge base. The "solution" is to continually improve the knowledge base (through basic and applied research and the dissemination of the results) and refine our interpretations of it, as well as to improve our micro- and macropolitical techniques. This understanding, in one variant or another, continues to be the dominant view.[11]

A wholly opposed view of the nature of the problem began to emerge strongly in the mid-1970s, arguing that schools could not build a new social order. The causal process works the other way round. Changing the socioeconomic order is a necessary pre- or co-condition for changing education in an egalitarian direction. Many scholars, particularly those arguing from a Marxist, neo-Marxist, or dependency theory approach, claimed that formal schooling could necessarily do little more than reproduce structural inequalities in existing societies, at least capitalist ones; this is its basic sociopolitical and economic function; this is inevitably part of the normal development of capitalist societies and of developing countries linked to such nations through dependent economic, political, and social connections.[12] This view gained considerable popularity among some sectors of the scholarly community and among some policy makers in developing countries and international aid agencies. However, it never became the predominant view. By the mid-1980s some of the academic proponents of this view began to significantly modify their earlier position, arguing that formal schooling could function *both* to reproduce existing structural inequalities and to produce structural change, at least in democratic societies.[13] Following the collapse of the former Soviet Union and its associated state socialist nations, new evidence has become available suggesting that structural inequalities in those societies have been very nearly as resistant to the meliorating influence of education as in capitalist nations.[14] This may suggest that the problem of resistant structural inequality is endemic across political-economic regime types and is created by some deeper pattern that we have not yet identified—it simply takes different forms and manifestations in different societies.

An intermediate view has also developed. It suggests that educational change *can* affect the social order but only under particular circumstances and only if the educational change program is carefully tailored to the particular circumstances. For example, Farrell and Schiefelbein have argued that the Chilean educational reform of the late 1960s was successful not only in increasing access to schooling for marginalized groups but in generating social mobility (more than 50 percent of the age cohorts most directly affected moved into occupational categories higher than those of their parents) only because parallel structural changes in the economy generated large numbers of new jobs in the higher occupational categories, into which these newly educated youth could be mobile.[15] Several observers have argued that the relative success of the Swedish secondary comprehensivization reform program is due to a particular set of historical conditions and political traditions in that society.[16] This can be seen as a profoundly pessimistic position in that the conditions for success are rare and idiosyncratic, and thus cannot be widely duplicated. A more optimistic take on this view has recently developed, arguing that the widespread failure has been due to a common tendency to try to design and implement (from whatever the-oretical/ideological point of view) universalistic "one size fits all" educational reform approaches and strategies. Thus success in using educational change to promote social equality is widely possible but is *contingent* on carefully tailoring the reform to the particular local conditions. Some scholars have begun trying to work out possible relationships between particular sets of conditions and potentially successful educational reform approaches. I have argued elsewhere that taking this point of view seriously fundamentally challenges almost the entire corpus of modernist theory that has informed comparative education over the past several decades.[17]

Changing Meanings of Educational Equality

Running through this broad theoretical debate has been a constant modification, amplification, and nuancing of what is meant by the term "educational equality." Next I shall briefly review these changes in meaning and introduce a model meant to bring together many of these changes in meaning in a way useful for thinking about the mass of accumulated evidence.

Categories of Differentiation

Thirty to forty years ago discussions of social equality tended to focus on a limited set of categories of differentiation then considered to be most important in determining or influencing (depending on how deterministic or contingent and loosely coupled a view of large-scale social interactions one held) how large numbers of people were able to live their lives in rich, industrialized nations (especially social class and race/ethnicity) and to apply these Western categories to developing nations. The understanding of such potential categories of differentiation is now much more complex. All extant societies have some form of internal social differentiation, with some members being valued or rewarded more than others. However, the degree of such differentiation and its significance for the way individuals and social groups lead their lives varies dramatically across societies. Moreover, there are many different bases or criteria for such differentiation. Among the most common are race, occupation, ethnicity, gender, regional origin, lineage, income, political power, and religion. Both across and within societies there is considerable variation in which one of these, or which set of them, is most powerful as a determinant of how different people can and do live their lives. Those of us who are creatures of the historical experience and intellectual traditions of the industrial nations of the West, whether we embrace some form of structural-functional or Marxist social theory, tend to collapse a

common set of these—particularly occupation, income, and political power—
into the notion of social class or social status. It is not at all clear now that these
theoretical constructs are the most salient for understanding social differentiation in rich nations (feminist scholars, for example, would generally argue that
gender is at least as important, if not more important, a category of differentiation) nor that they are directly applicable to all, or even most, less developed societies, either as accurate descriptors or as meaningful categories of social
thought and behavior among individuals in those societies. In many such societies the occupation or income of a child's parents may be much less salient as
a constraint upon his or her life chances than the parents' ethnic or tribal group,
their lineage, the geographical region of origin, or the child's gender.

As the list of potential categories of social differentiation has expanded,
some categories have come to be seen as more mutable or "disguisable" than
others, which has an effect on the degree to which they may constrain children's
life chances and what education can "do" about them. An instantly identifiable
basis of social categorization is, in general, much harder to overcome by educational (or, more generally, social) policy. Race and gender, for example, are
generally immutable and immediately identifiable characteristics. Religion is
generally much less easily identifiable, except when the observance of it involves locally unusual clothing or practices. Many people in many nations can
and do change their religion without necessarily changing their public appearance and hence their identifiability. This is why the Nazis in Germany required
all Jews to wear a yellow star and carefully traced family records to determine
who was counted as a Jew, whether or not they actually practiced that, or some
other, religion. As another example, the social class of origin of someone who
has used education (or some other means) to become upwardly mobile is frequently nonidentifiable unless he or she chooses to "advertise" it. It is a characteristic that is mutable and often easily disguisable. It is thus more easily altered by education than characteristics that are immutable and nondisguisable.
It has recently become apparent that consideration of the full implications of
this set of issues is complexly related to the question of identity—the identity
that people assign to themselves and the one that others assign to them. There
is not space here to work out the full implications of this. However, it can be
noted that some scholars, particularly those working from a postmodern feminist stance, are arguing that we must move from an idea of identity (as person-
ally understood or socially assigned) as something essential and fundamentally
unchangeable to a conception of identity, in both its senses, as something that
is multiple and malleable. That is, we must move from thinking of identity to
thinking of identities.[18] Other scholars working from the rapidly emerging field
of narrative theory and inquiry are arguing that identity consists of the stories
we tell to ourselves and others about ourselves, as well as the stories other people tell about us, and that these constantly and necessarily change through time
and circumstance.[19] These new ways of thinking about educational equality

represent a challenge to traditional modernist and grand theory approaches to comparative education, which are about as fundamental as the challenge represented by the contingency approach noted above. The implications of these ways of thinking for our understanding of educational equality are only beginning to be worked out, but it is becoming quite obvious that the meaning of the phrase is far more slippery and difficult to understand than we thought even a few years ago.

From Opportunity to Results[20]

The notion of educational equality, which grew originally with the development of systems of tax-supported public schooling, focused on opportunity. The general assumption was that the job of the state was to ensure that all children (with the exception in some areas of groups that were consciously excluded, on the basis for example of race or gender) had access to schools that were free of direct cost, with generally similar facilities and curricula, at least through the stage of compulsory attendance. It was assumed that it was the child's responsibility to use the opportunity thus provided. Responsibility for a child who did not do well in school, through lack of intelligence, diligence, motivation, and so on, rested with the individuals involved, not the state. Over the past several decades it has become increasingly apparent that large numbers of children are unable to use the educational opportunity provided because of their social origins. The concept of educational equality has gradually been extended to include some notion of equal educational results. The task of the state has been extended to include ensuring that all children, whatever their social origin, have an equal ability to benefit from the educational opportunity provided, in terms of what they learn and how they can use that learning in later life, particularly in the labor market.

Equality as Similarity or Equality as Valuation of Difference

Embedded within the standard discussions of equality of results is an even more complex set of questions: Do we really expect (indeed, do we want) the results to be similar, if not identical, for everyone? What do we actually mean by "results"? What do we mean by "an equal opportunity to benefit from" educational provision? Many discussions and arguments in both the scholarly and the popular literature imply quite directly that "equal results" means, for example, equal achievement test scores across social groups, schools, or nations (the "league table" approach), or equal access to particular highly valued occupational categories or salary levels. But it is increasingly argued that this view is too narrow and restrictive and that it is legitimate, indeed desirable, for different individuals and groups to want/need to learn different sorts of things and to use them for different life purposes. This alternative claim is expressed very strongly, for example, in many arguments for "relevant" education for particular subgroups within larger social/national groups (say, rural children in poor areas of developing nations).[21] This "valuation of difference rather than similarity" approach asserts that different types of learning, and ways of learning, as well as different uses of it throughout life, are equally (but differently) *valuable* socially and individually. If one accepts this concept of educational equality, it is not clear what "equality of results" might mean, let alone how we might assess it within or across societies. This consideration of value leads to another important distinction.

Equity or Equality?

A distinction has been drawn between equity and equality. As Bronfenbrenner has suggested, equity refers to social justice or fairness. It involves a subjective moral or ethical judgment. Equality deals with the actual patterns in which something (e.g., income or years of schooling) is distributed among members of a particular group.[22] The equality of an income distribution can, for example, be assessed statistically by measuring deviations from some hypothetically completely equal situation. But individual or group judgments regarding the equity or fairness of any given observed degree of inequality can and do differ; equity involves value judgments and differing understandings of what is normal or inevitable. Since societies, groups within societies, and individuals within those groups differ in their value systems, a given (even statistically measured) degree of observed educational or social inequality may be regarded as quite fair and reasonable, or equitable, by some as individuals or groups, and as very inequitable by others. Many of the most complex public political debates about educational equality, and what might be done for it in terms of public policy, revolve around differing equity-based interpretations of differing equality-driven statistical indices. Differing interpretations of rates of female participation in education and the labor force is a striking case in point.

A Review

The past several decades have been characterized by increasing conceptual confusion. This conceptual confusion has to a considerable degree resulted from the circulation of a bewildering quantity of comparative information regarding how different individuals and widely differing social groups utilize education and the effect it exerts on their destinies. Untangling some of that data and deriving meaning from it with respect to equality as a goal for education is the task of the remainder of this chapter. In the following pages I present a model for thinking about educational equality that summarizes much of what we now understand by that concept, and I use that model to organize and summarize what much of the now available comparative data tells us about education's role in equalizing the life chances of children born into very different social circumstance as they grow into adults.

A "Model" of Educational Inequality

When considering problems of educational inequality in recent years, we have come increasingly to view schooling as a long-term process in which children may be sorted at many different points and in several different ways. We recognize that schooling, whatever else it may do, operates as a selective social screening mechanism. It enhances the status of some children, providing them with an opportunity for upward social or economic mobility. It ratifies the status of others, reinforcing the propensity for children born poor to remain poor as adults, and for children born into well-off families to become well-off adults. Recognizing this, we need to address the following questions: At what points in the process, to what degree, and how are children of which social groups screened out or kept in? From this point of view, several facets of equality can be usefully distinguished:

1. Equality of access—the probabilities of children from different social groupings getting into the school system, or some particular level or portion of it.
2. Equality of survival—the probabilities of children from various social groupings staying in the school system to some defined level, usually the end of a complete cycle (primary, secondary, higher).
3. Equality of output—the probabilities that children from various social groupings will learn the same things to the same levels at a defined point in the schooling system.
4. Equality of outcome—the probabilities that children from various social groupings will live relatively similar lives subsequent to and as a result of schooling (have equal incomes, have jobs of roughly the same status, have equal access to sites of political power, etc.).

The first three types of inequality refer to the workings of the school system itself. Equality of outcome refers to the junction between the school system and adult life, especially (but not exclusively) the labor market. With reference to the first three, each represents a mechanism by which children are sorted and screened by the school, and all three occur at each level or cycle of the system (i.e., a child may or may not enter primary schooling, may or may not survive to the end of the primary cycle, may or may not learn as much, or the same things, as other students by the end of the primary cycle; having completed primary, a child may or may not enter secondary schooling, may or may not survive to the end of secondary, etc.). Thus in a three-level system (e.g., primary, secondary, higher) there are at least nine sorting points of children; in a four-level system (e.g., primary, junior secondary, higher secondary, higher) there are at least twelve sorting points. It should be noted that this classification of types of inequality is itself an oversimplification. For example, in systems that have different types of schools or "streams" at the same level (e.g., university-preparatory vs. technical secondary schools or streams, or universities vs. two-year technical colleges at the third level) the access question is not simply whether a student enters the cycle but the *type* of institution or stream to which the student is given access. We should also bear in mind that the same factors will not necessarily affect the destiny of children at all of the sorting points. Since children confronting a later sorting point are themselves "survivors" of earlier sortings, we can assume that factors which are critical at the earliest points may lose their significance at later points (having already had their effect), with new factors coming into play as the lengthy process moves along.[23] It should also be noted that although the focus here is on formal schooling for young people, the four general issues or questions can and should be asked of *any* organized learning program, formal or nonformal, for learners of whatever age. For example, it can be asked in regard to an adult literacy or vocational training program, Which people from which social categories have access to it? Which learners from which social categories "stay the course" to the end of the program? Which do not? Which learners from which social categories learn more or less of what is being made available to them? Which learners are more or less able thereafter to use their newly acquired knowledge/skills to improve their lives and to what degree?

What Do We Know?

Our task here is to try to make some sense of the welter of comparative data regarding educational inequality that have been developed during the past several decades. With respect to some aspects of the model just presented, the evidence is sufficient to permit a reasonably coherent summary; with respect to other aspects, the evidence is spotty or inconsistent.

Equality of Access

For the vast majority of children in developing nations, access is a problem at the primary level. As I noted above, a major objective of educational policy at the start of the 1960s was to provide school places sufficient to permit every child to have access to at least a few years of primary schooling. Although primary enrollment ratios have increased during the past thirty years in all regions of the developing world, these general figures mask what is in some nations, often very populous ones, a much grimmer reality. Consider, for example, the three nations of the Indian subcontinent, whose combined population of approximately 1,170 million is almost equal to that of China. Their net primary enrollment ratios in the early 1990s were 66 percent, India; 63 percent, Bangladesh; 29 percent, Pakistan.[24] Moreover, during the decade of the 1980s primary enrollment ratios actually declined in forty-five countries, leading many observers to refer to that period as a "disastrous decade for education."[25] A recent UNESCO publication notes the not-surprising principal causes for lack of access to primary education: "Where are the 'missing children'? Most live in remote rural areas or in urban slums. Most are girls. Most belong to population groups outside the mainstream of society: they pass their days in overcrowded refugee camps, displaced by man-made or natural disasters, or wander with their herds. Often [they are] marginalized by language, life-style and culture."[26] That same publication estimates that the number of such children will grow from 128 million in 1990 to 162 million in 2000 unless a breakthrough is achieved. Achieving such a breakthrough is highly unlikely. In order to meet the often cited goal of universal access to basic education by the year 2000 (as set, for example, by the World Conference on Education for All, held in Thailand in 1990), resources would have to be found, from shrinking national and international agency budgets, to create within the next few years almost as many new school places as were created in the twenty years between 1965 and 1985.[27] Given the fiscal conditions of most developing nations, that seems wildly improbable.

In the few developing nations that have achieved nearly universal primary education (24 have reached net primary enrollment rations of 90 percent or above), and in rich nations generally, the main access problem occurs at a later point in the schooling process. In the former nations it is generally at the entrance to secondary schooling (among those 24 nations the secondary enrollment ratios range from 33 percent [Paraguay] to 92 percent [Republic of Korea], but generally run between 50 percent and 70 percent).[28] In the latter, the key access question is the type or stream of secondary schooling into which youngsters are admitted. In very rich nations that have achieved nearly universal secondary education, the access question arises most seriously at the entrance to postsecondary education. Not even the richest nations have seriously contemplated the universal provision of that level of education. In all nations, rich or poor, there is some point (or points) in the educational system at which schooling (or some favored types of it) is a scarce good that not all can acquire. The ideal equality model then becomes one of random access, with the paradigm case being a fair lottery. The available comparative data (as outlined immediately above and earlier) indicate that the ideal random access situation is rarely even approximated. The same general set of factors that discriminate at the door of the primary school in poor nations simply operate in richer nations at a later point in children's lives.

It is commonly assumed that, particularly at the primary level, the problem of inequality of access is almost entirely a question of inadequate supply of schools and teachers; that an effective demand for primary schooling exists almost everywhere and that if the resources and political will can be found to provide an adequate number of primary schools, all children will attend. As I have shown, the obstacles on the supply side are indeed formidable. However, there are obstacles on the demand side as well. In most middle-income nations (and in some favored regions of low-income nations) there are more than enough school places, in the appropriate locations, for all age-eligible children. In such circumstances, when children do not attend school, and they often do not, it is because their parents will not send them. Parents may regard the education provided there as inappropriate (e.g., on religious or cultural grounds), irrelevant or of little use, or not worth the opportunity cost of the child's labor.[29] This is a particularly serious obstacle to the enrollment of girls in many nations.

Equality of Survival

Among middle-income developing nations between 70 and 80 percent of an entering grade-one cohort will complete the primary cycle. In low-income nations the completion proportions are even lower—just over 50 percent—and have actually been declining over the past ten to fifteen years.[30] In some very poor nations the primary completion ratios are far below 50 percent.[31] These high rates of nonsurvival are a result of the combined effect of (1) high repetition rates (Schiefelbein has estimated that repetition rates at the first-grade level in Latin America are over 50 percent,[32] and in some societies in other regions almost all children spend at least two years in grade one[33]) and (2) high proportions of children dropping out of school—frequently after having repeated an early grade one or more times. In many developing nations the survival rates at the secondary or postsecondary levels, for the very small proportion of the population who reach those levels, are also very low. However, the patterns at this level are highly variable. In some nations access to secondary schooling is very restricted and is based on scores on primary leaving examinations and/or socioeconomic privilege. The few who gain access to secondary or higher levels of schooling tend in large proportions to complete the cycle.

In richer nations survival becomes a serious policy issue at the point in the schooling cycle at which effective compulsory education ends, usually at some midpoint in the secondary cycle. Survival rates and patterns at this level vary greatly across such nations, in ways that are not easily accounted for. Policy expectations clearly have some effect. For example, in some nations all students are expected to complete secondary schooling. High "dropout" rates are considered a major problem, and various policies are put in place to "keep kids in school." These are sometimes quite successful. For example, in Canada the official dropout rate in secondary schooling is around 30 percent, and a variety of avenues have been developed to allow such young people to "drop back in" in ways that fit with their life needs. Following these various alternative tracks (a colleague has identified 19 such tracks in the province of Ontario[34]), roughly 85 percent of an age cohort have attained a secondary diploma or equivalent by age twenty-five. That is, about half of the officially identified "dropouts" eventually completed the cycle.[35] A roughly similar situation obtains in the United States.[36] On the other hand, in societies that do not expect all secondary-level students to complete the full cycle, dropping out is not seen as a policy problem but as a natural and normal circumstance. Here again we see the important difference between the concepts of equality and equity.

A survey of all available comparative evidence shows generally that in any given level of the educational system poor children are less likely to survive educationally than are well-to-do children; that children born in rural areas are less likely to survive educationally than urban children; that repetition and dropout rates are higher among girls than among boys. However, the evidence regarding the relationship between any particular aspect of a child's personal or family circumstances and the probability of completing a given level of education is so scanty and contradictory that general conclusions cannot be drawn easily. The patterns vary dramatically from country to country in ways that cannot be explained simply. Variations in the influence of gender on survival potential are particularly striking. For example, in a single geocultural area, the Arab Middle East, female enrollment as a proportion of total last year primary enrollment varies from 10.6 percent in the Yemen Arab Republic to 47.1 percent in Jordan.[37] Moreover, female enrollment ratios (compared with those among males) for the post-primary age group (12 to 17) varied in the 1980s from lows of 1.7 percent (vs. 14.9 percent males) in the Yemen Arab Republic, and 5.8 percent (vs. 22.3 percent males) in Chad, to highs of 79.3 percent (vs. 91.0 percent males) in Bahrain and 82.9 percent (vs. 83.1 percent males) in Chile.[38] Schiefelbein and Farrell have suggested that the best explanation of the Chilean pattern may lie in historical factors unique to that society.[39] An explanation for the unusually high female enrollment in a society such as Bahrain is not available in the literature.

It is important to bear in mind that survival rates, for entire populations or for subgroups thereof, can only be understood correctly with respect to educational policy by referring as well to access figures for the same societies. For example, in both Tunisia and Tanzania approximately 80 to 90 percent of children entering grade one will reach the end of primary schooling. In Tunisia almost all eligible children enter grade one, whereas in Tanzania just over half do so. In contrast, Malawi has about the same grade one access rate as does Tanzania, but only 46 percent of its entrants complete primary schooling.[40] In spite of their similarity on either equality of access or equality of survival, the interaction between the two types of inequality produces three very different educational situations by the end of primary schooling. It is especially important to note the interaction between access and survival for particular subgroups of a nation's population in trying to assess the overall educational equality situation. For example, if a particular group is heavily discriminated against in terms of access to schooling, those few of its members who do get into schooling (any particular level or type thereof), being themselves the winners in a very rigorous previous screening process, may (and often do) have a very high subsequent survival potential.

The combined effect of access and survival patterns determines the overall distribution of years of schooling attained within a society by various social groups. Some fascinating cross-national time-series evidence regarding equality of years of schooling attained was reported by Snodgrass some years ago. Using UNESCO data, he calculated Gini indexes of inequality[41] in the distribution of educational attainment for a large number of nations, ranging from the least to the most developed, at a number of different points in time, and related these to several other development indicators. Two interrelated findings are particularly noteworthy with respect to the comparative evidence and theoretical debate noted above. (1) There is a strong relationship between national wealth and mean years of schooling attained in a nation. Not surprisingly, richer societies can provide more education for their citizens than poorer nations. (2) There is a very strong negative relationship between the Gini index of inequality and mean years of schooling. That is, among societies in which the average educational attainment is very low, the distribution of years of schooling attained is very unequal. As societies become able, on average, to provide more schooling to their population, the degree of inequality in the distribution of educational attainment falls off systematically. This relationship holds both among nations and within individual nations over time. Even among those few developing societies that have relatively low inequality indexes (N = 19), most "would probably no longer be classified as developing countries today."[42] They are relatively wealthy. In sum, as more total education becomes available to a population, the equality of provision in the society increases. However, we live in a world in which the various fiscal and economic structural crises that are imploding upon many, if not most, nations make it less and less likely that they can in any near future "provide more total education" to their populations. In such a situation this research finding can be seen almost as a counsel of despair; of "what might have been" had we not lived through the desperate times of the last decades. It is also the case, however, that there were a few very poor societies that had quite low inequality of education indexes: Republic of Korea, 1953; the Philippines, 1956; Sri Lanka, 1969; Thailand, 1960; and Cuba, 1953.[43] Careful examination of these cases may provide some clues as to how or under what circumstances relatively equal access to or survival through schooling can be provided, when a society is not wealthy enough to improve the situation by increasing the overall provision of schooling.

Equality of Output

A system's output is whatever the system produces directly—in the case of an educational system, learning. Children with the same numbers of years of schooling (thus with equal access and equal survival) may have learned quite different things, or the same subjects to quite different levels. There is a substantial amount of cross-national evidence which indicates that differences in levels of achievement are systematically associated with differing social origins of children in a particular society. Generally, among those who have reached a given level of a nation's school system, children who are poor, rural, female, or from any other socially marginalized group, learn less. However, here too the differences among nations and cultures in the effect of such social characteristics on learning are impressive.

Given this comparative evidence, the following question has bedeviled educators: Considering the powerful influence of home background on relative levels of school learning, is there much if any room at all for changes in schooling policy and practice to improve the learning levels of socially marginalized children which will allow them, particularly as groups, to live better lives thereafter? Based on an increasingly large array of nation-specific studies, using many different methodological approaches and a smaller set of cross-national studies (many of which have turned out to be methodologically flawed),[44] scholars identified what appeared to be a quite clear pattern emerging in the 1970s and 1980s. The less developed the society, the less the effect of social origin on learning achievement, and the greater the effect of school-related (and thus social policy directed) variables.[45] However, the methodological critiques (particularly of those studies based on an "educational production function" approach) suggest that the overall pattern is not as clear as it once seemed.[46] Nonetheless, assessing all of the evidence, from several distinct methodological traditions, shows that the general pattern still seems to hold. Why should this be so?

Several different, and still quite tentative, explanations have been advanced. Quite early on, as the pattern was just beginning to become evident, Foster advanced the following:

> In broadest terms, as less developed nations "modernize" the pattern of "objective" differentiation of populations becomes more complex with the growth of a monetized economy and a greater division of labour. Not only this, possession of a "modern type" occupation becomes an increasingly important factor in determining the generalized social status of an individual. In other words, social strata defined in *objective* terms of occupations and income begin to emerge. Initially, however, this pattern of objective differentiation may not be accompanied by an equivalent degree of cultural differentiation as represented by increasing divergence of values, attitudes and life-styles among various subgroups. In time, however, this may occur and we move, in effect, toward a pattern of stratification that more closely resembles that obtaining in developed societies.[47]

For example, child-rearing patterns, attitudes toward schooling, aspirations, and other family traits that may affect a child's school success in a newly rich African family may differ little from those of families not yet participating in the cash economy, or participating at a much more marginal level, at least during the early stages of the social change process. What we may be observing here is the educational effect of the process of class formation (in the Western sense), as poor nations become more like Western societies. This explanation actually fits rather well within Marxist, neo-Marxist and traditional structural-functional understandings of social change (which may be rather annoying to singular minded and ideologically driven adherents of any of those theoretical stances). Of course, it is also observably the case that in societies in which standard Western indexes of social status are not (or are not yet) relevant to a child's educational destiny, other traditional stratification patterns may be very important, for example, caste, tribe, lineage.

A different but related explanation is that there is much greater variation in the availability of school resources in developing nations than in developed nations. For example, in rich nations almost all students have complete sets of textbooks, and the differences in the formal educational levels of teachers are relatively small. In developing nations, however, there are great variations in such indicators. In a poor nation, even modest increments in the provision of textbooks can thus have a major effect on student learning. In rich nations students are already abundantly supplied with books, and increases in learning require difficult and costly improvements in the quality of books—assuming knowledge of the aspects of book quality that actually influence student learning. In a poor nation many primary teachers have low levels of formal schooling and little if any pedagogical training. Thus a very modest change in pre-service or in-service training could significantly improve teacher performance and hence student learning. In a rich nation almost all teachers have university degrees, high-level pedagogical training, and many opportunities for in-service education, and thus even small improvements in teacher performance are difficult to achieve and hard to identify.

I have combined both of these explanations in a previous publication. In rich nations, which are close to the limits of perfectibility of the "standard model of schooling" as we know it, "even modest additional gains in achievement require very difficult and costly educational effort." In developing nations "even the very modest improvements in school quality which a poor nation can realistically contemplate have the potential for providing important increases in student learning," particularly among the most marginalized students.[48] The possibility of improving equality of output in developing nations, within the very modest resources available to them, is particularly important because the evidence indicates that levels of learning among students in developing nations are systematically lower than among students in rich nations. Cross-national comparisons of student achievement levels that have been carried out over these past decades, principally under the auspices of the International Association for the Evaluation of Educational Achievement (IEA), have consistently demonstrated that the achievement test scores of children from low- and middle-income nations are lower than those of children of comparable age or grade levels in industrialized nations. The differences are large in some subject areas and small in others, but they are consistent. Until quite recently these cross-national studies have compared young people at the secondary level, or in some cases the senior primary level. In most developing nations, as I noted above, children who are neither socioeconomically advantaged nor academically gifted do not typically survive to this level of schooling. Thus the differences in learning output could be expected to be even greater at the early primary level, which is as far as most youngsters in developing nations progress in their formal education. [49] Recently available evidence from an IEA study of reading levels among nine-year-olds in twenty-nine nations suggest that this may be the case. Unfortunately the number of developing nations in the sample is too small to firmly ground the conclusion.[50]

Much recently published evidence indicates that the fiscal crisis in most developing nations, combined with expanding enrollments, is dramatically decreasing the instructional resources available per student, which is in turn increasing the learning gap between students in rich and poor nations.[51] This has led many observers, including such powerful agencies as the World Bank, to conclude that in many poor regions, such as Africa, further progress in improving equality of access and survival may have to be sacrificed in order to restore at least minimal levels of learning output from the educational systems.[52] In sum, the argument is that neither individuals nor societies benefit from increasingly equal access to and survival through a schooling system in which students learn less and less as total instructional resources continually decline.

Equality of Outcome

Relatively equal distributions of access to, survival through, or learning within the formal schooling system is considered socially beneficial by many only if it pays off for the recipients in relatively equal access to life chances (particularly but not exclusively jobs) as adults. To what extent can, or does, education have an intervening effect on intergenerational status transmission? To what extent, and under what conditions, can it produce upward social mobility rather than simply ratify or reproduce existing patterns of structural inequality? Consideration of this question brings us back to the basic questions noted earlier in this essay. Can, or under what conditions, the school build a new social order? Can it at least provide opportunities for individual social mobility for at least some children of marginalized groups within a society? A huge amount of evidence has been generated over the past three to four decades regarding these questions, mostly within nations but occasionally comparatively across nations. The results are, at least in a comparative sense, systematic, but theoretically they are confusing. In 1975 Lin and Yauger reported data from a quite limited data set, from Haiti, from three Costa Rican communities at three levels of development, from

Britain, and from the United States, and concluded that "the direct influence of educational attainment on occupational status is curvilinearily (concave) related to degree of industrialization."[53] Schiefelbein and Farrell noted that data from Uganda at three points in time and from four Brazilian communities fitted the same pattern.[54] More recent results from Chile have reinforced the same pattern.[55] The general pattern seems to be as follows. In very poor societies almost everyone is engaged in subsistence agriculture, except for a few (typically young) occupants of newly created civil service posts and some commercial entrepeneurs. Education can have very little effect on occupational mobility because there are very few occupational destinations into which one could be mobile (partially explaining the lack of effective demand for education among such populations, as noted above). As the local economy grows and becomes more differentiated, it creates a variety of new job openings. In the absence of a traditionally dominant class or group that can exploit all of the new opportunities, formal education becomes a predominant influence on the level of job acquired. Significant numbers of even very disadvantaged children can use education to obtain positions in the "modern" economy. (In many developing societies the growth of the educational system has much surpassed the growth of the economy, producing a problem of "educated unemployment." Even in such societies youngsters often continue in school as long as possible because the potential payoff is high if, or when, they can obtain any job at all.) As societies become very developed, their economies become so complex and rapidly changing, and the possible avenues to economic success are so varied, that the independent effect of formal education begins to diminish.[56]

Evidence from the advanced state-socialist societies of Eastern Europe, which have recently collapsed, suggests that there too this general pattern has been evident.[57] Some economists have argued that in very advanced postindustrial economies the phenomenon of the "declining middle"—the elimination of well-paying industrial and middle-class jobs in favor of lower-paying service sector jobs—is reducing even further the mobility-generating potential of formal schooling.[58] Pushing this argument a step further, Farrell and Schiefelbein have claimed that *all* of the major studies that have provided data regarding the effect of education on intergenerational status transmission—which form the empirical foundation for the theoretical arguments on this question—are flawed and fundamentally uninterpretable because they fail to take into account long-term structural changes in the economy and how these necessarily constrain what education can do.[59] Beyond this, a new generation of "naturalistic" and "narrative" studies illustrate the ways in which youth from structurally disadvantaged backgrounds actually react to and use formal schooling. Their methods, which are wholly unfamiliar or foreign to typically middle-class university professors and ministry of education officials, further confound our understanding, from all traditional theoretical frames, of the ways in which young people are affected by and make use of schooling to ratify or improve their inherited life chances.[60]

However, in spite of this growing empirical and theoretical confusion, it is still clear that even in societies in which education has the weakest effect upon intergenerational status transmission, and the weakest effect upon social structural change, some individuals and social groups benefit from both its more widespread provision as well as increases in its quality. Rarely if ever does the provision of more formal education, or the improvement of its quality, have no mobility-generating or life-enhancing consequences for at least a few children of marginalized groups. Very recent analyses by Paquette and by Levin,[61] however, can be interpreted as suggesting that even that minimal effect of formal schooling on individual and collective life chances may be disappearing (or has already disappeared) in North American societies, and perhaps, by extension, in other societies as well.

Conclusion

In this final section I wish to apply the massive amount of comparative data analyzed above to the central theme of this book: the effect of *recent* educational reform movements, proposals, and occasionally enacted policies (e.g., privatization, decentralization, educational change for "global competitiveness," etc.) on equality of educational opportunity and outcome among the most marginalized members of the many societies of our world. This is necessarily a highly speculative enterprise. As we have seen, major educational change is generally a failure-prone, slow, and long-term process. It takes even longer to begin to really see and understand its eventual effects upon how today's students actually can and do live their lives. It has taken almost three decades for us to begin to really understand the results of the massive educational change efforts of the "optimistic sixties," and even now we are still arguing about the quality and completeness of the available comparative information and about how to interpret and understand it. We could hardly expect less with respect to the most recent waves of educational reforms. Moreover, local, regional, or worldwide events can significantly change the context of long-term reform efforts such that "results" can move in totally unpredictable directions. For example, if we had been creating this book fifteen years ago, none of the authors could have predicted the sudden demise of the former Soviet Union and its associated states, nor the consequences for our understanding of educational change and educational equality, which are still very unclear and will likely remain so for a long time. An ancient (probably apocryphal) proverb has it, "Prediction is always difficult, especially with respect to the future." A central lesson for the theme of this book from the comparative data assembled over the past several decades is this: Don't take seriously anyone who speaks with *certainty* about the probable effects of the current wave of educational reform proposals. We have, however, learned a few things since the end of the Second World War.

These lessons can provide us with some guidance regarding how to think about outcomes, if not how to predict them. A central lesson learned is the necessity of a high degree of intellectual and moral humility, as well as tolerance for a high degree of ambiguity.

Another lesson learned is that the common tendency over the past decades to centrally directed and command-driven forms of educational change, most commonly following national and international "faddism" and a "one size fits all" view of educational change, have poorly served the interests of those who might benefit from increases in educational equality. This applies equally as well to the current wave of educational reform "fads." The possible or probable effects of the current reform fashions on educational inequality depend on specific local conditions and history. For example, university education in many nations of Latin America has long been highly "privatized." The effects on educational inequality vary dramatically from nation to nation, depending on specific national conditions.[62] The effects of further privatization in any of these nations, however, would be almost certainly very different from privatization of higher education in the completely state-controlled higher education systems of many other nations. Similarly, as Mark Bray notes in chapter 8 of this volume, "decentralization" has different meanings and different possible long-term consequences, depending on where a particular nation starts on some sort of centralized-decentralized continuum.[63] Just as there are no universally applicable solutions to educational inequality, there are no universally applicable predictions of reform consequences. There is, however, one general claim that can be made. If the experience of the past forty years is any guide, it seems that the broad reform proposals now being widely discussed will in most cases not be enacted; if enacted, they will seldom be well or fully implemented; if implemented well, they generally will not have significant effect on equality of access, survival, or output (as discussed in the "model" presented above), at least for large numbers of youngsters; and if they do manage to improve these "within-school" aspects of equality, they are highly unlikely to have significant impact on equality of outcome by altering the life chances of large proportions of poor or marginalized children.

Overall, then, the picture appears rather bleak. There have been significant gains in educational equality over the past forty years, but they have been for the most part not the result of broad-scale, centrally driven, international-agency supported reform programs. Rather, they have been the result of economic growth or social structural change outside the realm of the school, or of an option that is now generally unavailable or that political leaders are unwilling to choose: massive increases in educational expenditure.[64]

However, I end this chapter on a hopeful note. Throughout the world, particularly the developing world, there are small and large attempts to fundamentally alter the traditional teacher-directed model of schooling. They typically use some or all of the following modalities: combinations of fully trained teachers, partially trained teachers, para-teachers, and community resource people; radio, correspondence lessons, television, and in a few cases computers; peer tutoring; self-guided learning materials; student and teacher constructed learning materials; multigrade classrooms; child-centered rather than teacher-driven pedagogy; free flows of children and adults between the school and the community; locally adapted changes in the cycle of the school day or school year. They typically spread not by a centrally planned and commanded reform plan but through an innovation diffusion process. They depend for their success not on the ability and willingness of teachers to "follow orders" from on high, but rather on stimulating and unleashing the creative energy, enthusiasm, and personal practical knowledge of teachers. Such change programs do not simply alter one feature of the standard school (e.g., change one part of the curriculum), strengthen one or several parts of the standard schooling model (e.g., add more textbooks or improve teacher training), or add one or two new features. Rather, they represent a thorough reorganization and a fundamental re-visioning of the standard schooling model such that the learning program, although often occurring in or based in a building called a school, is far different from what we have come to expect to be happening in a school. They tend to break down the boundaries between formal and nonformal education and to focus less on teaching and more on learning. Where they have been evaluated, the results have generally been very positive. New groups of learners are reached successfully, and the learning results are at least as good as, if not better than, those obtained in standard schools. And the costs are typically no more than, if not less than, those of the standard model. Moreover, because they serve the most marginalized, hardest to reach and teach (in the standard mode) students, the learning results from a value added perspective are quite spectacular.[65]

Some major examples of these model-breaking educational change programs include the *Escuela Nueva* program in Colombia, which has now reached close to 30,000 rural schools and has been adapted on a large- or small-scale basis in at least ten other Latin American nations;[66] various education for production programs in Latin America for disadvantaged youth who have been very poorly served by the standard schooling system;[67] the MECE Rural Program (Programa de Mejoramiento de la Calidad de la Educación para las Escuelas Multigrados Rurales) in Chile, which is now present in over 3,000 schools;[68] the Nonformal Primary Education program of the Bangladesh Rural Advancement Committee (BRAC), which operates in thousands of villages in that nation and is spreading into urban areas and parts of India;[69] a wide network of community schools supported by the Aga Khan Foundation in Pakistan and other developing nations;[70] and the Community Schools Program in rural Egypt, which is expected to be operating in thousands of schools within a few years.[71] What is important about such programs is that they focus on learning rather than teaching and provide a pedagogically superior experience for highly marginalized young people. In addition, they generally operate either outside

of or on the margins of the national school system (indeed, one of the major design issues with such systems, particularly at the early stages, is protecting or
insulating them from the heavy bureaucratic hand of the state schooling system).[72] They thus provide us with examples of successfully delivering opportunities for high-quality learning to the most disadvantaged children that *do not
depend on the eroding fiscal and managerial capacity of increasingly "fragile"*[73] *states.* They present us with an operationally successful vision of a more
hopeful future.

Even in these cases, however, it is far too early to tell whether these major
increases in the availability and quality of schooling for poor and marginalized
children will ultimately have any major effect on the socioeconomic and political structures that have created and maintained that poverty and marginalization in the first place. Indeed, ultimately we cannot know and predict that in advance. As I have argued elsewhere recently, human learning is, by its very
nature, not subject to coercion and control nor to prediction of its consequences.
In the final analysis all we can really do is enable it and hope for the best.[74] In
that context, whatever the ultimate effects of these new schooling programs on
the broad social structural level, significantly improving the availability and
quality of schooling is in and of itself a notable achievement and a very worthy
social goal.

Notes

1. A vast literature was generated during the 1950s and 1960s regarding the nature
of development, its causes, and education's presumed role in the process. Space here
does not permit a detailed analysis of the differing theoretical views that have been advanced, although it should be noted that almost all scholars at the time operated from a
consensus or equilibrium rather than a conflict model of social change. For a useful review of the general development literature through the mid-1960s, see C. E. Black, *The
Dynamics of Modernization* (New York: Harper and Row, 1966), esp. 175–199. For a
detailed review of what was then understood to be education's role in economic and social development, see, respectively, Arnold Anderson and Mary Jean Bowman, eds., *Education and Economic Development* (Chicago: Aldine, 1965); and Don Adams and
Joseph P. Farrell, *Education and Social Development* (Syracuse: Syracuse University
Center for Development Education, 1967).

2. For example, during the decade of the 1960s the province of Ontario, Canada, implemented a secondary education reform (the Robarts Plan) that aimed at (among other
things) allowing all young people to complete that level of schooling. It built enough
new universities and expanded the capacity of existing universities to more than double
the capacity at that level, and established an entirely new system of more than twenty
postsecondary colleges of applied arts and technology.

3. Jean-Pierre Jallade, "The Evolution of Educational Systems in Industrialized
Countries: A Summary," *Western European Education* 4, no. 4 (Winter 1972–1973):
330–336; Henry Levin, "The Dilemma of Comprehensive Secondary School Reforms in

Western Europe," *Comparative Education Review* 22, no. 3 (October 1978): 434–451; G. Neave, "New Influences on Educational Policies in Western Europe during the Seventies," in *Politics and Educational Change,* ed. Patricia Broadfoot et al. (London: Croom Helm, 1982), 71–85.

4. Data from the statistical division of UNESCO, as compiled at the World Bank. See *Education Sector Policy Paper,* 3d ed. (Washington, D.C.: World Bank, 1980), 103–106.

5. Philip H. Coombs, *The World Educational Crisis: A Systems Analysis* (New York: Oxford University Press, 1968).

6. World Bank, *Education Sector Policy Paper.*

7. Mitchell A. Seligson and John T. Passe-Smith, *Development and Underdevelopment: The Political Economy of Inequality* (London: Lynne Rienner, 1993).

8. Don Adams, "Development Education," *Comparative Education Review* 21, nos. 2–3 (June–October 1977): 299–300.

9. Joseph P. Farrell, "A Retrospective on Educational Planning in Comparative Education," *Comparative Education Review* 41, no. 3 (August 1997): 277–313.

10. George S. Counts, *Dare the School Build a New Social Order?* (New York: John Day, 1932).

11. The literature here is vast. For some recent and representative examples, see Marlaine Lockheed and Adrienne Verspoor, *Improving Primary Education in Developing Countries: A Review of Policy Options* (Washington, D.C.: World Bank, 1990); K. N. Ross and L. Mahlick, *Planning the Quality of Education* (Paris: International Institute for Educational Planning, 1990); K. N. Ross and L. Mahlick, *Education and Knowledge: Basic Pillars of Changing Production Patterns with Social Equity* (Santiago, Chile: UNESCO-CEPAL, 1993); J. M. Puryear, *Education in Latin America: Problems and Challenges,* Prealc Occasional Paper no. 7 (New York: Inter-American Dialogue, 1997).

12. For classic statements of this view, see Martin Carnoy, *Education as Cultural Imperialism* (New York: McKay, 1974); and Samuel Bowles and Herbert Gintis, *Schooling in Capitalist America* (New York: Basic Books, 1976).

13. See, for example, Martin Carnoy and Henry Levin, *Schooling and Work in the Democratic State* (Stanford, Calif.: Stanford University Press, 1985). See also Daniel P. Liston, *Capitalist Schools: Explanation and Ethics in Radical Studies of Schooling* (New York: Routledge, 1990). Although educators have learned much from comparative information over the past forty or more years, the fundamental debates about the possibility and desirability of using schooling as a form of social engineering go back a very long time. See P. S. Hlebowitsch and W. Wraga, "Social Class Analysis in the Early Progressive Tradition," *Curriculum Inquiry* 25, no. 1 (Spring 1995): 7–22.

14. Cesar Birzea, "Education in a World in Transition: Between Post-Communism and Post-Modernism," *Prospects* 26, no. 4 (1996): 673–681.

15. Joseph P. Farrell and Ernesto Schiefelbein, "Education and Status Attainment in Chile: A Comparative Challenge to the Wisconsin Model of Status Attainment," *Comparative Education Review* 9, no. 4 (November 1985): 490–506.

16. Arnold J. Heidenheimer, "The Politics of Educational Reform: Explaining Different Outcomes of School Comprehensivation Attempts in Sweden and West Germany," *Comparative Education Review* 18, no. 3 (October 1974): 388–410.

17. See D. Rondinelli, J. Middleton, and A. Verspoor, *Planning Educational*

Reforms in Developing Countries: The Contingency Approach (Durham, N.C.: Duke University Press, 1990); and Farrell, *Retrospective on Educational Planning.*

18. Joseph P. Farrell, "Narratives of Identity: The Voices of Youth," *Curriculum Inquiry* 26, no. 3 (Fall 1996): 1–12, plus the articles that follow this editorial essay. See also Elizabeth Ellsworth, "Claiming the Tenured Body," in *The Center of the Web: Women and Solitude,* ed. D. Wear (Albany: State University of New York Press, 1993), 63–74; S. K. Walker, "Canonical Gestures," *Curriculum Inquiry* 24, no. 2 (Summer 1994): 171–180; and Patti Lather, *Getting Smart: Feminist Research and Pedagogy within the Post-Modern* (New York: Routledge, 1994).

19. See, for example, Michael Connelly and Jean Clandenin, "Stories of Experience and Narrative Inquiry," *Educational Researcher* 19 (May 1990): 2–14; P. Spence, *Narrative Truth and Historical Truth* (New York: Norton, 1984); S. Gudmundsdottir, "The Teller, the Tale, and the One Being Told: the Narrative Nature of the Research Interview," *Curriculum Inquiry* 26, no. 3 (Fall 1996): 293–306; and Max van Manen, "Pedagogy, Virtue, and Narrative Identity in Teaching," *Curriculum Inquiry* 24, no. 2 (Summer 1994): 135–170.

20. A particularly useful historical analysis of early changes in conceptions of educational equality is found in James S. Coleman, "The Concept of Equality of Educational Opportunity," *Harvard Educational Review* 38, no. 4 (Winter 1968): 7–22.

21. V. J. Baker, "Education for Its Own Sake," *Comparative Education Review* 33, no. 4 (November 1989): 507–526.

22. M. Bronfenbrenner, "Equality and Equity," *Annals* 409 (September 1973): 5–25.

23. For an expansion of this discussion and an application of the "model" to the problem of educational equality over time in a particular developing nation, see Joseph P. Farrell and Ernesto Schiefelbein, *Eight Years of Their Lives: Through Schooling to the Labour Market in Chile* (Ottawa: International Development Research Centre, 1982).

24. UNESCO, *Education for All: Status and Trends* (Paris: UNESCO, 1993), 24–25.

25. UNESCO, *Education for All,* 17.

26. UNESCO, *Education for All,* 10.

27. Lockheed and Verspoor, *Improving Primary Education,* 31.

28. UNESCO, *Education for All,* 24–25.

29. For an extended analysis of these demand-side obstacles, see Mary Jean Bowman, "An Integrated Framework for Analysis of the Spread of Schooling in Less Developed Countries," *Comparative Education Review* 21, no. 4 (November 1988): 563–583.

30. Lockheed and Verspoor, *Improving Primary Education,* 13–14.

31. For example, Malawi, 28 percent; Ethopia, 40 percent; Mali, 20 percent; India, 38 percent; Lesotho, 27 percent; Mozambique, 26 percent; Pakistan, 34 percent; Nigeria, 31 percent. Kenneth King, "Donor Support to Literacy, Adult Basic and Primary Education," *NORRAG News* 7 (March 1990): 52.

32. Ernesto Schiefelbein, "Repeating: An Overlooked Problem of Latin American Education," *Comparative Education Review* 19, no. 3 (October 1975): 468–487.

33. Lockheed and Verspoor, *Improving Primary Education,* 14.

34. Saeed Quazi, personal communication with author, May 18, 1991.

35. Jerome Paquette, "Universal Education: Meanings, Challenges and Options into the Third Millennium," *Curriculum Inquiry* 25, no. 1 (Spring 1995): 23–56; Benjamin Levin, "Dealing with Dropouts in Canadian Education," *Curriculum Inquiry* 22, no. 3

(Fall 1992): 257–270; Joseph P. Farrell, "Educational Problems and Learning Solutions," *Curriculum Inquiry* 22, no. 3 (Fall 1992): 231–234.

36. T. Bailey, "Jobs of the Future and the Education They Will Require: Evidence from Occupational Forecasts," *Educational Researcher* 20, no. 2 (February 1991): 11–20.

37. Data from the Office of Statistics, UNESCO, as distributed at the World Conference on Education for All.

38. World Bank, *Education Sector Policy Paper,* 103–106. More recent data indicate that this unaccountable variation has continued. See Carol Bellamy, *The State of the World's Children, 1996* (Oxford: Oxford University Press, 1996), 86–87.

39. Ernesto Schiefelbein and Joseph P. Farrell, "Women, Schooling, and Work in Chile: Evidence from a Longitudinal Study," *Comparative Education Review* 24, no. 2 (June 1980): pt. 2, S160–S179.

40. Bellamy, *World's Children,* 86–87.

41. The Gini coefficient is a widely used measure of the degree to which the observed distribution of something (e.g., years of education) varies from an ideally equal distribution. Its values may range theoretically from zero (perfect equality) to one (perfect inequality). For a simple example of how it is calculated, see Donald R. Snodgrass, "The Distribution of Schooling and the Distribution of Income," in *Planning Education for Development,* vol. 1., ed. Russell Davis (Cambridge: Harvard University Center for Studies in Education and Development, 1980), 187–204.

42. Snodgrass, "Distribution of Schooling," 197.

43. That Cuba in 1953 had a relatively low degree of inequality in the distribution of years of schooling is an interesting datum to bear in mind when evaluating the educational accomplishments of the Castro regime since the revolution.

44. Riddell provides a particularly useful summary of the methodological critique and its implications for analysis. Abby R. Riddell, "Assessing Designs for School Effectiveness Research and School Improvement in Developing Countries," *Comparative Education Review* 41, no. 2 (May 1997): 178–204.

45. Stephen P. Heyneman and William Loxley, "The Effects of Primary School Quality on Academic Achievement across Twenty-nine High and Low-Income Countries," *American Journal of Sociology* 88, no. 3 (May 1983): 1162–1194.

46. Riddell, "Assessing Designs."

47. Philip Foster, "Education and Social Differentiation in Less Developed Countries," *Comparative Education Review* 22, nos. 2–3 (June–October 1977): 224–225.

48. Joseph P. Farrell, "International Lessons for School Effectiveness: The View from the Developing World," in *Educational Policy for Effective Schools,* ed. Mark Holmes et al. (New York: Teachers College Press, 1989), 14.

49. Joseph P. Farrell and Stephen P. Heyneman, eds., *Textbooks in the Developing World: Economic and Educational Choices* (Washington, D.C.: World Bank, 1989), 3–5. See also Farrell, "International Lessons," and Lockheed and Verspoor, *Improving Primary Education.*

50. W. B. Elley, *How in the World Do Students Read?* (The Hague: International Association for the Evaluation of Educational Achievement, 1992).

51. Farrell and Heyneman, *Textbooks in the Developing World,* 3–4; Farrell, "International Lessons."

52. "Symposium: World Bank Report on Education in Sub-Saharan Africa," *Com-*

parative Education Review 33, no. 1 (February 1989): 93–133. This possibly necessary trade-off was debated further at the World Conference on Education for All. See King, "Donor Support."

53. Nan Lin and D. Yauger, "The Process of Occupational Status Achievement: A Preliminary Cross-National Comparison," *American Journal of Sociology* 81, no. 6 (November 1975): 543–562.

54. Ernesto Schiefelbein and Joseph P. Farrell, "Selectivity and Survival in the Schools of Chile," *Comparative Education Review* 22, no. 2 (June 1978): 326–341.

55. Farrell and Schiefelbein, "Education and Status Attainment in Chile," 490–506.

56. For classic studies among the richest nations, see Christopher Jencks et al., *Inequality* (New York: Basic Books, 1972); R. Boudon, *Education, Opportunity, and Social Inequality* (New York: Wiley, 1973); and *Education, Inequality and Life Chances* (Paris: OECD, 1975).

57. Joseph Zajda, "Education and Social Stratification in the Soviet Union," *Comparative Education Review* 16, no. 1 (March 1980): 3–11; and Birzea, "Education in a World in Transition."

58. For an early statement of this position, see Bob Kuttner, "The Declining Middle," *Atlantic Monthly,* July 1983, 60–72; Bob Kuttner, *Economic Growth/Economic Justice* (New York: Houghton-Mifflin, 1984). For a more recent argument, see Paquette, "Universal Education."

59. Farrell and Schiefelbein, "Education and Status Attainment."

60. See, for example, Paul Willis, *Learning to Labour: How Working Class Kids Get Working Class Jobs* (Westmead, U.K.: Saxon House, 1977); J. C. Walker, *Louts and Legends: Male Youth Culture in an Inner-City School* (Sydney: Allen and Unwin, 1988); B. M. Bullivant, *The Ethnic Encounter in the Secondary School: Ethnocultural Reproduction and Resistance; Theory and Cases* (London: Falmer, 1987); R. N. Page, "Games of Chance: The Lower-Track Curriculum in a College Preparatory High School," *Curriculum Inquiry* 20, no. 3 (Fall 1990); Lois Weis, *Working Class without Work: High School Students in a De-Industrialized Economy* (New York: Routledge, 1990).

61. Paquette, "Universal Education," and Levin, "Dealing with Dropouts."

62. Daniel C. Levy, *Higher Education and the State in Latin America: Private Challenges to Public Dominance* (Chicago: University of Chicago Press, 1986); Joseph P. Farrell, "Higher Education in Chile," in *International Encyclopedia of Higher Education,* ed. Philip Altbach (London: Pergamon, 1991), 325–342.

63. Jennifer Adams, "Teacher Attitudes toward De-Centralization in a Decentralized and Centralized System: Ontario and France" (Ph.D. diss., Ontario Institute for Studies in Education, 1996).

64. There are of course exceptions, nations that have found the political will to significantly increase educational expenditures and effectively implement reforms that appear to be having a positive impact on educational inequality. Egypt is one such case. See *Review and Assessment of Reform of Basic Education in Egypt* (Paris: UNESCO, 1996); Joseph P. Farrell and Michael Connelly, *From a Massive Reform Model to an Innovation Diffusion Model of Change,* Report for UNICEF-Egypt (Cairo: UNICEF, 1994).

65. Ernesto Schiefelbein, *In Search of the School of the 21st century: Is Colombia's Escuela Nueva the Right Pathfinder?* (Santiago, Chile: UNESCO Regional Office for Education in Latin America and the Caribbean, 1991); George Psachoropolous et al., "Achievement Evaluation of Colombia's Escuela Nueva: Is Multigrade the Answer?"

Comparative Education Review 37, no. 3 (August 1993): 263–276; Ash Hartwell, *Evaluation of Egypt's Community School Project* (Cairo: UNICEF, 1995); M. Ahmed, *Primary Education for All: Learning from the BRAC Experience: A Case Study* (Dhaka: Abel, 1993). It is interesting to observe that the editors of the U.S. magazine *Education Week* reported on a 1991 survey of educators from that nation regarding their vision of "schools of the future." The reported "emerging oral concensus" closely approximates what these highly effective schools in developing nations are already doing. See *From Risk to Renewal: Charting a Course for Reform* (Washington, D.C.: Editorial Projects in Education, 1993), 27–31. In a similar vein, in a recent major analysis of the (generally failed) attempts at educational reform over the past century in the United States, Tyack and Cuban argue for an approach to educational change that these programs from the "developing" world are already implementing, conceiving effective educational change as not occurring from the "top down" or the "outside in" but from the "inside out," with teachers as the key protagonists. See David Tyack and Larry Cuban, *Tinkering toward Utopia: A Century of Public School Reform* (Cambridge: Harvard University Press, 1996). See also David Tyack, "Reinventing Schooling," in *Learning from the Past: What History Teaches Us about School Reform* (Baltimore: Johns Hopkins University Press, 1996), 191–216, esp. 211. This appears to be an area in which the aspiring educational reformers of rich nations could learn much from the successful practitioners of such reform in much poorer nations—if only they will listen and learn.

66. Schiefelbein, *In Search of the School.*

67. Oscar Corvalan-Vasquez, "Trends in Technical-Vocational and Secondary Education in Latin America," *International Journal of Educational Development* 8, no. 2 (May 1988): 73–98.

68. J. San Miguel B., "Programa de Mejoramiento de la Calidad de la Educación para las Escuelas Multigrados Rurales," *Formas y Reformas de la Educación* 1 (Trimestre 3, 1996): 18–24.

69. S. C. Sarkar, "The BRAC Non-Formal Primary Education Centres in Bangladesh," in *Partnerships and Participation in Basic Education,* vol. 2, ed. Sheldon Shaeffer (Paris: International Institute for Educational Planning, 1994), case 7; Suzanne Scott, "Education for Child Garment Workers in Bangladesh" (M.A. thesis, Ontario Institute for Studies in Education/University of Toronto, 1997); Madhumita Pal, "Voices from the Field: Alternative Education Strategies for Social Change" (M.A. thesis, Ontario Institute for Studies in Education/University of Toronto, 1996).

70. Huma Nauman, "The Need for Developing a Language Policy Common to Aga Khan Development Network Institutions" (paper presented at the annual meeting of education program officers of Aga Khan Foundation, Mombasa, Kenya, April 1996).

71. Malak Zaalouk, *The Children of the Nile: The Community Schools Project in Upper Egypt* (Paris: UNESCO, 1995).

72. Farrell and Connelly, *Massive Reform Model.*

73. Bruce Fuller, *Growing Up Modern: The Western State Builds Third World Schools* (New York: Routledge and Kegan Paul, 1991).

74. Farrell, *Retrospective on Educational Planning.*

Chapter 7

Women's Education in the Twenty-First Century

Balance and Prospects

Nelly P. Stromquist

Twenty years have elapsed since the international women's movement called attention to the social and economic inequalities confronting women. Over the two decades, substantial progress has occurred in problem definition and theorization of gender, including the role of education and schooling in the advancement of women. Less progress has taken place in the type and degree of change within formal school systems. Industrialized countries, with greater resources, more organized women's groups, and institutions more sensitive to public pressure have attained greater changes than the developing countries, but even in the former much work remains to be accomplished.

When discussing the connection between gender and education, it is necessary to make a distinction between education and schooling. Education is used herein to refer to the transmission of broad and specific knowledge that includes but also goes beyond that imparted by national school systems. Education may occur in formal situations, nonformal situations (programs and classes provided for adults by community groups, for instance), and informal situations (notably the knowledge conveyed within the home and through the mass media). Schooling relates specifically to the structured and institutionalized type of knowledge transmitted through formal educational institutions, mainly schools and universities. This distinction is important because, given the conservative nature of most schooling, it is within nonformal education settings that most gender-transforming processes have occurred and will occur.

This chapter discusses schooling and education in developing countries, focusing on their implications for and linkage to gender issues. It emphasizes developments in the 1990s and seeks to present an overview of the most recent developments along the lines of theory, policy, and practice.

Discussions of conceptual and practical changes must identify certain key groups involved in education, for their positions are not the same. Among governments and development agencies (both bilateral and multilateral), the question of women's education has moved from "invisibility" to explicit recognition of the need to consider it a priority. This priority, unfortunately, is not generally high. Official recognition tends to be more rhetorical than real and is so far based mostly on an understanding of women as important mediators in the modernization process—not yet on an understanding of women as autonomous citizens. International development agencies have continued their policy of dealing primarily with governments and in their actions tend to side with those governments. Their education efforts to promote women have generally focused on access to schooling and skills for production. Among groups within or closely associated with the women's movement, education is considered an important avenue toward empowerment, and valuable knowledge has been gained from experiences in this direction. Gail Kelly, one of the pioneer thinkers on the question of gender and education in the context of developing countries, admonished us to understand not only how education of women can improve society but how education can improve the lives of the women themselves.[1] This point has not yet been captured by either governments or international agencies.

Educational studies on gender in the 1970s concentrated on documenting sex inequalities in educational opportunity (primarily access to schooling). In the 1980s the studies expanded this focus to examine such issues as the determinants of these opportunities, the relationship between education and work/remuneration, and the benefits of women's education for society.[2] Later studies in the 1990s under the support of the World Bank have continued the line of exploration of barriers to girls' education and, particularly, the personal and social benefits derived from their education.[3] Such studies have been useful in highlighting the importance of education as a resource for women and the fact that it is neutral neither in its offerings nor in its consequences. A consistent finding has been that schooling increases women's earnings but does not remove their economic dependence on men. Women's years of schooling affects decisions on marriage, but there is no linear relationship between the two. These two critical shapers of women's lives indicate that whereas schooling is important for economic and social advancement, it is not sufficient to alter women's subordinate position. Even after higher levels of schooling, women have retained marginal positions in the political arena. Studies focusing on Latin America, a region in which gender parity is very close at all levels of education, have looked at issues beyond access and quality, such as the effects of coeducational settings on social outcomes, the participation and power of women in teachers' unions, student women in politics at the university level, and experiences in popular education for adult women.[4] A third generation of studies on gender and education has probed educational phenomena not often seen from a gender perspective, such as the role of women teachers in the process of educational change, the treatment of gender and ethnicity in history textbooks, tensions between the professional and personal identity of women teachers, and the contested experience of the incorporation of controversial subjects such as sex education in the curriculum.[5]

The Contributions of Feminist Theory to the Understanding of Educational Institutions

Society is based on complementary but hardly symmetric levels of reciprocity in social interaction. Several codes are used to create stable hierarchical social systems. Gender is not the only one but is pervasive as the main type of differentiation in all societies. Feminist theory seeks to place women and their lives in a central place to understand social relations as a whole. Feminism is best conceptualized as a form of critical theory and a movement that enables its member-users to see behind appearance and to understand the structure underlying it and giving meaning, albeit distorted, to their lives.[6] Through a gender lens we can understand mechanisms of oppression and identify forces that shape the apparent "free choices" that women and men make through various phases of their lives.

Feminist theory has highlighted the need to link analytically the micro and the macro: the personal/intimate and the institutional, the family and the community, the individual and her society, the school and the state. These settings are related in real life, and their connection should be recognized in examinations of institutions such as schools and universities.

Schooling presents a paradoxical situation in the process of gender transformation. Schooling is undoubtedly a major source of cultural capital, employment, and social mobility. Its importance is so widespread that most countries have moved into mandating compulsory public education for all. At the same time, however, educational institutions are conservative settings that reflect the values and rules of patriarchal society.[7]

Among gender scholars today, there is an increased understanding of the necessity to undertake a comprehensive analysis of educational institutions so that the various aspects that constitute the totality of the schooling experience—curriculum, instructional methodologies, peer relations, extracurricular activities—are investigated. Schooling is organized in gendered ways and has differential impacts on girls and boys. Studies in developed countries—which tend to have more open social systems than countries in the Third World—reveal school authority structures, teacher expectations and classroom practices, and peer exchanges that are organized along gender lines.[8] Knowledge about the gendered nature of schooling certainly existed in the 1980s, but in recent years more evidence has been accumulated to demonstrate the pervasive nature of these conditions and their existence despite variations in social class and ethnicity. The tools of qualitative research have been instrumental in documenting the everyday experience of students in educational institutions, noting the sometimes mild but cumulative nature of many events that gradually yet inexorably shape individuals' perception of self and their roles in society.[9] Also in recent years there has been greater conceptual attention given to the intersection between gender, social class, and ethnicity. These concerns, however, have not always materialized in actual studies because this type of research requires substantial financial resources, due either to more complex research designs or to the need to gain access to more heterogeneous school settings, which are not easy to find. The question of the intersection of social markers, although conceptually important, runs the risk of introducing innumerable differences that, although correcting the conception of the "grand narrative" so criticized by postmodernism, also threaten to depoliticize social issues through the introduction of multiple variability of situations and elusive complexity. This tension—acknowledging complex and fluid gender identities versus working with broad categories such as "women"—has not been satisfactorily resolved (see chapter 1 in this volume). It does appear that for purposes of strategic action and political mobilization it is essential to work with group definitions; we cannot operate politically on the basis of diffused identities. Although there are diverse experiences through which women live, they are simultaneously lived because of their sex.[10]

Gender theories today are more sensitive to power and the role of the state in shaping society. The extension of this understanding to schooling has highlighted the role that schools play in the creation of the binary categories of femininity and masculinity and how the state, through its quasi-monopoly of schooling, is implicated in this process. Thinkers such as Connell[11] have been instrumental in explicating the centrality of organized state power and highlighting the function of schools in the development of gendered subjectivities.

According to the analytical framework proposed by Althusser, schooling functions as an ideological apparatus of state. Yet it is also a space into which students bring their own preconceptions and make them a reality through the power of peer pressure. Schooling does not act by itself. Students and teachers bring into the classroom an array of values, attitudes, and beliefs they have learned in their homes and community. These become re-enacted in the school, through the treatment of women and men in textbooks, teacher-student interactions, peer-group transactions, and the school culture and organization in general.

A key feature of feminist theory is its emphasis on linking knowledge and action. Schools must be not only "understood" but seen as potentially transformative social spaces in which useful knowledge can be inculcated, reflection on existing knowledge and culture can take place, and alternative ways of being and living can be imagined and striven for. The dominant global public debate regarding education and women has accepted the importance of women's participation in schooling, at least in terms of access to basic education. This defense of women's right to education is certainly to be welcomed. At the same time, it has emphasized the aspect of access and has been rather unquestioning of other aspects of schooling—curriculum content, teacher-student interactions, and peer culture—that tend to reproduce a patriarchal social order. This definition of the situation creates a significant challenge for the women's movement. Without access, the question of the knowledge to be acquired is a moot point; without questioning existing educational institutions, the knowledge gained will tend to affirm the unequal and inequitable status quo.

In common with critical theory, feminist approaches are sensitive to the notion of individual and collective agency—the possibility of resistance by those oppressed, a phenomenon derived from the Foucauldian principle that power exists not only in official institutions and hierarchies but also through the multiple and lower-level interactions in our everyday lives. There is an increased emphasis on analyzing schooling as a contested terrain in which teachers and students try to create new definitions and personal identities and students do not passively accept dominant gender representations but argue about values and meanings. The potential of new teacher subjectivities and negotiations of the everyday life of schools is increasingly visualized as an avenue to attain the transformation of schooling.

In recent years, therefore, feminist work in schools and universities has moved toward more proactive strategies. At lower levels, these include bringing patriarchy, sexism, and racism into the context of the lives of young girls, creating spaces within schools and classrooms in which young girls can explore their experience and create situations of "equal exchange." At the university level, these practices include participation in the various women's studies courses and in the creation of mentoring mechanisms by which younger scholars (doctoral students and junior faculty) are helped by senior academic professors in ways that range from fostering research production to "learning the ropes" for promotion into tenured status.[12]

Models of the impact of the expansion of schooling on life chances are becoming more complete than they have been in the past. If before they included variables such as forgone earnings, current and future benefits, direct costs, supply of school facilities, and mass communication,[13] today they are more open to questions of patriarchal ideology reflected in such variables as early marriage and son preference. These variables do not directly address a society's belief in drastically distinct roles for women and men, but they do acknowledge that there are differential logics at work, rationales that are not necessarily economically based but reflect long-standing cultural norms. Researchers are also becoming more precise in their economic arguments. One example is Colclough, who remarks that rates-of-return analyses compare the cost of schooling to parents with the economic returns to the child, but in practice what determines schooling is the cost and benefits to parents of sending a child to school.[14] This observation illuminates why certain parents harm the educational opportunities for their children by depriving them of schooling in early years. Given the centrality of domestic work, and more specifically, the time invested in fuel and water fetching in rural households, it is becoming also increasingly clear that opportunities for greater access of girls to school will have to pass through greater investment in physical infrastructure by the government.

Ilon's study of macroeconomic and social variables[15] reinforces this point. She found that countries that become export intensive and improve their per capita GNP tend to increase the rate of females attending secondary school. This finding is compatible with the feminist argument and the empirical fact (observed in both the United States and Latin America) that women need more education to be as competitive as men in the labor force (reflected in women's need for about four more years of education than men to qualify for similar salaries). Also, as household incomes improve there is a diminished need for girls' domestic work.

In short, contributions from feminist perspectives to education underscore the need for holistic probing of the educational system, for a multidisciplinary analysis that considers influences at various level of social organization, and for policies or advocacy positions that exploit the opportunities for transformation within the narrow and somewhat temporary fractures that are possible.

The Conditions of Women's Schooling

Access to schooling has increased over time; comparisons of groups aged twenty to twenty-four with older cohorts invariably show higher levels of education among the younger generations. Some observers[16] note that the expansion of educational systems occurs independently of economic, political, and social factors within national borders, thereby suggesting that influential "transnational forces" are at work. Additional reasons for the expansion of schooling include international economic dynamics (i.e., countries becoming more export intensive or improving their per capita income, as shown by Ilon), social imitation, and, in the case of women's schooling, the increasing pressure of the women's movement. Supporting the latter assertion is the observation that over the past fifteen years the participation of women in education has been generally increasing faster than that of men, even though gender gaps remain and the pace of growth is exceedingly slow, at most 1.1 percent in favor of women during the 1988–1993 period.[17]

Table 7.1 indicates that women have closed the gender gap at all levels of schooling in the developed countries, representing 49 percent of the enrollment

Table 7.1
Female Enrollment as Percentage of Total Enrollment by Level
in Developed and Developing Countries, 1993

	Primary	*Secondary*	*Tertiary*
World Total	46	45	45
Developed Countries	49	50	52
Developing Countries	44	39	35

Source: UNESCO, 1995, 2–15, 2–16.

in primary education, 50 percent of the enrollment in secondary education, and 52 percent of the enrollment in tertiary education. In the developing countries, the situation shows marked disparities as women represent 44 percent of the enrollment in primary education but only 39 percent and 35 percent of the enrollment in secondary and tertiary education, respectively.[18] These statistics, based on gross enrollment rates, include repeaters and overage children; they also mask the large number of failures in terms of students who drop out of school and do not complete their respective educational cycle, many of whom are women. According to UNESCO data for 1993, there are 77 million girls of primary school age not in school compared with 52 million boys.[19] This is a statistic that powerfully predicts that the illiteracy rates of women will continue to exceed those of men.

Table 7.2 presents enrollment data by specific developing region. It also uses an equity index (E.I.) to show the enrollment of women compared to that of men; under ideal circumstances the index, representing the number of women for every hundred men, should be 1.0. Women are moving closer to parity in Latin America, but in the other developing regions there are substantial gender disparities; these disparities are considerable in secondary and tertiary levels, particularly in the case of sub-Saharan Africa, South Asia, and the Arab states (see relevant chapters in this volume).

Curiously, not everyone interprets the current statistics as indicating serious disadvantages for girls. In looking at regional averages, Knodel[20] contends that gender gaps have disappeared and remain substantial only in the Arab states and South Asia.[21] On the basis of this observation, Knodel goes on to assert that, first, "strong policy emphasis in closing the gap, as broadly advocated by the United Nations and other international development organizations, seems almost unnecessary" and, second, "it would be unfortunate to lose sight of the typically powerful effect of socioeconomic disadvantage on educational opportunities in the pursuit of promoting gender equality in schooling."[22] This argument assumes too readily that gross enrollment figures present a complete picture.

In several countries (e.g., Mauritius, Lesotho, Botswana, and Namibia in Africa; Mongolia and Korea in Asia; Jordan in the Middle East; and Honduras,

Nelly P. Stromquist

Table 7.2
Gross Enrollment by Region, Level, and Sex (in Thousands)

		Primary			Secondary			Tertiary		
		male	female	E.I.	male	female	E.I.	male	female	E.I.
Sub-Saharan Africa	1970	14,421	9,983	69	1,644	806	49	143	36	25
	1980	29,228	22,969	79	5,934	3,438	58	438	125	29
	1990	35,365	29,213	83	8,536	6,327	74	950	438	46
	1993	38,590	32,048	83	9,848	7,625	77	1,185	570	48
Latin America and Caribbean	1970	22,543	21,440	95	5,508	5,161	93	1,059	581	55
	1980	33,459	31,860	95	8,509	8,458	99	2,791	2,139	77
	1990	38,795	36,684	95	10,684	11,395	.07	3,966	3,450	87
	1993	41,265	38,743	94	11,660	12,527	.07	4,149	4,024	97
Eastern Asia and Oceania	1970*									
	1980	115,175	95,701	83	46,592	32,513	70	2,982	1,680	56
	1990	103,298	91,533	89	45,192	35,424	78	5,311	3,520	66
	1993	104,295	93,713	90	46,928	38,673	82	7,498	4,848	65
Southern Asia	1970*									
	1980	59,391	36,447	61	28,916	13,491	47	3,022	1,041	34
	1990	78,215	55,569	71	45,297	25,336	56	7,026	2,278	32
	1993	83,581	62,364	75	52,580	31,323	60	7,307	2,728	37
Arab States	1970	8,011	4,570	57	2,488	1,059	43	339	105	31
	1980	12,567	8,743	70	4,855	3,341	69	1,025	462	45
	1990	17,106	13,244	77	8,637	6,299	73	1,606	908	57
	1993	18,328	14,506	79	9,433	7,209	76	1,851	1,005	54

Source: UNESCO, 1982, 1995.
*Statistics for 1970 provide only a single "Asian" category and thus do not permit the distinction used in this table.
E.I. = Equity index, or the proportion of girls to boys, when boys are 100.

Jamaica, Colombia, and Argentina in Latin America) there are more girls than boys attending primary school. This greater participation does not reflect simply an absence of gender differences but rather the particular gender dynamics in those societies. For instance, in the case of Lesotho and Namibia, where men have more physical mobility than women, male labor is exported to South Africa, leaving more women behind for schooling. Some small islands such as Jamaica suffered the destruction of the family under slavery, with the consequence that women assumed more economic responsibilities and thus had a greater need for schooling. Mongolia is a cattle-herding country in which boys, because of the sexual division of labor and sexual norms, are considered more suitable for unsupervised work. Colombia and Argentina reflect a higher propensity for young men to be incorporated early in the urban labor force despite lower levels of education than women. These explanations are not based on detailed studies exploring such phenomena—those investigations have not been conducted. But it can be affirmed that women's greater access to the various levels of schooling does not automatically reflect the disappearance of gender as a discriminating marker in their respective society. If such were the case, there would be a much more even distribution in the salaries, professions, and political positions of men and women. One of the most accepted measures of equality between women and men in society, the Gender Empowerment Measure developed by the Human Development Report,[23] reveals that the country closest to such parity is Sweden, with an index of .76 (showing that Swedish women have two-thirds the access to economic and political power that men have). The highest GEM score among developing countries is .54, held by Barbados. Another important statistic concerns the number of children out of school. It is estimated that there are 110 million children not attending primary school, two-thirds of whom are women. And of the some 900 million illiterate youths and adults, also about two-thirds are women.[24] Table 7.3 represents a recent distribution of literacy rates by region. It shows a substantial gender gap in Asia and Africa.

Table 7.3
Estimated Proportion of Illiterate Population 15 Years and Over
in Developing Countries by Sex, 1995

	Percentage of Illiterates		
	Total	*Women*	*Men*
Africa	43.8	54.0	33.5
Asia	27.7	36.6	19.1
Latin America and the Caribbean	13.4	14.5	12.3

Source: UNESCO, 1995, 2–8.

Educational statistics combining gender with social class and ethnicity are lacking in many countries. Some notable exceptions are represented by studies in Brazil and India. The overall gross enrollment rate in the first five years of schooling in India is 115 for boys and 93 for girls, but in the case of its two main categories of minorities it is even lower. A study based on seven states in India found that enrollment among scheduled castes is 123 for boys and 91 for girls; among scheduled tribes it is 124 for boys and 89 for girls.[25] In general, 15 percent of the boys who enter first grade in India finish secondary school in India, but only 10 percent of the girls are similarly successful.[26] Brazil is a country in which some research on the intersection of race and gender has taken place. Rosemberg[27] found that the average years of schooling of a black woman from the northeast (the most rural area of Brazil, where African slave labor predominated until the late nineteenth century) is 2.1 years in contrast with 5.7 for a woman in the southeast (the most industrial and Europeanized area of the country) and 5.9 for a man of the same area. In a subsequent study focusing on preschool education in seven Brazilian states, Rosemberg detected that black children represented by far the largest group of preschool children over seven years of age. In her view, many black children are placed for several years in preschool with little possibility of access to primary school. Whereas all the preschool teachers were women, Rosemberg found that 85 percent of them had not received training as preschool teachers and that 79 percent had not finished primary school. In other words, black children in Brazil, the slight majority of whom are boys, seem to be trapped in dead-end schooling in Brazil being taught mostly by unprepared teachers. If one were to look merely at aggregate access indicators, without disaggregating by geographic region, age, and ethnicity, the complex manifestations of multiple forms of discrimination would not be visible.

Enrollment statistics may miss important additional aspects. Indian scholars report that a preappraisal mission by the World Bank (a prerequisite to granting loans) found that the state of Kerala was quite close to attaining universal primary enrollment. On the basis of this finding, the Bank declared that no gender interventions were required. Contrary to this declaration, fieldwork found a prevalence of dowry and women suffering the double burden of paid and unpaid work with no share in family or political decision making.[28]

Primary and Secondary Education

As the tables in this chapter indicate, access to schooling at primary education levels is moving toward gender parity, even though the pace is very slow and substantial differences between boys and girls exist in many developing regions. The ratio of girls to boys enrolled in primary school throughout the world (i.e., aggregating figures for developed and developing countries) has been increasing, from 65 girls per 100 boys in 1960 to 85 girls per 100 boys in 1990. In the developing countries, the average six-year-old girl in 1980 could expect to attend school for 7.3 years; by 1990 the figure had increased to 8.4 years.

Gender differentials had not disappeared, however. In 1990 the average six-year-old boy could be expected to attend school for 9.7 years.[29]

Equally important indicators of access to schooling are cycle completion, academic achievement, and transfer to a higher level of education (e.g., from primary to secondary school). These statistics are very scarce and, when available, seldom disaggregated by sex. Moreover, few countries have engaged in policies and activities specifically designed to enable girls and women to overcome social obstacles. A few exceptions do exist. In Guatemala scholarships for primary-school girls are being offered in the poorest regions of the country. In Bangladesh and Malawi stipends (to compensate in part for family forgone income) for secondary schoolgirls are being provided. Several of the development agencies funding the Bangladesh stipends affirm that a very large number of girls had enrolled. But the enrollment growth rate of girls has been uneven, increasing in some communities but not in others. These uneven results might be explained by the differences in implementation, which included varying amounts of stipends in the provinces in the study. An additional reason might be that this intervention was not accompanied by other supportive measures.

Another important policy focused on girls is being implemented in India, as the government has initiated the District Primary Education Program (DPEP), to pursue two objectives: access to quality education for all children and equality and empowerment for women. Gender studies in eight states to provide additional inputs for DPEP to address the issue of women's equality and empowerment more effectively found that in only two states (Maharashtra and Haryana) were the textbooks relatively free of gender bias.[30] Through structured interviews of a variety of school actors in more than 400 villages and urban slums, researchers found that girls' domestic work, sibling care, and helping parents in remunerative employment were the main reason for dropping out among girls. The same study found that the girls perceived their own illnesses as an important reason for dropping out in four of the eight surveyed states. Household poverty was strongly linked to girls' participation in schooling, but poverty in itself did not create cultural practices in favor of sons and boys. It simply made more acute the necessity of using girls and women in the biased division of labor. The study found that parents wanted girls to be educated, the most common reason given being that parents recognized that education prepares girls for economic contribution and that it develops a positive self-image and confidence among girls.[31] This finding corroborates another study in Balochistan, one of the least advanced provinces of Pakistan. Contrary to popular belief, including that of ministry of education officials, a large proportion of parents—especially mothers—recognized the importance of educating their daughters and were even willing to participate in the provision of school facilities.[32]

Another important insight regarding access to schooling comes from a study by Warwick and Jatoi,[33] based on a large survey of schools and teachers in Pakistan. The authors set out to trace the causes of low performance by girls in math.

Using hierarchical linear modeling, they were able to decompose effects and locate as the main cause the training of girls in multigrade schools in rural areas
staffed preponderantly by poorly trained women teachers. This finding verifies
the complex relations among gender, patriarchal ideologies, and educational
policies. Given patriarchal cultural norms, trained women teachers tend to avoid
the rural areas for reasons of distance from their families and safety. Although
more women are being trained as teachers, educational administrators' leniency
in assigning these women to urban areas reproduces a pattern of poorly trained
women teachers in rural areas, which make better trained women teachers avoid
the rural areas for reasons of safety and proximity to their families and lead educational administrators to allow this placement pattern.

The Content and Experience of Schooling

The discursive and material representation of women and men contributes to the
definition of self and others. The role of schooling in differential gender socialization can be captured through content analysis of textbooks and through observations and in-depth interviews with teachers, administrators, and students.
Studies of classroom dynamics and school climate, unfortunately, are very
scarce in developing countries, although steps have been taken to expand this
probe. Most of the educational investigations of this type have been conducted
through M.A. theses and Ph.D. dissertations. Since these products are not normally readily available in libraries, their contributions cannot be fully exploited.

   Studies conducted in the 1980s found that textbooks presented negative representations about women. As Smock observed then,[34] textbooks do not make
explicit statements on women's inferiority, but they present them in limited roles
and as reduced personalities. In a few countries receiving development assistance, efforts are under way to "eliminate sexual stereotypes" from the textbooks
and curricula (e.g., Pakistan, Malawi, Bangladesh, Mexico, and Sri Lanka). The
changes are operating at rudimentary levels of alteration. Three levels of textbook modification can be conceptualized. First, the gender-neutral approach, the
mildest effort, centers on the removal of biased language—excessive use of
masculine pronouns and examples depicting mostly men. Second, the nonsexist
approach eliminates stereotypical references to women and men in the work they
do, the roles they play in society, and the traits that supposedly characterize
them. Third, the antisexist approach presents alternative images of women and
men, and discusses ways to reach a different social organization.[35] As can be
surmised, the antisexist approach is the most transformative. Typically, the role
of governments in revising textbooks is limited to the first level of content
change, making the textbooks gender neutral. In a few cases, the efforts involve
the nonsexist mode. Introducing changes in language and in the representation
of women is not an easy matter, since it calls for modifying how we think and
requires a deep understanding of how language and images shape our thinking.

To assure the success of girls in schooling, careful monitoring of their every-day experience and their interactions with boy peers is needed. This type of research would not only produce rich insights into the creation of gender differences but would enable us to understand what is required to achieve transformative action. Some research along these lines is being funded, albeit in modest scale, by the Forum of African Women Educationalists (FAWE) in sub-Saharan Africa (see below).

In developed countries, research on girls' education has moved from documenting inequalities — which still exist — to (1) researching how these inequalities develop by looking at classroom situations, specifically the relations between students and teachers and among students, and (2) experimenting with how these inequitable situations can be transformed. In several school settings in the United States, new spaces are being created within schools so that lopsided patterns may be questioned and avoided and replaced with more equal relations. A number of feminist pedagogical efforts are seeking to incorporate the experiences and voices of students, promoting self and social empowerment, and making the classrooms less teacher centered. Recent efforts in U.S. schools have tried, for instance, to explore problems such as patriarchy, sexism, and racism in the context of the girls' contemporary lives. In contrast, in developing countries, engagement in this type of effort has been minuscule. There is increased understanding, however, that a curriculum content that acknowledges the body and sexuality and addresses citizenship in its widest meaning should receive early attention.

Some qualitative work is beginning to unveil gender practices in schools in developing countries. An ethnographic study of a Mexican high school focusing on how femininities and masculinities are created presents evidence that forceful groups of girls were called *marimachas* (tomboys) and that those who "excelled academically and aggressively pursued leadership roles took the risk of censure . . . from male and female classmates alike,"[36] even though these girls tended to defend their leadership on the ground of greater discipline and moral superiority. Levinson found a prevailing belief that girls were unfit to serve as student body president, to carry the flag during parades, or to fulfill leadership roles, areas for which masculine force was seen as essential. But he also found that the climate in the school was open to change. Levinson noted that the new high school leadership was causing transformations such as including girls in the flag escort and increasing participation of girls in classes and in activities traditionally associated with boys, which led him to become optimistic about the possibility of changing gender beliefs in schools.

In several countries, efforts to modify the existing curriculum to include sex education or a discussion of the social relations of gender have encountered significant opposition. Two pieces of evidence come from Latin America, a region relatively open to modernizing forces. In Argentina, the National Program for the Promotion of Women's Equal Opportunities in Education (PRIOM), operating within the Ministry of Education, was able to deliver a number of nonsexist and antisexist teacher training workshops on the question of gender and education for several years.[37] PRIOM also worked during an extended period on the production of a comprehensive women's studies curriculum that was to be incorporated into the overall curriculum at the primary-school level. PRIOM's curriculum also addressed linguistic sensibility and the unwarranted use of the masculine gender in words such as "citizen" (ciudadano), recommending instead collective nouns such as the "reading public" (el público lector) as opposed to "readers" (lectores) to make it easier to avoid the use of the masculine gender. Conservative parents and members of the Catholic Church accused PRIOM's staff of being antifamily and trying to introduce homosexuality in the schools, a complaint promptly heeded by the government. The document was reviewed to such an extent that PRIOM's technical team resigned. Persons closely involved in the development of the gender curriculum noted that the new document was not even concerned with nonsexist language.[38]

In Mexico, in a twist that divided parents and government officials, parents denounced and succeeded in removing a textbook coedited by a state branch of the Ministry of Education that would have addressed adolescent sexuality with a discussion of the positive and negative consequences of engaging in sexual behavior during adolescence. Conservative parents and high officials of the Catholic Church invoked instead the principle of abstinence and insisted that sexuality should be practiced "at the right time" and "within marriage," a discourse amply indifferent to the reality of the country.[39]

Interventions to increase girls' access to the secondary-school level are very infrequent. Those to modify content are even less frequent. In terms of access, a notable exception is a scholarship program for secondary-school girls in Bangladesh. When it was evaluated in its pilot version, it was able to double the participation of girls.[40]

Nonformal Education Programs for Primary School Children

A development of considerable importance in recent years is the use of nonformal education (NFE) settings to expand the education of girls. This approach is being tried primarily in populous Asian countries that have very low rates of school participation and sizable gender gaps in enrollment, notably Bangladesh, Pakistan, and India. The main NFE education program for girls in Bangladesh is being run by the Bangladesh Rural Advancement Committee (BRAC). This program covers about a million children (or about 8 percent of the total primary school enrollment in the country) through NFE "centers" in each of which a group of thirty to thirty-three students are served as a cohort that moves together from first to third grade. The BRAC program has been designed so that at least 70 percent of the students served in each center are girls. The curriculum is highly innovative and includes many activities aimed to promote the development of confidence and assertiveness in girls. The fact that, unlike the formal schools, most teachers are women provides the students with positive role models. The BRAC centers have been highly successful in cycle completion, but problems have emerged in transferring the students to regular schools to complete their primary education (grades four and five). According to a recent study, about 30 percent of BRAC girls do not advance to the next educational cycle, possibly due to early marriage or the distance of the regular public school.[41] In addition, BRAC girls drop out in the regular school at higher rates than BRAC boys (it is unclear whether this occurs because the students find the new environment hostile or because school distance or domestic work prevents them from further attendance).

The NFE programs in India—Shiksha Karmi and Lok Jumbish—present some of the features of the BRAC program, except that many of the rural teachers are men. On the other hand, the Indian programs cover the entire primary school cycle and the work is not done separately by NGOs but in conjunction with government officials. This joint participation assures a coordinated and mutually supportive plan of action. In Baluchistan the program is conducted by an NGO, also working in cooperation with the provincial government. By design, this program serves a large number of girls and uses locally hired women teachers. It offers a gender-sensitive curriculum and has succeeded in attracting the cooperation of parents in the running of the school. According to program statistics, girls have not only enrolled in large numbers but have shown good attendance rates. The participation of women as teachers and mothers in the running of Village Education Committees has provided new and alternative roles for women in their traditional communities.[42] Most of these projects operate with external support. Although governmental funds have been increasingly assigned to cover part of the costs, it remains to be seen whether the programs will continue without donor funds.

Higher Education

It might serve as a good point of contrast to remember that in May 1897, slightly over one hundred years ago, Cambridge University roundly defeated a resolution that would have given women the right to the bachelor of arts degree.[43] Such a position would seem bizarre in many countries today. Should people therefore conclude that the educational situation of women in higher education has dramatically improved?

In terms of numerical access to university, it is beyond doubt—as is the case for the other two levels—that tertiary enrollment of women has been expanding. What remains difficult to change is the concentration of women in typically feminine fields and, conversely, the overrepresentation of men in fields perceived as masculine, such as those dealing with science and technology. Despite the potential contribution of women's perspectives to such fields as agriculture and engineering, their representation in them remains insignificant. Women's choice of fields considered socially appropriate for their gender reflect the influence of multiple societal and cultural forces, but they also suggest that the academic experience of women reinforces this influence. There are very few instances of efforts to change the experience of women at the university level. One such exception comes from an incipient effort in Chile to begin exploration of gender bias and ways to make the curriculum more gender sensitive in the fields of education and journalism.

The most positive development in recent years within higher education in developing countries is the rapid expansion of women's studies programs and units. These can be quite extensive, as they are in India and Brazil, countries in which ties between feminist scholars and women in popular women's movements are strong. Women students in these universities are encouraged to produce master's and doctoral dissertations on gender issues, and they find intellectual spaces to discuss ways to analyze and combat gender discrimination.

Education for Adult Women

Since most formal education settings present endemic institutional barriers to gender-sensitive changes, it is essential to consider the transformative role of adult education, which lies outside the formal system. The increased gender awareness of such education not only affects the students but is transmitted to their children as well. Women, as key organizers of the household environment, can affect what their children do and learn at home.

Transformative work in women's education—in the form of both oppositional discourse and practical actions against inequities—has been undertaken mostly by women-based or feminist nongovernmental organizations.[44] The areas they have addressed have included such issues as empowerment, legal literacy, domestic violence, and income generation. A current theme within women-based NGOs in Latin America concerns citizenship training, lobbying and advocacy skills, health education practice, and the training of trainers. NGOs in Latin America are also moving from denunciation of women's unequal and exploitative situations to making proposals based on statistics and information, creating spaces for training, and making concrete demands on government.[45]

It is not easy to provide adult women with educational opportunities. Various studies focusing on the participation of low-income women in adult education programs have determined that women's domestic work, frequency of domestic violence, and the need for serving children and families leaves them with very little time and inclination for education, even though NFE programs often offer schedules and locations that make them accessible to the women.[46]

Important lessons have derived from these experiences. After many years of effort with literacy classes and condensed programs for which there were "no takers," Indian scholars and practitioners have learned that skills and education cannot be forced on women.[47] With the involvement of the Indian government and substantial funds coming from external sources, the Mahila Samakhya program has been implemented in India for several years. Women in this program were not offered literacy training but were given the opportunity to discuss in a social space their experiences and desires. Village-level forums were created exclusively for women, the assumption being that these women "in due time could emerge as strong pressure groups for raising genuine demands, fighting injustice and creating an environment for 'equal' treatment of women," and that these forums would enable them to "discover and re-discover their identities and problems as women, and mobilize around issues that were of priority to them."[48] By most accounts, the women in the Mahila Samakhya have succeeded in changing their self-concept and have made successful demands on their local government. These women have acquired the skills and insights to analyze their situation of subordination and, as one observer summarized it, they have been able to turn "fear" into "understanding."[49]

Adult education offers much potential for gender transformation. It tends to unite women from different social classes, with low-income women as beneficiaries and middle-income (but increasingly low-income) women as leaders and staff members of the NGOs. These groups are usually confronted with two demands: to address immediate problems, mostly linked with basic needs (what has been called women's practical needs) and to address macrolevel issues such as gender-fair legislation affecting the family, wages, access to credit, and so on (what is usually termed women's strategic needs).[50] The resolution of these tensions is not easy, yet there are encouraging examples of women being able to shift toward more encompassing and long-term objectives that will call for transforming institutions and enacting new policies. It is becoming increasingly clear to these women-based NGOs that formulating large-scale change within society will require influencing the state, which will require these NGOs to acquire mobilization and organization skills and engage in social action.[51]

In Latin America the unprecedented mobilization of women in the 1980s due to the economic crisis and the existence of dictatorial regimes provided unexpected skills for many of the low-income women, skills and practices they have retained—speaking in order to express an opinion, making demands, representing. They have also been able to produce more accurate evaluations of the social functions of interpersonal relations and of their own personal development.[52]

At present, NGOs in general and women-based NGOs in particular are making efforts to redefine such taken-for-granted concepts as "citizenship" and "social life," and introducing new ones such as "empowerment." The mutual recognition of women's great burdens and logistical problems in becoming NFE students and simultaneously their preference to learn through imitation and informal apprenticeships has prompted feminist adult educators to recognize the importance of "mediators" in the process of social learning. These mediators can play an effective role in the provision of training. Walters explains:

This approach refocuses the problem away from the masses of poorly schooled people to the mediators. It is up to the mediators to learn to serve people across class, language, culture, etc., so that learning can occur more effectively through everyday experiences.[53]

There are two instances in which NGOs are engaged in major efforts to improve schooling. FAWE (Forum of African Women Educationalists) is a group consisting of some forty-four women who hold key official educational roles in their country, such as ministers of education, vice-chancellors, and other senior policy makers. This group is engaged in projects that include, among others, examining girls' and boys' performance in math and science, providing gender sensitization to educational personnel, exploring the extent of sexual harassment in secondary schools, and addressing women's issues in teaching and education management. Because of its prominent membership, FAWE's work is expected to find a direct and relatively unblocked application in the school system. In Latin America, the Popular Education Network of Women (REPEM) is affiliated with the Adult Education Council of Latin America and the Caribbean (CEAAL). Comprising 150 women-based NGOS and committed to strengthening popular education with a gender perspective, REPEM is working very intensively on the development of nonsexist and antisexist educational materials.

The State and Women's Education

The state shapes education through policies governing tuition fees, books, uniforms, and other expenses that families must fulfill. State policy can also influence schooling by providing incentives such as scholarships or stipends for girls to counterbalance the opportunity cost to parents.

It has been noted earlier that despite the disadvantaged situation of girls in most educational systems, there are few official policies addressing this situation. Most projects focusing on girls begin and end as pilot projects supported by donor agencies and are rarely incorporated into national policies.[54] On the other hand, since 1985 states have committed themselves in a series of public and official meetings to work for the advancement of girls' education. This was explicitly acknowledged in the Forward-Looking Strategies signed in Nairobi at the end of the Third World Conference on Women (1985). The commitment was reiterated and expanded in the Platform for Action signed at the Fourth World Conference on Women in Beijing (1995). The proliferation of related documents is perhaps nowhere more visible than in sub-Saharan Africa. Since the "Education for All" Declaration in Jomtien (1990)—a document that is widely agreed to represent a breakthrough in terms of national and international support for basic education and girls—African governments have signed documents drafted at the International Conference on Assistance to the African Child (1992), the Pan-African Conference on the Education of Girls (also known as the Ouagadougou Declaration, 1993), the International Conference on Population and Development (1994), the African Common Position on Human and Social Development (1994), and the Fifth African Regional Conference on Women (Dakar, 1994). All of the documents approved at these conferences identify the education of girls as a top national priority. Some even call for affirmative action as a method of reducing the educational disparity that exists between boys and girls. There is a wide disjunction between rhetoric and actual action; it is to be hoped that as many of these documents are known and circulated, women and men who seek equality and equity in education will use these promises to force governments into compliance.

Donor Agencies and Their Support for Education

Following such major women's conferences as those in Nairobi and more recently Beijing, gender has become a more explicit policy objective of both bilateral and multilateral development agencies. In 1996, for instance, SIDA (Swedish International Development Agency) adopted gender as one of its six development objectives. The advocacy in favor of girls' education and the financial support of donor agencies have been instrumental in fostering attention to this issue, since, as noted earlier, governments are reluctant to invest their own funds on issues concerning gender, especially when such issues may incur strong opposition from certain segments of their constituencies. There is increasing support for girls' education among development agencies, although this support tends to be limited to basic education. Nonetheless, the strong leadership of agencies such as UNICEF and UNDP in favor of girls' schooling and the Dutch and Scandinavian agencies in support of women's education has made gender an unavoidable issue in national development politics. The influential *Human Development Report* for 1995[55] coined the slogan "if human development is not engendered, it is endangered," a phrase that seems to have lodged itself in the subconscious of many governments.

The actual performance of development agencies is contradictory. A substantial number of staff members within these agencies believe (erroneously, given the high number of national and international declarations of commitment to the education of girls and women) that to press for attention to gender issues constitutes a form of cultural imperialism. Several agencies are now working with new principles of international assistance, such as "recipient responsibility" and "program support," which might end up discriminating against women. These two principles call for much greater dialogue with governments and for greater discretionary powers by the recipient state. For many issues regarding national development, government autonomy is a desirable situation. But in the case of gender, this autonomy could easily result in the avoidance of gender issues. A very strong indicator that governments are not interested in the pursuit of gender issues is that almost all projects focusing on women's (or girls') education are funded through grants from international agencies, not loans. A further weakness in dealing exclusively with governments in the area of gender and education is that they tend to operate mostly on questions of access and, if curriculum and textbooks revisions are involved, changes operate at the gender-neutral (first) level.

Often development agencies present limited definitions of a situation even though their new principle appears on target. For instance, in recent years the World Bank has become very interested in the question of "good governance," a code phrase for countries eager to compete in the global economy. A 1995 World Bank publication on policies for gender equality identifies four areas affecting the welfare of women to be addressed through legal action: land and property rights, labor market policies and employment law, family law, and financial laws and regulations. But since the prescriptions to make reforms in these areas are not based on a profound and complete understanding of the causes of women's inequality, the recipient state is assigned—quite unproblematically—the implementation of these reforms. Even though NGOs are identified as important "players from civil society," there is no specific recognition of the role that women-based NGOs, and other elements in civil society clearly identified with the women's movement, can play in these socioeconomic transformations.

Today, however, women are much more aware of the institutions that conduct key work in social and economic policies. The World Bank is currently the object of strong feminist pressure. This emphasis started in 1995 at the Fourth World Women's Conference in Beijing when a letter signed by nine hundred women's organizations from around the globe was given to James Wolfensohn, the first president of the World Bank to attend a world women's conference. The letter requested that the Bank act toward increasing participation of grassroots women in the design of macroeconomic policies, institutionalizing the perspective of gender as a standard practice in its policies and programs, increasing the Bank's investments in the sectors of education, health, agriculture, land ownership, employment and financial services for women.[56] Since Beijing, the women have organized an umbrella group called Women's Eyes on the World Bank, with chapters in different parts of the world. In early 1997, this group wrote a second letter—widely circulated on the Internet—to President Wolfensohn stating that it had reviewed the Bank's initiatives during 1996 and found that "the admirable commitment from the top has yet to be translated into concrete action in the majority of Bank programs and operations, where there remains a lack of understanding among many Bank staff of gender inequities and their implications for development." A review of a specific project designed to improve the quality and efficiency of primary education, to address gender in training teachers and principals, and to provide education for girls, especially indigenous girls, found that the indicators on which performance would be based were not even disaggregated by sex.[57] Several observers of the World Bank's position in education criticize its "mercantilist conception of gender." Women are useful because the more educated the women, the fewer children they will have and the more they will participate in the labor force; infant mortality will be lower, and possibilities for work will increase, as will income. Instead, these observers call for more human and anthropological conceptualizing in which women are seen not as mere economic agents but as citizens.[58]

Commitments made at the Education for All Declaration signed in Jomtien in 1990 gave priority to girls' education. A recent review of actual resources indicated that the assistance to basic education from bilateral donors in the mid-1990s in real terms was lower than it had been before the conference. This study, based on a survey of twenty bilateral aid agencies, found that such assistance had increased in six of these agencies but remained static or fell in the other fourteen. The World Bank, which had been a major contributor in 1994 (US$2.16 billion), decreased considerably by 1996 (US$1.7 billion), according to Bennell.[59] Both governments and donor agencies have endorsed helping women, but primarily through skills training for the purpose of increased productivity. The overwhelming emphasis on productivity is rejected by feminist scholars. As Longwe states,

> On the contrary, gender training must be largely concerned with providing the analytical tools for participants to become dissatisfied with the current unequal gender division of society, which they (may have) previously accepted and taken for granted.[60]

Training should also enable women to generate mobilization around the analysis of gender issues and public action to address these issues.

Challenges in Developing Countries

In the past twenty years, women have been gaining increased access to education. In several parts of the world there is a clear tendency toward gender parity, at least at the elementary level. The positive content, experience, and outcomes of schooling are not so much taken for granted now, and efforts are taking place, albeit very modest vis-à-vis the nature of the problem, to advance the condition of women's education. Against this background, four major challenges remain.

The first is globalization, a process that is gearing all countries, and their school systems in particular, for economic competition and not for critical understanding. Globalization forces are promoting an increase in scientific and technological courses, yet it is not certain what efforts will be made to include women in this expansion. Competitiveness has created a demand for "quality" of education, an issue several observers see as comprising three dimensions: efficacy, process, and relevance. The positive side of efficacy resides in its focus on learning as opposed to merely attending school. The process dimension highlights the quality of inputs, such as good physical facilities, trained teachers, good textbooks, and adequate instructional methodologies, necessary for a successful learning process. "Relevance," however, introduces some conservative thinking in that it tends to emphasize the economic usefulness of education rather than the social and affective development of individuals. For instance, efforts to renovate the educational system in Latin America recognize the poor quality of the educational system in such areas as reading, math, and science; the neglect of the teaching profession; and the existence of inequities. Yet this last recognition tends to focus almost exclusively on social class, downplaying both gender and ethnic differences.[61]

Ironically, globalization, as it relates to women, seems to be based on an assumption similar to that first introduced by Marxist thought. The "woman question" in Marxism argued that women's oppression was rooted in their exclusion from productive participation in economic activity so that their incorporation in the labor force would make their subordination disappear. Globalization implies that if women were to join the labor market, multiple benefits would accrue to them and to society. In both cases, it is the labor market that creates transformation for women. Yet the unpaid work of women in reproduction, the gender division of labor and resources within the household and in society, and the role of patriarchal ideology are ignored in both perspectives.

The second challenge derives from the serious economic crisis that many developing countries still face and the simultaneous retrenchment of the state through the imposition by the World Bank and the International Monetary Fund of structural adjustment programs (SAPs). There is wide consensus that these programs have generated more poverty than in the past as increases in the price of basic goods and cuts in social services such as healthcare, family planning, child care, and education have affected poor and middle-class households. Women and girls have absorbed the heaviest burden of SAPs through their increased household work and participation in formal and informal labor markets.[62] Sub-Saharan African countries are particularly affected as they have entered a cycle of unpayable external debt characterized by more funds going abroad to pay the debt than financial resources moving into the region. Since 1987 the International Monetary Fund has received US$4 billion more from sub-Saharan Africa than it has provided in new finance.[63] The retrenchment of the state, which characterizes countries undergoing SAP policies, has negative consequences for women because the state is clearly a major institution capable of both applying pressure and creating large-scale change.

Comparisons between developing countries undergoing SAPs and those that are not have clearly shown that education budgets have suffered with SAP programs and that primary education levels (including teacher salaries) have suffered considerably.[64] Obviously, less public money for education investments also means a reduced ability and willingness to consider specific populations. Since the countries with the heaviest per capita burden linked to economic indebtedness are also those with the largest disparities between men and women, this forecasts a period of disregard for girls' and women's education.

The third challenge emerges from the paucity of educational research in developing countries. There are very limited national funds for research and development; most of the existing gender research has been conducted under the auspices of international assistance. Frequent calls by the World Bank and other institutions for developing nations to remove subsidies at the tertiary level of education and offer student loans instead suggests that funds thereby released may be used by educational systems to invest in other areas, research presumably being one of them. But several scholars doubt this. Colclough[65] contends that loans and scholarships involve higher administrative costs and are more expensive than the typical structure of subsidies. In his view alternative measures would be to create better and more progressive tax structures and to use private firms for the provision of education. In the case of women, a progressive tax structure would reduce the burden of social class, but the dynamics of privatization may be much less supportive. Since the education of girls and women tends to be seen as a consumption (not an investment) by many families, particularly low-income families, privatization might end up having harmful effects on their participation, particularly their participation in higher education. Research, especially of a qualitative kind, is needed to identify spaces of rupture of dominant gender norms and representations, and to document the instances in which agency is beginning to take place. The fourth challenge is perhaps the most significantly promising of the set. It concerns teachers. In critical theory literature, teachers are perceived as major change agents, with a tremendous potential for "border crossing"—their ability to bring themselves and their students to appreciate the position of other social and ethnic groups.[66] At the same time, since teachers, like everyone else, are products of their time and environment, many of them subscribe to traditional gender views. In several developing regions, Latin America in particular, women constitute the larger proportion of primary teachers. Teachers could be made to play a role in promoting reflection on society and gender roles; they could also be made to work on the transformation of gender representations and norms. To be successful, the teachers themselves would need to undergo a transformation; this would entail providing them with appropriate in-service and preservice teacher training and gender-sensitive curricula. Work on teachers is occurring in industrialized countries, but in developing countries this area has been considered only in exceptional circumstances (the Argentine case discussed above being one of them).

It might be suitable to complete this review of gender and education with a quote from the late Bella Abzug, a former member of the U.S. Congress and an extremely active feminist:

> In answer to those who think that women just want power for power's sake, it's not about that at all. It's not about simply main-streaming women. It's not about

women joining the polluted stream. It's about cleaning the stream, changing stagnant pools into fresh, flowing waters. Our struggle is about resisting the slide into a morass of anarchy, violence, intolerance, inequality, and injustice. Our struggle is about reversing the trends of social, economic, and ecological crisis.[67]

Notes

1. Gail Kelly, "Research on the Education of Women in the Third World: Problems and Perspectives," *Women's Studies International Quarterly* 1, no. 4 (1978): 365–373.

2. See, for instance, Audrey Smock, *Women's Education in Developing Countries: Opportunities and Outcomes* (New York: Praeger, 1981).

3. One of the best examples is Elizabeth King and Anne Hill, eds., *Women's Education in Developing Countries: Barriers, Benefits, and Policies* (Baltimore: Johns Hopkins University Press, 1993).

4. Nelly Stromquist, ed., *Women and Education in Latin America: Knowledge, Power, and Change* (Boulder: Lynne Rienner, 1992).

5. Nelly Stromquist, ed., *Gender Dimensions in Education in Latin America* (Washington, D.C.: Organization of American States), 1996.

6. John Wilson, "The Subject Women," in *Theory on Gender/Feminism on Theory,* ed. Paula England (New York: Aldine de Gruyter, 1993).

7. Gail Kelly and Ann Nihlen, "Schooling and the Reproduction of Patriarchy: Unequal Workloads, Unequal Rewards," in *Cultural and Economic Reproduction in Education,* ed. Michael Apple (London: Routledge, 1982), 162–180; Sara Longwe, "Education for Women's Empowerment—or Schooling for Women's Subordination?" (paper presented at the international seminar-workshop Promoting the Empowerment of Women through Adult Learning, Chiang Mai, Thailand, 24–28 February 1997).

8. See the series of studies on the United States sponsored by the American Association of University Women: American Association of University Women, *How Schools Shortchange Girls* (Washington, D.C.: American Association of University Women, 1992); American Association of University Women, *Hostile Hallways: The AAUW Survey on Sexual Harassment in America's Schools* (Washington, D.C.: American Association of University Women, 1993); Judy Cohen, *Girls in the Middle: Working to Succeed in School* (Washington, D.C.: American Association of University Women, 1996); Peggy Orenstein, *School Girls: Young Women, Self-Esteem, and the Confidence Gap* (New York: Doubleday, 1994); Valerie Lee et al., *Growing Smart: What's Working for Girls in Schools* (Washington, D.C.: AAUW, 1996).

9. For an ethnographic account of socialization at the college level, see Margaret Eisenhart and Dorothy Holland, *Educated in Romance* (Chicago: University of Chicago Press, 1990).

10. Kate Soper, "Postmodernism and Its Discontents," *Feminist Review* 39 (1991): 97–108.

11. Robert Connell, *Gender and Power: Society, the Person, and Sexual Politics* (Stanford: Stanford University Press, 1987); Robert Connell, "Poverty and Education," *Harvard Educational Review* 64, no. 2 (1994): 125–149.

12. See, for instance, J. Aaron and Sidney Walby, eds., *Out of the Margins: Women's Studies in the Nineties* (London: Falmer, 1991.

13. Mary Jean Bowman, "An Integrated Framework for Analysis of the Spread of Schooling in Less Developed Countries," in *New Approaches to Comparative Education,* ed. Philip Altbach and Gail Kelly (Chicago: University of Chicago Press, 1986), 131–151.

14. Christopher Colclough, "Education and the Market: Which Parts of the Neoliberal Solution are Correct?" *World Development* 24, no. 4 (1996): 589–610.

15. Lynn Ilon, "The Effects of International Economic Dynamics on Gender Equity of Schooling," *International Review of Education* 44, no. 4 (1998): 335–356.

16. Francisco Ramirez and John Boli-Bennett, "Global Patterns of Educational Institutionalization, in *Comparative Educa*tion, ed. Philip Altbach, Robert Arnove, and Gail Kelly (New York: Macmillan, 1982), 15–36.

17. UNESCO, *1995 Statistical Yearbook* (Paris: UNESCO, 1995).

18. UNESCO, *1995 Statistical Yearbook,* 2–15 and 2–16.

19. World Bank, *Toward Gender Equality: The Role of Public Policy* (Washington, D.C.: World Bank, 1995).

20. John Knodel, "The Closing of the Gender Gap in Schooling: The Case of Thailand," *Comparative Education* 33, no. 1 (1997): 61–86.

21. Knodel refers to figure 2.1 in the *1995 Human Development Report* (New York: UNDP, 1995). This table combines primary and secondary enrollment, a practice that tends to produce more positive accounts of girls' participation in schooling because primary rates, being higher than secondary, elevate the aggregate rate.

22. Knodel, "Closing of the Gender Gap," 83.

23. UNDP, *1995 Human Development Report* (New York: UNDP, 1995).

24. UNDP, UNESCO, UNICEF, and World Bank, *Education for All: Achieving the Goal: Final Report of the Mid-decade Meeting of the International Consultative Forum on Education for All* (New York: UNDP, 1996).

25. Scheduled tribes and scheduled castes represent ethnic minorities traditionally disadvantaged in Indian society and therefore constitutionally recognized to receive special compensatory measures in employment, education, and other areas.

26. National Council of Educational Research and Training, *Education of the Girl Child in India: A Fact Sheet* (Delhi: National Council of Educational Research and Training, 1995).

27. Fulvia Rosemberg, "Education, Democratization, and Inequality in Brazil," in *Women and Education in Latin America: Knowledge, Power, and Change,* ed. Nelly Stromquist (Boulder: Lynne Rienner, 1992), 33–46; Fulvia Rosemberg, "Educacion, Genero y Raza" (paper presented at the twentieth congress of the Latin American Studies Association, Guadalajara, 17–19 April 1997).

28. Usha Nayar, "Planning for UPE of Girls' and Women's Empowerment: Gender Studies in DPEP," in *School Effectiveness and Learning Achievement at Primary Stage,* ed. National Council of Educational Research and Training (New Delhi: National Council of Education Research and Training, July 1995).

29. World Bank, *Toward Gender Equality.*

30. Nayar, "Planning for UPE."

31. Nayar, "Planning for UPE."

32. Nelly Stromquist and Paud Murphy, *Leveling the Playing Field: Giving Girls an Equal Chance for Basic Education—Three Countries' Efforts* (Washington, D.C.: World Bank, 1995).

33. Donald Warwick and Haroona Jatoi, "Teacher Gender and Student Achievement in Pakistan," *Comparative Education Review* 38, no. 3 (1994): 377–399.

34. Smock, *Women's Education.*

35. Janice Streitmatter, *Toward Gender Equity in the Classroom* (Albany: State University of New York Press, 1995).

36. Bradly Levinson, "Masculinities and Feminities in the Mexican Secundaria: Notes Toward an Institutional Practice of Gender Equity" (paper presented at the twentieth congress of the Latin American Studies Association, Guadalajara, 17–19 April 1997).

37. Gloria Bonder, "From Theory to Action: Reflections on a Women's Equal Opportunities Educational Policy" (paper prepared for the expert group meeting on gender, education, and training, Division for the Advancement of Women, United Nations, New York, 10–14 October 1994).

38. Lea Fletcher, "No hemos hecho demasiado bien nuestra tarea," *Perspectivas* 5 (1997): 7–10.

39. Barbara Bayardo, "Sex and the Curriculum in Mexico and the United States," in *Gender Dimensions in Education in Latin America,* ed. Nelly Stromquist (Washington, D.C.: Organization of American States, 1996), 157–186.

40. Anne Hill and Elizabeth King, "Women's Education and Economic Well-Being," *Feminist Economics* 1, no. 2 (1995): 21–46.

41. Gajendra Verma and Tom Christie, "The Main-streaming of BRAC/NFPE Students" (paper prepared for the Manchester faculty of education, University of Manchester, December 1996).

42. Stromquist and Murphy, *Leveling the Playing Field.*

43. "1897: Degrees Denied," *International Herald Tribune,* 22 May 1997.

44. Many NGOs also provide maternal health and childhood clinics that serve as informal vehicles for the education of women. This type of education, though useful, is not gender-relations transformative. Women receive little education from agricultural extension workers. This type of education would enable women to increase their productivity, but, again, it usually is not transformative.

45. Celita Eccher, "The Women's Movement in Latin America and the Caribbean: Exercising Global Citizenship" (paper presented at the International Seminar-Workshop Promoting the Empowerment of Women through Adult Learning, Chiang Mai, Thailand, 24–28 February 1997).

46. Nelly Stromquist, *Literacy for Citizenship: Gender and Grassroots Dynamics in Brazil* (Albany: State University of New York Press, 1997); Shirley Walters, "Democracy, Development and Adult Education in South Africa" (paper presented at the international seminar-workshop Promoting the Empowerment of Women through Adult Learning, Chiang Mai, Thailand, 24–28 February 1997).

47. Sharda Jain and Lakshmi Krishnamurty, *Empowerment through Mahila Sanghas: The Mahila Samakhya Experience* (Tilak Nagar, India: Sandhan Shodh Kendra, 1996).

48. Jain and Krishnamurty, *Empowerment through Mahila Sanghas,* 13, 16.

49. Jain and Krishnamurty, *Empowerment through Mahila Sanghas,* 63.

50. Maxine Molyneux, "Mobilization without Emancipation? Women's Interests, State, and Revolution in Nicaragua," *Feminist Studies* 11, no. 2 (1985): 227–254; Marcy Fink and Robert Arnove, "Issues and Tensions in Nonformal and Popular Education," *International Journal of Educational Development* 11, no. 3 (1991): 221–230.

51. Renuka Mishra, "Promoting the Empowerment of Women through Adult Learning" (paper presented at the international seminar-workshop Promoting the Empowerment of Women through Adult Learning, Chiang Mai, Thailand, 24–28 February 1997).

52. Virginia Guzman, *Las organizaciones de mujeres populares: Tres perspectivas de análisis* (Lima: Centro de la Mujer Peruana Flora Tristan, 1990); see also Fink and Arnove, "Issues and Tensions."

53. Walters, "Democracy."

54. Hill and King, "Women's Education."

55. UNDP, *1995 Human Development Report.*

56. Laura Frade, "Women's Eyes on the World Bank," *Social Watch,* vol. 1 (Montevideo: Instituto del Tercer Mundo, 1997): 67–70.

57. Frade, "Women's Eyes."

58. Frade, "Women's Eyes."

59. Paul Bennell with Dominic Furlong, "Has Jomtien Made Any Difference? Trends in Donor Funding for Education and Basic Education since the Late 1980s," IDS Working Paper no. 51 (Sussex, U.K.: Institute of Development Studies, 1997).

60. Longwe, "Education for Women's Empowerment," 1997.

61. Jeffrey Puryear and Jose Joaquin Brunner, "An Agenda for Educational Reform in Latin America and the Caribbean," in *Partners for Progress: Education and the Private Sector in Latin America and the Caribbean,* ed. Jeffrey Puryear (Washington, D.C.: Inter-American Dialogue, 1997), 9–13.

62. Lourdes Beneria and Savitri Bisnath, *Poverty and Gender: An Analysis for Action* (New York: UNDP, 1996).

63. "Borrowed Burden," *Development and Cooperation* 2 (1997): 33.

64. Fernando Reimers and Luis Tiburcio, *Education, Ajustement, et Reconstruction: Options pour un Changement* (Paris: UNESCO, 1993).

65. Colclough, "Education and the Market."

66. See, for example, Michael Apple, "Work, Gender, and Teaching," *Teachers College Record* 84, no. 3 (1983): 611–628; and Henry Giroux, *Border Crossings: Cultural Workers and the Politics of Education* (New York: Routledge, 1992).

67. Bella Abzug, "Women Will Change the Nature of Power," in *Women's Leadership and the Ethics of Development,* by Bella Abzug and Devaki Jain, Gender in Development Monograph Series, no. 4 (New York: UNDP, 1996).

Chapter 8

Control of Education

Issues and Tensions in Centralization and Decentralization

Mark Bray

Debates about the appropriate locus of control in education systems are often heated and are usually difficult to resolve. The reasons for this are political as well as technical, for the nature and degree of centralization or decentralization influence not only the scale and shape of education systems but also the access to education by different groups.

Much can be learned from comparative study concerning the advantages and disadvantages of different arrangements. Comparative analysis can also enhance understanding of the reasons why some societies and systems have particular shapes and are moving in certain directions; and for politicians or administrators embarking on reforms, comparative study can demonstrate the need for certain preconditions and support systems.

This chapter commences by presenting some definitions, noting some of the motives for centralization and decentralization, identifying some models of governance, and outlining discussion on ways to measure centralization and decentralization. The chapter then turns to some specific domains to show variations in administrative systems in different places. The three domains chosen as examples are school-leaving qualifications, textbooks, and universities. The next two sections comment on the implications of different types of arrangements for efficiency and for social inequalities. The penultimate section notes some specific factors that must be taken into account during the design of administrative reforms, and the last section concludes the discussion.

Meanings, Motives, Models, and Measurements

Meanings

The words "centralization" and "decentralization" can mean different things to different people. This chapter must therefore begin by noting some possible meanings of the terms.

A starting point is to note that centralization and decentralization are processes—they are "-izations"—rather than static situations. This chapter is therefore concerned with a variety of starting points. It discusses centralization in systems that were previously decentralized; but it also discusses further centralization in systems that were already centralized. Similar points apply to systems in which control was centralized but is then made less centralized, and to systems which were already decentralized but become even more decentralized.

A second observation is that the terms "centralization" and "decentralization" usually refer to deliberate processes initiated at the apex of hierarchies. However, sometimes patterns change by default rather than by deliberate action. Also, power may be removed from the center either with the acquiescence of or in the face of resistance by the center.

Next it is necessary to distinguish between various types of centralization and decentralization. The literature on this topic is not entirely consistent, but there is general agreement on some major points.[1] Among them is the distinction between functional and territorial dimensions. *Functional* centralization/decentralization refers to a shift in the distribution of powers between various authorities that operate in parallel. For example:

• In some countries, a single ministry of education is responsible for all aspects of the public system of education. A move to split such a body into a ministry of basic education and a separate ministry of higher education could be called functional decentralization.

• In some systems all public examinations are operated by the ministry of education. Creation of a separate examinations authority to take over this role could be called functional decentralization, even if that examinations authority remained directly controlled by the government.

• In many countries, schools are operated by voluntary agencies as well as by governments. A loosening of government control on voluntary-agency schools could be called functional decentralization. Conversely, a tightening of control could be a form of functional centralization. Nationalization of voluntary agency schools, to place them under direct government control, would be an even more obvious form of functional centralization.

Territorial centralization/decentralization, by contrast, refers to a redistribution of control among the different geographic tiers of government, such as nation, states/provinces, districts, and schools. A transfer of power from higher to lower levels would be called territorial decentralization. This is a spatial conception of the term.

The category of territorial decentralization includes three major subcategories.

- *Deconcentration* is the process through which a central authority establishes field units or branch offices, staffing them with its own officers. Thus, personnel of the ministry of education may all work in the same central building, or some of them may be posted out to provinces and districts.
- *Delegation* implies a stronger degree of decision making power at the local level. Nevertheless, powers in a delegated system still basically rest with the central authority, which has chosen to "lend" them to the local one. The powers can be withdrawn without resort to legislation.
- *Devolution* is the most extreme of these three forms of territorial decentralization. Powers are formally held at sub-national levels, the officers of which do not need to seek higher-level approval for their actions. The subnational officers may choose to inform the center of their decisions, but the role of the center is chiefly confined to collection and exchange of information.

Some writers describe *privatization* as another form of decentralization.[2] Certainly privatization may be a form of decentralization in which state authority over schools is reduced. However, it is not necessarily decentralizing. Some forms of privatization concentrate power in the hands of churches or large private corporations. In these cases, privatization may centralize control, albeit in nongovernmental bodies.

Motives

The motives for centralization/decentralization of the control of education are commonly political but may also be administrative, or a combination of both. Politically motivated reforms aim to strengthen the power of the dominant group (in the case of centralization) or to spread power to other groups (in the case of decentralization). Administratively motivated reforms aim to facilitate the operation of bureaucracies. Often the origin of education reforms lies in wider political or administrative changes rather than in the specifics of the education sector.

Among the most dramatic examples of politically motivated reforms have been territorial decentralization schemes in the Philippines, Solomon Islands, Spain, and Sudan. Regionally based separatist movements in these countries were sufficiently powerful to threaten secession if not granted stronger autonomy. The central authorities conceded power in order to persuade the secessionist groups to remain within the national framework.

However, secessionist threats can lead to different reactions. For example, in

1961 the Ghanaian government reacted to separatist stirrings in the Ashanti confederacy by creating a strongly centralized unitary state. The Indonesian government reacted similarly during the 1960s to secessionist tendencies in the province of Irian Jaya. Alternatively, central governments may respond to secessionist threats with a strategy of "divide and rule." For example, when Nigeria's federal government was threatened by Biafran secession in 1967, it decided to split the country's four regions into twelve states. To respond to further political demands, the number of states in Nigeria was increased to nineteen in 1976, twenty-one in 1988, thirty in 1992, and thirty-six in 1996.

Other examples of political motivations include the desire through reforms to include or exclude certain groups from decision making. A 1972 decentralization reform in Peru attempted to strengthen the social participation of indigenous Indians and other disadvantaged groups,[3] and a 1989 Colombian initiative sought to promote unity by involving dissident groups and by incorporating all major segments of the population.[4] In contrast, decentralization in Mexico reduced the power of the teachers' union by transferring salary negotiations from the central to the state government level.[5]

On a more bureaucratic plane, both centralization and decentralization may be advocated in order to improve efficiency. The main centralizing argument is that operations can be directed more efficiently by a small group of central planners without cumbersome duplication of functions in parallel or subnational bodies. This has been a major factor underlying reduction in the number of municipalities in Denmark, Netherlands, and Sweden, for example.[6] The main decentralizing argument is that specialist parallel bodies are better able to focus on the needs of clients[7] and that territorially decentralized subnational units are closer to the clients and are better able to cater for local diversity.[8] The latter point has been elaborated upon by Winkler, who pointed out that efficiency arguments for territorial decentralization typically focus on the high unit costs of primary and secondary education provided by the central government. One explanation for such costs, he continued,

> is inadequate national government capacity to administer a centralized educational system. Another explanation is the costs of decision making in a system where even the most minor local education matters must be decided by a geographically and culturally distant bureaucracy in the capital city. Yet another explanation is the frequent application by education ministries of national standards for curriculum, construction, teacher quality, etc., thereby preventing cost savings through adjustments of educational inputs to local or regional price differences.[9]

Allied to this set of justifications are others based on cultural differences. Weiler points out that decentralization may be advocated in order to provide greater sensitivity to local variations in educational needs:

> Except in very small or culturally very homogeneous societies, most countries vary considerably across regions, communities, and language groups in terms of cultural and social frameworks of learning. The frames of reference for the study

of history, botany, social studies, and other fields vary obviously and significantly between southern and northern Italy, Alabama and California, or Bavaria and Berlin. Differences such as these, in countries such as the Federal Republic of Germany and the United States, historically have sustained the argument for a federal or local structure of educational governance and for varying degrees of cross-regional differentiation, as far as the content of education is concerned.[10]

In contrast, centralization may be advocated on the grounds that intranational diversity in the cultures of learning is excessive and that there is a need for standardization of at least the core elements in curriculum and instruction. This was among the justifications for partial centralization in the United States during the 1930s[11] and more recently has been a motive in England, the government of which introduced a centralizing national curriculum in 1988.[12]

Finally, one negative motive for decentralization is a desire by the center to reduce its responsibilities for education because of financial stringency. Central governments which realize that they do not have sufficient resources for adequate provision of services may choose to evade the problem by decentralizing responsibility to lower tiers or to nongovernmental bodies. This has been an underlying consideration of reforms giving subnational bodies greater responsibility for education in Argentina, China, and Kyrgyzstan.[13] It has also been a major motive in various privatization initiatives.[14]

Models

As already implied, the range of models for the governance of education is very wide. Decisions on the choice of models must be made in the context of political ideologies, historical legacies, and such factors as linguistic plurality, geographic size, and ease of communications.

An obvious starting point is with the overall structure of government. Australia, Canada, India, Nigeria, and the United States all have federal systems in which substantial powers are vested in state or provincial governments. The degree of provincial decision making in Canada, for example, is so great that the structure and content of education is substantially different in such provinces as Alberta and Quebec. Most obviously, in the former the education system is mainly conducted in English, whereas in the latter it is mainly conducted in French. Differences are not quite so marked between the different states of the United States, but they are still substantial in that country. These systems therefore appear to be highly decentralized.

Many unitary systems also appear to have high degrees of decentralization. For example, in 1976 Papua New Guinea adopted a quasi-federal system with nineteen provincial governments, each of which had considerable autonomy including in matters of education.[15] The United Kingdom, although not a federal system, has a strong degree of decentralization to its constituent parts — England, Northern Ireland, Wales, and Scotland. The education systems of England and Wales are closely linked, but Scotland and Northern Ireland operate separately.[16]

Some confederal systems have even greater degrees of decentralization.

Switzerland, for example, has twenty-six cantons, each of which has its own school laws and education system.[17] Cantonal authorities are empowered to decide on the structure of the system, the curriculum, the language of instruction, and the time spent on each subject in each grade. The national government plays hardly any role in the decision-making process.

Linguistic pluralism plays a major role in several of the countries already mentioned, particularly Nigeria, Canada and Switzerland. Belgium has parallel education systems serving French speakers and Flemish speakers, and linguistic pluralism was among the factors behind the territorial decentralization initiatives in Papua New Guinea. In Vanuatu, by contrast, efforts have been made to coordinate the separate English-medium and French-medium systems under a single ministry—an initiative which is a form of functional centralization.[18]

Concerning geographic size, one might be tempted to look at countries with large areas, such as Canada, India, Russia, and the United States, all of which have federal systems, and assume that all large countries have decentralized administrations. However, the fact that this is not the case is demonstrated by consideration of Indonesia and China, which until recently have had highly centralized administrations. Conversely, it cannot be assumed that small states necessarily have centralized systems. This is certainly true in some small states, such as Malta and Brunei Darussalam; but it is not true of St. Lucia and The Gambia. The latter two countries have district administrations and also permit some decision making at the school level.

The importance of the school as a level of consideration deserves emphasis. Since the mid-1980s, school-based management has received considerable emphasis in a wide range of countries. In New Zealand, for example, a far-reaching initiative was launched in 1988 under the heading Tomorrow's Schools.[19] The government's Department of Education was abolished, and school-level boards of trustees were formed. The boards were required to enter contractual agreements with their communities, and were empowered to manage school budgets and hire and fire teachers.[20] Similar initiatives were launched at about the same time in Australia, Canada, the United States, and the United Kingdom.[21] A reform in Spain took democratization to the extent of requiring School Councils to elect the principals of schools.[22]

Finally, models of administration are also influenced by the ease or otherwise of communication. In such countries as Cambodia and the Democratic Republic of the Congo, administration is decentralized by default simply because communications are poor. The center does not know what the periphery is doing, and the periphery would be unable to secure regular and detailed instructions from the center even if it wanted to. In other parts of the world, the advent of the fax machine and the Internet has greatly reduced remoteness and has permitted stronger central supervision.

Measurements

The complexities of centralization or decentralization become even more apparent when efforts are made at measurement. Many people suppose that countries can be ranked on a scale, with some having strongly centralized systems at the top and others having strongly decentralized systems at the bottom. However, attempts to create such rankings usually produce findings that are questionable and potentially misleading.

An initial problem arises from the custom of taking the nation-state as the unit for analysis. National boundaries are in most cases arbitrary, and they form countries of greatly differing sizes. Thus, to describe Japan (population 122,600,000) as having a centralized administration would mean something very different from describing Tonga (population 97,000) as having a centralized administration. Likewise, although the government of India has devoted much publicity to its decentralized District Primary Education Project,[23] the fact that some of these districts have populations above 5 million, which is considerably greater than the total populations of many countries, might make some observers feel that the unit of government is still very large.

Enlarging on this point, when the Soviet Union was a single country, the autonomy held by individual republics such as Azerbaijan, Georgia, and Latvia made the administrative system appear decentralized. Now that those republics are independent countries, the administration of their education systems, from the perspective of the nation-state, is commonly described as centralized. Conversely, when Hong Kong was a separate self-governing territory, its administration was widely described as centralized.[24] However, after the 1997 reincorporation of Hong Kong into the People's Republic of China, Hong Kong remained a Special Administrative Region with considerable autonomy which, at least from the perspective of Beijing, seemed a highly *de*centralized arrangement.[25]

A different difficulty in measurement arises from value judgments on the importance or otherwise of different powers. Thus the power to determine the structure of school systems, or the language of instruction, might be considered very important. In contrast, the power to hire school cleaners might be considered rather less important. This would require weighting within any model for measurement.

A further complexity is that reforms might move systems simultaneously in opposite directions. During the 1980s, the government in England greatly changed the nature of educational decision making.[26] As already noted, one component of reforms was the introduction of a national curriculum, which centralized power in the hands of the national government. Another component, however, was the requirement for all schools to have boards of governors that had considerable powers at the school level over such matters as budgets, recruitment of teachers, and facilities. The coexistence of trends that are both centralizing and decentralizing creates major difficulties for classification.

Also creating major difficulties is the fact that in some systems, the main balance of power is between the national and the school levels, with rather little power at intermediate provincial or district levels. One might ask whether such systems should be described as centralized or decentralized because they could seem to be both at the same time. Jamaica, for example, has elements of strong control in the Ministry of Education, combined with other elements at the school level and a generally weak intermediate regional level.[27] Related to this point is that the extent to which a system of government is centralized or decentralized cannot be prejudged from the existence or absence of sub-national institutions. Many constitutions give federal governments powers of veto which act as a considerable constraint on state or provincial governments, and which mean that the systems are not as decentralized as they appear at first sight. Also, the power of federal and quasi-federal governments is commonly strengthened by control of major sources of finance.[28] By contrast, even in countries with no state or provincial governments, national authorities may be willing to decentralize substantial powers to the school level.

Finally, while deconcentration is usually described as a form of decentralization, it can be a mechanism for *tightening* central control of the periphery instead of for allowing greater local decision making. When central government staff posted to the periphery are permitted to take local decisions to reflect local needs and priorities, then deconcentration may reasonably be described as a form of decentralization. But when staff in the periphery are responsible for tightening implementation of policies determined by the central government, deconcentration is more reasonably described as a form of centralization.

Yet despite all these complexities, and the questions they raise, some observers have persisted with efforts at measurement. One such attempt is presented in table 8.1. The figures led the authors to describe Zimbabwe as the most centralized of the ten countries covered, followed by Senegal and Malaysia. At the other end, the United States was described as the most decentralized, followed by the United Kingdom, India, and Nigeria.

Although these figures shed some light on the topic, they should be viewed with extreme caution. To establish the distributions, the authors counted functions, assigned each of them a score of one, and calculated percentage distributions at each level. Different total numbers for each country arose because in some cases functions were undertaken at more than one level. The authors made no allowance for the fact that some functions are arguably more important than others. Moreover, "local" may mean something very different in India and in Namibia. As such, the example shows the dangers as well as the benefits of efforts to place countries on a single continuum for comparison.

Themes and Variations

The factors behind different models, and the implications of different arrangements, may be further illustrated with a few examples. Three specific foci of decision making are presented here. They are school-leaving qualifications, school textbooks, and the operation of universities.

Table 8.1
Balance between Levels of Decision Making for Education in 10 Countries (%)

	Central		Regional		District		Local		Total	
	No.	*%*	*No.*	*%*	*No.*	*%*	*No.*	*%*	*No.*	*%*
France	24	59	4	10	9	22	4	10	41	100
India	16	38	16	38	4	10	6	14	42	100
Malaysia	26	63	4	10	4	10	7	17	41	100
Mexico	24	45	13	25	7	13	9	17	53	100
Namibia	25	57	2	5	6	14	11	254	4	100
Nigeria	21	42	20	40	0	0	9	18	50	100
Senegal	26	76	1	3	0	0	7	21	34	100
U.K.	16	36	3	7	11	25	14	32	44	100
U.S.	4	6	24	36	22	33	16	24	66	100
Zimbabwe	25	81	0	0	1	3	5	16	31	100

Source: William M. Rideout and Ipek Ural, *Centralised and Decentralised Models of Education: Comparative Studies* (Halfway House, South Africa: Development Bank of Southern Africa, 1993), 108.

Control of School Leaving Qualifications

Considerable diversity may be found in the control of secondary-school leaving qualifications. Table 8.2 highlights this diversity in the European context. In most countries the qualifications were dependent upon results in examinations, though in some cases they resulted from continuous assessment of various kinds. Among the twenty-six countries shown, the ministry of education set the examinations in seven cases, separate examination boards operated in four countries, and qualifications were determined through school-based assessment in fifteen cases. In two cases, other arrangements existed. Assessment was controlled by a curriculum and examination center in Latvia, and by a university board in Malta.

As with other aspects of administration, the factors underlying different arrangements reflected a combination of historical legacies and deliberate policies. The United Kingdom has a long tradition of independent examination boards, some associated with tertiary institutions such as the Universities of London, Oxford, and Cambridge, but others, such as the Associated Examining Board, operating with a different framework. This has fitted an educational culture that has permitted schools to determine their own curricula and approaches to education. Other countries, such as Poland, Romania and Russia, have more centralized traditions with examination units under direct government control in the Ministry of Education. Yet other countries, such as Iceland, Sweden, and Turkey, have no formal final examinations. Students in these countries are instead subject to school-based assessment throughout their secondary school careers. Institutions of higher education may set entrance

Table 8.2
Bodies Responsible for Administering and Awarding Secondary-School Leaving
Qualifications in 26 European Countries, 1994

Country	Ministry of Education	Examination Board	School	Other
Austria		*		
Belarus			*	
Bulgaria			*	
Croatia			*	
Cyprus			*	
Denmark			*	
Estonia			*	
Finland		*		
Germany			*	
Iceland			*	
Italy	*			
Latvia				*
Liechtenstein		*		
Lithuania	*			
Luxembourg	*			
Malta				*
Netherlands			*	
Norway			*	
Poland	*		*	
Portugal	*			
Romania	*			
Russia	*		*	
Slovakia			*	
Sweden			*	
Turkey			*	
United Kingdom		*		

Source: Sergij Gabršček, *Guide to Secondary School-Leaving Certificates in European Countries* (Cheltenham, U.K.: Universities and Colleges Admissions Service, 1996), 103.

examinations of various kinds, but that process can be a separate activity from certification of completion of secondary education.

Focus on examinations helps to show that the locus of real control over educational processes may be hidden. Examinations are a major determinant of actual (as opposed to officially intended) school curricula, and where there is a divergence between what is taught and what is tested, students generally pay greater heed to the latter. In England, where, up to 1988, schools had considerable freedom to determine their own curricula, the public examinations ensured some commonality, albeit with multiple centers of gravity.

Viewing the matter from a different angle, however, when the government of England wished to introduce a common national curriculum with a single center of gravity, it saw the existence of diverse examination boards as an obstacle rather than an asset. A mechanism had to be negotiated through which the various independent boards would come together to operate a new examination called the General Certificate of Secondary Education and operate "under the direction of the Minister" through a School Examinations and Assessment Council.[29]

For a rather different example of the dynamics of change, the Maltese case is interesting. Even for two decades after Malta's achievement of independence from the United Kingdom in 1964, most Maltese secondary school students sat for the school-leaving examinations of the University of Oxford or the University of London. Among benefits of this arrangement for Maltese candidates were access to professional expertise in examination design and administration, and international recognition of the qualifications.[30] However, a desire to localize processes and increase in-country control led to the creation in 1989 of an examinations board at the University of Malta. This change could not easily be called decentralization since, as noted above, that word usually implies a process of decision making at the top, and in this case the decision was made at the locality rather than at center. The effect was the same, however, for Maltese leaders asserted their autonomy and took charge of their own affairs. The fact that the Maltese initiative was based at the university rather than the Ministry of Education is also instructive. The decision was no doubt partly influenced by the fact that many examination boards in the United Kingdom were university based; but the arrangement encountered resistance from officers in the Maltese Ministry of Education, many of whom felt that they should have more direct control over this important aspect of the educational process. Sultana has indicated that ministry officials whom he interviewed "generally presented the University as 'an empire' dominating most aspects of the new examinations, and resented what was ultimately felt to be an impositional rather than a collaborative structure."[31] From the government viewpoint, therefore, the new situation seemed to have some continuity with the old one. Ministry personnel probably felt that they had more influence over the assessment system than before, but not as much as they would have liked.

Control of Textbooks

Commonality and diversity of textbook policies may be illustrated by comparing patterns in four parts of East Asia which themselves have much in common but also display major differences. The following account focuses on mainland China, Taiwan, Hong Kong, and Macau. All four are mainly inhabited by people of Chinese ethnicity, and their dominant cultures have Confucian roots. One has a communist government, whereas the other three have capitalist governments. Hong Kong and Macau share histories of colonization by European powers, but despite this commonality they have significant differences in the nature of educational provision.

The government of China, chiefly in order to spread the official ideology of communism, has held tight control over curricula and textbooks. Shortly after the foundation of the People's Republic in 1949, the government decided that only one basic set of textbooks, published in Beijing by the People's Education Press, would be permitted for use in schools. Since 1985, however, the central government has permitted increasing diversification in the production and contents of textbooks. The change has reflected the introduction of a market economy and increased tolerance of pluralism in both economic and social sectors. The relaxation of control began with Shanghai, which was followed by other economically advanced coastal areas and then by other regions.[32]

Taiwan contrasts with mainland China in many aspects of political ideology. Most obviously, whereas China became a communist society after the 1949 revolution, Taiwan remained a capitalist society which was strongly antagonistic to the political changes on the mainland. Yet despite this ideological difference, the Taiwanese authorities have been just as keen as their counterparts in mainland China to control the content of the curriculum. Textbooks are standardized and published by the National Institute for Compilation and Translation. Official goals for primary education include inculcation of patriotism and anticommunism, and textbooks are seen as a major vehicle for achieving these goals.[33]

Hong Kong, another society with long capitalist traditions, was a British colony between 1842 and 1997. As one might expect, the colonial authorities were also concerned about the content of textbooks, and particularly about the extent to which such books could disseminate ideas that conflicted with those promoted by the colonial government. However, the policies of the Hong Kong colonial government were not as rigid as those in China or Taiwan. The authorities only permitted schools to use books that had been placed on an official list, but the schools did have the scope to choose books produced by independent publishers and sold on the open market.[34]

Macau provides yet another model. Like Hong Kong, Macau has been a colony of a European power; but the administration within Macau has been much more laissez-faire than that in Hong Kong. Macau became a Portuguese colony in 1557 and remained under Portuguese administration for over four centuries. In 1987, the governments of Portugal and China agreed that sovereignty over Macau would revert to China in 1999, two years after the transition in Hong Kong. That political initiative did cause some changes in the education system, but the schools remained completely free to decide which textbooks on the market they wished to use. The government of Macau does not itself produce any textbooks for schools, and the lack of controls has resulted in considerable diversity in what is actually taught in different institutions.[35]

This set of examples shows on the one hand that similar administrative systems may be found in different political environments, and on the other hand that different administrative systems may be found in similar political environments. The governments of both China and Taiwan exerted tight control over textbooks, even though one was communist and the other, capitalist. China's move to a market economy was accompanied by some relaxation of control, and at that point contrasted with Taiwan which had always had a market economy but in which schools had never been permitted freedom of choice in textbooks. Hong Kong and Macau were both colonies of European powers, but the colonial government in Hong Kong only permitted schools to use books that had been vetted, whereas the colonial government in Macau adopted a complete laissez-faire policy. The difference in this case partly reflected the colonies' importance to the metropolitan authorities. Hong Kong was a sizeable colony in which the British government was anxious to maintain stability; Macau was a very small colony that had been important to the Portuguese empire up to the nineteenth century but subsequently declined in significance. The resulting neglect was evident in all sectors, including education.

Control of Universities

Concerning relationships between governments and universities, two main models may be identified.[36] The first is the state-control model, which is exemplified by higher education systems of continental Europe and particularly by that of France. These systems were created by the state and are almost completely financed by it. At least formally, the state controls nearly all aspects of the dynamics of these higher education systems. The national ministries of education regulate the access conditions, curriculum, degree requirements, examinations, and appointment and remuneration of academic staff. One objective of this detailed government regulation is the standardization of national degrees, which in several countries are awarded by the state rather than by the universities themselves.

In this state-control model, the power of the state is combined with strong authority at the level of senior professors. The latter hold considerable collegial power within the faculties and the institutions. This model is therefore characterized by a strong top (the state), a weak middle (the institutional administration), and a strong bottom (the senior professors).

In contrast is the state-supervising model, which was found in the United States and the United Kingdom up to recent times, as well as many former British colonies. In this model, senior professors have strong powers, while the institutional administrators have modest powers and the state also accepts a modest role. Each institution recruits its own students, hires its own staff, and determines its own curricula. Many systems influenced by the U.K. model have buffer bodies modeled on the University Grants Committee, which operated in the United Kingdom from 1919 to 1988. Table 8.3 summarizes information on buffer bodies in eight countries. Although the table shows variation in their roles, the bodies typically liaise between the institutions and the government, seeking on the one hand to respect institutional autonomy but on the other hand to secure accountability in the use of public resources. Also in the state-supervised model are systems such as that in the Philippines, which have large numbers of institutions which are private but which are to some extent regulated by the state.

Neave and van Vught highlight the merits of the state-supervising model in contrast to the state-control model.[37] They suggest that the former is more likely to permit and to stimulate the types of innovation within institutions that may be necessary to cope with rapidly changing circumstances. Because of this advantage, several higher education systems, including those in Chile, Argentina, and China, have moved in the direction of this model. However, Neave and van Vught recognize that the state-control model may also have advantages and that other higher education systems, for example in Kenya, Uganda, and Ghana, have moved in that direction. The reasons for this countermovement include a government desire to control high-level human resources output and to

Table 8.3
Functions of University Buffer Funding Bodies in Eight Countries

Country	Name of Body	Core Budget Allocations	Preserving Autonomy	Quality Control	Enrollment Determination
U.K.	University Grants Committee	x	x	x	
Nigeria	National Universities Commission	x		x	
Israel	Planning & Budgeting Committee	x		x	
New Zealand	University Grants Committee	x	x	x	
India	University Grants Committee			x	
Pakistan	University Grants Committee			x	x
Kenya	Committee on Higher Education			x	
Sudan	University Grants Committee				x

Source: Adrian Ziderman and Douglas Albrecht, *Financing Universities in Developing Countries* (London: Falmer, 1995), 117.

restrict political threats from universities, a legacy of centralized direction derived from theories of a planned economy and pressure on resources that requires a relatively elitist system. In this connection, movements in the United Kingdom are also instructive. In that country the University Grants Committee (UGC) was replaced in 1988 by a University Funding Council (UFC) through which the government can take much more direct control.[38] This was a form of functional centralization. It permitted the government to require institutions to conform to demands to measure their research output and the quality of their teaching. Just as the United Kingdom led parts of the world with its original model of the UGC, it has also led parts of the world with its new model of research assessment exercises and quality audits.[39]

Implications for Efficiency

As noted above, in various circumstances arguments for efficiency may be used to support both centralization and decentralization. These points deserve elaboration to identify the types of factors involved.

Experiences in Papua New Guinea provide a good starting point for discussion.[40] In 1977, the government of Papua New Guinea launched a major scheme for territorial devolution to nineteen newly created provincial governments. The reform was not without critics. For example, in 1978 the Leader of the Opposition highlighted the cost implications of an increase in the number of provincial-level politicians:

> Papua New Guinea is to have more than 600 paid politicians. We have three million people. Australia has about 600 paid politicians, and it has 14 million people. It took Australia almost 100 years to develop to the stage where it now has 600 politicians. It has taken us three years. Britain, which has a population of 40 million, has about as many politicians as Papua New Guinea. Does anyone seriously believe that a developing country like Papua New Guinea can afford that much government?[41]

Nevertheless, the reform went ahead. Provincial governments were formed with substantial responsibilities in most sectors including education—and including for each a provincial minister of education.

One result of the reform was a massive expansion of the bureaucracy. This was especially visible at the provincial level but was also evident at the national level, since more staff were required for coordination and training. In one province between 1977 and 1983 primary school enrollments expanded by 15 percent and secondary school enrollments expanded by 7 percent, but the number of senior administrative officers expanded by 208 percent. The smallest province had just 25,000 people (which elsewhere would have been equivalent in size to a small town) but nevertheless acquired a bureaucracy with the same major components as all other provinces. Moreover, at that stage in its development Papua New Guinea was severely short of skilled personnel. Given these circumstances, it is perhaps unsurprising that the whole reform encountered major problems and in the 1990s was reversed.[42]

However, other types of decentralization can increase efficiency. Among them are school-based management projects of the types launched in Australia, England, and New Zealand during the 1980s and early 1990s. Typical features of these projects included competition between institutions for pupils and teachers, and allocation of block grants to the school level so that principals and other administrators can switch between budget categories according to needs and priorities. Most schemes also allow some funds to be retained from one year to the next, which gives an incentive to school-level administrators to save money rather than simply disburse all surpluses towards the end of the financial year. Evaluations have shown increased personal stress at the school level, and critics have asserted that some of the pedagogic goals of school principals have been subsumed by the demands of managerialism. Nevertheless, it generally appears that the reforms have led to much greater consciousness of costs and of ways to improve efficiency.[43]

The government of Jamaica has similarly encouraged school-based management, though it has also attempted to improve efficiency through deconcentration of the Ministry of Education. Between 1990 and 1994, six regional offices were created with the goal of improving the delivery of services and supervising more effectively the educational process. In Jamaica, this was the second attempt at such structural reform, for the ministry operated branch offices from the mid-1970s to 1984. That initiative was abandoned because the regional offices

> did not have the information to make decisions or the authority to do so and were viewed as "post office boxes" for the central ministry. Financial constraints in combination with the concern that the operation of the Regional Offices increased administrative costs without increasing the efficiency of the system resulted in the closure of the Regional Offices.[44]

At least in its early years, the initiative of the 1990s also seemed problematic. Factors included reluctance of headquarters staff to relinquish authority, and general inertia within the system. This experience therefore highlights problems in implementation, and the fact that improved efficiency is certainly not an automatic outcome even of decentralization reforms that specifically aim at that goal.[45]

Also related to issues of efficiency is the need for coordination in decentralized systems. This may consume considerable time as well as labor. With reference to Switzerland, Gretler suggests that the decentralized structure creates close links between the people and their education systems. However, he adds, "since all important decisions are voted on by the population, the changes in the system of education are normally very slow."[46] The response from advocates of decentralization might be that the changes, although slow, are more likely to be solid because they would be grounded in general acceptance. This viewpoint implies that speed of change is only one indicator of efficiency and that effectiveness of change must be included as another. The example once again indicates the complexity of the subject and of the implications of administrative reform.

Taking another type of centralization/decentralization, it is useful to consider the functional as well as the territorial distribution of responsibilities. As noted above, one type of functional decentralization is the splitting of ministries to perform specialized tasks; and, conversely, combining separate ministries would be a form of functional centralization. The attraction of such splitting lies in the specialization that each body can achieve. However, separate bodies may find that their functions overlap, and that they cannot achieve economies of scale. It was partly for the latter reason that in 1990 the Ministry of Basic Education in Benin was merged with the Ministry of Secondary and Higher Education.[47] Likewise in Vietnam, four ministries were merged in 1987 to become two ministries, which in 1990 were themselves merged to form a single ministry.[48]

Implications for Social Inequalities

In general, decentralization is likely to permit and perhaps encourage social inequalities. Conversely, centralization provides a mechanism for reducing inequalities; but whether that mechanism is actually used depends on goals and willpower at the apex of the system. Commentary here will focus on geographically distributed inequalities and on socioeconomic inequalities within particular populations.

Concerning geographic disparities, discussion can usefully begin with territorial devolution to the provincial or state level. Such devolution permits subnational bodies to determine the nature and direction of development. Some bodies are likely to be more active than others, in which case regional disparities in the quantity and/or quality of education will increase. Further down the spatial hierarchy, the same point would apply to districts and to individual schools. Devolution is not usually just a matter of decision-making, it is also a matter of resource allocation. Highly decentralized systems commonly permit subnational bodies to retain most or all of the resources which they generate. Since prosperous communities can afford better quality and/or greater quantities of education, disparities remain or even widen.

To expand on the earlier example, one major part of the devolution package in Papua New Guinea was the provision for provincial governments to retain much larger proportions of locally generated revenue than had previously been permitted. The national government controlled external aid and various other revenues, and it was able through this mechanism to ameliorate some disparities. However, the national government was not able to make full compensation for the structural imbalances created by the devolution framework.[49]

Administrative structures have also created major imbalances in the United States, both within and between states.[50] The U.S. Constitution does not give a direct educational role to the federal government, though increasing federal funds have in fact been allocated to the education of disadvantaged groups. Within states, the problem is that some school districts are able much more easily than others to mobilize resources for education from property taxes and other sources. Taking a historical perspective, Table 8.4 shows the changing balance between federal, state, and local financing for elementary and secondary schooling during the present century. Whereas in 1919–1920 the bulk of revenue was raised at the local level, by 1979–1980 both federal and state government revenues were more prominent. This showed the existence of a mechanism to reduce some imbalances, though disparities remained to the extent that in 1989–1990, districts in Alaska had average per pupil expenditures of US$7,918, compared with an average of just US$2,606 for their counterparts in Utah.

Table 8.4
Sources of Revenue for Public Elementary and Secondary Schools,
USA (Percentages)

School Year	Federal	State	Local
1919–1920	0.3	16.3	83.2
1929–1930	0.4	16.9	82.7
1939–1940	1.8	39.3	68.0
1949–1950	2.9	39.8	57.3
1959–1960	4.4	39.1	56.5
1969–1970	8.0	39.9	52.1
1979–1980	9.8	46.8	43.4
1989–1990	6.1	47.3	44.2
1992–1993	6.9	45.6	44.7

Sources: Keith Hinchliffe, *Federal Finance, Fiscal Imbalance, and Educational Inequality* (Washington, D.C.: World Bank, 1987), 29; *Digest of Educational Statistics, 1995* (Washington, D.C.: U.S. Department of Education, 1995).

Inequalities may also be exacerbated within socioeconomic groups. For example, the literature on community financing of education points out that richer communities are more likely and better able to embark on self-help projects than are poor communities.[51] In Zimbabwe, for example, the policy of decentralization to the community level permitted the advantaged segments to retain their lead. As noted by Maravanyika:

Schools in former white areas established Management Agreements with government. These enabled Management Committees to levy parents so that the schools could buy additional school equipment and other teaching resources or recruit additional staff to reduce the government stipulated teacher/pupil ratio which some white parents considered too high for effective teaching, or introduced specialist subjects not covered by government such as music and computing.[52]

The large amounts charged by the management committees of these schools were generally out of the reach of ordinary black parents, and the system therefore perpetuated racial as well as socioeconomic inequalities.

In a very different context, a similar point has been made about New York City. In this case, reforms aimed to decentralize decision making to the community level with the idea that community boards would be more responsive to the immediate needs of parents and students. However, the politics of many communities proved at least as factionalized as citywide politics; and when factions assumed control, they were at least as exclusionary in their policies and practices toward minorities. As observed by Elmore:

> To be an African-American in East Harlem, where community politics is effectively dominated by Puerto Rican Hispanics, is to be an even smaller minority than an African-American would be in the city at large.[53]

He added:

> To say, then, that creating smaller institutions that are closer to "the people" is as often as not to substitute democratic sentiment for analysis. . . . There is no absolute presumption that "the people" at one level are any wiser, more informed, or better equipped to make decisions than "the people" at any other level; the only presumption is that factional interests will exert different influences at different levels of aggregation.[54]

Taking reforms of the opposite type, there is of course more scope for centralized authorities to oversee situations and to redistribute resources to those in need. This may happen, and it has been among the arguments used to support centralization in countries as different as Malta and China. However, much depends on the intentions of those in power, for of course centralized regimes are not necessarily more sensitive to the needs of disadvantaged groups.

Preconditions and Support Systems for Administrative Reform

The literature on administrative reform pays much greater attention to ways to achieve effective decentralization than to ways to achieve effective centralization. This probably reflects the value judgments of the individuals and

organizations producing that literature, though it may also reflect a perception
that decentralization is more difficult to achieve than centralization. As the examples in this chapter have pointed out, in some cases centralization is more
desirable than decentralization, and it should not be assumed that centralization can be achieved simply by issuing decrees.

Prawda has focused on lessons learned from decentralization efforts in the
education sector in Latin America.[55] He presents seven lessons, some of which
would presumably also apply to attempts at centralization. Successful decentralization, he suggests, requires the following:

1. full political commitment from national, regional, provincial, municipal, and local leaders;
2. a model addressing the issue of which educational functions and responsibilities could be more efficiently and effectively delivered at the
   central level, smaller decentralized government units, and/or the private sector, and explicitly defining the degree of accountability of the
   different participants;
3. an implementation strategy and timetable;
4. clear operational manuals and procedures;
5. continuous training for the skill levels to be performed at the central
   and decentralized units of government;
6. relevant performance indicators to be continuously monitored through
   a management information system by policy makers and senior government officials; and
7. adequate financial, human, and physical resources to sustain the process.

Turning to reforms of the opposite type, most analysts would consider the
most important requirements for centralization to be full commitment from the
central leadership, and acquiescence at lower levels. Questions about capacity
may be just as relevant to centralization as to decentralization initiatives, since
both may collapse if they fail to deliver promised benefits.

Missing from Prawda's list is a public relations campaign to explain the need
for reform, which would be equally valuable for centralization and for decentralization reforms. Allied to such a campaign would be the need to secure cooperation from teachers unions and similar groups.[56]

Also important in all reforms is the time element. The exigencies of political
forces sometimes require results before reforms have had time to become fully
effective. This is one reason for the swings evident in some countries from centralization to decentralization and back again. Prawda points out that the first accomplishments from decentralization in Mexico and Chile surfaced only five
years after the reforms had been launched.[57] However, such a period may be too
long for many political regimes. During the 1970s and 1980s, the average stay of
a minister of education in Colombia and Argentina was around sixteen months.

In Papua New Guinea, the pace of change was even more rapid. In the decade up to 1985, the country witnessed eleven changes in the national minister of education—quite apart from the multiple changes also occurring at the provincial level. This instability was also a factor in the policy swing in that country.

Conclusions

The political context of reforms is among the points most deserving emphasis. Although centralization and decentralization are often officially justified by technical criteria, political factors are usually the most important.[58] Centralization and decentralization are about matters of control, about the distribution of resources, and, in the education sector, about access to opportunities which can fundamentally influence the quality of life for both individuals and social groups.

For scholars who are more concerned with dispassionate analysis than with manipulation of variables, the first task in any review of centralization or decentralization is to identify precisely what is meant by the terms as used in each case. This chapter has shown that the words "centralization" and "decentralization" can have many different meanings. Not only are the terms vague, they may even have contradictory meanings depending on the circumstances and perspectives of the persons making the judgments. Deconcentration, for example, may seem like a form of decentralization when viewed from the central ministry but may be a mechanism to exert tighter control on the periphery and may thus be seen as a form of centralization from those who are distant from the ministry. Likewise, splitting of a single ministry into two parts may seem like decentralization from the perspective of those who are closely involved but may appear to make little difference to those who are more distant. Although attempts to empower local communities may appear to be laudable attempts at decentralization, the fact that such communities may be dominated by factional elites may leave other groups feeling at least as marginalized as before.

Also important to note are rather sober assessments about the impact of structural reforms on teaching and learning in classrooms. Tyack's review of debates and shifting patterns of control in the United States led him to conclude that "governance reforms have been mostly disconnected from what students learn."[59] A similar view has been presented by Elmore:

> Whatever the politics of centralization and decentralization is "about" in American education . . . it is not fundamentally or directly about teaching and learning. This disconnection between structural reform and the core technology of schooling means that major reforms can wash over the educational system, consuming large amounts of scarce resources—money; time; the energy of parents, teachers, and administrators; the political capital of elected officials—without having any discernible effect on what students actually learn in school.[60]

Although analysts in other parts of the world would recognize the thrust of these points, it would be an overstatement to suggest that shifts in the locus of control do not affect life in classrooms. Certainly the reforms may not be tied fundamentally or directly to teaching and learning, but many reforms have had marked impact on school curricula and on the access to education by different groups. Indeed it is mainly for this reason that the battles over control of education are so intense.

As was noted at the beginning of this chapter, comparative analysis can certainly highlight the advantages and disadvantages of different models of governance. It can also enhance understanding of the reasons why some societies and systems have particular shapes and are moving in certain directions; and for politicians and administrators embarking on reforms, comparative study can highlight the need for certain preconditions and support systems. However, it is impossible to reach a single recipe that will be appropriate for all countries. It does seem that societies with strongly entrenched democratic values and well-educated populations are more likely than others to demand decentralized systems and to make them work. But even this is a broad generalization which does not hold in all cases. The future, like the past, is likely to bring continued shifts in forms of governance in all parts of the world. Some of these shifts will be centralizing, others will be decentralizing, and yet others will be both centralizing and decentralizing at the same time. This need not be cause for bemusement or despair. Rather, it can be taken as part of the ever-present dynamic of human endeavor.

Notes

1. See, e.g., G. S. Cheema and D. A. Rondinelli, eds. *Decentralization and Development: Policy Implementation in Developing Countries* (London: Sage, 1983); Jon Lauglo, "Forms of Decentralisation and Their Implications for Education," *Comparative Education* 31, 1 (1995): 5–29; D. A. Rondinelli, J. R. Nellis, and G. S. Cheema, *Decentralization in Developing Countries: A Review of Recent Experience* (Washington, D.C.: World Bank, 1984); Jerry M. Silverman, *Public Sector Decentralization: Economic Policy and Sector Investment Programs,* Technical Paper no. 188 (Washington D.C.: World Bank, 1992); B. C. Smith, *Decentralization: The Territorial Dimension of the State* (London: George Allen and Unwin, 1985).

2. See, e.g., William K. Cummings and Abby Riddell, "Alternative Policies for the Finance, Control, and Delivery of Basic Education," *International Journal of Educational Research* 21, no. 8 (1994): 754–756; Rondinelli, Nellis and Cheema, *Decentralization,* 23–26.

3. Carlos Malpica, "Education and the Community in the Peruvian Educational Reform," *International Review of Education* 26, no. 4 (1980): 357–367; Nelly Stromquist, "Decentralizing Educational Decision-Making in Peru: Intentions and Realities," *International Journal of Educational Development* 6, no. 1 (1986): 47–60.

4. E. Mark Hanson, "Democratization and Decentralization in Colombian Education," *Comparative Education Review* 39, no. 1 (1995): 108.

5. Noel McGinn and Susan Street, "Educational Decentralization: Weak State or Strong State?" *Comparative Education Review* 30, no. 4 (1986): 486–497; Carlos Ornelas, "The Decentralization of Education in Mexico," *Prospects* 18, no. 1 (1988): 108–111.

6. Smith, *Decentralization,* 69.

7. See, e.g., Peter Harris, *Foundations of Public Administration: A Comparative Approach* (Hong Kong: Hong Kong University Press, 1990), 43–46.

8. See, e.g., Diana Conyers, *An Introduction to Social Planning in the Third World* (Chichester: John Wiley, 1982), 107–109.

9. Donald R. Winkler, *Decentralization in Education: An Economic Perspective,* Working Paper no. 143 (Washington, D.C.: World Bank, 1989), 2.

10. Hans N. Weiler, "Control versus Legitimation: The Politics of Ambivalence," in *Decentralization and School Improvement: Can We Fulfill the Promise?* ed. Jane Hannaway and Martin Carnoy (San Francisco: Jossey-Bass, 1993), 65.

11. David Tyack, "School Governance in the United States: Historical Puzzles and Anomalies," in *Decentralization and School Improvement: Can We Fulfill the Promise?* ed. Jane Hannaway and Martin Carnoy (San Francisco: Jossey-Bass, 1993), 3.

12. Chris Emerson and Ivor Goddard, *All about the National Curriculum: What You Need to Know, Why You Need to Know It* (Oxford: Heinemann, 1989).

13. Ministerio de Cultura y Educación, Transformación de la Educación Nacional (Buenos Aires: Ministerio de Cultura y Educacion, 1991); quoted in Hanson, "Democratization," 101; Cheng Kai-Ming, "The Changing Legitimacy in a Decentralising System: The State and Education Development in China," *International Journal of Educational Development* 14, no. 3 (1994): 265–269; Igor Kitaev, "Challenges of Realities: An Overview of Trends and Developments in Educational Finance in Central Asia and Mongolia," in *Educational Finance in Central Asia and Mongolia,* ed. Igor Kitaev (Paris: International Institute for Educational Planning, 1996), 74.

14. Mark Bray, *Privatization of Secondary Education: Issues and Policy Implications* (Paris: UNESCO, 1996); Mikolaj Kozakiewicz, "The Difficult Road to Educational Pluralism in Central and Eastern Europe," *Prospects* 22, no. 2 (1992): 207–215.

15. Mark Bray, *Educational Planning in a Decentralised System: The Papua New Guinean Experience* (Waigani: University of Papua New Guinea Press; Sydney: Sydney University Press, 1984); Y. P Ghai and A. J. Regan, *The Law, Politics, and Administration of Decentralisation in Papua New Guinea,* Monograph no. 30 (Waigani: National Research Institute, 1992).

16. Nigel Grant, "The British Isles as an Area of Study in Comparative Education," *Compare* 11, no. 2 (1981): 135–146; W. D. Halls, "United Kingdom," in *International Encyclopedia of National Systems of Education,* ed. T. Neville Postlethwaite (Oxford: Pergamon, 1995).

17. A. Gretler, "Switzerland," in *International Encyclopedia of National Systems of Education,* ed. T. Neville Postlethwaite (Oxford: Pergamon, 1995), 952.

18. Colin E. Hindson, "Educational Planning in Vanuatu—An Alternative Analysis," *Comparative Education* 31, no. 3 (1995): 327–337.

19. Government of New Zealand, *Tomorrow's Schools: The Reform of Education Administration in New Zealand* (Wellington: Government Printer, 1988).

20. R. J. S. Macpherson, "Administrative Reforms in the Antipodes: Self-Managing Schools and the Need for Effective Leaders," *Educational Management and*

Administration 20, no. 4 (1993): 40–52; David Mitchell with C. McGee, R. Moltzen, and D. Oliver, *Hear Our Voices: Final Report of Monitoring Today's Schools Research Project* (Hamilton: University of Waikato; Wellington: Ministry of Education, 1993).

21. Clarrie Burke, "Devolution of Responsibility to Queensland Schools: Clarifying the Rhetoric, Critiquing the Reality," *Journal of Educational Administration* 30, no. 4 (1992): 33–52; B. Lingard, J. Knight, and P. Porter, eds., *Schooling Reform in Hard Times* (London: Falmer, 1993).

22. E. Mark Hanson and Carolyn Ulrich, "Democracy, Decentralization, and School-Based Management in Spain," *La Educación: Revista Interamericana de Desarrollo Educativo* 38, no. 2 (1994): 324.

23. N. V. Varghese, "Decentralisation of Educational Planning in India," *International Journal of Educational Development* 16, no. 4 (1996): 355–365.

24. See, e.g., P. Morris, "Identifying the Strategies of Curriculum Development within a Highly Centralized Education System," *International Journal of Educational Development* 6, no. 3 (1986): 171–182; P. Morris, *The Hong Kong School Curriculum: Development, Issues, and Policies* (Hong Kong: Hong Kong University Press, 1996), 91–95.

25. See Mark Bray and W. O. Lee, eds., "Education and Political Transition: Implications of Hong Kong's Change of Sovereignty," special issue of *Comparative Education* 32, no. 2 (1997).

26. W. D. Halls, "United Kingdom," 1031.

27. Lorraine Blank, "Education Decentralization in Jamaica" (Washington, D.C.: World Bank, 1994).

28. Keith Hinchliffe, *Federal Finance, Fiscal Imbalance, and Educational Inequality,* Report no. EDT 72 (Washington, D.C.: World Bank, 1987); Donald R. Winkler, "Fiscal Decentralization and Accountability in Education: Experiences in Four Countries," in *Decentralization and School Improvement: Can We Fulfill the Promise?* ed. Jane Hannaway and Martin Carnoy (San Francisco: Jossey-Bass, 1993).

29. Max A. Eckstein and Harold J. Noah, *Secondary School Examinations: International Perspectives on Policy and Practice* (New Haven: Yale University Press, 1993), 82.

30. Ronald Sultana, "Malta," in *Examination Systems in Small States: Comparative Perspectives on Models and Operations,* ed. Mark Bray and Lucy Steward (London: Commonwealth Secretariat, 1998).

31. Sultana, "Malta," 133.

32. John Cleverley, *The Schooling of China: Tradition and Modernity in Chinese Education* (Sydney: Allen and Unwin, 1991), 244; Keith M. Lewin, Xu Hui, Angela W. Little, and Zheng Jiwei, *Educational Innovation in China: Tracing the Impact of the 1985 Reforms* (Harlow, U.K.: Longman, 1994), 147–162.

33. Yi-Rong Young, "Taiwan," in *Education and Development in East Asia,* ed. Paul Morris and Anthony Sweeting (New York: Garland, 1995), 120.

34. J. A. G. McClelland, "Curriculum Dissemination in Hong Kong," in *Curriculum Development in East Asia,* ed. Colin Marsh and Paul Morris (London: Falmer, 1991), 113.

35. Mark Bray and Philip Hui, "Structure and Content of Education: Evolution and Reform in the Transitional Period," in *Macau: City of Commerce and Culture,* ed. R. D. Cremer, 2d ed. (Hong Kong: API Press, 1991); Mark Bray and K. C. Tang, "Imported Textbooks, Non-Interventionist Policies, and School Curricula in Macau," *Curriculum and Teaching* 9, no. 2 (1994): 29–43.

36. Guy Neave and Frans van Vught, "Government and Higher Education in Developing Nations: A Conceptual Framework," in *Government and Higher Education Relationships across Three Continents: The Winds of Change,* ed. Guy Neave and Frans van Vught (Oxford: Pergamon, 1994), 9–11.

37. Guy Neave and Frans van Vught, conclusion to *Government and Higher Education Relationships across Three Continents: The Winds of Change,* ed. Guy Neave and Frans van Vught (Oxford: Pergamon, 1994), 309.

38. Geoffrey Walford, "The Changing Relationship between Government and Higher Education in Britain," in *Prometheus Bound: The Changing Relationship between Government and Higher Education in Western Europe,* ed. Guy Neave and Frans van Vught (Oxford: Pergamon, 1991).

39. See, e.g., University Grants Committee of Hong Kong, *Higher Education in Hong Kong: A Report by the University Grants Committee in Hong Kong* (Hong Kong: University Grants Committee, 1996).

40. Bray, *Educational Planning in a Decentralised System,* 99–114.

41. Iambakey Okuk, "Decentralisation: A Critique and an Alternative," in *Decentralisation: The Papua New Guinean Experience,* ed. R. Premdas and S. Pokawin (Waigani: University of Papua New Guinea, 1978), 21.

42. Constitutional Commission, Papua New Guinea, *NEC [National Executive Council] Endorse Changes to Provincial Governments System* (Waigani: Constitutional Commission, 1994).

43. Audit Commission, *Adding Up the Sums: Schools' Management of their Finances* (London: Her Majesty's Stationery Office, 1993); Hedley Beare and William Lowe Boyd, eds., *Restructuring Schools: An International Perspective on the Movement to Transform the Control and Performance of Schools* (London: Falmer, 1993); Rosalind Levacic, "Assessing the Impact of Formula Funding on Schools," *Oxford Review of Education* 19, no. 4 (1993): 435–458.

44. Blank, "Education Decentralisation," 13.

45. For an instructive view on this topic of patterns and changes in Australia, see Fenton Sharpe, "Towards a Research Paradigm on Devolution," *Journal of Educational Administration* 34, no. 1 (1996): 4–23.

46. Gretler, "Switzerland," 952.

47. R. Sack, "Benin," in *International Encyclopedia of National Systems of Education,* ed. T. Neville Postlethwaite (Oxford: Pergamon, 1995), 101.

48. D. C. Bernard and Le Thac Can, "Vietnam," in *International Encyclopedia of National Systems of Education,* ed. T. Neville Postlethwaite (Oxford: Pergamon 1995), 1063.

49. Bray, *Educational Planning in a Decentralised System,* 72–87; Ghai and Regan, *Law, Politics and Administration,* 233–283.

50. William T. Hartman, "District Spending Disparities Revisited," *Journal of Education Finance* 20, no. 1 (1994): 88–106; Linda Hertert, Carolyn Busch, and Allan Odden, "School Financing Inequities among the States: The Problem from a National Perspective," *Journal of Education Finance* 19, no. 3 (1994): 231–255.

51. Mark Bray with Kevin Lillis, eds. *Community Financing of Education: Issues and Policy Implications in Less Developed Countries* (Oxford: Pergamon, 1988); Mark Bray, *Decentralization of Education: Community Financing* (Washington, D.C.: World Bank, 1996).

52. O. E. Maravanyika, "Community Financing Strategies and Resources within the Context of Educational Democratization" (paper presented at the conference on Partnerships in Education and Development: Tensions between Economics and Culture, University of London Institute of Education, London, 1995), 12.

53. Richard F. Elmore, "School Decentralization: Who Gains? Who Loses?" in *Decentralization and School Improvement: Can We Fulfill the Promise?* ed. Jane Hannaway and Martin Carnoy (San Francisco: Jossey-Bass, 1993), 45.

54. Elmore, "School Decentralization," 46.

55. Juan Prawda, "Educational Decentralization in Latin America: Lessons Learned," *International Journal of Educational Development* 13, no. 3 (1993): 262.

56. See, e.g., Mitchell Tracy, "To Transfer Power or to Transfer Responsibility: Educational Decentralization in Venezuela," *International Journal of Educational Development* 17, no. 2 (1997): 153–154.

57. Prawda, "Educational Decentralization," 262.

58. See Edward B. Fiske, *Decentralization of Education: Politics and Consensus* (Washington, D.C.: World Bank, 1996).

59. Tyack, "School Governance," 1.

60. Elmore, "School Decentralization," 35.

Chapter 9

Beyond Schooling

Adult Education in Postcolonial Societies

Anne Hickling-Hudson

This chapter considers experiments in adult education in order to explore its role in national development, particularly in postcolonial societies that were until relatively recently part of the former European empires, attaining their independence only with the ending of World War II. Using a case study approach, the paper discusses lessons that postcolonial societies can learn from comparing the Caribbean experience of two approaches to adult basic and popular education. The main question is that of the potential—or lack thereof—of adult education to make a social difference, not in the sense of providing catch-up schooling on the cheap but in the sense of helping participants play a political role in challenging the structures of injustice, inefficiency, and dysfunctionality that are still entrenched in most societies. The case of Grenada, a microstate of about 90,000 people, helps to explore this because of the comparative analysis made possible by its socialist-oriented revolution (1979–1983), the overthrow of this process of change, and the return to a traditional path of market-led development in the past two decades.[1] The discussion in this chapter compares two models of adult education: one designed within the context of postcolonial socialist orientation, and the other tending to characterize postcolonial capitalism. It argues that in spite of some strengths both models have flaws and that we need to go beyond them to meet today's imperatives.

A postcolonial perspective pays particular attention to understanding the ideological power of the colonial historical context, how this power continues to influence material conditions across the globe, and how it is challenged. It explores the extent to which the colonial is embedded in the postcolonial, in economies, societies, and ideologies, and is acutely aware of contradictions. During the early postindependence period some Caribbean economies moved from the predominantly plantation model that had prevailed during colonial times to a model that sought modernization along lines advised by Western governments. There was the development of industries such as bauxite in Jamaica and Guyana, oil refining in Trinidad, and tourism and light manufacturing, assembly-type industries in virtually all Caribbean countries. In general, the modernization model has not served the region well. Though it has enriched elite minorities, it has brought about crippling national debt and widespread environmental pollution. Plantation-style agriculture remains the basis of sugar cane, banana, coffee and spice industries, and the region still suffers from overdependence on raw material exports at low prices, from dependence on imports (many of which could be produced regionally), from adverse terms of trade, and from the continuing underdevelopment of its productive potential. Social institutions, including education, reflect and reproduce economic underdevelopment.[2] Yet the beliefs of modernism, which characterized colonialism, are still entrenched—faith in Western "reason," the Western metanarrative, or all-encompassing story, that progress is brought about by the adoption of a consumerist economic model. Postcolonial ideas are challenging the modernist assumptions of this model and are helping to reshape the identity of ethnicities that have emerged from the diasporic movements started by European colonialism. Colonial-derived institutions are being analyzed, challenged, and modified, but at this point only partially, and often ineffectively. To the extent that education, and particularly adult education, falls into the category of an inappropriately modified institution, it is all the more urgent to recognize the limits and weaknesses of reform in order to move forward.

Literacy, Literacies, and the Postcolonial Context for Education

A theory of literacy and literacies embedded in a sociopolitical framework is necessary for analyzing issues in the practice and improvement of adult education. This section briefly outlines a literacy theory that facilitates comparison of the conservative, system-maintenance role of adult education with the role that it would play were it to make a significant difference in contributing to change in the society. The term "adult education" is used in this chapter as a comprehensive reference to compensatory or second-chance schooling and vocational training (basic education), and community education organized in voluntary structures accessible to all citizens (popular education). The term "nonformal" is not used, since not all components of adult education are nonformal in the sense of being informally structured, or outside of the formal education sector. The following questions are explored in this chapter. Do adult "basic" and "popular" education structures reflect and reinforce stratification? Or do they challenge it with a view to establishing greater democracy? Or perhaps some combination of these? Why is it so difficult to achieve democratic change in and through adult education? How might such change be pushed forward?

Scholars of literacy see it not as a unitary skill of reading and writing but as a set of discourses and competencies applied to tasks in a given culture. They demonstrate that people are initiated into these discourses in different ways according to their socioeconomic and cultural status and that literacies are practiced along a continuum that ranges from basic to critical and powerful.[3] It is inadequate to assume that literacy is, by its very nature, empowering. As Lankshear argues, for claims of empowerment to be clear they should spell out at least four variables: the subject of empowerment (person or group), the power structures in relation to which, or in opposition to which, that subject is being empowered, the processes through which empowerment occurs, and the sorts of outcomes that can or do result from being thus empowered. The outcomes of acquiring literacy competencies are not necessarily empowering—people can acquire disempowering or "subordinate" literacies rather than powerful or "dominant" ones.[4]

The model put forward by McCormack is useful in conceptualizing literacy as comprising at least four domains, each of which embodies a type of knowledge and a set of competencies.[5] The domain of epistemic literacy refers to the uses of written text associated with formal knowledge conceptualized along the lines of traditional academic disciplines. Technical literacy is interpreted as procedural knowledge in areas of practical action. A high degree of technical literacy in the modern workplace would demand competence in technology-based forms of creating, storing, and conveying information, although in developing societies technical and mechanical skills are still as economically important as the skills of information technology. Humanist literacy refers to the ability to construct narratives that enable individuals to conceptualize, explain, and draw strength from their cultural, social, and gender identities. Public literacy is seen as the ability to participate in the public sphere, understanding and being able to contribute to opinion, debate, political judgment, and the shaping of collective identity.

Putting this model of literacy domains into a framework of social class analysis would demonstrate that deeply stratified education systems such as those in the Caribbean and similar postcolonial societies in Africa and Asia inculcate these literacy domains into citizens along social class lines. Through schooling, people are placed on a certain track or channel in the educational hierarchy. Some are initiated by their education and upbringing into the content and techniques of dominant literacy in each domain, which is then used to justify their continuance in the elite educational channel (lined by the best schools and colleges) and their socioeconomic dominance and political power. Others are denied this initiation. Instead, they are shunted into the less adequate, often grossly underresourced and neglected educational channels that provide subordinate literacies, which are then penalized as being of inferior worth and status in the society.[6] The "literacies" of these economically poorer people may be functional for survival in the disadvantaged layers of society[7] but do not gain them any systematic access to the corridors of power or the levers of political change. This stratified model of literacies exists in any class-divided society, but the divisions are deepest, and the barriers to mobility highest, in postcolonial societies whose recent colonial history left them with maldeveloped and distorted economies subordinated in the world capitalist system. Across the Caribbean region, although functional literacy is widespread, it is at a minimal level for the majority (with the possible exception of Cuba). Adult education, with its catch-up schooling to a primary level and its vocational training for subsistence jobs, is too underdeveloped to provide adequate opportunity for adults either to gain the education necessary for well-paid employment and social mobility or to gain the political skills necessary to put consistent pressure for democratic change on the system. Instead, it entrenches them in their position in the lowest levels of the socioeconomic pyramid. Thus the social role of adult education is arguably largely a system-maintenance one.[8]

When a political process is serious about putting in place change with equity, it has to learn how to change the stratified nature of these literacies. In postcolonial experience it tends to have been socialist-oriented regimes that have taken this task seriously, since it has been in their interest to provide conditions, including more and better education, that will encourage people to support and defend revolutionary change.[9] The option of socialism in its twentieth-century form has been largely superseded, but seeking radical change remains vital for people marginalized by social injustice. This includes acquiring literacies that are powerful enough to enable them to critique negative social patterns and help to change them. From the perspective of striving for social justice, education should be contributing toward improving the material base by helping people to establish viable self and group employment projects and to demand from the state a commitment to development policies that are fair, sustainable, and accountable. It should be changing the contextual pattern of stratified channels of education and occupation so as to help reduce the hierarchical barriers that sustain an obscene level of inequality between social classes, strata, and gender groups. Politically, education should prepare people to assess the quality and performance of their political systems, to be aware of international changes together with the continuation of patterns of injustice, to hold politicians accountable, to discuss and experiment with problem-solving, both nationally and in alliance with international movements, to run for local and national political office on the basis of informed and creative platforms. To consider the potential of adult education for playing such roles, experiments need to be examined for their strengths and limitations, and new ones designed on this basis. This analysis needs the tools of literacy theory, but a political economy framework must also be clear.

Grenada's revolution, although brought to an end by fratricidal conflict that paved the way for invasion and overthrow by the United States in October 1983, left a social legacy of deep significance. The path of socialist transition tried there was an example of an alternative development model that made a start, and looked likely to succeed, in restructuring and revitalizing the stagnant economy, establishing better social services in health and housing, implementing legislation that sought new rights for disadvantaged groups, especially women and workers' unions, massively expanding education for adults, and forging communities and groups into alliances for improving community life and articulating a more culturally confident national vision. However, the weaknesses of the party structure, with its highly restricted membership and inadequate structures of public accountability, proved a poor foundation for supporting such changes and ultimately contributed to the collapse of the revolution.[10] After this experiment, the society returned to the regional model of dependent capitalism, which is aggressively advocated and endorsed by the United States and other governments of the North for developing countries. This neoliberal model opens the economy even further to "free" trade and foreign capital seeking cheap and minimally protected labor, maintains traditional export agriculture and tourism, and cuts back public sector employment and state services, including education. So far it has widened the gap between already impoverished majorities and wealthy minorities.[11] Like nearly all Caribbean people at the current juncture, Grenadians vote for the various parties that sustain the neoliberal model in a context in which there appears to be no other viable option but globalizing capitalism. This swing back to tradition is inevitable, given the general failure of socialist revolutionary leadership globally to have established a consistently participatory and viable change process or economic model. However, in Grenada, in spite of the overthrow of the revolution, the reversal of most of its programs, and the swing to conservative capitalism, the memory of its social achievements has not been erased, and this kind of memory may also be important in informing future political development in other parts of the formerly socialist world.[12] The next sections discuss the revolution's experiments in adult basic and popular education, and the strengths and limitations of these experiments compared to those in the neoliberal model.

Adult Basic Education: Structural and Curriculum Issues

Educators in the Grenadian revolution designed a completely new structure to provide adult basic education for impoverished people, mostly subsistence farmers and seasonal agricultural laborers. The new structure became known as the Center for Popular Education (CPE) and initially attracted 4,000 learners to enroll — about 24 percent of the approximately 17,000 adults assessed as ranging from nonliterate to minimally literate. Many postcolonial societies, including several Caribbean ones, have designed and implemented structures and programs of compensatory and vocational adult education, but there were unusual features in how Grenada's CPE tackled the problems of articulation of levels, access, and program design. First, a new and completely government-funded program was created, with one educational level leading to another (literacy, primary, secondary, postsecondary, and tertiary). Second, the program was intended to be equivalent to but not the same as schooling. It had a specially designed curriculum geared to adult interests and maturity. Third, each level from primary onward included compulsory vocational education and certification that prepared adults for jobs. Fourth, successful completion of the secondary level of the program could lead into scholarships for vocational or university education either at home, where the tertiary education level was being expanded, or abroad, most likely in Cuba, which was assisting the Grenadian government through tertiary education scholarships. And fifth, the political ethos of the program, illustrated in its newly designed textbooks, reflected the government's desire to contribute to the confident and creative reconceptualization of cultural and national identity. The impetus of the revolution led to a high degree of community participation by adult education students in organizing CPE programs and extracurricular activities in their neighborhoods.[13]

All of these new features disappeared with the demise of the CPE and the discarding of its textbooks after the collapse of the revolution and the U.S. invasion. Adult education was then taken over by a department within the newly amalgamated Grenada National College, and it was redesigned along the lines of the old traditions common to the rest of the anglophone Caribbean. The focus shifted to the preparation of fee-paying adults for retaking the annual secondary-school-leaving exams set by the Caribbean Examinations Council or the British General Certificate of Education. In 1992–1993, there were about eight hundred students in these programs, mostly people who had attended high school but failed or dropped out of their final exams. There is relatively minor attention given to the most disadvantaged adults, those who seek literacy and the primary level of education—the people who had received the most attention during the revolution. Adult literacy is now a minimal program involving fewer than a hundred learners, and with no provision of specially designed literacy materials. Adult primary education is no longer conceptualized as a special program but is the same as the "senior primary" (all age) program for adolescents who were denied entry to secondary schools. Only about ninety-eight adults a year sit for the "senior primary" school-leaving exams.[14]

The CPE, for all its innovative programs and its enrollment of more than four thousand adult learners, had serious weaknesses that should be examined if an effort is to be made to understand the lessons of the model in order to develop a more appropriate one in the future. There was a dropout rate of about two-thirds, a common feature of adult education programs throughout the world.[15]

This was partly because the CPE structure was larger and more complex than available government resources could handle efficiently, which puts immense strain on both volunteer teachers and economically impoverished learners. It may be that the revolutionary government should have considered making the CPE a statutory body with the independence to invite philanthropic assistance from NGOs and other bodies, and to seek funding from more countries than Cuba (which had helped with the production of materials). The complete dependence of the CPE on the revolutionary state made it vulnerable to being erased with a change of government.

But the CPE's failure to have more than average success might also have something to do with another, more qualitative factor — the new adult education structure did not challenge many of the entrenched, elitist assumptions of the colonial model of education because it did not even recognize them. Stratification is so entrenched that often even the most radical of educators do not know exactly how to change things. After all, they were socialized within the old, constrained metanarratives of Western education. Among these metanarratives are traditions of prescriptive rather than critical content, didactic pedagogy based mainly on written text, and the necessity of "schooled literacy" in sequential stages similar to those of the formal education system. This was as characteristic of the CPE as it was of the adult continuing education programs in Grenada after it. The CPE organizers put forward a Freirean-style "critical literacy" as their aim but were, on balance, unable to achieve this. In practice, the texts and exercises only rarely allowed for critical learner discussion of themes, and it is unlikely that the volunteer teachers were sufficiently developed to encourage a critical literacy approach outside of the texts. Although CPE teachers increasingly encouraged the use of the Creole language of the majority in oral interaction, the ingrained assumption underlying the program was that serious study necessitated the use of formal, high-status standard English, written in authoritative texts. This assumption, widespread across the Caribbean, means that most educators are reluctant to recognize and encourage as a basis for learning the discourses of orality in the vernacular languages of the majority. Although the picture painted in the adult basic education programs of the new cultural and national possibilities for revolutionary Grenada was inspiring in many ways, in several places the material went overboard toward prescriptive and annunciatory revolutionary propagandizing. The dangers in a politically prescriptive curriculum are that people's willingness to attend classes may be reduced if they find the ideology of curriculum content offensive or overdone, that a high dropout rate could in turn discourage volunteer teachers, and that a partisan curriculum may be discarded by subsequent regimes. Such factors could help to explain the high dropout rates of students and teachers during the revolution and the discarding of the CPE structure and materials after the revolution's collapse.

The CPE was like the new wine of radical content and participatory structures being poured into the old bottle of a restrictive educational philosophy particularly unjust for the majorities brought up in a folk tradition rather than a middle-class one. The philosophy assumes the necessity of formal, institution-alized education peddling a formalist type of scribal literacy. It may be that this explains the low attractiveness, relative to need, and high dropout rates common in adult education programs. Even if adults gain a certain degree of epis-temic and technical/vocational literacy through them, it is not likely to be the dominant literacy that enables them to surmount the barriers to social, political, and economic mobility, far less the powerful literacy that can empower them to make structural changes that would remove these barriers. The traditional model, which does not respect or build on vernacular "literacies," stultifies the radicalizing potential of new content and structures.

It is for this reason that I argue that popular education based on the develop-ment of political and cultural capacities in local communities, compared to adult basic education that provides individual catch-up schooling and job training, has more immediate potential to carry out some of the radicalizing aims outlined above. This is not to say that basic education is not necessary; it is to say that *it needs to be redesigned* within the nourishing context of a popular education structure. In the next section I lay the basis for discussing this by considering the strength and limits of popular education as it was experienced in Grenada.

Popular Education in Grenada: Strengths and Limitations

To what extent can the experiences of popular education contribute to trans-forming the power relations within civil society? Can participants take the op-portunities for growth offered to them by leaders who are usually middle class and "run with them" in creative ways that are not necessarily directed?[16] If they could learn this role, and help others to learn it, it would indeed have the po-tential to become part of a cultural revolution or the kind of "cultural action for freedom" that Freire describes.[17] Light is thrown on these questions by the at-tempt during the Grenadian revolution to mobilize a level of popular involve-ment in community education and social reform that had never been experi-enced in Grenada, indeed, in the Caribbean, before. This popular education movement was led by the New Jewel Movement (NJM), the revolutionary po-litical party from which most of the members of the government were drawn. The goal was to create a tradition of educated activism in community-based and workplace-based groups *outside of* educational structures that promoted formal and vocational knowledge, that is, outside of the CPE and vocational training programs of a quasi-school nature. Since the new groups involved a broad cross section of the population and combined political and educational aims, I shall refer to them as community associations and to their educational aspect as the popular education process. There were two categories of community associa-tion representing two types of activity. First, communities of citizens gathered to discuss and contribute ideas to local and national goals and policies of trans-formation. In this category were nationwide peoples' councils (comprising as-sociations called Workers' Parish Councils and Zonal Councils) and the peo-ple's budget process in which local communities all over the country met politicians and technocrats to help plan the national budget.

Second, interest groups worked for improvements in their particular group, on a national rather than a local scale. These were called mass organizations and were grouped around women, youth, farmers, and trades union members.[18]

The political role of the community associations was inextricably linked to their role in developing public and humanist literacy. They were the chief means of giving Grenadians a new voice in national affairs traditionally han-dled by the government. Through the associations, the broad population got in-creasingly pulled into an ongoing cultural revolution in an experiential way that involved affect as well as intellect.

"Humanist" Literacy and Cultural Identity

The role of the community associations in developing humanist literacy was to contribute to challenging traditional images related to social class roles, gen-der, and national identity and reshaping them in new ways. For example, the preconceptions about stratified economic roles started to be reshaped. Through the activities of the community associations, all became "workers." Middle-class professionals were seen as "intellectual workers," and they frequently met and interacted with manual workers in the same discussion groups. Political and social roles started to be reshaped in that people from different social class groupings had to learn how to interact—cooperating in identifying, prioritiz-ing, and carrying out tasks, listening to and communicating with each other. Most of the members of the community associations would not have attended elite schools and would therefore have been deprived of the chance to acquire skills in the public and humanist literacy domains that are provided for in the curriculum and extracurricular activities in elite schools. The community asso-ciations helped give them "public" and "humanist" knowledge, supplementing the education provided through the CPE, which had its main focus on the epis-temic and technical domains of literacy.

The community associations were the main locations in which people could engage with what it meant to develop a self-confident national identity in a global context. Through them, people experienced visits and speeches from famous in-ternational figures associated with political transformation, such as Jamaica's Michael Manley, Mozambique's Samora Machel, African-American activists Harry Belafonte and Angela Davis, and those associated with cultural trans-formation such as Barbadian novelist George Lamming and Guyanese poets Martin Carter and Robin Dobreau. They listened also to their leaders' explana-tions of international events, and they became associated with campaigns such as fund-raising to assist countries that had experienced natural disasters. In the collectives Grenadians worked closely and became friendly with many internationalist workers from other countries in the Caribbean and beyond, who had also joined these groups. National identity was increasingly expressed through the cultural activities of the community associations, especially the mass organizations, which were the chief vehicles in the communities for organizing cultural events that publicized the unprecedented outpouring of artistic expression in vernacular Creole poetry, drama, and music that was taking place.[19]

In the sphere of gender identity, it proved necessary to persuade some women as well as many men that women were entitled to equal rights with men. New images of women's social and political roles took shape through the community associations, especially the National Women's Organization (NWO), which at one time had some eight thousand members.[20] There was a long way to go before some men yielded to this challenge, but it started. The NWO played a key part in mobilizing women, regardless of traditional political divisions, to articulate and represent to the government the legal and social changes for women that they wanted. The uneven process of development showed in the fact that on the one hand, the government passed laws such as those institutionalizing paid maternity leave without loss of job, a minimum wage, and equal pay for women, and those that imposed sanctions on the sexual exploitation of women workers in an attempt to bring this to an end. On the other hand, sexism continued to exist in the NJM itself. Male double standards in sexual behavior was rife, and NJM men refused on several occasions to make any concessions to the women in consideration of their extra burden of domestic responsibilities. Further problems of sexism that had to be overcome were male reluctance to take on equivalent responsibilities for the financial support of all of their children, and their overwhelming predominance in employment and leadership positions.[21] Yet even the initial and tentative nature of the women's confrontation of many spheres of gender inequality, the fact little attention was given to reconceptualizing "masculinities," and the middle-class, didactic conception of leadership education could not blunt the real achievements and the powerful potential of the organization as one that could substantially increase the strategic power of Grenada's women to make changes benefiting the whole society.

"Public" Literacy and Political Participation

Community associations played an enormous role in developing public literacy. Reflection on their work facilitates a deeper and more complex conceptualization of this literacy region than that put forward by McCormack. Public literacy can be understood to have at least three major aspects. One aspect relates to the image of what political parties do and how they operate. Another is the development of participation, responsibility, and leadership. Another has to do with power relationships between social classes. The development of critical competencies in all of these aspects is what would lead to a high level of public literacy. In turn, it was envisaged that this would lead to a theoretical understanding of "the nature and structure of opinion, political judgement and political argument, the dynamics of political action, the forms of political consciousness, and the way a political community appropriates its past, projects its future, and conceptualises its historical continuity."[22]

In the anglophone Caribbean, the traditional political parties, shaped by the British model of parties as electoral vehicles, tend to be hostile to each other — in Jamaica, sometimes to the point of hundreds of murders being committed in the tense run-up to elections. In contrast to this neocolonial tradition of political socialization within competing and hostile party organizations, the mass organizations, citizens' councils, and worker education classes developed in Grenada sought to involve and unite broad cross sections of Grenadians in educational, social, and political activity regardless of their past or current political allegiance. Some mass organizations, such as the National Women's Organization, were more successful than others in achieving this goal. Other mass organizations were less successful in uniting a political cross section. The National Youth Organization and the Productive Farmer' Union, for example, had a reputation of consisting mainly of members and supporters of the NJM.

The community associations were the vehicles which achieved people's engagement in shaping change structures, speaking at meetings, becoming leaders. This affected both privileged and less privileged classes. For working-class and agricultural workers, the associations provided an opportunity for participation open to everyone, not just those who had registered as adult learners in the CPE. As far as middle-class people were concerned, the community associations pulled more of them into political activity than is usual in Caribbean multiparty systems. Workers' parish councils were regular meetings between NJM politicians, government officers, and local communities to discuss their needs, as well as to shape policy ideas in the context of social and economic developments in the nation. At one meeting, for example, the manager of Grenlec, the newly established state electric company, explained the problems of the old electric equipment and the policies of repair and development. At another, the government town planner explained some of the present regulations and future plans for land use. These representatives would then have to answer the people's questions, write down their concerns, and respond to any challenges. At each meeting, the NJM leader who was present would have to explain to the people what progress had been made on attending to matters brought up at a previous meeting. A workers' parish council meeting had the right to request in advance the presence of any government official it wished to question. Within a year, attendance at these meetings had grown so large that there was no hall big enough to hold the hundreds who wanted to get in. The workers' parish councils were then subdivided into zonal councils, the zone being a cluster of villages in a parish. At the high point of development, there were about thirty-six zonal councils.[23]

Although the government was willing to listen to and assist with local suggestions for change, funds were scarce, and it became clear that little could be achieved without a national volunteer effort. The importance of volunteer donations of time and effort was highlighted. Taken together, the CPE, the parish and zonal councils, and the mass organizations involved thousands of Grenadians in voluntary work and activities that not only started to raise their levels of education but also mobilized their hope and power to confront poverty and begin the long and complex process of working to eradicate it.

The political activity that took place in the parish and zonal councils and the mass organizations ensured the success of the PRG (People's Revolutionary Government) "People's Budget," unique and unprecedented in the Caribbean. This transformed the annual, traditionally secretive and technocratic exercise of making a national budget, controlled by the Ministry of Finance, into a planning operation that directly involved the participation of the masses of the people. Launched in 1982 and repeated in 1983, the People's Budget exercise was an extended procedure lasting about three months, during which the national economic plan was presented to communities all over the country for their study, criticisms, and recommendations. Then it was modified in the light of this interaction between politicians, technical advisers, and people:

> First, expenditure requests from all government departments were studied by the Ministry of Finance, headed by Bernard Coard. A preliminary draft was then submitted to the PRG Cabinet for discussion. This was followed by a period during which officials from the ministry went before the trade unions, mass organisations, zonal and parish councils to discuss the draft with them. The high point . . . was the national conference on the economy, which was attended by delegates from all the mass organisations. Breaking up into workshops devoted to specific areas of the economy, the delegates made detailed comments and criticisms on the draft proposals. The budget then went back to the Ministry of Finance for final revisions and then to the cabinet for approval. Finally, a detailed report was made to the people by the ministry and an explanation was given as to which recommendations had been rejected and why.[24]

Personal involvement in these activities is at the basis of my understanding of them as being a deeply educative process. I attended all of the large workers' parish council meetings in the parish of St. George's as well as many of the smaller zonal council meetings in our area to discuss local community matters and the budget draft. It was possible to merge anonymously with the crowded audience at the workers' parish council meetings and simply listen with interest to the proceedings in which government officials explained national programs, answered questions, responded to criticism, and noted suggestions from members of the crowd. But mere listening was not possible at the smaller zonal council meetings. These involved our neighbors and the people in our local district, and discussion was lively. We divided ourselves into small groups to read the budget proposals, questioned the visiting government representative about them, discussed them thoroughly, and contributed suggestions. In our small groups we had to help each other come to terms with economic concepts like gross domestic product, inflation rate, real growth, balance of trade, the social wage, and many others. At the end of an evening's discussion, there was a real feeling not only of having learned something significant about the country's economic processes but also of having learned it through dialogue with people from farming, fishing, and craft backgrounds with whom we did not often have the chance to interact. The dialogic nature of these kinds of meetings, and their interaction with text, make them examples of "literacy events" that raised the political competence of participants. Attending the National Budget Conference involved us further in the dialogue between people and government leaders. The climax was the realization that

> what was eventually passed as the national budget was the product of a unique three month process of consultation involving a broad spectrum of social interests and strata in which public technocrats were required to describe the economic situation in language accessible to the masses; and the people in turn were challenged to grapple with national development issues.[25]

The third major aspect of public literacy relates to power relationships between privileged and less privileged social strata. Community associations went beyond the CPE's circumscribed sphere of teaching and learning, in which middle-class teachers had, compared to the learners, demonstrably more power derived from their high-status cultural capital and their dominant role in shaping the CPE materials and controlling the pedagogy. A contribution of the community associations to public literacy, then, was their role in gradually reshaping this traditional, stratified relationship. The associations were a forum in which people who had been marginalized learned to recognize and value their contribution to shaping change and middle-class people started learning how to share power. The mutual interaction involved in community and political work was a process in which teachers and other educated volunteers learned immensely from the people they were teaching. A teacher involved in the process of community consultations on the preparation of the national budget had this to say:

> What I found out was that once you speak in a simple language the ordinary person is able to take part and participate and they have lots of good ideas. I think it was an eye-opener when you realized that these people who did not go to a secondary school and did not have a degree had such good ideas.[26]

Angus Smith, a young Grenadian who at the age of twenty-three was appointed Accountant General in the Ministry of Finance, described how his own development was enhanced by the process of interacting with community groups in discussing the People's Budget:

Like many others, I was surprised at the high level of consciousness of the people throughout the budget process, at their knowledge of general affairs and their eagerness for involvement. Numerous practical and useful ideas were constantly coming out, things that technicians like ourselves would never have thought about, things which gave us a much wider perspective of the issues and ideas in the minds of the people around the country. . . . The experience brought home to us the need for our technicians to have a much wider view of things, to look at the country from the widest possible angle, and not just from behind a desk. Everybody in our society has a viewpoint and we must pool all these together. For us it was genuinely exciting to be able to translate these budget figures that pass across our desks every day into the living reality of people's lives, and doing so learn more and more about how our people live.[27]

The community associations showed the importance of the language question. A wider range of middle-class people than literacy teachers were involved in them, and had to start to grope for an appropriate form of communication—perhaps not in the vernacular Creole, as some critics[28] felt should be the case, but at least in the sense of struggling to get away from jargon and elitist language. This was particularly evident in the People's Budget process. Ministry of Finance technocrats were given the responsibility of compiling a book that set out information about the economy and the budget issues for the community meetings at which they were to discuss the issues. They sought help from educators at the Teachers College in doing this, and the budget books were compiled only after these educators had helped them make the language more direct and clear. Using the books assisted the discussion groups, and the discussion groups forced Ministry of Finance facilitators to clarify concepts even further.

The community associations had immense democratic potential, but they also had problems associated with being at the beginning of a change process. They were to a large extent dependent on the leadership of the NJM, although local, nonparty leadership was starting to emerge. There was a tendency for many group leaders to expect members to listen to sessions based on prepared texts that sought to promote the messages of the revolution. A didactic communication process usually characterized occasions when the leaders sought to implement classes of "political education" based on their often inflexible images of socialist vision. This sometimes occurred in spite of the fact that the teachers gained a lot of knowledge from listening to the people with whom they were interacting in community work. In a paper analyzing some of the weaknesses of the NJM leaders, Charles Mills[29] argues that many of them seemed to regard their political analysis of the Grenadian situation as the only correct interpretation, based as it was on the "scientific thought" of Marxism. This argument holds that NJM philosophy, in spite of some strengths, did not take enough into account the contribution of local Caribbean thought and popular traditions. It failed to heed Gramsci's observation that a philosophy of praxis must, dialectically, both criticize and incorporate common sense and must base itself on common sense in order to demonstrate that everyone is a philosopher. "It is not a question of introducing from scratch a scientific form of thought into everyone's individual life, but of renovating and making critical an already existing activity."[30] If the NJM, as Mills suggests, failed in some important areas of activity to achieve this pedagogical dialectic, "this would inevitably have contributed to that distancing from the population, that partial estrangement from popular discourse and ways of seeing things, that is both the strength and potential danger of Marxism."[31]

This narrow social vision is one of the serious weaknesses of the modernist tradition, which assumes that a single prescriptive voice can (and has the right to) shape the answers to social problems. This afflicts both the "left" and the "right" side of politics, with the result that people have not been able to achieve grounded critique or strive for the powerful synergies of blending several visions of change. This insight throws light on areas of failure in many revolutions, including the one in Grenada. The Grenadian revolutionary party's internal conflicts over strategy, leadership structure, and pace of reform were not resolved because each faction, convinced it had the correct view, took this to the point of armed struggle against each other. Too late, Bernard Coard, one of the imprisoned survivors of the struggle, reflected on how the potential power of the community associations could have been further tapped:

> I have thought, often, over the past five years what would have happened if either the minority of the majority faction had taken the matter in a principled manner to the masses. And what better fora for doing it than the Zonal Parish and Workers, Women, Youth . . . Assemblies (and) meetings? With copies of all relevant minutes printed and distributed to the people; with representatives of both trends in the leadership putting their view forward to the people in the Assemblies . . . and being questioned and grilled by the people in return and hearing their views . . . what better way could there have been for resolving our differences?[32]

Comparing the revolution's popular education process with the traditional approach reverted to after the revolution throws light on the significant issues that need to be considered in striving for the improvement of popular education. The new community structures in the revolution sought what should be the basic thrust of popular education—to produce a reorganization of the social basis of power in the communities, and on this foundation, in the overall society. Marginalized people were educated into adopting more powerful ways of behaving politically—articulating demands, building organizations to carry out specified purposes, exchanging views with educated government officials and party politicians, holding these people accountable for the carrying out of their promises, uniting across the partisan divisions of the past. The associations reflected both the strengths of genuinely participatory learning and leadership and the weaknesses of didactic authoritarianism that were contradictory facets of the process. Their potential for change was weakened by flaws that contradicted the rhetoric of people's power, for example, by the fact that the accountability of national leaders was limited by a lack of electoral processes and by the secrecy of a Marxist-Leninist style centralist political organization.[33]

In traditional politics, electoral processes maintain a much more open, competitive government-versus-opposition structure that allows for a multitude of rival political parties (in Grenada there have been nine political parties jostling for power since the 1983 U.S. invasion)[34] but provides little potential for cooperation between adherents of these groups. Popular education is on a minimal scale rather than a national one. Instead of being multiclass, it is directed at the economically disadvantaged. It takes the form of consciousness-raising about specific, narrowly defined social problems and carries out some pressure-group advocacy through religious groups, drama groups, and a few fragmented women's groups. Limited political information giving, such as talks about current events, occurs in some groups, for example, in Grenadian groups funded by the Agency for Rural Transformation, an NGO that was one of the few institutions established during the revolution that survived. In general, there is minimal development of education that develops political and humanist literacy, encourages public and community voice, or facilitates collective political activism for change within the prevailing structure. The challenge for the future is to find a way of balancing an open electoral process with the kind of popular education that promotes participatory democracy—collective activism for meaningful community development on a national scale—and through this, the production of powerful, transformational knowledge.

Adult Education: Ways Forward

A comparative view of Caribbean experiments in adult basic and popular education in the Grenada revolution and in traditional polities provides postcolonial societies with clues about how adult education can seek ways forward out of the model that consigns it to being the minimalist educational channel at the bottom of the social hierarchy.

First, the context. What pushed forward educational change in the Grenada revolution was a combination of the political goals of a socialist-influenced vision and the correlating economic changes that increasingly required skilled and educated workers. Such workers are even more urgently required in today's context, as postindustrial changes and new trade blocs are making the neocolonial, dependent economic model redundant. A socialist-oriented path based on the classical model of revolution is not viable in most of the postcolonial world, but the answer does not lie in neoliberal capitalist structures such as the ones that continue in the Caribbean. Only a minority is highly developed for the new opportunities in the high-tech and global markets, and the majority remains in an exploited or marginalized position. Change is needed that draws on two strands of thought. One strand is based on social justice ideas searching for a mode of economic organization and work conditions that facilitate more widespread and sustainable employment, and greater political power, for those unjustly marginalized. Another strand foregrounds the ideas of economists stressing the urgent need for a creative and educated response from entrepreneurs and workers ready to seize new global, postindustrial opportunities in new enterprises and niche markets. Transforming a weak postcolonial economy depends on better articulation among the productive sectors, the governmental system, and the society's educational and research-and-development institutions.[35] It also needs a continuing and united pressure on the international economic system for changes in structures that maintain injustice for impoverished countries.[36] No section of the population can be omitted from the educational change that would be an integral part of this vision of interrelated political, economic, and cultural activism. Governments can be pushed into supporting the kinds of changes needed if articulate social groups among the population are informed and motivated enough to push them. Social alliances in civil society could more effectively engage in local action for change if they joined forces with global transformative movements such as those for ecologically sustainable development, feminism, literacy, and media reform. It is these kinds of activities that would be supported by a combination of basic and popular education, each informing the other.

Second, rethinking is needed about the structure and goals of adult education. What varieties of institutions and groups, in what arrangement relative to each other and relative to employment, would best form this combination of basic and popular education? Although details cannot be prescribed, the principles of an empowering adult education structure—basic education and popular education nourishing each other—will understand the importance of developing all of the literacy regions toward the "powerful literacy" that facilitates critique and activism. It will not simply provide instrumentalist education for practical subsistence needs or train semiskilled workers, which appears to be the main function of much contemporary basic adult education. It will provide a host of opportunities for *combining* an academic and a practical education with a sophisticated and activist general and political knowledge.

A Brazilian example of the kind of structure that could promote such education challenges the familiar shadow-schooling-for-subordinate-literacies approach of adult education in the contemporary Caribbean. The Cajamar Institute was founded by workers in a region of northeastern Brazil dominated by plantation agriculture. Paulo Freire was elected president of the council of this institute in 1986. He describes how workers managed to acquire a 120-room building that used to be a motel and created there the Cajamar Institute as an organization for the "training of the working class, peasants and the urban workers under their responsibility." Seminars and courses were offered to workers, some on a weekend basis. The staff included teachers from the working class and teachers from the university—intellectuals, says Freire, whose political choice coincided with their (the workers') choice, also, "who don't think that they possess the truths to give to the workers. Intellectuals who respect the workers' process of knowing and who want to grow up with the workers." The programs were oriented toward developing a critical understanding of Brazilian history and society, and particularly of the struggles of the Brazilian working class. Freire saw the institute as a kind of seed for a popular university that would be able to depart from the formalism of the traditional model and play the important role of being "a theoretical context *inside* of which the workers can make a critical reflection about what they do *outside* of the theoretical context." Worker institutes such as Cajamar could play the role of allowing men and women to achieve the distance from their daily work that facilitates studying society theoretically, "in order to understand the reason for the struggle and to make better methods for this struggle, and how to choose."[37]

Adult education organizers, to achieve such goals, probably have to assume that in the present political context of cash-strapped, timid, conservative governments, the best hopes of development lie outside of government control or interference, and beyond the limited horizons of narrow, instrumentalist adult education institutions, whether state controlled or private. Several excellent independent NGOs with an adult education component already exist in the Caribbean, for example, the Folk Research Center in St. Lucia and the Social Action Center in Jamaica.[38] They could form the basis of a potentially powerful alternative adult education movement. Existing and new groups could be strengthened by interacting with each other regionally for systematic knowledge exchange and development and by drawing on the support of international institutions and networks. This networking would be a source of empowerment and independence outside of the parameters of state control. Adult educators need, in addition, to develop their fund-raising skills in order to draw on the goodwill of wealthy strata, both nationally and internationally. Funds would be urgently needed to acquire or construct buildings for worker-peasant education, to pay for the development of libraries, staff, and resources, and to support the economic and cultural projects necessary for grounding adult learning in a material basis so as to meet the practical needs of people who have been marginalized. These needs include training in modern communications technology (especially the Internet) that can enhance local and international activist links. Training adult learners in the skills of radio production and community radio is, arguably, particularly important for impoverished communities that depend largely on the radio for information and entertainment.[39] Sometimes funds from unlikely sources can be used for genuinely popular education. USAID funds have been used in Central America to establish a community education program regionally organized across three Central American countries, Costa Rica, Honduras, and Guatemala. This program of education for participation

(PEP) aimed to develop among participants in local communities the knowledge and skills that would enable them collectively to use popular processes effectively in improving their life circumstances, for example, by (1) making claims on public resources and services and (2) engaging in local and national political life. A detailed evaluation led by Robert Arnove reported on the ways in which the program had achieved and sometimes surpassed its major objectives. It did this by working within the progressive Latin American tradition of popular education which, although not necessarily involving formal skills of reading and writing, nevertheless created a participatory education approach that enabled community organizations in impoverished and marginalized communities to define their problems and design and implement action strategies for tackling them.[40]

A third essential element of the way forward for adult education is that there needs to be a reconceptualizing of the literacy-and-education nexus. A fundamental task for adult educators is that of "rewriting literacy," that is, critiquing, restructuring and redeveloping the learning activities offered by educational institutions, whether basic or popular. The foundation is to understand the domains, the philosophical qualities and discourses, the social practices, and the dynamic potential of literacies. At the stage of development that characterized the CPE educators during the Grenadian revolution, educational transformation was seen as combining socialist ideals of highlighting worker/peasant roles and middle-class conceptions of epistemic literacy. The stage of development necessary now would have to expand equity goals to include educational respect for orality, folk discourse, and the "border crossing" flexibility that empower learners to experiment with a range of perspectives and learning experiences. Popular education of the type experimented with in the Grenadian community associations has strong potential for building humanist literacy as the foundation of a self-confident cultural identity, without which few challenges to negative aspects of tradition can be mounted. This is the first step toward rewriting epistemic literacy for most postcolonial countries in which the literacy of the folk roots has been subordinated. Fashioning epistemic literacy anew requires blending a people's literacy with postcolonial epistemological advances such as those contained in the work of C. L. R. James, Walter Rodney, and Paulo Freire. Validation of vernacular or Creole literacy for serious study rather than informal communication and entertainment is essential for this.[41] Another necessity is the pedagogy of participatory education characterized by the Freirean approach of the learner as subject rather than as the object into which predetermined content is "banked." Education as communication praxis, which combines the voices of learners and teachers into a cycle of social analysis, social activism, and reflection, must became part of the philosophical base of teachers and learners.[42] Yet another essential for rewriting literacy is the incorporation of a feminist perspective that challenges the older concept of integrating women in development (given the socially and ecologically disastrous impact of the present development model of international capitalism) and replaces this with a search for gender-sensitive and sustainable development.[43] Finally, reconceptualized literacies and pedagogy need not depend on the kind of text-based, school-imitative adult education model taken for granted in most post-colonial countries. Adult education can be creatively located as one component of economic, cultural, or political projects. It does not have to take the form of a unitary national system that shadows the centrally designed curriculum levels, texts, and examinations of schooling. Each project could have an education team that designs learning experiences related to the project, to participants' levels of education, their aspirations, and other needs that they may express. Methods and ideas do need to be coordinated between projects, but in such a way that there is an enriching relationship between local and central concerns in a search for effective socioeconomic development.

Conclusion

Nonformal and popular education, particularly in impoverished countries, has to facilitate the development of approaches for tackling material and cultural problems simultaneously. There is the need, for example, to balance culturally the growing power of global mass media with confidence in the best of local culture, design small-scale enterprises that suit both local and global niche markets, seize work opportunities with international concerns while protecting worker rights and the environment, and utilize governments and international agencies while not relying on them. Such goals require crossing boundaries of class, gender, and location in sharing and extending knowledge. They can be better sought by collective networks of like-minded people operating globally and locally. It is more necessary than ever to draw on and rework the best of the revolutionary changes implemented by Grenada's Center for Popular Education and the community associations in order to challenge the Caribbean tradition of separating dominant, exclusionary literacy from subordinate literacy. Structures of adult education need to be based on the shaping of material change, as well as on involvement in pressure-group politics and other types of political activism. They can promote an alternative, politicized curriculum, a deep exploration and appreciation of culture, alternative forms of assessment and recognition, and the integrated rather than marginal use of vernacular languages as well as English. Changes such as these can give people the confidence to demand the end of the stratification of education channels so firmly entrenched in societies of the "South." Considering the adult education experiments in Grenada helps us to draw from their strengths but also to see beyond them in the search for education strategies to overcome disadvantage.

Notes

1. Two in-depth studies of adult education in the Caribbean are those by Didacus Jules, "Education and Social Transformation in Grenada" (Ph.D. diss., University of Wisconsin, 1992); and Anne Hickling-Hudson, "Literacy and Literacies in Grenada: A Study of Adult Education in the Revolution and After" (Ph.D. diss., University of Queensland, 1995). Both writers are Caribbean educators who worked in Grenada during the revolution and have had extensive experience in education in other Caribbean countries.

2. The crises of development underlying Caribbean economies and institutions are discussed in Carmen Deere et al., *In the Shadows of the Sun: Caribbean Development and U.S. Policy* (San Francisco: Westview, 1990); and *Caribbean Economic Development: The First Generation,* ed. Stanley Lalta and Marie Freckleton (Kingston, Jamaica: Ian Randle), esp. pt. 4, "The Path Forward."

3. James Gee, "What Is Literacy?" and "Discourse Systems and Aspirin Bottles: On Literacy," in *Rewriting Literacy: Culture and the Discourse of the Other,* ed. Candace Mitchell and Kathleen Weiler (New York: Bergin and Garvey, 1991), 3–12, 123–138; Peter Freebody, *Research in Literacy Education: The Changing Interfaces of Research, Policy and Practice* (Brisbane: Griffith University, 1994); Daniel Wagner, "Literacy Assessment in the Third World: An Overview and Proposed Schema for Use," *Comparative Education Review* 34, no. 3 (1990): 112–138; Ian Winchester, "The Standard Picture of Literacy and Its Critics," *Comparative Education Review* 34, no. 1 (1990): 21–40.

4. Colin Lankshear with James Gee, Michele Knobel, and Chris Searle, *Changing Literacies* (Buckingham, Milton Keynes, U.K.: Open University Press, 1997), 63–79.

5. Rob McCormack, "Framing the Field: Adult Literacies and the Future," in *Teaching English Literacy in the Pre-Service Preparation of Teachers,* ed. F. Christie et al. (Darwin: Northern Territory University, 1991).

6. This argument is developed in detail in Anne Hickling-Hudson, "Literacy and Literacies in Grenada" 117–133. Figures showing the immense disparity in levels of formal educational attainment between the highly educated minority (about 3 percent) and the less schooled majority are set out in *Time for Action: Report of the West India Commission,* ed. S. Ramphal (Jamaica: The Press, University of the West Indies, 1993), 237.

7. A study that emphasizes the concept of the functional practice of literacies in local contexts is *The Social Uses of Literacy: Theory and Practice in Contemporary South Africa,* ed. Mastin Prinsloo and Mignonne Breier (Capetown: Sached Books/John Benjamins, 1996).

8. The system-maintenance role of adult education is explored in *Nonformal Education and National Development,* ed. John Bock and George Papagiannis (New York: Praeger), 3–20; Thomas LaBelle and R. E. Verhine, "Nonformal Education and Occupational Stratification: Implications for Latin America," *Harvard Educational Review* 45 (1975): 161–190; Robert Arnove and Harvey Graff, "National Literacy Campaigns in Historical and Comparative Perspective: Legacies, Lessons, Issues," in *Emergent Issues in Education: Comparative Perspectives,* ed. R. Arnove, P. Altbach, and G. Kelly (Albany: State University of New York Press, 1992).

9. Joel Samoff, "Education and Socialist (R)Evolution," *Comparative Education Review* 35, no. 1 (1991).

10. See Anne Hickling-Hudson, "Literacy and Literacies in Grenada," 254–256; Fitzroy Ambursley and James Dunkerley, *Grenada: Whose Freedom?* (London: Latin American Bureau, 1984); Gordon K. Lewis, *Grenada: The Jewel Despoiled* (Baltimore: Johns Hopkins University Press, 1987), chap. 7; Tony Thorndike, "People's Power in Theory and Practice," and Paget Henry, "Socialism and Cultural Transformation in Grenada," in *A Revolution Aborted: The Lessons of Grenada,* ed. Jorge Heine (Pittsburgh: University of Pittsburgh Press, 1991), 29–50, 51–82. Jamaica in the 1970s and Guyana from 1979 to 1990 were the other English-speaking Caribbean countries that experimented with variants of a socialist orientation. Economic and ideological weaknesses meant that the approaches could not be sustained. See "National Experiments: The Radical Options," in Clive Thomas, *The Poor and the Powerless: Economic Policy and Change in the Caribbean* (New York: Monthly Review Press, 1988), 210–237, 251–264.

11. In Grenada, GDP per capita in 1988 was US$1,346. The average for the Commonwealth Caribbean, excluding the Bahamas, was about $2,254. See Deere et al., *In the Shadows of the Sun,* 6.

12. Joel Samoff, "Education and Socialist (R)Evolution," 1.

13. Hickling-Hudson, "Literacy and Literacies in Grenada," chap. 6.

14. Hickling-Hudson, "Literacy and Literacies in Grenada," chaps. 8–9.

15. See Robert Arnove and Harvey Graff, "National Literacy Campaigns in Historical and Comparative Perspective: Legacies, Lessons, and Issues," in *Emergent Issues in Education: Comparative Perspectives,* ed. R. Arnove, P. Altbach, and G. Kelly (Albany: State University of New York Press, 1992), 287.

16. Carlos Alberto Torres, "Education and Social Change in Latin America," *New Education* 12, no. 2 (1990): 2–6.

17. Paulo Freire, *Pedagogy of the Oppressed* (Harmondsworth, U.K.: Penguin 1972), 81–82.

18. These adult education associations are described and analyzed by Didacus Jules, "The Challenge of Popular Education in the Grenada Revolution," in *Critical Literacy: Policy, Praxis and the Postmodern,* ed. Colin Lankshear and Peter McLaren (Albany: State University of New York Press, 1993), 133–166; Thorndike, "People's Power in Theory and Practice"; and Hickling-Hudson, "Literacy and Literacies in Grenada," chap. 7.

19. See Chris Searle, *Words Unchained: Language and Revolution in Grenada* (London: Zed, 1984).

20. David Franklin, "The Role of Women in the Struggle for Social and Political Change in Grenada, 1979–1983" (B.A. diss., University of the West Indies, Mona Campus), 73.

21. NJM Women, "Proposals for Women with Children within the NJM" (report for the New Jewel Movement, Grenada, 1983); Charles Mills, "Getting Out of the Cave: Tensions between Democracy and Elitism in Marx's Theory of Cognitive Liberation" (paper presented at thirteenth annual conference of the Caribbean Studies Association, Guadeloupe, May 25–27, 1988).

22. Rob McCormack, "Framing the Field," 32.

23. Tony Thorndike, "People's Power in Theory and Practice," 41.

24. Ambursley and Dunkerley, *Grenada: Whose Freedom?* 38.

25. Jules Didacus, *Education and Social Transformation in Grenada* (Madison: University of Wisconsin Press, 1992), 183, 327.

26. Ibid., 327.

27. Angus Smith, quoted by Chris Searle and Don Rojas in *To Construct from Morning: Making the People's Budget in Grenada* (St. Georges, Grenada: Fedon, 1982), 56–58.

28. Hubert Devonish, the major critic of the language policy of Grenada's revolutionary government, argues that although educators encouraged the vernacular Creole more than before, they continued to relegate it to the inferior status of oral expression (or, at the most, as being a bridge to learning high-status English) instead of promoting it as a serious medium of communication. Hubert Devonish, *Language and Liberation: Creole Language Politics in the Caribbean* (London: Karia, 1986).

29. Mills, "Getting Out of the Cave."

30. Antonio Gramsci, *Selections from the Prison Notebooks* (New York: International Publishers, 1971), 120.

31. Mills, "Getting Out of the Cave."

32. Bernard Coard, *Village and Workers, Women, Farmers and Youth Assemblies during the Grenada Revolution: Their Genesis, Evolution, and Significance* (London: Caribbean Labour Solidarity and the New Jewel Movement/Karia Press, 1989), 10–11.

33. Brian Meeks, *Caribbean Revolutions and Revolutionary Theory* (London: Macmillan, 1993), 153, 160–165.

34. See James Ferguson, *Revolution in Reverse* (London: Latin American Bureau, n.d.), 41–65.

35. Clive Y. Thomas, "Alternative Development Models for the Caribbean," in *Caribbean Economic Development: The First Generation,* ed. Stanley Lalta and Marie Freckleton (Jamaica: Ian Randle, 1993), 326.

36. Trevor Farrell, "Some Notes towards a Strategy for Economic Transformation," in *Caribbean Economic Development: The First Generation,* ed. Stanley Lalta and Marie Freckleton (Jamaica: Ian Randle, 1993), 330–342; and A. Sivanandan, "New Circuits of Imperialism," *Race and Class* 30, no. 4 (1989): 1–19.

37. Myles Horton and Paulo Freire, *We Make the Road by Walking: Conversations on Education and Social Change* (Philadelphia: Temple University Press 1990), 213–214.

38. Hickling-Hudson, "Literacy and Literacies in Grenada," 360.

39. The importance of radio education and development in the Nicaraguan revolution is discussed by Penny O'Donnell, *Death, Dreams, and Dancing in Nicaragua* (Sydney: Australian Broadcasting Corporation, 1991), 110–141.

40. Robert Arnove, *An Evaluation of the Program of Education for Participation (PEP)* (Washington D.C.: United States Development Agency, Bureau of Latin America and the Caribbean, 1989).

41. See Hubert Devonish, *Language and Liberation;* and Nan Elasser and Patricia Irvine, "English and Creole: The Dialectics of Choice an a College Writing Program," *Harvard Educational Review* 55, no. 4 (1985): 399–415.

42. Anne Hickling-Hudson, "Towards Communication Praxis: Reflections on the Pedagogy of Paulo Freire and Educational Change in Grenada," *Journal of Education* 170, no. 2 (1988): 9–38.

43. Peggy Antrobus, "Gender Issues in Caribbean Development," in *Caribbean Economic Development: The First Generation,* ed. Stanley Lalta and Marie Freckleton (Jamaica: Ian Randle, 1993), 144–159.

Chapter 10

The Political Economy of Educational Reform in Australia, England and Wales, and the United States

Edward H. Berman

The ideological underpinnings of the educational reform efforts in Australia, England and Wales, and the United States over the last fifteen years are strikingly similar despite these nations' differing political structures and the varied organizational patterns of their respective school systems. The common element linking reform efforts in all three locales is the attempt to weaken public control over education while simultaneously encouraging privatization of the educational service and greater reliance on market forces. Proponents contend that these reforms will enhance efficiency within individual schools while providing students with the requisite skills to make them more productive when they move into the workforce.

Undergirding these beliefs is the acceptance of the principle of economic rationalism, whereby decisions concerning national economic growth become the determining factor in all public policy decisions, including those affecting education. Issues of political democracy increasingly are defined as economic equations to be calculated and evaluated. Economic rationalism, in turn, draws on an updated version of human capital theory, which holds that contemporary economies can only be viable if based on the foundation of an educated, skilled, and technically competent labor force. There is a major difference between today's infatuation with this theory and its initial appearance in the 1960s, however. As Simon Marginson notes, "In the free market climate now prevailing, the emphasis is on private rather than public investment."[1]

This emphasis is hardly surprising, given the degree to which politicians of various persuasions in all three countries denigrate the public sector's role while ascribing almost mystical and liberating powers to the invisible hand of the market. This neoliberal commitment to market forces and minimalist governments has led to a reduction of state ownership of major resources and a concomitant increase in the privatization of services that once fell within the public domain, for example, railroads, utilities, and health care, to name the most obvious. The success of the Thatcher/Reagan agenda in shifting the balance between the public and private sectors decidedly in favor of the latter, and its durability even some time after its authors left office, helps to explain the concerted attack on continuing public control of the school, which after all is the epitome of the state sector.

The assault on the public sector has been accompanied by efforts to reduce government bureaucracies, which are accused of being both bloated and inefficient. Critics insist that centralized decision making has been too far removed from local communities, which need greater voice in matters concerning their well-being. Within educational systems this rationale has led to a managerial revolution that has reduced the authority of central bureaucracies while devolving responsibility (but not necessarily authority) for school activities down to the local level. This in turn has led to an increase in local control over school finances, more school-based decision making, and more active efforts to involve community groups in school affairs. A cursory examination of these new arrangements might lead to the belief that these efforts represent movement toward a more participatory and thus democratic form of school governance. This would be an incorrect reading of the situation, however.

In practice central authorities have successfully established policy outcomes without having devolved true power to the local level or community. Individual schools are indeed given greater autonomy in budgetary matters, but they have no voice over the size of the outlay they will receive; budgetary allocations continue to be determined centrally. At the same time schools are required to provide additional student performance data to central offices; increased student testing at various levels is seen as a way to accomplish this. There is greater movement toward centrally derived national curricula. But perhaps the most important issue that continues to be determined centrally is the very reason why schools need restructuring at all. The justification driving school reform efforts in Australia, England and Wales, and the United States is unambiguously instrumental, although this is now increasingly obscured by the current emphasis on the reform process. Educational reform proponents argue its necessity to ensure economic competitiveness in the global economy. Nothing more.

This shift in public policy discourse in a decidedly rightward and instrumental direction is not as seamless as its advocates hope nor can it mask numerous contradictions. As mentioned above, the neoliberal commitment to market forces and minimalist government has been accompanied by an increase rather than a reduction in the power of central governments over educational decisions. The Australian Commonwealth (federal) government in Canberra, for example, has assumed a role in educational policy unprecedented in that nation's history. The Thatcherite reforms in Britain have concentrated more power in central government ministries in London while considerably weakening the influence of the democratically elected Local Education Authorities. At the same time, central government fiat a decade ago seriously undermined the universities' traditional autonomy while simultaneously strengthening the oversight powers of a government-dominated regulatory body. Reforms in the United States have resulted from the advocacy of a coalition of corporate executives and state functionaries who maintain that America's continuing global hegemony rests on massive school restructuring. This has been accompanied by calls for a standardized national curriculum and the implementation of mandatory testing measures to ascertain the efficacy of the far-reaching reforms; both changes would seriously undermine the long tradition of local control of school affairs.

The effort to "downsize" the public sector while simultaneously lessening government oversight of market activity represents an effort to reinvent a nineteenth-century laissez-faire political economy characterized by a class of robust capitalist entrepreneurs assured of a supportive investment climate and a plentiful and pliable labor force. It also represents an effort to return to a time before the majority of citizens had access to such social welfare services as medical care and educational opportunity. The economic rationalist's argument concerning the primacy of material interests leaves little room for such issues as participation, equity, social justice, or even democracy. Educational reforms in Australia, England and Wales, and the United States shed considerable light on the degree to which, and the manner whereby, concerns over property rights have come to challenge, if not to supplant, concerns over citizenship rights. The abbreviated case studies that follow demonstrate how the latter have been subordinated to the former in current educational policy formulation, and they demonstrate as well how an overarching ideological proclivity has played itself out so similarly despite the considerable cultural and political differences that characterize these countries.

The Federal Government Forces Australian Educational Reforms

The individual states traditionally played the major role in Australian education; however, during the last twenty years there has been a marked increase in the involvement of the Commonwealth government in educational activities at all levels, especially in higher education. There has also been a decided shift in the issues that have engaged educational policy makers during the last generation. Until about 1970 the issue of state aid to nongovernment (particularly confessional) schools was both recurring and contentious, and a regular feature in electoral campaigns. By the late 1960s the Labor Party had joined the other major parties in agreeing to provide state aid for nongovernment schools, thereby obviating this once divisive issue.

The accession to power in 1972 of the Labor Party was followed by increased attention to educational matters. Initially this centered on the creation of a (Commonwealth) Australian Schools Commission. The impetus to overhaul at least some aspects of the system was furthered by the commission's publication the next year of a report authored by respected academic Peter Karmel. The Karmel Report focused on the underdeveloped secondary system and the steps required by government to make it more accessible to underrepresented segments of the population. Another Commonwealth initiative was the creation of the Curriculum Development Centre, whose primary function was the production of curricular materials that might one day be incorporated into a unified national curriculum.

The issue of educational access was less featured at the Commonwealth level after the 1975 defeat of the Labor Party and its replacement by the more conservative Liberal-Country Party coalition government. The coalition was more concerned with schooling outcomes than with who entered the system. This shift of emphasis was attributable to a combination of ideology and a deteriorating economic situation. Youth unemployment was particularly disturbing. The government of Prime Minister Malcolm Fraser charged that Labor policy had provided additional school places (at great expense), but students leaving school were unfit to assume a productive role in the labor market. This led the government to reduce federal expenditures for education while increasing pressure on the schools and the colleges of Technical and Further Education (TAFE) to refocus their programs so that graduates would leave school with better skills and appropriate workplace attitudes. The government drew its justification largely from a 1979 report entitled *Education, Training, and Employment.* This study recommended a more vocationally oriented school focus, especially at the secondary level, together with a rationalization of the postsecondary system, which had grown significantly since the end of World War II.[2]

Later that year the Commonwealth launched its School-to-Work Transition Programme, which was jointly funded and administered by the states. It focused on the upgrading of young people's technical and vocational skills. Two years later the government turned its attention to the higher education sector. Numerous Colleges of Advanced Education were closed or incorporated into other institutions, the emphasis on teacher education and liberal studies was reduced considerably, and institutions were put on notice that scientific, technical, and applied fields would be favored in future funding cycles. This initial government reorganization of the higher educational system was noteworthy for its lack of consultation with members of the academic community; it also set the pattern for the significant changes in the tertiary sector that continue to this day.[3]

It was not until 1983 that the Labor Party again formed the national government in Canberra, where it remained in office through 1995, by which time major structural changes had been effected in the Australian education system. The transition from the coalition government to the Australian Labor Party did not signal an abrupt change in the direction of national educational policy. Indeed, what is so striking about the changes in Australian education in the last quarter century is the shared view by politicians of both major parties concerning the direction that educational policy should take. Although the two major national parties do not always agree on particulars concerning education (e.g., public support for private schooling), it was soon clear that the Labor Party of the mid-1980s shared its predecessor's view that the Australian educational system needed to be more closely aligned with national economic requisites and the global capitalist market.

Recession and the resulting faltering economy were major issues when Labor returned to power in 1983. Inflation was high; unemployment was rising, a result both of deregulation efforts and the depressed price of mineral exports; the foreign debt was mounting rapidly because of the decline of exported manufactured goods. The government was being pressured by corporate interests to improve the economy while simultaneously curbing the influence of the nation's powerful unions. The deteriorating economic situation led both the Commonwealth and state governments to reduce expenditures. Although the Labor government had encouraged increased outlays for education during its tenure in the early 1970s, it found itself in the paradoxical situation the next decade of continuing its advocacy for educational expansion while reducing considerably government's contribution to the education sector.[4] This awkward situation was glossed over by the government's decision to direct educational policy in a manner intended to realize greater productivity from schools at all levels. It was argued that the education sector must be more closely aligned with a national economic strategy that emphasized technologically driven exports to augment the undependable natural resource sector.

The reasoning was quite straightforward. The strong linkage between national economic well-being and education necessitated expansion of the educational system so that more students could gain the requisite skills enabling them to contribute to economic growth. The schools as structured had insufficiently developed students' human capital. Given the country's economic plight, however, educational institutions had to produce better results with fewer resources. Policy makers insisted that this was possible because of the notoriously lax managerial practices that characterized schools and particularly the postsecondary system.

In 1986 the Business Council of Australia published a report critical of the nation's educational system. Students' basic skill levels had declined, the report claimed, and the schools needed to give greater attention to workplace issues and less to nonproductive academic subjects and custodial care. The skills decline was attributed to the system's rapid expansion and to progressive educational practices. Similar arguments were advanced by a network of conservative think tanks, especially the Centre for Policy Studies and the Institute of Public Affairs. The fact that these claims were not substantiated by empirical data in no way lessened their impact on the public's perception of an inadequate education system. It also suited government officials hopeful of coupling school and workplace more tightly. Basic skills needed to be better taught and testing instruments devised to measure exactly how school personnel were performing. In this way schools could be held accountable while the business sector would be assured of getting an ample supply of skilled workers. Prime Minister Bob Hawke's Labor government championed these arguments in the mid-1980s. In practical terms this led to efforts to increase school retention rates, especially at the upper secondary level, with the launching of the Participation and Equity Programme, which sought to encourage students to stay in school while equipping them with marketable skills.[5]

By 1985 Hawke, the former leader of the Australian Council of Trade Unions, had moved noticeably rightward; Labor Party policies became increasingly pragmatic under his leadership. He reassured the business community that the unions could cooperate with management and that reconciliation between the two sides was not only possible but necessary to address the nation's considerable economic problems.[6] The key issue was clear: how to guarantee the conditions to make possible capital accumulation while ensuring labor peace and worker reliability. An overhauled educational system was deemed crucial to greater labor productivity. At the same time, this system needed better direction so that it was more aligned with national economic priorities. In political terms this necessitated a revamping of the education bureaucracies in Canberra.

Hawke moved swiftly after winning a second term in 1987. The Commonwealth Department of Education was integrated into a newly created Department of Employment, Education, and Training, headed by former finance minister John Dawkins. This merger, coupled with the fact that Dawkins was a senior minister with strong views concerning education's role in the production of human capital, signaled that the educational system would be a centerpiece in the government's efforts to address the nation's economic problems. Further evidence of this can be drawn from the fact that a large number of senior staff in the new department were trained economists.[7]

Dawkins wasted little time in implementing policies to bring the educational system, at all levels, into line with national economic policy. He tapped a former secretary of trade who had served under him in the Ministry of Finance to run the newly integrated department. The autonomous Australian Schools Commission was abolished, as was the Commonwealth Tertiary Education Commission. This latter body had long served as a buffer against the politicization of higher education while being vigilant in defense of institutional autonomy. The functions of these two commissions, together with those of the Australian Research Council, were transferred to a newly created National Board of Employment, Education, and Training, whose brief was to provide policy advice to the minister of the new "mega" department—Dawkins. This new organizational arrangement was designed to provide the mechanism whereby greater control over educational and research decisions could be exercised by one ministry.

It needs to be noted in passing that the Commonwealth government's role in educational reform initiatives far exceeds its direct financial contribution to the system. This is the case because the majority of the funds allocated by the individual states for educational provision are encumbered, for example, for teacher and staff salaries, transportation expenses, supplies, and the like. Moneys earmarked for educational purposes from Commonwealth funds, on the other hand, can be directed toward whatever program/concern the granting agency perceives to be valuable at the time. Such discretionary funds, consequently, can play a significant role in both influencing educational decisions at the state and local levels while at the same time attracting funds from other sources that might otherwise be directed to basic educational services.

Perhaps the most striking changes in Australian education since the mid-1980s have been at the tertiary level. It is here as well that we see most clearly the effort to corporatize the educational infrastructure while aligning it with national economic priorities. The government's plans for higher education were contained in the 1988 white paper, *Higher Education: A Policy Statement*. This document called for the closure of smaller institutions or their amalgamation with those larger and more financially viable; the incorporation of the entire higher educational network into a single unified system controlled by the Ministry of Employment, Education, and Training; and the institutionalization of procedures to make research funding from the Australian Research Council more competitive. Annual appropriations and recurring moneys would be determined by a central authority, calculated on the basis of various performance indicators, measures of institutional efficiency, student completion rates, and a loosely defined series of evaluations and reviews of individual sites. Taken together, these several measures would provide the data to enable Canberra planners to assess each institution's degree of efficiency/effectiveness.[8]

Meanwhile, Commonwealth appropriations for tertiary education were reduced and savings derived from a combination of internal budgetary reallocations and institutional amalgamations. Funds realized from these savings were designated for the national research pool, to be available to individual institutions on a competitive basis. Part of the reduction in government appropriations was to be offset by a sharp increase in student fees after 1987.[9]

Concomitant with the sweeping changes initiated by the recommendations in this policy document, there has been a growing effort to market Australian higher education overseas, thereby attracting additional fee-paying students into the system. To a considerable extent this strategy has been successful.[10]

The Dawkins approach has explicitly encouraged the tertiary sector to form alliances with business and industrial concerns, while at the same time establishing a formal mechanism, the Council for Business/Higher Education Cooperation, to enable the private sector to exert its influence on Australian higher education. Not surprisingly, the decade since the implementation of the Dawkins plan has been marked by a significant increase in the growth of business and administrative studies within the tertiary sector and a corresponding decrease in more traditional liberal arts and educational studies enrollments.[11]

The issue of state aid to private (particularly religious) schools has become potentially divisive once again. From the mid-1970s the Commonwealth government increased funding for all private schools. Both major political parties agreed that the main criterion for school aid should be economic resources— or their lack—and that children attending private schools should have the same level of support as did children in the public sector. The Commonwealth government(s) correspondingly took greater responsibility for subventions to private schooling, while the public sector remained almost the exclusive responsibility of state governments. More recently this issue, which initially focused on school resources, has been conflated with the debate over the relative merits of public versus private schooling. Critics of the public sector argue that government domination of the schooling process not only has failed to halt a decline in academic standards, thus hindering economic growth and individual social mobility, but has removed as well the locus of control from its rightful site—the local community and stakeholders. The solution to this problem calls for the removal of government from the educational system and its replacement by a market-based system featuring school vouchers that would enable parents to choose their children's school. The work of John Chubb and Terry Moe is regularly cited in support of this approach.[12]

The reforms enacted in the 1980s established new, more instrumental norms for the Australian educational system during the subsequent decade. Changes at the primary and secondary levels generally resulted from pressures emanating from Canberra *and* at least concurrence at the state level concerning the need for revamped practices. The movement from policy statement to implementation can be tracked in the effort to establish a national curriculum that delineates eight "areas of knowledge" that students must master before being credentialed. The debate over this proposed change coincided with demands by state education departments for greater accountability from individual schools. Compulsory testing at various levels is a common way to achieve this end. Disagreement over the issue of testing to determine school results is rife, as evidenced by the controversy in the state of Victoria when the General Achievement Test was introduced in 1994. There a coalition of principals and teachers objected to government's efforts to quantify school outcomes by means of paper-and-pencil "objective" multiple-choice tests, arguing, among other things, that such instruments failed to measure what was actually learned in school and that these testing devices further disadvantaged students for whom English was not the first language. The head of the Victorian Secondary Principals Association noted that the state government was using these tests for narrowly economic purposes, while hoping "to be able to measure performance and to demonstrate—by producing figures—that people are getting value for money."[13]

A more rancorous debate was widely reported in early 1994 when the Commonwealth government issued its rankings of the nation's universities. The publication of this first "league ladder" was an outgrowth of the 1988 white paper on higher education, which argued that national economic considerations dictated a more streamlined, focused, and productive higher education system. The publication of the government's quality review involved more than institutional prestige: Funding formulas determined by Canberra rewarded those universities highly ranked while penalizing those judged of lower quality. This was a high stakes endeavor indeed. The University of Melbourne, for example, was ranked in the top tier and received some $7.5 million, while the sixth-ranked (bottom tier) University of Southern Queensland received only some $300,000 in Commonwealth funding. The message was unequivocal: Funding from Commonwealth sources is to be directly related to research productivity as determined by politicians and policy planners in Canberra.[14]

In March 1996 the Labor government lost the national election to a conservative coalition made up of the Liberal and National Parties. The new government wasted little time in making known its agenda for Australian education. Prime Minister John Howard announced plans to reduce considerably the expenditures for higher education authorized by the former Labor government; he also proposed a 12 percent staff reduction at the federal Education Department. Major tuition increases for university programs expensive to mount, in the sciences, engineering, and technology subjects, have been imposed. The ironic outcome of this action has been a significant reduction in the number of applicants to these programs and the acknowledgment by several institutions that they have lowered their admissions criteria to compensate for the dearth of qualified students.[15]

The Thatcher Educational Revolution in England and Wales

The government of Prime Minister Margaret Thatcher passed the omnibus Education Reform Act during the summer of 1988, after prolonged and acrimonious debate.[16] The provisions of this act cannot be separated from the larger Tory economic and social agenda that Mrs. Thatcher initiated after forming her first government in 1979. Government heralded its bold efforts in both education and the economy in the language of expanded consumer choice and as representing a return to traditional values, while simultaneously increasing its reach through centralized government agencies. The Thatcherites rolled back the state's regulatory oversight function in the economy, while encouraging the invisible hand of the marketplace, unencumbered by government interference, to restore Britain's fiscal health and to play a greater role in social welfare provision, including schooling. The Thatcher years were marked by an assault on the public sector, the concomitant privatization of various sectors of the economy, and a severe reduction in the influence of British unionism. These steps were part of a larger effort to arrest the advances made since 1945 by women, minorities, and the working class.

The 1988 Education Reform Act (ERA) was in some ways only the culmination of a series of efforts by the Thatcher government to align the educational system with its socioeconomic agenda. Beginning in the early 1980s the government began to reduce the autonomy of the nation's universities through a series of severe budgetary reductions. These measures were mild indeed compared to the fate awaiting the universities at decade's end. In 1983 the government abolished the Schools Council, which had long given advice on curricular matters. In March 1987 the Conservative-dominated parliament passed the Teachers' Pay and Conditions Bill, which effectively abrogated teachers' bargaining rights, which had been enshrined for years in a cumbersome but workable group called the Burnham Committee.[17]

For Thatcherites the fiscal crisis of the state was in large part due to too much state intervention in economic matters, which had the effect of discouraging the entrepreneurial spirit required to build an economy for the next century. This situation was exacerbated by the fact that the broad range of welfare programs in place since 1945 had made the British too dependent on the state, with the effect that the requisite traits required to compete in the new global economy had been vitiated. Successful entrepreneurship in the nineteenth century was not hobbled by an organized working class. Mrs. Thatcher was determined to destroy the strong British union movement.

The 1987 Teachers' Pay and Conditions Bill was passed despite a threatened nationwide teachers' strike, which was not long in coming. When schools across the country were disrupted, the government used the opportunity to direct parental anger against the union movement, while simultaneously deflecting attention from the teachers' professional concerns, which were many and very real. Mrs. Thatcher's action was calculated to engender hostility toward British middle-class unionism, thereby reducing the movement's appeal and legitimacy in the eyes of many affected parents.

Government's decision to push ahead with the ERA the next year needs to be located in the context of the hostility between the Thatcherites on the one side and the teachers unions and Local Education Authorities (LEAs) on the other. The Thatcher governments were dedicated to a reduction of union influence in general, which they perceived as a brake on economic growth. The long-standing and close relationship between unions and LEAs, especially in urban areas, was fortuitous in some ways for the Thatcherites, since it provided a convenient way for them to undermine union influence while simultaneously attacking a cumbersome bureaucracy that, according to government's repeated pronouncements, had grown unwieldy and no longer served its constituents' interest. Shortly after the passage of the ERA the Inner London Education Authority was dismantled and its many responsibilities distributed among smaller LEAs and to individual schools. This largest and most innovative of all English LEAs was closely associated with the British Labour movement. Labour-dominated LEAs, like the ILEA, tended to spend more than wealthier councils on social and welfare services for their constituents, both out of ideological commitment and because of the fact that urban areas, like that served by the ILEA, are home to heavy concentrations of low-income and minority groups. The Thatcher government contended that the ILEA mismanaged its funds while emphasizing "progressive" educational activities for low-income and minority children at the expense of more traditional curricular content and appropriate educational practices.

The ERA reduced significantly the power of the Local Education Authorities, which had controlled education at the primary and secondary levels for most of the twentieth century. Schools can now "opt out" of LEA control either by vote of their governing bodies or, under certain conditions, by a minority vote of parents with children in the school. Schools choosing this route can seek grant-maintained status from the central Department of Education and Science, thereby enabling them to be self-governing without government oversight while ensuring their financial security. A corollary to this governance model is that schools can be selective in their admissions procedures, admitting some students while rejecting others. Opponents argue that such procedures are little more than an attempt to reintroduce selective education, which had been on the decline nationwide, in a surreptitious manner.[18]

The opting-out model serves to reduce union domination of the teaching cadres (schools can select their teachers with less regard to union regulations), while at the same time reducing the LEAs' influence. Finally, the opting-out principle in theory makes available more school choice and greater diversity through the establishment of private alternatives and the quest for nongovernmental funding to support them.

The outline and rationale for the opting-out principle was mooted in a 1986 pamphlet entitled *Whose Schools? A Radical Manifesto,* issued by the Hillgate Group, a well-connected clique of right-wing intellectuals and free marketeers. *Whose Schools?* maintained that schools should be owned by private trusts, released from oversight of the LEAs, and funded directly by the central government. Teachers would then be employed by individual schools, freeing the process from meddlesome government interference. It was argued that school choice—a manifestation of individual freedom—could be expanded in this way while control over educational matters could be reclaimed simultaneously from state functionaries and restored to the people.[19]

The establishment of City Technology Colleges was seen by the Thatcher government as another way to afford more choice while moving both toward school privatization and a solution to Britain's economic malaise. This effort was already under way when the ERA became law in 1988, but provisions in the act did ensure future central government support for the initiative. These new institutions grew out of the belief in government circles that the educational system put too little emphasis on technical education, which needed to be upgraded if the country's economic performance were to improve.

In the autumn of 1986 Secretary of Education and Science Kenneth Baker announced the creation of a network of twenty secondary-level technical colleges, to be funded by the central government. The next spring Tory policy makers revealed another aspect of their platform when they approached representatives of the Industrial Society, a consortium of influential industrial and financial institutions, with the suggestion that a large part of the funding for these colleges should come from those interests most likely to benefit—British industry and commercial interests. The response was far from enthusiastic. Society representatives urged the government to reconsider its plans, seeking ways instead to help their members strengthen the relationships that many already had achieved with inner-city schools. This course of action held little appeal to Tory policy makers, however, since it failed to accomplish two important items on their agenda: the undermining of the LEA's influence in educational matters and the privatization of the educational system at large.[20]

Secretary Baker's enthusiasm for this concept was reinforced by a trip to the United States, where he toured a number of so-called magnet schools in several large cities. Just as these magnet schools provided specialized programs for secondary-level students, so too would the City Technology Colleges perform a similar function. A major difference, however, was that the English school would be independent of local oversight, since they would have their own governing boards and would not report to the LEAs. The other major difference was that Baker and colleagues hoped that in the future major funding for these institutions might yet come from the private sector; American magnet schools, on the other hand, remained within the public sector.[21]

Another key provision of the ERA was the development of a common core curriculum for all schools in England and Wales and the establishment of a mandatory system of national assessment (testing) to be administered to children at the ages of seven, eleven, fourteen, and sixteen. The government's rationale was that a national curriculum would for the first time establish uniform and quantifiable standards to replace the more subjective evaluation measures generally used, thereby ensuring all children comparable educational experiences. Teachers were wary of this step, seeing in it yet another effort to undermine their influence in and control over various aspects of the school process. At the same time there was concern that a national curriculum, and its corollary testing instruments, represented yet one more step in the process of centralizing educational decision making while decreasing local involvement in educational matters, rhetoric to the contrary notwithstanding.[22]

By the mid-1990s it was apparent that the new education legislation had not achieved all the goals that its proponents had claimed when it was introduced. The expanded curriculum was in many instances unwieldy and impossible to implement by teachers who were asked to accomplish more without a commensurate increase in resources. At the same time there was growing concern that the emphasis on assessment was leading to a situation whereby testing was increasingly driving classroom instruction.[23] An outgrowth of the emphasis on assessment and school outcomes was a directive that gave the education secretary authority to take over a failing school from the LEA. The decision to determine which schools did not measure up to standard was given to the standards and effectiveness unit. It is hardly surprising that this action was strongly opposed by the teachers unions when it was introduced by the Conservative education secretary. Nor is it surprising that it was also opposed at the time by the opposition Labour Party and its supporters in local government. It is noteworthy that after sweeping to power in May 1997 the "new" Labour Party of Prime Minister Tony Blair quickly sought to extend its authority to intervene in the affairs of schools that did not measure up to standard.[24]

The impact of the 1988 Education Act on tertiary education was dramatic. Three major changes were advocated for the university system: (1) the abolition of academic tenure, (2) the replacement of the central funding agency, the University Grants Committee, and (3) differentiation among universities in a manner designed to concentrate research in several institutions while simultaneously substituting a competitive, grant system of payment in lieu of the traditional formula whereby all institutions received a lump sum.

Secretary of Education and Science Baker announced that no academic appointments would be tenurable after the government filed its Bill in Parliament in November 1987. The universities were subsequently charged to rewrite professorial contracts in keeping with the new government policy, a step necessitated by the fact that the universities' charters and statutes theretofore governed such issues as tenure and conditions of service.[25]

Throughout much of the twentieth century universities in England and Wales were insulated from undue political influence in their internal affairs by the presence of the University Grants Committee, a nonstatutory body that played a key advisory role in the allocation of the government's share of the universities' budgets. The role of the university vice-chancellors was central to the committee's deliberations. The University Grants Committee was replaced by the University Funding Council which, unlike its predecessor, reports directly to the secretary of state for education and science. The influence of academic personnel has been severely reduced accordingly, while that of government and segments of the corporate and financial sectors have increased commensurately. In keeping with the Tories' free market approach, proponents of educational reform in the late 1980s argued that British universities relied too heavily on the national exchequer and that in the future they needed to pay more of their costs. To accomplish this, the government simultaneously reduced appropriations for the universities while encouraging them to seek outside research funding. The government institutionalized a ranking system whereby universities would be rewarded according to their research productivity. These assessments occur every four years and are coordinated by the Higher Education Funding Council for England. Government funding is directly related to these quadrennial assessments and, unsurprisingly, they are perhaps even more controversial today than when they were introduced a decade ago.[26]

Universities costituted only part of the tertiary sector, albeit the most prestigious part. The 1988 ERA provided for the restructuring of twenty-eight polytechnical institutes. The polytechnics were responsible to local county councils from their founding in the 1960s. The ERA created the Polytechnics and Colleges Funding Council which, like its new university counterpart, reports directly to the secretary of state for education and science. This council, which allocates funds among these institutions, draws its members largely from the industrial, commercial, and financial sectors. This new arrangement is intended to centralize control of the polytechnics and colleges in the hands of the government, while eliminating the influence exerted by the local Labour-dominated urban councils. It is also seen as a way to enable the corporate sector to influence the technical side of higher education in a manner that will push the institutions to support the needs of British commercial and corporate interests, whom the Thatcherites see as crucial to the revival of the nation's economic fortunes.[27]

The 1988 Education Reform Act was the most significant piece of educational legislation passed in Britain since the 1944 Butler Act, which expanded the secondary system and made it more accessible to groups formerly excluded. The corollary to the Butler Act was the significant post-World War II expansion of higher education, whose primary beneficiaries were members of those groups most underrepresented earlier: women, minorities, working-class youngsters. The 1988 act has engendered much bitter hostility, from school practitioners, academics, and lay commentators. On the other hand, it has also won considerable praise as a farsighted and innovative approach to school reform that breaks the traditional mold while promising significant structural reform of a system that has seemed almost impervious to more than superficial alteration. Counted among the ERA's most vocal supporters are American researchers John Chubb and Terry Moe, whose ideas about school reform have been influential both in Australia and in the United States.

In a 1992 review they were enthusiastic about the changes effected by the 1988 act, especially in their analysis of several City Technology Colleges.[28] These seem to be singled out less for what they had actually accomplished when Chubb and Moe visited in 1991 than by the fact that they afford an alternative to the public system and receive private support. The authors were favorable as well about the opting-out concept and the resulting grant-maintained schools. Again, the reasoning for this support appears to be grounded more in ideology than in outcomes.

Chubb and Moe argued that opting-out "attacks the system head on" (as if it were the enemy). At the same time they maintained that these schools achieve better results (a claim not documented), despite the fact that they do not receive more funding than LEA schools. This is inaccurate; grant-maintained schools do receive supplemental funding. It is clear from their analysis that they were attracted to the reforms contained in the 1988 act because they reflected their own views concerning schooling in the United States. According to them, schoolchildren in both locales would be better served by a reduction of educational (and governmental) bureaucracies and state involvement in schooling, more choice in school selection, and greater involvement of market forces in the educational system. Taken together, these factors would unleash unrealized student potential to contribute both to individual mobility and to national economic productivity. The reforms effected by the 1988 act in Britain seem designed to address these concerns. They feel that the United States does not seem to be as responsive to such innovative measures.[29]

State and Private Interests Push Educational Changes in the United States

Contemporary school reform efforts in the United States date from the issuance in 1983 of a spate of reports highly critical of the nation's educational system. The reports appearing then and over the next few years were sponsored by a variety of organizations—federal government agencies, consortia of corporate and financial institutions, major foundations. Their overriding message was similar despite the varied sponsorship: The security of the United States was threatened by a deeply entrenched economic crisis, and the nation's educational system was central to reversing this situation and restoring the nation's economic prosperity. Some commentaries even suggested that the schools had caused the downturn, but past errors could be overlooked if the schools would now reform themselves by recognizing the realities of the new global marketplace and the productivity needs of American capitalism. Translated, this meant that school reform should proceed in a manner that would provide youngsters with those skills and traits required to make them more productive upon graduation into the labor market.[30] The Reagan administration strongly supported such sentiments, and joined as well in the rising chorus of criticism that located the nation's economic malaise in the schools rather than in corporate sector practices.

American education is the responsibility of individual states; the federal government's contribution totals less than 10 percent of annual school appropriations. Accordingly, the influence both of Washington, D.C., agencies and of such external agencies as corporations and foundations is limited to advice and exhortation, while state legislatures retain statutory authority over educational matters. (There are several obvious exceptions to this generalization, however, the significant role played by the federal government in extending educational opportunities for handicapped children being one.) Having said that, however, I need to note that this diffused educational decision-making process has never been immune from external pressure groups seeking to organize schools in one manner or another. In the present context the series of reports issued by federal government agencies, corporations, and major foundations helped to establish the parameters of debate within state legislatures regarding the direction that school reform should take. One brief example serves to illustrate how this process operates in the United States.

Tennessee governor Lamar Alexander had been importuning his legislature to overhaul the state public education system even before the appearance of several education reports in 1983. His argument was that the perilous state of the Tennessee economy necessitated foreign investment, but what sensible investor, foreign or domestic, would locate a manufacturing or assembly plant in a state with such a lamentably poor educational system and consequently low level of worker literacy? Members of the state legislature initially ignored the governor's admonitions, that is, until the first education reports appeared in 1983. Alexander then brandished them at balking legislators, arguing that the reports of these prestigious corporate bodies, foundations, and federal agencies reinforced his contention that the state educational system needed overhauling to stimulate the economy. The Tennessee legislature soon passed a bill mandating a thorough restructuring of the state's public education system.

The perspective of the organized corporate community was unequivocal concerning what was required of American schools. A representative report, *Investing in Our Children: Business and the Public Schools,* was issued in 1985 by the Committee on Economic Development, a consortium of the nation's largest corporate and financial institutions. This document noted, among other things, that "economic productivity and the quality of education cannot be separated" and that "human resources [education] are more important than physical ones." Data collected by committee staffers confirmed suspicions about the inadequacy of America's human resources, especially compared to the nation's main European and Asian competitors. The solution to this problem was clear. What was required was "nothing less than a revolution in the role of the teacher and the management of the school."[31]

A key figure in the corporate offensive to overhaul the nation's schools was David Kearns, one-time head of the Xerox Corporation and an influential member of the Committee on Economic Development. In 1991 he became assistant secretary of education in the Bush administration. Several years earlier he had coauthored a book entitled *Winning the Brain Race: A Bold Plan to Make Our Schools Competitive.* Many of the Bush administration ideas concerning education were drawn from this volume and from John Chubb and Terry Moe's *Politics, Markets, and America's Schools,* which appeared in 1990. Kearns's perspective on the role of American schools, together with his reasons for encouraging reform, was succinctly summarized in a 1987 newspaper interview in which he denounced the public schools as "a failed monopoly" guilty of producing workers "with a 50 percent defect rate."[32]

In September 1989 President George Bush summoned the fifty state governors to discuss the problems besetting the educational system. The outcomes from that meeting formed the basis for the Bush administration's proposals for school reform, which appeared in April 1991 under the title *America 2000: An Education Strategy*. Pulling together the conferees' generalities into a coherent strategy was one of the initial responsibilities of President Bush's new secretary of education, former Tennessee governor Lamar Alexander.

Some of the proposals in America 2000 were as widely accepted as they were innocuous, for example, the suggestion that all children come to school ready to learn. Opposition began to mount around other aspects of the Bush administration's proposals however, particularly those that would encourage privatization of large parts of the school system, and related choice and voucher provisions. Proposals for a national curriculum and mandatory standardized testing of schoolchildren also engendered opposition.

The Bush Education Department included among its staff a group of neoconservative intellectuals who increasingly despaired of effecting meaningful reform within the public system. The most vocal of these, Chester Finn and Diane Ravitch, occupied influential policy positions within the bureaucracy. Ideas and proposals regularly filtered into the department from a handful of like-minded associates, many affiliated with one of the Washington, D.C., conservative think tanks (e.g., the American Enterprise Institute, the Heritage Foundation, the Hudson Institute). John Chubb and Terry Moe were among this group, as was Denis Doyle, who coauthored with David Kearns the 1988 book *Winning the Brain Race*. Doyle's perspective on the role of schooling in America is both straightforward and representative of the advice influencing educational policy during the Reagan and Bush administrations. In a 1994 article he wrote that "public schools must learn to take a page from other organizations' books and squarely address the question of productivity." Competition, private initiative, reduced government involvement, market forces: these are the factors required to get America's schools back on the right track.[33]

The Bush administration made several attempts to effect school reform directly, despite the traditional limits on federal educational initiatives. In mid-1992 the New American Schools Development Corporation announced its first grants for innovative educational projects. The corporation had been organized as a private foundation by business leaders at President Bush's behest, and its funds solicited from private sources. The corporation's chief executive was a former secretary of labor in the Reagan administration. The Bush team had less success with another effort, however, the so-called 435+ Bill, which would have given $1 million to any of the nation's 435 congressional districts supporting innovative school programs.

The Clinton administration's approach to schooling issues did not repudiate all its predecessor's educational initiatives. This is understandable in view of the fact that as governor of Arkansas in the late 1980s, Bill Clinton played a key role in drafting documents that subsequently formed the basis for President Bush's America 2000 plan. Clinton's staff merely refashioned the Bush program, adding something here while removing a particular emphasis there; the Goals 2000: Educate America Act was signed into law by President Clinton in 1994. Taken together, this act, the pronouncements of influential policy advisers such as Secretary of Labor Robert Reich, and the president's emphasis in his second inaugural address in January 1997 leave no doubt concerning the rationale for school reform as seen from the White House. The nation's schools need to be aligned with the realities of the new global economy. Or, as succinctly summarized by Clinton's assistant secretary of education in 1995, "The primary rationale . . . for the concern about human capital [within the administration] was based on the ever-present challenges of international economic competition and a changing workplace."[34]

This official emphasis on aligning education more closely with the nation's human resource needs enjoys, unsurprisingly, strong support within the American corporate and financial community. Representatives of these sectors have long attempted to influence the direction of American public education. It is only recently, however, that its concerns have been so coincident with official educational policy statements as articulated both at the federal and state levels. The past fifteen years has also seen a notable increase in the amount of direct private involvement, as well as investment, in the public school system. In late 1989, for example, the RJR Nabisco Foundation announced a $30 million program to identify and fund a number of innovative schools, private as well as public. Fifteen schools were selected during the next three years and awarded grants up to $250,000 annually as part of Nabisco's Next Century Schools Project. Secretary of Education Lamar Alexander served on the project's advisory board, as did his deputy David Kearns and the latter's coauthor, Denis Doyle.[35]

The twelve years of the Reagan and Bush administrations were marked by regular official pronouncements denigrating the role of government agency while sanctifying that of the marketplace and the private sector. It is not coincidental that this same period saw a notable increase in direct corporate penetration of the nation's public school system. Corporations have been involved in public education for at least fifty years, although this involvement was always peripheral. The post-World War II efforts to promote Junior Achievement are well-known, as are more recent programs featuring corporate-school "partnerships," for example, Chicago United, the Atlanta Partnership, the Boston Compact, and the more ubiquitous Adopt-a-School program.[36] Contemporary efforts, however, are marked by both a quantitative increase in program proliferation and a heightened degree of receptivity by local school districts that either welcome private sector initiatives into the educational process or simply take them for granted, as if they are just the "normal" way to operate a school system. Examples abound, but mention of several will illustrate the magnitude of the issue.

The operation of the Chelsea, Massachusetts, school district was taken over in 1989 by Boston University, a private institution that was awarded a ten-year contract by the state to manage the public system in this greater Boston neighborhood. The initial management team was organized by a former ranking Education Department official in the Reagan administration. The record since the initiation of this arrangement has been mixed: Standardized test scores have not risen as project administrators predicted, student dropout rates continue to be high, and staff morale has plummeted. University administrators dismiss these findings, contending that the entire process has been politicized by "liberal" elements that have their own agenda.[37]

A clear example of the degree to which the private sector has penetrated public education is offered by the chequered story of Whittle Communications, a unit of the Time-Warner media conglomerate. In the late 1980s entrepreneur Chris Whittle began to distribute posters to public schools, gratis. They featured barely disguised advertisements for various products in addition to uplifting slogans. Several years later Whittle started a national news program anchored by student announcers. His corporation agreed to provide participating districts with some $50,000 worth of telecommunications equipment in exchange for agreement from individual schools that they would make the program mandatory for all students. This highly controversial Channel One venture featured a daily ten-minute news program, several minutes of which were given over to advertising products especially appealing to youngsters. Revenues to finance this expensive project came from fees paid by corporate sponsors who wanted their products beamed to student audiences.

This venture was less ambitious than Whittle's subsequent effort to influence America's public education system. The Edison Project envisioned the creation of some 1,000 for-profit schools by the year 2010. The tuition charged to attend would approximate that spent by the average American school district per child each year, roughly $5,500. Edison spokespeople boldly announced that this venture would afford students a superior education, bolstered by the latest technological advances and low student-teacher ratios. They envisioned an assured funding source after the passage of federal legislation establishing a voucher system, which would give parents credit that could be exchanged for educational services at any school, public or private. The Edison Project received a significant boost in 1992 when Yale University's president resigned his position to become its chief executive officer.

The list of those involved in this project reads like a Who's Who drawn from the staff of the Reagan and Bush Education Departments. Chester Finn was a close adviser to Whittle during the project's formative stages; he is perhaps best known as a strong proponent of choice and voucher schemes. Other advisers included John Chubb and Terry Moe. The whole scheme began to unravel in 1994 with the collapse of Whittle Communications, the project's primary financial supporter. Allegations of financial mismanagement and tax irregularities over a number of years served to undermine investor confidence in the entire undertaking. Project staff increasingly tried to distance themselves from Chris Whittle's now embarrassing and overly visible involvement in daily affairs. The project was subsequently scaled back drastically; current efforts concentrate on operating a handful of schools in several locations.[38]

Yet another manifestation of corporate efforts to penetrate the public school system is represented by the appearance during the last decade of a host of management companies seeking to administer entire school districts. The number of these "contracting-out" arrangements, whereby the administration of public districts become the responsibility of for-profit corporations, has increased considerably. Among the best-known companies are the Nashville-based Alternative Public Schools and the Minneapolis-based company Educational Alternatives Inc. These arrangements have frequently proved contentious and litigious as school districts in Baltimore, Maryland, and Hartford, Connecticut, for example, have alleged that the management companies have failed to increase student "outcomes" (i.e., learning) as promised or have reneged on contractual agreements to provide greater capital expenditures on school facilities.[39]

Concluding Observations

The similar processes followed to overhaul national education systems are perhaps easiest to observe when comparing events in Australia with those in England and Wales. The Australian decision to abolish the Commonwealth Tertiary Education Commission and locate its responsibilities in a ministerial portfolio parallels the British decision to terminate the University Grants Committee and replace it with the University Funding Council, which also is subject to political control. These efforts were part of a larger undertaking to reduce institutional autonomy while concentrating greater power in government ministries.

After 1945 the British government invested massively in higher education expansion; the reasons for doing so were both ideological (an extension of limited social goods to those groups formerly lacking access to these) and instrumental (economic growth necessitated a more highly educated labor force). The Australian government embarked on a similar course twenty years later. Today both countries find themselves with dramatically expanded higher education networks that politicians in particular argue are poorly articulated with national economic requisites. The British government has been very explicit on this point recently. A February 1997 policy statement by the Department of Education and Employment noted that "there is a limit to how many extra graduates the economy can absorb before the increased productivity they generate starts to decline."[40] The solution? Implement measures to force students out of higher education by (1) increasing fees while simultaneously (2) reducing the number of available places by slashing university budgets, which has the effect of forcing institutions to so reduce staff that student intake must be curtailed. Those students most affected by this approach are those least able to afford the increased tuition fees or accelerated loan repayment scheme. A 1997 report commissioned by the Higher Education Funding Council for England spoke to the implications of this approach. It noted, in part, that "the wealthiest quarter of young people . . . have about a 50 per cent chance of becoming undergraduates before the age of 21. The poorest quarter . . . have an 11 per cent chance."[41] A variation on this theme was captured by an Australian student leader when, commenting on his government's proposals (since enacted) to raise fees selectively in 1995, he observed that soon "postgraduate education . . . [will] rapidly become the preserve of the rich."[42] An earlier ideological commitment to afford greater opportunity to those most disadvantaged has been subordinated to instrumentality in today's market-driven socioeconomic environment. It is clear that the current Australian government will continue this trend. The British Labour government of Tony Blair will do so as well, as was made clear with its mid-1997 announcement that tuition would be imposed at the nation's universities for the first time by 1999.[43]

It is at this juncture that recent proposals for higher education funding in the United States warrant mention. After noting education's importance for U.S. national security, President Bill Clinton in his January 1997 State of the Union message to Congress advocated a tax deduction of up to $10,000 to offset college tuition fees. Families spending such sums on their children's higher education are likely to pay to send them to college whether they receive a tax break or not. Clinton's proposal is a subsidy for middle-class parents whose children will benefit from the status conferred by a university degree. It is of course to state the obvious to note that few working-class families can afford to pay $10,000 per annum for their children's higher education.[44]

In all three nations attention focuses on such issues as a national curriculum and regular testing to measure reform's efficacy. The language of reform is regularly couched in metaphors drawn directly from the workplace. This was also the case early in the twentieth century, at least in the United States, when F. W. Taylor's principles of scientific management, which were designed for the factory floor, were widely heralded as the panacea for the nation's educational ills.[45] In today's reform climate schools are told to develop performance indicators, their detailed plans should be as efficient and effective as they are quantifiable, and rewards should be reserved for those who successfully enhance productivity (i.e., student learning). Alliances between school districts and business interests are encouraged in all three locales, as is school privatization, which is frequently conflated with efforts to introduce choice and/or voucher programs. Higher educational institutions are also strongly encouraged by public agencies to seek additional corporate sponsorship. Policy advice regarding the appropriate direction for educational reform is provided by a network of right-wing think tanks, which emphasize a reduction in government services and ownership and the enforcement of market discipline in school matters. In Australia these sentiments are regularly articulated at the Centre for Policy Studies, the Institute of Public Affairs, and the Centre for Independent Studies; in England such advice emanates from the Centre for Policy Studies, the Institute of Economic Affairs, and the Hillgate Group; while in the United States these pronouncements are the common mantra at the Heritage Institute, the American Enterprise Institute, the Hudson Institute, and, most recently, the Brookings Institution.

Reductions in social welfare expenditures in all three societies have coincided with robust economic expansion at the national level and a correspondingly inequitable distribution of wealth. A result of this, in the United States at least, is a notable increase in the number of children living in poverty, now generally agreed to be one in four. Schools and universities are asked to perform the same (or additional) services with reduced budgets; the outcomes are predictable. For example, a 1994 survey in Australia's second-largest state, Victoria, found that "about 70 per cent of government schools have scaled down education programs because of funding cuts." At the same time 17 percent had either abolished or reduced remedial educational programs.[46] The dismantling of the Inner London Education Authority in 1989 had a similar impact on those populations most vulnerable and in need of special services, for example, a reduction in English as a Second Language programs for newly arrived immigrants whose mother tongue was, say, Chinese or Bengali. Such issues appear to be of little concern to growing numbers of parents who can afford private education for their children or lobby to have public subsidies, in the form of vouchers, subvene their children's private schooling.

Educational reform efforts in Australia, England and Wales, and the United States can only be understood in the context of concerted efforts by neoconservatives to return their nations to more halcyon days before a newly emergent middle class of women and people of color began to demand their citizenship rights. These efforts coincide with attempts to roll back the influence of the state and replace it with a form of "free market" competition that neoconservatives imagine existed at an earlier, less complicated time. In educational terms this leads to calls for greater competition among educational purveyors as a mechanism to enhance consumer "sovereignty," more choice in school placement, the minimization of government influence in educational provision, and the simultaneous maximization of market principles. Evidence to support the superiority of such arrangements is readily available in the form of reputedly "objective" social science research data as collected in, say, Chubb and Moe's *Politics, Markets, and America's Schools.* Jim Carl recently summarized the issue succinctly: "Central to New Right school reform is the construction of an ideology that equate[s] public education with bureaucracy and inferior schools and associated private education with the marketplace and superior schools."[47] This equation does not augur well for those groups who, especially since 1945, have relied on the public sector, including its schools, to gain a voice in their nation's affairs. The right wing's continuing assault on and downsizing of the public sector can only impede the advance of those traditionally marginalized.

Notes

1. Simon Marginson, *Education and Public Policy in Australia* (Cambridge: Cambridge University Press, 1993), 40.

2. Committee of Inquiry into Education, Training, and Employment, *Education, Training and Employment* (Canberra: Australian Government Printing Service, 1979).

3. For specifics, see Marginson, *Education and Public Policy in Australia,* chap. 6; and Susan Lee Robertson, "The Corporatist Settlement in Australia and Educational Reform (Ph.D. diss., University of Calgary, 1990), passim, but especially chap. 5.

4. Marginson, *Education and Public Policy in Australia,* 85, notes that Commonwealth spending on education fell from 9.6 percent of the total budget in 1974–1975 to 6.8 percent in 1986–1987, both periods when Labor was in power in Canberra. Similar decreases are noted in state spending as well. In 1975–1976 the proportion of states' budgets committed to education was 28.8 percent; in the 1986–1987 budget year the figure was 19.8 percent.

5. For specifics on the Participation and Equity Programme, see Robertson, "Corporatist Settlement in Australia," 175–180.

6. This modus vivendi between management and labor is generally known in Australia as the Accord. Its consolidation is seen by many as an unambiguous effort to more closely integrate Australia into the rapidly expanding global economy. See Robertson, "Corporatist Settlement in Australia," passim.

7. Don Smart, "Reagan Conservatism and Hawke Socialism: Whither the Differences in Education Policies of the US and Australian Federal Governments?" in *Education Policy in Australia and America,* ed. William L. Boyd and Don Smart (London: Falmer, 1987); and Marginson, *Education and Public Policy in Australia,* 26.

8. Grant Harman, "Institutional Amalgamations and Abolition of the Binary System in Australia under John Dawkins," *Higher Education Quarterly* 45 (Spring 1991): 176–198; David Mahoney, "The Demise of the University in a Nation of Universities: Effects of Current Changes in Higher Education in Australia," *Higher Education* 19 (1990): 455–472; Neil Marshall, "End of an Era: The Collapse of the 'Buffer' Approach to the Governance of Australian Tertiary Education," *Higher Education* 19 (1990): 147–167.

9. Lesley Vidovich et al., "Australian Higher Education Policy and Practice: Effects of Economic Rationalism and Corporate Managerialism" (paper presented to the Canadian Society for the Study of Higher Education, Calgary, June 1994); Jan Currie, "The Emergence of Higher Education as an Industry: The Second Tier Awards and Award Restructuring," *Australian Universities Review* 35, no. 2 (1992): 17–20.

280 *Edward H. Berman*

10. The number of fee-paying students increased from 622 in 1987 to 20,219 in 1991. Marginson, *Education and Public Policy in Australia,* 186.

11. Between 1979 and 1990 course completions in business/administrative studies in Australian higher education increased by 130 percent while those in arts/humanities/social sciences increased some 46 percent. During the same period enrollments in education studies declined by 4 percent. Marginson, *Education and Public Policy in Australia,* 131.

12. Cf. Sheena MacLean, "A Private Obsession with Class," *The Age* (Melbourne), 24 May 1994, 14; John Chubb and Terry Moe, *Politics, Markets, and America's Schools* (Washington, D.C.: Brookings Institution, 1990).

13. On the curriculum debate: Cherry Collins, "Curriculum and Pseudo-Science: Is the Australian National Curriculum Project Built on Credible Foundations?" (unpublished manuscript, Murdoch University, January 1994). The quote over the testing debate: Sheena MacLean, "Teachers' Unease Grows over GAT and Testing," *The Age,* 19 April 1994, 15.

14. Sheena MacLean, "Fissure over a League Ladder for Universities," *The Age,* 11 March 1994, 17; Sheena MacLean, "Quest for Quality Splits Tertiary Ranks," *The Age,* 15 March 1994, 16; Sian Powell, "Low-Ranked Universities Slate Quality Report," *Australian* (Canberra), 16 March 1994, 21.

15. Geoffrey Maslen, "Australia's New Government Pushes for Cuts in Spending on Colleges," *Chronicle of Higher Education* 3 May 1996, A45; Geoffrey Maslen, "Applications to Australian Universities Drop," *Chronicle of Higher Education,* 7 February 1997, A47.

16. The educational systems of England and Wales are subject to the same political forces and administrative arrangements; those of Scotland and Northern Ireland are both politically and administratively separate.

17. For specifics on the events leading up to passage of the Education Reform Act, see Denis Lawton, ed., *The Education Reform Act: Choice and Control* (London: Hodder and Stoughton, 1989); Geoff Whitty, Towards a New Education System: The Victory of the New Right? (London: Falmer, 1989).

18. Phillipa Cordingley and Peter Wilby, *Opting Out of Mr. Baker's Proposals* (London: Education Reform Group, 1987); Geoffrey Walford, "The Privatisation of British Education" (paper presented at the meeting of the Comparative and International Education Society, Cambridge, Mass., 1989); "ILEA Plan Secret Job Cuts," *Time Out,* 25 March–1 April, 1987, 8–9; "Keep ILEA," *Economist* 30 January 1989, 15–16.

19. Members of the Hillgate group had close contacts with several of Prime Minister Thatcher's inner circle, especially onetime minister of education and science Keith Joseph. The most influential members of the group included Caroline Cox, Roger Scruton, John Marks, and Stuart Sexton.

20. Edward Vulliamy, "Industrialists Attack City Colleges," *Guardian,* 16 March 1987, 1; and Ian Nash and Barry Hugill, "Industrial Giant Spurns Baker CTC Approach," *Times Educational Supplement,* 27 May 1988, A1.

21. Stuart Maclure, "A Radical Proposal for English Schools," *New York Times,* 17 January 1989, education supplement, 57–61.

22. Geoff Whitty, "The New Right and the National Curriculum: State Control or Market Forces?" *Journal of Educational Policy* 4, no. 4 (1989): 329–342; Susan Chira, "A National Curriculum: Fairness in Uniformity?" *New York Times,* 8 January 1992, A1, B9.

23. David L. Silvernail, "The Impact of England's National Curriculum and Assessment System on Classroom Practice: Potential Lessons for American Reformers," *Educational Policy* 10, no. 1 (March 1996): 46–62.

24. Donald MacLeod, "Hit Squads to Be Ordered into Schools," *Manchester Guardian Weekly,* 18 May 1997, 11.

25. David Walker, "British Parliament Votes to End Tenure for New Faculty Members at Universities," *Chronicle of Higher Education,* 26 July 1988, A1, A10.

26. Alina Tugend, "In Britain, Research Assessments Can Make or Break a University's Reputation," *Chronicle of Higher Education,* 28 February 1997, A48; Martin McLean, "Higher Education in the United Kingdom into the 1990s: Shopping Mall or Reconciliation with Europe?" *European Journal of Education* 25, no. 2 (1990): 157–170.

27. See, for example, "Mr. Baker's Take-over," *Times Educational Supplement,* 23 April 1987, 7; David Walker, "Prime Minister Thatcher Moves to End Local Control of Britain's Polytechnic Institutes and College," *Chronicle of Higher Education,* 30 September 1987, A39, A41.

28. *A Lesson in School Reform from Great Britain* (Washington, D.C.: Brookings Institution, 1992).

29. For an assessment of their analysis, see Geoffrey Walford, "The Real Lessons in School Reform from Britain," *Educational Policy* 7 (June 1993): 212–222.

30. The first report issued was probably the most influential: National Commission on Excellence in Education, *A Nation at Risk: The Imperative for Educational Reform* (Washington, D.C.: Government Printing Office, 1983). See also Carnegie Corporation of New York, *Education and Economic Progress* (New York: Carnegie Corporation, 1983).

31. The quotes appear on pages ix–xx, 10.

32. Pat Ordovensky, "Failed Monopoly: 'Defect Rate' 50 Percent from Public Schools," *USA Today,* 27 October 1987, 1A.

33. Denis P. Doyle, "The Role of Private Sector Management in Public Education," *Phi Delta Kappan* 76 (October 1994): 132.

34. Marshall S. Smith and Brent W. Scoll, "The Clinton Human Capital Agenda," *Teachers College Record* 96 (Spring 1995): 390. For a commentary on the direction of Clinton's educational initiatives as sketched out in his inaugural address, see "Mr. Clinton's Challenge on Schools," editorial, *New York Times,* 18 February 1997, A14.

35. Lee A. Daniels, "New Corporate Effort to Aid Innovative Schools," *New York Times,* 1 November 1989, A2.

36. Kathryn Borman and Joel Spring, *Schools in Central Cities* (New York: Longmans, 1984).

37. "Urban Education Experiment Stumbles in Boston Suburb," *New York Times,* 6 September 1992, A15.

38. Susan Chira, "Reading, Writing, and Broadcast News," *New York Times,* 6 March 1990, B1, B3; Stuart Elliot, "Whittle Communications' Fall Dissected," *New York Times,* 24 October 1994, C10; James B. Stewart, "Grand Illusion," *New Yorker,* 31 October 1994, 64–81; Sam Howe Verhovek, "First Edison Schools Open in Texas," *New York Times,* 1 March 1996, A1, B12.

39. Isabel Wilkerson, "A City Is Letting a Company Run a School District," *New York Times,* 22 April 1992, B7; William Celis 3d, "School Management Company

Admits Overstating Results," *New York Times,* 8 June 1994, C18; George Judson, "Private Business, Private Schools: Why Hartford Experiment Failed," *New York Times,* 1 March 1996, A1, B12. Cf. Phyllis Vine, "To Market, to Market . . . The School Business Sells Kids Short," *Nation,* 8–15 September 1997, 11–17.

40. Reported in John Carvel, "Britain to Squeeze Student Numbers," *Manchester Guardian Weekly,* 16 February 1997, 1.

41. John Carvel, "University Intake Tilted toward Rich," *Manchester Guardian Weekly,* 27 April 1997, 12.

42. Simon Vanderaa, president of the Council of Australian Postgraduate Associations, as quoted in Geoffrey Maslen, "Students across Australia Protest against Higher University Fees," *Chronicle of Higher Education,* 7 April 1995, A40. Cf. Geoffrey Maslen, "Applications to Australian Universities Drop: Major Tuition Increases . . . Are Seen as the Chief Cause," *Chronicle of Higher Education,* 7 February 1997, A47. On the comparable situation in England and Wales, see Alina Tugend, "Financial Crisis May Force British Universities to End Tradition of Free Higher Education," *Chronicle of Higher Education,* 12 July 1996, A39.

43. Sarah Lyall, "For First Time, British Students Face Tuition," *New York Times,* 24 July 1997, A1; David Walker, "British Government Plans to End Free Tuition at Universities," *Chronicle of Higher Education,* 1 August 1997, A35.

44. Martin Walker, "Clinton Pins Colours to Education Crusade," *Manchester Guardian Weekly,* 16 February 1997, 6.

45. The particulars are the subject of Raymond Callahan, *Education and the Cult of Efficiency* (Chicago: University of Chicago Press, 1962).

46. Sheena MacLean, "Schools Axe Programs as Cutbacks Bite: Survey," *The Age,* 16 March 1994, 1; Joanne Painter, "Classes Get Bigger as Subjects Get Cut: Study," *The Age,* 23 May 1994, 6.

47. Jim Carl, "Parental Choice as National Policy in England and the United States," *Comparative Education Review* 38, no. 3 (August 1994): 304.

Chapter 11

Higher Education Restructuring in the Era of Globalization

Toward a Heteronomous Model?

Daniel Schugurensky

Any attempt to examine international trends in higher education in a few pages inevitably implies a high degree of generalization and simplification. A global analysis of this type cannot account for the significant differences in models of national development, in the history and organization of every national higher education system, and among and within individual institutions. It can, however, describe some universal trends and discuss them in terms of the context of the world system.

As the century comes to an end, higher education systems continue toward institutional diversification, regionalization, and vocationalization. In many countries, the typical student is neither male, upper class, nor young, as women, minority groups, and mature students have entered the system in increasing numbers. Technological advances are nurturing unprecedented innovations in the transmission of information, greatly affecting the quantity and speed of knowledge production and transfer.

The end of the century is also witnessing the continuation of important social, cultural, economic, and political developments that affect higher education. Prominent among them are the globalization of the economy, the decline of the welfare state, and the commodification of knowledge. Since the fall of the Berlin Wall in 1989, there has been a deepening of the shift from Keynesianism to neoliberalism, and with it a wave of privatization and an increasing presence of market dynamics in social exchanges.

The impact of these developments on the university is reflected in a new discourse that emphasizes value for money, accountability, planning, cost-efficiency, good management, resource allocation, unit costs, performance indicators, and selectivity. Tenure is under attack, and disciplines must prove their worth by their contribution to the economy. The fiscal crisis of the state, resulting in budget cutbacks, generates an increased reliance on private sources of revenue · (through links with the business sector and user fees), restrictions on enrollments, growth of private institutions, deregulation of working conditions, and faculty entrepreneuralism. Like a chain reaction, these developments impact many others. Changes in the origin of university revenues (e.g., higher fees and more service to industry) may have serious implications for accessibility and autonomy. Limited accessibility, in turn, can lead to the reduction of student diversity and to the proliferation of second-class institutions, creating two, three, or more tiers in the system. Likewise, a reduction in autonomy may have an impact on areas like governance, curriculum, and research priorities. In general, most of these changes are expressions of a greater influence of the market and the government over university affairs. Overall, in terms of its long-term implications, probably the most significant trend worldwide during the 1990s is the drastic restructuring of higher education systems. In essence, at the core of the restructuring process is a redefinition of the relationship between the university, the state, and the market, and a drastic reduction of institutional autonomy. Although advocates and detractors of the current higher education restructuring may disagree on a number of issues, most of them would likely agree that such restructuring will alter not only the historical modus operandi of the university but also its social purpose.

What is most striking about the current higher education restructuring is the unprecedented scope and depth of changes taking place as well as the similarity of changes occurring in a wide variety of nations having different social, political, historical, and economic characteristics. Although the pace and the dynamics of this change vary according to the specific historical conditions and social formation of each country, any review of recent policy initiatives implemented by governments throughout the world shows that the direction of the change follows an unmistakably similar path. On all continents, a myriad of government plans, constitutional reforms, legislative acts, regulations, and recommendations are moving universities closer to the demands of the state and the marketplace. This has serious consequences for the financing, governance, and mission of higher education, and ultimately for the degree of autonomy enjoyed by individual institutions to proactively define their agenda.

This restructuring (also referred to as repositioning, reengineering, streamlining, downsizing, adjustment, etc.) is not so much a genuine reform as it is a response. Although both involve change, reform is active and by choice, whereas response is reactive and of necessity.[1] In most cases, university restructuring is not emerging from democratic deliberation among internal actors but from external pressures emanating from socioeconomic and political developments such as the globalization of the economy, the dismantling of the welfare state, and the increasing commodification of knowledge. Restructuring is often implemented in spite of considerable opposition from the academic community, reflecting the increasing power of international and domestic political and economic forces in influencing higher education policy.

The Context of University Change: The Era of Globalization

The changing role of the university at the end of the twentieth century cannot be isolated from the emergence of a postindustrial economy, in which productivity relies predominantly on science, technology, knowledge, and management, rather than on the amount of capital or labor. This is particularly clear in advanced countries, in which the new economy is increasingly based on information-processing activities. The new economy is also abandoning the Fordist principles found in standardized mass production and moving into a customized, flexible, "just in time" model known as Toyotism. Most important, the new economy is global. Production processes, markets, capital, management, telecommunications, and technology bypass national boundaries. Although nation-states are still important centers of power, national economies are now subsumed in real time with (and increasingly dependent on) the global economy.

Globalization, a dynamic that has economic, political, social, and cultural ramifications, implies the intensification of transnational flows of information, commodities, and capital around the globe (eroding technical, political, or legal barriers), the development of new trading blocs, and the strengthening of supranational governing bodies and military powers.[2] This increasingly globalized economy is largely controlled by a transnational elite composed of the G-7 countries, international financial institutions, and multinational corporations.

Parallel with globalization is the retrenchment of the welfare state, which is being replaced by a neoliberal state geared at promoting economic international competitiveness through cutbacks in social expenditure, economic deregulation, decreased capital taxes, privatization, and labor flexibilization.[3] This new state abandons its role as direct economic agent (producer of goods and services) and as regulator of economic life (minimum wages, maximum prices, protectionism, subsidies, etc.), becoming instead a subsidiary agent whose main function is to guarantee a social and economic environment propitious for capital accumulation. For the average person, the dismantling of the welfare state results in higher unemployment rates, lower wages, and less job security. It also implies the withdrawal of the state from the commitment to universal provision of public services such as education, health, housing, and social security, which are now becoming increasingly regulated by market dynamics. This withdrawal, coupled with increasing incentives to capital via lower taxes and labor flexibilization, is referred to as a shift from social welfare to corporate welfare.

The transition from the welfare state to the neoliberal state implies not only structural changes but also ideological ones. Growing public deficits and declining economic growth provide fertile soil for the cultivation of conservative ideology. Fostered mainly by the business community, this ideology attributes economic problems to excessive state expenditure and to an oversized state bureaucracy and calls for drastic cutbacks in university funding. The progressive, optimistic view that links investment in education with economic growth and democratization of society is being replaced by a much tougher view based on the assumption that the private sector creates wealth whereas public expenditure based on high taxation fuels inflation and discourages entrepreneurs.[4]

Amid globalization pressures and welfare state retrenchment, inequalities between and within nations are increasing. At the global level, there is a growing concentration of capital and power in multinational corporations, international agencies, and supranational organizations over sovereign nation-states and labor organizations.[5] Currently, six hundred major multinational corporations control 25 percent of the world economy and 80 percent of world trade. Likewise, there is an ever growing financial and technological gap between more developed and less developed countries. In an increasingly knowledge-based society, the average proportion of researchers per million people in developed countries reaches 850, whereas in developing countries it is 127, and the percentage of the GNP allocated to research and development is 1.78 and 0.45 respectively.[6] Some analysts are talking about the emergence of a fourth world, a category including those pauperized economies that, as they become marginalized from the world system, shift from a structural position of exploitation to one of irrelevance.[7] At the national level, many countries, rich and poor alike, are experiencing higher levels of social and economic polarization.[8]

In developing countries, governments are pressured by lending agencies to implement austerity programs in order to be eligible for emergency loans at the same time that the redistributive role of the state is reduced and societal exchanges are increasingly ruled by the market. These programs, known as structural adjustment programs (SAPs), recommend liberalization of imports, elimination of subsidies, privatization of public enterprises, user fees in public services, and drastic cuts in government expenditures in areas such as health, education, housing, sanitation, transportation, and environment. Privatization proposals, generally defended on the grounds that they promote efficiency, equity, and decentralization of decision making, usually result in the disentitlement of large sectors of the population to services that once were considered an inalienable right.

At the same time, both production and dissemination of knowledge are increasingly commodified. Commodification of cultural goods is changing the way knowledge is produced and distributed. As cultural and scientific endeavors must become profitable activities, cultural goods become commercial products, the public is redefined as customers, the university becomes a provider, and the learner, a purchaser of a service. Technological advances go hand in hand with the ascendance of "home delivery" electronic cultural goods (cable TV, Internet, videos, instruction, etc.), the predominance of cultural mega-industries in the production and distribution of cultural goods, and a time-space compression of human interaction.

Public universities are not immune to this new climate. During the Fordist period universities were perceived as the most vital of public investments, whereas in the post-Fordist era they are seen as a major part of the economic problem. The aims of accessibility, social criticism, cultural development, and institutional autonomy are being subordinated to the three Rs of the economic crisis (recession, rationalization and restraint), further aggravated in many developing countries by the R of repayment of the external debt. Since the decline of state funding for public universities has been in many cases very noticeable, many students and faculty tend to equate the current university crisis as a financial crisis. But budget cuts, although they constitute a serious problem, represent just one element of the ongoing restructuring process. In other words, it is not that universities must do the same with fewer resources but must do different things and in different ways.

The scope and depth of university restructuring throughout the world, with the adoption of similar ideologies and policies in so many different settings, cannot simply be attributed to a spontaneous upsurge of mass disaffection with higher education. It is neither an inevitable nor an impersonal process but the product of a double process of consensus and coercion carried out by concrete social actors. On the one hand, simultaneous developments in a variety of countries reflect a common response to common problems. To some extent, higher education restructuring results from technical analysis and its ensuing recommendations, which flow from country to country (usually from developed to developing ones) in a process of cultural diffusion through networks of experts who borrow what they perceive as the most sensible alternatives. This process is usually piecemeal and works through arenas such as demonstration effects, conferences, debates, literature, and study abroad programs.

On the other hand, restructuring is part and parcel of a conscious effort on the part of powerful interest groups to adapt the university (and education in general) to the new economic paradigm. This effort is organized through institutional arrangements that put together business and government representatives who pressure academic institutions to redefine their priorities and adopt new operational principles. Those institutional arrangements have different expressions in core and peripheral countries. In the former, the interests of the corporate sector are advanced through a bevy of business–higher education fora, joint research groups, government-industry conferences, and the like. In the latter, they are advanced by what Samoff calls the "intellectual/financial complex of foreign aid."[9] Prominent among this network are international financial institutions like the World Bank, which have the means to concentrate research, funding, and policy formulation under one roof.

In spite of the fact that these donors and lenders have become hegemonic powers in influencing educational policy in the developing world, this does not mean that restructuring measures are applied consistently in every country. Although most higher education systems are moving in a similar direction, the transition is full of adaptations, partial rejections, and conflicts. In each national formation, which has its own history and educational traditions, local actors actively struggle over policy recommendations emanating from the world system. Furthermore, even in the same country, restructuring processes vary according to the unique features of each individual institution.

Higher Education in the 1990s: Major Trends

Convergence and Marginalization

The trend toward convergence pointed out at the beginning of this decade by Philip Altbach, one of the pioneers in the field of comparative higher education, is intensifying.[10] This convergence does not mean that all higher education systems are one and the same, but that they are increasingly governed by similar pressures, procedures, and organizational patterns. As the fiscal crisis of the state continues, universities all over the world are still affected by deep financial constraints. The budget cutbacks of recent years have forced public universities to reduce costs through a variety of means and to seek private sources of revenue. This has enhanced university-business linkages in teaching and research and has prompted institutions to rely more on fund-raising activities and increased (or imposed, if they did not exist) tuition and fees.

However, privatization is not only expressed in the introduction of private elements in public institutions but also in the rapid growth of the private sector. Moreover, with the increased direct and indirect state financial support of private institutions, what is emerging in many countries is a hybrid system that combines public and private features in all institutions, to the point that, if the tendency continues, in a few years it will be difficult to distinguish, at least in terms of funding, a private university from a public one. The shift from a dual public-private system toward a hybrid model is one among several elements of a general trend toward the Americanization of higher education systems. This trend is not necessarily new. For different reasons, the U.S. system has constituted the dominant higher education paradigm for the past several decades. Back in the 1970s, Altbach asserted that "there is no question that higher education planners and others often look to the United States as the most relevant model for academic development in their countries."[11] What is new is the widening and intensification of this convergence process.

The convergence of higher education systems at the global level is related to at least three related phenomena: the influence of international and national organizations on higher education policy, the consolidation of regional blocs, and a broader consolidation of international epistemic communities. First, the role of international foundations and financial institutions on higher education policy is an important element to consider in understanding the direction of university systems, particularly in developing countries. These organizations have great coercive power over nations in need of funding, and this power is exercised not only through conditionalities to access credit (structural adjustment policies based on budget cuts and promarket reforms) but also through agenda setting, collection and interpretation of data, workshops and conferences, recommendations and consulting, and so on. In developed countries, the role of these international organizations is fulfilled by a variety of think tanks, state-industry committees, and business–higher education fora that typically advance a pro-corporate agenda.[12]

The process of world convergence among higher education systems is also assisted by a process of regional convergence, which occurs as nation-states integrate into economic communities and regional trading blocs such as the North American Free Trade Agreement (NAFTA), the Mercado Común Sudamericano (Mercosur), the European Union (EU), the Association of South East Asian Nations (ASEAN), or the African Economic Community (AEC). These common markets, with their political, legal, economic, and cultural requirements and their need for regional harmonization, create new demands on universities. For instance, agreements on labor mobility lead to stricter recognition of credentials and transfer of equivalencies, which in turn influences the homogenization of curricula and the standardization of educational experiences, particularly regarding professional programs. At the same time, the consolidation of these regional communities has prompted a wave of institutional cooperation, joint projects, and student and academic exchange programs.

The convergence of higher education systems is also related to a broader consolidation of international epistemic communities (networks that generate more or less consensual definitions of problems and solutions across a variety of fields) that rapidly accelerates the convergence of scientific discourses. Although academic elites continue circulating their ideas through the traditional avenues (conferences, seminars, journals, study abroad programs, etc.), the proliferation of list-serves, newsgroups, teleconferences, Internet colloquia, and the universalization of English as the academic lingua franca in academic discourse and among symbolic analysts has considerably speeded up the process.

However (and paradoxically), at the same time that a relatively small number of symbolic analysts are able to interact more fluidly in closed networks, a large contingent of academics and students in poor countries who have restricted access to up-to-date computer technologies are likely to be marginalized by this interaction. If they live in non-English speaking developing countries, the process of marginalization is compounded, as translators have difficulty keeping pace with the increasing number of volumes published every

year. By the time a work is translated and published, it has already been superseded by new works that render the original material obsolete.

Language, Science, and Dependency

Dependence on English as the primary language of scientific communication
not only raises concerns about exclusion and lagging behind but also about inclusion. In addition to the general issues of neocolonialism and cultural imperialism, in some national settings (such as the Arab countries or the Philippines), specific concerns have arisen regarding the most appropriate language
of instruction at the university level. These concerns are not only about pedagogy, textbooks, and proficiency of students and faculty but also about a potential detrimental impact of these practices on the preservation of domestic
languages. This preoccupation is not exclusive of poor nations. In France, for
instance, reservations against the Internet were advanced on the grounds of the
preservation of local language and culture. In Holland, the issue of the potential disappearance of Dutch as a national language and its possible replacement
by English has led the Dutch Ministry of Education and Science to express in
the national press its strong commitment to "a flourishing Dutch culture and,
consequently, to the survival of Dutch as the language of instruction in schools,
the government and the courts," while recognizing that this will not be an easy
task, since "the internationalization of higher education and research make the
use of other languages beside Dutch indispensable."[13] For universities in developing countries, the language situation is a symptom of a deeper issue. With
a few exceptions, the production and distribution of knowledge is still concentrated in core countries.

Indeed, peripheral countries are basically consumers of knowledge, especially
in the areas of science and technology. The knowledge produced in Latin America, for example, represents less than 3 percent of the world's scientific production, which is not surprising in light of its low investment in research and development. The public expenditures in R&D of all Latin American countries
together are equivalent to the expenses in R&D of a couple of multinational corporations.[14] In the two leading countries of the region in terms of scientific production (Brazil and Mexico), R&D expenditures as percentage of GNP are 0.4
and 0.3 respectively, a low proportion when compared to the 3.0 allocated by
Japan and the 3.5 by Sweden. These differences in resource allocation are reflected in the critical mass of researchers. In Mexico and Brazil there are only 95
and 165 scientists and engineers per million people, respectively, whereas in
Sweden there are 3,714 and in Japan, 5,677. The Latin American situation is no
different from that in other developing regions. To take two examples from
Africa, Nigeria allocates to R&D only 0.1 percent of the GNP and the Central
African Republic, 0.2 percent, with 15 and 55 scientists per million, respectively.
In Asia, Thailand assigns to R&D 0.2 percent of the GNP, China, 0.6 percent and

India, 0.8 percent, with 73, 537, and 151 scientists per million, respectively.[15] Likewise, Sweden and Japan are not atypical examples of advanced countries, in which the figures for resource allocation are usually above 2.5 percent of the GNP, and the number of scientists and engineers per million is close to 3,000.

The current model of development implemented in most developing countries, highly dependent on foreign capital and technology, does not provide the most propitious conditions for the production and application of indigenous knowledge. In many of these countries, scientific dependence is indirectly assisted by higher education systems that do not pay enough attention to research and development. In many developing countries, for instance, in spite of current efforts to increase the proportion of full-time academic staff, most professors still work part time or by the hour, which in many cases limits the possibilities of developing a critical mass of researchers. Likewise, the emphasis of academic activities rests largely with the professional training of undergraduate students. Although graduate programs have recently expanded and multidisciplinary programs are growing, the experience of most students is confined within the narrow limits of their disciplines. This professional orientation provides little room for a flexible curriculum. Students specialize in their discipline from the first year and in general terms are not prepared with the research tools and interdisciplinary skills that are required in graduate programs.

The technological dependence of developing countries and the relatively low incomes of scientists, among other factors, contribute to the continuation of human capital transfers to more developed countries. Continuous impoverishment and deterioration of living conditions in developing countries, coupled with the scarcity of relevant employment opportunities for university graduates, result in an escalation of the brain drain, which in turn aggravates the cycle of technological and scientific dependency. As long as the gap in scientific development and working conditions in both settings persists, the exodus is likely to continue.

Technology and Instruction

Higher education instruction is being affected by the rapid development of new interactive technologies, which are impelling quantitative and qualitative changes in distance education programs. These programs are not only growing but are being reconceptualized, from correspondence or one-way televised courses to a much more sophisticated model of immediate interaction between instructors and students, particularly through the use of the Internet. The growth of virtual courses is so impressive that it has been speculated that the technological advances could eventually lead to the consolidation of virtual universities, in which students can complete a degree online without setting foot on campus. The area of distance education that is expected to have the most growth in the upcoming years is the one of asynchronous (anytime/anywhere) courses, offered not by interactive video but also by software that can be used by students at their preferred time and place. This emerging model of "flexible learning" is receiving special attention from governments because it promises three goals that usually are not found together: cutting costs, improving quality, and broadening access to instruction.

The Impact of Cutbacks

The unprecedented expansion of the 1960s, 1970s, and early 1980s raised concerns among a variety of actors, particularly when enrollments were not matched by appropriate budgetary increases. Although several university systems have moved successfully from elitism to massive access during the postwar period, the expected transition to universal access has been interrupted by stricter admission policies and higher tuition and fees.[16] Expansion was brought to a halt because it has allegedly led to a quality decline, and financial resources could not continue growing indefinitely. As the welfare state retrenched, government financial cutbacks became a reality, and higher education institutions were forced to reduce enrollments, increase revenues, and/or save costs. Many universities, then, began to selectively cut certain programs and services as well as diversify their revenue sources, including contracts with the business sector, client fees, alumni contributions, and donations. Self-recovery programs were encouraged, and fund-raising activities came to the forefront. Cost savings were achieved through a variety of strategies, including the replacement of high-paid faculty by less expensive staff, early retirement packages, attrition, larger classrooms, outsourcing, interruption of library subscriptions, cancellation of major renovations of facilities, and reductions in equipment acquisition. Administrators are also reducing labor costs and labor conflicts by contracting out a variety of services previously performed by staff directly employed by the university.

The new rules of the game are not being accepted without conflict. Budget cuts, restrictive entrance requirements, and new or higher fees, for instance, have prompted a new wave of faculty and student militancy in different parts of the world, particularly in developing countries. At the moment of this writing, massive student protests over these issues are taking place in sites as distant as Nicaragua and Kenya, and in both cases the clashes between students and police are reaching violent dimensions. However, in spite of occasional student resistance, user fees are becoming part of the reality in many countries with a long tradition of free higher education. This constitutes a considerable departure from just a decade ago, when the possibility of charging students for attending public universities was unthinkable. Tuition and fees, then taboo issues, are now openly debated and often implemented in a variety of developed and developing countries.

To cope with social demands for accessibility, many governments are encouraging the expansion of nonuniversity postsecondary institutions. This institutional diversification allows governments to cope with the new cohorts of high school graduates, shifting resources from universities to lower-cost institutions such as technical institutes, regional universities, community colleges, and professional training programs. The effects of institutional diversification are still to be seen. On the one hand, the proliferation of nonuniversity postsecondary institutions provides greater choice and increased accessibility to the system. On the other hand, it could lead to a further stratification of higher education, in which the mechanisms of closure are redefined and masked under a facade of democracy and meritocracy.

To further reduce pressures for accessibility without incurring budgetary increases, many governments (particularly in Latin America, Asia, and the former socialist bloc) have allowed (and in many cases encouraged) the growth of private higher education. A case in point is Chile, where, as a result of the growth of private institutions, public expenditures on higher education decreased from $171 million in 1981 to $115 million in 1988.[17] The private sector not only absorbs the social demand for higher education when it exceeds the public supply, but it also reduces political conflict due to limited student activism and increases the availability of choice by providing different content and (theoretically) better quality. Although the introduction of market dynamics in higher education promotes competition and could raise efficiency and quality, it could also lead in some cases to a dual structure, with an expensive and high-quality education for the elites and a deteriorating and impoverished education for the masses.[18]

In many developing countries, both elite and nonelite private universities continue their steady growth. The demand for these institutions comes from those who believe that the quality of public universities has declined, those who are dissatisfied with its excessive politicization, those who believe that private credentials are more marketable, and those who are rejected by public universities on academic grounds.[19] Although in most developing countries the contribution of private universities to national development is acknowledged, the public sentiment toward some of these institutions is not always positive, particularly when they are perceived as profit-seeking businesses in which financial considerations are more valued than academic ones. This perception is reinforced by the fact that in some countries a significant proportion of private universities tend to invest almost exclusively in programs that are marketable, require low infrastructure, and have fast rates of return. In addition, research activities are scarce and quality standards are usually unregulated, partly because strict accreditation mechanisms are seldom in place.

Vocationalization

In many countries, rich and poor, the relationship between higher education and labor markets shows less-than-perfect correlations. Enrollment expansion and economic slowdown have led to significant numbers of educated unemployed and underemployed (performing tasks below their qualifications or, as a sort of internal brain drain, in fields different than those from which they graduated), and to an escalation of credentialism (by which higher degrees are required to perform essentially the same jobs). This situation has provided a fertile soil for the vocationalization of higher education. Pressures for vocationalization come from students who become more pragmatic and focus on material rewards and remunerative job prospects, from business and industrial groups demanding a curriculum that is responsive to the needs of the workplace, from governments demanding a closer connection between education and economic development, and from opinion leaders (mainly politicians and the media) accusing universities of irrelevance and esoterism.[20] The growth of vocational and professional programs undermines the tradition of liberal education (the idea that knowledge is a worthwhile end in itself) and the image of the community of independent scholars pursuing truth. A strong emphasis on a restrictive version of vocational education may be counterproductive, given the difficulties of forecasting labor needs in a constantly changing labor market. It may also backfire against employers and limit the employment prospects of students, as graduates of these programs will lack the problem-solving skills and the flexibility to adapt to changing situations and new technologies typical of a post-Fordist work environment.

Diversification and Restratification of the Student Body

In terms of demographics, the traditional higher education student population has changed, with increasing participation by female, minority, and mature students. In many countries, women now represent approximately 50 percent of enrollments. However, although expansion has improved accessibility, a full democratization of higher education has not occurred. The system is stratified, with female and minority students underrepresented in high-status, high-paid fields, and overrepresented in low-status careers and institutions.

In higher education institutions that have implemented positive discrimination policies, an increase in the representation of disadvantaged groups has taken place. These progressive policies, established during the 1960s and 1970s under the "principle of redress," aimed at equalizing opportunity and increasing access and successful participation of underrepresented groups, and gave rise to a variety of programs such as affirmative action, need-based grants and scholarships, subsidized student loans, and so on. Today, in an environment dominated by conservative thought, these policies are being challenged ideologically and legally. Their critics contend that affirmative action has been abused, that unfair quotas have been established, and that it has contributed to an alleged quality decline. In some cases, the attack on affirmative action has been successful through political and legal actions, with a negative impact on equity and accessibility.

The Academic Workforce and Accountability Pressures

The increasing flexibilization of labor is also present in universities, as a re-composition of the academic workforce is taking place. This is particularly noticeable in countries in which academic staff has traditionally enjoyed stability and good working conditions. During the last decades, the proportion of full-time faculty has shrunk considerably, whereas the number of staff holding part-time or nonpermanent appointments (sessionals, readers, adjuncts, lecturers, etc.) has increased at unprecedented rates. As in other labor markets, academic workers are being restratified and segmented into a small group of core workers (with high stability and good working conditions) and a large army of low-paid flexible workers perpetually haunted by the ghost of labor insecurity. In the emerging division of labor, the core workers are likely to be tenured professors who concentrate on the coordination of research projects and graduate teaching. The contingent workers are more likely to teach undergraduates and collaborate in research projects on a temporary basis. Part and parcel of labor flexibilization are attacks launched on tenure, on the grounds that its original purpose (protection of academic freedom) has been distorted into job security for faculty members. Pressures for the elimination of tenure have been occasionally successful (in Britain it has been already abolished), but so far, the academic community has been able to preserve it or at least negotiate it (e.g., at the University of Minnesota). However, in spite of the preservation of tenure codes, university administrators are enjoying increasing managerial flexibility in firing human resources based on new clauses such as financial exigency or program redundancy.

The calls for the elimination of tenure, together with the intensification of the academic workforce, are part of a larger pressure from governments to make universities more efficient and accountable. In times of budget constraints, there is a widespread assumption among state officials that universities are not cost-effective institutions and that they are irresponsive to societal needs. As a result, there is an increasing importance attributed to the evaluation of university activities. In general terms, the evaluation of the quality of higher education institutions is shifting from an approach exclusively based on inputs (academic credentials of faculty members, library resources, laboratories and research facilities, teacher/student ratios, academic/nonacademic staff ratios, per-student expenditures, etc.) to one that also includes processes and outcomes. However, outcomes are generally measured in terms of performance indicators (program completion rates, levels of satisfaction of graduates and employers, etc.) that tend to disregard qualitative data and ignore the particular "historic missions" of individual institutions.

Although performance indicators are broadly accepted in the political and administrative discourse as the most adequate tools to evaluate universities (in teaching, research and service), in practice they mainly provide statistical measures of efficiency, speed, and productivity. Although there is a general agreement that university activities should be accounted for and evaluated, controversies have arisen about the differences between evaluation and assessment, the definition of quality and the best indicators to evaluate it, and the criteria to measure efficiency. Debates consider not only the technical dimension of evaluation but also the political one, usually addressed in terms of who carries out the evaluation, and for what reasons. For instance, disputes have taken place on the most appropriate evaluating entity (whether the evaluation should be best carried by the government, an internal body of the university, a team acceptable to both parties, etc.) and on the purpose of the evaluation (to assist universities in improving their performance or to provide governments with supposedly objective information to reward and punish with the power of the purse).

Higher Education Restructuring: Toward a Heteronomous Model?

The common denominator of current higher education changes worldwide is the gradual loss of institutional autonomy. Autonomy allows institutions to set, collegially and free from external interference, their own objectives and missions, content and methods of instruction, evaluation criteria, admission and graduation requirements, research agendas, promotion and demotion procedures, and the like. Since its medieval origins, and in spite of considerable tensions with the church and the state, the university has enjoyed a large degree of autonomy. It was recognized early on by its ecclesiastical masters that the university, as a self-governing community of scholars, warranted independence from external powers. The assumption was that scientific knowledge is most effectively produced, maintained, and disseminated in institutions that are relatively autonomous and whose members enjoy a high degree of academic freedom. In addition to institutional autonomy and academic freedom, the medieval university was characterized by a participatory approach to learning and inquiry, a collaborative internal government, open admissions, and a belief in knowledge for its own sake.[21]

Today, in the midst of globalization pressures, market-friendly neoliberal reforms, state adjustment, and calls for accountability, the principle of autonomy is being challenged and drastically redefined. Like most public institutions, the university has begun to suffer the effect of a deep, unrelenting recession. However, its situation is aggravated by a generalized distrust of its contribution to economic development, by the growth of educated unemployment and underemployment, by the widespread belief that it is a luxurious "ivory tower" disconnected from the real world, by complaints about waste and mismanagement, by suspicions about the productivity of tenured academics, and by the problems related to student unrest.

In this context, universities are experiencing a transition (sometimes voluntary, usually forced) toward a heteronomous model.[22] Following Weber, an institution can be considered heteronomous when its mission, its agenda, and its outcomes are defined more by external controls and impositions than by its internal governing bodies. Thus, a heteronomous university is one increasingly unable to proactively design its itinerary, and whose success derives from its effective and rapid response to external demands. Whereas autonomy implies self-government and refers to the quality or state of being independent, free, and self-directed, heteronomy, by contrast, implies a subordination to the law or domination of another. The available evidence indicates that a significant number of universities throughout the world are increasingly forced to reduce their margin of autonomy by reacting both to market demands and state imperatives.[23]

The heteronomous university stems from the combined effect of two apparently contradictory dynamics: laissez-faire policies and state interventionism.[24] Indeed, the emerging model encompasses two university models usually addressed independently in the literature on the topic: the "commercial" model and the "state-controlled" model.

The commercial dimension includes a variety of policy instruments promoting the spread of private institutions, corporate-like management, faculty entrepreneurialism, client fees, consumer-oriented programs, contracts with industry, and a multiplicity of fund-raising, cost-recovery, and cost-saving mechanisms. At the same time, the state is able to influence the university's behavior through budget cuts and new funding mechanisms based less on enrollments and more on performance evaluations and institutional competition. In the commercial university, the institution becomes an enterprise, faculty become entrepreneurs, and students and research products become outcomes for industry—the ultimate customer of the service. As traditional values and organizational patterns are replaced by those of the marketplace, the university enters full-fledged into the phase of academic capitalism.[25] This includes an unprecedented growth of administrative structures separated from the academy; consequently, managerial professionalism becomes the ultimate model in decision making.

The corporate rationality is also expressed in mergers among departments, faculties, and institutions, in departmental structures that promote autonomous units, in reward mechanisms, and in hiring, promotion, and firing criteria. As mentioned above, the logic of the market is also expressed in contracting out, in a general emphasis on efficiency and cost-reduction strategies, and in an increasing institutional diversification of the system, encouraging differentiation and choice. It is also noticeable in an increasing vocationalization of the system, with the introduction of short cycles closely connected with labor market requirements that sometimes lead to an excessive utilitarianism. As well, more restrictive admission policies, with a rhetoric of excellence and an explicit rejection of models based on open access or compensatory justice for disadvantaged groups (i.e., affirmative action), are creating a swing back in the long dated quality versus equality debate.

At the same time, individual professors, departments, and schools of public and private universities must engage in competitive behavior similar to that prevailing in the marketplace for funding, grants, contracts, and students. Among academics, entrepreneurship is greatly promoted, tenure is endangered, and the proportion of part-time faculty increases. Education is considered more as a private consumption or investment than an inalienable right or a search for disinterested knowledge. As a language that centers on user fees, rational choices, job prospects, and private rates of return becomes increasingly hegemonic and the commercial model becomes paradigmatic, attacks on competing models escalate. The "academic haven" model (scholars seeking truth in an uncontaminated environment) is perceived as an irrelevant ivory tower, the "human capital" model that led to the educational expansion of previous decades is discredited after the recurrent failures of labor forecasting, and the "social transformation" model that had so many sympathizers during the 1960s and 1970s is now portrayed as cheap populism that leads to an extreme politicization of academic activities.[26]

The commercial model is complemented by an increasing number of control mechanisms designed and implemented by the state. Indeed, it is important to note that the consolidation of academic capitalism does not mean a total withdrawal of the state. The withdrawal is more financial than anything else, and decreasing state appropriations—contrary to the expectations of some observers—do not necessarily grant universities greater autonomy. One of the paradoxes of the heteronomous model is that governments tighten controls and regulations of higher education outcomes even as they demand higher education institutions to rely more and more on private sources of revenue (fees, donations, research contracts, etc.). The leverage exercised by the state in defining the direction of the system as a whole, including each individual institution, is largely augmented by linking a shrinking budget to performance evaluations based on debatable criteria.

Under a new model known as "distance evaluation," universities maintain autonomy to decide on internal matters and the means to achieve stated goals (process control) while the state retains the power to decide those goals (product control).[27] This conditional funding (which is defended by state officials on accountability grounds) increases the university's procedural autonomy while reducing its substantive autonomy[28] and allows the state to play a key role in determining enrollments in different areas, the type of skills delivered, the kind of postsecondary institutions to be strengthened, the resources for research across disciplines, the number of staff per students, and so forth. As part of state funding conditions, universities must make tough choices, such as cutting programs with low enrollments or in vulnerable (low marketable) fields such as the humanities and creative arts, or cutting library acquisitions and research and instructional equipment.

Summary and Conclusions

During the postwar period, the most important single trend worldwide in higher education was undoubtedly the expansion of the system. At the turn of the twentieth century, however, the most significant trend is probably the shift from autonomy to heteronomy. A comparative analysis of contemporary developments suggests that this shift goes beyond conjunctural changes in a given university or in a particular country, becoming structural in nature and global in scope. The context of this shift is a rearrangement of economic, ideological, and political forces. Among them are the globalization of the economy, the implementation of neoconservative and neoliberal policies, the consolidation of international corporate powers, and a redefinition of the role of the state. The impact of these factors on the university is reflected in budget cutbacks, an increased reliance on private sources of revenue, a growth of private institutions, the deregulation of working conditions, and in general a greater influence of the market and the government over university affairs. The heteronomous model tends to be imposed upon the university community rather than designed by choice, and the new rules of the game not only change the university's relationship with the state and the market but also its goals, its agenda, and the way it manages its internal affairs.

Although university transformations are largely propelled by external forces, they are mediated by university actors who support and resist them. However, the very nature of the changes under way makes universities less autonomous and therefore makes their members not only less resistant and more receptive to further changes in the same direction but also unable to formulate an alternative policy. Visions contending that the university should be the critical consciousness of society, the engine of new knowledge, and the guardian of the long-term interest of the community are being displaced, as are concerns about the environment or inequitable models of development. Likewise, the idea that evaluation should be used to diagnose problems and to provide feedback to improve is overshadowed by accountability measures, performance indicators, and strategies of reward and punishment.

The heteronomous university is a Pandora's box. In the best-case scenario, government regulations can help monitor standards, avoid duplications, and improve efficiency and social responsibility; market practices and values can promote the adoption of better managerial procedures and a closer relationship with business in which both partners benefit equally. However, in a different scenario, the heteronomous model can also lead to the erosion of important values and traditions such as the social mission of the university, its institutional autonomy and academic freedom, its pursuit of equity and accessibility, or its disinterested search for the truth.

What would the university of the future look like in this scenario? Taking into account current trends, it is possible to expect that linkages with the market will be intensified, entrance requirements to high-quality institutions will be higher, quotas will be imposed on programs with limited employment opportunities, students will pay higher fees, more faculty will be seconded to government and business, and research activity will be linked more directly to industrial application, with an increase in joint ventures between industry and university. Public universities will accrue more revenue from private sources; private institutions will receive more subsidies from government and will expand in size and number. In terms of hiring policies, it is possible to expect a reduction in the proportion of career academics with full-time contracts and an increase in the proportion of part-timers and sessionals hired only to teach specific courses. A decline in faculty salaries will discourage professors from remaining in public universities.

Continuing with this scenario, changes in curriculum will take place, with a stress on instrumentalism and the marginalization of courses related to social critique. Lower ranked universities to which restrictions on enrollment are not applied will be characterized by overcrowded classrooms and labs, although this will be compensated by distance education and the intensive use of media. Collegial decision making will be reduced to a minimum, replaced by managerial processes based on a corporate rationality. Changes in the organization of academic work will continue to reformulate the balance between teaching, research, and extension in elite universities in fields closely tied to the market with a reward structure placing even more emphasis on research and publications. Finally, the university agenda will be increasingly shaped by market dynamics and state control, and its activities and products will primarily benefit powerful economic, social, and political groups. In spite of its appeal to the common good, the heteronomous university may serve primarily the sectorial interests of industry, the political agenda of the government in place, and the social and economic aspirations of the upper classes.

Indeed, the general direction of external funding and pressures may often be in disharmony with the historical social and academic priorities of the public university, limiting the range of choice that academics have over priorities and methods of work. For instance, the work process of university environments, characterized by self-paced work, discretion over organization and management of research, freedom of communication and publication and the like, could be replaced by the logic of business, which emphasizes profit and commercialization, deadlines, secrecy, proprietary rights, a competitive edge in the marketplace and so on, and the logic of government, which emphasizes cost-effectiveness, budget reduction, and short-term political opportunism. As a result of the new pressures and drastic changes in the production and distribution of knowledge, universities will be forced to establish new priorities that can erode their commitment to accessibility, their reliance on open debate, and their critical voice in society. Greater dependency on external powers can lead to a factory-like model in which the bottom line is acquiescence and cost-effectiveness, learners are outputs, and intellectuals become entrepreneurs. It can lead to an erosion of the academic environment, to more cases of censorship and conflict of interests, to an emphasis on vocational and professional disciplines, to lower support for basic research and nonmarketable disciplines, and to further exclusion of disadvantaged groups.

The two logics—market pressures and state controls—are often complementary but can occasionally lead to contradictory developments. On the one hand, the university must satisfy the demands of students and business, who act as consumers and demand value for money, and, on the other, must fulfill the performance indicators developed by the government. This can open doors to new problems. For instance, students/customers may demand lower teacher-student ratios and higher contact time with professors. When a university adjusts to these two pressures, the logical consequences are higher per-student costs and lower number of faculty publications in academic journals, which leads to government punishment in terms of funding cuts.

Responding to short-sighted market demands could also have implications for long-term development. Examples of this situation are the elimination of unpopular courses in enrollment terms (but perhaps important in terms of strategic needs) and the reduction of basic research, which in turn will decrease the capacity of the state to develop long-term plans in terms of both professional training and research and development. In this context, the main challenges for universities are how to contribute to economic development while preserving integrity, autonomy, and community interests, how to balance an efficient management with democratic governance, how to expand while protecting quality, and how to engage in scientific and technological ventures that are guided by human and ethical values.

A pessimistic reading of reality suggests that the heteronomous agenda has achieved incontestable hegemony, as the university as an institution has become too weak to contest outside forces, and most faculty and administrators feel that they are unable to mount a credible defense. However, although universities seem to be less capable than ever of defining the ways in which they are distinct from other institutions, of articulating how the principles on which they operate differ from those of business and government, and of explaining to society why they should enjoy special privileges, it is important to remember that nothing in history is a final script. The depth and pace of the restructuring is contingent on the political economy and the historical traditions of each nation-state and each individual institution. In many countries, the pervasive dimensions of the heteronomous model are being confronted by concrete social actors who oppose and resist it, and eventually may advance alternative projects. At the beginning of the century, in spite of academic freedom, J. McKeen Cattell was fired by Columbia University because of his progressive ideas. One of those ideas was the call for "a democracy of scholars serving the larger democracy."[29] Today Cattell's call is more urgent and more relevant than ever.

Notes

1. Following Cerych and Sabatier, a "reform" is a planned and intentional process consistent with a set of values shared by a given community, whereas a "response" is something that must be done in reaction to a situation. See L. Cerych and P. Sabatier, *Great Expectations and Mixed Performances: The Implementation of Higher Education Reforms in Europe* (Paris: Trenharn, 1986).

2. David Held, "Democracy, the Nation-state, and the Global System," *Economy and Society* 20, no. 2 (May 1992): 38–72.

3. The welfare state refers to the intervention of the capitalist state in the form of social policies, programs, standards, and regulations in order to reduce class conflict and provide the conditions for the long-term reproduction of the capitalist mode of production. The welfare state intervenes in five main areas of social reproduction: (1) physical reproduction of the working class (universal health care, subsidized housing, and social benefits for mothers and children such as subsidized child care, child or family allowance, food stamps, etc.); (2) preparation of the new generations for the labor market through the provision of certain skills and attitudes (universal and cost-free basic education, technological and vocational institutes, etc.); (3) provision of adequate labor supply and working conditions (subsidized public transportation, regulations on minimum wage, work hours, child labor, retirement age, training, injury insurance, immigration, etc.); (4) provision of an institutional framework for class conflict (collective bargaining rights, recognition of unions, employment and health and safety standards, etc.); and (5) provision of income for the "unproductive" and retired (unemployment insurance, old-age pensions, etc.). See Gary Teeple, *Globalization and the Decline of Social Reform* (Toronto: Garamond, 1995); and Claus Offe, "The German Welfare State: Principles, Performances and Prospects after Unification" (paper presented at the annual colloquium series The End of the Nation-state? University of California at Los Angeles, 1997).

4. Offe, "The German Welfare State."

5. According to World Bank data, the sales of foreign affiliates of these corporations currently exceed the world's total exports. Multinational corporations are also creating their own education and training systems, including costly and well-equipped postsecondary institutions.

6. José J. Brunner, *Educacion Superior en América Latina: cambios y desafíos* (Chile: Fondo de Cultura Económica, 1990).

7. Manuel Castells, "The Informational Economy and the New International Division of Labor," in *The New Global Economy in the Information Age,* ed. Martin Carnoy et al. (University Park: Pennsylvania State University Press, 1993).

8. During the last three decades, the ratio of the income share of the richest 20 percent to that of the poorest 20 percent has more than doubled from 30 to 1 to 61 to 1. The poorest 20 percent saw their share of global income decline from 2.3 percent to 1.4 percent over the last thirty years. World poverty is increasing at about the same rate as world population. The World Bank recently estimated that 1.3 billion people survive on less than a dollar a day, and the number of people with incomes of less than $750 per year, hardly more than $2 per day, is about 3.3 billion people, or 60 percent of humanity. Between 1960 and 1993 total global income increased sixfold to $23 trillion, and the average world per capita income tripled, but three-fifths of humanity still lives in poverty. Today, the assets of the world's 358 billionaires exceed the combined annual incomes

of countries accounting for nearly half, 45 percent, of the world's people. See *United Nations Development Project Report* (New York: UNDP 1996).

9. Joel Samoff, "The Intellectual/Financial Complex Of Foreign Aid," *Review of African Political Economy* 53 (March 1992).

10. Philip Altbach, *Patterns in Higher Education Development: Toward the Year 2000,* in *Emergent Issues in Education: Comparative Perspectives,* ed. Robert Arnove, Philip Altbach, and Gail Kelly (Albany: State University of New York Press, 1992).

11. Philip Altbach, *Comparative Higher Education: Research Trends and Bibliography* (London: Mansell, 1979), 28.

12. For an expansion of this argument, see D. Schugurensky, "Global Economic Restructuring and University Change: The Case of Universidad de Buenos Aires" (Ph.D. diss., University of Alberta, 1994).

13. Ministry of Education and Sciences of the Netherlands, *Information on Education,* no. 0–02-F, February 1992. Cited by Zaghloul Morsy in introduction to *Higher Education in International Perspective,* ed. Zaghloul Morsy and Philip Altbach (Paris: UNESCO, 1993).

14. Mario Albornoz, editorial, *Redes: Revista de Estudios Sociales de la Ciencia* 2, no. 3 (April 1995).

15. See UNESCO *1996 Statistical Yearbook* (Paris: UNESCO).

16. See Martin Trow, *Problems in the Transition from Elite to Mass Higher Education* (Berkeley: Carnegie Commission on Higher Education, 1973). In Trow's classification, higher education systems are considered "elite" when they enroll less than 10 percent of the age-group, "mass" when enrollments are above 15 percent of the age-group, and "universal" when more than 50 percent of the age-group enters higher education.

17. E. Schiefelbein, "Chile: Economic Incentives in Higher Education," *Higher Education Policy* 3, no. 3 (1990): 21–26. See also E. Schiefelbein, "The Chilean Academic Profession: Six Policy Issues," in *The International Academic Profession: Portraits of Fourteen Countries,* ed. P. Altbach (Boston: Boston College Center for International Higher Education, 1996).

18. J. Tilak, "Privatization of Higher Education," in *Higher Education in International Perspective: Toward the Twenty-first Century,* ed. A. Morsy and P. Altbach (Paris: UNESCO, 1993), 59–71.

19. This situation is particularly clear in Latin America. See Daniel Levy, *Recent Trends in the Privatization of Latin American Higher Education: Solidification, Breadth, and Vigor,* Higher Education Policy no. 4, 1993.

20. Philip Altbach, "Patterns in Higher Education Development: Toward the Year 2000," in *Emergent Issues in Education: Comparative Perspectives,* ed. R. Arnove, P. Altbach, and Gail Kelly (Albany: State University of New York Press, 1992).

21. Ronald Barnett, *The Idea of Higher Education* (Buckingham: Society for Research into Higher Education/Open University Press, 1990).

22. See Schugurensky, "Global Economic Restructuring," 33–45.

23. Some clarifications regarding the term "heteronomy" are pertinent at this point. First, it is true that universities have been conditioned by state and private interests before; however, the emerging pattern constitutes a new structural and globalized model of dependency to the market and subjection to the state that goes beyond the classic control of a specific institution by a business person through endowments or donations, and

beyond conjunctural infringements on institutional autonomy by the government in a particular university or nation-state. Second, the term "heteronomy" as used in this context does not imply that universities are being (or are going to be in the near future) stripped of any vestige of institutional autonomy. It rather indicates that this space is being reduced, and gradually taken over, by external powers that are increasingly capable of imposing their own logic and interests. It is not so much that the university is operated by nonacademic actors as that its daily practices (its functions, internal organization, activities, structure of rewards, etc.) are subsumed into the logic imposed by the state and the market. Third, heteronomy is used here as an abstract concept, and hence its application to the analysis of a specific reality should be appropriately contextualized. Finally, the transition to the heteronomous university is not a smooth, linear, and consensual process, welcomed by all members of the academic community; this process is usually obstructed by resistance from advocates of alternative visions of the university.

24. In this unusual combination of market liberalization and state interventionism, the state pulls out of education funding and market takes its place, but at the same time that economic controls are relaxed, ideological controls are strengthened. See Adriana Puiggrós, "World Bank Education Policy: Market Liberalism Meets Ideological Conservatism," *NACLA Report on the Americas* 29, no. 6 (May–June 1996).

25. Sheila Slaughter and Larry Leslie, *Academic Capitalism: Politics, Policies, and the Entrepreneurial University* (Baltimore: Johns Hopkins University Press, 1997).

26. For a detailed description of these models, see J. Newson and H. Buchbinder, *The University Means Business: Universities, Corporations, and Academic Work* (Toronto: Garamond, 1988).

27. G. Neave and F. Van Vught, eds., *Prometheus Bound: The Changing Relationship between Government and Higher Education in Western Europe* (New York: Pergamon, 1991).

28. Berdhal distinguishes between substantive and procedural autonomy. Substantive autonomy refers to the power of the university to determine its own goals and programs, whereas procedural autonomy is the power to determine the means by which its goals and programs are pursued.

29. J. McKeen Cattell, *University Control* (New York: Science Press, 1913), 61–62.

Chapter 12

Education in Latin America
at the End of the 1990s

Robert Arnove, Stephen Franz, Marcela Mollis,
and Carlos Alberto Torres

In order to understand education in the region of Latin America in the late 1990s, it is necessary to view the nature of the state and how international economic and political forces influence the governance, financing, workings, and outcomes of school systems. After defining the state and its relationship to education, we make the case that the state in Latin America is further conditioned by the neoliberal economic and social policies being followed by countries in the region in order to gain access to international capital and markets. After discussing enrollment patterns, we examine how the structural adjustment policies recommended by the World Bank, the International Monetary Fund, and national technical assistance agencies like USAID have affected educational provision and practice. We argue that gains made in extending education to previously neglected populations during the period from the late 1960s to the mid-1980s have been substantially eroded by the introduction of market-based policies designed to decentralize and privatize education. At the same time, we provide examples of grassroots movements that counter education policies that serve elite interests. Such programs provide an alternative to externally imposed and top-down reforms, while equipping individuals and their collectivities with the means to articulate their interests and gain access to needed resources and services.

Defining the State and Its Relationship to Education

Generally, we view the state as a pact of domination, as an arena of conflict, and as a purposeful actor that must select among competing political projects. We agree with Cardoso that the state should be considered the "basic pact of domination that exists among social classes or factions of dominant classes and the norms which guarantee their dominance over subordinate strata."[1] As an arena of confrontation, the state displays the tensions and contradictions of competing political projects as well as the political agreements of civil society. Moreover, social class, racial, ethnic, gender, geographical, ethical-moral, and religious factors influence the actions of the state in legislating and executing social policies.

Although the state in a capitalist society, by its very nature, favors policies that are directed toward the constitution and reproduction of the capitalist system,[2] it also is the representative of the nation as a whole and, in liberal democratic societies, is a proponent of the extension of personal rights and greater mass participation in the determination of public policy.[3] Hence, as noted above, the state has a dual character: It is both a pact of domination and a contested terrain. Various groups intervene to shape public policy to serve their interests. Although education can be used to legitimate a political system, it also can serve to interrogate it; although an education system may function to perpetuate the social division of labor, it also can equip individuals with the skills and knowledge to humanize the workplace and change the class structure of a society by those in power.

The "Conditioned" State

Education policies and programs are further limited in their ability to bring about fundamental social change or improvements in the lives of the majority by the fact that Latin American countries, with the exception of Cuba,[4] are dependent or "conditioned" capitalist states. According to Cardoso, an "associate-dependent development" has characterized Latin America.[5] As he notes, the economic systems of Latin America are built upon an alliance among the state bureaucracy and state managers, the multinational corporations, and the highest strata of the national bourgeoisie. Not only multinational corporations but U.S. hegemony exercised in the region for the past one hundred years—a hegemony that has involved frequent military interventions, particularly in the Caribbean region and Central America—has thwarted alternative and more independent models of economic development.[6] The typical political economy of Latin America strengthens a more concentrated economic system that is inherently less redistributive and increasingly excludes the subordinate classes.

According to Carnoy, the educational implications of dependent capitalism in Latin America are that "(l) the state is often unwilling or unable to mobilize enough resources to make public education (state-defined knowledge) generally available; and (2) even if education is made generally available, the private production sector and the state are often unable to provide sufficient wage employment to absorb those with average education—this tends to make the average level of public schooling (and therefore the average level of knowledge) insufficient for integration into the regularly employed labor force."[7]

Education and Enrollment Patterns

Although Latin America, historically, has had a greater percentage of children and youth enrolled in schools in other developing areas of the world, enrollment patterns reflect the particular history of the region (table 12.1).

In a number of countries, there is a bimodal distribution of enrollment: Large numbers of students from the least privileged sectors of society do not attend or complete primary schooling while a substantial number of students attend universities, often at rates exceeding those of European countries.[8] For example, in 1995, Costa Rica, Argentina, and Peru respectively had twenty-nine, thirty-one, and thirty-three students per 1,000 inhabitants enrolled in higher education, compared with Germany, the United Kingdom, and Hungary, which respectively enrolled twenty-six, thirty-one, and fifteen.[9] These figures provide a striking contrast with the average amount of schooling of the adult population (15 to 64 years of age) in Latin America which, in the 1992, was 5.6 years; for developing regions the overall average was just over 4.5 years.[10]

Table 12.1
Percentage of Appropriate Age-Group Enrolled in Different Levels of Education, for All Developing Areas and Latin America, 1975, 1985, and 1995

	Level 1	*Level 2*	*Level 3*
All Developing Areas			
1975	92.8	31.4	4.1
1985	98.6	37.6	6.1
1995	99.1	49.2	8.9
Latin America			
1975	96.6	36.9	11.8
1985	105.9*	51.1	15.6
1995	110.4*	56.6	17.3

Source: UNESCO, *1997 Statistical Yearbook,* table 2.10.
*These figures are largely explained by high repetition rates and the substantial number of overage youths who were absorbed into the school system when opportunity was extended to previously excluded populations.

Different Access and Outcomes

In most countries, a majority of students who enter the first grade do not complete the period of "compulsory" schooling, which is usually a six-year period (table 12.2). There are significant differences in access to, participation in, and returns to education depending on social class, ethnicity, geography, and gender.

Social Class

Income inequality is greater in Latin American and the Caribbean than in most developing regions. For example, United National Development Program data on six Latin American countries reveal that the disparity between the highest 20 percent of households to that of the lowest 20 percent ranges from ten to one in Guatemala to twenty-six to one in Brazil.[11] Social class influences educational attainment, which in turn has a determining impact on life chances of individuals. According to Psacharopoulos et al., "Education [in Latin America] is the variable with the strongest impact on income inequality."[12]

Table 12.2
Latin American Repetition and Completion Rates in Primary Education in 1989 by Percentage

Country	First Grade Repeaters	Sixth Grade Graduates	Sixth Grade Nonrepeating Graduates
Argentina	31	83	17
Bolivia	33	47	9
Brazil	53	34	1
Chile	10	85	41
Colombia	31	87	26
Costa Rica	22	79	31
Dom. Rep.	58	38	3
Ecuador	33	81	34
El Salvador	54	50	4
Guatemala	55	59	9
Honduras	53	66	12
Mexico	33	77	23
Peru	28	76	21
Panama	–	86	33
Paraguay	33	71	20
Uruguay	15	91	54
Venezuela	28	62	14

Source: Laurence Wolff, Ernesto Schiefelbein, and Jorge Valenzuela, *Improving the Quality of Primary Education in Latin America and the Caribbean* (Washington, D.C.: World Bank, 1994), 31.

The poor are systematically at a disadvantage relative to the rich at all levels of education. This is the case even in countries such as Chile, which historically has had one of the most developed educational systems in Latin America. In the 1980s, a mere 28 percent of lower-income students completed primary education.[13]

Urban/Rural

In addition to social class factors, there are significant urban/rural differences in equality of educational opportunities and outcomes. In Mexico, for example,

> only a small proportion of the rural schools offer a full six years of primary education, whereas nearly 90 percent of urban schools offer the first six years. There are still 25,000 rural primary schools in which children can't progress beyond the third grade. In some remote rural areas, primary schools consist of a single grade.[14]

Similar problems exist in Bolivia. The educational system consists of three three-year cycles. In both rural and urban areas, 90 percent of students complete the first three grades. In urban areas, the vast majority move on to the second cycle. However, in the rural areas, 90 percent of the students drop out. Thirty-eight percent of the rural population twenty-five years of age and older have no schooling at all, and for females the rate is 51 percent, as compared with only 13 percent of the urban population as a whole, and 18 percent of urban women.[15]

Rural/urban completion rates are also skewed for El Salvador and Colombia. Forty-seven percent of urban Salvadoran children complete the primary education. Only 19 percent of rural children complete the first six grades. In Colombia, 60 percent of urban primary students complete the sixth grade. Seventeen percent of rural children finish primary education.[16]

In contrast with the urban elites, the masses in rural locations are politically weak and disorganized. Historically, their interests have been poorly served by educational systems. Rural areas have the highest illiteracy rates, often two to three times greater than that of cities; they have fewer primary schools, inadequate school resources, and often no form of secondary or higher education at all.

Rural schools in Latin America, typically, are dilapidated and overcrowded, and they lack educational materials. Rural teachers are as a rule the least qualified, the most overburdened in terms of student-teacher ratios, and the most poorly paid. The textbooks (when in sufficient supply) and the curriculum contain little to engage the interest of children in rural areas. This problem is particularly acute in countries that have substantial indigenous populations, such as Bolivia, Peru, Ecuador, and Guatemala.

In most Latin American countries, students are required to pass standardized national examinations at various stages in the educational system to continue on to the subsequent stage. Given the disparity in the quality of education pertaining to rural and urban areas, many rural students (as well as those students who attend

inferior urban schools) fail to pass these examinations and either drop out or repeat the same grade. This pattern is evident from the beginning of primary school.
It is not uncommon for one-fourth of the students to repeat first and second grades
and for one-half of the students to not even finish their primary education.

To advance through the educational system in Latin America, an academically talented or socially ambitious youth will have to go to the cities, for that
is where most secondary schools are located. In a number of countries, well
over 90 percent of all educational facilities are located in urban areas, and a
handful of cities contain the bulk of secondary schools.

Gender

There are gender differences in literacy levels and educational attainments, but
over the years women have been making substantial gains, especially when
compared with women in other regions of the world. For example, in 1995, illiteracy figures for developing countries were 29.6 overall and 38.3 for females,
whereas the corresponding figures for Latin America were 13.4 overall and
14.5 for females.[17] From 1980 on, the rate of increase in female enrollments at
all three levels of education decelerated in developing regions; in the 1990s,
there has been almost no increase in enrollment rates: 46 percent at the primary
level, 43 percent at the secondary level, and 40 percent at the tertiary level. By
contrast (and rather surprisingly), female enrollment rates for Latin America
are on a par with those of "developed" countries: 48 percent at the primary
level, 52 percent at the secondary level, and 51 percent at the tertiary level. In
Argentina, Cuba, Brazil, Colombia, El Salvador, Nicaragua, and Panama
women comprise 50 percent or more of higher education students.[18]

In Latin America, despite increasing access to education and the narrowing
of the percentage difference in illiteracy by gender, there were still approximately 23 million illiterate women in the region in 1995.[19] When the combined
effects of social class, region, and gender are taken into account, the highest illiteracy rates are found among poor women living in rural areas. Gender differences in literacy attainment become even sharper when ethnicity is taken
into account. For example, Venezuelan illiteracy rates are as follows: 7.1 urban
and 26.7 rural, 9.1 male and 10.8 female, and 5.9 urban male and 28.0 rural female. In Bolivia, which has a very large indigenous population, illiteracy rates
are 8.9 urban and 36.1 rural, 11.8 male and 27.5 female, and 3.7 urban male and
49.4 rural female.[20]

Ethnicity

Indigenous populations or "first peoples" are the most discriminated against
populations with regard to access to educational services for two reasons. First,
they are commonly located in the most impoverished and underdeveloped

regions of their countries and, second, the language of instruction is invariably Spanish (Portuguese in Brazil). Even when efforts are made to begin instruction in maternal languages during the first year or two of schooling, Spanish (or Portuguese) becomes the language of instruction as one progresses through the education system. The countries with the largest indigenous populations—Bolivia, Peru, and Guatemala—have the highest illiteracy rates. Figures for countries like Mexico, which have a fairly low overall rate of illiteracy (13 percent in 1990), do not reveal the high illiteracy in regions with large concentrations of indigenous populations. Similarly, Panama, with an overall illiteracy rate of only 12 percent, has illiteracy rates of over 63 percent for its indigenous groups. It is not uncommon to find illiteracy rates greater than two-thirds to three-fourths of indigenous women living in rural areas.[21]

Advancing through the System

In recent decades, the great demand for secondary education has led to an impressive numerical expansion at this level of schooling. In 1950, approximately 10 percent of fifteen- to nineteen-year-olds attended secondary education; by 1995, 56.6 percent attended.[22] However, secondary education often has functioned as a "bottleneck" in a number of countries, not providing sufficient access for primary school graduates. In comparative perspective, Brazil, Guatemala, and Venezuela have enrollment ratios nearly 15 percent below that of international benchmarks.[23] Moreover, when we examine secondary student enrollments as a percentage of total enrollments, Latin America lags behind developing areas. In 1995, 22.3 percent of students in Latin America were enrolled at the secondary level, as compared with 30.2 percent for all developing areas.[24]

According to Behrman, secondary education also is a bottleneck in the sense that in countries such as Brazil and Venezuela, it is not producing sufficient numbers of graduates who are able to contribute to their competitive positions in the global economy.[25] As the United Nations Project on Development and Education in Latin America and the Caribbean notes, quantitative change generally has not been matched by a qualitative change in the aims, content, and pedagogy of secondary education. Secondary education, developed long after university and primary school education, has traditionally served as merely a junior appendage to university education, providing elite youth with the prerequisite educational background.[26] In time, a second branch of secondary education developed, consisting of technical, commercial, and normal (teacher training) schools. This vocationally oriented sector of secondary education has primarily served children of the lower middle class and the upwardly mobile working class. In many cases, it is of a terminal nature, that is, it does not lead to higher education. Thus it contributes to the dual-track character of schooling.

With the increasing demand for further education, the first cycle of secondary education—in most countries grades seven through nine—has become
an integral part of an introductory or "compulsory" cycle of six to nine years
of schooling. Latin American countries are increasingly moving away from
channeling postprimary students by means of tests. In fact, the trend is toward
"homogenization" of the different branches of secondary education with regard
to content and function up to grade nine.[27] General, university-preparatory
studies have become standard. Such studies represented over 70 percent of secondary school enrollment in 1950 and over 80 percent by 1988.[28] This pattern
has unfortunate consequences for the substantial number of students who drop
out or are otherwise unable to go on to higher education. And these students are
ill prepared to enter the workforce.

At the Top: Characteristics of Higher Education

A recent report of the Latin American Studies Association (LASA) Task Force
on Higher Education examines the functions, financing, and governance of tertiary education, as well as efforts to privatize and professionalize it.[29] The
report concludes that although democratization has often rescued higher education from government neglect, market orientations have not produced a
coherent reform agenda. It further notes that the reform agenda is highly polem-
ical, with supporters arguing that neoliberal reforms have not been sufficiently
implemented and opponents arguing that they should be postponed. Critics
maintain that the neoliberal agenda compromises the autonomy of higher education institutions while diverting their attention from the overriding tasks of
contributing to the strengthening of democratic government and addressing issues of increasing poverty and inequitable distribution of income.

An ironic pattern becomes apparent. Until recently, students who attended
private high schools frequently went on to a public university, where tuition
fees were nominal because of generous public financing. In effect, the children
of the middle and upper classes were subsidized by the government to attend
public universities and thereby to confirm their higher social status.

This pattern has begun to change as increasing numbers of students attend
private institutions of higher learning. Although higher education has grown
faster than primary or secondary education (and its growth rate in Latin America is the highest for any region of the world, approximately 3 percent annually
between 1975 and 1990), it is the private sector that registered the most dramatic gains. In the 1970s, approximately 5 percent of higher education students
were enrolled in private institutions; today over 30 percent attend private universities and colleges. Enrollment in private universities in Brazil is the highest in Latin America. At 61.5 percent, it is double the average figure for Latin
America.[30]

Overall, the growth rate of higher education in Latin America in the post–World War II period has been remarkable—in absolute terms and with regard to the corresponding age group. In 1950, there were approximately 1.5 million students in higher education; in 1995, more than 8 million.[31] In 1950, there were 105 universities in Latin America. By 1990, there were over 700 universities and altogether more than 2,500 institutions of higher learning, including teacher colleges, technical institutes, and junior colleges.[32]

Among the factors behind the growth of higher education, especially in the private sector, are overall population growth and the increasing numbers of students at the lower levels of education. More students, with their parents' encouragement, are demanding access to higher education, which is widely viewed as the gateway to the modern sector of the economy and to more prestigious and higher-paying jobs. Coupled with the social demand for education are government perceptions that economic development will require human resource development, especially high-level professionals and skilled technicians. Today, although in some countries 80 to 90 percent of university students still come from the middle and upper classes, increasing numbers of "popular sector" or lower-middle-class and working-class youths are gaining access to higher education institutions—notably the public universities.[33] For example, a study by Reimers showed that in Venezuela, 36 percent of university students came from the working classes.[34] Many believe that the rapid expansion of higher education has led to a deterioration of quality and a devaluation of education credentials throughout the region. Such fears, together with ongoing upheaval and student political activism in public institutions, have led to a movement of elites to private institutions. Thus, there has emerged a stratified system in which students from non-elite backgrounds attend two- or four-year public institutions and colleges and a variety of nontraditional "open universities" or "universities without walls" (which use radio and television transmissions and correspondence materials). At the same time, those from elite backgrounds attend more prestigious institutions that are often private or, if public, organized along the lines of private universities (e.g., Simón Bolívar University in Venezuela).

There are, of course, differences in public-private higher education from country to country. For example, the quality of private education in Brazil, Colombia, Mexico, Chile, El Salvador, and Costa Rica has declined due to easy private institutional accreditation policies.[35] These institutions absorb students who have failed to pass rather rigorous public university entrance examinations, and/or do not have the time to study on a demanding, full-time basis.

Public-private differences also emerge with regard to field of study. Most medical students are enrolled in public institutions because the cost of facilities adequate to prepare physicians is very high and usually must be borne by the state. Conversely, fields requiring minimal expenditure, such as the social sciences, are disproportionately represented in private institutions. Increasingly,

Table 12.3
Most Commonly Studied Fields in Latin America, 1960, 1975, 1989, 1993

Rank	1960	1975	1989	1993
First	Medicine	Social Sciences	Business Admin.	Business Admin.
Second	Law	Medicine	Engineering	Engineering
Third	Social Sciences	Education	Education	Education
Fourth	Engineering	Humanities	Medicine	Medicine

Sources: 1960 and 1975 data from UNESCO/CEPAL/PNUD, *Desarrollo y Educación en América Latina: Sintesis General,* informe final 4 (Buenos Aires: Projecto Desarrollo en América Latina y el Caribe, 1981), tables VII-12 and 16; 1989 figures from James Wilkie, ed., *Statistical Abstract of Latin America, 1995,* vol. 31, pt. 1 (Los Angeles: UCLA Latin America Center Publications, 1995), table 912; 1993 figures from *Statistical Abstract of Latin America, 1997,* vol. 33, table 908.

the study of economics, business, and administration takes place in the private sector. Engineering tends to be equally divided, more or less, between public and private universities.

The above discussion is pertinent to changing enrollment patterns, by discipline, over the past three decades. Table 12.3 illustrates changes in enrollment patterns since 1960. For each time period, medicine ranked among the most studied fields. It is particularly important to note the recent and rapid increase of enrollments in business administration.

Enrollment patterns by field of study bear little relation to the so-called human resource needs of Latin American countries. Despite the agricultural basis of many Latin American economies, often fewer than 5 percent of students are enrolled in courses in agricultural sciences. Late 1980s Cuba and Nicaragua, with university admissions quotas geared to national economic plans, were possible exceptions. Enrollments in agriculture, forestry, and fishery studies in Cuba constituted 10 percent of total enrollments (11,606 out of 115,529 students), whereas in Nicaragua, 15 percent of total enrollments (4,065 out of 26,878 students) were in agriculture, forestry, and fishery studies.[36]

One consequence of these enrollment patterns is that graduates in overpopulated fields such as business administration have great difficulty finding employment. Only graduates from the most prestigious institutions and fields—and in many cases with the traditional advantage of family connections—may be able to find employment to suit their expectations. One familiar outcome of these frustrated expectations is the "brain drain" of high-level talent to the metropolitan centers of North America and Europe. On the other hand, in new fields of development (e.g., petro-engineering), countries are forced to import experts from abroad.

Defining Education and Development

Fuenzalida has noted that in the post-World War II period, definitions of the term "development" passed through at least three stages.[37] During the first stage, development was defined primarily in terms of the expansion of an economy, to growth in the gross national product (GNP) of a country, which, in turn, was heavily dependent on acquiring the advanced scientific and technological knowledge of the industrialized countries of the North. By the end of the 1960s, a second stage emerged, in which development was viewed not only in terms of the expansion of the productive capacity of a country but also with regard to (1) the more equitable distribution of the expanded output of goods and services and (2) the democratic participation of the majority of citizens in decisions concerning the direction and nature of change. During this stage, attention also was given to the notion of preserving national culture and safeguarding the political sovereignty of a country. In the 1970s (the third stage), development was further defined to incorporate ideas of respect for the environment and conservation of nonrenewable natural resources as well as more equitable relations between the countries of the South and those of the North.

As international definitions of development have changed, so have conceptions of the role of education in society.[38] In Latin America, the goals of education from 1950 to 1970 tended to emphasize the importance of technology and the sciences in national development. Attention was given more to quality of education than to equality of educational opportunity, and higher education was emphasized. By 1970, it was evident that the goals of national development were better served by expanding access to schooling and democratizing opportunities for previously excluded populations to advance to the highest levels of education. In the 1970s and early 1980s, priority was accorded to provision of primary education and the first years of secondary education as well as literacy and adult basic education. However, the international debt crisis of the 1980s and 1990s hampered the achievement of these goals. In recent years, the notion of efficiency has achieved preeminence, attention being given to social rates of return to investments in different levels of education. As a result of such analyses, higher education and adult education do not enjoy the priority they were accorded in previous decades.[39]

Education and the Debt Crisis

The 1980s have been termed the "lost decade" for development in Latin America. Economic expansion, experienced at high rates from the 1950s through the 1970s, slowed considerably in the 1980s and 1990s. In the 1960s, the average annual GNP growth rate for Latin American economies was 5.7 percent. In the 1970s, the growth rate was 5.6 percent, despite difficulties caused by the oil crisis. By the 1980s, the average annual GNP growth rate for Latin American countries dropped to 1.3 percent.[40]

The falling gross national product translated into decreasing per capita income for the majority of Latin Americans. On average, Latin American per capita incomes fell 9 percent. In Argentina, per capita income fell 22 percent, whereas in Brazil per capita income fell only 5 percent.

In response to the ever deepening economic crisis, most Latin American governments adopted the neoliberal fiscal stabilization and economic adjustment policies promoted by international donor agencies like the International Monetary Fund (IMF) and the World Bank. The term "neoliberal" derives from the neoclassical economic theories expounded by these agencies and their consultants. The theories are based on the work of the classical economists Adam Smith and David Ricardo, who believed that the role of the state consisted in establishing the conditions by which the free play of the marketplace, the laws of supply and demand, and free trade based on competitive advantage would inevitably redound to the benefit of all. Government policies based on these notions have led to a drastic reduction in the state's role in social spending, deregulation of the economy, and liberalization of import policies. The educational counterparts of these policies have included moves to decentralize and privatize public school systems.

Although neoliberal policies are designed to reduce a country's fiscal deficits and external debt while bringing inflation under control, they also have contributed to deepening poverty in the region. In many countries, the social safety net provided by government subsidized services in health, education, and other basic services has been removed. Consequently, social class differences have intensified. In the 1980s in metropolitan Buenos Aires, 25 percent of the poorest households lost 15 percent of their income, whereas 5 percent of the richest households increased their income by almost 20 percent. In the metropolitan areas of Rio de Janeiro and São Paulo, 25 percent of the poorest households lost almost 13 percent of their income, whereas 5 percent of the richest gained approximately 25 percent. However, income losses were not only experienced by the poorest of the poor; 50 percent of the households located in the middle of the scale lost between 3 percent and 10 percent of their income.[41] As a result, class structures in Latin America have become more polarized, with rich and poor sectors separated by an increasingly wider gap. This is also true in Mexico and Chile, which have served as models of structural adjustment for other countries in the region. Despite the apparent economic success of Chile in particular, and Mexico until recently, the poor are becoming poorer and more numerous, and the gap between rich and poor is growing.[42]

With the economic downturn, all Latin American nations experienced decreases in educational expenditures in terms of gross national product and total governmental expenditure (TGE) (table 12.4). For example, in Ecuador both the GNP and the TGE were cut by nearly 50 percent. Education's percentage of the

Table 12.4
Education as Percentage of Gross National Product (GNP) and Total Governmental
Expenditure (TGE)

Country	% GNP 1980	% GNP 1995	% TGE 1980	% TGE 1995
Costa Rica	7.8	4.5	22.2	19.9
El Salvador	3.9	2.2	17.1	N/A
Bolivia	4.4	6.6	25.3	8.2
Chile	4.6	2.9	11.9	14.0
Ecuador	5.6	3.4	33.3	17.5*

*Figure is for 1991.
Source: UNESCO, *1997 Statistical Yearbook,* table 4.1.

GNP in Ecuador fell from 5.6 percent in 1980 to 3.4 percent in 1995. The percentage of TGE fell from 33.3 percent to 17.5 percent between 1980 and 1991.[43]

Under neoliberalism, significant improvements in education spending made during the 1960s and 1970s were effectively negated by drastic spending cuts in education. According to Reimers,

> On average, (unweighted) per capita expenditures in education in Latin America increased by 4.29 percent per year between 1975 and 1980, while they decreased by 6.14 percent between 1980 and 1985. The progress in educational finance made in the seventies was undone in the eighties.[44]

For example, in Bolivia, between 1975 and 1980, per capita expenditure on education increased at an annual rate of 3.62 percent. But between 1980 and 1985, per capita expenditure on education decreased at an annual rate of 42.03 percent.[45]

The spending cuts in education in Latin America first affected recurrent expenditures like the purchase of teaching materials and the maintenance of school buildings. Due to lack of funding, reforms designed in the 1970s and early 1980s were not implemented. Thus in the late 1980s and early 1990s teachers were working from curricula developed in the 1960s and with pedagogy designed to confront the challenges of the 1960s classroom.

Decreased expenditures, outdated pedagogies and curricula, and restricted access all contributed to the general decline in the quality of education. But neoliberal state policies have not gone uncontested. In Argentina, for instance, unionized state teachers, such as those who belong to the CTERA (Argentina Confederation of Educational Workers), jointly with one of the two larger general confederations of workers, the CTA (Confederation of Argentine Workers), have opposed the neoliberal reforms of the Peronist government. The recent elections, in which the government lost control of the lower house of parliament to an alliance of opposition parties, testifies to the effectiveness of the opposition of teachers, who have consistently been among the most visible and vocal challengers of the neoliberal agenda.

Low teacher salaries also affect education quality. The real value of teachers' salaries decreased steadily as currencies were devalued and inflation increased during the economic turmoil of the late 1980s. In many Latin American nations teachers were paid little more than domestic employees (Nicaraguan teachers receive less than domestic employees).

Unable to support their families, teachers throughout the hemisphere have regularly gone on strike to demand higher wages. On average, for all Latin American nations, teacher salaries fell 34.8 percent between 1980 and 1989. In El Salvador, teachers' annual salaries fell 68.4 percent, from $7,980 to $2,514. In the Dominican Republic, teacher salaries fell 60 percent, from $2,432 to $974.[46]

In recent years, many teachers have left the profession for higher-paying jobs. Many of the resulting vacancies are filled with teachers who lack a teaching credential. This is most unfortunate, as during the period between 1950 and 1985 there were substantial gains in the percentage of certified teachers, from 65 percent to 83 percent in Spanish America.[47] Throughout this period, male-female ratios in the teaching profession remained fairly constant, with women composing more than three-fourths of primary education and nearly one-half (46–49 percent) of secondary education teaching staff.[48] The secondary education figures compare favorably with those for developing regions, in which females make up only 32 to 40 percent of teaching staff.[49]

The exodus of teachers and the weeks and months of classroom time lost in strikes intensified already difficult circumstances in most Latin American classrooms. Overcrowded classrooms and the lack of up-to-date textbooks exacerbated the educational problems caused by the debt crisis. Moreover, teachers often have to spend time engaged in bureaucratic paperwork and carrying out the community outreach and assistance functions of schools, especially in poor neighborhoods (since schools there are social centers and nutritional centers), thus further reducing real teaching time.

As the debt crisis worsened and it became clear to education ministries that future funding would be limited, many ministries began to pursue other means of financial support. Primary among these options were privatization and decentralization. These two policies are favored methods of improving educational efficiency commonly sponsored by international donor agencies such as the World Bank and the International Monetary Fund. International donor agencies provided essential financial support to many Latin American nations in the 1980s and 1990s. Consequently, education ministries were, to an extent, obligated to subscribe to donor agency policy. As a result, "[donor agencies] have advocated a decrease in the amount of government involvement in the education process, an increase in the private sector's role, and greater application of market principles to the organization of Third World educational systems."[50]

Privatization

Privatization, most basically defined, is the investment of private money in previously public institutions. It entails either converting some public institutions into private institutions or charging user fees in public schools that were previously free of charge.

As the educational sector turned toward private interests to fund educational endeavors, policy planning changed to accommodate private investors. Parallel to education ministries' desire to conform to private interests was their need to create self-supporting school systems. This does not mean that education ministries abandoned the finance and support of public education. Rather, education ministries allowed for accelerated development and accreditation of private institutions (primary, secondary, and higher education). Private institutions were also attractive to middle- and upper-class students because high-quality ones offered smaller classes, improved facilities, and an overall atmosphere that was more conducive to learning.

The number of private schools in Latin America mushroomed in the past fifteen years. For example, in 1989, in Brazil, 14.5 percent of primary school students were enrolled in private schools, 34.6 percent of secondary school students, and 61.5 percent of university students. According to Plank and colleagues,

> there are two distinct kinds of private schools in Brazil. High-quality, high-cost primary and secondary schools serve the children of the middle and upper classes, while low-cost schools serve poor children in areas where the public provision of schools is inadequate. Secondary schools predominate among low-cost private schools, which are found mainly in rural areas and on the urban periphery. Both kinds of schools receive public subsidies, which are essential to the survival of many low-cost schools.[51]

Brazilian public authorities have adopted educational policies that, through governmental subsidization, support the privilege of middle-class parents to send their children to superior private schools. As a result, middle-class parents are no longer limited in their choices to send their children to public schools or low-quality private schools.[52] Such policies and practices have negative effects on the public schools. When middle-class parents leave the public school system, the most vocal advocates for quality in the schools disappear. The lower classes, although constituting the majority of the population, lack the political and economic clout necessary to promote quality in the public school system. Without middle-class support, and facing decreased funding, many public school systems have fallen into decline. Both educational quality and facilities have deteriorated significantly.

Decentralization

Another option pursued by educational ministries in response to financial crisis was decentralization. Decentralization is essentially the practice in which municipalities are given responsibility for governing the educational sector (finance and curriculum). Unlike the highly decentralized U.S. school system, education in most Latin American nations is dominated by a strong central education ministry that controls all budgetary and curricular issues. In the past ten years, there has been considerable debate surrounding the issue of decentralization. Many nations have pondered decentralizing their educational systems, shifting many financial and curricular planning responsibilities to the municipalities. To date, the countries that have implemented a national decentralization policy are Colombia (1968 and 1986), Argentina (1976), Mexico (1978), and Chile (1981).[53] Local municipalities have been given primary funding responsibilities for local schools. The idea is that schools considered superior in quality and services can attract more students and thereby increase their funding capacity. The state partially subsidizes education, but the municipalities are responsible for paying the balance. For example, in Chile, at the preprimary and primary levels (grades 1 and 2), the government subsidized 46 percent of education costs. Grades 3–5 and 6–8 were subsidized at 52 and 56 percent, respectively. General secondary education was subsidized at 63 percent and technical secondary education grades 1–2 and 3–5 were subsidized at 37 and 63 percent, respectively.[54]

This system may be successful in middle-class, suburban municipalities, but it presents serious problems for lower-class municipalities and rural areas. These areas do not have the resources necessary to make up for educational costs not covered by government subsidies. Nor do they have the same resources to make informed decisions regarding market mechanisms and cost-containment incentives introduced by the government as new educational practices.[55] Both privatization and decentralization exacerbate preexisting socioeconomic inequalities in the education system. Although the elite continue to benefit from quality education, the marginalized sectors of the population are disproportionately the victims of the growing educational crisis.

Popular Education and Other Innovations

In contrast to state-sponsored education programs, there are a number of grassroots education programs in Latin America that form part of a "popular education" movement. Although limited in resources and small in scope, these programs nonetheless are significant in that they offer an alternative model of education that empowers individuals and communities to place demands on national governments for social services and resources that should be the right of all citizens of a country.

Since the 1960s, nonformal and popular education programs have been important alternatives to the formal education sector. Nonformal education implies an educative experience that occurs outside the standard education sphere. Popular education, a subset of nonformal education, is distinguished by its pedagogical and political characteristics.[56]

Pedagogically, popular education programs emphasize nonhierarchical learning situations in which teachers and students engage in dialogue, and learners' knowledge is incorporated into the content of instruction. According to Torres, "education appears as the act of knowing rather than a simple transmission of knowledge or the cultural baggage of society."[57]

Politically, popular education programs tend to be directed at meeting the special needs of marginalized sectors of society (women, unemployed, peasants, and indigenous groups). Popular education programs have offered marginalized sectors in Latin America opportunities for personal growth and socioeconomic and political participation. They have played a significant role in facilitating the development of collective survival strategies to confront the economic crisis of the 1980s and 1990s in the region. Furthermore, the ultimate aim of many popular education programs is not just adaptation or survival for hard-pressed populations but sweeping social change that leads to more just societies.[58]

Examples of popular education programs include Peru Mujer (Peru Woman) and the Center for Women's Action (CEPAM) in Ecuador. Both programs attempt to organize and educate women in the fields of discriminatory labor codes and practices, inheritance and family law, and domestic violence issues. These programs meet the demands of women for greater equality and opportunity and the chance to participate actively in the formulation of alternative social change strategies.

Although popular education programs are generally effective on the community level, they often fail to bring about change at the level of governmental policy. In one extremely interesting case, a leading proponent of popular education, Paulo Freire, had an opportunity to effect large-scale educational change.

For the past thirty years, the late Paulo Freire, as a theorist and an innovator, has redefined what educators all over the world think about the potential of education to contribute to social change. Freire's theories articulate the intimate relationship between education and development, particularly the connection between individual empowerment and democratic ideals. Freire was involved in designing and implementing literacy campaigns and popular education programs in countries worldwide. As municipal secretary of education between 1989 and 1991, Freire was involved in the development and implementation of numerous programs in São Paulo (South America's largest city, with a population of over 14 million people). The popular education programs put in place were designed to (1) increase access to schooling, (2) democratize school administration, (3) improve instructional quality, (4) expand educational opportunity for working youths and adults, and (5) contribute to the formation of critical and responsible citizens.[59]

Despite the egalitarian intent of Freire's program, several studies point out the limitations of such efforts. Stromquist analyzed the literacy and adult education component (MOVA, Movimiento de Alfabetização de Jovenes e Adultos) of the overall reform effort. She found a number of problems in moving from the notion of a liberating education to the actual classroom practices and materials that would enable individuals to develop reading and writing habits leading to personal fulfillment and social action, especially for women. Personal case histories revealed the disjuncture between the political goals held by those planning literacy programs and the personal goals motivating women to acquire literacy.[60] At the macrolevel of policy formulation and implementation, Lindquist Wong's study indicates that implementation of the reform program became mired in local politics and bureaucracies.[61] Yet Lindquist Wong's overall assessment is that the model of educational reform during Freire's administration has been one of the most successful in terms of its process and outcomes.

Of concern to those committed to the cause of literacy, adult basic education, and various forms of popular education is that state funding for such programs has begun to dry up in recent years. National school systems are increasingly focusing their literacy efforts on school-aged children or adults under thirty-five years of age. Governments such as Nicaragua (1990 on) have largely abandoned the state's role in meeting the educational needs of out-of-school youths and adults to the civil sector. However, if universal literacy and comprehensive lifelong learning systems are to be achieved, the state and the civil society will have to work in tandem rather than in opposition.[62]

There are, nonetheless, examples of ambitious state-sponsored educational innovations that do benefit traditionally underserved populations. One example is Fe y Alegría (Faith and Happiness). This Venezuelan NGO began in 1955 with educating one hundred children in a single room. By 1992 the program had expanded to twelve countries with a total of 509 centers and more than half a million students. According to Reimers, the mission of Fe y Alegría is to "provide quality education to the poor as expressed in their motto 'Where the asphalt road ends, where there is no water, electricity or services, there begins Fe y Alegría.'"[63] Although there is no "systematic evaluation" for Fe y Alegría, parents claim that these schools provide a better education than public schools. In 1989, 85 percent of Guatemalan students who entered Fe y Alegría at the preschool level completed primary education within seven years, as opposed to 34 percent in government schools.[64] Reimers states that innovative programs such as Fe y Alegría are usually not embraced by Latin American ministries of education until they have proven themselves. Fe y Alegría was initially privately funded but went on to secure substantial government funding in most cases. For example, 80 percent of the program budget is now funded by the government in Venezuela.[65]

Another example of a state-sponsored innovation is La Escuela Nueva (the New School) in Colombia, which is designed to meet the special needs of rural schools and communities by creating a curriculum that emphasizes communal needs and values. The New School reform actively encourages a strong relation between schools and communities, and a flexible school calendar and promotion policy that is adapted to local agricultural production cycles. One of the goals of the New School is to teach civic values by encouraging both student and parent participation in important decisions concerning local educational policy.[66] Between its creation in 1989 and 1992, the program expanded from 8,000 to over 35,000 schools.

Finally, it is necessary to point out the important role that universities, through their research, development, and dissemination activities, can play in regard to the most disadvantaged members of their societies. In this role universities can contribute to income and job generation to overcome the devastating effects of the debt crisis and the economic restructuring to control inflation and fiscal deficits. Higher education leaders like Xabier Gorostiaga of the Central American University (UCA) of Nicaragua have proposed a vision of a new role for "universities of the South." His vision calls for utilizing existing university departmental extension programs and research and development institutes affiliated with the UCA as nuclei for experimentation, training, and popular education. Building a university education around the knowledge generated by rural-based centers would contribute to the formation of professionals who, because they had a more realistic understanding of their society, would be better prepared to address its most pressing problems. Moreover, the work of such centers would contribute to empowering the "producing majority" to become major historical actors involved in the transformation of an unsatisfactory status quo that has marginalized and exploited them. According to Gorostiaga, "All of these experimental nuclei offer an ideal place for our professors and students to bring their theoretical knowledge down to earth, to participate in research projects that directly benefit civil society" and to extend education to the majority of people excluded from secondary and higher education.[67] Such efforts are critical to the development and dissemination of appropriate and self-sustainable technologies, and they offer prospects of collaboration between universities of the North and the South.[68]

Conclusions

The implementation of structural adjustment policies to liberalize the economies of Latin America and integrate them more tightly into the world capitalist system has provoked a number of crises throughout the region. In diminishing the role of the state in the provision of basic social services—part of the cost-cutting policies recommended by the World Bank and the IMF—the social safety net provided the most marginalized populations has been effectively removed. The distance between the wealthy and the poor is increasing.

Moves to decentralize and privatize economies are paralleled by initiatives to dismantle centralized ministries of education and charge user fees for educational services that once were provided free to all. Although such measures contain an element of justice in that the wealthy may have to pay a fairer share of the costs of their education—costs once borne by the public at large—for the poor the picture is bleak. Their hope that education can provide a means of mobility for their children to climb out of poverty appears to be thwarted by the imposition of fees they are unable to pay.

These fiscal austerity and structural adjustment policies have resulted in growing social unrest and mass demonstrations that have threatened and toppled governments, as in Venezuela. In the education field, the introduction of these neoliberal economic policies and a conservative ideological agenda into the education system has led to numerous protests—teacher strikes and student and parent occupations of schools and Ministry of Education offices in countries like Nicaragua. As Arnove has documented in his case study of Nicaragua, these initiatives have polarized education, despite the ostensible goals of government to use education as a means of achieving social consensus.[69]

There is now widespread recognition by international donor agencies (such as the Inter-American Development Bank), national governments, and NGOs—the various protagonists and antagonists—that there is a need for consensus around a model of national development and around the education system itself. Achieving consensus concerning how education will be governed and financed and what will be taught is extremely important if education systems are to play their role in contributing to preparing individuals to exercise citizenship rights in a democracy and providing them with the knowledge and skills to contribute to sustainable economic development that benefits all.

It is possible, but unlikely, that consensus around education can be achieved without a national agreement being reached around a model of economic development. This model must be based on protecting the autonomy and sovereignty of individual countries to devise economic and social policies that are reflective of their individual histories, social and cultural dynamics, rather than economic agendas determined in Washington, D.C., Rome, or Paris. It would be a model that recognizes and supports autonomous, sustainable development at the grassroots level and in the informal sectors of the economy, the so-called industries of the poor, that provide employment for as much as one-half of the workforce of many Latin American countries.[70] It would be a model that draws upon features of a free-market economy to generate goods and services but also upon those of social democracies that provide a social safety net—the basic conditions for all to live decently.

Such a model obviously requires all major stakeholders to engage in a dialogue on how their various strengths can complement one another in achieving the goal of sustainable and equitable economic development. Although this vision is utopian in many respects, it nonetheless offers a more realistic route out of present and impending crises than do current political and economic policies that further condition the dependent state in Latin America and contribute to increasing social inequalities, political instability, and economic stagnation.

Notes

1. F. H. Cardoso, "On the Characterization of Authoritarian Regimes in Latin America," in *The New Authoritarianism in Latin America,* ed. David Collier (Princeton: Princeton University Press, 1979), 33–57.

2. Claus Offe, *Contradictions of the Welfare State* (Cambridge, Mass.: MIT Press, 1984); Claus Offe and V. Ronge, "Theses on the Theory of the State," *New German Critique* 6 (Fall 1975): 137–147.

3. Martin Carnoy and Henry Levin, *Schooling and Work in the Democratic State* (Stanford: Stanford University Press, 1985); Samuel Bowles and Herbert Gintis, *Democracy and Capitalism* (New York: Basic Books, 1986).

4. Sheryl L. Lutjens, *The State, Bureaucracy, and the Cuban Schools: Power and Participation* (Boulder: Westview, 1996).

5. F. H. Cardoso, "Las Contradicciones del Desarrollo Asociado," *Desarrollo Económico* 14, no. 53 (1974); F. H. Cardoso, *Political Regime and Social Change: Some Reflections Concerning the Brazilian Case* (Stanford, Calif.: Stanford University/University of California, Berkeley, Stanford-Berkeley Joint Center for Latin American Studies, 1981), 28–29.

6. See, for example, Walter LaFeber, *Inevitable Revolutions: The United States in Central America* (New York: Norton, 1993).

7. Martin Carnoy, cited in Carlos Alberto Torres, *The Politics of Nonformal Education in Latin America* (New York: Praeger, 1990), x.

8. Robert Arnove, Stephen Franz, and Kimberly Morse, "Latin American Education," in *Latin America: Perspectives on a Region,* 2d ed., ed. Jack W. Hopkins (New York: Holmes and Meier, 1998); Jere R. Behrman, "Investing in Human Resources," in *Economic and Social Progress in Latin America: Annual Report* (Inter-American Development Bank, 1993), 206.

9. UNESCO, *Statistical Yearbook 1997* (Paris: UNESCO, 1997), I-5 through I-9.

10. Behrman, "Investing," 205.

11. *UNDP Human Development Report 1992,* table 17; cited in Behrman, "Investing," 196–197.

12. George Psacharopoulos et al., *Poverty and Income Distribution in Latin America: The Story of the 1980s* (Washington, D.C.: World Bank, 1992); cited in Behrman, "Investing," 196.

13. George Kurian, ed., *World Education Encyclopedia* (New York: Facts on File, 1988), 197.

14. Kurian, *World Education,* 864.

15. UNESCO, *1996 Statistical Yearbook,* table 1.3.

16. Kurian, *World Education,* 123, 1498, 242, respectively, by country.

17. UNESCO, *1997 Statistical Yearbook,* table 2.2.

18. UNESCO, *1997 Statistical Yearbook,* table 3.10. It should be noted that al-

though current data are not available for Argentina and Panama, in the mid-1980s, female enrollments in those countries were respectively 53 percent and 58 percent. Also noteworthy is that in Nicaragua, in the 1980s, women made up 56 percent of enrollments; this figure reveals not only the commitment of the Sandinista government to expanded educational opportunity but the existence of a civil war and a military draft.

19. UNESCO, *1997 Statistical Yearbook,* table 2.2.

20. James W. Wilkie, ed., *Statistical Abstract of Latin America,* vol. 32 (Los Angeles: UCLA Latin American Center Publications), pt. 1, 1996, table 900. Figures for Venezuela and Bolivia are based on 1990 and 1992 data, respectively.

21. James W. Wilkie, ed., *Statistical Abstract of Latin America,* vol. 31 (Los Angeles: UCLA Latin American Center Publications), pt. 1, 1995, table 900.

22. UNESCO, *1997 Statistical Yearbook,* table 2.10.

23. Behrman, "Investing," 206.

24. UNESCO, *1997 Statistical Yearbook,* table 2.5.

25. Behrman, "Investing," 205.

26. UNESCO/CEPAL/PNUD, *Desarrollo y Educación en América Latina: Síntesis General,* informe final 4 (Buenos Aires: Proyecto Desarrollo en América Latina y el Caribe, 1981), vii–1.

27. Ibid.

28. UNESCO, *World Education Report* (Paris: UNESCO, 1991), 33.

29. Latin American Studies Association Task Force on Higher Education, "Higher Education amid the Political Economic Changes of the 1990s," *LASA Forum* 24, no. 1 (Spring 1994): 3–16; also see Noel McGinn, "The Implications of Globalisation for Higher Education," in *Learning from Experience: Policy and Practice in Aid to Higher Education* (The Hague: CESO, 1995).

30. David Plank, José Amaral Sobrinho, and Antonio Carlos da Ressurreiçao Xavier, "Obstacles to Educational Reform in Brazil," *La educación* 1, no. 117 (1994): 83.

31. UNESCO, *1997 Statistical Yearbook,* table 2.4.

32. Orlando Albornoz, *Education and Society in Latin America* (Oxford: Macmillan, 1993), 136; Latin American Studies Association Task Force on Higher Education, "Higher Education," 3–4.

33. UNESCO/CEPAL/PNUD, *Desarrollo y Educación,* vii–1.

34. Fernando Reimers, "The Impact of Economic Stabilization and Adjustment on Education in Latin America," *Comparative Education Review* 35, no. 2 (1991): 339.

35. Latin American Studies Association Task Force on Higher Education, "Higher Education," 11.

36. Wilkie, *Statistical Abstract,* 1995, table 912.

37. Edmundo Fuenzalida, "Development and Education," in *International Encyclopedia of Education,* ed. Torsten Husén and T. Neville Postlethwaite (New York: Pergamon, 1985), 3:1374–1379.

38. Robert Arnove, Stephen Franz, Kimberly Morse, and Carlos Alberto Torres, "Education and Development in Latin America," in *Understanding Contemporary Latin America,* ed. Richard S. Hillman (New York: Lynne Rienner, 1996).

39. George Psacharopoulos, "Economic Aspects of Educational Planning," in *Economics of Education: Research and Studies,* ed. George Psacharopoulos (New York: Pergamon, 1987), 311–314.

40. CEPAL, *Transformación productiva con equidad* (Santiago de Chile: Comisión Económica para América Latina, 1990); CEPAL, *Panorama social de América Latina* (Santiago de Chile: Comisión Económica para América Latina, 1991); World Bank, *Brazil: Public Spending on Social Programs: Issues and Options,* World Bank Report 7086-BR (Washington, D.C.: World Bank, 1988).

41. CEPAL, *Panorama social.*

42. Jorge Castañeda, *La utopia desarmada* (Mexico: J. Mortiz/Planeta, 1993).

43. UNESCO, *1997 Statistical Yearbook,* table 4.1.

44. Reimers, "Impact of Economic Stabilization," 322.

45. Ibid.

46. Laurence Wolff, Ernesto Schiefelbein, and Jorge Valenzuela, *Improving the Quality of Primary Education in Latin America and the Caribbean* (Washington, D.C.: World Bank, 1994), 154.

47. See Carlos Newland, "Spanish American Elementary Education, 1950–1992: Bureaucracy, Growth, and Decentralization," *International Journal of Educational Development* 15, no. 2 (1995): 108.

48. UNESCO, *1997 Statistical Yearbook,* table 2.7.

49. Ibid.

50. Edward Berman, "Donor Agencies and Third World Educational Development, 1945–1985," in *Emergent Issues in Education: Comparative Perspectives,* ed. Robert Arnove, Philip Altbach, and Gail Kelly (Albany: State University of New York Press, 1992), 69.

51. Plank et al., "Obstacles to Educational Reform," 81.

52. Plank et al., "Obstacles to Educational Reform," 82.

53. Cuba, as part of its 1986 "rectification" overhaul of centralized government, also initiated a process of decentralization in education. Unlike municipalization plans in other Latin American countries, it tended to shift more power to local school councils and various forms of "popular power" (see Lutjens, *State, Bureaucracy*).

54. Patricia Matte and Antonio Sancho, "Primary and Secondary Education," in *The Chilean Experience: Private Solutions to Public Problems,* ed. Christian Larroulet (Santiago: Editorial Trineo S.A., 1993), 106.

55. Juan Prawda, "Educational Decentralization in Latin America: Lessons Learned," *International Journal of Educational Development* 13, no. 3 (1993): 262.

56. Marcy Fink and Robert Arnove, "Issues and Tensions in Popular Education in Latin America," *International Journal of Educational Development* 11, no. 3 (1991): 221–230; Cyril Poster and Jorgen Zimmer, eds., *Community Education in the Third World* (New York: Routledge, 1992).

57. Carlos Alberto Torres, "Paulo Freire as Secretary of Education in the Municipality of Sao Paulo," *Comparative Education Review* 38, no. 2 (1994): 198–199.

58. Carlos Alberto Torres and Adriana Puiggrós, "The State and Public Education in Latin America," *Comparative Education Review* 39, no. 1 (1995): 26.

59. Pia Lindquist Wong, "Constructing a Public Popular Education in Sao Paulo, Brazil," *Comparative Education Review* 39, no. 1 (1995): 120; see also Rosa María Torres, "Illiteracy and Literacy Training in Latin America and the Caribbean: Between Inertia and a Break with the Past," *Prospects* 20 (1990): 464.

60. Nelly Stromquist, *Literacy for Citizenship* (Albany: State University of New York Press, 1997).

328   *R. Arnove, S. Franz, M. Mollis, & C. A. Torres*

61. Wong, "Popular Education."

62. Moaçir Gadotti, "Latin America: Popular Education and the State," in *Community Education in the Third World,* ed. Cyril Poster and Jürgen Zimmer (New York: Routledge, 1992), 170–184; Rosa María Torres, *Para Rejuvenecer la Educación de Adultos* (New York: UNICEF, 1995).

63. Fernando Reimers, "Role of NGOs in Promoting Educational Innovation: A Case Study in Latin America," in *Education and Development: Tradition and Innovation,* vol. 4, *Non-formal and Non-governmental Approaches,* ed. James Lynch, Celia Modgil, and Sohan Modgil (London: Cassell, 1997), 35.

64. Reimers, "Role of NGOs," 38.

65. Reimers, "Role of NGOs."

66. Henry Levin, "Effective Schools and Comparative Focus," in *Emergent Issues in Education: Comparative Perspectives,* ed. Robert Arnove, Philip Altbach, and Gail Kelly (Albany: State University of New York Press, 1992), 229–245; Carlos Newland, "Spanish American Elementary Education, 1950–1992: Bureaucracy, Growth, and Decentralization," *International Journal of Educational Development* 15, no. 2 (1995): 103–114.

67. Xabier Gorostiaga, "New Times, New Role for Universities of the South," *Envío* 12, no. 144 (July 1993): 24–40.

68. Robert Arnove, "Partnerships and Emancipatory Educational Movements: Issues and Prospects," *Alberta Journal of Educational Research* 42, no. 2 (June 1996): 170–177.

69. Robert Arnove, *Education as Contested Terrain: Nicaragua, 1979–1993* (Boulder: Westview, 1994).

70. Gorostiaga, "New Times."

Chapter 13

Asian Education

Zhixin Su

Asia is the largest and the most populous continent in the world. Home to some of the world's oldest cultures, Asia has long been of great interest to the rest of the world. There are two definitions of Asia. In the classical sense, Asia extends east as far as the Pacific Ocean, north to the Arctic Ocean, and south to the Indian Ocean and the islands of Southeast Asia. The five major regions, Russian Asia, Southwest Asia, South Asia, Southeast Asia, and East Asia, into which classical Asia is divided are distinguished primarily by culture, history, political development, and, to some extent, natural environment. Modern geographers, however, often define Asia in a narrower sense. This smaller Asia is based on the region's more recent political, cultural, and economic changes. Thus modern Asia excludes two subregions, Russian Asia and Southwest Asia. Remaining in the modern version of Asia are three subregions: South Asia, Southeast Asia, and East Asia.[1] This chapter describes and discusses educational trends and changes in modern Asia because 2.2 billion people, or 85 percent of the Asian population, live within the modern limitations of Asia. The modern definition is also the one commonly used by comparative researchers and international organizations.[2]

In ancient times, merchants carried silks, spices, and other exotic products from Asia westward to Europe. This trade benefited Asian economies, and it also brought knowledge about Asia to the outside world. Unfortunately, that knowledge led eventually to the European colonial takeover of much of Asia by the nineteenth century. By World War I, most of Asia was under European control. Asian traditional societies proved to be no match for the militarily and technologically superior Europeans.

After World War II and between 1945 and 1975, colonialism ended and virtually all the countries of Asia became independent. In 1997, Hong Kong

returned to China peacefully; in 1999 the last relic of the colonial era—
Macao—is scheduled to revert to China's control. The contemporary political
economic systems in Asia vary significantly from one country to another. Some
are market economy democracies, some have had socialist/communist governments with centrally planned economic systems, some are still ruled by kings,
and some have a mixed system of hereditary kings and democratically elected
rulers.[3] Asia has some of the world's poorest countries, such as Bangladesh and
Nepal. In fact, two-thirds of the world's poor live in the region of South Asia.
Yet many Asian nations (e.g., South Korea and Singapore) are well developed
and fall into the category of middle-income countries.[4] The foremost and earliest success in Asia was Japan, which had to rebuild itself after the devastation
of World War II. By the late 1970s Japan had become the economic giant of
the Far East, carving out market shares for its products in all parts of the world.
By the 1980s Japan's success was being emulated by the "Four Little Tigers"
of Asia: Taiwan, South Korea, Hong Kong, and Singapore. By 1990 even larger
areas were undergoing significant economic development. Among these were
Indonesia and Malaysia. Both of these multi-island nations are very populous,
and development was uneven. The most surprising change took place in South
China. Guangdong province, just north of Hong Kong, had become one of the
fastest growing economies in the world by 1992. There has been tremendous
change and growth in education and schooling in many of the Asian nations
since World War II. Today one out of every two students in primary and secondary schools, and one out of every three students enrolled in higher education in the world, is in Asia. The rate of growth in enrollments in primary education has been the highest among the world regions. Enrollment growth in
secondary and higher education is also higher than the world averages. Many
Asian nations, especially those with rapidly expanding economies, have started
to invest heavily in research and development, and universities have played a
central part of this expansion of research.[5] Although many regions are still undeveloped, Asian universities located in major cities are becoming centers of
research and development, some at world-class levels. As Tilak observes, the
world education miracle can even be called the "Asian Miracle."[6]

Nevertheless, the growth in education is highly uneven in Asia, and there is
a clear contrast between the East Asian and South Asian regions. Moreover, the
impressive progress in education appears less impressive when adjusted for an
increase in population. Asia's population growth rate is the highest in the
world. Consequently, even though literacy rates increased over time, the number of illiterates also increased. In fact, half of the out-of-school children and
four-fifths of the illiterates in the world can be found in Asia.[7] In addition, male-
female inequalities in education are rather high in Asian countries. Female literacy rates are about half the male literacy rates in South Asia, and about three-
fourths in East Asia. Female enrollment ratios in education in all Asian nations
are lower than male enrollment ratios. Gender discrimination seems to be in-

creasing at higher levels of education, though they are declining over time at every level of education.[8] The following discussion of the similarities and the differences in educational development in Asian nations is divided into three sections: South Asia, Southeast Asia, and East Asia. The discussion in each section includes illustrations of selected critical issues in education from selected nations. I emphasize the effect that recent reform efforts in education have had on equality of opportunity and outcomes for the most disadvantaged groups in different Asian nations.

South Asia

South Asia is often referred to as the Indian subcontinent. It consists of modern India, which has a dominant presence, plus the smaller nations of Pakistan and Afghanistan to the west, Bangladesh to the east, Nepal and Bhutan to the north, and the island nations of Sri Lanka and the Maldives to the south. The northern boundary of South Asia is the great Himalayan mountain chain, which forms the southern border of Tibet, a part of China. Nepal and Bhutan are landlocked mountain states with limited agricultural potential. The same is true of Afghanistan, though it has a much larger territory.[9] All of South Asia was controlled by the British as part of their worldwide colonial empire until independence was granted in the late 1940s. The great diversity of peoples, languages, and religions in South Asia, combined with overpopulation and extensive poverty, left the region with many problems in national and educational development. Since independence, there have been many improvements characterized by growth of industry, mechanization of agriculture, urbanization, and an increase in literacy. Table 13.1 shows the current educational performance figures in selected South Asian nations. It indicates some achievements in universalizing primary education, but modest and varied gains in developing secondary education. Higher education is available only to a small percentage of the population, and the adult illiteracy rate, especially among women, is still very high. In Pakistan and Bangladesh, about two-thirds of the adults (nearly 80 percent of women) are illiterate, and in Nepal, 74 percent of the adults (87 percent of women) are illiterate.

India, with more than 800 million people and a rich history of culture and religion, is the giant nation in South Asia. It has gained considerable economic growth and has made large-scale investment in education, and has established a well-developed educational infrastructure as well. Table 13.1 shows that India has universalized primary education and has sent 49 percent of the age-group to secondary schools. However, there is still a very high rate of adult literacy (48 percent overall; 62 percent for women), and a substantial gap exists between urban and rural areas. This disparity presents the fundamental challenge to Indian educators.[10] India's higher education system, a legacy of the

Table 13.1
South Asia

	Afghan-istan	Bangla-desh	India	Mal-dives	Nepal	Paki-stan	Sri Lanka
Government expenditures in education (% GNP) 1992	n.a.	2.3	3.7	6.6	2.9	2.7	3.3
Primary students 1992 (Gross enrollment ratio %)	31	79	101	130	109	44	105
Secondary students 1992 (Gross enrollment ratio %)	15	19	49	44	35	21	74
Tertiary students 1992 (Gross enrollment ratio %)	n.a.	4	n.a.	n.a.	7	n.a.	6
Adult illiteracy 1995 (%)	68.5	61.9	48	6.8	72.5	62.2	9.8
Female adult illiteracy 1995 (%)	85	73.9	62.3	7.0	86	75.6	12.8

Sources: Michael Westlake, ed., *Asia 1996 Yearbook* (Hong Kong: Far Eastern Economic Review, 1996), 14–17; UNESCO, *World Education Report 1995* (Paris: UNESCO, 1995).

colonial period, has grown into the second largest in the world in the past half century, providing many people with access to higher education. It has developed a small number of excellent centers of learning. Nevertheless, it has also produced a very large number of poor-quality products from the "academic slums."[11] In addition, a large number of university graduates remain unemployed because college and university education has expanded much more rapidly than the economy. Serious reform to solve these problems is under way in a World Bank–sponsored project on higher education reform in India.[12] The reform attempts to reduce government control, grant autonomy to colleges, create resources, and develop a new general degree program for the mass of students who are presently shunted off into the traditional arts, science, and commerce courses. The smaller nations in South Asia have also tried to develop and modernize their own educational systems. In the tiny isolated kingdom of Bhutan, secular education is still very young and has been highly dependent of

Indian traditions. In the late 1980s, educators in Bhutan initiated a reform movement called the New Approach to Primary Education, which has achieved remarkable success and radically changed the nature of primary education in Bhutan. In contrast to traditional monastic education, the new curricula are much more closely oriented to the reality of Bhutanese society. Passive rote learning has been largely replaced by a much more active, inquiry-based approach.[13] Another notable example in educational advancement in small nations can be found in the pear-shaped island nation, Sri Lanka. Table 13.1 demonstrates that in contrast to the very high illiteracy rate in all other South Asian nations, including the more economically developed India, Sri Lanka has reduced its illiteracy rate to only 10 percent (13 percent for women). Schooling is free and compulsory for children aged five to thirteen. Free secondary and college and university education are also available, although only 6 percent of the people in that age-group are studying in tertiary institutions. Among those attending colleges and universities, there has been a steady increase of women, from 10.1 percent in 1942, when the first university in Sri Lanka was established, to 42.9 percent in 1990. Still, women are underrepresented in technology-related fields, and female enrollment is relatively low in postgraduate institutions.[14] The experience in Sri Lanka suggests that even in economically poor and developing countries, it is possible to universalize primary schooling, achieve adult literacy, and provide more equal education for women.

Despite moderate to great successes in educational development in some areas, educators in South Asian nations have experienced numerous difficulties in their reform and modernization efforts. Several factors have been recognized as obstacles to educational development: war, rapid population growth, natural calamities, and constant political instability.[15] In recent years, although some improvements have been reported in terms of the alleviation of poverty, South Asian nations still rank among the least developed nations in the world.[16] Regardless of the obstacles and difficulties they face, the nations of South Asia have become increasingly open to the outside world and interlocked with extranational social and cultural systems. Moreover, they are beginning to regard themselves as newly democratizing countries (NDCS) and have strong faith in the power of education to engineer social change. How much to change and how much to keep in the way of traditional educational practices remains a constant challenge. As Regmi, a leading scholar in Nepal, states, "Their interests lie typically in using education as a means of producing a fairer, more equitable society."[17]

Southeast Asia

Southeast Asia consists of two parts: mainland and insular (largely the island area). The mainland is composed of parallel mountain ranges and river valleys that run south and southeast out of the Tibetan plateau and surrounding highlands. Thus the mainland nations of Myanmar (formerly Burma), Thailand, Laos, Cambodia (Kampuchea), and Vietnam consist of a central river valley in which most of the people live. Insular Southeast Asia consists of the Malay peninsula and the many islands that make up the nations of Malaysia, Singapore, Indonesia, Brunei, and the Philippines.

All of Southeast Asia was under colonial rule or influence until the end of World War II. Since becoming independent, these countries have struggled to develop their natural resources, industries, and educational systems. Singapore and Jakarta have already become modern industrial centers, and other nations are catching up. The Indochina conflict that raged from World War II until the mid-1970s hampered progress in the states of Indochina, of which Vietnam has become perhaps the most powerful. Political turmoil disrupted education in the region, especially in Cambodia, further complicating economic and educational growth.[18] In 1967 the Association of Southeast Asian Nations (ASEAN) was founded, which included all of the insular nations plus Thailand. Vietnam joined ASEAN in 1995. Over the last three decades, ASEAN has maintained close ties to the West and now has a combined population of 420 million people, which makes it a strong political, economic, and trade group. The organization's goal is to become a ten-nation bloc by the year 2000. In the 1970s, all ASEAN nations participated in a basic education movement to improve their primary- and secondary-school education. Emphasis was placed on reading, writing, and numeracy, as well as citizenship education. The reform movement was later criticized for ignoring other important elements of the curriculum, but it did succeed in laying a strong educational foundation for each of the ASEAN nations. In addition to formal schooling, ASEAN countries also developed a variety of nonformal education programs targeting literacy, women's education, agricultural education, and vocational-technical education.[19]

Table 13.2 shows education performance figures in selected Southeast Asian nations. Although all nations have recognized education as a crucial element in the modernization process, the governments in Singapore, Thailand, and Malaysia have spent comparatively more on schooling than other nations in the region. Primary education has been universalized, and secondary education has served more than one-third of the age cohort in most nations. Higher education is available only to a small percentage of the population in all Southeast Asian countries with the exception of the Philippines, where 28 percent of the age cohort attend tertiary institutions. Adult illiteracy, especially among females, still exists in most Southeast Asian nations, although at a much lower rate than that of South Asia.

The most economically developed nation in Southeast Asia is Singapore, one of the "Four Tigers in Asia." Singapore's experience in higher education development offers useful lessons to other developing Asian nations. Since its independence from British rule in 1959, education has played a key role in nation

Table 13.2
Southeast Asia

	Indonesia	Laos	Malaysia	Philippines	Singapore	Thailand	Vietnam	Myanmar
Government expenditures in education (% GNP) 1992	2.2	2.3	5.5	2.9	n.a.	4.0	n.a.	2.4
Primary students 1992 (Gross enrollment ratio %)	114	104	93	112	107	99	108	105
Secondary students 1992 (Gross enrollment ratio %)	43	24	60	77	68	39	32	23
Tertiary students 1992 (Gross enrollment ratio %)	10	n.a.	7	28	n.a.	19	2	n.a.
Adult illiteracy 1995 (%)	16.2	43.4	16.5	5.4	8.9	6.2	6.3	16.9
Female adult illiteracy 1995 (%)	22	55.6	21.9	5.7	13.7	8.4	8.8	22.3

Sources: Michael Westlake, ed., *Asia 1996 Yearbook* (Hong Kong: Far Eastern Economic Review, 1996), 14–17; UNESCO, *World Education Report 1995* (Paris: UNESCO, 1995).

building and economic development in Singapore, enabling the country to maintain international competitiveness in the global economy alongside the developed nations and the other newly industrialized nations. At the same time, sustained economic growth over the past three decades has also generated increasing social demand for access to quality education, especially higher education. Thus access and equity issues have become a major concern for policy makers and education reformers. Although primary schooling is free and secondary education is also available to most people in the country, access to higher education is relatively restricted and selective. Many students have had to turn to overseas institutions. In the early 1990s, the government initiated a plan to increase substantially the proportion of each age cohort in higher education. Consideration has also been given to those who cannot afford the cost of overseas studies. The goal for the year 2000 is to have 40 percent and 20 percent of each age cohort in the polytechnics and the universities, respectively, compared to 20 percent and 15 percent, respectively, in 1991. However, it has become increasingly difficult for the government to influence enrollment patterns by controlling access to various courses in higher education institutions. A related issue is the disproportionately high number of highly educated and skilled people among the ranks of emigrants.[20]

Gender and ethnicity also complicate access issues in Singapore's higher education development. Although female participation in higher education has increased dramatically since 1960, there is still a lack of female representation in certain fields such as medicine, dentistry, and engineering. The government has created deliberate policies to require relevant universities programs to achieve a certain proportion of women students. For example, in medicine and dentistry, the proportion of female students has been maintained at about one-third since 1979. However, the government has explicitly rejected the idea of using admission quotas as a means of redressing ethnic disparities in educational achievement. Instead, it has encouraged the formation of (and provides financial and intrainstructional assistance to) several ethnically based self-help organizations whose mission is to improve socioeconomic and educational achievement in the respective ethnic communities.[21] Although 78 percent of Singapore's population is Chinese, 14 percent is Malay, 7 percent is Indian, and 1 percent belongs to other ethnic groups. There are four official languages — Malay, Chinese (Mandarin), Tamil, and English. The government stresses the need for bilingualism and encourages it in all educational institutions.

In comparison to the Singaporean approach, the Malaysian government has developed a different policy in addressing the equity issues for the nation's female population and ethnic minorities. A developing middle-income country, Malaysia has undergone rapid technological advancement and economic growth since World War II. The availability of schooling has also grown dramatically. The government has expanded educational opportunities through an active school building program, particularly in remote areas. By 1976, primary education was universalized[22] and by the mid-1980s, the majority of primary school graduates continued on to secondary school. Such rapid expansion brought about phenomenal gains by historically disadvantaged ethnic Malays and by girls, who previously had attained fewer years of schooling than boys.[23] A recent survey of a sample of 1,508 teenagers (aged 15 to 19) in Malaysia shows that a higher percentage of girls (59 percent) than boys (52 percent) attended school. Malay students also have a higher participation rate than Chinese students (59 to 52 percent, respectively), although Indian students have a comparatively lower rate of school attendance (47 percent).[24] Ethnic minorities make up 22 percent of the population in Singapore, and in Malaysia more than 60 percent of the population is composed of native ethnic groups, including 55 percent Malays, 10 percent Indians, and 1 percent "others" (Sri Lankans, Eurasians, and other communities). The Malaysian government views access to higher education as a means of restructuring the society to eliminate the identification of ethnic community with economic functions. This has been one of the primary objectives of the New Economic Policy implemented in 1970, which involves providing more educational opportunities to the minority students so that there will be greater minority representation in the various professions and occupations in the modern society. To achieve this objective, the government implemented the racial quota system whereby the ethnic composition of the student population in the universities as a whole and in each of its faculties should reflect the ethnic composition of the country. The government even established a central university admission unit, whereby admission to the country's universities was tightly controlled and based on racial quotas. The implementation of this policy has eroded one of the deeply entrenched university traditions in Asian nations, that is, the admission of students based on merit. In addition, the government has provided special assistance and financial aid to minority students from the poor and rural areas, and this policy has been hailed as extremely successful in increasing minority participation in tertiary education. However, the preferential treatment policy in favor of minority students has also generated interethnic conflict and tension, and greater intraethnic inequalities. It has denied university access to many qualified mainstream students, who have sought overseas opportunities for higher education. Moreover, the positive discrimination policy has been found to award scholarships more to students from rich and powerful families than from poor families.[25]

Rural-urban equity is another challenge facing Asian educators. Many developing Asian nations are still dominated by agricultural economies. In general, children from the rural areas have less access to quality schools and teachers and are more discouraged from attending schools than children from the urban areas. For example, in an evaluation study of the preprimary education in Thailand, Raudenbush and colleagues found that 50.3 percent of urban children attended preprimary schools in 1982, whereas only 28.8 percent of the rural children had any preprimary experience. Moreover, the effect of preprimary education was estimated to boost test scores by 68 percent, on average, in urban as compared with rural schools in math achievement and by 65 percent in the case of Thai language achievement.[26] Researchers suggest that in order to reduce urban-rural achievement disparities, there is a need to increase access to preprimary education and to improve the quality of preprimary education in rural areas.[27] These are useful lessons for most other Asian nations that have a large rural population.

East Asia

The modern version of East Asia includes the nations of Japan, North and South Korea, China (including Taiwan and Hong Kong), Mongolia, and the colony of Macao. An old term for the region is the Far East, dating from earlier history when the area was "far" from Europe and "east" of Europe in terms of traveling time and direction. East Asia is the most populous region in the world, with about 1.4 billion people—more than a quarter of the world total. More than 1.2 billion people live in China alone. Population densities in East Asia are also among the highest in the world.[28]

After World War II, the East Asian region was among the poorest of the world, characterized by high levels of illiteracy and ravaged by the aftermath of wars and civil conflicts. Since then, the East Asian countries have experienced rapid economic and technological growth, which has significantly and positively affected the development of education in this region. From 1965 to 1990, the economy of East Asia grew faster than all other regions of the world, and this growth was achieved along with considerable improvement in the distribution of income and other measures of human welfare.[29] As shown in table 13.3, primary education has been universalized in most of East Asia and secondary education has become available to the majority of the age cohort except China. In higher education, however, there is considerable disparity. Although 32 percent of the age cohort in Japan and 42 percent of the age cohort in South Korea attend colleges and universities, only 2 percent of the age cohort in China has an opportunity for higher education. There is also a fairly high rate of adult illiteracy, especially among women, in China.

In ancient times, China was the first predominant civilization in the region. Much of the history, tradition, language, and culture in East Asia (as well as the rest of Asia) can find its roots in ancient China and Confucian ideology. In the more recent past, China was weakened by wars and explosive population growth. Political movements such as the disastrous Great Proletarian Cultural Revolution (1966–1976) created instability in the society and resulted in stagnation in educational development. Since the late 1970s, China has experimented with various social and economic reforms. It is decentralizing management and using wage bonuses to encourage production. China is also

Table 13.3
East Asia

	China	Hong Kong	Japan	Mongolia	South Korea	Taiwan
Government expenditures in education (% GNP) 1992	2.0	n.a.	4.7	8.5	4.2	6.2
Primary students 1992 (Gross enrollment ratio %)	120	102	100	97	103	99
Secondary students 1992 (Gross enrollment ratio %)	54	n.a.	96	86	91	85
Tertiary students 1992 (Gross enrollment ratio %)	2	20	32	14	42	26
Adult illiteracy 1995 (%)	18.5	7.8	n.a.	17.1	2	7
Female adult illiteracy 1995 (%)	27.3	11.8	n.a.	22.8	3.3	n.a.

Sources: Michael Westlake, ed., *Asia 1996 Yearbook* (Hong Kong: Far Eastern Economic Review, 1996), 14–17; UNESCO, *World Education Report 1995* (Paris: UNESCO, 1995).

stressing production of consumer goods to meet the needs of its huge population. A market economy and private enterprise are permitted along with a socialist planned economy and government-run enterprises.

Political and economic change have had a powerful impact on the development of education in China, which aims to universalize nine-year compulsory education by the year 2000. In fact, the goal has already been reached in major cities. The major challenge to Chinese educators is to extend quality basic education to the huge rural areas and to close the gap between the urban and the rural areas. The government has identified three problem areas in education for rural transformation in China: relocation of highly trained individuals from the urban to the rural sectors; development of educational resources within the rural areas; and continuing high levels of illiteracy.[30] Although the obstacles to reform are great, impressive progress has been made in many rural areas, especially in the more developed regions such as Guangdong and Shengzhen in which schools benefit directly from the booming economy. In return, the educational system has produced educated and skilled personnel needed by both the urban and rural economy.[31]

Huge regional disparities, however, continue to exist. Although the richest counties, such as Fanyu County in Guangdong, can now afford to send school principals to U.S. universities for professional development training, schools in Tibet and other remote rural areas are still struggling to improve the basic conditions for teaching and learning. Providing quality and equal education to all school-age children in China remains a difficult task for both policy makers and education reformers. The return of Hong Kong to China and the increasing marketization and privatization of education in China add both stimulation and challenge to this task.

Japan's impressive record of educational development and achievement is well known to educators outside of Asia.[32] By the 1980s, Japan was by far the most successfully industrialized Asian country. It has been recognized that education has played a key role in Japan's modernization process. However, Japanese leaders are not satisfied with these accomplishments, and several major educational reform movements have been pursued since the 1980s. First, forward-looking educators feel an urgent need to prepare young people to meet new challenges in the twenty-first century. Second, there is a recognition that lifelong learning must replace the previous emphasis on credentials and individuals' general educational background. Third, there is a proposal to increase quality and creativity at all levels of schooling, particularly higher education, focusing more on the individual than was done previously. Also, the effective utilization of educational technology is being promoted in different educational settings. Japan's technological advancement provides ideal conditions for this reform. There is a common consensus that the central examination system needs to be challenged, and a credit system has been suggested for use in upper secondary schools.[33] There are increasing concerns that the younger generation in Japan is not upholding traditional Japanese values. The National Council on Educational Reform even describes the present condition of education as "an educational wasteland" and argues that the country is experiencing a crisis of "desolation in education," the symptoms of which include bullying, school violence, and excessive competition in examinations.[34] Thus many challenges and difficult tasks in educational development continue to exist even in the most developed nation in Asia.

Little information is available about education in North Korea, which is one of the few remaining closed societies in the world. But in the past few decades there has been much discussion about educational expansion and accomplishments in South Korea. Today South Korea provides compulsory education up to middle school, at least to children in the rural areas. As of 1993, the enrollment rate was over 100 percent for primary schools, 96 percent for middle schools, 90 percent for high schools, and 44.8 percent for tertiary education.[35] However, research studies have found that Korean women still have unequal access to education, as is true in many other Asian nations. About 40 percent of South Koreans over sixty think that women's work should consist only of housework, which does not require higher education. The rate of return to education for males is expected to be greater than that of females because even women with higher education receive lower wages than their male counter-parts. It has been criticized that even the state has played an important role in conveying patriarchal attitudes through the educational system.[36] Korean women, as well as women in most other Asian nations, have a long way to go to achieve equality in education and work.

Conclusion

Several important factors have affected the quality and development of educa-tion in Asia. In the more developed countries, especially Japan, there are high standards for education and health care. Most of the developing nations of Asia, however, face major problems in improving education and health care for their large populations. Overpopulation remains the chief obstacle to improving the lives of the people. This is not only because of the large populations within each nation. It is also because a large proportion of the population is young. In many parts of Asia, it is not uncommon for 40 to 50 percent of the population to be under twenty-one. Subsequently, there is an enormous demand for education. The demand for health care and various other social services is growing con-tinually. Population control is generally recognized as a major requirement for solving these health and education problems in Asia's poorer countries.

Economic development is another important factor shaping the advancement of education. Great poverty contrasted with great wealth characterizes Asia's economies. Asian economic growth, the fastest in the world, was 8.6 percent in 1994.[37] Parts of Asia, such as Japan, Singapore, and some of the Middle East oil-rich nations, have a standard of living equal to that of most Western coun-tries. Other parts of Asia, such as Indonesia, Myanmar, Indochina, and Bangladesh, have much lower standards of living. Many of the people live in poverty. Within many of the countries of Asia, there are great gaps in income levels, with a relatively small and wealthy elite living beside large masses of people who struggle to survive. Many factors account for this inequality; prob-ably one of the most important is that Asia's people still depend largely on agri-culture for their living, and so a middle class has not been able to develop through industrial growth. What limited industrialization there is in most Asian countries tends to be concentrated in a few large cities. The wealth produced by such urban-centered industry tends not to spread evenly throughout the countries.

The most recent financial crisis in Asia, which began in early 1997, also has powerful implications for education development in Asia. First, several lead-ing conglomerates in South Korea, once deemed role models for economic de-velopment in other Asian countries, collapsed under billions of dollars in debts. Then large financial and banking systems in Thailand, Malaysia, and the Philip-pines failed, which triggered the "East Asian crisis" and led to the devaluation of currency in many Asian nations and regions including Indonesia, Taiwan, and Hong Kong. When the Hong Kong stock market suffered its heaviest drubbing ever in October 1997, it produced the single-biggest point loss ever in the Dow Jones Industrial average on the Wall Street and a very heavy fall in Japan's benchmark Nikkei 225-share index. Even some big banks in Japan collapsed under the weight of bad loans. The currency of certain Asian nations depreciated as much as 50 or 60 percent. The economic crisis immediately affected study abroad opportunities for students in these Asian countries. Their parents had to spend more than before in local currencies to buy the same amount of U.S. dollars to support their education in the colleges and universities in the United States, Australia, and other Western nations. Consequently, many had to interrupt their children's education abroad. Meanwhile, severe economic crises have given rise to social and educational unrest in some of Asia's most populated countries. For example, hundreds of students in Indonesia took to the streets in March 1998 to demand that the government curb excessive price hikes on food and other staples. Although there has not been much discussion of the educational implications of the financial crisis in Asia, it is expected that the crisis will force major changes in Asian countries' educational planning and development in the next decade.[38]

Moreover, Asia's traditional societies, reluctant to change their customs, also foster inequality in basic education and work. Although some Asian nations (e.g., Japan, China, Korea, and Singapore) are known for placing a high value on education and producing high achievement rates,[39] in reality, young people in many regions, especially girls in rural and minority areas, receive only a primary school education in less than adequate schools. A lucky few go on to high school, and even fewer, to college. Opportunities for higher education are very limited and entrance to college is often controlled by restrictive national examinations. Therefore, despite efforts to universalize basic education in the past several decades, the literacy rate in Asia is still 65.5 percent. In some of the poorest Asian nations, the adult illiteracy rate is well over 50 percent, with more females being illiterate.[40]

Asia's rapid social transformation and economic growth have had a positive impact on the development of higher education. At the same time, higher education is expected to play a significant role in national development. Today Asia has the world's fastest-growing academic systems. Many Asian nations, especially those with rapidly expanding economies, have started to invest heavily in research and development, and universities have played a central role in this expansion.[41] Although many regions are still undeveloped, Asian universities located in major cities are becoming centers of research and development, some at world-class levels. They are increasingly part of the world academic system and have established numerous ties and exchange programs with the outside world. The unfinished tasks of educational development in Asia include universalization of primary education, particularly in South Asia, reduction in gender and ethnic inequalities in education in all nations, and closing of the gap between rural and urban education in the developing nations. With a clear vision for reform and tireless efforts to change, Asian educators will continue to impress the outside world with their progress and accomplishments.

Notes

1. J. F. Williams, "Asia," in *Compton Interactive Encyclopedia,* ed. D. Good et al. (Cambridge, Mass.: Softkey Multimedia, 1996).

2. See, for example, G. A. Postigilone and G. C. L. Mak, eds., *Asian Higher Education* (Westport, Conn.: Greenwood, 1997); and John N. Hawkins, "Education in Asia," in *Encyclopedia of Educational Research,* ed. M. Alkin (New York: Macmillan, 1991), 87–92. International organizations such as the Asian Development Bank, the UNESCO Regional Office for Education for Asia and the Pacific, and the World Bank all use the modern definition of Asia in their work.

3. J. B. G. Tilak, *Education for Development in Asia* (London: Sage, 1994).

4. World Bank, *World Development Report* (Washington, D.C.: World Bank, 1990).

5. Philip G. Altbach, foreword to *Asian Higher Education,* ed. G. A. Postigilone and G. C. L. Mak (Westport, Conn.: Greenwood, 1997), viii–xi.

6. Tilak, *Education for Development,* 42.

7. United Nations Development Program, *Human Development Report* (New York: Oxford, 1990).

8. Tilak, *Education for Development,* 50–51.

9. Williams, "Asia."

10. Hawkins, "Education in Asia."

11. N. Jayaram, "India," in *Asian Higher Education,* ed. G. A. Postigilone and G. C. L. Mak (Westport, Conn.: Greenwood, 1997), 75–92.

12. P. Altbach and Suma Chitnis, eds., *Higher Education Reform in India: Experience and Perspectives* (New Delhi: Sage, 1993).

13. M. Bray, "Educational Reform in a Small State: Bhutan's New Approach to Primary Education," *International Journal of Educational Reform* 5, no. 1 (January 1996): 15–25.

14. S. Jayaweera, "Sri Lanka," in *Asian Higher Education,* ed. G. A. Postigilone and G. C. L. Mak (Westport, Conn.: Greenwood, 1997), 325–143

15. See discussions of the social contexts of education in K. P. Chowdhury, "Bangladesh," in *Asian Higher Education,* ed. G. A. Postigilone and G. C. L. Mak (Westport, Conn.: Greenwood, 1997), 1–20; and M. P. Regmi, "Nepal," in *Asian Higher Education,* ed. G. A. Postigilone and G. C. L. Mak (Westport, Conn.: Greenwood, 1997), 217–230.

16. World Bank, *The World Development Report* (Washington, D.C.: World Bank, 1993).

17. M. P. Regmi, "Nepal," in *Asian Higher Education,* ed. G. A. Postigilone and G. C. L. Mak (Westport, Conn.: Greenwood, 1997), 217–230.

18. Williams, "Asia."

19. Hawkins, "Education in Asia," 89.

20. E. T. J. Tan, "Singapore," in *Asian Higher Education,* ed. G. A. Postigilone and G. C. L. Mak (Westport, Conn.: Greenwood, 1997), 285–310.

21. Tan, "Singapore."

22. D. D. Tray, *Schooling in Malaysia: Historical Trends and Recent Enrollments,* Rand Report no. R-2011-AID (Santa Monica, Calif.: Rand, 1984).

23. *Fifth Malaysia Plan, 1986–1990* (Kuala Lumpur: National Printing Department, 1986).

24. S. L. Pong, "School Participation of Children from Single-Mother Families in Malaysia," *Comparative Education Review* 40, no. 3 (August 1996): 231–249.

25. E. T. J. Tan, "Singapore"; V. Selvarantnam and S. Gopinathan, "Higher Education in ASEAN: Toward the Year 2000," *Higher Education* 13 (1984): 67–83.

26. S. Raudenbush, S. Kidachanapanish, and S. J. Kang, "The Effects of Preprimary Access and Quality on Educational Achievement in Thailand," *Comparative Education Review* 35, no. 2 (1991): 255–273.

27. Ibid.

28. Williams, "Asia."

29. P. Morris, "Education and Development," in *Education and Development in East Asia,* ed. P. Morris and A. Sweeting (New York: Garland, 1995), 1–18.

30. J. N. Hawkins, "The Transformation of Education for Rural Development in China," *Comparative Education Review* 32, no. 3 (August 1988): 266–281.

31. For an insightful discussion of the development of education in the Pear River Delta region, particularly Guangdong, see K. H. Mok, "Retreat of the State: Marketization of Education in the Pear River Delta," *Comparative Education Review* 41, no. 3 (August 1997): 260–276.

32. See, for example, the descriptions of excellence in Japanese education in M. White, *The Japanese Educational Challenge* (New York: Free Press, 1987); and H. Stevenson and J. Stigler, *The Learning Gap* (New York: Summit, 1992).

33. J. N. Hawkins, "Education in Asia."

34. W. O. Lee, "Japan," in *Asian Higher Education,* ed. G. A. Postigilone and G. C. L. Mak (Westport, Conn.: Greenwood, 1997), 19–39.

35. C. S. Ihm, "South Korea," in *Asian Higher Education,* ed. G. A. Postigilone and G. C. L. Mak (Westport, Conn.: Greenwood, 1997), 125–148.

36. J. S. Chung, "Women's Unequal Access to Education in South Korea," *Comparative Education Review* 38, no. 4 (November 1994): 487–505.

37. International Monetary Fund, *World Economic Outlook* (New York: International Monetary Fund, 1995).

38. References for the discussion on the Asian financial crisis appeared in such publications as *Business Week, Wall Street Journal, New York Times,* and *Los Angeles Times* between January 1997 and April 1998.

39. See, for example, Harold Stevenson and James Stigler, *The Learning Gap* (New York: Summit, 1992).

40. J. F. Williams, "Asia."

41. Altbach, foreword to *Asian Higher Education,* viii–xi.

Chapter 14

Education in the Middle East

Challenges and Opportunities

Rachel Christina, Golnar Mehran, Shabana Mir

Education has long been a source of both power and promise in the Middle East. Control of information by the educated (or their employers) in the region's pre-Islamic civilizations shaped the economic and social development of both western and eastern civilizations: Pharaonic, Phoenician, Persian, Greek, Roman, and Byzantine cultures around the Mediterranean dominated, in turns, the intellectual, social, and economic worlds of their times. With the advent of Islam and the Qur'anic injunction "Read, in the name of your Lord!" (*Surat Al-'Alaq*), the pursuit of knowledge, as an obligation "of every Muslim" (Sunan Ibn Majah), began to move away from the purview of the very few and into the common consciousness of the region's population. The underlying power of Islam's regard for learning remains, to this day, an integral component of the educational culture of the countries in which it has taken root. The blossoming of Middle Eastern education and scholarship under the Muslim caliphates and the concurrent role of regional institutions in preserving the legacy of Western classical knowledge are well documented in the history of education. Unfortunately for the region's population, these years of glory were followed by a five-century decline, and the dawn of the twentieth century found most Middle Eastern education in a state of disarray.

This chapter examines the current status of Middle Eastern education as the product of repeated and dramatic changes in the region within this century: the establishment of independent nation-states, the boom and decline of Arab oil wealth, and a series of wars, internal conflicts, and revolutions, all of which have redefined the dynamics of power within the region and between the region and the rest of the world. The modern history of the Middle East is complex, and the interaction of its social, economic, and political changes with education is equally so. The legacy of colonialism and dependency on Western aid for development have colored Middle Eastern education, but they are not the only factors to be considered: Nationalism, pan-Arabism, and Islam have all left their stamp on the educational systems of the various countries in the region. Middle Eastern education is now in a period of transition and transformation, characterized by a reevaluation of its form, content, and function, and our analysis explores some of the complex tensions that are currently influencing change across this diverse and dynamic region. Essentially, we view the current debate over education as a reevaluation of the equation of development with modernization and a critical assessment of the primacy of economic as opposed to social welfare foci in development efforts. The infusion of moral and social concerns into the development plans of the region has not been absent from the educational arena, and it is an increasingly important element in the reform of Middle Eastern educational systems.

In our analysis, we first present an overview of historical trends in Middle Eastern educational development and then examine the current status of schooling across the region. To highlight the challenges facing Middle Eastern educators and policy makers, we examine three areas in which the tension between traditional and innovative forces is promoting a rethinking of structure and content in the interest of equitable and empowering development: early childhood education, the education of girls and women, and higher education. Early childhood education is increasingly seen as a significant point of leverage for breaking the cycle of poverty in the region and is therefore being targeted for expansion and reform, with a redirection of services in the interest of the most disadvantaged of children as at least the rhetorical goal. Girls' education has been shown to be a key factor in successful development efforts, and it is a focus for the promotion of gender equity and the reduction of discrimination against women. Higher education in the Middle East has been a major contributor to indigenous national and regional development and has served to promote the autonomy and identity of states within the region; preserving its role as a democratizing and empowering institution in a period of financial crisis and declining quality is a key challenge for Middle Eastern educational policy makers. How these various and competing agendas will be addressed in the future is uncertain, but our discussion highlights some of the possibilities inherent in current reforms, and the effects those reforms may have on the region as a whole.

In this discussion we use the term "Middle East" to refer to the twenty-one members of the League of Arab States (Algeria, Bahrain, Djibouti, Egypt, Iraq, Jordan, Kuwait, Lebanon, Libya, Mauritania, Morocco, Oman, Palestine [West Bank and Gaza Strip], Qatar, Saudi Arabia, Somalia, Sudan, Syria, Tunisia, United Arab Emirates, and Yemen), and to the non-Arab countries of Iran and Turkey. This is consistent with UNESCO, UNICEF, and World Bank designations for the region and allows for relative comparability in analysis. Nevertheless, the region itself is notably diverse in terms of income, culture, and status of development, and any exploration of Middle Eastern education must take this diversity into account.

Countries of the Middle East have been grouped in various ways by scholars studying the region. Cultural designations often divide the area into the Eastern Mediterranean, North Africa, and the Arabian Peninsula. The first and second groups have relatively higher levels of contact with other cultures and as a result greater internal diversity; the peninsular countries, by virtue of their relative isolation, are more homogeneous and consistent over time.[1] Economic designations evaluate wealth, sources of income, and development status, and they generally group countries into categories such as the least developed states (low income, poor in natural resources and manpower, e.g., Sudan and Yemen), middle income non-oil states (human resource based, with large populations and few natural resources, e.g., Egypt, Jordan, and Tunisia), and oil states with small populations and high surplus that often finance development in other parts of the Middle East (e.g., Kuwait, Saudi Arabia, and UAE).[2] Indeed, although the region as a whole is considered to be part of the developing world, it contains some of the world's wealthiest states, whose per capita income is as much as seventy-five times that of the poorest in the region.[3] The resultant differences in local capacity and priorities are important to remember. Our discussion of Middle Eastern education, although general, should be read in the context of these cultural and developmental differences among the states in the region.

With the establishment of independent nation-states across what had previously been the Ottoman Empire, "development" of the Middle East took on new energy. Commitments to welfare state models, supported both by the influence of Western state theories and the social welfare ethos within Islam, were common across the emerging political systems in the area, and the provision of free public education was quickly established as a responsibility of the state and a right of the citizenry. Education was seen by all emerging governments as one of the keys to modernization and economic growth (the primary goals of development according to the Middle Eastern model), and the resultant expansion of the region's school systems was dramatic. Between 1955 and 1984, double- and triple-digit increases in enrollment across the region were the norm. The oil producers demonstrated the greatest gains (Saudi Arabia's 58.1 percent per year average increase is staggering), but even in non-oil countries the gains were significant (Syria averaged a 15.6 percent per year increase over the same period).[4]

It was the oil boom of the 1970s, however, that had the greatest effect on the development of education in the Middle East. As Badran notes, "the great regional inflow of oil revenues in the 1970s, both directly to the Arab oil producing countries as well as indirectly through grants and the transfer of workers' salaries to non-producers, fueled a tremendous investment increase in education."[5] Between 1970 and 1985, 80,000 new primary schools, 10,000 new secondary schools, and 32 new universities (or major extensions of existing facilities) were built in the Arab states alone, and enrollment rates nearly doubled.[6]

A significant characteristic of this period was the massive transfer of educational labor within the region, as well as a sharp increase in interregional and international migration of students and faculty. The education boom that occurred across the region was most noticeable in the newly rich oil-producing states, and the resultant demand for educational personnel in countries with insufficient numbers of qualified local educators resulted in a dramatic increase in migration from the human resource–rich states (such as Egypt, Lebanon, and Palestine) to the human resource–poor oil states. At its height, such migration was incredibly lucrative for those who moved. El-Din notes that "an Egyptian professor [migrating to the oil states] would earn in only four years twice as much as would be earned in 30 years of a professional career in Egypt."[7] The prospects for primary and secondary school teachers were equally bright.

By the 1980s, however, the fortunes of states in the region had taken a turn for the worse. Decreased demand for oil and a decline in prices led to a "'loss' to those countries by 1985 of over half their earnings as they stood in 1980,"[8] and the 1980s witnessed the emergence of the Arab states as a "major indebted group of countries in the Third World."[9] Patterns of high consumption of imported goods and staples, combined with high levels of military spending and a lack of reinvestment into local systems, left governments scrambling to cover their expenditures, and social services, including education, suffered as a result. This pattern of consumption and spending overreaching resources also had negative outcomes in Turkey, and certainly the 1979 Iranian revolution was in part a reaction to conditions of poverty and inequity that resulted from the extravagance of the Shah's regime.[10]

With the decline of the oil market, Middle Eastern states found themselves dependent on external aid for the maintenance and support of their social networks. Consistent with the principles of donor assistance in the 1980s, recipient states embarked on programs of structural adjustment and fiscal austerity designed to bring national economies more in line with those of the developed world and stimulate sustained economic growth. At the same time, Middle Eastern countries were encouraged to continue to expand their primary education systems toward a goal of universal primary education (UPE) and to redesign their secondary and tertiary systems to more effectively address the manpower needs of the region. The long-term outcomes of these policies in the region are still unclear, but it has been argued that although a reassessment of the form and content of Middle Eastern education was necessary, the particular responses advocated by international donors (primarily privatization and decentralization) have reinforced existing inequities in the system and in many cases have limited the access of poorer populations to the education that is supposed to serve as their ladder out of poverty.[11]

What is certain is that in spite of the region's impressive gains in educational provision over the century, quantitative expansion has come largely at the expense of educational quality, and the prevailing conditions of education leave much to be desired. This is true whether one examines educational provision from a social justice or an economic growth standpoint. In the first case women, rural populations, and the poor are not well served and in the second the models in place do not meet the human resource needs of the region. Expenditure on education in the Middle East, although higher than in any other region, has simply failed to produce a system that is an effective contributor to national and human development.

Although enrollment continues to increase, the region's school systems have not kept pace with population growth, and demand outreaches supply. Although the primary enrollment ratios in Arab countries average 85 percent, and in Turkey and Iran stood at 97 percent in 1993 and 101 percent in 1994 respectively, class sizes in most countries continue to grow, dropout rates are climbing, and the number of out-of-school children continues to increase.[12] The region's high dependency ratio places increasing pressure on the formal education system, and the goal of UPE is unlikely to be reached within the next decade.

Adult illiteracy is also a problem, as educational development efforts have tended to focus on educating children in the formal system, and adults have received little attention. Exceptions to this policy include a generally unsuccessful literacy campaign in Iran prior to the 1979 revolution,[13] and more successful programs in Iraq (prior to the Gulf War of 1990–1991), Egypt, and Sudan.[14] Currently, however, only South Asia has a poorer standard of literacy than the Middle East. In the Arab states, for example, 42 percent of the population is illiterate, and women account for two-thirds of that figure.[15] Although literacy efforts are increasing in many Middle Eastern countries, emphasis by national governments and donor institutions on expanding primary education continues to divert funding and attention away from the needs of the illiterate in most cases.

Funding and administration are also areas in which Middle Eastern education is subject to criticism. Although many governments cite poverty as a major factor in the failings of their schools, Richards and Waterbury argue that "lack of spending is not the major problem with most educational systems in the region. . . . The real difficulty is in how the money is spent."[16] Middle Eastern education systems are, as a rule, heavily centralized and bureaucratic, and appointments are often based on connections and influence. As a result, administration is unidirectional (top-down), there is a physical and conceptual separation between administration and instruction, instructional supervision is limited and ineffective, and the administrative cadre is often unqualified and untrained.[17] Planning is unorganized and incoherent, and funds are ineffectively allocated, with rural and poor populations continuing to receive less priority than urban and wealthy groups, and funding across the system skewed in favor of higher education.

Finally, instruction and curricula are unsuited to either economic or social justice models of education for development. Rote learning and lecturing are the norms in Middle Eastern classrooms, and the authoritarian structure of the system as a whole is devolved to the level of student-teacher interaction; democratic interaction and critical inquiry are not fostered by instructional methods or by school culture. Many teachers are poorly trained, and teaching as a rule is a low-status, low-pay occupation. Resources and materials are costly and limited in availability, and the examination focus of the system works against creativity and innovation in the classroom.[18]

Faced with these weaknesses in their education systems, governments in the Middle East are in the process of reexamining the nature and extent of their commitment to education as a vehicle for national development. Economic growth and modernization models continue to remain powerful in terms of policy and planning, but there is also a growing consensus that such models need to be more carefully integrated with the cultural norms of the region. The resurgence and politicization of Islam in the 1980s and 1990s has been a significant factor in this reassessment of educational policies and practices, as have secular calls for movement away from dependency on the West and Western-dictated development agendas. A general feeling of "disenchantment with the west [and] disillusionment over pervasive social and political decline" has generated a "quest for identity and authenticity—new indigenously-rooted answers for pressing problems."[19] These solutions range from extreme rejectionism to democratic and cooperative efforts across the region to devise development solutions that promote human development in addition to economic growth.

As Badran notes, "there is great concern about the appropriateness of western education in a region with a predominantly Muslim population who have been raised in religious traditions that cannot immediately be reconciled with the western culture inevitably introduced along with western educational methods."[20] Concerns about a moral and spiritual vacuum in education and a desire to have educational systems reflect local identity are salient issues for the Middle Eastern states. Iran's Islamic revolution attempted to "correct" for the negative influences of the West by radically transforming the philosophy and organization of the country's education system.[21] Turkey's long tradition of forced secularization and westernization in education has also given way in recent years to efforts at reintegrating its Islamic heritage with modernization[22] (efforts that are a source of contention within Turkish society), and in some Arab states, Islamism has been seen as "a factor of modernization permitting local cultures to equilibrate their own heritage with new social and political evolutions."[23]

Suggestions for ways in which the traditional institutions and cultural norms of the region may be used to support education have included a revitalization of the traditional Qur'anic schools to serve as a nonformal extension of the formal education system, and an exploration of the humanistic and critical tradition of early Islamic education. Many regional educators argue that tensions between religion and secularism, autocracy and democracy, and authority and liberty, as identified by critics of educational development in the Middle East, are not as explicit as is claimed, and that integration of regional with certain international norms is not only possible but imperative.

How this integration will occur in the context of MENA states' subscription to the Jomtien Declaration on Education for All and international agreements on human rights and education remains to be seen. Policy and practice, in the Middle East no less than in the rest of the developing and developed worlds, remain largely nonsynchronous. In addition, application of new philosophies is inconsistent across sectors and may have very different effects, depending upon the target group. The rest of this chapter will explore in greater detail the context for reforms and their potential effects on three segments of the region's population: women and young children (traditionally disempowered and underserved populations), and university faculty and students (the traditional elite). It will illustrate the variety of ways in which Badeau's question, "How shall we, the ancient peoples yet new nations, of this area, modernize ourselves and our society?"[24] is being answered across the Middle East.

Early Childhood Care and Education

Early childhood care and education in the Middle East have traditionally been privileges of the elite. Nevertheless, recent conclusions by donor agencies and promoters of early childhood education worldwide that "investment in [early childhood] education . . . yields a far higher rate of return than does equal investment in secondary or higher education" and that "integrated early childhood development programs may be the single most effective intervention for helping poor children, families, and communities break the intergenerational cycle of poverty"[25] are beginning to turn the tide of early education program development in the direction of those who need it most. All MENA governments have expressed a desire to expand and equalize access to their limited early childhood programs, yet as in other areas, financial and human resource constraints may limit the extent to which rhetoric will be accompanied by practice.

The adoption by MENA member states of the U.N. Convention on the Rights of the Child in 1989 and the Jomtien Declaration on Education for All in 1990 have provided conceptual underpinnings for recent early childhood reforms. Article 5 of the Jomtien Declaration's statement that "learning begins at birth" and the Convention on the Rights of the Child's article 18 provisions for the development of institutions and services for the care and development of children are rallying cries for early childhood educators in the region. Bolstered by a growing body of evidence that early childhood programming is a key to long-term school success and community development, these advocates continue to argue that the years prior to a child's entry into the formal school system are of signal importance and should be given appropriate consideration within the educational policy-making arena. Nevertheless, emphasis by local governments and international funding agencies on basic education[26] and a persistent perception of early childhood issues as falling outside the purview of the government have created an imbalance between policy discourse and practical developments through which the early childhood sector continues to lag behind other sectors in growth, to suffer from sharp inequities along lines of gender, income, and location, and to remain primarily the product of nongovernmental initiatives.

At the state level, support for early childhood programming is increasing. The majority of Arab governments have adopted social and educational policies that are favorable to early childhood initiatives,[27] and the 1996 regional conference on EFA recommendations included the injunction that "special attention should be paid to the promotion of early childhood care and development, especially through low-cost alternatives which involve schools, communities, families and mothers. . . . Emphasis should be placed on encouraging local traditional institutions to fulfill their roles more effectively with this age group."[28] Turkey has implemented a strongly supportive framework for early childhood that incorporates optional public preschool, community education, and the provision of child care; Iran provides limited state subsidies for early care and education programs, both through the Ministry of Education's public early childhood institutions and through support for workplace child care.[29] Nevertheless, policy is still generally based on what Khattab calls a principle of "noninterference" by government, resulting in an inconsistent vision of early childhood care and education across the region, and strongly varied and conflicting approaches to practice in a broad constellation of private and civil-sector service providers.[30]

A 1995 UNESCO survey of early childhood care and education organizations in the Arab states illustrates this diversity. Its analysis of the orientations and services of sixty-four organizations (including women's groups, charitable societies, religious organizations, social service wings of political parties, research centers, nonaffiliated nonprofit organizations, and universities) found that programs cluster around three primary foci—the child, the family, and the community—and that activities within these arenas vary from a strong emphasis on care to a strictly academic conception of early childhood education. Child-centered programs are the most narrowly focused, addressing in relative isolation issues of children's health and development or academic preparation for children over three. Family-centered programs incorporate children's issues, addressing family health care and welfare, parent education and awareness about issues of child development and socialization, the needs of families at risk (i.e., in situations of poverty, dislocation, or single-parent status), and general advocacy supporting the rights and priorities of families. Community-centered programs are the most broad based, integrating education and health services, women's income-generating projects and environmental protection campaigns, and community advocacy in favor of the protection and rights of children as the basis for the community's future.[31]

These differing orientations and programs reflect the diversity of resources and priorities within the region. They also reflect the significant influence of trends in international development assistance. The early childhood care and education sector in the Middle East is heavily dependent upon the financial and moral support of international actors in the field of ECE, including UNICEF, UNESCO, Save the Children, the Bernard van Leer Foundation, the High/Scope Foundation, and the World Bank. Programming in the region has developed in layers that largely reflect the priorities of these various agencies.

Until the 1980s, many international early childhood care and education agendas were centered around child survival, viewing survival and development as separate and sequential processes, and care and education as distinct issues.[32] The MENA states have embraced maternal and child health and nutrition initiatives wholeheartedly and with great success, reducing child mortality there faster than any other region of the world (from an under five mortality rate of 25 percent regionally in 1960 to one of 7 percent in 1993) and doubling primary immunization rates to an average of 84 percent in 1993, with rates as high as 95 percent claimed by Iran, Jordan, Kuwait, Oman, and Tunisia.[33] Philosophical and conceptual changes in the early childhood arena, which include emotional and social dimensions along with the physical and extend concepts of learning and cognitive development from birth to age eight, however, have been less uniformly embraced,[34] and transition to integrated care and education programming is uneven across the region. Separation between care-based (mainly for the under-four age group) and academic preschool preparation (for four- to six-year-olds) programs continues, and early childhood programs and the first years of primary school remain vastly different in conceptual terms. The overall level of service to children in the preprimary years is very low. Twenty percent of four- to five-year-olds are enrolled in preschools regionally, but only 3.3 percent of MENA children are served from birth to school entry, with a high of 35 percent in the UAE and a low of 0.3 percent in Djibouti. Services remain biased toward the wealthy.[35] Calls at the global level to increase provision internationally with preference for the least advantaged of children, however, have been echoed by early childhood advocates in the Middle East, as well,[36] and growth in programs integrating community development, caregiver education, and multifaceted service delivery may serve to address some of the inequities that currently characterize the ECE system in the region.[37]

As discussed elsewhere in this chapter, processes of modernization and democratization and the rise and decline of the regional economy have altered family structures within Middle Eastern societies; transformed the position of women within the economic, political, and social spheres; and challenged "traditional" understandings of child rearing and education.[38] The extended family, the dominant model in much of the region, has begun to give way to smaller family units, with the nuclear family (father, mother, and children) as the base unit becoming an increasingly common structure, particularly in urban areas. Rural-to-urban and international migration and the inability of infrastructure and social service development to keep pace with changes in demographics have contributed to a widening gap between the rich and poor, and it has lessened the ability of traditional social networks to meet social needs. More and more Middle Eastern women have moved into the formal labor market and into positions of prominence in political and civil circles, and the traditional understanding of a woman's primary role as "housewife/lactating mother"[39] has been dramatically challenged. Ultimately, as UNESCO notes, these "changes in family structures and socio-economic levels in the region have led to changes in values, attitudes and child-rearing habits [and] families have had to look for alternative ways of taking care of their children."[40] Early childhood providers have responded to the challenge, but the solutions they have generated are as yet unequally distributed across the population.

In addition to being primarily urban (more than two-thirds of ECE services are provided in urban areas, according to Khattab),[41] early childhood programs are also largely biased in favor of middle-class and upper-middle-class populations. Their primarily urban location and primarily fee-based admission structure make access for these groups easy, while raising both the real and opportunity costs of enrollment for others. Programs also tend to serve a higher proportion of male than female children, both in care-based programs and in preschools.[42] The 1994 UNESCO statistics for the Arab states, for example, show an increase of 6 percent from 1980 in the percentage of female children aged four to six enrolled in preprimary education, but they still make up only 42 percent of the total of enrolled preprimary students. When reviewing services for birth to age six, the imbalance increases to 70 percent in favor of males.[43] In a sector with already limited gross provision, the minority status of females is significant. If early childhood programs do indeed lay a foundation for success in future schooling, selection against long-term female success may well begin here.

A turn toward a community focus in expansion of ECCE programs is characteristic of many current reform initiatives in the Middle East.[44] In addition to considerably diversifying the populations served, these programs, it is hoped, will also improve the "fit" between programs and the local context. A concern for modernization and development's effect on "the erosion of culture . . . with the influence of outside cultures replacing existing beliefs, attitudes, and practices with modern ideas [and] disorienting the community"[45] has led to initiatives intended to rejuvenate and incorporate traditional institutions into the ECCE framework. These include programs that attempt to strengthen community and family support for children, drawing on extended family/community patterns of child care and working away from center-based methodology to de-

velop more flexible and accessible programs (particularly for rural populations). Qur'anic schools, which have provided religious-based early education
for generations of Middle Eastern children, are also being explored as a potential low-cost, value-centered venue for ECCE programs.[46] These schools can
be modernized, it is argued, "without detracting from their spiritual standing or
their original educational role," and are particularly well suited to "reaching
children at risk in rural and remote areas."[47] Whatever the direction and success of reforms at the community level, however, their going to scale will depend largely on the mobilization of political will and support within governments to act in conjunction with nongovernmental agents who are designing
and providing early childhood services. The policy-practice dialectic, in this
arena no less than in formal education, remains the key to change.

Women's Education

Any analysis of women's education in the Middle East must include a discussion of the role and status of the Muslim woman. Although it is true that not all
Middle Eastern women are Muslim and that not all Muslim women are treated
alike or behave in a similar fashion, any discourse about female education in
the Middle East must take into consideration the fact that the teachings of Islam, combined with indigenous customs and traditions, play a crucial role in
determining the status of women and their education in the region.

Middle Eastern countries are dissimilar in their levels of political development, economic prosperity, and educational achievements; these dissimilarities
contribute to marked differences in the roles and status of women in each country. However, they share the continued dominance of religious law, and this law
is variously interpreted in ways that can be either constraining or empowering
for women. This governance of religion in the public realm distinguishes Muslim societies from states in which the jurisdiction of religious law is limited to
the private lives of citizens. In Muslim societies, traditional practices and beliefs regarding the roles and status of women interact with religious interpretation to create a unique dynamic; in fact, it may be argued that it is the continued presence of a "moral order"[48] in Middle Eastern societies that distinguishes
them from the "modern" states of the West. This is not to say that modern societies cannot be moral or that morality is in conflict with modernity. What is
implied here is that the principles of the moral order are different from those of
the modern, especially where women and their education are concerned.

The educational experience of women in the Middle East is thus determined
by the interplay between tradition and modernity, as well as by political and
economic forces, and it varies greatly across the region. The experience of
women in countries with a long history of educational provision for them, such
as Egypt and Lebanon, is different from that of women in countries in which

female schooling is a relatively recent phenomenon (such as Kuwait and Oman). And there are marked differences between rich oil-producing states and poor countries such as Djibouti.[49] The colonial experience in Morocco, Algeria, and Tunisia and the revolutionary ideology in Libya have left their imprint on female education, as has the push toward modernization and secularization in countries such as Turkey and Iran before the 1979 revolution.[50] The traditional attitude toward women in Saudi Arabia, Islamic revival, the battle against westernization in postrevolutionary Iran, and the struggle for national liberation in Palestine have also contributed to the diversity of women's education in the region.[51]

Middle Eastern women do, however, share the basic moral order that has determined the quantity and quality of service they receive relative to men. We deliberately use "moral" as opposed to "religious" order to differentiate between Islamic teachings, which do not discriminate against women in the realm of education, and the prevailing moral code, which mingles interpretations of religious law with traditional practices and attitudes regarding the appropriate amount and kind of schooling for women. In principle, there are no restrictions imposed on Muslim women in the area of education, and, contrary to widespread belief, Islam has never prevented women from pursuing learning. None of the reasons given by parents in Middle Eastern societies for not sending their daughters to school—including the charges that girls may learn new and challenging ideas in school and that it is better to invest in education for boys rather than for girls because girls enrich only their husbands' households, whereas boys provide returns to their immediate family—are based on Islamic law. Such statements merely reflect the persistence of traditional beliefs about women's economic value and social roles (beliefs that are not limited to the Muslim countries of the Middle East).

Islamic faith has not prevented women from receiving education in traditional *kuttab*s or *maktab*s, or from private tutors in the home. Women have attended *madrase*s and Islamic colleges. Muslim girls were not prevented from entering the Christian missionary schools established in the region in the late nineteenth and early twentieth centuries, and they were even sent abroad to study when no indigenous options were available.[52] The introduction of modern public schools along with nondiscriminatory compulsory education laws in the twentieth century further facilitated the education of girls. Traditional customs and beliefs particular to populations within the region have, however, limited women's enrollment at various levels and have restricted and/or redirected their fields of study. This is where the moral order is in command.

In general, recent expansion of women's involvement in education in the Middle East has been favorable when compared to the rest of the developing world. The average increase in female enrollment in the Arab states between 1990 and 1994, for example, was 4 percent, as compared to 3 percent in developing countries as a group.[53] Increases in the number of female teaching staff have also been higher than the developing country average: 4.7 percent (2.4 percent for the developing countries) at the first level and 5.2 percent (as compared to 3 percent) at the secondary level from 1990 to 1994.[54] However, there is still a significant gender gap in education in the region, and female gross enrollment rates are higher only than those of sub-Saharan Africa and the least developed countries at both the first and second levels of education.[55] In 1994, male gross enrollment rates in the Arab states, for example, were 62.1 percent at all levels, compared to 50.8 percent for women.[56]

Therefore, despite significant quantitative expansion in recent years, there is still room for improvement in female education in the region. Many girls are still left out of the school system and many girls repeat grades. At the primary-school level the repetition rate varies from 2 percent in Jordan to 17 percent in Mauritania.[57] Finally, many girls (up to 28 percent by grade four in Yemen)[58] drop out of the formal system, particularly at the primary level and among nomadic and rural populations. These figures are alarming not only because they indicate serious educational inefficiencies and high rates of wastage but also because fourth-grade dropouts in the region are unlikely to have acquired sufficient competencies to remain literate.

Many female primary school graduates in the Middle East fail to enter secondary school.[59] Even when the transition to education at the secondary level is made, a significant number of girls choose traditionally "female" fields of study. The reason is not simply because they are uninterested in "male-oriented" specializations or are unqualified to enter them, but rather because doing so is not deemed appropriate within the social norms of the region. According to El-Sanabary, curriculum bias is mild in academic secondary programs, yet "females are more likely than males to choose the humanities and social sciences track."[60] Gender bias is more pronounced in the technical and vocational schools because gender role types have limited women's access to "male programs" and have restricted them to "female crafts" such as home economics, nursing, typing, shorthand, and simple bookkeeping.[61] Nevertheless, once girls are allowed access to male-dominated fields, they have an equal and at times higher rate of success than boys. Girls have, for example, achieved higher scores than boys on secondary examinations in selected Arab countries and have performed better than boys in all science subjects (excluding mathematics) in traditional societies such as Kuwait.[62]

Middle Eastern women have had access to modern higher education since the 1920s. Such a long tradition may account for the fact that the percentage of Arab women studying at institutions of higher learning (9.7 percent) is considerably higher than the rate for developing countries in general (6.8 percent). Yet available statistics on female participation in third level education reveals significant diversity in terms of gender inequity in the region. Women constitute only 16 percent and 17 percent of university students in Mauritania and Yemen, respectively, whereas 71 percent of students are female in third level institutions in

Qatar.[63] Ironically, women's participation at universities is significantly lower in countries with a long tradition of female higher education (Egypt, 39 percent; Syria, 38 percent; Iraq, 32 percent) than in the Gulf states, where women were only admitted to universities as late as the 1970s. Societies such as Kuwait and Saudi Arabia, which are known for their traditional attitudes toward women, are among those with the most significant level of female enrollment at the tertiary level (with 67 and 44 percent, respectively).[64] It should, however, be noted that the high rate of female enrollment in the Gulf states may result from the fact that male students are often sent abroad for study.

As in secondary education, gender disparity in higher education is also reflected in the fields of study chosen by students. The traditional fields of the humanities, education, and medicine were long deemed "appropriate" for women in the region since they led to respectable, sex-segregated employment for them in the future.[65] Thus societal norms and limited job opportunities determined not only the specializations offered to women but also the ones chosen by them as a result of a realistic assessment of sociocultural taboos and labor market conditions.[66] Recent studies, however, are pointing to a shift in emphasis toward science and technology, even in such male-dominated fields as engineering and agriculture. A combination of increased employment opportunities and an increase in female role models in science-related professions has led to a higher proportion of Middle Eastern secondary- and tertiary-level females choosing science and mathematics; higher, even, than their Western counterparts.[67]

Clearly, women's education in the region is at a pivotal point, and increasing attention is being devoted in policy circles to improving quality and opportunity for female students. But the barriers to increased participation and equity remain strong. The available literature on female education in the region points to a number of obstacles to greater integration of women into the educational system, including the absence of political commitment to implementing gender equity in education and in society,[68] the type of schooling, curricula, and teaching methods common to systems in the region,[69] and economic constraints faced by poor and working-class families.[70] In-school and out-of-school factors both have bearing on girls' success and access. In-school factors include the school, classroom, teaching style, and examinations and assessments of student achievement; out-of-school phenomena encompass the social, economic, political and cultural milieux in which girls live. Essentially, Middle Eastern female students are subject to three sets of hindering forces: school-centered push-out factors that act to push girls out of the educational system; family-centered factors that pull girls out of the system for socioeconomic reasons or as a result of cultural beliefs; and child-centered reasons that eventually lead girls to drop out of the system in a final surrender to push-and-pull factors.[71]

Various solutions, based on these analyses of the obstacles to women's education, have been proposed for the region. Legal recommendations include legal reforms that facilitate women's access to education, based on research findings indicating a strong correlation between restrictive legal systems and limited female school enrollment in Muslim countries.[72] International donor agencies are recommending remedial measures that make schools more "girl friendly"[73] such as "providing schools within walking distance, boarding facilities or school busing, relevant curricula, school-lunch programs, adequate sanitation, and expanded teacher training."[74] Those who view the existence of discrimination in teaching and gender bias in the curriculum as the causes of persistent problems in female education recommend gender-sensitive teacher training and the elimination of sex stereotypes in textbooks.[75]

The academic success of girls in the Middle East, especially at the secondary level, at which single-sex education prevails, has led to critical reflection upon and reappraisal of the "separate is rarely equal" principle of the UN/UNESCO Committee on the Elimination of Discrimination Against Women. The principle that "cultural, family, or religious pressure for separate forms of education should not be tolerated"[76] is not necessarily valid in countries in which single-sex education is the only alternative open to girls. Maintaining a delicate balance between the ideal, in which "girls and boys, men and women . . . interact in the freedom of the academy," and the real, in which the school doors are open to women only if the schools are segregated, has become a challenge to those who would use education to empower women without destroying their progress toward equal opportunity.

What other factors are there that cause Middle Eastern women to remain behind in the educational arena, and what else needs to be done? We contend that a major cause of limited female participation in education is the reign of a moral order that bestows second-class status on women and leads them to believe in their "inferiority." Thus solutions cannot be limited to restructuring institutional arrangements or changing public attitudes toward women.[77] Clearly, rearranging unjust social, political, and economic structures is crucial in bringing about equality and social justice in the region. But equally important is the assertion of the dignity of Middle Eastern women, and an affirmation of their pride in themselves and their abilities. This can be achieved if education is seen as a means of empowerment. In the past schooling has acted as an agent of stability, preserving the nonthreatening roles of women as mere wives, mothers, sisters, and daughters rather than as independent individuals in their own right. Nevertheless, the educational system can and should have an empowering effect by stimulating the intellectual growth of Muslim women, raising their consciousness, and enabling them to reflect on their status in society.

Higher Education

The dilemma of dramatic growth and poor quality besets higher education in the Middle East, as it does in many other regions of the world. Increasing access to higher education has often facilitated state legitimation and relative equity, but economic pressures and declining quality have led to a reexamination of the feasibility of public higher education. In addition, exclusive state provision has resulted in a tightening of centralized control and a concomitant restriction of academic freedom. Democratization of higher education therefore stands in a problematic relationship with educational quality.

In the past several decades, higher education in the Middle East has expanded phenomenally. In the 1940s there were eight universities. In 1985 the number of institutions offering some form of postsecondary education in the Arab world was estimated at about four to five hundred.[78] In 1994 total higher education enrollment was 2.9 million. Although the general rate of growth has been considerable (total enrollment grew by 6.3 percent between 1980 and 1985, and 3.5 percent between 1990 and 1994), the actual numbers are still far behind those of developed countries.[79] Moreover, even the spectacular expansion of higher education facilities may not be able to meet the demand for higher education, as it increases with demographic change. (An estimate of the Arab states' population in 1980, for example, was roughly 168 million; this jumped to 249.6 million in 1994.) In Iran, population increase, urbanization, industrialization, and economic development between 1960 and 1979 increased the need for qualified expertise, and the state machinery engaged in expansion and modernization of higher education. After the revolution, especially during the war with Iraq (1980–1988), no further growth took place.[80] In Turkey, where the dramatic increase in enrollments is characterized as a "burning issue," the number increased from 177,281 in 1974 to 635,828 in 1990.[81] Clearly this increasing demand confronts countries in the region with questions regarding means of provision.

Most higher education in the Middle East (60 out of 72 universities in the Arab world, almost all in Iran, and all but one in Turkey) is controlled and financed by the government. Lebanon is the only Arab country in which most higher education is private. The central role of the state in planning, financing, and administering educational programs is common across political systems, including "traditional" Saudi Arabia, socialist Libya, and the Islamic state of Iran,[82] reflecting the expectation that education was a basic service that the state should provide. In the Arab world, the concerned ministry generally ensures that the university system operates according to state policy. There is strong state involvement in the appointment of heads of universities. In Turkey, four major laws reflecting varying degrees of centralization have been passed to systematize higher education, in 1933, 1946, 1973, and 1981. The most recent law places higher education under strict centralized control with regard to finances, recruitment and promotion of faculty, structure of the curricula and approval of course offerings, selection and placement of students. However, centralization was planned carefully so as not to disturb the delicate balance with academic autonomy of individual universities, since each university has its own governing body and can formulate its own curricular regulations.[83]

Trends toward centralization and bureaucratization work against university autonomy and academic freedom. Despite historical Arab traditions of higher learning, modern Arab universities have been strongly influenced by the colonial model based on centralized administration. "A conflict developed between governments that wanted universities to adhere strictly to civil service rules and policies and universities striving for academic freedom and autonomy." Consequently, affairs that could lie within the jurisdiction of a university council or senate tend to become a state concern. With some exceptions, there is no statutory basis for faculty participation in decision making through a university body.[84]

Political centralization and the growth of the bureaucracy have seriously affected academic freedom in the Middle East. According to Shamsavary, "Iran's higher education has seriously suffered from lack of academic freedom in both pre- and post-revolutionary Iran." Under the Shah, policies of academic repression and secularization were followed. After the Islamic revolution (for about fifteen months before the Cultural Revolution) Iranian higher education "enjoyed an autonomy not previously seen in the history of these universities." Later, faculty supportive of the Shah were purged and a Cultural Revolution staff was appointed to supervise higher education. Considerable centralization of authority resulted, which nevertheless permitted a level of local autonomy that did not threaten the central authority.[85]

The state's role in education expanded under the influence of common perceptions of state responsibility as well as of the effect of education on the economic welfare of the masses. It has been argued that the university model is based on the need for governments to "enhance the welfare of their people by creating an environment of equal opportunity" to "provide avenues for people to improve their standard of living." Government investment in education, it was believed, would help create the infrastructure for more equitable income and wealth distribution and would help generate more wealth in the future.[86] The population explosion and the consequent increase in demand over recent decades led to democratization, and open admissions in the 1950s and early 1960s led to mass higher education in, for example, Egypt, Syria, Iraq, Algeria, and Morocco. The mainly academic and college-bound secondary education in the Arab world, however, led to severe pressures on universities, and the association of a university degree with upward social mobility no longer remains universally valid.[87]

Faculty members' motivation to work toward high professional standards is generally low in the Middle East, in view of high faculty-student ratios, economic pressures, low salaries, the lack of academic freedom, and poor infrastructure and research facilities. Moreover, there is considerable lack of uniformity in the academic structure of universities across the Arab world. French, British, American, and mixed models are used in different universities and even in the same university in different departments. The lecture-hall model of teaching has been promoted in Middle Eastern universities by several factors, including dramatic increases in student enrollment unaccompanied by corresponding increases in competent faculty and facilities, and the lack of general academic freedom, which filters into transmission modes of teaching.[88] The average faculty-student ratio in humanities colleges at Mansoura University, Egypt, is said to be one to eighty-five, and the overall average in the university is one to 452, the highest in the country. Science and technology faculties, perhaps due to strict admission requirements, have lower ratios. Though universities in the oil-rich countries have modern, high-quality facilities, overcrowding at most Middle Eastern higher education institutions has affected their ability to provide adequate classroom space, science laboratories, libraries, and other facilities. The King Saud University Library has 1.1 million volumes, whereas Ain Shams University, with the largest student body in the region, has only 92,000.[89]

A different state of affairs prevails in the oil-rich Gulf states, where the scale of educational provision relative to the size of national populations is too large and gives rise to "an education system top-heavy with misdirected, poor quality students, despite high drop-out rates from the bottom, primary levels of the system." Maintaining lavish education systems may not be feasible, particularly when oil revenues begin to diminish.[90]

Lecture-centered modes of teaching, inadequate facilities, and centralized educational administration have led to theoretically based educational experience for the average Middle Eastern student. The consequent lack of training in practical skills and training causes employment prospects for graduates to be limited. Many graduates, especially in theoretical disciplines, cannot be easily absorbed in the workplace. National needs for trained technicians and management to assist development remain unfulfilled. Across the Middle East, like many countries in the world, "socioeconomic pressures of society have led to the creation of 'degree mills' rather than universities, which flood the market with incompetent degree holders."[91]

In spite of sustained efforts to open enrollments, participation in higher education remains relatively difficult for people of lower socioeconomic status, people from rural areas (because most universities were established in metropolitan centers), and women. Though tuition is free at most state universities, students from poorer or rural backgrounds generally cannot afford housing, even if subsidized.[92]

The crisis of higher education has drawn two main responses: blaming the use of Western institutional models in non-Western societies or blaming state inefficiencies. A World Bank publication points out that higher education is in a state of crisis with worldwide fiscal constraints. During the past twenty years government subsidization of higher education has generated fiscally unsustainable enrollment growth and declining quality. To the World Bank, this indicates the need for private educational provision.[93] Badran agrees, citing large public debts and growing demand to show that the public sector would not be able to assimilate the same proportion of students that it did in the past. However, he emphasizes the state's crucial role in providing guidelines for and monitoring higher education to ensure quality and equity, since private institutions are flourishing regardless of the predominant state role in educational provision. In Jordan, for example, inadequate higher education provision has bred a number of community colleges. The standard of private institutions is often superior to their public counterparts. Many educationalists contend, however, that privatization and decreased state investment in education may aggravate inequalities that already exist. Increasing access to education is widely believed to promote growth and equality and to have long-term positive effects in terms of human welfare.[94] In view of the existing inequalities in the Middle East, it appears wise for governments to follow policies of protection, or even expansion, of investment in postprimary education through a combination of state and private enterprises.[95]

Although most Middle Eastern countries "seek to meet the rising demand for higher education by going down the well-trodden path of creating universities," demographic change, improved economic feasibility, and socioeconomic and political pressures have increased awareness of the need to create such alternative formal institutions as community colleges, teacher training institutes, and vocational schools. Other ways of cutting the cost of education have also been recommended, including maximizing the use of facilities by holding classes in shifts. In Egypt the same school may be used for up to three shifts each day. Innovative use of the mass media is another cost-effective way to increase access to higher education. Turkey is making productive use of television in its Open University program. The Arab world, with a common language, can use it with even more utility and cost-effectiveness.[96]

Large sections of Middle Eastern populations have been unable to benefit from higher education, and class differences have been exacerbated. Benefits have flowed mainly toward the upper classes and the urbanized middle class. Yet problems related to the unplanned growth of higher education will not be solved simply by restricting higher education.[97] In Iran after 1979 private institutions were nationalized and almost all tuition fees were also abolished. Selection criteria were changed to allow a quota of students from poorer families who participated in the Islamic revolution to pursue tertiary education, resulting in a partial collapse of barriers of class and privilege. Yet the discrepancy in enrollments from different socioeconomic backgrounds in the Middle East amply bears out the fact that open admissions and state-sponsored education will not suffice by themselves. A "diversified system that reaches all strata of society, providing relevant education that will produce productive members in their own communities" is the need of the hour.[98] In the meantime, however, such factors as gender, socioeconomic status, religion, and political affiliation continue to limit access to higher education for certain sections of the population across the Middle East today.

Conclusion

The variety of political, social, economic, and cultural realities in countries of the Middle East make it necessary to guard against a monolithic view of educational conditions in that region. Complex and multifaceted realities in the various levels and fields of education have created a moment of educational promise as well as decline in the Middle East. The situation appears to warrant a thorough review of the direction that educational provision has been taking in the Middle East. The drive to expand educational provision, which needed no justification some decades ago, has not reduced educational inequities by gender, class, rural-urban distribution, and region. Impressive and beneficial in many significant ways though it has been, the recent expansion of public educational provision in the Middle East may not even be economically feasible for some countries in the region. Though poor quality increases the difficulty of keeping education on the list of public priorities, the demand for it continues to be on the increase. The expansion of education has benefited many of the traditionally disadvantaged, notably women. We have shown that apart from educational provision, legal, structural, and attitudinal change must accompany such provision to render it effective. In the wake of post-Gulf war financial and political strains, the need to address socioeconomic and cultural relevance in education has become more pressing than ever. The necessity of ensuring that such relevant education is also made available to the sections of Middle Eastern populations hitherto deprived of such education has come to the fore in most countries of the region.

Notes

1. Nicholas Kittrie, "Responsibility for Education: A Social, Religious, and Economic Partnership," in *At the Crossroads: Education in the Middle East,* ed. Adnan Badran (New York: Paragon, 1989), 3–17; Byron Massialas and S. A. Jarrar, *Arab Education in Transition* (New York: Garland, 1991); Saad Eddin Ibrahim, *The New Arab Social Order: A Study of the Social Impact of Oil Wealth* (Boulder: Westview, 1982).

2. Kunibert Raffer and M. A. Mohamed Salih, "Rich Arabs and Poor Arabs," in *The Least Developed and the Oil-Rich Arab Countries,* ed. Kunibert Raffer and M. A. Mohamed Salih (New York: St. Martin's, 1992), 1–12; Stephen Heyneman, "Human Development in the Middle East and North Africa Region," in *Economic Development of the Arab Countries,* ed. Samih El-Naggar (Washington, D.C.: International Monetary Fund, 1993); A. Richards and J. Waterbury, *A Political Economy of the Middle East* (Boulder: Westview, 1996).

3. International Monetary Fund, 1996, cited in Patricia Alonso-Gamo and Mohammed El-Erian, "Economic Reforms, Growth, Employment, and the Social Sectors in the Arab Economies," in *The Social Effects of Economic Adjustments on Arab Countries,* ed. Taher Kanaan (Washington, D.C.: International Monetary Fund, 1997), 15.

4. Nathir Sara, "Administrative Aspects of Education in the Arab Countries," in *At the Crossroads: Education in the Middle East,* ed. Adnan Badran (New York: Paragon, 1989), 253–255.

5. Adnan Badran, in *At the Crossroads: Education in the Middle East,* ed. Adnan Badran (New York: Paragon, 1989), 159.

6. Abdulaziz Saqqaf, "Educational Expenditure Patterns in Arab Countries," in *At the Crossroads,* 170.

7. El-Din, cited in Ibrahim, *New Arab Social Order,* 69.

8. Yusif Sayigh, *Elusive Development: From Dependence to Self-Reliance in the Arab Region* (London: Routledge, 1991), xi.

9. Abbas Alnasrawi, *Arab Nationalism, Oil, and the Political Economy of Dependency* (New York: Greenwood, 1991), 175.

10. Robert Looney, *Economic Origins of the Iranian Revolution* (New York: Pergamon, 1982), 12–25.

11. Abdelatif Benachenhou, comment in *The Social Effects of Economic Adjustments on Arab Countries,* ed. Taher Kanaan (Washington, D.C.: International Monetary Fund, 1997), 184.

12. UNESCO, *Statistical Yearbook, 1996* (Paris: UNESCO, 1996), table 3.2; International Consultative Forum on EFA, *Regional Policy Review Seminar on Education for All in the Arab Region* (New York: ICF on EFA, 1996), 4.

13. Naz Rassool, "Theorizing Literacy, Politics, and Social Process: Revising Maktab Literacy in Iran in Search of a Critical Paradigm," *Comparative Education Review* 15, no. 4 (1995): 423–435.

14. Byron Massialas, "Arab Countries: Adult Education," in *International Encyclopedia of Education,* vol. 1, ed. Torsten Husen and T. Neville Postlethwaite (London: Pergamon, 1994), 324–326.

15. UNICEF, *State of the World's Children* (New York: UNICEF, 1996); International Consultative Form on EFA, *Regional Policy Review.*

16. Richards and Waterbury, *Political Economy,* 117.

17. Sara, "Administrative Aspects," 253–255.

18. Massialas and Jarrar, *Arab Education,* 32–49.

19. Esposito, cited in Massialas and Jarrar, *Arab Education,* 16.

20. Badran, ed., *At the Crossroads,* 1.

21. Bahram Mohsenpur, "Philosophy of Education in Post-Revolutionary Iran," *Comparative Education Review* 32, no. 1 (1988): 76–86.

22. Sabahaddin Zaim, "The Impact of Westernization on the Educational System in Turkey," in *At the Crossroads: Education in the Middle East,* ed. Adnan Badran (New York: Paragon, 1989), 18–42.

23. Burgat, cited in Tuomo Melasuo, "Maghreb Conflicts, Socioeconomic Crisis, and Unity," in *The Least Developed and the Oil-Rich Arab Countries,* ed. Kunibert Raffer and M. A. Mohamed Salih (New York: St. Martin's, 1992), 52.

24. Sami Hajjar, ed., *The Middle East: From Transition to Development* (Leiden: Brill, 1985), 3.

25. Mary Eming Young, *Early Childhood Development: Investing in the Future* (Washington, D.C.: World Bank, 1996), 12.

26. World Bank, *Priorities and Strategies in Education* (Washington, D.C.: World Bank, 1995); International Consultative Forum on EFA, *Regional Policy Review;*

Ministries of Education, MENA Member States, "Country Reports: Middle East and North Africa," in *Proceedings of the International Conference on Education* (Paris: IBE, 1994).

27. UNESCO, "Early Childhood in the Arab States: Challenges and Opportunities," in *Directory of Early Childhood Care and Education Organizations in the Arab States* (Paris: UNESCO, 1995); Ministries of Education, MENA, "Country Reports."

28. International Consultative Forum on EFA, *Regional Policy Review,* 9.

29. Tanju Gurkan, "Early Childhood Education in Turkey," in *International Handbook of Early Childhood Education,* ed. Gary Woodhill, Judith Bernard, and Lawrence Prochner (New York: Garland, 1992), 481–489; M. Sorkhabi, "Preacademic and Academic Education in Iran," in *International Handbook of ECE,* 293–297; Z. Sabbaghian, "Kindergarten and Primary Education in Iran," in *International Handbook of ECE,* 299–305; Ministries of Education, MENA, "Country Reports: Turkey and Iran."

30. Mohammed Khattab, *A Comprehensive Survey of the Status of Early Childhood Care and Education in the Middle East and North Africa* (Amman, Jordan: UNESCO, 1995).

31. UNESCO, "Early Childhood Care and Education in the Arab States: Survey Findings," in *Directory of Early Childhood Care and Education Organizations in the Arab States* (Paris: UNESCO, 1995).

32. Robert Myers, *The Twelve Who Survive* (London: Routledge, 1992).

33. UNICEF, *State of the World's Children.*

34. Khattab, *Comprehensive Survey.*

35. Mohammed Khattab, "Early Childhood Education in Eighteen Countries in the Middle East and North Africa," *Child Study Journal* 26, no. 2 (1996): 149–159; UNESCO, *Early Childhood Care and Education: Basic Indicators on Young Children—Arab States* (Paris: UNESCO, 1995).

36. Indu Balagopal, *Report on Dialogue '95: First Annual Consultative Days of the Arab Resource Collective Regional Consultative Resource Group on Early Childhood Care and Development* (New York: Consultative Group on Early Childhood Development, 1996); International Consultative Forum on EFA, *Regional Policy Review.*

37. UNESCO, "ECE Challenges and Opportunities."

38. Richards and Waterbury, eds., *Political Economy;* Samih Farsoun and Christina Zacharia, "Class, Economic Change, and Political Liberalization in the Arab World," in *Political Liberalization and Democratization in the Arab World,* ed. R. Brynen, B. Korany, and P. Noble (Boulder: Lynne Riennier, 1995), 261–283; Elizabeth Warnock Fernea, "Childhood in the Muslim Middle East," in *Children in the Muslim Middle East,* ed. Elizabeth Warnock Fernea (Austin: University of Texas Press, 1995), 3–17; Ibrahim, *New Arab Social Order,* 92–93.

39. Ghanem Bibi, cited in UNESCO, "ECE Challenges and Opportunities," 29.

40. UNESCO, "ECE Challenges and Opportunities," 29.

41. Khattab, "Early Childhood Education in Eighteen Countries," 157.

42. UNESCO, *Statistical Yearbook, 1996* (Paris: UNESCO, 1996), table 2.3.

43. Khattab, "Early Childhood Education in Eighteen Countries," 156.

44. C. Kagitcibasi, *The Early Enrichment Program in Turkey* (Paris: UNESCO-UNICEF-WFP, 1991); Early Childhood Resource Center, *Towards the Year 2000* (Jerusalem: ECRC, 1995); Myers, *Twelve Who Survive.*

45. Balagopal, *Report on Dialogue '95,* 2.

46. Khattab, *Comprehensive Survey;* Myers, *Twelve Who Survive.*

47. Khattab, *Comprehensive Survey,* 96.

48. Afsaneh Najmabadi, "Iran's Turn to Islam: From Modernism to Moral Order," *Middle East Journal* 41 (1987): 202–217.

49. Edith A. S. Hanania, "Access of Arab Women to Higher Education," in *Arab Women and Education,* Monograph Series of the Institute for Women's Studies in the Arab World, no. 2 (Beirut: Beirut University College, 1980), 24–28; N. El-Sanabary, "Women's Education, History of: Islamic Countries," in *International Encyclopedia of Education,* 2d ed., ed. Torsten Husen and T. Neville Postlethwaite (Oxford: Pergamon, 1994), 6753–6761; H. A. S. Khattab, "Female Education in Egypt: Changing Attitudes over 100 Years," in *Muslim Women,* ed. F. Hussain (New York: St. Martin's, 1984); Jonathan P. Berkey, "Women and Islamic Education in the Mamluk Period," in *Women in Middle Eastern History: Shifting Boundaries in Sex and Gender,* ed. Beth Baron and Nikki R. Keddie (New Haven: Yale University Press, 1991), 143–157; May Rihani, *Learning for the 21st Century: Strategies for Female Education in the Middle East and North Africa* (Amman, Jordan: UNICEF, 1993); Sheikha Al-Misnad, *The Development of Modern Education in the Gulf* (London: Ithaca, 1985), 172–188; UNICEF Sudan and the Ministry of Education, the Republic of Sudan, *Report on the Study of Girls' Education in Sudan* (Khartoum: Undersecretariat for Educational Planning, Ministry of Education, 1993); Fathi Salem Abdou, *La Scolarisation des Enfants dans la Republique de Djibouti* (Djibouti: UNICEF, 1994).

50. Marie Thourson Jones, "Educating Girls in Tunisia: Issues Generated by the Drive for Universal Enrollment," in *Women's Education in the Third World: Comparative Perspectives,* ed. Gail P. Kelly and Carolyn M. Elliot (Albany: State University of New York Press, 1982), 31–50; Massialas and Jarrar, *Education in the Arab World,* 252–258; F. Ozbay, "The Impact of Education on Women in Rural and Urban Turkey," in *Women in Turkish Society,* ed. N. Abadan-Unat (Leiden: Brill, 1981); Handan Kepir, "Turkish Women in an Era of Transition," in *At the Crossroads: Education in the Middle East,* ed. Adnan Badran (New York: Paragon, 1989), 113–120; Jospeh S. Szyliowicz, *Education and Modernization in the Middle East* (Ithaca, N.Y.: Cornell University Press, 1973); David Menashri, *Education and the Making of Modern Iran* (Ithaca, N.Y.: Cornell University Press, 1992).

51. Nagat El-Sanabary, *The Saudi Arabian Model of Female Education and the Reproduction of Gender Divisions,* Center for Near Eastern Studies Working Paper, no. 16 (Los Angeles: UCLA Press, 1992); Jacquiline Rudolph Touba, "Cultural Effects on Sex Role Images in Elementary School Books in Iran: A Content Analysis After the Revolution," *International Journal of Sociology of the Family* 17 (1987): 143–158; Golnar Mehran, "The Creation of a New Muslim Woman: Female Education in the Islamic Republic of Iran," *Convergence* 24 (1991); Nesta Ramazani, "Women in Iran: The Revolutionary Ebb and Flow," *The Middle East Journal* 47 (1993): 412–413; Agustin Velloso, "Women, Society, and Education in Palestine," *International Review of Education* 42 (1996): 524–530.

52. Hanania, "Access of Arab Women to Higher Education," 16–19, 29–31.

53. UNESCO, *1996 Statistical Yearbook,* table 2.4.

54. UNESCO, *1996 Statistical Yearbook,* table 7.

55. UNESCO, *1996 Statistical Yearbook,* table 6.

56. UNESCO, *1996 Statistical Yearbook,* table 9.

57. UNESCO, *1996 Statistical Yearbook,* table 7.

58. Golnar Mehran, *Girls' Drop-Out from Primary Schooling in the Middle East and North Africa: Challenges and Alternatives* (Amman, Jordan: UNICEF, 1995), 13.

59. UNESCO. *Development of Education in the Arab States: A Statistical Review and Projection* (Paris: UNESCO, 1994).

60. El-Sanabary, "Women's Education," 6758.

61. Massialas and Jarrar, *Education in the Arab World,* 239.

62. A. E. Al-Methun and W. J. Wilkenson, "In Support of a Sociological Explanation of Sex Differences in Science and Mathematics Achievement: Evidence from a Kuwaiti Study of Secondary School Certificate Examinations," *Research in Science and Technological Education* 6 (1988): 91–101.

63. UNESCO, *1996 Statistical Yearbook,* table 10.

64. UNESCO, *1996 Statistical Yearbook,* table 10.

65. Audrey C. Smock and Nadia H. Youssef, "Egypt: From Seclusion to Limited Participation," in *Women: Roles and Status in Eight Countries,* ed. Janet Z. Giele and Audrey Smock (New York: Wiley, 1977), 59.

66. Massialas and Jarrar, *Education in the Arab World,* 242.

67. El-Sanabary, "Women's Education," 6758.

68. El-Sanabary, "Women's Education," 6756.

69. Massialas and Jarrar, *Education in the Arab World,* 233–245.

70. Nagat El-Sanabary, "Middle East and North Africa," in *Women's Education in Developing Countries: Barriers, Benefits, and Policies,* ed. Elizabeth M. King and M. Anne Hill (Baltimore: Johns Hopkins University Press, 1993), 153–154.

71. Mehran, *Girls' Drop-Out from Primary Schooling,* xi.

72. Elizabeth H. White, "Legal Reform as an Indicator of Women's Status in Muslim Nations," in *Women in the Muslim World,* ed. Lois Beck and Nikki Keddie (Cambridge: Harvard University Press, 1978), 63–67.

73. UNICEF, *Strategies to Promote Girls' Education* (New York: UNICEF, 1992); Karen Tietjen, *Educating Girls: Strategies to Increase Access, Persistence, and Achievement* (Washington, D.C.: Creative Associates International, 1991); Rihani, *Learning for the 21st Century;* Rosemary T. Bellew and Elizabeth M. King, "Educating Women: Lessons from Experience," in *Women's Education in Developing Countries: Barriers, Benefits, and Policies,* ed. Elizabeth M. King and M. Anne Hill (Baltimore: Johns Hopkins University Press, 1993), 285–326.

74. El-Sanabary, "Women's Education," 6757.

75. J. Abu Nasr et al., *Identification and Elimination of Sex Stereotypes in and from School Textbooks: Some Suggestions for Action in the Arab World* (Paris: UNESCO, 1983).

76. United Nations Committee on the Elimination of Discrimination against Women in Cooperation with the United Nations Educational, Scientific, and Cultural Organization, *Towards a Gender-Inclusive Culture through Education: Principles for Action* (Paris: UNESCO, 1995).

77. Munir Bashshur, "Arab Women and Education," in *Arab Women and Education,* Monograph Series of the Institute for Women's Studies in the Arab World, no. 2 (Beirut: Beirut University College, 1980), 70.

78. George E. Za'rour, *Universities in Arab Countries* (Washington, D.C.: International Bank for Reconstruction and Development/World Bank, 1988), 3, 80; Munir Bashshur, "Similarities and Constraints in Patterns of Higher Education in the Arab

World" (paper delivered at the Nordic Conference on Higher Education in the Arab World and the Middle East at Lund University, Sweden, 28 March 1985), 1.

79. Massialas and Jarrar, *Arab Education,* 49; Byron G. Massialas, "The Arab World," in *International Higher Education: An Encyclopedia,* vol. 2, ed. Philip G. Altbach (London: Garland, 1991), 981; Mohamed I. Kazem, "Higher Education and Development in the Arab States," *International Journal of Educational Development* 12, no. 2 (1992): 116.

80. Badran, "Meeting the Demand for Higher Education," in *At the Crossroads: Education in the Middle East,* ed. Adnan Badran (New York: Paragon, 1989), 248–249; Riad Tabbarah, "Population, Human Resources, and Development in the Arab World," in *Population and Development in the Middle East* (Beirut: UNECWA, 1982), 26; P. Shamsavary, "Iran," in *Encyclopedia of Higher Education,* vol. 1, *National Systems of Education,* ed. Burton R. Clark and Guy Neave (Oxford: Pergamon, 1992), 327–331.

81. E. E. Taylan and C. Taylan, "Turkey," in *Encyclopedia of Higher Education,* vol. 1, *National Systems of Education,* ed. Burton R. Clark and Guy Neave (Oxford: Pergamon, 1992), 750.

82. Massialas and Jarrar, *Arab Education,* 193. Massialas, "The Arab World," 987. Taylan and Taylan, "Turkey," 745; Shamsavary, "Iran," 327; H. M. Al-Baadi, "Planning Education: Arab World," in *International Encyclopedia of Education,* 2d ed., ed. Torsten Husen and T. Neville Postlethwaite (Oxford: Pergamon, 1994), 4484.

83. Massialas, "The Arab World," 987–988; Taylan and Taylan, "Turkey," 749–751.

84. Massialas and Jarrar, *Education in the Arab World,* 193, 196.

85. Shamsavary, "Iran," 332; Asghar Rastegar, "Health Policy and Medical Education," in *Iran after the Revolution: Crisis of an Islamic State,* ed. Saeed Rahnema and Sohrab Behdad (London: Tauris, 1995), 220; Nancy W. Jabbra and Joseph G. Jabbra, "Education and Political Development in the Middle East," in *The Middle East: From Transition to Development,* ed. Sami Hajjar (Leiden: Brill, 1985), 87; Rastegar, "Health Policy," 221.

86. Badran, "Meeting the Demand," 244–245.

87. Massialas and Jarrar, *Education in the Arab World,* 203–204.

88. Massialas and Jarrar, *Education in the Arab World,* 214–220; Massialas, "The Arab World," 990; Za'rour, *Universities in Arab Countries,* 8; Massialas and Jarrar, *Education in the Arab World,* 219.

89. Massialas, "The Arab World," 990.

90. J. S. Birks and J. A. Rimmer, *Developing Education Systems in the Oil States of Arabia: Conflicts of Purpose and Focus* (Durham, England: University of Durham, 1984), 27–31.

91. H. M. Al-Baadi, "Planning Education," 4484. Massialas, "The Arab World," 985–986; Badran, "Meeting the Demand," 250.

92. Massialas, "The Arab World," 984. Massialas and Jarrar, *Education in the Arab World,* 217.

93. S. Schwartzman, "Non-Western Societies and Education," in *Encyclopedia of Higher Education,* vol. 2, ed. Burton R. Clark and Guy Neave (Oxford: Pergamon, 1992), 974; World Bank, *Higher Education: the Lessons of Experience* (Washington, D.C.: World Bank, 1994), 2–3.

94. Badran, ed., *At the Crossroads,* 250, 316; Alonso-Gamo and El-Erian, "Economic Reforms, Growth, Employment, and the Social Sectors in the Arab Economies," 13.

95. Jacques Van der Gaag, "Social Development during Adjustment in the MENA Region: Contradiction or Opportunity," in *The Social Effects of Economic Adjustments on Arab Countries,* ed. Taher Kanaan (Washington, D.C.: International Monetary Fund, 1997), 147.

96. Badran, "Conclusion: Considerations for the Future," in *At the Crossroads: Education in the Middle East,* ed. Adnan Badran (New York: Paragon, 1989), 316.

97. Massialas and Jarrar, *Education in the Arab World,* 217. Schwartzman, "Non-Western Societies," 973–974; Sofronis Sofroniou, statements in discussion in *At the Crossroads: Education in the Middle East,* ed. Adnan Badran (New York: Paragon, 1989), 306.

98. Shamsavary, "Iran," 330–331; Massialas and Jarrar, *Education in the Arab World,* 217.

Chapter 15

Russia and Eastern Europe

Maria Bucur and Ben Eklof

With the demise of the Soviet empire, the vast social and political landscape of
Eurasia has been fundamentally altered. The political monopoly exerted by the
Communist Party has been eliminated and state monopolies on the economy
and the press have been challenged; even the political map of the region has
been redrawn as new (or newly reconstituted) states have emerged. The enormous energies released in this process have undoubtedly benefited some regions or countries as a whole. But uncertainty, impoverishment, and marginalization have also been the lot of many millions. In the former Soviet Union, for
example, some 80 million blue-collar workers have seen their living standards
plummet as their factories have closed or have failed to pay wages for months
on end. Disproportionately, women have found themselves out of work. And
perhaps 25 million Russians living in the non-Russian republics of the former
Soviet Union have suddenly discovered they were foreigners or minorities in
countries now detached from their Russian homeland. Border disputes proliferate, and a plutocracy built out of the Soviet Union's old informal networks
linking the criminal underworld and the party bureaucracy has emerged to feed
on the carcass of the Soviet economy. Whether this plutocracy is actually generating new wealth or simply reaping windfalls from the virtually untaxed export of extracted natural resources and sweetheart privatization deals is unclear.
Elsewhere, Hungary, the Czech Republic, Slovenia, and Poland seemed better
prepared to deal with the challenges of transition. Albania, Bulgaria, Romania,
and Slovakia have encountered more difficulty, and Yugoslavia has descended
into a bloody civil war.

Since 1989, educational reform has also swept across Eastern Europe and the
former Soviet Union. Attempts have been launched to dismantle the Soviet
legacy and to bring schools in line with European and American practices. At

the same time, reformers have turned to older, national and imperial legacies from the Ottoman, Austro-Hungarian and Russian empires for inspiration and emulation. Broadly speaking, reformers have pushed for democratization of governance and classroom practices, for diversification and choice, and for decentralization (or even privatization) of education. This ambitious agenda has achieved notable success in some areas. But elsewhere drastic reductions in education budgets undercut many programs. Precipitous decentralization led to chaos and undermined efforts to coordinate reform. And as if these problems weren't enough, growing ethnic and economic polarization has been reflected in tensions over school admissions and curriculum policy. In general, schools now seem to be exacerbating instead of mitigating society's inequities. At the same time, the prestige of a diploma has rapidly fallen; it appears that the generation of "post-Fall" citizens will be much less well educated than previous generations. Some economists have argued that this generational loss of human capital, in combination with the emigration of close to 100,000 highly trained scientists will, in the long term, inflict a greater body blow to the postsocialist economy than even the virtual collapse of the manufacturing sector. Finally, as a reaction to the inequities, to the friction and chaos that reform introduces, many voices have been raised for reviving those elements of the Soviet-type system of education worth saving.

This chapter surveys educational change since 1989 in Russia and Eastern Europe, with only brief mention of the newly independent states of the former Soviet Union. The discussion highlights general trends and acknowledges differences observed from region to region and from country to country. But the reader should recognize the shortcomings of this approach. First, a common nineteenth-century European educational tradition shaped pedagogy throughout the area covered in this chapter and provided a commonality of school practices and discourse. Second, the Soviet-type schools and administrative practice introduced in Eastern Europe after World War II imposed a new and different layer of uniformity across state borders. And finally, the underlying cultural diversity of the region was never fully eradicated in the schools. The cultural mosaic of Eastern Europe is no secret to the educated reader; fewer readers may be aware that Russian traditions vied with Baltic, Muslim, Turkic, and other legacies beneath a sometimes weighty, sometimes superficial veneer of communist beliefs and practices. Thus, separating the educational narrative into Russian and Eastern Europe educational histories both exaggerates and understates differences. Moreover, although school reform accelerated after Gorbachev came to power in 1985, much discussion and experimentation had taken place before that date. So we must begin with legacies and vastly simplify our presentation to preserve even a semblance of cohesion.

Finally, the political rhetoric of transition in Russia and Eastern Europe has detached terms such as liberal and conservative, progressive and democratic from their traditional moorings. Russians talk of an "ideology" of reform, but to them this means an explicit conceptualization, not a political agenda, as we think when we hear that word. Yet when they talk of "depoliticizing" the school curriculum, many Western observers see such talk as naive, for all educational reform involves political choices, however explicit. Thus our task of description is complicated by lexical as well as boundary confusion.

Old Regime Schools

It is not possible to speak of a single precommunist legacy in Eastern Europe with regard to education. Before 1918 this area was divided among three empires with very different outlooks on education—The Hapsburg, Ottoman, and Russian empires. Since the middle of the eighteenth century the rulers of the Hapsburg empire had become interested in providing basic education for all subjects as a means of creating a cohesive empire. Primary education served to imbue pupils with feelings of loyalty toward the Crown and the values for which it stood. Catholicism was an important element of this education, serving thus as an important counterforce against the threat of nationalism and ethnic challenges. Over the nineteenth century the Hapsburgs offered ambitious students of all nationalities the opportunity to study in its reputable schools (e.g., the Theresianum) or to become part of the officer corps, another important education institution in the empire. At the same time, authorities made it increasingly difficult for students who wanted to study in their own local language—be it Slovene, Croat, or Romanian—limiting their subventions only to schools that used German or (after 1867, especially) Hungarian as their primary language. Be that as it may, the empire offered many people (not just its German- and Hungarian-speaking populations) an opportunity to study in reputable Viennese universities and other schools abroad. The level of literacy and general education were higher here than elsewhere in Eastern Europe.

No such cohesive policy developed in the Ottoman Empire. The authorities were uninterested in the local administration and education of the non-Muslim populations. Instead, through the millet system each religion recognized under Islam—Orthodox Christian, Catholic, Protestant denominations, and Judaism—ruled over their respective flocks with little interference from the outside. The Orthodox Church, which came to dominate the lives of most Balkan Christians, had few education goals beyond the training of parish priests. As the empire waned in the face of challenges from the growing nationalist movements, the various ethnic groups in the Balkans began building education institutions that would ensure the creation of autonomous educated elites. Education reform proceeded from the top down, starting with the creation of elite schools and academies and only slowly spreading throughout the rest of the population. In addition, a small number of schools for vocational training appeared. The legacy of Ottoman rule for the development of education in the Balkans was meager, in part because the Orthodox Church lacked interest in education that was not strictly canonical. The various newly independent states tried to make up for these inadequacies but had a hard time catching up with the institutions, personnel, and other resources available in the Hapsburg lands. After 1918 the newly independent Balkan countries succeeded in passing legislation that made education compulsory to the fourth grade, although its implementation was rather haphazard. The illiteracy rate remained very high in this part of the world.

In the Russian empire, which at its zenith encompassed roughly one-sixth of the earth's land surface, eighteenth-century rulers made education a state concern by establishing universities, an academy of science, and then secondary schools. The Orthodox Church also founded seminaries, many of whose graduates later became prominent civil servants or revolutionaries. The Ministry of Education was created in 1802, and the Great Reforms of the 1860s included legislation encouraging state schooling for the newly liberated serfs and expanding opportunities for women at the secondary level. Trying to finance an army to support Russia's imperial and great power ambitions on the basis of a backward economy, the state had little left to spend on basic education. However, in the quarter century before World War I, a combination of societal and state initiative gave an enormous boost to public schooling for the lower classes, and educators hoped to achieve universal literacy in the empire by 1922.

Russian pedagogy and classroom practices were derivative of European, especially Prussian, approaches. Universities, though plagued by issues of autonomy and political freedom, made substantial contributions to world science; at the secondary level the atmosphere was formal, discipline often harsh, and the curriculum rigorous. At the primary level, however, Tolstoyan child-centered practices were influential, and after the turn of the century progressivism made deep inroads into educational practice. Dewey's democratic classroom became part of a powerful radical democratic and socialist movement against autocracy, in which redistributive justice was combined with decentralization and political freedom; indeed self-government, or *samoupravlenie*, came to be seen as a panacea in education: if only the oppressive weight of the central state could be removed, popular initiative would be unleashed and Russia catapulted into a better world.

Religion and language were problems for educators, whether oppositionist or autocratic. Most progressives insisted on the right to use local languages in the schools, yet most also believed in the civilizing mission of empire and argued that Russian should also be taught. Reformers were overwhelmingly secular in orientation and believed that the Orthodox Church had no place in the schools. Yet many, believing in cultural autonomy, argued that local populations should be allowed to establish private confessional schools, whether Catholic, Muslim, or (Orthodox) Old Belief. The practical problems involved in implementing such policies (teachers facing a classroom with children from a half dozen minority groups, for example) were never confronted, and tensions over ethnic and linguistic issues mounted in Russia's borderlands after 1900.

Socialism and the Stalinist School

World War I led to the collapse of the Ottoman, Austro-Hungarian, and Russian empires and the emergence of numerous new states, many having ethnically and religiously diverse populations and sharply contrasting rural and urban cultures.

From 1918 all Eastern European countries focused on building a strong educational infrastructure. Education policies had been important in the nationalist debates in the nineteenth century, and political leaders recognized the power that such institutions had to create a loyal, mobilized community of citizens. Furthermore, as these states had significant minority populations, education institutions and curriculum development became one of the main venues for constructing a homogeneous national identity. Policy makers favored highly centralized models over regional administrative and curricular autonomy, since they appeared to be destabilizing centripetal forces.

The practical challenges faced by all Eastern European countries had to do primarily with financial resources. Ambitions for creating a comprehensive primary education system and a secondary system with possibilities for vocational and theoretical education were high among most policy makers. They also encouraged the growth of higher education institutions, with growing diversification among the liberal professions from engineering to law and social sciences. Demography, anthropology, and sociology came to displace the central position held by philosophy and history among the humanities. These multiple agendas for developing various levels of education suffered especially after the Great Depression. Unfortunately for the bulk of the population, compulsory primary education suffered most. In Romania, for instance, the shrinking education budget prompted the minister of education to reduce the number of state-paid teachers by 2,000 in 1934, whereas university research institutes retained most of their state funding. This abatement of primary education was not as marked in places in which higher education was not as significant to the policy makers, such as Bulgaria. Finally, Czechoslovakia was able to weather the 1930s better, since it already had a well-developed primary and higher education infrastructure, inherited from the Hapsburgs, and an economy less vulnerable to a depression than that of other Eastern European countries.

By the end of the 1930s, all Eastern European countries except Albania had an integrated education system that included university and other higher education institutions. Czechoslovakia led the rest of the region in both extent of institutional development and diversity. It also had the highest rate of literacy. Throughout the area the state had become the most important agent for the dissemination of knowledge through schools at the expense of the Catholic and Orthodox Churches especially. Independent education institutions did survive, especially those funded by religious denominations—Christian and Jewish. Efforts were also made by different nongovernmental organizations to develop vocational schools and schools for women. Access to education, especially at the post-primary levels, was still very difficult for women, and none of the Eastern European states made a very sustained effort to eliminate the institutional, economic, and cultural obstacles faced by women who wished to engage in education.

Meanwhile, the Russian Revolution of 1917 had swept away the old Tsarist order, and the new Bolshevik leaders, borrowing heavily from Dewey, set about creating a new, secular, democratic, and progressive school system without uniforms, grades, textbooks, or conventional disciplinary boundaries. Open access to all levels of the school "ladder" was guaranteed for workers and peasants, and the walls separating school, work, and community were to be broken down. A genuine effort was launched to promote local languages and foster indigenous elites on the borderlands, though Enlightenment presumptions of Europe's civilizing mission remained deeply entrenched in the mind of Russian leaders. In 1921, as part of the introduction of a mixed economy in Russia, school financing was made the responsibility of local government. The result was chaos, since four years of revolution and civil war had destroyed the Russian economy, and its people were cold, hungry, and diseased. By the end of the first decade of Soviet rule, when the economy had rebounded to its prewar level, the democratic and decentralized school had been thoroughly discredited.

In 1929 Stalin swept away the mixed economy; he also inaugurated a new era in the schools. The Stalinist school system created after 1931 imposed a breathtaking uniformity and hierarchy upon education across the vast territories and ethnically diversified populations of the Soviet Union (by now approximating the boundaries of the old Tsarist empire). Stalinist education was nominally egalitarian as well as "polytechnical," and strongly "collectivist" in that it discouraged individual initiative or choice. Textbooks were restored to their traditional place, the authority of the teacher was reinforced, uniforms were reintroduced, and rote learning once again reigned supreme. Rapid expansion of education did provide opportunity for millions of peasants and workers, many of whom gained a secondary technical education and rose to positions of power and status. But the genuinely emancipatory and redistributive aspects of socialism, not to mention the learner-based tenets of democratic education, were scarcely evident in this system. All were cogs in a wheel, some were more equal than others, and everyone—teacher, student, administrator—knew his or her place in a "command system." After graduating, students were assigned jobs by the state. In reality, the system was not foolproof, and millions of enterprising individuals managed to beat the rules to get the education and career *they* wanted, regardless of the state's plans for them; but individual choice was not prominent. Stalinism also meant the ruthless suppression of local languages (and often those who spoke them) in an attempt to establish a "New Soviet Person" implicitly dominated by Russian culture. By 1953, whether in Ukraine, Russia, Central Asia, or Moldova, all schools looked alike, all textbooks were the same, and all teachers followed the same lesson plans. In this system an insidious ideology of bombast, distortion, and untruth corrupted the teaching of history and literature, and it profoundly compromised the singular achievement of unprecedented educational expansion, the other hallmark of Stalinism.

In Eastern Europe, the Communist regimes established after World War II did not completely do away with existing education legacies and institutions. Many qualified educators were purged between 1948 and 1956. Faculty in higher education institutions suffered the most. Taking their cue from the Soviet Union, the East European Communists used education as a tool for legitimizing their control on ideological grounds. Studying Russian became compulsory for all students, and dialectical materialism became the basis for all social sciences. The applied sciences became a priority, and many of the new specialists from these countries received their training in the Soviet Union.

In their efforts to modernize and remain ideologically untainted, policy makers had to choose between replacing certain structures, institutions, and programs for the sake of ideological purification, or preserving them, if in an ideologized fashion, for the sake of economic progress. In Czechoslovakia, Hungary, and especially East Germany (where the existing institutions for technical education were already well developed, especially at the higher levels) the Communists used these assets in their plans for modernization. It was different in Bulgaria and, to a great extent, in Yugoslavia and Romania, where it was the Communists who created many of the technical education schools.

Achievements and Problems of the Soviet School

The achievements of the Soviet-type school were considerable. First, it was effective in delivering full literacy under Stalin and, under his successors, a complete secondary education to the population of a far-flung and linguistically diverse country. By the 1980s access to higher education lagged only behind that of the United States: vocational and technical schools, one network of special schools for the gifted and another for children with special needs, boarding schools, a vast network of preschool and extramural institutions—all enhanced opportunity and recruited talent. The Communist regimes also opened up greater access to all levels of education for women. Illiteracy was greatly reduced, save in Albania. The state also provided some education for minority groups in their maternal language.

As for the quality of this education, there is no simple formulation. Graduates of Soviet schools who have emigrated to the West often praise the education they received and speak of caring and highly competent teachers; émigré children who enroll in American schools tend to be two to four years ahead of their cohorts in science and math, and they are far better read. Many Soviet and East European schools developed innovative art and music programs in the 1970s and 1980s. According to a World Bank study, students in Soviet-type schools, although excelling at the awareness of facts, fared less well in their application, and did poorly at using knowledge in unanticipated settings. Preschool institutions were woefully overcrowded, vocational schools had severe discipline problems, and 70 percent of all university graduates earned engineering degrees of questionable worth. Children with special needs were isolated, gender stereotyping was ubiquitous in textbooks, and minority cultures were paid only lip service.

Fitting the curriculum of the humanities and social sciences into the straitjacket of Marxism-Leninism had a stupefying effect. Even in the better schools a "conceptually overtaxing" curriculum (stemming, ironically, from the so-called Zankov reforms initiated in the 1960s, which sought to modernize instruction and enhance independent thinking) resulted in first-grade children having up to three hours of homework daily, widespread falsification of records, and social promotion (*protsentomania*). Bribes flourished as competition for places at universities intensified.

By the end of the Brezhnev era (1966–1982), planners in the Soviet Union and Eastern Europe were aware that their schools were in trouble. Seemingly intractable social and pedagogical issues were exacerbated by chronic underfunding. As a proportion of national income, investments in education lagged and schools declined. Rural schools lacked all amenities; overcrowded and crumbling urban schools met in two and sometimes three shifts daily; science laboratories were antiquated; underpaid and overworked teachers left in large numbers. Structural rigidities made it difficult to adapt schools to the changing needs of the economy, and the area's primitive communications infrastructure created daunting obstacles to participation in the information revolution by Soviet schools. Finally, an expensive network of research institutions under the various academies of science made only a limited contribution to economic growth; in Eastern Europe a growing brain drain stunted any significant contributions to research and development.

In Russia and Eastern Europe, women were relegated to secondary positions in all branches of the economy and administration, in spite of academic performance equaling that of men. Schools for minorities were supported in an inconsistent manner. In Romania, for instance, support for such schools rose and then fell with the waves of defensive nationalism among the Romanian leadership. In most cases special education remained limited to providing spaces for isolating individuals with physical and mental handicaps from the "normal" population. In Czechoslovakia, traditions in developing special education programs that focused on integrating these individuals in society as full participants were replaced by a policy of isolating individuals with mental handicaps and ignoring the needs of individuals with physical handicaps. This attitude was typical of all Soviet bloc countries.

In the Eastern European bloc, one of the most important weaknesses of the Communist education policy was the centralized nature of its allocative distribution powers. This system fostered the continuous dependency of local educators in budgetary and curriculum matters on the local representatives of the party and, in turn, on the higher chain of command that led to the top of the party hierarchy. During the 1980s the quality of basic education, research, and development, as well as the training of technical and humanities elites, steadily declined, not only in comparison with Western Europe but also in the context of the goals and expectations of the education policy makers in each individual country. The intellectual brain drain that started in the 1970s and intensified in the 1980s due to waves of emigration among the educated strata also deprived Eastern Europe of some of its best and most educated minds. Although this phenomenon has been present in other developing countries with non-Communist regimes, such as India, Eastern Europe's patterns of emigration are particular in their one-way direction. The intelligentsia that has left Eastern Europe since the 1970s has not in most cases returned and has not maintained close professional relations with colleagues there, at least before 1989.

The same strict, top-down control that fostered emigration also led to pedagogical restraints against creative and critical thinking among those who remained. By the early 1980s, the economic and administrative infrastructure in Eastern Europe had reached a level of modernization yet was incapable of generating the type of creative, dynamic change needed to compete in international markets. The more advanced countries, Hungary, Czechoslovakia and Poland, attempted to address these problems as early as the 1970s, with reforms similar to the Zankov initiative in Russia. The Gierek regime attempted to reduce the ideological content in all disciplines in Polish education. The Hungarian leadership also attempted such a change after Janos Kadar came to power, but it took another thirteen years from the initial resolution in 1972 before any substantial change occurred. In 1985 the Education Act was passed, which finally decentralized administrative, budgetary, and, to some extent, curriculum matters. With this legislation, which transferred some responsibilities from the ministerial level to local administrators and teachers, Hungary became the first East European country to understand and grapple with the educational inadequacies of the Communist regime. Another remarkable development occurred in Poland starting in 1980, when the Polish church, in collaboration with Solidarity, established alternative education institutions, such as primary and secondary schools under the administrative control of the Catholic Church. This development was essential to fostering values, goals, and attitudes divorced from the Communist order.

Reform and the Collapse of the Soviet Empire

In the Soviet Union in 1986, a year after Gorbachev came to power, a powerful reform movement emerged in education, with roots in Estonia, Georgia, and Russia. So-called Eureka initiative groups of parents and teachers, supported by the country's leading educational newspaper, *Teachers' Gazette*, as well as innovators in the Academy of Pedagogical Science, promoted a "pedagogy of cooperation." For a brief period education was a topic of genuine public interest, and in the rhetoric of reformers the belief grew that new schools could transform society. Through learner-based instruction children would grow into critically thinking, self-aware, and democratically inclined citizens to replace the "cogs" and "drones" of the totalitarian system. Between 1988 and 1990 the reformist platform of decentralization, differentiation, democratization, and enhancement of the humanities in a humanized school won official endorsement. Radical reformer Edward Dneprov was catapulted into national office as minister of education (1990–1992) in a highly centralized state.

With the dissolution of the Soviet Union in 1991, Dneprov found himself in charge of Russia's newly independent schools, and Boris Yeltsin's Decree 1 proclaimed education a top priority of the state. Yet Dneprov confronted a dilemma. He believed profoundly in decentralization as the key to unleashing public initiative, but he also saw that the only way to overcome the stifling inertia of a monolithic bureaucracy was to use his "fists" as minister to achieve a "breakthrough" and make reform irreversible. To his dismay, he learned that only a minority of teachers and parents actively supported the reformist agenda. Worse yet, he presided over school reforms as Russia spiraled into an economic collapse that dwarfed America's Great Depression in scale. As in the aftermath of the Russian Revolution, energetic, progressive reformers found empty coffers.

In a situation of growing disarray and disillusionment, Dneprov's reformers pursued a three-stage agenda of reform: conceptualization, legislation, and implementation. They believed that the conceptualization stage had been completed by 1990; their chief mission now was to promote a foundational law on education, which was promulgated to great fanfare in 1992. Reformers did not expect every article of the law to be implemented immediately, but they hoped that in the long run it would serve as a cornerstone for a profound transformation of attitudes and practices in education.

Dneprov promoted privatization, which won him many enemies; he also insisted on keeping the church out of state schools and fought against military training in the schools, which won him other enemies. He was replaced in 1992, but by then he had launched a major shake-up of the Russian school system, including curriculum, structure, and governance. But when he left office, the Ministry of Education had significantly diminished in power and influence. A policy of decentralization as well as a sharply reduced Kremlin budget for education contributed to a historic shift in control over schooling to Russia's regions, as part of an even larger transformation of Russian politics, from a highly centralized to a federal system.

The fall of the Communist regimes in Eastern Europe since 1989 has had a tremendous impact on education institutions in these countries, especially in regard to their role in society in the post–cold war era. Change in this sector of public life has varied, as countries of the former bloc have adopted their own particular strategies. The success of these policies in meeting the current economic and political challenges has been uneven in this region as well. However, some of the main problems faced by all of these countries were similar in kind, if not in degree.

Changes in Structure and Governance

In the Soviet-type school, legislation was a fig leaf hiding administrative chains of command through which directives were issued to run the system. Directors and inspectors were charged with ensuring compliance; professional unions were also controlled by the party-state, though they occasionally defended teachers. Forums to bring teachers and parents together often turned into shaming sessions for parents who were not bringing up their children properly. Budgets for individual schools were controlled in the smallest detail by the central authorities. And the "central authorities" were overwhelmingly male. Although women made up a majority of state employees in the education system, men dominated the middle and upper levels of the administrative hierarchy. Corruption and inefficiency, and perhaps the more decent side of human nature, made the running of these schools far less rigid and monolithic than is sometimes claimed. Still, this was what local reformers would call an "administrative-command" system rather than a "law-abiding" system. "Structural rigidities" were a reality as ugly as the term itself.

Attempts to turn to a law-governed system, to practice negotiation and adjudication, and to keep accurate accounts for outside observers have had to come to grips with the lingering command culture and its remaining personnel. In Russia, programs have been set up with Western aid to teach more flexible management approaches. Gradually, agreements are being reached among Moscow, the regions, and municipalities to share authority in decision making, and various collegial bodies have been established for resolving issues among the various authorities.

At the international level, some success has been achieved in re-creating a "common educational space," or agreements among the states of the former Soviet Union to promote cooperation and to establish equivalencies. At the local level, the school boards created in the early stages of reform have not proven their viability, but school principals undoubtedly enjoy more autonomy than before. As for alternative education, private schools, gymnasia, and the like have clearly established a foothold in Russian education but still account only for 1–2 percent of all schools. The 1992 law endorsed a limited privatization of education facilities and provided for setting up state-subsidized experimental schools. Reformers also flirted with the notion of vouchers. But in 1995 a Duma hostile to privatization forced revisions to the law prohibiting privatization of state school property. And there is widespread hostility among teachers to breaking up the state's monopoly over schooling.

In Eastern Europe policy makers began to explore institutional reform at an early stage, but change has been slow in coming for a variety of reasons. Initially, discussion centered around issues of decentralization and local autonomy in a visceral reaction to the centralist setup under communism. Decentralizing was identified with rejecting communism.

When policy makers began to discuss the effects of decentralizing the administration and budgets of education institutions more systematically, it became apparent that the quality of education might suffer from such changes. How could they monitor the quality of instruction without retaining control over the purse? The debate concerning local institutional autonomy vis-à-vis ministerial control has not yet been resolved, and it has not helped that a tug-of-war has ensued among bureaucrats at the center fearful of losing their positions and bureaucrats on the periphery hoping to increase their paltry salaries.

In some cases the debate over decentralization has had a political and especially nationalist side. In Romania, for instance, leaders of the Hungarian minority have relentlessly called for a comprehensive reevaluation of minority education, with the hope of reinstating locally administered Hungarian-language primary and secondary schools wherever Hungarians are the majority. Most Romanians are skeptical of the loyalty of the Hungarian minority, so Bucharest has been reluctant to agree to such demands. Because the ministry has until recently identified local autonomy with nationalist threats, both Hungarian and Romanian schools have suffered. Similarly, in now separated Czechoslovakia, debates between the Czechs and Slovaks about ending Prague's control over Slovak schools played an important role in the partition. Since the separation, nationalist trends have only grown in Slovakia, and the government has subsidized the attempts by a nationalist organization, Matica Slovenska, to prepare textbooks in history, language, and literature.

Independent schools have added a new dimension to the debate over authority by introducing a market component of choice for the consumer. Since 1990, the Catholic Church has provided the most sustained challenge, creating a number of schools in Poland and Hungary at both primary and secondary levels. These schools are now recognized as equal competitors with the state schools. Nonreligious private establishments such as Montessori schools have opened as well, but the general public's unfamiliarity with them, as well as high tuition rates, have limited their growth.

Marketization of school has met a mixed reception in Eastern Europe. In Poland, nongovernmental education institutions can benefit from state subsidies of up to 50 percent of their operating costs. This has encouraged a proliferation of such schools and has enhanced their credibility among parents. In Hungary, by contrast, the state is still reluctant to subsidize independent schools; in Bulgaria and Romania the state cannot find enough money to meet its commitments to state schools, much less consider financing independent institutions. Moreover, commissions set up in Eastern Europe to monitor the quality of private schools have often abused their power for the sake of personal interest by practicing favoritism. As a result, the integrity of private schools as institutions of learning has been called into question. The uncertainty is even greater in that parents cannot be sure their child's degree will be recognized upon graduation. Thus public reluctance, to some extent fostered by the behavior of official commissions, has reinforced the position that the central offices of the ministries of education need to retain budgetary and administrative control.

These discussions of administrative and budgetary autonomy as well as the role of private schooling have not yet led to comprehensive legislative reform anywhere outside the former Soviet Union. In Hungary a debate still smolders over national curriculum standards that would enable schools, private or public, to make changes in curriculum independently, provided their actions conform to the national standard. In Romania and Bulgaria no such legislation has even come under discussion. In Poland and the Czech Republic, legislative change has taken place in a piecemeal fashion without an overall agenda. The entire area is still in transition, experimenting with different policies from year to year but unwilling to settle on a set direction at this point.

Curriculum Reform

After 1989 educators in Russia and Eastern Europe sought to "de-ideologize" the curriculum by allowing a choice of textbooks and free discussion of long forbidden topics in history, eliminating "scientific communism," "scientific atheism," and introducing sociology, civics, global education, and even religion. In Eastern Europe, the dismantling of old curricula took place almost spontaneously, before the formulation of any projects for legislative reform. Hungary and Poland began the process before the rest of the bloc countries, and by 1990 reformers had removed many of the humanities textbooks of the old regime, as well as mandatory courses such as political economy. Czechoslovakia soon followed, with Romania, Bulgaria, and Albania lagging behind. Another symbolically powerful change was eliminating Russian language study from most of the other countries' curricula. Central authorities have allowed the regions and municipalities to choose what they will teach and how they will teach it, and many schools now offer students a range of electives in Russia and the Commonwealth of Independent States (CIS). As Steve Heyneman has emphasized, in theory at least, a major "paradigm shift" from teacher-based to learner-based approaches has occurred everywhere, and the promotion of academic freedom and choice has been a genuine achievement of the past decade. In Romania, Bulgaria, and Albania, by contrast, discussions about fostering a pluralist political culture have led to few significant changes. The governments here have not encouraged the founding of alternative institutions at the level of secondary education. These countries have only recently begun their own active campaign to produce reforms in teachers' understanding of pluralist values and their ability to foster such a spirit in the classroom.

At the same time, these advances have been limited if not crippled by economic constraints, the inertia of tradition, and outright resistance. They have proceeded unevenly in different regions and at different levels. Even where academic freedom has struck deep roots, it has often been with deleterious consequences.

Economic constraints, palpable in all areas of schooling, have wreaked the most damage. Despite generous funding by George Soros, producing adequate numbers of new textbooks (often in several languages) has proven a daunting task, and in Russia three out of four schools still use Soviet-era books. In Eastern Europe, the textbook situation is brighter. Change occurred first in Hungary and Poland, which eliminated old textbooks by 1990. Most of the other countries in the former Soviet bloc had introduced new textbooks by 1997.

Retraining teachers is an expensive and lengthy process that involves in-service release time and support, as well as an overhaul of pedagogical institutions. Learner-based and problem-solving instruction also call for smaller classes, but low salaries (often months in arrears) have caused widespread flight from the teaching profession. Many empty slots have been filled by retired teachers unable to live on their meager pensions, but these pensioners tend to be conservative and wedded to the old ways of rote instruction. Teachers who do not leave and are not ill-disposed to innovation often are simply too overworked and exhausted from the daily stresses of an impoverished existence to make major changes in their routines. By all accounts, rote learning in large classrooms continues to prevail in all but a few elite schools and institutions throughout Eastern Europe.

Even with European markets pressuring Eastern Europe in regard to the need for better training in managerial, business, and high-tech skills, curriculum reformers are driven by the desire to offer more humanities courses and fewer science courses in primary and secondary schools. Because Soviet-era educators had packed the curriculum with up to sixteen different disciplines for each academic year, the initial reaction against this overburdening of students was to eliminate disciplines "tainted" by ideology. More high schools have begun to focus on applied disciplines—computer science, business, accounting—at the expense of theoretically oriented high schools. In Poland and the Czech Republic at the moment, however, there is an effort to return to a focus on individual development, on humanizing students instead of accumulating technical knowledge.

One important element of this new emphasis on personal rather than professional growth has been the inclusion of religion in the compulsory curriculum, starting with primary education. Outside the former Soviet Union, all Eastern European countries, save Albania, teach religious studies from the primary level onward in both state and private schools. Countries with a predominantly

Catholic population (Poland, Slovakia, and Hungary) have offered a more ecumenical version of religious studies, but Orthodox countries (Romania in particular) offer students little unbiased information about other religions.

The resurgence of nationalism in all humanities disciplines has been a prominent feature of curriculum reform in the area. Focusing on national traditions at the expense of a comparative international framing of knowledge has been especially popular among the older generation of policy makers and teachers. In Hungary, for instance, a large contingent of specialists voiced their criticism against a 1991 reform project because it seemed too immersed in the challenges of the globalized economic market and not mindful enough of national values. Romanians have embraced this nationalist outlook even more fervently. Since 1989 Romania has pursued reforms regarding education opportunities for its ethnic minorities in their own language more because of international pressures than because of an earnest desire to deal with these issues.

Language, religion, and history everywhere present especially thorny problems for educators. Decentralization and pluralism allow local minorities to teach more fully and truthfully their own languages, history, and culture. In language instruction, however, this often disenfranchises other resident minorities. Russians have a notoriously poor record of learning local languages, whether they live in Riga or Bishkek. Being forced to learn (or even study) a local language, as students now are in Tallin, is perhaps long overdue. Yet multinational communities, especially large ones such as Russia, must have a lingua franca for the courts, army, and scientific institutions, whether it be Russian, German, or French. Finding a realistic way to encourage a flowering of tongues as well as a common language (not to mention training teachers and generating textbooks for schools balancing these needs) will be no easy task, even with the best of intentions, which are sometimes in short supply.

In history, narratives of conquest, expropriation, deportation, exploitation, and even genocide were long banished from school textbooks, and the creation of empires was described in fairy-tale terms. But the Bashkirs and Tatars and dozens of other ethnicities in Russia, the banished populations of the Crimea, Caucasus, the Roma, and others now want their stories told in the schools, and they want the creation of empire presented as an unqualified evil. Religious conflict is also part of the narrative, not only the suppression of religion as such but also the collaboration of a dominant church (often Orthodoxy) in the persecution of "sects" (Protestantism) or non-Christian faiths, whether Judaism, Islam, or Buddhism. Yet instruction in religion, especially in Eastern Europe after 1989, has often been treated as an integral part of national and spiritual rebirth in the aftermath of communism. In some areas (a prominent example is Bosnia and Herzegovina), new textbooks have "increased ethnic divisions, exacerbated differences, and prevented social cohesion."

Thus decentralization and emancipation have had ugly consequences in some communities. Educators as well as international organizations are concerned that schools are now being used to sustain ethnic grievances rather than promote citizenship tenets, reconciliation, and development of the "social capital" societies need to prosper in a global market environment. History's didactic function of building consensus around common myths, which sometimes conflicts with seeking the truth, is at issue. Civic education courses, energetically promoted by various international organizations, may play a significant role in resolving conflicts now evident in the teaching of history, language, and religion. But these subjects will be a source of contention for some time to come.

Not all the news is bad. Many individuals and organizations in the Baltics, Russia, and Eastern Europe are working actively to promote social reconciliation. In one notable case, Central Asia, the ministers of education from neighboring countries signed an agreement (1992) to create schools for the large mix of ethnic groups from surrounding states and to allow textbooks to be imported across borders for local minorities; thus Uzbeks in Kazakhstan can use textbooks imported from Uzbekistan. The ministers also agreed to meet annually, recognizing that tolerance and mutual understanding are crucial for the survival and stability of the entire region.

International pressures have become important factors in the debate over curriculum reform everywhere in Eastern Europe, but perhaps less so in Russia. The prospect of becoming part of the European Union has become a prominent factor in the education policies of these countries since in the early 1990s. In Hungary, for instance, as early as in 1991, one criterion for education reform was to "link up to the European education standards," with the hope of having degrees conferred in Hungary recognized everywhere in Europe. Similar ambitions have dominated discussions about reform after the initial period of transition in both Poland and Czechoslovakia. As these three countries prepare to become members of the European Union, curriculum reformers here are paying increasing attention to the structure and content of curriculum in Western European schools, especially from the secondary level up. In the rest of Eastern Europe, concerns about such competitiveness are still premature, since most graduates are content to be able to compete for economic and professional opportunities inside their own countries.

Other curriculum issues have been created by decentralization and pluralism. How, given the primitive state of licensing and certification, can quality be measured? How can the rights of students to receive a decent education and to transfer from school to school or region to region be protected? The Russian Ministry of Education has worked hard to develop a choice of syllabi for schools, in the hope that schools will avail themselves of one of these choices. In addition, the ministry has issued "minimal competencies" and has propagated the notion of standardized testing. A lot of creative thinking has gone into developing a three-tiered core curriculum with national, regional, and local school components. Progress has been made, but there is widespread suspicion that Moscow wants to use standards to reimpose central control. Nevertheless, dozens of regions have worked out agreements with Moscow on this issue.

Economic Issues

Economic pressures have deeply compromised reform efforts in every area of education. Even before the economies in this region began their sharp decline, education was underfunded in per capita terms, and it made up a declining proportion of gross domestic product (GDP). For example, the Soviet Union spent 7 percent of its GDP on education in the 1970s, but this declined to less than 4 percent by the late 1980s. According to official data, in 1988, 21 percent of all Soviet schoolchildren attended schools in buildings without central heating, 30 percent were in schools lacking indoor plumbing, and 40 percent studied in schools with no access to sports facilities. By 1996, education funding in Russia and Ukraine had dropped to 3 percent of GDP. Romania, Slovakia, Bulgaria, and Albania have suffered from similar declines. In the Baltic states education expenditure has recovered to 6 percent of GDP, and Poland, the Czech Republic, Hungary, and Slovenia, preparing for membership in the European Union, have had to show a willingness to increase per capita expenditures on education. Except in Poland, however, economic production throughout the region has declined by as much as half from 1989 and thus *real* outlays on education by the state have declined precipitously. Education officials in Russia estimate that the schools currently receive less than half the sum needed for a minimally adequate schooling.

All sectors of education have suffered, but preschool programs have suffered most. This is particularly unfortunate, since unemployment and impoverishment have severely strained family life, and the need for intervention programs has only grown. The decline in health and nutrition programs, as well as in support for children with special needs, is an especially bitter pill to swallow. In the Soviet era more than a quarter of all public expenditures on education went to preschool programs, compared to 4 percent in Japan, 6 percent in the United States, and 5 percent in the United Kingdom.

During the Soviet era, family income and occupation affected children's opportunities to gain admission to prestigious schools; bribes, personal connections, and private tutors hired to prepare students for entrance examinations were all widespread. Nevertheless, children from less fortunate families could take advantage of special schools for the gifted and a well-developed network of free extramural enrichment programs. Those who won admission to an accelerated school, professional and technical institute, or university paid no tuition fees and received free housing as well as small stipends for living expenses. But now access to education has narrowed. The sharply curtailed availability of inexpensive child care has reduced women's opportunities to study or take part in professional retraining programs. Tuition has been introduced in elite secondary schools; even where schooling is nominally free, parents have been dragooned into paying large sums for "optional courses," "special services," or capital improvements. Despite efforts to introduce standardized exams, bribery persists in admissions to higher education, and private tutoring continues to privilege children of wealthier families, especially when "tutors" also sit on admissions committees. In 1998 Alexander Tikhonov, minister of education, openly admitted to the editor of *Teachers' Gazette* that bribes prevail in competition for admission, and not only to the most prestigious institutions. The same problems persist throughout Eastern Europe.

Special education has been the Cinderella of education reform in Eastern Europe. In the early stages of reform much attention was devoted to improving the quality of special education, and in 1991 Poland passed a comprehensive law making special education an integral part of the school system, "mainstreaming." But elsewhere financial constraints have generally led to a decline in the quality of special education programs. Credit belongs to the many international organizations that have worked to educate policy makers, train families of children with handicaps, and provide direct aid for such children. Equipment such as wheelchairs, virtually unavailable a decade ago, have now appeared, again partly thanks to international efforts.

The market has also created obstacles for reformers devoted to humanizing the curriculum and helping children to become well-rounded adults with a pronounced civic ethos. Instead, parents and children want training that leads directly to lucrative jobs. In their eyes the liberal arts and humanities, except for foreign languages, are an unaffordable luxury. By contrast, programs in law, economics, business administration, and computer technology have become growth industries. Yet the same market forces have made it very hard to retain teachers of foreign languages in the schools. Vocational education has suffered greatly in the past decade, since most of its programs prepared students for jobs that are no longer available in the manufacturing sector. To survive, vocational schools must undergo expensive reforms. But how can programs in banking, marketing, commerce, or computer training be established just as funding from the state and bankrupt enterprises is drying up? Remarkably, enrollments at vocational schools remained steady during the past decade of upheaval in Russia, but this was largely because the state feared the societal consequences of releasing thousands of largely unemployable youth onto the streets and continued their stipends. In this period, vocational schools performed a largely social rather than economic service, and their future is now imperiled.

Finally, other areas of education have been especially hard hit by marketization. Research has proven to be very expensive and very difficult to sustain. Russia's central education bureaucracy has only a handful of statisticians collecting and analyzing data, so the ministry must often make crucial decisions without adequate information. Sociological surveys are usually carried out only when supported by international organizations. The tradition of promoting research in specialized academies is withering away for lack of funding, but only a handful of universities (twelve in Russia according to one estimate) are capable of supporting basic research. A decade ago, laboratory equipment in Soviet-style institutions lagged far behind the West. Accelerated technological change and collapsing budgets have made that gap even greater, and thousands of scientists have left, compounding the decline by removing human capital. Virtually everywhere libraries are in woeful shape. A valiant effort has been made to address these problems by creating access to information resources through the Internet. Hungary, the Czech Republic, and Poland have been most successful; elsewhere electronic links are prohibitively expensive, unreliable, or simply not available.

Universities

Universities share, as well as inherit, the problems confronting lower-level schools, but the post-Soviet period has been especially turbulent for higher education. Of the more than five hundred higher education institutions functioning in Russia today, under a dozen can properly be called research oriented, and the academies of science traditionally responsible for the production of knowledge are crumbling. Enrollments in higher education institutions were expected to plummet after 1991, as the value of a college degree declined. Instead, enrollments have surged, but only in new, market-oriented fields of study. Everywhere fee-paying students have replaced those enrolled with merit-based stipends. At the university level living stipends have dwindled to the point that most high school graduates now apply only to universities that allow them to continue to live at home. This has had the paradoxical effect of reducing applications to more prestigious institutions located in the expensive large cities and boosting enrollments in run-of-the mill institutions.Once the state covered all tuition fees, but now fewer than half of all students receive scholarships, and "tuition has become an essential part of public institutions." Yet tuition fees exceed annual average income by almost 200 percent. To meet this changed environment, the concept of student loans was introduced in the 1992 Law on Education, but no practical loan schemes have yet been proposed (much less funded) in Russia. Private universities now exist, but many are phantom institutions, existing in a parasitic relationship with state facilities; endowments, critical to long-term stability and autonomy, are virtually unknown. In Russia's regions, local VUZY (higher education institutions) are often consolidating, since agricultural, pedagogical, and humanities-oriented institutions see their survival in reorganizing as comprehensive (called "classical") universities. Interestingly, many regional universities now compete successfully with Moscow and St. Petersburg for the best students, since families find it financially impossible to support their children away from home.

In terms of governance, the post-Soviet transition brought autonomy from the state to universities. Academic freedom has been achieved across the East European plain, and in a handful of locations changes have created vibrant institutions of higher learning. But in most Russian universities demoralization prevails. Generous amounts of Western aid have been funneled into a select number of programs (assuming a long-term trickle-down effect), and some rectors are paid thousands of dollars monthly. But most faculty, like teachers in schools, are paid a starvation wage and must teach a double or triple load (sometimes moonlighting at "private" institutions using the very same classrooms). Merit-based competition for research money and peer reviews are virtually unknown, and accounting procedures are laughable; instead patronage and clientalism prevail as most institutions are ruled by the heavy hand of Soviet-style bosses and fixers. Teachers show little interest in university affairs outside the classroom, and faculty governance bodies now exert little influence. Inside the classroom, a culture of rote instruction to bored students survives from the Soviet era. According to OECD/World Bank specialists, little change has taken place in the humanities curricula, though new programs in business, marketing, and law are springing up like mushrooms. Facilities are in shocking disrepair, and university communities must often cope without heat, light, or running water.

In Place of a Conclusion

A decade after revolutionary change in Eastern Europe that shook the world, the schools remain in an unsettled state. Change has occurred much more rapidly and profoundly in some areas than in others. Internationalization has left a mark, but much less so in, say Kazan, than in Prague. Freedom and opportunity beckon, but equity has declined. Corruption, bribery, incompetence, and lip service to reform can all be found, but so can remarkable dedication and a capacity for innovation even in very difficult circumstances. A revival of national and imperial traditions proceeds, but a fascination with Western approaches also persists; textbooks fomenting xenophobia and ethnic animosities can be found along with others promoting reconciliation and tolerance.

Looking ahead, we anticipate Russia and Eastern Europe taking two divergent paths. Since August 1998 the Russian economy has collapsed, with deleterious consequences for education. In many areas schools have been forced to retreat from their educational mission in order to meet children's basic social needs. At the apex of the education system, universities function only in name.

As Russia struggles for survival, Eastern Europe is in a relatively more advantageous position, with the countries of this region continuing the catch-up game with the European Union. However, global economic and social forces, such as the Asian crisis, will condition the success of this effort, as well as Russia's attempts to climb out of the abyss into which it has fallen. Thus the future of education in Russia and eastern Europe will be shaped by the interplay between the local dynamics described in this chapter and the broader context of globalization.

Bibliography

Bain, Olga. "The Costs of Higher Education to Students and Parents in Russia: Tuition Policy Issues." *International Higher Education,* no. 11 (Spring 1998): 6–8.

Bartz, Brunon, and Zbigniew Kullas. "The Essential Aspects of Education Reform in Poland." *European Education* 25, no. 2 (Summer 1993): 15–26.

Baskerville, Stephen. "East Central Europe: The Future of American Higher Education?" *Academe* (November-December 1997): 22–26.

Bollag, Burton. "Nationalist Group Gains Power over Slovakian Education." *Chronicle of Higher Education* 28 (February 1997): 49.

Bolotov, Victor, et al., eds. "The Reform of Education in New Russia: A Background Report for the OECD Review of Russian Education." *ISRE Newsletter on East European, Eurasian, and Russian Education* 6, no. 1 (1997): 4–21,and no. 2 (1997): 9–62.

Education in Russia, the Independent States, and Eastern Europe. Biannual publication of the United Kingdom Study Group on Education in Russia, the Independent States, and Eastern Europe.

Eklof, Ben, and Edward Dneprov, eds. *Democracy in the Russian School.* Boulder: Westview, 1993.

Gutsche, Marta. "The Hungarian Education System in the Throes of Change." *European Education* 25, no. 2 (Summer 1993): 5–11.

Heyneman, Stephen P. "From the Party/State to Multi-Ethnic Democracy: Education and Its Influence on Social Cohesion in the Europe and Central Asia Region." *International Journal of Education Development* (forthcoming).

———. "Education and Economic Transformation." Papers presented to the National Academy of Sciences, Washington, D.C., September 1996.

———. *Russia: Education in the Transition.* Washington, D.C.: World Bank, 1995.

Holmes, Brian, Gerald H. Read, and Natalya Voskresenskaya. *Russian Education: Traditions and Transition.* New York: Garland, 1996.

Jones, Anthony, ed. *Education and Society in the New Russia.* New York: Sharpe, 1994.

Kirk, Mary, and Aaron Rhodes. "Continental Responsibility." *European and International Support for Higher Education and Research in East Central Europe.* Vienna: Institut für die Wissenshaften von Menschen, 1994.

Kodin, Evgenii. "Problems of Private Higher Education in Russia." *International Higher Education* 6 (December 1996): 11–13.

Mitter, Wolfgang, et al., eds. *Recent Trends in Eastern European Education.* Frankfurt: German Institute for International Educational Research, 1992.

Muckle, James. *Education in Russia: Past and Present: An Introductory Study Guide and Select Bibliography.* Nottingham: Bramcote, 1993.

———. *Portrait of a Soviet School under Glasnost.* New York: St. Martin's, 1990.

Organization for Economic Cooperation and Development. *Secondary Education Systems in PHARE Countries: Survey and Project Proposals.* Paris: OECD, 1996.

Prucha, Ian, and Eliska Walcherova. "Czechoslovak Education within the Broader Social Framework." *European Education* 25, no. 2 (Summer 1993): 27–35.

Tjeldvoll, Arild, ed. "Education in East/Central Europe: Report of the Oslo Seminar." *Special Studies in Comparative Education* 30 (1992). University of Oslo Institute for Educational Research and State University of New York at Buffalo.

Valery, Soyfer. "Who Offers a Better Education—The USA or Russia?" *Izvestiia*, November 15, 1995. In Russian.

Verdery, Katherine. *National Ideology under Socialism: Identity and Cultural Politics in Ceausescu's Romania*. Berkeley: University of California Press, 1989.

Wanner, Cathy. "Educational Practices and the Making of National Identity in Post-Soviet Ukraine." *Anthropology of East Europe Review* 13, no. 2 (Autumn 1995).

Watson, Peggy. "Gender Relations, Education, and Social Change in Poland." *Gender and Education* 4, no. 2 (1992): 127–147.

Weselowsky, Tony. "Russia: Costs Render Educational Reforms Almost Prohibitive." *Radio Free Europe/Radio Liberty*, Prague, 12 February 1998.

Chapter 16

No Teacher Guide, No Textbooks, No Chairs

Contending with Crisis in African Education

Joel Samoff

The sense of excitement, hope, and anticipation in African education has been replaced by widespread dismay, disappointment, and discouragement. Earlier, expectations were unbounded:

> We in Zambia are immensely proud of our University. This pride is not simply that this is our first and only University. It is also because the university of Zambia is our own University in a very real sense. . . . Humble folk in every corner of our nation— illiterate villages, barefooted school children, prison inmates and even lepers—gave freely and willingly everything they could, often in the form of fish, or maize or chickens. The reason for this extraordinary response was that our people see in the University the hope of a better and fuller life for their children and grandchildren.[1]

Initial postcolonial progress was clear and dramatic:

> Around the time that most countries of Sub-Saharan Africa gained independence from colonial rule, the region lagged far behind the rest of the world on nearly every indicator of Western-style educational development. Efforts since then have been truly dramatic. . . . The record of this period is a tribute to the determination of African leaders and the sacrifices of African parents in their quest to provide a better standard of living for their children's generation.[2]

Today, the most common refrain is crisis. Education in Africa, at all levels and in all its forms, is in dire straits, we are told. With few exceptions, both schools and learning have deteriorated, and the situation is continuing to worsen. Recent detailed studies of the education sector have been especially pointed. A sampler:

> The universities of Africa are in crisis. Enrollments rise as capacities for government support decline. Talented staff are abandoning the campuses, libraries are out-dated, research output is dropping, students are protesting overcrowded and inhospitable conditions, and educational quality is deteriorating. The need for action is urgent.[3]

> The quality of primary education is at present unacceptably low. . . . The physical conditions of most schools are unacceptably poor.[4]

> Great shortages of qualified and trained teachers . . . a generally poor and non-stimulating learning environment.[5]

> A large number, possibly the vast majority, of primary school buildings and many teacher houses are in a very dilapidated state of repair.[6]

> [University of Ghana and University of Cape Coast are] a mere shadow of their earlier glory; drained of teaching staff, lacking in equipment and teaching materials, housed in degenerated infrastructure, surrounded by an air of demoralization and incipient decay.[7]

Not only is there crisis, but national authorities seem to be unable to deal with it effectively:

> Most of the Sahelian countries do not have qualified personnel or adequate facilities for planning, administration and management of basic education. Where these facilities exist, rational working methods for the release of viable statistics and data on education are inexistent. Up to date, none of the member States is capable of correctly planning and evaluating its basic education programmes.[8]

> The crisis in Senegalese higher education reflects the lack of any discernible expenditure strategy in the past decade.[9]

> Le système éducatif togolais a été caractérisé dans le passé récent par le manque d'une politique sectorielle cohérente et focalisée. [The Togolese educational system has been characterized in the recent past by the lack of a coherent and focused sectoral policy.][10]

Imaginative responses to crisis and "remarkable resilience" notwithstanding, no end is in sight for the decay and disarray:

> In the 1990s and beyond, institutions of higher education in Africa, especially the universities, must contend with several interrelated major problems, whose combined effect threatens to strangulate them. . . . To say that higher education in Africa is in

crisis does not mean simply that the funds available to run higher education institutions are grossly inadequate. . . . More than that, African countries and societies are going through a period of economic uncertainty, political and social upheavals, plus other contortions, and higher education has become a victim of the prevailing state of affairs. The situation is likely to remain so, well into the twenty-first century.[11]

Yet Africa has also been the site of imaginative experiments, innovations in the content and forms of education, and critical reflections on the role of education in society. Long before Europeans arrived, and to this day, Africa's intellectual contributions have had global influence.

How, then, to make sense of this transition from expansive expectations to pervasive degeneration, from promise to progress to crisis? Like education itself, the analysis of education in Africa requires attention to both content and forms, and especially to context and process. In the remainder of this brief overview, I explore major issues and themes in education in contemporary Africa,[12] considering both outcomes and analytic frameworks.

"Education in Africa," like "African education," is of course a simplification fraught with risk. For most purposes, neither exists. With care, it is possible to study education in Guinée and to explore the unique characteristics of, say, Ghanaian education. But since the diversity within countries is vast and most countries are themselves of very recent origin, it is foolhardy to speak in general terms about a continent comprising more than fifty countries. Still, the craft of comparative education requires just that. Identifying and understanding similarities and commonalities sometimes requires deferring attention to individual variations. Our continuing challenge and responsibility is to use each sort of analysis—detailed examination of what is unique at the small scale and synthetic overview of what is common at the larger scale—to illuminate and strengthen the other. Hence, as we consider shared patterns across Africa, we must at the same time constantly recall and respect Africa's rich diversity.

Education in Africa at the Century's End

The 1990s have been a period of reflection and reevaluation for African development. The optimism that accompanied the decolonization of the late 1950s and early 1960s has been displaced by a deep dismay at persisting poverty and a profound pessimism about the viability of any strategy of social transformation. For many, the objective is no longer broad improvement in the standard of living or self-reliance but simply survival.

Education too has experienced a similar transition. Earlier, education (formal and nonformal) was expected to be the principal vehicle for social change, both helping to define the new society and enabling its citizens to function effectively within it. Not only were the illiterate to learn reading and writing, but they and other newly educated were also to foster innovation, accelerate the generation and diffusion of ideas and technologies, and monitor and manage a responsive political system. Education was to be the vehicle for redressing discrimination and inequality, both in daily practice and in popular understanding.

There has been progress and, in some countries, very substantial achievements. Still, in much of Africa, many children get little or no schooling, illiteracy rates have ceased to decline (or have begun to rise), school libraries have few books, laboratories have outdated or malfunctioning equipment and insufficient supplies, and learners lack chairs, exercise books, even pencils. As I have noted, nearly all observers characterize contemporary African education as being in crisis. Many, both inside and outside Africa, are pessimistic about the ability of national authorities to address the crisis effectively.

In this setting, recourse to foreign aid has become a way of life. Almost without exception, education reform proposals are presumed to require external funding. In some, perhaps many, countries, even the day-to-day operation of the education system depends on overseas support.

As the general crisis has unfolded, external aid agencies have increasingly come to provide development advice as well as finance. Notwithstanding its critical role, their funding remains a very modest portion of total education expenditures. Consequently, their influence may be far greater than the absolute value of their aid suggests. Indeed, some agencies, and especially the World Bank, currently assert that their development expertise is even more important than their funds. "[The World Bank's] . . . main contribution must be advice, designed to help governments develop education policies suitable for the circumstances of their countries."[13]

The increased reliance on foreign aid to support education innovation and reform has been accompanied by another transition, from understanding education as a human right and general good to viewing it primarily in terms of its contribution to national development through the development of the knowledge and skills societies are deemed to need. Occasional voices continue to insist that education is liberating and that learning is inherently developmental. Most often, however, education is regarded as distinctly instrumental, an investment in a country's future, a production system that (more or less successfully) turns out people with particular competencies and attitudes, and a delivery system that transfers wisdom, expectations, ways of thinking, and discipline to the next generation.[14] As we shall see, these two currents—on the one hand the expanded role for foreign aid and its providers and with it the tendency to address education through the prism and with the tools of finance and, on the other, the understanding of education primarily as preparation for the world of work—reinforce each other with enduring consequences for education in Africa. In the following section I briefly review that trajectory, from education as social transformation, broad development engine, and foundation for self-reliance to aid dependence and education as targeted skills formation.

Toward Education for All

Nearly all African countries started with an inherited education system that excluded most of the population. In Tanzania (then Tanganyika), for example, both Christian missionaries and the British government operated schools. But at independence in 1961 those schools accommodated less than half the country's children. For most, the course of study was four (or fewer) years. As former Tanzanian president Julius Nyerere notes, at independence "85 percent of [Tanzania's] adults were illiterate in any language. The country had only two African Engineers, 12 Doctors, and perhaps 30 Arts graduates."[15] Although the schooled population was larger in a few African countries, many faced the new era with as few educated citizens as Tanzania.

If education were to transform society, access to it had to be expanded massively and rapidly. Indeed, expanded access had become both a popular demand of the anticolonial nationalist movement and a promise of the newly installed leadership. The premise was personal as well as political. Access to education was the primary route by which nearly all of Africa's initial leaders escaped (or rather mitigated) the discrimination and domination of European rule. Where there was a clear effort to reject race and other ascriptive criteria for employment and promotion, education's selection role became even more important. And opening schools in urban neighborhoods and rural villages was the most readily achievable and visible manifestation of the new government's accomplishments. Progress in this regard was indeed remarkable.

Unfortunately, before turning to the data on African education, it must be recognized that the apparent precision provided by numbers is often fundamentally misleading. Put sharply, the margin of error on reported African education data is often far larger than the observed variation. Hence, an apparent change over time, say, in enrollment or public spending, may not be a change at all.

The problems are several. Available figures are often inaccurate, inconsistent, and not readily comparable. Schools, districts, and other sources provide incomplete and inaccurate information. Sources differ on periodization and on the specification of expenditure categories. Especially common are the confusion of budget and actual expenditure data and the comparison of budget figures in one year with expenditure reports in another. Recurrent and development (capital) expenditures are treated inconsistently. Often the available data do not include individual, family, local government, and direct foreign spending. Discussions of the cost of education in fact generally refer to government expenditures on education. Inflation, deflation, and exchange rates are treated inconsistently. Data series are frequently too short to be sure that observed variation reflects significant change.

One example of this problem must suffice as the caveat for the data that follow.[16] How many children are in school? Or, more importantly, what percentage of the relevant age-group is in school? Table 16.1 lists the primary gross enrollment ratio for sub-Saharan Africa (recall that available data generally exclude North

Africa) in 1970, 1980, and 1990, as reported in several widely used sources. Notice that the reported figure for 1970 varies from 46 percent to 50 percent—nearly a 9 percent difference—in different editions of the World Bank's own annual publication. Similarly, in this very limited sample, the reported figures for 1990 vary from 66 percent to 76 percent, a 15 percent difference. What happened over those two decades? Did primary enrollment increase by two-thirds (from 46 percent to 76 percent) or by half that (a 32 percent increase, from 50 percent to 66 percent), or something in between? From the available data, we cannot be sure. What we can probably say with some confidence is that (1) fewer than half of school-aged children were in school in 1970, (2) by 1980 progress had been substantial, with some three-fourths in school, and (3) there had been a significant decline by 1990.

The implications seem clear. First, it is essential to take the margin of error seriously, that is, to treat most national education statistics as rough approximations. Second, small observed changes may be more apparent than real. Even changes on the order of 5–10 percent (or greater) may reflect nothing more significant than random fluctuations, annual variations, and flawed statis-

Table 16.1
Africa Education Statistics

	Primary Gross Enrollment Ratio (%)[a] Sub-Saharan Africa		
Source	1970	1980	1990
UNESCO, *World Education Report 1991*	46.3		76.2
UNESCO, *World Education Report 1993*		77.5	68.3
World Bank, *Education in Sub-Saharan Africa*[b]	48.0	76.0	
World Bank, *African Development Indicators 1994–1995*		77.0	66.0
World Bank, *World Development Report 1993*[b]	46.0		68.0
World Bank, *World Development Report 1995*[b]	50.0		
World Bank, *World Development Report 1996*[c]		80.0	
World Bank, *World Development Report 1997*[c]		79.0	

[a]School enrollment as a percentage of the relevant age group.
[b]Weighted average.
[c]Weighted average; male and female combined.

Table 16.2
Enrollment Growth Sub-Saharan Africa, 1960–1980 (Thousands and Percentage)

	1960	*1970*	*1980*	*Average Annual Growth Rate, 1960–1980*
Primary	11,853	20,971	47,068	7.1
Secondary	793	2,597	8,146	12.4
Tertiary	21	116	337	14.9

Source: World Bank, *Education in Sub-Saharan Africa,* tables A-1, A-2, and A-4. (Average annual growth rate is a weighted average.)

tics. Consequently, apparent changes of that magnitude are a weak foundation for broad inferences and for public policy. Third, both researchers and policy makers must reject statistics whose underlying assumptions require a level of precision, linearity, or continuity that the data do not reliably support. Finally, effective use of available data requires seeing through the facade of precision and demystifying the use of statistics. A profusion of numbers neither makes a particular interpretation more valid nor renders a policy proposal more attractive. Indeed, the numeric halo may well obscure far more than it reveals.

Duly cautious, let us consider the accomplishments. Primary school enrollments nearly quadrupled from 1960 to 1980 (table 16.2). In the same period, secondary enrollments increased tenfold, and tertiary enrollments grew sixteen times. In societies in which less than a tenth of the population was deemed literate at the end of colonial rule, illiteracy steadily declined (table 16.3). Comparable figures for the number of schools opened, postsecondary institutions created, and new teachers recruited show similar substantial growth. Clearly, access to education expanded dramatically and rapidly.

But those growth rates could not be sustained. Indeed, some measures showed important reversals where progress had seemed assured (table 16.4). For many

Table 16.3
Estimated Adult Literacy Rate, Sub-Saharan Africa, 1960–1990 (Percentage)

	1960	*1970*	*1980*	*1990*
Adult Literacy	9.0	22.6	40.2	47.3

Sources:
1960: World Bank, *Education in Sub-Saharan Africa,* table C-4.
1970: UNESCO, *World Education Report 1991,* table R8.
1980: UNESCO, *World Education Report 1995,* table 3. (UNESCO, *World Education Report 1993,* gives 32.5 percent for 1980.)
1990: UNESCO, *World Education Report 1993,* table 3.

Table 16.4
Primary Gross Enrollment Ratio, Sub-Saharan Africa, 1970–1990 (Percentage)

1970	1980	1985	1990
46.3	77.5	76.1	68.3

Sources:
1970: UNESCO, *World Education Report 1991,* table R4.
1980: UNESCO, *World Education Report 1993,* table 6.
1985: UNESCO, *World Education Report 1998,* table 6.
1990: UNESCO, *World Education Report 1993,* table 6.

countries the primary enrollment ratio stagnated or even declined, one indication of the deterioration of public services and of the inability of governments to meet their commitment to move toward schooling for all their citizens. At the same time, the supporting infrastructure for the rapid expansion was also sorely stretched. In many places buildings were not maintained, crash teacher recruitment programs were not accompanied by in-service professional development opportunities, low salaries forced teachers to look outside their classrooms to supplement their incomes, curriculum revision and textbook preparation proceeded slowly if at all, and morale plummeted. By the late 1980s African education was in crisis:

> It is not uncommon to find a teacher standing in front of 80–100 pupils who are sitting on a dirt floor in a room without a roof, trying to convey orally the limited knowledge he has, and the pupils trying to take notes on a piece of wrinkled paper using as a writing board the back of the pupil in front of him. There is no teacher guide for the teacher and no textbooks for the children.[17]

For at least some countries the situation has continued to deteriorate, with a decline in the absolute number of children enrolled in schools. Overall, the proportion of Africa's school-aged children actually in school now is smaller than it was at the beginning of the 1980s.

In 1990 governments and international and nongovernmental organizations enthusiastically committed themselves to Education For All.[18] Though it shared that commitment, indeed was and is one of its principal arenas of action, Africa found itself moving in the opposite direction. Far from being an engine for social transformation, Africa's education systems found it increasingly difficult to provide even basic schooling.

Large Commitments, Little Wealth

What had happened? In Africa as elsewhere it is common to blame governments for education problems. What is particularly striking, however, is the extent to which governments maintained their commitment to education even in

periods of dire economic distress. Many African governments adopted structural adjustment programs with a larger or smaller role for the International
Monetary Fund and the World Bank. Often termed "liberalization," these programs generally emphasized substantial devaluation, decreased direct government role in the economy (especially in productive activities), reductions in the
size of the civil service, encouragement of foreign investment, and support for
privatization of many activities, including public services. Nearly everywhere
the implementation of these policies meant increased prices for consumer
goods and new or increased fees for social services, including education. Pressures to constrain or reduce education spending notwithstanding, for example,
by employing paraprofessional or other lower-paid instructional personnel,
many African governments maintained their basic commitment to funding education. Expressed as a percentage of the national budget, spending on education did not decline (table 16.5). Indeed, in terms of the overall economy, the
level of spending on education in much of Africa is comparable to or greater
than that in the world's most affluent countries (table 16.6).

Even a large part of a small budget, however, is still small. In Africa, government revenues did not permit a continuing increase in enrollments or even
the maintenance of per capita spending that is very low in international terms.
Over several decades, international terms of trade have generally worsened for
Africa. In some countries, servicing the national debt requires a share of the national budget comparable to that of education. Although Africa's relative
spending on education was high, the actual amounts spent were very small. By
1995, sub-Saharan Africa was spending $87 per pupil, North America was
spending $5,150, Europe, $4,552, and Latin America and the Caribbean, $444

Table 16.5
Public Expenditure on Education as a Percentage of Total Government Expenditure
Sub-Saharan Africa, 1970–1995 (Percentage)

1970	1975	1980	1985	1990	1995
16.7	16.6	16.2	15.0	16.7	17.6

Sources:
1960–1980: World Bank, *Education in Sub-Saharan Africa,* table A-14 (weighted mean).
1985: UNESCO, *World Education Report 1998,* table 10.
1990: Association for the Development of African Education, *A Statistical Profile of Education in
Sub-Saharan Africa, 1990–1993,* table A-14.
1995: UNESCO, *World Education Report 1998,* table 10.
Note: In view of my earlier comments about unreliable data and in view of the multiple sources of
error in these derived figures, I present them reluctantly. Since the margin of error is likely to be
large, the most reliable interpretation is that these data suggest that there has not been significant
change in the proportion of sub-Saharan Africa's national budgets allocated to education over this
25-year period.

Table 16.6
Estimated Public Expenditure on Education, 1980–1995,
as Percentage of Gross National Product

	1980	1985	1990	1995
Sub-Saharan Africa	5.1	4.8	5.1	5.6
World Total	4.9	4.9	4.9	4.9
North America	1.2	5.1	5.4	5.5
Europe	5.2	5.2	5.1	5.4
Latin America and Caribbean	3.8	3.9	4.1	4.5

Source: UNESCO, *World Education Report 1998,* table 12.

(table 16.7). Equally dramatic, while per capita education spending increased 66 percent in North America between 1985 and 1995, 152 percent in Europe, and 110 percent in Latin America and the Caribbean, in sub-Saharan Africa during the same period the per capita spending declined 5 percent. That African countries came to independence with few educated people and a very small education infrastructure and have a school-aged population that is larger than that of other areas makes the comparison even more stark. Thus the principal constraint has been total government revenue, not a lack of commitment or a failure of leadership or inefficiency, although there has clearly been ineffective and inefficient education (and national) management. Increasing indebtedness, another consequence of aid dependence, consumes an increasing portion of the revenue that is available. Even with great sacrifices, in absolute terms there was little money for education.

Education was to be the developmental engine, the principal strategy, for eliminating poverty and closing the gap between the most and least affluent countries. In order to play that role, however, education required resources that were simply not available. A consequence of this dilemma is that for poor countries (and most of the world's poorest countries are in Africa), the development gap is likely to continue to expand. Education for all remains a distant and apparently receding goal.

It is useful to note here that within countries, differences in communities' and individuals' ability to invest in education are constrained by redistributive education financing. Though the specific mechanisms vary, the common general principle is that the most affluent segments of the population bear the largest share of supporting the education system, including the education of the poorest children. The contemporary fascination with globalization notwithstanding, there has yet to emerge a serious proposal for establishing that pattern globally, that is, for internationally redistributive education funding. To date, foreign aid provides a very small percentage of Africa's total spending on education,[19] and whatever its magnitude, much of the aid to African education is in fact spent

Table 16.7
Estimated Public Current Expenditure on Education, 1985, 1995
Per Pupil and as a Percentage of GNP Per Capita (US$ and Percentage)

	1985		*1995*	
	US$	*% of GNP per capita*	*US$*	*% of GNP per capita*
Sub-Saharan Africa	92	29.0	87	30.4
World Total	683	22.4	1,273	22.0
North America	3,107	19.0	5,150	22.0
Europe	1,803	22.1	4,552	22.7
Latin America and Caribbean	211	11.7	444	12.9

Source: UNESCO, *World Education Report 1998,* table 13.

on personnel, services, products, and scholarships in the aid-providing country. Hence, in at least some settings, far from redistribution toward Africa, foreign aid may in fact function to generate a net outflow of both capital and skills from Africa.

Desegregation and Resegregation

Along with expanded access, the second major commitment of Africa's post-colonial leadership was to desegregated schools and desegregated curriculum. Progress in this area has been substantial. Formal racial restrictions were eliminated immediately. Informal barriers weakened as senior civil servants and other more affluent Africans moved into formerly white neighborhoods and sent their children to elite schools. Although the most egregious elements were addressed immediately, for example, teaching the history of Europeans in Africa as the history of Africa itself, revising the general curriculum has taken longer and has proved more difficult. Postcolonial education systems had few African staff with relevant expertise and experience, and in any case revising instructional materials and teacher guides is a time-consuming and often expensive process. Equally important, since curriculum revision revolves around issues of quality and standards, proposed replacements for the inherited materials were often sharply debated. The persisting powerful role of national examinations, widely accepted as the official and formal measure of the quality of education and revised much more slowly and less radically than instructional materials, continues to be a brake on curriculum revision.

At the same time, there are clear indications of the reemergence of racial differentiation in at least some African countries. The combination of a deterioration (actual and perceived) in school quality and a financial crisis has led to efforts to transfer a larger share of the cost of schooling to students and their families, generally through school fees and, in some countries, an expanded role for private schools. High-fee schools, whether public or private, can offer better prepared and better paid teachers, well-equipped and adequately staffed libraries, laboratories, and computer centers, and, frequently, increased likelihood of success at the next selection point. Where that occurs, schools become stratified. Commitments to equal opportunity notwithstanding, in practice access to elite schools is a function of disposable resources. The differentiator is money rather than race, but the two are related, and thus racial distinctions have reemerged, in some countries even within government schools. Ironically, where the (formerly) white schools are perceived to provide the highest-quality education, the newly admitted African elite often becomes the staunchest defender of its privilege. This problem will prove to be a particularly daunting one for South Africa, where decentralized authority provides some protection for white parents who seek to preserve their better-funded, better-staffed, and better-equipped schools.

Equality and Equity

A third commitment of the postcolonial leadership was to use the education system to address inequality. Expanded access was an important but insufficient step in that direction. At a minimum, schools were to stop reproducing and reinforcing the inequalities and injustices of the larger society. Nondiscriminatory recruitment and meritocratic selection were to redress the inherited inequities.

Historically, schools had been primary agents in reproducing a sharply unequal social order. Limited recruitment and severely constrained academic pathways restricted most Africans to less-skilled and lower-paying jobs and to their concomitant social status. There were important exceptions. A few Africans did reach the highest levels of the education system, surpassing many of their European peers. A few poets, novelists, and playwrights found ways to publish their work. A few West Africans were elected to the French parliament and served in the cabinet. Especially in places that had a longer history of missionary education, a few families could point to several generations of university graduates. Even if schooling was not fully racially exclusive, however, it was nevertheless not egalitarian. Most Africans simply never had a chance to go to school. Most of the few who did soon found they could no longer proceed further in the system. Hence, to convert schools from institutions for creating and maintaining inequality into vehicles for achieving equality would require a fundamental transformation. What in fact has occurred in this regard? In developing an answer to this question, I must first clarify several issues of terminology and public policy.

First, common to much of the analysis of education in Africa is a confusion of *equity* and *equality*. This confusion is potentially quite problematic for public policy. Although equity generally requires equal treatment, in some circumstances achieving equity may require differentiated treatment. One manifestation of the equating of the two terms occurs in the World Bank's 1995 review of education policies, which assigns equity a high priority and defines it in terms of access to school.[20] Basic education should be universal, and "qualified potential students [should not be] denied access to institutions because they are poor or female, are from ethnic minorities, live in geographically remote regions, or have special education needs." That is, equity means equal treatment.

Equality has to do with sameness, or, in public policy, with nondiscrimination. Equality has to do with making sure that some learners are not assigned to smaller classes, do not receive more or better textbooks, or are not preferentially promoted because of their race, gender, regional origin, or family wealth. Although there may be valid educational grounds for differentiating among students, equal access requires that status differences not function to limit or guide admission, promotion, and selection.

Equity, however, has to do with fairness and justice. And there is the problem. Sometimes the two do not go together, at least in the short term. A history of discrimination (which is true of essentially all former colonies) may mean that justice requires providing special encouragement and support for those who were disadvantaged in the past. Given its history, what is equitable education in postapartheid South Africa? Clearly, repealing discriminatory laws will not in itself achieve equality of access any time soon. Nor will the discriminatory elements embedded in curriculum, pedagogy, and examinations disappear of their own accord. The circumstances in which focused attention and additional assistance are required and appropriate are and ought to be a matter of public debate. But wherever it is deemed reasonable, affirmative action may involve pursuing policies that treat different groups of people in somewhat different ways. The point, of course, is not to keep the advantaged group out but rather to help the disadvantaged group to join in.

Achieving equity—justice—may require structured inequalities, at least temporarily. Achieving equal access, itself a very difficult challenge, is a first step toward achieving equity. But to define equity as equality distracts attention from injustice instead of exploring and addressing the links between discrimination and injustice.

Even when equity is specified as equality, what is generally envisioned is equality of opportunity. But how is it possible to know whether or not opportunities have been equal without considering outcomes? A careful study might, for example, find no visible gender discrimination in selection to primary school or in the primary school pedagogy. But if that study also finds that attrition and failure rates are much higher among girls than among boys, it might be concluded that opportunities were not equal after all. Similarly, if regional origin, race, or ethnicity is clearly visible in examination results, notwithstanding the lack of obvious regional or racial or ethnic discrimination, it might again be concluded that in fact opportunities were not equal. That is, measures of access are insufficient for assessing equality of opportunity. Discovering and redressing inequalities of opportunity require considering outcomes as well as starting points. (See chapter 6 in this volume.)

Second, discussions of equality and equity commonly assume a fundamental tension between growth and equity. African countries must choose, commentators often assert, between allocating resources to promote growth or using them to achieve equity. Although African governments must make development choices, it is far from clear that growth and equity are alternatives, especially in education. Where inequality is associated with the concentration of wealth and persisting poverty for the majority, for example, limited consumer demand may constrain the expansion of production and productive capacity. If competencies and understandings are not widely diffused, there may be chronic difficulties in filling skilled labor posts and thus continued reliance on much more expensive expatriates, and it may be correspondingly difficult to reorient the workforce as forms and circumstances of production change. Intensified inequality is both a barrier to broad participation in democratic governance and a breeding ground for socially disruptive discontent. Though less often argued, there is a strong case for the view that growth and equity are not alternatives but are mutually dependent, each requiring and advancing the other.

Third, as access has expanded, in part because of the massive resources required to transform primary education for a selected elite into basic education for all, the broadened base has narrowed into a highly selective education system in most of Africa. The exclusion point has moved farther along in the school cycle. As table 16.8 shows, in all of sub-Saharan Africa, fewer than one-fourth of those who start school proceed beyond the basic level and only 2.5 percent reach tertiary education. Comparable percentages for Latin America and the Caribbean are 31.6 percent and 9.9 percent, and for North America they are 88.1 percent and 61.0 percent. These continental figures surely obscure significant variations among African countries. Still, they show clearly that for most Africans, schooling is a process of ever narrowing selection, with only a few learners proceeding to the advanced levels.

Fourth, although earlier discussions of (in)equality and (in)equity in education were generally concerned with region (a surrogate for ethnicity and, more commonly, tribe), in recent years the principal focus has shifted to gender. Explaining that transition in focus and exploring its consequences is beyond the scope of this chapter. It is important to note, however, that there is substantial and reliable evidence that access to and success in school is, in many places, sharply differentiated by region, religion, race or national origin, and class. Learners from one area of the country, for example, are more likely to be

Table 16.8
Enrollment and Selection Education in Sub-Saharan Africa, 1995

Level	Total Enrollment (millions)	As Percentage of Preceding Level	As Percentage of Primary Enrollment
Primary	76.5	—	—
Secondary	18.8	24.6	24.6
Tertiary	1.9	10.1	2.5

Source: UNESCO, *World Education Report 1998,* tables 6, 7, 8.

selected and to do better than their peers from other areas. Available data indicate that Christian communities generally have more schools, more children in school, and more graduates than Muslim communities. Within Africa, Qur'anic and other Muslim schools have not been a serious academic alternative to secular (i.e., Western and at least unofficially Christian) education. When relevant data are collected, the systematic finding is that children from more affluent and higher status families are more likely to find places in school and to proceed to higher levels. The ample evidence of these inequalities notwithstanding, they are far less often the focus of discussion and systematic research than gender differentiation. Several countries have adopted gender affirmative action programs. But there seem to be no comparable initiatives to assist prospective learners who are discouraged or disadvantaged by region, ethnicity, race, national origin, religion, or socioeconomic status. Earlier age-related affirmative action, for example, mature-aged entry schemes for higher education with reserved places for older applicants, seems to have been deemphasized or discarded.

Efforts to encourage and support girls to enter and succeed in school have not been entirely successful. Table 16.9 shows that the percentage of literate adult females in sub-Saharan Africa has more than tripled over the past quarter century; nevertheless, half remain illiterate, whereas two-thirds of adult males are literate. Although progress has clearly been made toward equal gender access to primary school, in the countries of sub-Saharan Africa as a group, females do not yet constitute half of the enrollment (table 16.10). From lower starting points (one-fourth of the secondary school population and one-tenth of tertiary enrollment in 1960), there has been similar progress at secondary and tertiary levels. Still, by the mid-1990s females constituted only slightly more than one-third of total tertiary enrollment. The variation among African countries is substantial. At the primary level, for example, the female gross enrollment ratio in 1995 varied from 22 percent (Niger) to 134 percent (Namibia).[21] In the same year, female gross enrollment ratio at the secondary level varied from 4 percent (Chad and Malawi) to 88 percent (South Africa), and at the tertiary level from 0.1 percent (Chad and Tanzania) to 15.2 percent (South Africa).[22]

Table 16.9
Estimated Adult Literacy Rates in Sub-Saharan Africa, 1970–1995 (Percentages)

Year	Total	Female	Male
1970	22.6	13.2	32.5
1980[a]	32.5	22.3	43.2
1980[b]	40.2	29.2	51.8
1985	45.6	34.9	56.7
1990	47.3	35.6	59.5
1995	56.8	47.3	66.6

Percentage of literature adults in the population aged 15 years and older.
Sources:
1970: UNESCO, *World Education Report, 1991,* table R8.
1980[a]: UNESCO, *World Education Report, 1993,* table 3.
1980[b]: UNESCO, *World Education Report, 1995,* table 3.
1985: UNESCO, *World Education Report, 1998,* table 3.
1990: UNESCO, *World Education Report, 1993,* table 3.
1995: UNESCO, *World Education Report, 1998,* table 3.

A recent research overview concluded that

although tremendous gains have been made since the 1960s in most places, participation levels of girls still remain lower than those of boys. Repetition, drop-out and failure is very high among girls, beginning at the primary level and continuing throughout the system: many girls remain outside the formal education system. The small number of girls who remain in the system tend to be directed away from science, mathematics and technical subjects. . . . Consequently, female participation in the [formal] labour market is limited. . . . Female illiteracy remains high.[23]

It is striking that in a very short period women's experiences in education have become a central focus of education analysis and, in at least some countries, of education policy and planning. A review of nearly 150 broad studies of African education undertaken during the late 1980s found little explicit attention given to the education of girls. A review of some 240 students completed in the early 1990s found that essentially all addressed that topic.[24] That increased attention has been accompanied by the development of organizations, institutions, and networks concerned with the education of girls at the continental, national, and local levels. Several external funding agencies, international, national, and nongovernmental, many within the context of their own gender or women in development programs, provide significant support for efforts to increase the recruitment of girls and their school success.

Some dissonant voices, however, believe that the differential experiences of males and females simply reflect deep characteristics of human society and

Table 16.10

Female Enrollment by Level, as Percentage of Total Enrollment
in Sub-Saharan Africa, 1960–1995 (Percentages)

Year	Primary	Secondary	Tertiary
1960	34	25	10
1970	39	31	16
1980	43	34	21
1985	45	41	25
1990	45	40	26
1995	45	44	35

Sources:
1960 World Bank, *Education in Sub-Saharan Africa,* tables A-1, A-2, and A-4 (weighted average).
1970 World Bank, *Education in Sub-Saharan Africa,* tables A-1, A-2, and A-4 (weighted average).
1980 UNESCO, *World Education Report, 1993,* tables 6, 7, and 8.
1985 UNESCO, *World Education Report, 1995,* tables 6, 7, and 8.
1990 UNESCO, *World Education Report, 1993,* tables 6, 7, and 8.
1995 UNESCO, *World Education Report, 1998,* tables 6, 7, and 8.

therefore cannot be modified dramatically. Others see concern with gender as yet one more value and priority imported to Africa and imposed by outsiders, often as a condition for foreign aid. Still others accord gender no special prominence, insisting instead on addressing gender as part of a broader focus on equality and equity. (For further discussion, see chapter 7 in this volume.)

The dominant research orientation in this arena clearly reflects both the dominance and the limitations of what has come to be the standard model for social science research. Generally, the starting point is a set of instrumental assumptions about the value and importance of educating women, especially expanding and strengthening workforce skills, increasing employability, improving family health, and reducing fertility. If educating women produces clear social and individual benefits, why do they not constitute half the school population? In response to this question, researchers seek to identify factors that explain lower enrollment or higher attrition, both in and out of school. The candidate causes are by now well-known: parental attitudes, gender-differentiated expectations for future income (based at least in part on gender-differentiated salary scales), the labor and household responsibilities of women, the absence of role models at home and in school, explicit and implicit discouragement for pursuing particular courses of study, parents' educational achievement, family religious and moral precepts, sexual harassment and early pregnancy, and more. Much of this commentary talks of bringing women into the development process.

Some analysts, however, stress that women, as primary producers of agriculture and reproducers of the family, are already at the core of the development process. In that view, the problem involves power and authority relations, not exclusion. From this perspective, schools reflect the social order in which they function, and thus it is not surprising that societal gender distinctions infiltrate and orient the schools. That is, to confront gender inequality in education requires not so much identifying individual causative factors but reconstructing social, and therefore economic and political, relations. In this approach, schools must become locations and agents of social transformation instead of trying to incorporate females more efficiently into a nonegalitarian society. This understanding of the problem, though forcefully presented in the general literature on African development, is with few exceptions little evident in studies of African education, which for the most part continue to list variables and attempt to test their relative importance.

Education and Development

Understandings of the role of education in African development diverge sharply, with important educational and political consequences. Efforts to expand access, desegregate schools and curriculum, and promote equity reflect the premise and promise of decolonization. Viewed from that perspective, education has a broad and transformative mission. Parallel to that orientation and often in tension with it is a narrower view of the relationship between education and development (understood broadly as an improved standard of living and the economic changes required to achieve that). Often mechanically economic, this view assigns primary importance to the instrumental role of education in expanding production and productive capacity and generally considers other education objectives to be societal luxuries that must be deferred as currently unaffordable. However desirable, the humanist aspirations of liberal education, the moral obligation to redress inequalities, the expected social benefits of promoting equity, and the potential power of political mobilization and expanded democratic participation all must wait or, alternatively, must be achieved as by-products of insisting that schools focus on preparing the next generation for its expected role in the national and global economies. These are indeed difficult choices, its advocates insist, but unavoidable for poor countries.

That orientation is reinforced by widespread concern with what is generally termed "educated unemployment." The widespread adoption of this terminology is itself revealing. What in fact is the problem here? What distinguishes the unemployment of the more educated from the joblessness of those with little or no schooling? Surely neither the society at large nor the young people who cannot find jobs would be better off if they were illiterate as well as unemployed.

That young people who finish school are frustrated in not finding jobs (or not finding the jobs they think they should have) is primarily a function of job creation (understood broadly) and not of schooling. Although those in power may feel threatened by rising levels of education among the unemployed, that is primarily a problem of politics, not education.

It is commonly assumed that modifying the content and practice of education will either increase employability or alter expectations, or both. But even with better trained and better paid teachers, less crowded classrooms, and sufficient instructional materials, the education system cannot single-handedly overcome the consequences of a stagnant economy. Revising curriculum and pedagogy is unlikely to have much impact on this phenomenon. If job seekers outnumber job openings, a modified school curriculum may affect which students find employment but not how many. Life experiences, far more than school lessons, shape expectations. Efforts to reduce unemployment among those who finish school, as well as to reduce their frustration and alienation, must focus on job creation (including providing tools, start-up capital, and the like) instead of on schooling. In the absence of more jobs (i.e., economic growth), neither the subject content taught in schools nor the political education they provide will do much to reduce frustration or relieve the anxiety of the political elite.

Together, the common view of education's role in development and the concern with educated unemployment have generated a series of efforts to link education closely with perceived skills needs. Over time, strategies for forging that link have evolved. An earlier notion was "manpower planning," which relied on projected labor needs as the major determinant of current education programs and allocations. That approach is still widely used, although it has been widely criticized. It is difficult and perhaps impossible to develop precise projections of needed skills very far into the future. That is especially problematic in a growing economy undergoing rapid industrial and technical change. Just a few years ago, human resources planners in Africa had no entries in their job lists for computer programmer, microelectronics technician, or education technology instructor. Yet today every African economy needs those skills. This approach commonly underestimates the extent and rapidity of career changes. Since it understands education primarily in terms of its skills training consequences, it tends to disregard intellectual growth, the development of critical and problem-solving ability, the encouragement of creativity and expression, and many other dimensions of education that have no immediate and direct vocational outcome.

In part a response to humanpower planning, an alternative approach emphasized society's broad interest in access to education and used social demands to shape education programs. This approach too has been both widely practiced and widely criticized. Focusing on demand enables education institutions to be sensitive to changing perspectives and preferences in the population. But this approach is also subject to misunderstandings, fashions, and special circumstances that make it difficult to develop a coherent and integrated national education agenda. A different response to humanpower planning was to locate principal programmatic decision making within education and training institutions. Clearly, this supply orientation maximizes institutional autonomy. If institutions are especially sensitive to their economic, political, and social context, that autonomy may be very desirable. At the same time, this approach is not readily compatible with efforts to set national policies and priorities. Nor does it facilitate coordinating the activities of different institutions. And when institutions are primarily responsive to their own internal pressures for new and enlarged programs, the risk of a mismatch between labor market demand and graduates' specializations is very high. Most recently, decentralized education decision making has received attention, and I shall turn to that subject shortly.

The effort to link curriculum and the education system more generally to the labor market has also led to the regularly reiterated charge that schooling is too academic and too humanist. Education must be, the constant refrain goes, relevant to national needs. In this view, national needs, relevance, and the curriculum implications of this claim tend to be construed very narrowly. Beyond a rate and pattern of economic growth that enables people to improve their standard of living and develop spiritually as well as materially, what exactly are national needs?[25] Steel mills and a microelectronics industry? More village boreholes and grain mills? What about reliable, high-quality public services? Or the demand—often termed "need"—for more video recorders and other consumer goods? And what of the need for moral and ethical behavior, nonviolent conflict resolution, and the equitable treatment of all our citizens? Where to rank cultural, aesthetic, and literary needs? All societies continually redefine their needs and priorities. In all societies, some groups assert that their needs are the national needs. Education surely has a role in both shaping and addressing national needs, but equally surely has no linear paths to be followed.

Relevance makes sense only in terms of context and process. Often, for example, the observation that most people in Africa are rural agriculturalists leads to the assertion that education should focus on the tools and skills of farming. From that perspective, schools that teach languages to introduce young people to other cultures or assign books intended to expose learners to new ideas and different ways of thinking or insist that students use microscopes to understand and master systematic observation and comparison are wasting time with irrelevant programs. If so, how will Africa ever escape its dependence on the ideas and technologies of others? How will Africa move beyond exploiting nonrenewable resources to creating and developing new resources? If no Africans experiment with subnuclear particles, write new computer programs, or devise new approaches to dysentery, malaria, and AIDS, how can Africans assume responsibility for their own direction? How will Africa prepare the next generation to innovate, to invent, to create? If education is to expand horizons rather than limit them, determining what is relevant requires not a simple statement of the obvious but an ongoing engagement with values, expectations, and constraints in each society. Relevant programs emerge not from an authoritative decision but from collaboration and negotiation.

In practice, however, the narrow construction of needs and relevance has generally prevailed. Unemployment is attributed to miseducation, this is, to studying history and language rather than chemistry and accounting. Reflecting that view, Namibia's recently adopted scheme for higher education student support seeks to shape choice by assigning priority points to particular fields of study, with teaching, medicine, and agriculture at the top, and humanities, culture, and the arts at the bottom.

In summary, two sharply divergent perspectives on education and development have developed in Africa. In one, education's role is transformative, liberating, and synthetic. Education must enable people to understand their society in order to change it. Education must be as much concerned with human relations as with skills, and equally concerned with eliminating inequality and practicing democracy. Education must focus on learning how to learn and on examining critically accepted knowledge and ways of doing things. Favoring innovation and experimentation, that sort of education is potentially liberating, empowering, and, as such, threatening to established structures of power, both within and outside the schools. This orientation has remained the minority view.

Occasional initiatives to redefine the core and practice of education notwithstanding (e.g., education for self-reliance in Tanzania and production brigades in Botswana), the dominant perspective understands education primarily as skills development and preparation for the world of work. The emphasis on relevance assigns low priority to educating historians, philosophers, and poets, and thereby to cultivating the historian, philosopher, and poet in all learners. Fearing unemployed graduates, leaders expect schools to limit learners' aspirations. Shaped by national examinations, curriculum revolves much more around information to be acquired than around developing strategies and tools for acquiring that information, generating ideas, or crafting critiques.

Experimentation and Innovation

Like much of education, experimentation and innovation are contested terrain. As I have noted, Africa has witnessed important experiments and innovations in education. In the late 1960s Tanzania rejected manpower planning in favor of education for self-reliance. At independence the pressing national need, it was thought, was to have Tanzanians with higher-level skills filling the posts of departing Europeans and branching out in new directions. Since available resources did not permit rapid expansion in all fields, allocations were to be directed by projections of specific skills needs. As the 1960s proceeded, Tanzania's leaders became increasingly critical of that approach, primarily because it constrained the expansion of primary education, the most visible of the fruits of independence. The country was focusing major resources on a small part of the population, Tanzanian president Julius Nyerere noted, creating an arrogant elite detached from their social roots. Scarce resources ought to be directed toward those having little or no education rather than those who have the most (and the most alienating) education. Reversing the earlier orientation, Nyerere's widely read and cited *Education for Self-Reliance* shifted the emphasis to primary and adult education.[26] Schools were to become community institutions, intimately connected with the patterns and rhythms of the local setting. Schools were also to have farms and workshops, both to value directly productive activities and to generate supplementary income. Production brigades in Botswana sought to integrate learning and the local setting by creating community schools in which learners and teachers were also producers.[27] In an effort to expand access rapidly, several African countries experimented with different models of preservice and in-service teacher education. Others—Zimbabwe's efforts stand out—explored how to draw effectively on the local setting to develop lessons and materials for teaching science despite nonexistent or poorly equipped laboratories. More recently, dispersed and locally managed resource centers for teachers have proved to be an effective strategy for providing continuing support to instructional staff. Imaginative and energetic literacy campaigns have brought rapid progress in several countries. Building on its own literacy mobilization, Tanzania created district Folk Development Colleges, in part modeled on Scandinavian folk high schools and intended to provide continuing education for adults who completed basic literacy programs. These institutions offered specialized short and long courses and served as sites for a wide range of community activities. Innovative community-based nonschool education programs have emerged across Africa, often with the support of a local or international nongovernmental organization.

Though materially poor, several of Africa's higher education institutions are intellectually rich, exploring ideas and constructs with contacts and influences around the world. Ghana, for example, nurtured the rejuvenation of studies and debates about pan-Africanism. Through seminars, research, and major student holiday research projects scholars at the University of Dar es Salaam explored the claims and problems and refined the methods of oral history, thereby joining and advancing an international debate among professional historians.

Recognizing the importance of interchanges across Africa, especially since it has often been easier for African scholars to communicate with colleagues in Europe than with colleagues in a neighboring country, researchers have established several continent-wide organizations. Founded in Dar es Salaam in 1973, the African Association of Political Science has regularly brought scholars together, published a journal, provided modest funding to assist participation in international meetings, and generally challenged Africa's political scientists to be critical and to cooperate. Two parallel networks link education researchers in West and Central Africa and in Eastern and Southern Africa, concerned especially with the role of research in making public policy. Several research institutes and centers have sought to provide a venue for critical research and debate and to support both established and younger scholars, among them the Council for the Development of Economic and Social Research in Africa (Dakar) and SAPES Trust (Harare).

Despite a parched and bleak landscape, education innovation and experimentation have periodically flourished in Africa. Some initiatives have won wide recognition and influence. Most, however, have found it difficult to survive after the founders departed or after initial funding was exhausted. Although foreign funds have periodically supported reforms and experiments, rarely has that support been directed toward initiatives with strong local roots and effective organic local participation. Indeed, overall, aid dependence has generally discouraged experimentation, especially activities that are oriented toward broad national political and social goals rather than more narrowly defined instructional tasks.

Setting Education Policy

Education policy and agenda setting in Africa have taken many forms, from broadly inclusive to narrowly authoritarian.[28] The inherited model was distinctly bureaucratic, oriented more toward control and management than innovation and development, a pattern that has been widely retained and reinforced. In some countries key individuals (often the education minister but occasionally the head of state) have played the central role in defining problems and charting directions. In other countries, select commissions, sometimes composed primarily of educators and other times of senior politicians, have gathered evidence, commissioned studies, and recommended new policies. In still other settings, a major national conference (in francophone Africa, états-généraux) provided opportunities for the diverse interests of the education community to present their views and construct coalitions to support particular policies. Some countries have employed several different strategies.

Tanzania's experience is instructive in this regard.[29] Both the policies and the policy-making process reflected the changing times, influences, and balance of forces. With a very small pool of educated officials at its independence in 1961, Tanzania, like many other African countries, sought external advice and assistance in setting priorities and developing concrete plans. Guided by consultants recruited by the World Bank, Tanzania decided initially to emphasize postprimary education and to implement a manpower planning approach. With the publication of *Education for Self Reliance,* the priority shifted to primary and adult education. Earlier, the principal education policy advisers had been external experts. By the end of the 1960s, the influential voices were those of the president and Tanzania's single political party.

Tanzania's all-out effort to achieve universal primary education and its mass adult education campaigns both had positive and very visible results. Rapid expansion at the primary level, however, shifted the pressure for expanded access to secondary school. As public discontent and especially middle-class protest mounted, President Julius Nyerere appointed a national commission to review education policy in the early 1980s. Individuals with significant political constituencies made up its membership; educators composed its professional staff. The commission was responsible to the president, and through him to the cabinet and the National Assembly on the one hand and to the party on the other. After a two year-effort that included an extensive national tour, numerous public and private hearings, and a mountain of commissioned and unsolicited documents, the Presidential Commission on Education offered analyses, projections, and recommendations. Publicly released and then abruptly withdrawn, it initiated a national debate. Several issues were especially contentious, including the introduction of secondary school fees.

Thus the education policy-making process had again been modified. Whereas in the preceding decade the president and the party had initiated the new policies, by the 1980s the circle of participants in policy making had expanded to include the parliament, major national figures, and local constituencies. The presidential commission strategy recognized and legitimized multiple poles of power, including the president, the party, the elected political leadership, and education administrators.

By the early 1990s, the situation had again changed. A new national review of education policy was commissioned. This time the initiative lay with the Ministry of Education and Culture, and the principal participants were academics, not politicians.[30] Its chair, the dean of the education faculty at the University of Dar es Salaam, relied largely on external funding to support his commission's research, deliberations, and publications. Eventually this commission too produced its vision of education, with much less fanfare and public debate than had characterized the 1980s effort. This represents yet another approach to formulating education policy, one in which the central roles are played by certified education experts who report to the education bureaucracy. This orientation was quite consistent with the general 1990s trend of seeking to depoliticize the public policy process in the expectation that relying on research and technical expertise would yield better policies. That orientation in turn coincided with the vastly increased role of the World Bank in Third World education research and policy making, a role that was particularly evident in Tanzania in the early 1990s.

In short, over the years Tanzania experimented with several different policy-making models: reliance on externally recruited experts, initiative by the president and the party, consultation managed by an inclusive and distinctly political national commission, and, most recently, renewed recourse to education experts, this time Tanzanian, though heavily dependent on external funding.

Policy is also made through practice. Indeed, it is essential not to equate policy with official statements that may have little or no influence on what actually occurs. Most of the writing on public policy focuses on formal pronouncements by authoritative institutions. Since making policy is assumed to be the prerogative of those in power, the literature of policy making studies elites and formal documents. Most often, this perspective understands policy making as a sequence of activities and feedback loops, moving from vision to formulation to negotiation to policy specification and announcement to implementation to evaluation. This understanding of policy is widespread and regularly asserted in Africa.

Yet policy is made as much (or often a good deal more) in practice as by pronouncement. Consider, for example, policy on language of instruction. The ministry responsible for education may have formal rules, publicly announced and officially recorded, specifying that instructors are to use a particular language to teach certain subjects. Suppose, however, that an on-site study shows that 90 percent of the instructors use other languages to teach those subjects. When asked, a school principal might say that "our policy in this school is to use the language that our students understand. To do otherwise will make their examination marks even worse." What, then, is the *policy*? From one perspective, the policy is what the ministry has promulgated, and what the teachers do is a deviation from official policy. From the other perspective, the actual policy (i.e., the working rules that guide behavior) is what the teachers are doing. In this view, the ministry documents are just that: official statements that may or may not be implemented and certainly not guides to what people actually do. *Stated policy* may thus be very different from *policy in practice*.

Recognizing that policy results from practice as well as from official pronouncements helps identify other major influences on education policy in Africa. Increased reliance on foreign funding has expanded the direct role of both the finance ministry, which generally manages all external aid, and the funding and technical assistance agencies, whose own agendas have come to guide and constrain education initiatives and reforms in Africa. Explicit conditions attached to foreign aid may require particular policies or priorities, for example, attention to educating females. Even if there are no explicit conditions of that sort and foreign aid is a very small portion of total national spending on education, external influence can still be decisive. Consciously or unconsciously, African policy and decision makers shape their programs and projects, and thus policies and priorities, to fit what seems most likely to secure foreign funding. As the director of planning in Tanzania's education ministry explained, planning had in fact become marketing.[31] His task was less a process of exploring needs and developing strategies to address them than an effort to study the market of prospective funders. He then identified its priorities and value points, using that market knowledge to craft, advertise, and sell projects and programs. That strategy was perhaps an effective one for coping in difficult circumstances. Nevertheless, it entrenched the role of the funding agencies in setting national education policies and priorities. It also reinforced the status and influence of a particular set of actors within the country, not those with the clearest or most dynamic education vision or those with the most solid national political base but rather those who proved to be most effective in securing foreign funding. In these ways aid dependence becomes a vehicle for internalizing within African education establishments externally set policies, priorities, and understandings. Although human capital theory and thus an approach to education as an investment in the development of human capital have clearly external origins, Africa's educators are among their most energetic advocates.

Education and the State

The state in Africa has come to play a major role in the processes of accumulation and legitimacy.[32] Sometimes on behalf of an emerging indigenous bourgeoisie and often in the absence of local capitalists capable of controlling the national political economy and in the context of a continuing dominant role for foreign capital, the state in Africa assumes responsibility for fostering and managing the accumulation and reinvestment of capital that are essential both for economic growth and development and for the security of the tenure of the national leadership. In practice, that often requires the African state to manage conditions for accumulation that are largely specified externally (structural adjustment programs are the most recent example). As it does so, the African state must at the same time maintain its own legitimacy. As students of industrialized capitalist states have stressed, there is a necessary tension between legitimacy and accumulation. (For further discussion, see chapter 3 in this volume.)

Within a peripheral capitalist economy with fragile political authority, accumulation requires a relatively weak, poorly integrated, and politically disorganized labor force. A liberal democratic capitalist system requires even more: a state that can successfully present itself as a representative of the popular will and not an agent of the dominant class(es). The policies the state pursues to maintain its universalist image, however, threaten its ability to manage, or even assist, accumulation. Each arena in which citizen participation is encouraged, and thus some degree of democratic choice is permitted, becomes a point of potential vulnerability for the state itself, and for the capitalist order. Promoting legitimacy through controlled democratic practice—which surely has been occurring in Africa—risks threatening the accumulation process. Empowered peasants may organize and demand greater control over both the organization of production and the distribution of wealth. At the same time, facilitating accumulation by constraining participation—which has also occurred in Africa—undermines legitimacy.

Accumulation is particularly problematic for the leadership of peripheral conditioned capitalist states.[33] As Fanon foresaw, the structural interests of

Africa's postcolonial leadership maintained and reinforced their dependence.[34] The rhetoric of decolonization notwithstanding, the agenda of most who assumed office after the European rulers left was neither radical transformation of the peripheral economy nor the risk taking required for capitalist innovation. Fragile states with insecure elites were disinclined or unable to take a long-term view of what national development would require and reluctant to make a continuing investment in a skilled, disciplined, and accountable public service.[35] One consequence has been a constellation of interests and power that found it difficult to create conditions conducive to accumulation and sustained investment in the development of new production and productive capacity. Another consequence has been a generally inefficient and not infrequently corrupt administration. For education, this situation has been manifested in the ineffective use of limited resources. Facilities are poorly maintained. Even when prepared and printed, instructional materials often do not reach students. Funds are poorly managed, both nationally and locally, with little accountability and reliable oversight. Inefficiency becomes normal, both expected and tolerated.

This tension between accumulation and legitimacy is regularly reflected in education policy, perhaps the most contested of public policies. Establishing and managing the conditions for accumulation favor regarding education instrumentally, primarily as a set of institutional arrangements concerned with preparing the future labor force, which includes developing both skills and work discipline. That orientation reinforces the inclination to link schooling with projected labor needs, to emphasize acquiring information, to regard teachers as transmitters of knowledge and students as receivers of it, and to rely heavily on examinations and other selection and exclusion mechanisms. The commonly asserted view that young Africans must be prepared for their role in the global economy (i.e., that their jobs and the skills those jobs require are likely to be defined not within the country but at distant centers of economic and political power) bolsters the external orientation of this instrumental view of education. Schools, it is argued, need to prepare workers who will, say, assemble automobiles more efficiently than automobile workers elsewhere.

Legitimacy, however, is rooted in popular participation and consent. Maintaining the legitimacy not only of particular officeholders but of governing arrangements more generally requires the active involvement of an informed public that is aware of the power that it wields and is willing to use it. From this perspective, education must be concerned with, and must be seen to be concerned with, encouraging participation, redressing inequality, promoting social mobility, and fostering cooperation and nonviolent conflict resolution. This orientation reinforces the inclination to regard learners as active initiators, not passive recipients. And opening new schools throughout the country has been one of the clearest and most tangible manifestations of the provision of services to the populace.[36]

In short, as it struggles with its own fragility, the state adopts two different (at times incompatible) postures toward the education system. Most often its orientation is functional and technical. Periodically, however, its expectations for schools are more liberal and humanist. The appropriate institutional configurations, even spatial arrangements, for these two orientations also differ. The school-as-factory architecture so common throughout the world—classrooms with the teacher-authority at the front, separated by a buffering space from students in orderly rows, and hierarchical administrations within schools and school systems—reflects the instrumental role of schooling. Open classrooms, activity-group seating patterns, and shared leadership responsibilities generally reflect a preference for the liberal and humanist perspective.

At work here are two related but distinct tensions. One is confronted in the political system as the state works to promote both accumulation and economic growth and at the same time to establish and reinforce its legitimacy. The second is confronted in the education system, which is charged both with preparing students for the world of work and at the same time with nurturing the development of individual potential, intellectual critique, and societal well-being. Each with its own characteristics, participants, institutional configurations, and consequences, these two tensions are interdependent but not identical. Although they intersect frequently and are often mutually reinforcing, neither fully determines the other.

Understood somewhat more broadly, education in Africa has a dual charter. Its major task is to reproduce the economic, political, and social order.[37] Schools assume responsibility for developing requisite skills (training), which is generally assumed to require assigning students to ability groups (tracking). Schools then become the mechanism by which society selects young people who will proceed far in their education (as well as those who will not) and certifying the accomplishments of those who succeed. The internalization of the reasonableness of that certification is crucial. For schools to serve their reproductive role, students who fail must attribute their problems to their own lack of skill or application, to circumstances beyond their control, or perhaps to bad luck. What the schools must avoid is the understanding that tracking, achievement, and certification, and their consequences for subsequent life chances, are planned and controllable outcomes of schools and schooling. (Consider for a moment teachers whose students all receive high marks. The immediate assumption is that the teacher must be doing something wrong, since the classes of teachers who behave appropriately have both successes and failures.) Schools must legitimize as well as track, select, and certify. Their assessments must be accepted as just and appropriate and internalized. Where significant unemployment and underemployment exist, lengthening the course of study, ostensibly to enable graduates to be better prepared and thus more employable, delays their entry into the workforce. When they do not secure the jobs they seek, that emphasis on schooling as job preparation also functions to direct their frustrations away from the economic and political system that has not created sufficient jobs and toward the education system that has apparently failed to prepare them adequately.

Reproducing the social order in a capitalist world system, however, also requires critique and innovation. To survive in a fiercely competitive environment, national economies must have some people who reject the old ways of doing things, insist on looking for better alternatives, and are willing to run the risks associated with criticism and innovation. Hence, schools have a radical and a conservative role. They must enable and encourage at least some students to ask difficult questions, to be impatient with the answers they receive, to trust their own judgment at least as much as their teachers' opinions.

The education system is thus charged with contradictory tasks in reproducing society: preserving and protecting the major features of the social order and at the same time challenging and changing them.[38] Commonly, education systems try to manage that combination by separation—emphasizing the conservative role in most schools for most students and encouraging critique in a few schools, generally for elite students. In practice, that separation is difficult to establish and maintain. Each orientation is corrosive of the other. Critique and innovation have a momentum of their own. Schools become sites for rebellion, indirect (withdrawal, rejection) and direct (militant organization).

During the nationalist and liberation struggles, education emphasized its critical role. After minority rule was dismantled and the new order emerged, education in Africa turned back to its conservative charter, more concerned with preserving order than with challenging common understandings and forging new paths. In the circumstances of the peripheral conditioned state and dependent legitimation, accumulation is deemed more important than redistribution.

Decentralization

The widespread sense of crisis in education in Africa, combined with the perceived failure of central institutions, has fueled a fascination with decentralization.[39] A late 1980s World Bank report on education exemplifies the widespread optimism by declaring "decentralization . . . the key that unlocks the potential of schools to improve the quality of education."[40] The rationales for decentralization are multiple. Some are explicitly philosophical and ideological. Greater local autonomy is deemed inherently desirable on human, societal, and intellectual grounds: the development of human potential, the intrinsic— as contrasted with instrumental—value of democracy and thus citizen participation in governance, and the inescapable limits on the ability of any individual or agency to command and manipulate the necessary information. A second set of rationales for decentralization is political. The devolution of authority is deemed essential to maintaining and expanding political power or control, or, from the opposite perspective, for challenging and reforming the political system. Decentralization can permit expanded access to decision-making arenas. As previously excluded groups develop a stake in the political system and thus a rationale for working within and maintaining it, they are less likely to seek to overthrow or destroy it. A third set of rationales, the most commonly asserted in the education literature, focuses on organization and administration. Assigning decision-making authority to local officials supposedly moves authority to those likely to be better informed and more sensitive to the local setting, reduces bureaucratic delays, improves the capacity of local government institutions, facilitates the effective integration of isolated rural areas into local and thus regional and national development programs, increases efficiency by relieving the central government of unnecessary tasks and reducing diseconomies of scale inherent in the (over)centralization of decision making in the national capital, fosters greater coordination between central and local agencies, permits administration that is more flexible, more creative, and more innovative, encourages small-scale experimentation, and enables more effective monitoring and evaluation.

Experiences with decentralization in education have been mixed, often disappointing.[41] Expected benefits, from improved administration, increased efficiency, and reduced bureaucracy to enhanced democratic participation and empowerment, have proved illusory. In part, the rhetoric of decentralization has not in practice been accompanied by real transfer of authority. Recall that the inherited model of government was highly centralized and authoritarian. Emphasizing the importance of concentrating skills and resources and avoiding regional particularisms and divisiveness, national leaders, sometimes with local support, have been reluctant to devolve responsibility and have generally opposed enabling local authorities to generate and manage their own income.

In part, regarding decentralization primarily as a strategy for improving administration and implementation has itself been self-limiting. Decentralization is inherently a political process concerned with specifying who rules in broader or narrower settings. The institutional arrangements are only a part of the determination of who rules. Indeed, there is no absolute value in either central direction or local autonomy. Both are more or less important at different moments. (See, for example, chapter 8 in this volume.) They must coexist. It is commonly asserted that decentralization empowers citizens, especially disadvantaged groups, in their relationship to large, bureaucratic, and distant government, yet neither centralization nor decentralization necessarily benefits the disadvantaged. If privilege is maintained by strong central authority, increased local autonomy may create room for some groups to transform their circumstances. If inequality is maintained by local authorities, however, disadvantaged groups may seek intervention by the national government to constrain the action of local institutions. Which is preferable? The answer is always a function of the answers to two more questions. First, what priorities are to be assigned to the different interests involved (i.e., *whose* interests are to be ranked highest)? And second, what are the characteristics of the specific situation? It is not surprising that ostensibly similar institutional arrangements can serve very different goals and move in very different directions.

To the extent that decentralization strengthens local interests and their institutions, it obstructs redistribution. Parents may be willing to pay more for their children's education. But except in unusual circumstances they are generally reluctant to see their increased school fees used to improve the schooling of other children elsewhere. As recent experiences in South Africa have shown, local control permits advantaged communities to entrench their privilege and resist change.

South Africa

Until recently, South Africa's experiences were generally excluded from discussions of education in Africa. The extremism of apartheid and South African politics more generally were reflected in the extremism of its education. Though extreme, South Africa was perhaps never as unique as was commonly thought. The use of education to structure economic, political, and social roles (in South Africa, to segregate and subordinate) is common throughout the world. Central to maintaining minority rule and to organizing and managing a sharply differentiated society, education was at the same time an escape valve for a selected elite. Education has also been a sharply contested terrain, manifested repeatedly in South Africa, including student uprisings in Soweto in 1976. Indeed, several of the themes addressed in this chapter, and in other chapters in this volume, are as relevant to South Africa as they are to other settings. The delayed and very dramatic transition to majority rule in South Africa combines with its more developed productive capacity and infrastructure, and therefore available national and individual wealth, to extend and entrench South Africa's influence across the continent. Several major currents in South African education are of interest here.

Like colonial education elsewhere in Africa, education in apartheid South Africa sought explicitly to structure roles and relationships in society. Especially as the education philosophy was elaborated and articulated by the National Party government that came to power in 1948, most Africans were to receive little education, if any at all, focused on the basic literacy, numeracy, and other skills deemed necessary for the labor force in the country's industrializing economy. Educators were cautioned to avoid raising expectations in students that education would lead to "greener pastures." At the same time, a small segment of each subordinate group was to have access to more advanced education, to provide the administrative staff, the teachers, the nurses, even a few doctors and lawyers, that the system required. Hence, a few Africans were admitted to elite schools, generally church or other private institutions. As elsewhere in Africa, then, from that elite came both the lower-level officials and administrators of minority rule and the activist leaders who militantly opposed it.

When education is primarily concerned with structuring roles, it is the experience of schooling that matters, not learning. As the critics of apartheid education highlighted its shortcomings, they sought also to shift its emphasis from schooling to learning. That distinction was posed sharply in the debates on strategies for addressing the education of older and younger adults who had never been to school or whose schooling had been truncated by apartheid and the anti-apartheid struggle. Amid repression and challenge, a wide range of community groups developed programs intended to enable adults to continue their education in diverse nonschool settings. As the anti-apartheid struggle intensified, education became a mobilization strategy as well, concerned with raising political consciousness and enabling disadvantaged groups to seize the initiative and reclaim their rights as citizens. In this domain too South African experiences paralleled those in other countries. During their struggles, for example, liberation movements in Zimbabwe, Mozambique, and Namibia recognized the importance of education as mobilization and politicization. Schools in war zones were mobile community centers concerned with confronting not only the military power of their opponents but also the internalization of subordination within the African population. In the initial years of majority rule, however, the emphasis has perceptibly shifted from learning and mobilization to schooling. Schools are the markers of modernity, the entry gates to desired futures, the fruits of the defeat of the old order. With a long history of attention to examinations and certification, the education system and its officials are more comfortable dealing with schooling than with learning. The widely heralded efforts to restore the culture of learning have in practice had more to do with reestablishing the discipline of schooling than with nurturing and harnessing curiosity and the intrinsic rewards of the learning process. Like other African countries in an earlier era, South Africa has apparently moved from education as politics to education as administration.

In part, the marginalization of political initiatives for education reflects a shifting center of gravity in political leadership specific to South Africa's setting. Primarily concerned with the education of exiles, earlier the African National Congress (ANC) education department did not play a strong role in the formulation of postapartheid education policy. Student uprisings in the mid-1970s and protests and boycotts continuing into the 1980s seized the initiative in education away from the apartheid state. But critical as these actions were, they were not enough to set and lead a new agenda for transforming education. With the formation of the National Education Co-ordinating (formerly Crisis) Committee (NECC) in 1985, a student-teacher-parent antiapartheid education alliance with strong community roots, this protest became focused, coordinated and directed at the establishment of an alternative, democratic, critical, empowering, nonracist, and nonsexist education. The NECC thus became the political center of a national initiative to chart a new education agenda that included a broadly based review of policy options. At its height, the NECC was expected eventually to become the nucleus of a new education ministry. Unbanned early in 1990s, the ANC relocated its education department to Johannesburg and increasingly assumed organizational leadership from the NECC. As it did so, however, the ANC both reflected and led the transition from the focus on opposition and then policy to an overarching concern with planning. Although it was central to drafting the education component of the ANC's manifesto for the 1994 majority rule election, the ANC education department often followed the lead of trade union education activists and by then had already begun to reduce its staff. Very quickly, it ceased playing the active leadership role.

Following the majority rule election, the new education leadership did not assume the mantle of radical and militant educators. The two former university rectors, who are now the new education minister and the senior civil servant, were drawn from neither the ANC's education leadership nor those directly involved in the earlier mobilization and organizations. They moved cautiously as they entered an education department still staffed largely by the creators and maintainers of apartheid education. New appointments and new initiatives were delayed, reinforcing the opposition to change within the education department and in privileged communities throughout the country. The implementation plans created by the democratic movement to guide the new leadership were extensive and detailed, more a menu of choices than a clear agenda that could be implemented energetically and rapidly. Although several senior education activists were among the members of South Africa's new parliament, they found themselves unsure of their role and generally waited, sometimes in great frustration, for leadership from the education ministry. Whereas the period before the majority rule election was marked by the energy, dynamism, populism, and urgency of the education democratic movement, the immediate postelection period was remarkable for its uncertainty and for the absence of a visible, energetic, and purposive leadership.

That became even more consequential as South Africa struggled to decentralize responsibility for education, a constitutional compromise forged to secure broad participation in the majority rule election. That is, the earlier expectation that the multiple, racially differentiated education authorities would be integrated into a strong national ministry notwithstanding, all but higher education became the responsibility of the nine new provinces. Since only a few of those provinces had the infrastructure, staff, and experience to manage an education system and since no one had experience with decentralized education authority, the initial consequence of this extensive decentralization was to blunt still further the radical education initiative. As people scrambled to implement the new pattern, it became clear that decentralization has provided an extended lease on life for the old education authorities and has offered to advantaged communities a new framework for preserving privilege.

At the same time, the inherited inequalities combined with the commitment to national reconciliation, in part manifested in a postapartheid government of national unity, to generate a financial crisis for education in a relatively affluent country. The general agreement was to expand access without reducing quality, understood to mean maintaining spending in elite schools and affluent communities. The recognition that there were limited available resources for a reform agenda fueled an inclination—as in the rest of Africa—to seek external funds. With those funds came ideas about what is desirable and appropriate for the country's postapartheid education agenda and how to achieve it.

Education had been at the center of the anti-apartheid struggle. Its task, everyone agreed, was social transformation. As the new government assumed power, responding to both general and specific pressures, it moved from mobilization to planning to implementation. As elsewhere in Africa, its principal concerns were expanded access, desegregation, and the redress of inequality. In the context of a constitutionally required fundamental decentralization, education debates focused less on learning and liberation and more on schooling and examinations, and more generally on education as preparation for the world of work. With surprising speed, education's conservative charter once again became paramount.

From Education as Social Transformation to Education as (and for) Production

It is time to take stock. African countries came to independence with high aspirations and expectations. For capitalists and socialists alike, education held the promise of national development, community improvement, and individual social mobility. Nearly everywhere schools mushroomed and enrollments increased. Community centers, radio, television, and village newspapers were employed in efforts to enable older learners to participate in the march toward education for all.

In much of Africa, the rate of education expansion could not be sustained. Facilities deteriorated, worn-out textbooks were not replaced, libraries had few books, laboratories had little equipment, and gross enrollment ratios stagnated or declined. Measures of education quality, school efficiency, and teacher and learner satisfaction showed similar distress. By the end of the twentieth century, spending per pupil in affluent countries was forty to sixty times higher than comparable spending in most of Africa. Imaginative experiments continued, but in general promising innovations were localized and often did not survive the departure of their founders.

As they confronted this education crisis, whose roots lay in poverty, the international division of labor, fragile dependent states, and deteriorating public service, African countries turned increasingly to foreign funding. Innovation and reform, and in some countries even textbooks and desks, were assumed to require external support. With the foreign funding came ideas and values, advice and directives on how education systems ought to be managed and targeted. Although external resources amounted to a very small portion of total spending on education, their direct and indirect influence on policy and programs was often substantial. A wide range of approaches to setting education policy notwithstanding, their imprint on education agendas and priorities is clearly visible across the continent. As external agencies undertook research, as well as providing funding and development advice, their perspectives on scholarship and science shaped approaches, methodologies, and the definition of universities' missions and more generally the scientific enterprise. Throughout Africa, unable to find local support, education researchers became contracted consultants. As they did so, those imported understandings of research, from framing questions to gathering data to interpretive strategies, were internalized and institutionalized, no longer foreign imports but now the apparently unexceptional everyday routines of universities, research institutes, and indeed informed discourse.

We see here international convergence at several levels. Increasingly, the specification of education quality is presumed to be universal rather than nationally, culturally, or situationally specific. As such, it is amenable to measurement through the standardized assessments that seek to compare, say, reading ability among fourth-grade students in England, Korea, and Zimbabwe. Similarly, notions of effective schools, good school management, and community participation are also treated as universals.

Note that I have not applied the term "globalization" to this process. Wallerstein notes that

> as used by most persons in the last ten years, "globalization" refers to some assertedly new, chronologically recent, process in which states are said to be *no longer* primary units of decision-making, but are now, only now, finding themselves located in a structure in which something called the "world market," a somewhat mystical and surely reified entity, dictates the rules.[42]

Clearly, the international integration of goods, technology, labor, and capital has a long and energetic history. Throughout that period controllers of capital have been powerful decision makers, not infrequently determining state behavior. New technology permits instantaneous transmission from one end of the world to the other and enables researchers in Africa to consult the same electronic databases as researchers in, say, Sweden, Japan, or the United States. Yet the movement of labor remains sharply controlled and restricted by nationally set rules. Colonial rule was, among other things, a general strategy for integrating Africa into the global political economy on terms set largely in Europe. Formally managed by the World Bank and the International Monetary Fund, structural adjustment plays a similar role.

In a context of persisting poverty, aid dependence, increasing debt, and powerful pressures from within and without to adopt a particular understanding of development, African governments have been inclined to emphasize accumulation over legitimation. Similarly, though pockets of innovation and radical reform persist, the trajectory of education policy and practice in Africa has generally been to discard or devalue education's role in economic and social transformation in favor of education's role in maintaining particular patterns of economic, social, and political organization. In practice, the productivist and conservative charter for education contributes to entrenching still further the conditioned state and Africa's dependence. Within Africa it means acquiescing in (even seeing as necessary) fundamental societal inequalities and the politics they breed.

Consistent with that conservative role for education, attention has increasingly focused on efficiency, quality, and school improvement, often modeled on approaches and experiences elsewhere. The rhetoric of liberation and empowerment notwithstanding, the commonly held view is that education must enable Africa to run faster as it tries to catch up with those who are ahead rather than forge new paths or transform the international economy and Africa's role in it. Scrambling to catch up always leaves those presumed to be in front to determine where they, and thus everyone else, are going.

Notes

1. President Kenneth Kaunda, at the chancellor's installation banquet of the University of Zambia, 12 July 1996, quoted in J. F. Ade Ajayi, Lameck K. H. Goma, and G. Ampah Johnson, *The African Experience with Higher Education* (Accra: Association of African Universities; Athens, Ohio: James Currey/Ohio University Press, 1996), 28.

2. World Bank, *Education in Sub-Saharan Africa: Policies for Adjustment, Revitalization, and Expansion* (Washington, D.C.: World Bank, 1988), 11.

3. Ismail Serageldin, ed., *Universities in Africa: Strategies for Stabilization and Revitalization* (Washington, D.C.: World Bank, 1992), vii.

4. *Zambia. Primary Education Sector. Report of a Preliminary Fact Finding Mission* (DANIDA: April 1993), 1.

5. *Zanzibar. Proposed DANIDA Support for Educational Development and School Building Activities* (DANIDA: December 1991), 4.

6. *Tanzania. Proposed DANIDA Assistance to the Primary Education Sector: The Establishment of a Teacher Support Structure* (DANIDA: August 1991), 6.

7. Esi Sutherland-Addy in World Bank, *Revival and Renewal: Reflections on the Creation of a System of Tertiary Education in Ghana* (Washington, D.C.: World Bank, 1993), 1.

8. *Project on Sahel Sub-Regional Programme in Support of Education for All by the Year 2000* (UNESCO and Permanent Inter-State Commission on Drought Control in the Sahel, 1992), 12.

9. World Bank, *Revitalizing Higher Education in Senegal: The Challenge of Reform* (Washington, D.C.: World Bank, 1992), i.

10. World Bank, *Note sur le Secteur de l'Éducation République du Togo* (Washington, D.C.: World Bank, 1991), 1.

11. Ajayi, Goma, and Johnson, *African Experience with Higher Education*, 145.

12. As we shall see, beyond the mystification and exoticism associated with the "dark continent," the terminology commonly employed regularly structures the discussion in ways that are not immediately apparent, even to careful readers and active participants in policy debates. The specification of what is "Africa" is an instructive case in point. Nearly all World Bank documents on Africa, as well as many others, include a note that indicates, "Most of the discussion and all of the statistics about Africa in this study refer to just thirty-nine countries south of the Sahara, *for which the terms Africa and Sub-Saharan Africa are used interchangeably*" (this example is from World Bank, *Education in Sub-Saharan Africa,* viii; emphasis added). That is, "Africa" is not the Africa specified either by geography—countries on the African continent and its adjacent islands—or by African states themselves—membership in the Organization of African Unity—but rather a subset of those states grouped to reflect the foreign policy interests and categories of the World Bank, the United States, and other countries of the North Atlantic. Unfortunately, there is currently no straightforward resolution to this dilemma. Much of the most readily available data on education in Africa come from publications of those organizations, and to date no one has systematically revised those data to include North Africa or reorganized other data that do include North Africa to make them directly comparable. In this discussion, other than explicitly noted exceptions, my comments generally refer to the entire continent.

13. World Bank, *Priorities and Strategies for Education* (Washington, D.C.: World Bank, 1995), 14.

14. For a fuller discussion of these understandings of education, see Joel Samoff, "Institutionalizing International Influence," chapter 2 in this volume.

15. Julius K. Nyerere, "Africa: The Current Situation," *African Philosophy* 11, no. 1 (June 1998): 8.

16. I addressed this problem in more detail in "The Facade of Precision in Education Data and Statistics: A Troubling Example from Tanzania," *Journal of Modern African Studies* 29, no. 4 (December 1991): 669–689.

17. The country is Tanzania. UNESCO, *United Republic of Tanzania: Education in Tanzania,* vol. 1, *Overview* (Paris: UNESCO, 1989), 15.

18. Inter-Agency Commission, World Conference on Education for All (UNDP, UNESCO, UNICEF, World Bank), *Final Report, World Conference on Education for All: Meeting Basic Learning Needs* (New York: UNICEF, 1990).

19. Unfortunately, there have been few systematic studies of aid to African education and especially of its volume and its impact on the direction of capital flows. For South Africa in 1993, foreign aid was estimated to account for less than 1.5 percent of total spending on education. See Baudouin Duvieusart and Joel Samoff, *Donor Cooperation and Coordination in Education in South Africa* (Paris: UNESCO, Division for Policy and Sector Analysis, 1994).

20. World Bank, *Priorities and Strategies for Education,* 113.

21. UNESCO, *World Education Report 1998,* table 4. The broad age range of enrolled students permits figures greater than 100 percent.

22. UNESCO, *World Education Report 1998,* tables 6, 8.

23. Adhiambo Odaga and Ward Heneveld, *Girls and Schools in Sub-Saharan Africa: From Analysis to Action* (Washington, D.C.: World Bank, 1995), 14.

24. See Joel Samoff, with N'Dri Thérèse Assié-Lumumba, *Analyses, Agendas, and Priorities in African Education: A Review of Externally Initiated, Commissioned, and Supported Studies of Education in Africa, 1990–1994* (Paris: UNESCO, 1996).

25. I draw here on discussions of education and relevance in two major Namibian policy statements, *Toward Education for All* (Windhoek: Ministry of Education and Culture, 1993), and *Investing in People, Developing a Country: Higher Education for Development in Namibia* (Windhoek: Ministry of Higher Education, Vocational Training, Science, and Technology, 1998).

26. Julius K. Nyerere, *Education for Self-Reliance* (Dar es Salaam: TANU, 1967); reprinted in Julius K. Nyerere, *Freedom and Socialism/Uhuru na Ujamaa* (Dar es Salaam: Oxford University Press, 1968), 267–290.

27. Ingemar Gustafsson, *Integration between Education and Work at Primary and Post-Primary Level—the Case of Botswana,* Working Paper Series, no. 95 (Stockholm: University of Stockholm, Institute of International Education, 1985). For a parallel effort in Zimbabwe, see Ingemar Gustafsson, *Zimbabwe Foundation for Education with Production. ZIMFEP. A Follow-Up Study,* SIDA Education Division Documents, no. 29 (Stockholm: Swedish International Development Authority, 1985).

28. Two recent collections of case studies address education policy making in Africa: David R. Evans, ed., *Education Policy Formation in Africa: A Comparative Study of Five Countries,* Technical Paper no. 12 (Washington, D.C.: USAID, Bureau for Africa, 1994), and Association for the Development of African Education, *Formulating Education Policy: Lessons and Experiences from sub-Saharan Africa* (Paris: Association for the Development of African Education, 1996).

29. I draw here on Joel Samoff, "Education Policy Formation in Tanzania: Self-Reliance and Dependence," in *Education Policy Formation in Africa: A Comparative Study of Five Countries,* ed. David R. Evans (Washington, D.C.: U.S. Agency for International Development, 1994), 85–126.

30. It is important to note here that I do not use the term "politicians" pejoratively but simply to refer to individuals who hold political office or whose concerns and activities revolve around the expression, confrontation, integration, and mediation of political interests. Nor do I assume that education policy *ought* to be set by professional educators or that decisions guided primarily by the findings of education researchers will necessarily produce *better* policy.

31. Joel Samoff, with Suleman Sumra, "From Planning to Marketing: Making Education and Training Policy in Tanzania," in *Coping with Crisis: Austerity, Adjustment, and Human Resources,* ed. Joel Samoff (London: Cassell, 1994), 134–172.

32. Since an extended discussion of the state in Africa is far beyond the scope of this chapter, I limit my attention here to the tension between accumulation and legitimation and its implications for education. For a more extended development of these and related themes, see Martin Carnoy and Joel Samoff, *Education and Social Transition in the Third World* (Princeton: Princeton University Press, 1990), especially part 1, and Martin Carnoy, "Education and the State: From Adam Smith to Perestroika," in *Emergent Issues in Education: Comparative Perspectives,* ed. Robert F. Arnove, Philip G. Altbach, and Gail P. Kelly (Albany: State University of New York Press, 1992), 143–159.

33. Martin Carnoy, "Education and the Transition State," in *Education and Social Transition in the Third World,* by Martin Carnoy and Joel Samoff (Princeton: Princeton University Press, 1990), 63–96.

34. Frantz Fanon, "The Pitfalls of National Consciousness," in *The Wretched of the Earth* (New York: Grove, 1963).

35. The World Bank and other external agencies have recently focused major attention on problems of governance and administration, though generally without addressing the structural roots of managerial inefficiency and the lack of transparency and accountability. For example, see Mamadou Dia, *A Governance Approach to Civil Service Reform in Sub-Saharan Africa,* Africa Technical Department Series Technical Paper no. 225 (Washington, D.C.: World Bank, 1993); and World Bank, *Sub-Saharan Africa: From Crisis to Sustainable Growth* (Washington, D.C.: World Bank, 1989).

36. Hans Weiler explores what he terms "compensatory legitimation" in "Education and Power: The Politics of Educational Decentralization in Comparative Perspective," *Educational Policy* 3, no. 1 (1989): 31–43.

37. Samuel Bowles and Herbert Gintis have developed and refined the notion of the correspondence between school and society. See "Education as a Site of Contradictions in the Reproduction of the Capital-Labor Relationship: Second Thoughts on the 'Correspondence Principle,'" *Economic and Industrial Democracy* 2 (1981): 223–242.

38. Carnoy and Levin characterize this tension as between education as a democratizing force (social mobility, public education as an equalizing experience, instruction on the democratic ideal) and education as a mechanism for reproducing capitalist inequalities (class, race, or gender division of labor, unequal access to knowledge): Martin Carnoy and Henry M. Levin, *Schooling and Work in the Democratic State* (Stanford: Stanford University Press, 1985).

39. The literature has mushroomed. For an overview of major issues, see Joel Samoff, "Centralization: The Politics of Interventionism," *Development and Change* 21, no. 3 (July 1990): 513–530.

40. Marlaine Lockheed et al., *The Quality of Primary Education in Developing Countries* (Washington: World Bank, 1989), 1.

41. For an overview of problems drawn from Latin America, see Juan Prawda, *Educational Decentralization in Latin America: Lessons Learned* (Washington, D.C.: World Bank, 1992).

42. Immanuel Wallerstein, "The Rise and Future Demise of World-Systems Analysis," *Review* 21, no. 1 (1998): 107.

About the Contributors

Robert F. Arnove is Professor of Comparative Education and Coordinator of the doctoral program in Education Policy Studies, Indiana University, Bloomington. He is Vice-President/President-Elect of the Comparative & International Education Society.

Edward H. Berman is recently retired from his position as Professor of Education, University of Louisville.

Mark Bray is Director of the Comparative Education Research Centre at the University of Hong Kong. He is also Assistant Secretary General of the World Council of Comparative Education Societies and in 1998 was elected President of the Comparative Education Society of Hong Kong.

Maria Bucur is Assistant Professor of History and John W. Hill Chair of East European History at Indiana University, Bloomington.

Rachel Christina is a doctoral student in the Education Policy Studies Program of Indiana University, Bloomington.

Ben Eklof is Associate Professor of Russian History and Director of the Institute for the Study of Russian Education, Indiana University, Bloomington.

Joseph P. Farrell is a Professor in the Comparative, International, and Development Education Centre of the Ontario Institute for Studies, University of Toronto. He is a past President of the Comparative & International Education Society.

Christine Fox is Senior Lecturer and Director of Primary Education, Faculty of Education, University of Wollongong, Australia.

Stephen Franz is a doctoral student in the Education Policy Studies Program of Indiana University, Bloomington.

Anne Hickling-Hudson is Senior Lecturer in Cultural & Policy Studies, Faculty of Education, the Queensland University of Technology, Brisbane, Australia. She is a past President of the Australian and New Zealand Comparative & International Education Society.

Vandra Masemann, an independent consultant living in Toronto, Canada, is Secretary General of the World Council of Comparative Education Societies. She is a past President of the Comparative & International Education Society.

Golnar Mehran is Lecturer in the School of Education, Al-Zahra University, Tehran.

Shabana Mir is a doctoral student in Education Policy Studies at Indiana University, Bloomington, and an Assistant Professor at Eastern Illinois University.

Marcela Mollis is Professor of Comparative Education and History of Education, Faculty of Philosophy and Letters, the University of Buenos Aires, Argentina.

Raymond Morrow is Professor of Sociology at the University of Alberta, Edmonton.

Joel Samoff is Consulting Professor at the Center for African Studies, Stanford University.

Daniel Schugurensky is Assistant Professor in the Department of Adult Education at the Ontario Institute for Studies in Education, University of Toronto.

Nelly Stromquist is a Professor in the School of Education, the University of Southern California. She is a past President of the Comparative & International Education Society.

Justine Zhixin Su is Professor of Education and Director of the China Institute at California State University, Northridge.

Carlos Alberto Torres is a Professor in the Graduate School of Education and Director of the Latin American Center, the University of California, Los Angeles. He is a past President of the Comparative & International Education Society.

Anthony R. Welch is an Associate Professor in the School of Social and Policy Studies in Education, the University of Sydney, Australia.